REAPING THE WHIRLWIND

~~~

Israel sows the wind and reaps the whirlwind.

HOSEA 8:7

REAPING
THE WHIRLWIND

A Christian Interpretation of History

LANGDON GILKEY

A Crossroad Book

THE SEABURY PRESS • NEW YORK

In gratitude for the life and thought of
REINHOLD NIEBUHR
and
PAULUS TILLICH

The Seabury Press
815 Second Avenue
New York, N.Y. 10017

Printed in the United States of America

LIBRARY OF CONGRESS CATALOGING IN PUBLICATION DATA

Gilkey, Langdon Brown, 1919–
Reaping the whirlwind.

"A Crossroad book."
Bibliography: p.   Includes index.
1. History (Theology) I. Title.
BR115.H5G54   231'.7   76–29738   ISBN 0–8164–0308–2

CONTENTS

PREFACE

This work, even more than its companion volume, *Naming the Whirlwind*, is the result of a long, often interrupted process of study, thought and reformulation. Direct research into conceptions of history and of providence began somewhat euphorically as long ago as 1960 with a Guggenheim in Munich; out of that study was to come a "doctrine" of providence as a companion piece to a preceding volume on creation. That enterprise, however, quickly experienced its own nemesis. Not only did I find my thinking devoid of an available method and my mind empty of relevant and credible concepts, but, even more, during that time my own life seemed to fall apart into meaningless pieces—surely a liability for one seeking to pen a theory (especially an "existentially relevant" theory) of providential meaning in history! The project was shelved and not taken up again until a decade later.

By that time, thanks partly to the "shock" of the radical theologies, an apparently more viable method and a more useful set of ontological and theological categories had appeared on my own theological scene; and, much more important, new possibilities in personal and family existence had begun to be actualized. In both arenas, contingency, fragility, risk and the threat of renewed nemesis continue to be present, but some actuality of intelligibility and meaning had mysteriously been "given" in the interim. Consequently, in 1970–71, on a sabbatical in Holland, study on history and providence was resumed, intellectually inspired this time by the appearance of the exciting political-liberationist theologies. And thus the present work began to take shape.

The first public form of these reflections appeared that spring (May 1971) in four lectures delivered under the auspices of the Disciples Student Center in Tübingen, one of which was a lecture for the Faculty of Theology of the university itself. Then in the next year (1972) these were expanded into the seven Annie Kinkead Warfield Lectures at Princeton Theological Seminary. Subsequent reformulations of these materials provided the bases for a number of such lectureships in the ensuing years: the E.T. Earl Lectureship at the Pacific School of Religion; the Larkin-Stuart Lectures at Trinity College, Toronto; the Iliff Week of Lectures; the Willson

Lecture at the Earlham School of Religion; the Carver-Barnes Memorial Lectures at Southeastern Baptist Theological Seminary; the Smyth Lectures at Columbia Theological Seminary; and in their final form, the Thomas White Currie Lectures of Austin Presbyterian Theological Seminary. Mention should be made of the fact that selected aspects of these reflections, in single lectures or in a short series, have been presented at Hamma School of Theology, at the Theology Institute of Villanova, at Garrett-Evangelical Theological Seminary and at General Theological Seminary. Finally, after the text was almost completed (in February 1975), the whole was rewritten in the form of five public addresses delivered in Kyoto in the spring of 1975 under the auspices of the Department of Religion in the Faculty of Arts and Letters of Kyoto University. I wish at this point to express my gratitude to each of these institutions, and to those who represented them, not only for their original invitations to speak, but even more for their interest, their challenging questions and for their warm hospitality.

This volume has been dedicated to Reinhold Niebuhr and to Paulus Tillich. The reasons for this are both personal and intellectual. It was Reinhold Niebuhr who first quickened my interest in Christian symbols, and so in theological reflection, as illuminative of our social and historical, as well as of my own personal, existence. It was under his personal and intellectual influence, therefore, that all my earliest attempts to do theology were undertaken and so to him that any adequacy in these attempts is deeply and permanently indebted. With the need for "reconstruction" referred to above, I found—to my own initial surprise—the influence of my other theological teacher and friend, Paulus Tillich, steadily growing. As this volume will abundantly show, by now the influence of both on whatever creative elements there may be in these reflections is so thoroughly intertwined that I would myself find it impossible clearly to disentangle the strands. So deep and by now unconscious has been this dual influence that—to my continual embarrassment—I find, whenever I reread their writings, that ideas and phrases long thought to be my own turn up uncomfortably on the pages of their works! Whether these quite diverse forms of thought have here come together into a creative and coherent "synthesis" or merely into an eclectic hodge-podge I cannot say. In any case there is hardly a page of this volume that does not represent the insights of one or of both of these two thinkers, and thus is this volume appropriately dedicated in gratitude to the memory of both of them

Two further influences should be cited—besides that of Augustine. First of all, as noted, I wish to express my indebtedness to the political-eschatological theologies of the recent period. In the work that follows some rather pointed theological criticisms are offered of these theologies, at least in the forms in which they originally appeared in the published materials. I wish here to state as clearly as possible that this theological critique does not, and cannot be made to, imply a critique of "political theology" as such, nor of its practitioners' inspiring efforts to rethink theology "politically," nor of the particular political judgments (especially those emanating out of South America) that also inform these theologies. To me—and this volume will seek to give theological grounds for this—political theology, while not exhausting the scope of the gospel, is a genuine expression or fulfillment of it. Consequently, to me any theology without critical and transformative political implications is insofar an *inadequate* theology. That these theologies have reminded us all of this truth, and so have turned our concern back to social issues and to historical developments, is all to their credit—and personally I am greatly in their debt.

Finally, in the following effort to sketch out an ontological conceptuality adequate to the symbols of providence and of eschatology the significant influence of Whitehead's philosophy will be obvious. Again, an important critique of and differentiation from Whitehead's view of God appears, namely, that I do not follow him in the metaphysical distinction on which he insists between "creativity" as the "ultimate" and God as the nontemporal actual entity. However, despite this obvious and momentous difference, my indebtedness to other important aspects of Whitehead's metaphysics is very real indeed and should be appropriately acknowledged. In sum, the modes of recent conceptuality that are here hopefully brought together, and for each of which I am grateful, are the theologies of Reinhold Niebuhr and Paulus Tillich, the political eschatologies of the present and the metaphysical vision of Whitehead.

I wish to express, as I have before, my gratitude to my colleagues at the Divinity School, both faculty and students, for their interest in and criticism of these reflections when they have been presented; to Anne Grant for her typing and retyping of the manuscript; to Father Jack Shea of St. Mary of the Lake Seminary for his work on the index; and to my wife and children for providing daily embodiment not only of the ambiguity common to us all, but even more of the excitement, the meaning, the intercommunion, the joy and the love possible for human existence in time.

The Divinity School   LANGDON GILKEY
The University of Chicago
May 26, 1976

PART I

Historical Passage: A Prolegomenon

1

CHANGE, POLITICS AND THE FUTURE:
THE HISTORICITY OF HUMAN BEING

Human Historicity and Social Change

Change is basic in human experience and in the world that is experienced. To be in time, as we in our world are, is to be subject to changing moments as day replaces day, to new relations between the moving things in our world, to new and so to surprising combinations of what is around us. And often there are unpredicted developments out of the old, a sudden, unheralded introduction of the radically new, the appearance of the utterly unexpected or improbable.[1] These forms of change, the object of an entire history of awed and puzzled reflection since human beginnings, appear in bewildering mixture in our own most concrete experiences of ourselves and our world. Time and change set the limiting frame for all of human reflection on the being which we experience and know.[2] They also provide the most fundamental structure and tone of our experience of our own existence. To experience change is to experience with inner immediacy our immersion in history. To understand and to deal with the change in which humans are engulfed, the passing of the old and the appearance of the new in time, to affect the shape and direction of historical process, are inescapable requirements for human thought and for human life alike. We can neither escape time and change, nor easily subdue and control them—nor in the end can we acquiesce passively in them, and remain human.

This experience of change has always been an important part of human existence. I believe that for a variety of reasons it is quite dominant in the modern consciousness, and that a sharpened apprehension of basic change and awareness of the future into which change is moving us is the peculiar character of modernity, a character that has increased in intensity in this century. It is, I shall argue, the source of our most fervent hopes and our deepest anxieties, and it sets for us our most important spiritual tests and dominates our politics. The experience of change, and especially of social and historical change, is the way we apprehend our temporality. In experiencing change, we feel what it is "like" to be in history. To be immersed in

3

historical process, and to experience that movement into the social future as menace or as promise, is, therefore, constitutive of what we mean by our "historicity." Human existence as temporal, as a project into the future, is no individual journey in time;[3] rather, man's historicity cannot be comprehended except in the environment of social process, in the environment of historical passage. Thus theology in speaking of human existence, its problems and their redemption, must speak of change, of social process and of history realistically and intelligibly if it is in our time to have any relevance or creativity. Correspondingly, as we shall seek to show, no human can exist serenely and creatively amidst temporal passage without raising questions about the historical future, about the direction and course of that passage, and so about the nature and meaning of history itself.

The experience of change begins with the passing of days, each of them different from the last, a world filled with familiar things but always slightly new, often fresh, often broken. Then on a deeper level as we grow older, we know and feel changes in ourselves, in the self in that moving world. An older and so new, and so different self appears when we find ourselves at another stage: in a different place, in a different community, in a different role; as we move from house to new house, from home to college, and possibly to graduate school; as we progress from school to vocation and job, from dater to lover to mother or father.

The experience of change, however, can go even deeper than these experiences of change in ourselves and in the places and roles we occupy. Nature changes around us in the sun and the rain and in the seasons; our whole world seems continually to become different as it moves on the belt of time. For men and women in the past these changes in the nature around them have been of overwhelming importance, at one moment threatening their life and at another replenishing it. Natural changes became for humans the focus of their deepest terrors and of their most exultant joy, gratitude and hope. Slowly through this bewildering sequence an order and harmony within natural change appeared, especially in the farmland, on the sea, in the recurrent cycle of stars, of seasons, of birth, growth, death, and new crops and new life. This intuition of a regular, recurrent order within natural change has been the basis for much traditional religion and, later as reflection developed, for the attempts of philosophy to understand change and of reflective "practice" to deal with it.[4] In the modern period this same intuition of an intelligible order in a changing natural and social world remains as the often unspoken basis of our physical and social sciences, and of much of our present confidence in our ability to control the moving, shifting environment of events in which we live.[5] One question which will occupy us in this volume is whether the social and cultural changes that make up *history* and that form the central environment of change within which we now live can be understood, or dealt with, on the inspiration and the model of the undoubted regularities and so intelligibilities of natural changes.

The deepest experience of change for most modern people is not the experience of the recurrent changes in nature, nor even of the changing self in a seemingly changeless world. Rather, it is the even more fundamental experience of change in the social world around us, in the world humans have created for themselves to live in, the world of history and of history's institutions. For two centuries or more our culture has been increasingly aware that the seemingly most permanent structures of our social world are by no means everlasting, changeless orders established by God or inherent in the grain of things. Rather, they too, like the people who create and inhabit them, are historical, creations of time and place and so subject to continual if often unpredictable transformation. Historical awareness has grown and spread among us.[6] Few are unaware that our Western political institutions have moved from monarchy to democracy, and in some cases to fascism and communism; and our economic institutions from agrarian, feudal structures to bourgeois capitalistic ones, and then in some cases to socialistic and communistic ones. And it has been part of the experience of only two generations that our social institutions of family, guild, church and nation, our social convictions, values, and habits—styles of life— have moved radically from grandfather's to father's to our own. Modernity, both in its feelings and so in its social and philosophical reflections, has been suffused with this sense of the process, the becoming, the fluidity and the transitoriness of its social and historical institutions. This deep experience of flux and passage in the social world around us has been further deepened by the twin forces of modern industrialism and technology that spread forth a deliberate and so a pervasive and an accelerated change over everything that surrounds our existence—cars, planes, new products, new buildings, new techniques—and transform our homes, our towns, our landscapes, our ways of living. A technical culture has now weirdly and even frighteningly caught nature itself in *linear* change, and so nature is swallowed up in history —perhaps to its destruction. Thus our basic experience of change is now correlated directly not with the experience of nature but with that of history, of changing events in our social world. And thus is our sense of time, both as we primordially feel it in ourselves and as we reflect upon it, linear and moving forward into the future rather than cyclical and returning always to the natural past.

Modern men and women have lived and live in an accelerating kaleidoscope of social change in which they are themselves caught up. Everything is transformed literally before their eyes—the natural world around them, their cities, the way they live, where they live, their roles in the world, their sexual and family life patterns. To their dismay they feel that their own inner personness, their values and even their identity inexorably change and can even be disintegrated and lost entirely. They seem on a moving and accelerating belt leading they know not where and becoming persons they feel they will hardly recognize or even be able to find at the end.[7] As opposed to what we can presume to be the experience of former historical epochs, in which change in the "world" was so slow as to be almost imperceptible, so that the sense of continuity was dominant, to us stability of structure appears to be an abstraction, and change or process the basic reality of all things. This apprehension of the reality of ourselves and of our world as in process is accurately reflected, as we shall see, in almost all modern ontologies, theologies and social theories.[8] Consequently on both the theoretical level of understanding change, and on the existential level of experiencing and dealing with it, process, history, the new and the future have become characteristic preoccupations of modernity.

The process of social change, change on the level of history, which we have here sought to describe—and which each of us feels in various tones of expectancy or of anxiety—is an exceedingly complex matter, never an easy object for intelligent comprehension. Initially, and so to speak on the surface, even our brief discussion has uncovered two quite different processes or strata of change: there are first the slow, gradual changes in technology and tools (means of production), and in social forms and institutions, a process which, to be sure, may accelerate but which basically consists of small mutations and shifts that become perceptible as a new form or institution in history only when they result in a cumulative aggregate.[9] Typical examples of these gradual but "natural" processes of social development are: developments in technology and tools, developments in economic and political institutions, growth in the size, shape, and breadth of communities and corporations, changes in family structure, macroscopic changes within social structures from status to contract societies, Gemeinschaft to Gesellschaft, and so forth. In relation to these fundamental processes of change, the contingent events of historical life and the intentions and policies of history's significant actors seem at best arbitrary elements that are clearly secondary and even replaceable.[10] Certainly the plans and decisions of men, however important, seem hardly crucial or determinative in any such major social or institutional shift. The changes, say, from a nomadic to an agrarian culture, from agrarian to an urban industrial society, from feudalism to capitalism, from a society with hierarchical personal authority to one with a unified bureaucratic rationalized authority, and so on, appear obviously to be neither intended in the main nor, on the other hand, to be completely arbitrary or accidental.

Now although these gradual and cumulative changes happen in this way, "behind the backs" of politicians and statesmen, intended by no particular political policies or action, still it seems evident that in some measure they embody a knowable pattern and so are capable of being comprehended by careful inquiry and judicious hypothesis. If they can be thus rationally comprehended, they must in some sense reflect what is "natural" to social organisms, namely a steady, immanent, continuous and even necessary pattern of change that can be formulated into a "law."[11] Thus appear those twin modes of understanding history's mysteries, which, as is so often the case, seem to each other to be antithetical but from a wider perspective are clearly siblings. These siblings are, first, speculative philosophy of history that seeks to uncover by reflective thought the a priori, rational order or pattern of a changing social process, and, secondly, social science insofar as it seeks to uncover by empirical investigation the universal or natural laws or patterns characteristic of every society at the various stages of its development. In both cases, however different their modes of rational inquiry, history is understood more or less on the model of our understanding of nature. That is to say, historical passage is assumed to be made up of a complex series of events in sequence which, however contingent and even arbitrary the sequence may seem at first to be, is, when subjected to the proper inquiry, shown to represent a realm of rational order, a sequence ruled by universal laws or patterns of change. It has been on the basis of such "insight" into the efficacy of laws in social and historical process, the discovery of universally relevent and effective variables, that not only most modern social science, but also—ironically—our dominant modern mythologies of history—evolutionary progress and the Marxist dialectic—have been built.[12] It is also on this intuited basis that our present scientific "seers" into the mystery of the future project their alternative worlds to come.[13] Thus have some of the lineaments of modern religious myth and practice been constructed, as Stephen Toulmin has said,[14] out of materials forged in the laboratories of physical science and in the surveys of social science.

There is, however, another side entirely of the social changes we have been briefly viewing. For in the process of transformation which we have as a culture lived through, everything has by no means been a matter of slow, gradual, continuous, cumulative and necessary changes. And none of it, not even the most ineluctable developments, had the feel of necessity about it when it happened. Rather, the large and crucial events, such as the revolutions, the domestic social and political reforms and the international wars that have accompanied this gradual process of social transformation, make evident that there have been significant turning points in this story. Such "turning points" are occasions when the outcome of significant trends and their dominance in the future hang in the balance; where obvious alternative courses of action and alternative consequences of action were present; where informed judgments and brave, often risky, decisions have had to be made; where unforeseen factors and unexpected combinations of forces completely changed the landscape and to which immediate and creative response was called for.[15] One cannot read the social, economic and political history of America since 1900 without being vividly aware of the crucial role of contingency (an unplanned constellation of factors) and of political judgment and decision in fundamentally shaping this process of social change. In such historically important situations, contingency rather than necessity seems to be the name of history, and far from being ruled by either transcendent or subpersonal "laws," events seem to be the product of good or bad policy on the part of actors blessed with very good luck or cursed with very bad fortune.

Historians are on the whole very aware of *these* factors of contingency and decision as important ingredients of history.[16] When an event has happened, they tell us, it becomes a necessary basis for subsequent events. In its happening, however, it was flanked by real alternatives. Thus is its outcome the result of the combination of (1) contingent constellations of factors unique to that situation,[17] and (2) judgment, decision, policy and action on the part of the people involved. History reflects a fundamental structure in which (1) temporality creates a *modal* change from possibility to necessity; and there is (2) a "given" presented to each moment to which there is the response of freedom, of intelligence and of will to that given: out of this union of what we shall call destiny and freedom appears the historical event.[18]

Some historians will further argue that the contingent and volitional character of history holds not merely for its great events where good fortune and good policy (or their opposites) are evident. It also characterizes even those very slow, gradual cumulative changes in the institutional habits of people which the social philosopher and social scientist view as ruled by law or by overarching patterns. For on analysis it is clear that social institutions which "gradually evolve" are not *entities* in their own right which could "change." They are, on the contrary, abstracted congeries of the habits of behavior of individual men and women. Because institutions are composed of people who even in their social behavior are never fully necessitated, rationally ordered or totally predictable, so correspondingly the process of the social development of institutions, in which inescapably individual people are the sole actors, is likewise free of a rigid and determined necessity.[19] Viewed from this perspective, therefore, history is constituted at its most concrete level not at all by necessitating general laws or patterns of change or development. Rather is it an open drama whose constituent elements are contingent events and human decisions, where possible alternatives impinge on every moment and every action, whose ontological structure is that of the polarity of destiny and freedom—and so where exhaustive comprehension through a speculative or an empirical discovery of law is logically impossible and humanly irrelevant.[20] The question of how history, if in this way both contingent and free, may be comprehended, remains one of the points of continuing debate in modern life. And the more serious existential question how radical social change, which engulfs us in a "new" that has little necessity, less predictability and so meager security in it, may be borne and creatively formed, poses on the level of feelings and of practical politics perhaps our deepest spiritual problem.

As the social changes we have described offer themselves to our comprehension in two quite diverse ways, so the apprehended reality of social change in our common experience impinges itself upon us in two quite different moods. The fact of change, as we have intimated, is spiritually and politically of immense importance, for change ushers men and women into a new world, and that experience is what requires, impels and drives political action. The apprehended *quality* of change, however, the mood it generates, the apparent character of the world it ushers us into, determines the character of the future we expect and so is of even more importance to our common existence. For that "future world" can be exciting and buoyant, full of infinite possibilities for human life, or it can be dark and threatening. On that qualitative tone of the future portended for us by change depends much of the character of our personal spiritual and our public political life.

When the awareness, described above, of significant and accelerating change in our social world and so in our social selves first appeared in modernity, it was welcomed by the rising middle classes with joy and with expectation. These classes saw in the breakup of an old order indifferent to their talents and oppressive of their interests an opportunity for a new status, a new wealth and a new security. Thus to them change meant social "progress" or "growth." It meant a new freedom from old, traditional structures that favored other groups, and that were now disappearing, and it meant the possibility of creating a new world, more efficient, more secure, more comfortable, more humane for all who had suffered in the old world of the past. Since the rising classes saw social change as the opportunity for their own, and with them humanity's, expansion, it is not surprising that in adopting this biological analogy of "growth" as the clue to all of history's movement, they quietly dropped out the other, polar element in all natural growth, namely decline, decay and death: history, they said, involves rising without falling, growth without decay.[21] As we shall see later, many thinkers expressed this sense that historical change is progress in reflective philosophical and theological form; and even today many scientists and social scientists still assume it in their thoughts about history. For the past two centuries most of the middle classes have *felt* it. In sophisticated and popular culture alike, change and the changing future were greeted with enthusiasm, buoyancy and hope. This was for good reason especially true in America, where a fundamental change from the old European order was continually supplemented by the ever-present reality for many, and the possibility for all in the new land, of change for the better in social and economic status, and if necessary in space.

In our own day this confidence that history illustrates and enacts a law of growth or of progress has largely dissipated.[22] Since we shall review in some detail later the rise and fall of the progressivist understanding of history, there is no need here to rehearse the complex factors: world wars, the rise of totalitarianisms and their brutalities, the frequent disarray of capitalist societies, and so on, that led to the demise of this confidence.[23] At the moment we are concerned with the loss of faith in progress insofar as it concerns our present emotional apprehension of historical change, the way the prospect of radical change and so of a new future impinges on us now. For the way we as a people respond to the future is the key element in the health or the sickness of our political and so our public life. Our basic moods with regard to social change and the historical future shape the most essential modes of our existence or being, the *way* we are immersed in time and in history, the *way* we are human. Human existence is "historical" in the fundamental sense that change in the history in which humans are immersed affects at the deepest level the character of their existence, its relation to its future, its courage or anxiety, its serenity or its panic, its temptations to sin or its possibilities of virtue. The temporality of human being is a social and historical temporality. For this reason the way social change, and the history it illustrates, is understood and symbolically thematized is a large part of our essential human self-understanding. Without symbols expressive of the nature of the history in which we are immersed, we are on the one hand vulnerable and helpless and on the other demonic in our inescapable rush into the future. Human temporality in its changing historical context sets the conditions for the way we are human; it thus also sets the conditions for the way we are or are not religious. Our humanity, our action, our religiousness and thus our theology are essentially intertwined with our historicity.

Promise and Menace in Our Future

The following analysis of areas of change in our present makes no attempt to be an exhaustive survey of our immediate social and political situation as it moves into the future. What I have tried to do is to locate those larger areas of significant change which open up in our future radically new possibilities for our human existence. As we noted, ours is a moment of vast change; the possibilities that impinge on us do represent very different "worlds" than our present, accustomed one. This is, I believe, *felt* by all; it is also objectively borne out by analysis.

What is significant for the loss of faith in progress is that these possibilities of the new are, as we shall see, both creative and threatening. The loss of faith in progress is not only dependent on the political and social turmoil of the already past first half of the century; it is also dependent on the potential menace of our own impinging future. Of equal significance, the mood with which these possibilities for our future are greeted depends largely on one's status in our present world. There is not only a sociology of knowledge—an analysis of the social roots of ways of knowing.[24] There is also a sociology of anxiety and of expectancy. Radical change to established, affluent groups comes as anxiety, as the dark threat of the loss of precious values and of stabilizing orders. Radical change to oppressed groups comes as new creative possibilities, as the possibility of liberation and of justice—as our own example of the rising middle classes of the seventeenth and eighteenth centuries shows.[25] Ironically, power and property do not seem to bring with them hope and confidence in the future but precisely their opposite—*if* change is abroad in the land. It should be recalled, therefore, that this account of changes impinging on our present—as with this attempt to think about history—is conceived by a member of the present world's most powerful and affluent society, and that it will suffer from much of the bias that such membership entails. These same changes, seen from the perspective of other groups, will wear a different hue. Both hues are, however, spiritually and politically important. For the powerful to be gripped by anxiety is to impel the world toward tyranny; for the weak to be without hope is to make impossible many necessary creative changes. For both groups confidence in the future is crucial. For both groups the possibilities of the future must be viewed in the light of the threatening as well as the liberating characteristics of present social changes. Thus for both groups powerful, intelligible and credible symbols illuminating the open and so uncertain history into which they move—historical self-consciousness in that sense—are necessary.[26]

There can, I believe, be little doubt that the future—however euphorically our traditional technologists or our new-style eschatologists may on quite different grounds picture that future—impinges on us in the West differently than it did on our fathers and grandfathers. To many in our present Western culture, change portends the threat or at least the possibility of the loss of treasured values, not inevitably their increment. To be sure, we all feel it is a realm of possibility, of the creative new. But an undertone of anxiety is also present as we become aware of the future that is coming. The possibilities are, so to speak, "open" and not merely in a buoyant confident sense. Rather are they dual, ambiguous. Evil possibilities are seemingly there marching toward us as well as good, and probably we are as a generation as prominently aware of the former as our forefathers were of the latter. Hence it is that theories of progress seem so anachronistic to us, so much the product of another age with another future than ours. I shall discuss four factors in the American, and probably the Western, experience of the present, four areas where basic change is taking place, which portend ambiguous possibilities for our future. They give not only a tone of anxiety as well as of expectancy to our apprehension of our immersion in history—an immersion which always hurls us willing or unwilling into the unknown that is to come. Thus do they force us to ponder the meaning of the future and of history. Paradoxically they also present us when we dare to face them with almost insurmountable problems, theoretical and existential, when we try to understand the course of history theoretically or to give grounds for hope for the future.

The Ambiguity of a Technological Society

1. The technological society in which we increasingly live—and on whose developments the confidence in progress of the preceding generations was largely based—now presents to us a different, much more ambiguous face. Its necessity for our survival, its inevitability in our future, its benevolence to us in feeding, housing, warming, educating and organizing the growing and concentrated populations of modern life, are undeniable. We could not eradicate technology and the technological society it breeds even if we would; and no future is conceivable which does not take account of it. Nonetheless it does have elements of menace for the humans it supports and pampers. The apprehension of these elements is new and peculiarly characteristic of the affluent world.

Our social world, organized more and more thoroughly on a rational, systematic basis, appears to us now as a vast, integrated, predetermining and all-determining system of technological production, a system in which we must participate or die.[27] By this systematization of life I mean the transformation of every creative activity in our social world: economic, political, educational, professional—into an aspect of a system of rationalized interrelations, rationalized in the sense that common goals are presupposed and that common means are organized and governed with regard to their efficiency in gaining these goals. Such a systematization of our common institutions and through them of our active public life in the world is paradigmatically seen in an army or navy; but now it also appears in the areas of production, distribution, government, academy, medical and even ecclesiastical work, wherever modern industrial and technological methods have taken over. Such rationalization has as its obvious goals the unification of common effort toward one shared goal, the achievement of efficiency and integration of common effort, the complete control by practical intelligence over all forms of incoherence, and the eradication of the varieties of inefficiency that incoherence brings with it. More specifically it seeks by means of an all-encompassing pragmatism and a total rational organization to diminish all that is wasteful and irrelevant by unification and integration of efforts, to eradicate the incoherence resulting from the contingent or the accidental in life, and to reduce inefficiencies resulting from the personal weaknesses, the pronenesses to error, and the arbitrary whims of individual people. The values of such total rationalization or organization are undeniable, and every developing country in our century of necessity immediately seeks to rationalize and organize its basic functions into an effective system in order to feed, clothe, support and defend itself. America has been the symbol, to itself and to the world, of this organizational efficiency, both of machines and of men, in all walks of life. Thus did such technical rationalization of life, making every means more efficient in gaining assumed and desired ends, seem to harbinger a creative future.

As every advanced technological society has discovered, however, human beings are now not so much the masters as the servants of the organizations they have created, servants in the precise sense that they find themselves "caught" and rendered inwardly helpless within the system insofar as they participate in it at all. By caught and rendered helpless I mean that they experience their personness, their individuality, their unique gifts, creativity and joy—their sense of their own being —as sacrificed to the common systematic effort, an effort in which all that their own thought and ingenuity can contribute is to devise more practical means to an uncriticized end. Any considerations they might raise concerning creativity, aesthetics or ethics, that might compromise the efficiency, the smooth functioning of the whole team, are "impracticable" and so irrational. Thus do their own individualities lose their transcendence over the system: their mind and conscience cease to be its master and become its servants, devoted only to its harmony and to its success. Humans here are, and are creative, only as parts of a system; their worth is judged only with regard to their contribution as an efficient part. The problem of technology is not so much that humans in their active work in the world are made subordinate to their machines as that they are lured into being *parts* of a machine.

The system has, moreover, proved ruthlessly destructive of many of the other, less public grounds of our identity as persons. It uproots us from that in which much of our identity, or sense of it, is founded, namely, our identification with a particular place and with a particular community.[28] For it gathers us into ever larger groups of people similarly organized, and then it moves us about from here to there, from these people to those, within the larger society. It rewards and satisfies us only externally by giving us things to consume or to watch. After all, such things are all that efficient organization can produce. Having dampened our creative activity in the world into the rote work expected of a mere part of a system, it now smothers the intensity of our private enjoyments by offering us the passive pleasures of mere consumption. Thus does it stifle our inwardness.

Realizing subconsciously that in our rationalized communal work individuality, self-determination and critical personal judgment are less and less appreciated and possible, our technological society has more and more referred these crucial aspects of our personal being, our freedom, our transcendence and so of our humanity to our "leisure time," the private life of each individual and family separated from their public work. But as our analysis shows, this is not only dangerous for the human character of our public life in the world; it is also an illusion. For increasingly that leisure, as a consumer's leisure, is itself void of active individuality, of creative self-determination and of critical, personal judgment. Dominated by the family den's tyrannical "set," it produces a passive, consumptive mode of being human.[29] Moreover, by this concentration of "meaning" away from the qualitative values of creative labor either in public or in private in favor of quantitative consumption, a technological culture has helped to make material affluence rather than internal creativity the top priority in the search for worth in life. This not only creates inner emptiness, as we have noted; it even more exacerbates the growing ecological crisis that threatens us all. If as more and more people become "technologized," they all come—as we have long since come—to desire material affluence above all else, then surely the race is doomed.[30] As an African sardonically remarked to the author: "The world can only stand one America!"

In sum, a technological society makes us live and work publicly in ever larger corporate systems to whose demands we must conform if we are to participate. To them we subordinate our individuality, our conscience, our creativity, and our powers of self-expression and creative decision—those aspects of our humanity which make us human, whose loss strips us of our human being, and whose absence in the public life of society spells the doom of freedom and so of genuine participation in that society. It tends, unless resisted, to make our private leisure world equally empty of personal, individual and creative content, a passive, senseless world devoid of spirit.[31] In large offices, in commuter trains, in unweildy communities, schools, and corporations, and in the darkened "family room" these threats of a technological society have been *felt.* Much of our art, our films and literature have reflected these experiences of contemporary people. The portent of change in this case has here a menacing side: will the technological future that is coming be one in which human beings lose rather than gain themselves? Will the landscapes of the future technological society be filled not only with dreary stretches of similar Dairy Dips and look-alike cottages, but also more and more with look-alike consumers inside?

On the other hand, if real progress in human well-being and so in justice is to come to our world as a whole, technology and its benefits in goods and services, and the benefits of rational, efficient organization must spread more and more throughout not only our society but the world. There are immense possibilities of a fuller human life for countless people—the oppressed in our land and around the world —in these developments. To be sure, fundamental political and economic changes are also necessary if this "progress" is to be possible. But such political and economic "liberation" would be futile were it not for the fundamental capacity that alone a more just use of technology offers to us to feed, clothe and sustain ourselves with comfort and dignity. The first deep ambiguity of our future and so of our present history lies here: the technological society that we must retain and develop if economic and political justice are to mean anything in our future is itself a threat to the humanization of man. Must man die inwardly if he is to live outwardly in the future? An old question, but one very much alive in our changing future. Again, the private, spiritual, personal existence of persons in our future is inevitably correlated with the character of the social changes that our future portends: existence and history cannot be sundered but belong together.

The Travail of Social Change

2. Industrialism and technology have caused cumulating and accelerating changes, planned as a whole by no one. These are changes in techniques and forms of production, in economic institutions, in population concentrations, in social associations and modes of life. These changes in turn have transformed the character of our landscapes, of our towns and especially of our large cities. Such basic transformations in their turn have generated *new* social problems that grow like cancers almost before we are aware of them, much less in control of them. Examples are the rapid decay of our cities into jungles of violence and destitution, and the enormous and sudden ecological crisis. Now the point is that these fundamentally institutional and social changes that have, so to speak, merely "happened" without intention, demand from us an intentional response, a response of intelligent *policy* in new economic and political actions.[32] Here clearly, as in every case of unintended and cumulative social change, we can see the intertwining of unplanned destiny (the changes that have "happened") with human intentionality and response (policies directing, diverting or accelerating these changes) to create together historical change. Concretely, these massive social changes demand first of all new policy and action to control technical and industrial development. Let us note in this connection how technological development by its own logic demands more and more rationalization, more "technology" in the broadest sense, if it is in the wider social context itself ever to be controlled, tamed and so made "rational." They also demand new and stringent controls over the use of available natural resources; they demand new projects—economic and political—in our cities and among our poor; they require new social arrangements of our housing, our transportation and communal living—and the list at this writing could be indefinitely extended—unless our cities and the nature on which they depend are to die. The problems raised by industrial and urban change, by an interlocking technological society, inevitably force us into increasingly "corporate" responses if we are to survive in that new world. All this is obvious: in ordinary life anyone knows that a new situation demands a new response, often a totally new response, and that any new response, if it is to be effective, requires open inquiry, common judgment, communal decision and finally creative political action.

New responses in our domestic life, however, involve not only technical and pragmatic policies to settle new problems. They also involve new views on the part of both leaders and people of our economic and political institutions, a new understanding of what social responsibility and the welfare of the community entail, and back of all this a new understanding of the rights of people, of property, of the role of government and of the priorities of the community. In demanding new political action, cumulative social changes require new views of our social structures. They demand reconsideration of an almost forgotten category: the public good, the good of the community as a whole and so of all of its members. Immediately, therefore, we are embarked on the necessity of changes, not merely in social techniques and habits, but even more in our legal, even constitutional structures, changes in our social convictions, our ideas, values and norms, and ultimately changes in our moral and humanistic concepts—in short, changes in all our most fundamental social symbols. For in the end such "new views" presupposed by new pragmatic policies involve a reassessment of the role and the fulfillment of men and women in community, of what fulfills humanity and therefore what historical communities are ultimately for. New policies call for new symbolic interpretations of history at its most fundamental level, a reassessment of what authentic humanity and authentic community are and how they may in history be embodied.[33]

If, moreover, the growth and expansion of technological organization to every corner of our social existence characterizes our present and increasingly our future —and there seems little doubt that this is in fact our "fate"—then this too has immediate repercussions on our traditional and cherished social symbols. Men and women are creative and active in our world insofar as they participate. Nothing is done alone or by oneself, *a se*, whether one is a worker, a manager, an owner, a civil servant, a professional. Thus the symbol of the self-made man, the self-created man of power and of property, is in our present world more and more a false myth. Every position of eminence, of privilege and of power is created, sustained and made possible by *communal* work, not by individual vitality and ability alone—and all property is likewise the product of communal, participatory labors. No doctor or professor is self-made: his or her education, instruments, knowledge, place of work are produced and made possible by communal funds. In effect, he or she is a "public servant," created by participatory labors, and so responsible to the public not out of benevolence and so for a fee but out of fundamental obligation and debt.

In a participatory culture, a technological culture, self-made roles and powers, self-created properties and so private property rights in their traditional form are anachronistic, unrelated to social actuality, rationalizations through which the privileged classes grasp for themselves illegitimately the rewards and privileges of common labor. And their results in an interdependent society in terms of massive poverty, urban decay and an expanding proletariat are evident on every hand. A technological culture requires out of its own historical logic a massive reevaluation of social, economic and political symbols away from their traditional capitalistic and individualistic emphasis on the rights of private well-being in a sea of misery, of private property and privilege, toward the socialist rights of the whole community, the obligation of sharing, and so of the more equal distribution of commonly produced goods and services.

Lest, however, the tone of these remarks seems to have shifted from black to red, let me add that in a technical, organized society, where systems of rationalized conformity (economic, political, academic and social) dominate us all, our own traditional symbols of individuality, of individual rights, of individual conscience and initiative—of the protection and nurture of the person against the overwhelming force of the collective—will have increasing relevance to the survival of the human being.[34] Thus is our democratic tradition from the eighteenth century (and the seventeenth) by no means to be rejected in a future apparently dominated by the corporate nineteenth. It must be *retrieved* and *reinterpreted* in a communal setting, forced on us by technological developments. Both traditions, the capitalist-democratic and the socialist, have failed to deal creatively with the social demands of technology. *Our* essential individualism has led to economic injustice toward the community and an inability to deal with its large social problems; *their* political collectivism has led to massive political oppression of the individual. What is needed, then, in the light of technological developments, is a retrieval and a reworking of political, economic and social theory on both sides, new forms of syntheses of corporate responsibility and individual rights, so that personal humanity is possible in our participatory future. Policy decisions are, to be sure, of the gravest importance in the social future. However, new policies to meet new problems require new evaluations and new creative reworking of fundamental symbols—and thus political and economic *reflection* as well as political and economic *techne*.

Although again this seems obvious, this unavoidable move to new forms of social understanding gives any society pause. The reason is that these required economic and political changes, these new social responses forced on us by industrial and technological change, contradict and so threaten many of our older and cherished ways of doing things, and more important, many of our older values and symbols reflective of those ways of doing things. Images like that of the self-made man, values like the sanctity of work and of property earned by work, overriding priorities such as personal economic success and individual fulfilment—the right of private well-being even in a sea of misery and discontent—these symbols and values, enshrined in much of the older American way of life, are, as we have noted, suddenly themselves threatened. Thus as in the case of the problem of a technological society, a new dilemma on the level of the spirit joins the social decay of our cities and of nature as we face the future.

If we let these traditional symbols of the American way of life go, are we not headed for a terrifying nowhere? And yet if we hang desperately on to them in untransformed forms, we cannot, even if we would, respond in new ways to our current problems. In that case, can we possibly prevent the further depredation of the land, or prevent the further deterioration of our cities—and so ultimately the revolution or at least the radical social upheaval that is bound in the end to come? Everything seems to slip: our landscape, our institutions, our values, our way of life —and so the security and meaning, the sense of being at home in a world we can understand and deal with, that they brought. Much of modern American life as it faces the immediate future is caught in this dilemma: it feels its personal identity dissolving in a technological, mass society, and it finds the symbolic "world" it understood and felt at home in likewise dissolving. In fact, the impact of change on Western modernity is having much the same effect as the impact of modernity on traditional cultures outside of the West, namely, that of threatening familiar roles, personal identity and social symbolic world—and the three are intrinsically related—at one and the same time.[35]

Our analysis of the contemporary experience of social change, of history and the impinging future has uncovered another level of the process of change. First, we have pointed to a basic level of gradual, cumulative, orderly change, subject possibly to some regularity and even necessity and so to scientific analysis. Secondly, we have indicated a level of contingency, of "freedom" and so of intelligent response, of political judgment, policy, decision and action. And now there has appeared as ingredient in all social change a level of values or convictions expressed through social symbols.

As the study of religion, developments in anthropology, and now many, if not most, forms of theoretical sociology have clearly established, every society is constituted not only by its shared space, its common history, its organic relations, its shared habits and techniques, its common neighbors and its needs of defense. It is also constituted, preserved and controlled by the symbolic world which is shared by its members.[36] As Peter Winch puts it: "A man's social relations with his fellows are permeated with his ideas about reality. Indeed, 'permeated' is hardly a strong enough word: social relations are expressions of ideas about reality."[37] The role of such ideas or symbols constituting a social world is therefore crucial. All our modes of social interaction, even the smallest, are shaped and controlled by such a social world. Our own acts within that world, and our expectancies of the acts of others, what we are to do and why and how we are to do it, all of these forms of habitual and unhabitual acts are molded by the interlocking system of meanings expressed in symbols that make this society possible. That a man seeks to make money, i.e., what he considers of worth in life; how he goes about it, relates to others and models his decisions, i.e., what he considers appropriate and inappropriate, right and wrong in behavior; what he expects from others in behavior and interactive services; what he hopes for and is sad about—these are all channelled along lines set up by the symbolic structure, the system of meanings, that constitute his society. At the center of this entire interlocking system of meanings, on which the roles and patterns of behavior in society depend, stand the views of human nature, human society and the modes of the fulfillment of each which form the heart of a culture's life. As the historian Gordon Leff notes: "If men govern the rest of nature in virtue of their reason and technical power, they are themselves governed by their beliefs."[38]

These symbolic structures that cohere, form and direct humans within a social whole are, moreover, fundamental for all forms of social change. The unconscious gradual and necessary processes of change which move a society; the most habitual actions of people expressive, if anything is, of social laws of behavior which account for its stability; and the conscious "policy" decisions, creative and uncreative, innovative of new social forms and so of new habits and modes of behavior—these are all three in the end based on the system of meanings, of value expectancies and of beliefs, i.e., on the social symbols, expressive of *that* culture's view of human being and of the social world. Finally, there are no "entities" in the social world except people, and so no "causes" or "factors" except those that work in and through people. As a consequence, because men and women are beings who structure their world and act within it in terms of meaning, values and goals expressed through symbols, all social and historical change, and all social and historical stability, are qualified, shaped and in part determined by these symbolic universes of the communities in question. The identity and communal role of every person in the society and the political decisions of the community are alike referent to the social symbols that structure that community's life. Thus, as Leff argues, all social understanding depends on historical understanding, since these symbols, constitutive of a society's trends as well as of the contingent events and intentional acts that help determine its history, vary not only from place to place but from historical epoch to historical epoch. Thus the most fundamental structures of any society and of the changes it undergoes must be understood by *historical* inquiry. By implication, therefore, all "general laws" of such change subsist in any meaningfully concrete form only within specific cultural and so historical communities, and must be comprehended with the help of the methods of the historian.

Finally, as our original discussion of modern American culture and its future intimated, a basic shift in the structure and stability of such a symbolic world and a fortiori the threat of its loss or breakup through the processes of social change and of political history, can be an overwhelmingly upsetting event for a society that has achieved some stability.[39] The "world" in which people live a meaningful life begins to fall apart, and so their identity and role, their "place" in their world, seem to be vanishing. A substantial change in the symbolic system makes relative strangers of everyone used to the old; a lonely, frightened, displaced situation in which one's sense of identity and one's security are alike vastly reduced.[40] A much more substantial change or "real revolution" in the norms, values and symbols of a culture's life —or the fear of it—poses almost an ultimate threat, as in an earthquake when the very ground on which one stands breaks apart. Then there is no longer an authentic world in which I myself can be authentic, and great anxiety results, an anxiety that in turn breeds significant and often menacing political and social consequences for the future.[41]

All over our present world the breakup of older symbolic social symbols and the societies dependent on them, as well as the spread of technology and organization, opens up vast possibilities of justice and of liberation. Domestically nothing could be more creative for our common life than new views of poverty and the responsibilities of the community towards poverty, a new view of minority groups and their rights in the common life, a new view of material property and fundamental services as "common," at least with regard to the obligation for minimal subsistence, security and the benefits of the common social effort—in sum a new appreciation of the public as well as of the private good. And internationally every oppressed people calls out for a new understanding of the right and the necessity of self-determination, not only as in 1918 against the political and social power of dominant nations, but also against the economic power of the mighty. Thus does the creation and spread of new social symbols, new "ideologies," push forward and accelerate the processes of change, and bring excitement, hope and confidence in liberation and fulfillment, in humanization. As every oppressed group, class or nation knows, "self-consciousness" is utterly necessary on the part of that group if it is to take effective political action. Such political self-consciousness means the adoption and interiorization of a new self-understanding expressed in terms of new symbols which articulate the problems of the present and the hopes for liberation.[42] To those whose dominance, affluence and security are threatened by these changes, however, who wish for no new world but only for a continuation of the old, the threat of such changes in fundamental social symbols causes deep anxiety, and the defense of its symbolic world becomes in turn an integral part of the defense of its life.[43] Symbolic worlds are, therefore, crucial in history. They not only hold a society together, help to defend it, and so give it stability. They also are instruments in dismantling the old and initiating the new.[44] Thus do ideologies clash in history. And so their creation and revision, their victories and their defeats, their waxings and their wanings—and hopefully, their mutual accommodation into higher syntheses—are as significant a part of historical change as are the "laws" or patterns of social development to which human intentions and meanings respond and which they seek to direct.

There appears, then, a second dilemma of social change on the level of symbol. On the one hand, society is, as we have seen, *constituted* by its symbolic heritage, a "gift" of its inherited past that makes both inner and outer cohesion—social existence—possible. On the other hand, cumulative changes, an ineradicable aspect of our social temporality, mean the necessity of the *reinterpretation* of symbols, their transformation into new forms and so embodying new possibilities to meet new situations. How is such a reinterpretation possible without the loss of the constitutive conditions for social existence?—so ask conservative voices. How is it avoidable without the disintegration of a nonresponding society?—so ask the liberals. How is a reinterpretation—in effect a *re*-constitution—possible without both loss of nerve and unending conflict? On the basis of what standards or norms is a reinterpretation, even a retrieval, of older symbols to be made? Clearly these questions, arising ineluctably out of the reality of social change, deal with the relation of given actuality to new possibilities, of "destiny" to "freedom," and they ask the further question about a norm for our response. If we are later to speak of the work of providence in history, it must be in terms of both the role of the constitution of society and its continuance in terms of continuing symbols, and of the reconstitution of society in terms of new possibilities—and it must provide norms for this continuing process of change.

Power, Justice and the Loss of World Dominance

3. When Americans and Westerners take a wider look beyond their borders, and so beyond the domestic problems of technology, industrialism and urban society

requiring new responses, new values and new social symbols, they find the realities of present change in the international order even more shifting and fluid than at home. Furthermore, the long-term situation, while full of new creative possibilities, also possesses threatening and ominous possibilities from the viewpoint of a once-dominant West and a still-dominant America. At this writing, the economic disease of inflation made into a running fever by the beginnings of a fuel shortage seems the first hint of that "new future" of reduced production and lower standards of living prophesied by many. On the other hand, at present a balance of forces seems to have been reached among the great contending powers, and the immediate threat of nuclear war between ideological blocs has vastly lessened—thanks to good sense on all sides and the good luck or the common grace of the mutual desire for trade and so for peace.[45] I refer here, therefore, not to the immediate scene but rather to the more general balance of dominance among the powers and so to the longer prospects vis-a-vis the position and role of Western culture and so of America in the world as a whole. On this level a vast change has already taken place, and further changes are portended[46]—and such changes raise deep moral and religious, as well as policy, issues for us all.

In principle, since the end of World War II, and in fact in the last two decades, the relative power of America and of the European West as a whole has dramatically slipped, and in all probability it will in the foreseeable future slip much much more in relation to the world's other powers. For three and a half centuries the West totally dominated the entire world. Western powers, varied among themselves but representing one common civilization and culture—and so in the end one set of norms, values and goals—could subdue opposition where they would, take territory, resources and privileges where they willed, and above all guarantee and uphold their peace in the world—a peace which not only favored their interests but guaranteed them for the future. European powers might threaten each other, but no alien culture or civilization could challenge them from the outside. No wonder they thought that history represented a benevolent progress, since it had for those who thus viewed it effectively dissolved all power alien to their civilization, and all mortal threats to their most cherished values.

After World War II, however, European power if not influence almost vanished. America then inherited and even increased this domination of European Western culture. For a brief two decades America alone could in principle do, and in many cases in fact did, what Europe collectively had done, namely, dominate most of the world. In the short era of the Pax Americana, the United States could establish and maintain a world order favorable to its own interests and those of its allies, and thus could determine in the direction of *its* norms, values and goals the outcome of most of that period's contingent events. This was called, of course, "maintaining the peace"—and it was. But it was a peace in which we and our values were obviously secure, in which our present and our future seemed to be ordered because our domination was unchallenged; therefore, it was a peace that was in many important respects unjust to others and so potentially unstable. In the last decade and a half it has become visible to all that this clear domination has gone. The United States is still the strongest power—but barely. Put more precisely, it is now *one* of the great powers in the world. As the United States has learned painfully in South East Asia and the Middle East—and as I hope soon learns in South America—it cannot, as it and Europe once did, so dominate any situation in the world as to control and direct it simply as it judges expedient and wise. Henceforth the outcome of events will not depend solely on the American will—and so on its interpretation of Western values and norms. The outcome of events will depend on the contingent results of negotiations and contests of power among a multitude of other nations and cultures whom no Western nation or even group of nations can dominate and so whom they can in no way control. Whatever peace and order are to emerge in our future will not be *our* peace or *our* order but a peace and order that is the result of many interests and many wills.

Even more significant, the unchallenged role of Western values, norms and goals —that structure of social symbols for Western civilization as a whole, our "ideology," which we uncovered in the preceding point—has also lost its dominance. Such dominance in the world on the part of a system of symbolic forms (a "way of life") connotes the power to grasp men and women so that they structure or wish to structure their world by these same symbols. Thus symbolic forms can be dominant within a culture and also outside the natural orbit of that culture which gave it rise. On this internal dominance of symbolic forms depends the unity and strength of a culture; on its external dominance depends much of its power in the world.

This dominance of the symbols of Western culture has been challenged, first of all, by the appearance in power of other ways of life, expressed in other systems of social symbols, as potent alternatives to those of the West. China has joined Russia in incarnating in its life a quite different ideology than our own. However antithetical they may be, together these two powers represent fully half the world's potential technological, military and economic power; and together they represent a very different symbolic world. When one also considers that Japan has become the fourth major power, a culture which has adopted many of our significant social symbols but which nonetheless has its origins in a tradition totally unlike ours, one can realize the scope of the change in the role of Western culture to which we refer. During the eighteenth, the nineteenth and the early twentieth centuries, England, Germany, France and possibly later the United States, all representatives of Western social symbols, were the "world powers," and every non-Western nation that wished to become "a power" had to adopt Western social symbols as the pass necessary for entrance into what was in fact the Western club. Correspondingly, it could reasonably be assumed until the second half of this century that whatever the future held, it would manifest the continual dominance of that same culture: in technology, in science, in politics, in economic goals and values, in morals and in religion. All these assumptions are now infinitely problematic, as Communist social theory, Eastern religions, and Asiatic economic and military power begin to appear as major forces in world—and even in American—culture. Now the West is merely one cultural and

ideological bloc among many others, each bloc possessing comparable power and
each of equal stature and value in its own eyes.

Perhaps most significant of all is the undeniable fact, equally disquieting to the
Western sense of security, that our social symbols: our social goals, values and norms,
no longer grasp the minds or express the growing hopes and aspirations of people
outside the orbit of Western culture, namely, the Third (or the undeveloped)
World.[47] This is surely partly because these social symbols, arising among the
growing middle classes in the sixteenth, seventeenth and eighteenth centuries, have
little lasting relevance or possibility of incarnation in agrarian, feudal and especially
tribal cultures—as was finally evident even to us in China and South East Asia, and
will become increasingly evident in South America and Africa. To try to defend or
enforce these symbols in an alien context does not help either the spread or the
security of these symbols. As the bitter experiences of the Viet Nam war and the
U.S.-inspired coup in Chile show, "the defense by force of democracy in an *alien*
cultural environment effects only the support of the fascist and totalitarian remnants
of the older feudal hierarchies presently there, or helps in the creation of new ones
out of advancing bourgeois classes."[48]

Thus we are led to the second point: these symbols have lost their power over
men's hopes and aspirations also because in the past half century—at least both
when they were embodied by European colonialism and by present American
economic colonialism—they have become symbols expressive of dominant economic
and political privilege rather than of revolutionary, oppressed voices. Power corrupts
symbolic structures as well as men, as the history of a dominant Christianity shows
exceedingly clearly. When social symbols become the ideology of the dominant class
or culture, the use made of those symbols can become contradictory to their original
intent. For example, our use of our traditional symbols of freedom, of private
property, of individual rights, of the limitations on government action, of individual
well-being, has recently been more that of the buttress of unjust privilege and power
for the few than that of generating, as once they sought to do, universal justice,
equality and well-being. And, as noted, our use in Asia and in South America of the
symbols of free elections, of the right of political opposition, and of a free press has
been evidently more to prevent socialist reforms, economic independence, and the
loss of dominance of U.S. firms than anything else. Clearly this use is precisely the
opposite of the use made of these symbols by the revolutionary forces that originated
them. The meanings of symbols, in politics as in speech, depends on their use in
the community, and their use in social affairs depends largely on the power they
represent. Thus (as we shall reiterate in Chapter 6) is the ethical and political *use*
of theological symbols—the praxis intrinsic to them—one of the most important
aspects of their meaning; incorrect usage and changes in their usage effect drastic
changes in their meaning. And thus have the symbols of Western culture, embodied
primarily in American forms in the twentieth century, lost their attractive or mag-
netic power over men and women elsewhere in the world—and over much of the
youth at home.

No longer the vassal of our interests as it once was, the Third World may well come quite voluntarily to embody an entirely different set of values, norms and goals, a set strange and alien to our own. Unless, therefore, the use that we make of our inherited symbols domestically and internationally changes significantly, they will increasingly lose their creative and constitutive role in world affairs. The future might well be one where most of mankind, far from joining Western technological, libertarian, democratic and capitalistic—"free"—society, follows other ways of life entirely different from our own. The permanent future and ultimate victory of European civilization, which the West once took quite for granted, now seems an improbable dream. Since the view of progress generated in the Enlightenment was founded on the certainty that the future would develop and not dissolve Western culture (that was in fact what progress *meant*), this diminution of the role of the West in present history is one of the reasons for our loss of the sense of progress. At best the Western world (but only if it reassesses the use as well as the present relevance of its symbols) may be able to preserve its culture as a part, and probably by no means the major part, of a quite new world. At worst its symbols may in the future be merely the anachronistic ideology of waning pockets of privilege despised and ridiculed by the advancing forces of the world.

This loss of dominance in the wider world is a new experience for the West, and certainly for America. And to find their symbolic structures, once revered and copied, now weak, often despised, and frequently attacked—not only by official communists but by most everyone else except the few privileged classes around the world—will seem strange indeed. Americans have spoken easily and patronizingly of the problem which Europeans have had to face in becoming "second class powers," and noted the psychological and political strains involved therein. On the world scale, and especially ideologically, we are about to go through the same abrasive and intensive spiritual test. It is no easy matter for Westerners, and now especially for Americans, being used to the enthusiastic adulation of the rest of the world for the West's most fundamental practices and ideas, to face the prospect that tomorrow it may wake up in an alien world, possibly dominated by alien people and determined by a cluster of totally strange ideas and norms. This is indeed radical social change, hardly slow and cumulative, and certainly not expected; nor will any social law here save us or what may be of value in our tradition as we face this new prospect. Sadly, only by embodying the classical human and social virtues: humility, serenity, wisdom, self-understanding, self-control, courage and very great forbearance in the use of our remaining power, can we in this potentially anxious situation retain our humanity and the real values of our culture. Certainly if we use our waning preponderance of power in a fit of anxiety, pride and the lust to remain dominant and secure, we shall only bring down ourselves, our world and the noble house of our traditional cultural life the more quickly. Change, symbols, political decisions, and the requirements of political and so human virtue are strangely mixed as we move into the unknown future.

In this analysis of the changing role of the West and of America in the world as a whole, we have uncovered another factor or category crucial to the comprehension of change, politics and the shape of the future. This factor is that of power. Power is fundamentally an ontological category, but in this context it is a social and historical category. As an *historical* category, power is communal power, the power of a group; politics is its instrument; its aim is the public or communal good. It involves some ability on the part of a person or a group not only to be, to express its being, but also to continue to be in the future. Thus power implies the capacity to control, direct and determine at least in part the shared events of the immediate future. It connotes the capacity of a group to realize its being and so its will or interest within the social sphere. On the deepest level, therefore, as Tillich rightly notes, power is an ontological category, equivalent to the being or reality of an entity and thus unquestionably in that sense a "good."[49] As a result, power is closely associated not only with the category of "legitimate authority" in social existence but also with freedom and self-determination in the face of the "given" in life. Power, as we shall seek to interpret it, is the ground both of genuine authority and of creative freedom. It is, therefore, essential to both authority and freedom and thus essential to any full realization of personal and communal humanity.

Power has two manifestations in the social sphere.[50] Power is necessary and evident first of all in establishing and maintaining the unity of any given social group, and through that unity the ability of the group to act as one or with one social will in the face of contingent events in its future. Expressed through government, power in this form is the first requirement of communal life in space and time; centered unity is necessary to the continued life of any organization or group.[51] In turn, since preponderant power is essential in order to effect and maintain that centered unity, governmental power must always be greater than the other powers in the community. Again because of the necessity of unity to its continuing being, the government is invariably given innumerable social, moral and religious sanctions by the group. It stands inevitably for the public good in the face of all the contingencies of the social future. The goal of the exercise of such power is a just order; its norm is a rule of evenly applied law; and its tasks are to prevent the vitalities of the community from fundamentally disrupting the unity of the group and so threatening its being, and to protect the being of the group in its relations with others. But the seeds of totalitarian tyranny lie in the social necessity of unity and defense and in the reality of preponderant power. One centralized power in a society threatens to dispose of all subsidiary centers of authority and power; thus it tends, on the one hand, to appropriate to itself a relatively infinite power and, on the other, to leave the individual unprotected by other forms of association from the one central authority.[52] The perennial danger inherent in governmental power is, therefore, the subordination and suppression of the vitalities, groups and associations of the community in the name of unity and order.[53]

Secondly, power is manifested in the interaction of persons and groups within a wider community. Here an intramural group or community has power insofar as within the community of other powers it can defend its being and interests and can exert its will on other groups and on the common effort. Clearly such power is essential to the health of a group, lest it be a helpless pawn to the interests of other communities, and lest the central unifying power of the state be the only power in the social scene. Such groups, guilds, professional groups, classes, religious associations and so on, also give identity, role, and so authenticity and dignity to individuals and in fact protect them from both the formless mass of their peers and from the supreme authority of the State. But equally such power when expanded poses a threat not only to the competing groups that surround it or are beneath it, but also to the order, peace and unity of the wider community as a whole. And the more such established ranks and classes in a society gain an internalized and so legitimate "authority" within the society—as in a feudal hierarchy or a caste system—the more those on the lower levels, while granted unambiguous identity and role, are nevertheless shorn of freedom and subjected to fate. Associations and communities *within* a social order are essential to its creative life and to the individuality, dignity and status of its members. But they must be qualified and balanced, not only by each other, but by the unifying power of the group as a whole in the interests of smaller communities with neither authority nor power. The goal of power in this case, therefore, is the integrity, freedom and self-determination of the group, and so of all groups in society; the power, that is, to share in the shaping of their own common destiny; and the norm of such power and of its exercise is equal justice, a balance of power in the community as a whole that will allow every community and vitality to express itself without anarchy and conflict, and so without threat to the unity of the life of the wider community.[54]

Social power in both of these fundamental forms, as the power of government over the whole group and as the power of each group within the whole over against other groups and against the unifying power of government in a wider community, includes both the capacity to control and to use materials and resources, and the ability more or less to direct or influence other competing human wills and thus to shape the common destiny. Such control and/or domination usually involve, therefore, both force and persuasion, the ability to compel others through economic, political or military means, and the ability to elicit their consent, support and alliance.[55] A government or a person, class or nation is powerful in history partly because they have access to the various sources of compulsion: economic, political and military. But they are also powerful when their symbols grasp others, when their goals and intentions are shared and so supported by other wills. Thus, as we noted, a government is powerful not only when it has techniques of coercion but when its majesty and legitimacy elicit "consent" and "support," both from its own citizens and from those who share with it a wider community of purposes. For this reason Western and American power in the world were dependent both on military and economic predominance on the one hand, and also on the "grasping power" of Western democratic and capitalistic symbols to elicit the alliance of other groups.

Power, as the influence of any being over other beings, is morally a very ambiguous factor in social and political affairs, and this ambiguity affects both forms of power: the power of force and the power of symbolic persuasion.[56] Many theoreticians and moralists find the category of power or of force negative because both connote to them exclusively the power of the state over against all its members or of one dominant group over another, and so heteronomous, crushing and arbitrary dominance. However, analysis shows that what is really evil in any situation of dominance is that the oppressed group has no power: no power to sustain itself, to exert in some measure its will, and so in some measure the power to direct its own destiny. In such circumstances of powerlessness, the group is literally helpless with regard both to its existence and to its welfare. Being helpless, it is subject to the decision, passions and whims of another group, and its destiny is directed toward their interests alone. It is then subject to fate, and incapable of self-determination and of freedom; it can barely "be" because it has no power, and thus is the situation unjust. Consequently, it is the total loss or lack of power on the part of any group and the total accession to power of either the whole or of some other group within the whole that are here the most significant grounds of evil. In a situation of oppression, it is the radically unequal balance of power that is at fault, not the fact or presence of power. Correspondingly, it is by a redress in that balance of power, a gaining of significant power by those who lack it, not by an evacuation of power from the scene, that social justice or "liberation" will be achieved. Every contemporary political drive towards liberation and justice, whether on the part of the middle classes, the workers, the blacks, women or the South American nations recognizes this fact and makes the achievement of self-determination through the gaining of relevant power the direct goal of every important political action.[57]

The distribution of power in a social situation is thus very closely tied with issues of identity, freedom and of justice. Freedom and identity in a social context *mean* power requisite for shaping one's own destiny; justice *means* a tolerable or equal distribution of such power. It is for this reason that, if love be defined as total self-giving and consequently if love be perfectly symbolized in social history as powerlessness, justice as the equal distribution of power and liberation as the gaining of a requisite or just power have a strange and dialectical relation to love. Powerlessness is, as we shall see, the ultimate symbol of goodness and of hope in concrete history. *Initially* in social analysis, however, powerlessness represents the most significant cause of injustice, of suffering and so of evil in social history. Justice has been and can be defined in many ways. Surely one significant definition is such a distribution of power in the social situation that each relevant group or community can sustain its own being in the present and share significantly in the direction of its own destiny into the future and in so doing experience its own identity and dignity. Contrary to much of historic Christian sentiments on this issue, therefore, morality relates itself to social affairs more essentially in terms of the character of the *structure* of a social situation, the mode of its distribution of political, economic and symbolic power, than it does on the level of the personal morality of the individuals within a given structure—though, as we shall see, both forms of morality are essential.

The importance of the category of power to our present subject of historical change is that significant social changes involve inevitably the redistribution of power. Pervasive social changes accumulate gradually, by small continuous mutations in economic, political and social habits. Each minute development may have been in part intended, but the entire sweep of social transformation was not the result of any decision or plan; it just happened. Examples we have already seen of this sort of social change are the rise of industrialism, the spread of technology, the emergence of the rationalization of life, the proliferation and decay of cities, the transformation and exhaustion of the landscape, the coming to dominance of the West and of America, and the present loss of that same dominance.

Our present point is that each of these fundamental changes raised and raises crucial questions of power: questions of the loss of power to some dominant group and of its accession to some formerly underprivileged or oppressed group. Thus is added to even the most steady cumulative and so "predictable" changes in social history an explosive, contingent and unpredictable element: the loss of old power and the consequent grasping for new power.[58] For the loss of power by a dominant group will in all probability be *resisted* by all of the resources of its economic, political and symbolic might. And the accession to power by oppressed groups promised by social change will be *advanced* politically and so accelerated by competing classes or nations. Thus do "developments" in technological, economic, political and other institutions—in effect the elements of "social evolution"—become *history*. What is for abstractive analysis a steady process of gradual change becomes in the concrete a drama with involved actors, and laws of development become at best vulnerable and mortal trends.[59] For now arise struggles for power, clashes between symbols, issues of policy, and out of all of this, political intentions, decisions and actions—and unexpected alliances and mortal conflicts. These in turn interact with the developing trends in a maze of historical events, twisting these trends, accelerating them, slowing them down, or even bringing them in a given place to a partial halt—as the outcome, either way, of a war or of a political revolution can surely do.[60] We noted before that social changes create new problems and call for new political policies and political actions. Thus do steady, cumulative changes cause an always passionate and often violent interaction between traditional symbols and new symbols. Now we have added the dimension of power and the desire for power, making this political and symbolic interaction between groups explosive and so contingent, a clash of anxieties and of hopes, a matter of ultimate concerns and so of cruel force, of fanaticism and of unlimited courage.

Again, the reality of deep social change, this time in the balance of power (political, economic and symbolic), in the world as a whole, opens up new possibilities of creative life for much of the world's underprivileged. It is hard for Western and American minds to accept this, but it is true. The loss of colonial domination around the globe, and the prospect of the loss of American economic and political domination, especially in South East Asia and South America, has been and is one of the most "hopeful" portents of liberation and so of justice. Insofar as our present use of American power effects largely the perpetuation of older class structures, of new tyrannies of the army and of the wealthy classes, and the dominance of our predatory corporations, the loss of that power in the world can realistically speaking only be an "opening" of history for a better future—though it would surely be of little help to change the yoke of the American corporation boardroom for that of the Kremlin or the Forbidden City. It is also true, however, that most if not all of the goals and the norms of such movements of liberation around the globe have found their origin in the cultural tradition of the Western world. They will (I believe) also find their continuing substance in many of its most significant symbols: of personal and political rights, of shared power in the community, of the limits of communal power over private associations and over the individual. The eclipse in the future of these Western values and symbols, therefore, may contain as much of a menace to the forces of genuine liberation as for the forces of reaction. As we have noted, in the increasingly unified and centrally controlled world that technolog-ical and economic developments seem inexorably to be effecting, the goals of individual self-direction, of individual freedom to be what one is, of diversity of opinion and of lifestyle, the right to dissent against the centers of power, and the right to influence politically the common movement of the future may, strangely, seem radical and not conservative, and—like two centuries ago—their use may become revolutionary rather than reactionary.

The final point about the existential meaning of this loss of power is that it faces those nations which have had great power with a crucial spiritual challenge. The threat of the loss of significant power invariably produces great anxiety: for one's security, for one's dominance over events, and for the perpetuation of one's set of social and political values. A national, class or racial group permeated with such anxiety is tempted to use its remaining power with increasing injustice, and ulti-mately with ruthlessness and cruelty, in order to maintain its dominance. Thus, for example, a dominant nation may well be led or tempted to secure its own interests by defending ever more blindly its vassals around the globe. These vassals in the present world are the governments of dominated states which represent more the interests of their upper classes and of the dominant external power than they do their own people. Such vassal governments, driven themselves to become more and more tyrannical, function for the dominant nations as outposts against the advancing forces of reform, of liberation or self-determination. Both Russia and America have defended such "vassal" governments, Russia in Eastern Europe, and the United States in South East Asia and in South America. The perpetuation of such a course, as America slowly loses its predominant power, would, obviously, be fatal to the real interests of democratic America, but even more fatal to prospects of world peace and world justice. Perhaps the greatest spiritual test of America in the immediate future is the challenge to recognize realistically its loss of dominance, to combine this recognition with serenity, wisdom and forebearance, and to refrain, as it has not done in the last decades, from those last-ditch efforts at defense. Social change and the future it brings create not only new opportunities for liberation and so for greater justice. They also create anxiety in dominant groups, and thus present a temptation to chaos as well as new possibilities of creative adjustment.

The Finitude of Nature and the Infinity of Greed

4. A fourth change or trend active in our present—quite new to our consciousness —is of even vaster importance for the future we face, the future in our presently unified world of all mankind. This is the crisis in the earth's resources, the probable depletion, in relation to the globe's expanding population, of the means of sustenance.[61] Not only does the recently discovered finitude of these resources imply a necessary end of the growth in the world's standards of living. Even more it seems to necessitate, in the surprisingly near future, an actual diminution in the standards of living of all affluent powers. This interaction between finite resources, an expanding population, and an accelerating industrial consumption has been abstracted by scientific inquiry and subsequent mathematical elaboration into predictive curves and graphs. Such abstraction through the methods of science has been of immense importance and value because otherwise this "not yet" problem and its imminent challenge to us would never have been known beforehand at all. In this sense science alone can tell us of a problem that scientific and industrial technology has created. But when these cool graphs and the impersonal processes they picture are made concrete into historical events involving concrete people in their communities, they are transformed. Like the processes of decline in the power of the West, they then become intermixed with passionate struggles for survival, for well-being and so for power, with issues therefore of oppression, exploitation and injustice, and so with conflicts of social and moral symbols.

In every group the drive for survival more than competes with, if it does not quite overwhelm, the claims of others for justice. Thus when the great powers fully realize the radical precariousness of their future in the light of these shrinking resources, it is not inconceivable that they may, as an ironic result of detente, expropriate for themselves these resources on which they mutually depend rather than rigidly controlling their own use down to a limited portion of those resources. Made concrete or historical in this way, these impersonal changes or processes of development become immediately fraught with all sorts of political potentialities; these alternatives include, to be sure, wise and just resolutions, but they also include new alternatives of domination, oppression and conflict on a world scale. On a raft or in an internment camp, people do not change their essential character for the worse when their supplies become dangerously short and their life and welfare become thereby increasingly threatened. But there is no doubt that their anxieties about their own security and comfort rise. As a result, the difficulties of being rational and just to the less powerful on that raft or in that camp multiply. It is harder to share when you are hungry, or fearful of being hungry, than when you are full.[62] Our world in the future may well face this prospect on a global scale: a rapidly diminishing supply of resources may create the possibility that the powerful, fearful of the gradual loss of their higher standards of living, will grasp for their own use alone the earth's remaining resources.[63] Furthermore, in order to succeed in this theft, they would then be forced to smother dissent from within and challenge from without in a veritable orgy of tyranny and injustice. There is no "fatedness" or necessity that predetermines this grim future; this is not an ineluctable historical law. We are dealing, as always in history, with real alternatives for political judgment, decision and action in the face of the limits and conditions out of the past that are given to us.[64] The difficulty is not an external fate but the fallibility of our own freedom —and it will be only our own use or misuse of our freedom that will precipitate such a catastrophe.

Two preliminary conclusions may be drawn from this last aspect of change that we have discussed. The first is that it is a dramatic reminder to us of our continual embeddedness in and dependence on nature, the interpenetration of history and nature in all of historical process. It has been fashionable in many of the most perceptive modern discussions of history, both philosophical and theological, to minimize or deny this interdependence. The separation of history from nature has been made firstly in order precisely to separate historical studies within theology from those of science and the philosophy of science, and so to free the former for their own appropriate methodologies. Secondly, it has been made in order to reject any hint of natural necessity or determinism in the career of mankind.

The ecological crisis reveals that this separation between history and nature is both partly right and partly wrong. It is right in that it has been man's freedom that has created the crisis in nature. This has been freedom in several of its dimensions: the freedom to create technology and industrialism; the freedom to make of himself an insatiable consumer; the freedom consequently to consume nature limitlessly by transforming it into an infinity of consumable goods; and so the final freedom to ravage the earth of its resources. Together it has been these forms of freedom, capacities of man's creative intellect and will, that have, in creating and abusing technology, generated the problem, a problem which ironically only these same capacities of "spirit," namely, man's intelligence and his moral will, can resolve.[65] The separation of history from nature is on the other hand wrong because the human freedom to use, dominate and control nature, thence to create and transform society and so to move into history, is not the freedom to escape nature or to transcend human dependence on it. To our surprise, after centuries of unconcern with nature except to use it, the ultimate problems of history in the future may well again concern our common relation to nature. That "return to nature," let us hope, will not, as in the distant past, be as a child in nature, dominated by her cycles and her strange powers; nor will it be as a thoughtless and greedy "steward" of an alien, merely material or "object" reality concerned only with potential goods for his own comfort. Possibly it may be a return to nature on a higher level, as a part, albeit the highest member, of a natural order, a member related internally and essentially to every other member in that natural order, dependent therefore on that order and on each of its members, and thus responsible for it and for them. Certainly a new historical sanity is required if our race is to continue: a sanity qualified at last by consciousness of nature's finitude, of the infinity of our own greed and anxiety, of our ultimate dependence on nature, and so of our obligations both to it and to one another in relation to it. Somehow a new level of religious consciousness, a sense of the union of nature, history and human being, is necessary if any of the three are to survive at all. We must see the world as a whole once more, that is, religiously, if we are not to die; we must see finite being as an aspect of the whole unity of being.[66]

Secondly, this prospect of nature's depletion sets, perhaps unfortunately, a stern limit to the chorus of euphoric hope for the future that both a naive technology and a too abstract theology have sounded. The phenomenal growth of technology has created a problem which in this case technology alone is powerless to resolve. As the example of the raft indicates, a future dominated by this crisis will find the moral problem of economic and political justice exacerbated rather than eased by the coming of the future. Moreover, the political and economic solutions to our problems, for example, even a socialist redistribution of wealth and of corporate ownership in a given community, will not by themselves solve *this* problem. For a community, whatever the mode of ownership of its means of production, will struggle for its own when common supplies begin to run short. Here the concept of the public good (of *our* good) can, unless made wide enough, itself become demonic. Likewise, religious grounds for political hope—"God's new" in the future—viewed as purely eschatological, extrahuman and so extrapolitical answers to the problem, seem empty theologisms at best in the face of the hard limits of natural supplies and the resultant temptations to vast sin that these limits imply.[67]

Facing our race with an apparently dour if not hopeless future of overcrowding, scarcity, want, authoritarian control and potentially more and more violent conflict, the ecological crisis in its widest extent raises the question of the meaning of history and of the future as no other issue has done. The self-destructive character of greed —or better, of concupiscence, long considered the primal form of sin—is here manifested on a global scale in the potential self-destruction of the race and of the nature that produced the race. If religion and theology are to speak a word of hope to mankind, it is to this issue that they must address themselves. But by the same token, if there are to be grounds for hope, and I believe there are, even in the face of these four—and especially the fourth—elements of menace in our future, they must be based on the forces of redemption and renewal at work in the *historical* life of man and so creative of his *social* and *political* intelligence and will. The concrete future is in actuality menace as well as promise, and our choices can be disastrously wrong and sinful. It is *this* future arising out of trends in our present, and these responses of ours arising out of our freedom, that will determine of what sort that future is. Thus we must speak of providence, the work of common grace, and the present activity of the spirit acting in our history and in our responses— as well as of God's future eschatological activity—if we would have grounds for hope in our human future. For this reason among others this book on history, politics and the future concerns itself with providence as well as with eschatology.

CHANGE, HISTORICAL EXISTENCE AND RELIGION

In this chapter our discussion of the four areas of problems and promise in our impinging future has uncovered five fundamental factors or categories involved in social change and so necessary for its comprehension: (1) cumulative changes in technology and in social forms; (2) human intentional, "political," responses to these changes to divert, direct or refashion them; (3) the symbolic structures of our "world" which maintain relative stability amid change, which are threatened by change, and which provide the ultimate basis for our creative or uncreative, conservative or radical responses to change; (4) the factor of power and with it the issues of security and well-being, a factor which interacts with the above three to render historical existence explosive and intense, and which continually raises the moral questions of justice and injustice, equality and inequality, freedom and order; and finally (5) the factor of nature and her resources upon which the existence of men and women, and of their future, depends. Insofar as these factors in historical process have been discriminated and brought into provisional conceptual unity concerning what history is, that is, what some of the elements which constitute history are, our discussion has been philosophical and gives us the basis for further intelligible talk about history and the future.[68] Also we discussed the "existential" issues raised by social change: the mood of expectation or anxiety accompanying change, the temptations and spiritual problems with which change faces us, and the moral issues of right and wrong ingredient in responsible thought and action in the face of change. Since it deals with the "meaning" of historical change, this aspect of our analysis might be called "theological," though clearly no transcendent dimension present or effective in historical life has as yet been uncovered.

It might be well, in concluding this chapter, to enlarge briefly on the theme that will concern us in the next, namely the intrinsic relation between political experience and religion, both set as we see in an inexorable and accelerating process of fundamental social change. As is clear from our analysis, the situation of being immersed in radical change in these five areas creates the context for our most basic political and economic—and so personal—issues. Shall we respond politically to each of these "futures" in terms only of our old political goals and so of our old symbols: desiring only the increased material well-being that technology can bring to us and so forfeiting our humanity; defending our rights of private property and the accumulation of individual wealth amidst a morass of poverty and urban deterioration; protecting our nation's past dominance and security in a world struggling for new forms of liberation; and finally, in the name of our own national security and standard of living, grasping and hoarding all the earth's shrinking resources to ourselves? Or will we be willing to move politically into a new future in which we are certainly less dominant, possibly less affluent and secure, with courage and with openness? Change poses life and death political questions to all of us, questions of ultimate seriousness, of ultimate danger and of ultimate possibility. The character of our inner and outer, our private and our public life, is effectively shaped by the character of the changes we undergo and of our political responses to them. As we have sought to show, the new world of our future, as possibility or as deadly menace, will depend as much on the way we respond politically as a people as it does on the silent inexorable processes of technology and social transformation. Correspondingly, the kind of private or inner life characteristic of our future will be determined by these larger historical forces and by our political actions in relation to them. Historical change and individual "existence" can, therefore, not be separated; as history reshapes our spiritual characteristics, so the stature of our spiritual life and thus of our political responses in turn shape history. Change as it moves through historical time creates, transforms, engulfs and possibly destroys both individual, personal and inner existence—ourselves as persons—and also social structures and social symbols—our society as a society. These in turn are created, shaped, maintained or lost by the creative or destructive, wise or foolhardy, interpretations, decisions and actions of men and women. Through the instrument of social change, the creative work of providence both as social constitution and as new possibility enters history. Person and community are polar and cannot be separated: the individual and the social world he or she inhabits dance *together* down the corridor of time. Our society, and through it history, and through both of them nature form our true home, giving to each of us as persons the form of our identity, our place, our role, setting before each of us the shape of our ultimate concerns, and thus presenting each with his or her task—all that we really are and will be as individuals in history. Historical destiny and personal existence, social transformation and personal ethics, are thus inextricably intertwined. It was only in a stable (or seemingly so) society that Protestantism could develop an individual Christian ethic interested only in personal vices and virtues, and a theology concerned with inner personal piety alone.

Historical change, moreover, reveals and exacerbates evils long present yet possibly hidden. By shifting the balance of power and so uncovering the oppression and injustice hidden by that stability, change brings to the surface both the decay of life and the injustice lying back of that decay. Change opens up the festering sores of history's body and lays the raw flesh bare—in our cities, in Asia, in Africa, in South America. Through the instrument of change, the divine judgment in history, a crucial aspect of God's providence, does its destructive and creative work. Correspondingly, change claims from us the political response of concern, courage and action to transform the social reality that is ours. It instigates the call to mission; it evolves and requires the symbol of the kingdom—as it always has done. And in thus impelling us to political action for the future, historical change raises critical questions about the adequacy and justice of our most fundamental social concepts, the social structure that undergirds our social world with all its values and its disvalues. Change and movement in time, therefore, relate us "christianly" to our world: to God's work in that world of constitution and of new possibility, of judgment and of liberation, of justice, peace and human authenticity. Through change the call to the kingdom is sounded, and new visions of possibility for future life are made visible. Historical change is, therefore, for us as for previous cultures, a religious phenomenon, one of the most deeply religious factors in ordinary experience. From the point of view of faith, it is the strange face of the hidden God constituting, upsetting, destroying, challenging, judging, re-creating and calling.

Our sustained—though by no means "tight"—argument throughout this book is that historical change can neither be intellectually comprehended, existentially borne, nor politically and ethically dealt with, without a theological and a Christian interpretation of it. More than any other element of our being it poses and exemplifies our existence as a question. It challenges our moral intentionality, as it does our powers of intelligent comprehension, and forces us to creative historical action, to politics. It ignites and fuels our awareness of our ultimate dependence upon God if we would understand and bear change, and if in active participation in change we would be our own authentic, historical selves. As we have seen, change represents both opportunity and possibility, terror and anxiety. It demands both creative response at the same time that it tempts to tragic sin. And we must respond, for change is not to be avoided, nor can we fail to act. Even running away is a response, though a fatal one, to our being in history.

Change in the social world around us is, then, the *way* we experience our immersion in history; it is the way history comes immediately and existentially to us. In showing the depths of this relation of social change to our being as persons—in the shape of our character, our roles, our moods, our desires, our crises, our temptations —we have thus uncovered the way we *are* as historical beings, and the absolute importance of the relation of history and the future to both our humanness and to our religious existence. Thus it cannot be questioned that as an authentic human is *historical,* deeply related intentionally and unintentionally to social changes in which he or she is immersed, so an authentic religion and a valid theology must be historical. This is no proof of the validity of the Christian gospel (though it is a help); but it surely is a warning to those interpretations of Christianity which tend to ignore the social and historical worlds of history in favor of the private world of the individual. As men and women are historical and political if they are to be human in time, so accordingly their faith (and their God) must be historical and political. In the character of their responses to historical change, the meaning or the meaninglessness, the fullness or the emptiness, of the religious existence of men and women will be manifested. We *are* what we are in time and in history; and likewise since we are historical, our religion *is* only if it qualifies creatively our responses to the promises and the menace of historical change.

Correspondingly, the ambiguity of change and of the future it presents means, as we have intimated all along, that in the long run it is impossible for men and women to ignore the final shape of this historical horizon in which they move. To be human is to be conscious of one's situation in change, of one's role and possibilities within it, and to respond to that world. Thus to be historical is to be conscious of one's immersion in social history, of one's immediate destiny, and so of one's roles and possibilities within that destiny. No one can be a human without asking questions about the future, and so questions about the character of history and its

movement into the unknown. This whole chapter has shown why. Modern intellectual life has, as we shall see, largely regarded questions of the ultimate nature of
history as "mythical," questions of the direction and goal of history as fantasies, and
both as frivolous luxuries an empirical age of inquiry and practical work can well
ignore. The evidence shows, however, that they were able to ignore the question of
the course of history—and so philosophy and theology of history—only because they
so firmly believed their own progressive view of it, namely, in the efficacy of inquiry
and technology in history. Having already answered the question of history in terms
of what they thought was obvious, they regarded any further pressing of that
question as superfluous and gratuitous. Contemporary history has shown that their
ultimate faith in technology was not only a false faith but also a demonic one. In
destroying that faith it has posed again with the utmost urgency the perennial
question of the meaning of human life within the temporal process that it inhabits.[69]
Once again, history has a religious dimension for those who exist within it: it not
only shapes them, sets before them issues of ultimate concern, faces them with deep
anxiety, tempts them to sin, and calls forth their courage, creativity and compassion.
It also poses for them the deepest of reflective issues concerning human existence
in time, the form of history's events, and the shape of the ultimate horizon of
temporal being. On the most existential level it calls for a philosophy or a theology
of history.

2

ULTIMACY IN HISTORICAL
AND POLITICAL EXPERIENCE

We are, whether we will or no, driven in our day to a consciousness of history. Rumblings of fundamental change and even of revolution are heard on our every horizon. The hungry and oppressed in lands beyond our borders, the hungry and oppressed within our own soulless cities, feel the injustice of our culture's life as we do not, and call for its radical transformation if not for its overthrow. History, not our psyches, is our current problem, and the unknown shape of our future our burning concern.

I do not speak here necessarily of what we or youth are in fact consciously concerned with. A lack of interest in historical change will not make it go away. Conceivably, as one reaction, men and women stopped speaking of the weather as the last Ice Age descended. I speak of the social facts of our time, all of which, as we noted in the last chapter, point to radical change. This new world we must seek to understand if we are to live creatively within it, and especially if we are to provide it with relevant social thought, theology, preaching or leadership. In particular this means for theology that its consciousness must be historical and therefore political. For politics is the handle with which communities attempt to grasp and to direct historical change. History becomes an overwhelming fate for those who seek neither to understand nor creatively to direct it.

The problem of history is by no means a new focus for twentieth-century theology. The theological liberalism of the last century was, as we shall subsequently see, grounded on a particular and a very positive view of historical development. And for the neo-orthodox theology of the first half of this century, at least English and American "neo-orthodoxy," the question of history and its meaning continued quite to dominate theology[1]—until, that is, existentialism, psychoanalysis, and the secluded community of the church or cell group removed it. That theological interest in history in the 1930s and 1940s, however, was different and not so radical as is our present one. Its primary concern was the Fascist and Stalinist threats to the values of democratic or Western culture, and men and women wondered what meaning history could have if Western culture's obvious "developments" in science, knowledge and technology could have produced these sorts of demonic social orders. The present concern is quite different. It is our own Western culture that now appears demonic, stale and dying, and not from external threat but from inward loss of creativity, from injustice and from aesthetic and moral decay. Thus our age speaks not of "defense" but of "revolution."[2] This different experience of historical chaos, the one threatening from without and the other from within, helps illumine not only the "generation gap" between World War II fathers and Viet Nam and Kent State youth. It also clarifies the differences between neo-orthodox views of history and those of contemporary eschatological radicalism, the theologies of liberation.[3]

In any case, we find ourselves now trying to talk theologically about history and its changes, and I suspect that for all of us this task is difficult. Part of the problem is that theologians and churchmen and women also are in many ways "secular" in their orientation, probably as much toward changes in society and in history as toward nature and its changes.[4] Most of them, when they are honest, tend to understand and to analyze contemporary politics and the prospects for the social future in thoroughly humanistic or secular terms. Thus we are not sure why it is necessary or even possible to deal with a changing history or the impinging future *theologically.* What are the grounds, in the subject matter of historical change and of political action themselves, that call for religious response and so for theological comprehension? We know we may wish to be "revolutionary," or at least politically active in response to social problems—but why be theological, or even peculiarly Christian, about them? In this chapter I shall try to answer part of that question by showing that any examination of our historical, and especially our political, experience, reveals a dimension of ultimacy in that experience that must be understood, illumined and dealt with in terms of religious symbols. Otherwise the real horizon of historical experience remains unclarified and so unknown, the deeper terrors of history and of political life unexpressed and so unconquered, and the necessary and creative grounds for hope and for constructive action in historical passage unknown and so uncelebrated.

ONTOLOGICAL ELEMENTS OF HISTORICAL PROCESS

History is the history of communities or groups.[5] They, not individual men and women, are the subjects of historical life, and it is *their* history that is here our primary concern.[6] Individuals, to be sure, are the sole creaturely agents in historical action.[7] But the actions of individuals become *historical,* achieve effectiveness and significance on the plain of historical life, only insofar as they are received by, affect and so mold the life of communities.[8] This is self-evidently true for men and women with political or economic abilities and powers; it is also true for other forms of creative cultural activity. No scientific discovery, new form of artistic, philosophical, literary or religious view becomes important or relevant to historical change unless it is appropriated by and forms the life and mind of a community, and is embodied there socially.

To put the same point another way, human being is social being, and through its social context it becomes historical being. The personness, its shape and form, and so even the uniqueness of an individual come to be in, and are formed and upheld by, the surrounding community.[9] Correspondingly, his or her actions—and so the creative work and objective meaning of each individual's life—issue forth in communal labor and influence, whether it be the wide communities of nation and city, the small communities of town and family, or the esoteric circles who read professional monographs. Creative freedom, the inner spiritual existence of men and women, objectifies itself in communal work, in the creation and recreation of things, organizations and activities relevant to some community's life. Thus we are individual persons in community, hence in society, and, as Pannenberg argues this point,[10] hence within the whole stream of history. Our relation to history is *through* the communities in which we participate; as we saw in the last chapter, we each experience history immediately and directly ("existentially") through the social changes in which we participate as members of our communities.

This deep, ontological interaction of individual and community—veritably a historical doctrine of internal relations—means first of all that it is possible, even without the ontological confusion of calling communities "real entities," to speak of "social experience" and not just of "private experience." For in speaking of experience, of what we perceive and feel as individual entities, we include much more than what is often called private experience or individual experience. Of course in some sense, all experience, even political experience, is both private and individual, i.e., the experience of someone. Few even among the idealists or the sociologists have argued that society as a whole has experience or "acts" as an experiencing and effective "entity."[11] But all private experience is itself social and historical, cultural in character; the sharp division between inner experience and objective social reality is on three counts a false division.

1. The *ways* we experience our world even on the most individual level are determined for us socially, i.e., by the forms of experiencing and interpreting that experience which are characteristic of our society. This social influence on individual experience is utterly foundational, beginning with the structuring of experience through language and the categories of being, action and value enshrined in language. The sense of reality, of value and of validity by which every individual lives is given him or her by their social environment—and this influence is never lost however creative the individual may later be.

2. A great deal of what we experience individually during the course of our life is experienced by us *because* we are members of a certain group. It is felt by us because of our internal relations with the society in which we live. Thus is each individual given status, identity and role by the structured forms of his or her society, and every change in that social structure reverberates in the internal, personal existence of each individual.[12] Every victory or blessing of our group, every defeat or woe, is, moreover, felt by each member as his or her own experience. Thus can these shared experiences legitimately be called "social experience," experience enjoyed by individuals *as* members of a given society.

3. Finally, much of what we call the objective social world, a given social order, is a "world" formed by human consciousness and intentionality. This social "world" is a system of meanings, values, norms and expectations reflective of a view of nature, of community, and of men and women in their social roles, that is shared by the individual consciousnesses of all the members of that society.[13] Thus the internal relations of individual to society run both ways: the content and tone of the individual's experience is continually qualified and shaped by the structure and by the shared experiences of the group, and the social reality in which he or she lives is constituted by the shared consciousnesses of that society's individuals. It is this sort of experience of ourselves as participating members of an historic community, and of groups as projected meanings of individual consciousnesses, about which I wish in this chapter to speak.

Further, this ontological interaction of individual with social communities means that there is a correlation between the modes of existence: of being, activity and effectiveness, of substance and of causality, between individual persons and social communities. This correlation means in turn that the life of groups and so their history exhibit the same fundamental categorical structure as do the lives and the histories of individual persons, though, of course, with some significant differences which shall be noted.[14] Overlooking the *human* character of communities and their history is the basic error of all mechanistic or deterministic theories of history, all "natural histories" of history, based on some concept of natural law or on some analogy of natural growth and decay.[15] Since ontologically the only finite "substances" or "entities" in historical being are human persons,[16] we can understand the life of groups only if we apply to them in some analogical form the modes of understanding appropriate to personal existence. Hence the methods of history provide a more helpful empirical base for a philosophical understanding of the nature of historical change and the categories appropriate to it than do those of the social sciences. The reason for this preference is ontological, namely that the "objects" of the inquiries of the social sciences are the ontologically more abstract institutions and social systems (nexūs) within which concrete men and women, the real and active "entities" in history, live and act; in isolating for its study social systems devoid of individual actors, social science not only abstracts away from contingency and deviance, it also abstracts away from concrete reality.[17] On the other hand, as in individual life so in social existence, a great deal is determined by unconscious processes or trends concomitant with and resulting from human actions —and so the social sciences are a necessary supplement to historical inquiry.[18] In either case, however, the analogy with the understanding of man himself is basic to and determinative for the understanding of men and women as social beings in time.[19]

It is also, as Tillich points out,[20] important to note that the correlation between individual and community creates at best only an *analogy* between individual and group that allows for and emphasizes real differences as well as similarities at certain significant points. If, as we are arguing, the analogy is important in recognizing and understanding the *human* character of groups and so of historical passage, the differences are equally important for both reflection and for political praxis. Because of the internal relations of an individual to his or her society, the group helps to "create," fashion, sustain the individual; thus it can be likened to an "organism" with organic parts, the life, identity and function of which parts are totally dependent on the larger organism. But this analogy, while as we have argued, significant for understanding groups, is *only* an analogy. The individual is also independent of its group in many important aspects; to be totally dependent, as an organ is on its larger organism, is to sacrifice its critical and creative individuality. Thus the view that society is an organism represents a conservative ideology dangerous to both individual and community. Individual and community are *interdependent* in their interrelationship; individuals are both independent and dependent in relation to society; and the strength and health of the community depends as much upon their realization of that independence of its individuals as it does on their realization of their dependence. Society is ontologically not a person; at best it is like the persons who in their communal internal relations alone give to society reality, power and meaning. It is, then, both an ontological and a political error to speak of society as an organism possessing a "mind," "will," in effect a "self," a self that creates the selves that make it up and that functions for and in their name. Each group must, as we have noted, have some effective center, namely the center established by government through political action. But that center is a political and not a biological or psychological center; that is, it is always one ruling group within the wider community, a relatively independent *part* of the community, not the biological or psychological center of the community as a whole. It represents, therefore, its own concerns as much or more than it does the concerns of the entire community. The political center of any society or any class, therefore, is not at all "the real self" or "the real conscience" of the members of their society, and thus is it capable, as no organism's principle of unity is capable, of following and enacting its own special interests even against the interests of the community as a whole. Tyranny, revolution and anarchy are *political* problems, not biological ones—except again by analogy. The analogy of human being and community is, therefore, an analogy and not an identity, important for understanding groups insofar as they are communities of persons, but reflectively false and politically dangerous if taken literally. History is not the story of groups as ontic entities but of individuals *in* communities. Now let us return to this analogy to see its fruitfulness in understanding history.

We have already uncovered in the last chapter several factors or elements in historical social being that correlate with analogous factors in individual human being: (1) a "given" that is the deposit of the continuities and cumulative changes of the past and which must be now dealt with; (2) the necessity of intentional response to that given in comprehension, judgment, decision and action; thus the primacy of politics as the arena in which communal judgments, decisions and actions are achieved and enacted; (3) the role of inherited symbols in both the processes of comprehension and of decision; (4) the factor of power, of security, of well-being and of control; (5) and the omnipresent dependence on nature. Now let us proceed to outline other elements important to the comprehension of communal histories where traits analogous to the characteristic structures of individual human existence also appear.

First of all, and most important, there is on the part of the group (or of individuals as members of the group) a measure of self-awareness, and insofar, of self-transcendence, a sense of its own individual being as a group, of its own unique qualities, history and destiny. Such an awareness grows in intensity—as it does in individuals —in situations of conflict or of danger when the existence of the group is threatened. It is, however, present implicitly throughout the group's life, expressed powerfully in the numerous rituals, symbols and myths essential to the community's being. As we noted, a group is in a sense the shared consciousness of itself, of its structures, norms, expectancies and goals; in turn this common shared consciousness, defining the group and its individuals alike, is enshrined in its shared "stories" about itself in ritual and myth. The symbolic structure constitutive of the group, the being of the group among other groups, and its self-awareness of itself as a being in history are all three, therefore, intimately related. Many important consequences follow from this: (1) As essentially related to that fundamental social symbolic structure, religion is inevitably correlated with both community and politics, with both the permanent being of the group and its capacity to act. Rulership and power are religious matters—as the history of tribes and nations surely shows.[21] (2) No group can easily exist over time or maintain a creative self-awareness without a fundamental symbolic structure expressing its view of its being and role in history. (3) Since the group exists in a wider history and is self-aware of itself as so existing, it structures its sense of its own identity in terms of its understanding of its role in wider history. Consequently its symbolic structures quickly move to encompass not only the grounds of its own political life, but also history as a whole, i.e., to include explicitly religious elements and so to entail implicit "theologies" or at least "philosophies" of history. We shall enlarge on these points later in the chapter.

Meanwhile, through this common awareness of its own being, structured by its most important symbols, each group can bring to consciousness its immediate problems, its ways of dealing with problems, and its needs and possibilities for the immediate future; and through self-awareness each group comes to feel its relatedness to, and relativity in, the community of other groups. Such self-awareness or sense of identity in community, in relation to its own passage in time and in relation to other groups in space, is the sole ground for common political action, for concerted action of the group as a group.[22] As persons become themselves and are enabled to act authentically in relation both to themselves over time (memory), in relation to a community of other persons in space, and in relation to possible projects for their future, so a group is aware of its identity, its autonomy and its relativity in its memory of its own past, in its consciousness of the wider community of other groups, and in its awareness of its role and its possibilities in the impinging future. Out of this awareness of itself a community senses the threats to its life, its possibilities for greater power and life, its moral obligations (such as they are), and its own unique strengths, weaknesses, purposes and role. Thus does it speak of its "way of life" and its "destiny"; through self-awareness a group becomes *historical* and so *political.* Through its individual members the group can and does feel its relation to wider history and so can be aware of its own ultimate place and significance in that history, or, alternatively, of its own insignificance or possible mortality there—most crucial capacities of self-transcendence for its political existence.

In turn, time in group experience becomes a wider time than *my* past or future in personal memory and expectation. It is the time of the family, the tribe, the city, the nation, the wider culture or, possibly, of all of history. The past history of that community enshrined in group memory is felt to be as relevant to me as is my own personal history, and the common future of my group is for political and historical life *my* future. Space likewise is no longer merely the space of my home and street; it is by the group *felt* to be the whole space of the historical community in which we exist in relation to the spaces of other groups. National borders are felt as bounding *our* space with the same intensity as the home fence is felt to bound *my* space. Individuals live in their awareness and their identity within the community as participating members of it.

Correspondingly, communities live, analogously to individuals, with the powers of self-understanding, awareness of their own identity, their vocation, their destiny, their time, their space—and their potential death. Thus the bearers of history, its groups, participate and live from the whole range of dimensions of human existence: the physical and organic being of men and women expressed through the issues relevant to the group's political and economic security; the practical genius of men and women creative of technologies and organizations expressed in the economic and social structures of the group; the moral goals, ideals and purposes of people expressed in the common social symbols of the group; and the self-transcendence of people expressed in the group's sense of its own relation to time, to change, to the future, and to possible mortality or possible glory in that future—altogether forming its crucial sense of itself, its identity, its value and its significance as a mode of historical being in the human story as a whole, its "way of life."[23]

Crucial to the understanding of history is, of course, the discussion of historical causality, i.e., the factors in temporal social process, whatever they may be, that bring events about. We shall return to this important topic frequently. Suffice it here to make the basic point that since communities are human beings in time and in relation to each other, and since all that happens in social change is therefore ultimately what *people* do, historical causation reflects the same multiplicity and complexity of *kinds* of factors that is characteristic of individual human action.[24] Thus first of all, human intentions and motives—what Alfred Schutz calls "in order to" motives, projective actions that have a goal—are factors in the coming to be of an historical event. The philosopher of history R. G. Collingwood made this element within historical causality, namely, thoughts or intentions embodied in actions, the *sole* object of historical inquiry, the only relevant causes in historical events.[25] While most others concerned with this problem qualify this extremely idealistic view of historical causation sharply in various ways, few disagree that historical events are massively influenced by the "free" judgments, decisions and consequent actions of people.[26] It is an optical illusion, a subversion through massive numbers, to think that while individuals may act "freely," as centered beings responsible for what they do, groups of people do not; no social scientist believes this about himself or his community of social scientists—at least about the grounds for holding his or her own theory—but he or she can easily hold it about other large groups of people.[27]

At best so-called determinating factors provide conditions *for* and so set limits *to* human actions.[28] Human beings, and so their groups as well, for example, are in truth driven by hunger and by insecurity, but how and how far they are so driven is never determined finally by the conditions. What humans in fact *do*, which alone is causative of historical events, is determined only within the mysterious interaction of these given limits and conditions with their own needs, desires, intelligent judgments, intentions, norms, goals and resulting decisions. Thus there are always alternatives in history; and events are historical in that until they happen, they *need* not have occurred.[29] All here is finally contingent. Put another way, nothing is a *cause* in history unless it evokes a human response. And no situation merely in itself is determinative; only the way people "take" it, i.e., the way they understand it, interpret its meaning for themselves and their future, and so deal with it.[30] Thus are modes of interpretation (social symbol systems, norms and goals), desires, motives, purposes, intelligence and comprehension, and finally the mystery of decision and of enaction, all significant, not to say basic, factors in historical events. These "inner" factors alone mediate into event the effects of what might seem in retrospect to be necessary trends and conditions. As in individual existence, the fundamental ontological structure for groups and so for historical passage is the polarity of destiny and freedom, the inherited "given" from the past on the one hand, and the present human response in the light of possibilities for the future on the other.

As our discussion has made plain, besides the factor of human intentionality or freedom, namely, comprehension, judgment, decision and enaction, there are also unintended and impersonal factors at work in any historical situation. These are, I believe, composed of four quite different sorts of processes, which form the "given" and thus set the limits and pose the conditions for human response. (1) First there is the material environment, both natural and social, and the natural resources and technical tools of the society. Changes in this material environment will of course create important historical effects and thus are important conditions of historical events. (2) Secondly, there are habitual modes of relationship and of behavior established in the social system governed by the symbolic "social world" participated in by all the members. This symbolic world structuring the social order in a qualified sense predetermines or better limits the modes of individual and corporate behavior in a society. (3) There are, then, the slow, unintended changes (for example, the growth of industrialism or the spread of rationalization) within this interlocking system of natural resources, tools, modes of behavior and social symbolic system, changes which when their effects become visible become "causes" or better, "conditions," in that they necessarily evoke new responses in terms of patterns of behavior and above all new corporate political responses. (4) Finally, there is the contingent (unplanned and unnecessary) coming together of a multiplicity of innumerable factors into a new constellation of conditions. This new constellation of factors is drawn from all four of the above in various sorts of mixture, and also from present (or radically recent) responses of other persons or other groups to these same or other conditions. All of these factors together make up the unexpected, unplanned constellation of the present. This present, this "given" arising, seemingly, out of all the infinity of past actuality, includes in itself both traditional continuities and unexpected changes, both unplanned and planned acts. Thus despite its "necessity" for us, its unavoidable and unremovable character, in itself it has no necessity, no all-determining reason for the strange character it possesses. This given, contingent in itself, but necessary for us, sets the stage for our response, and is thus the ground and limit for our freedom. This given we are here calling "destiny"; it is one pole, we are arguing, of the basic ontological structure of history and of temporal being and so a most significant factor in our awareness of history.

Meanwhile, let us note how primordial and yet how important this factor of destiny is. We do not create these conditions; they are given to us; we are, as Heidegger says, "thrown" into them.[31] All that we are and so all we can do arise out of this given as our source and matrix. Consequently, we cannot overreach the real limits these conditions set, both in our imaginative powers of projection of a new course, or in our powers to remove or eradicate this given. It is with *this,* and with nothing else, that our own being in time begins. It is with these conditions therefore that we must work in history, and which all political action must honor. Thus does the given determine in large part, sometimes more, sometimes less, what we are able to do and so what history becomes. Because the possibilities of the future are bounded by the realities of the given in the present, creative politics is rooted in the present situation with which enaction, reaching into the future, begins. Insofar as it is "historical," therefore, the new cannot come entirely from the future any more than it can be entirely the product of the past. The new in historical action arises out of the union of destiny with freedom, of given actuality with relevant possibility. To understand events or history either in terms solely of determining continuities from the past, of destiny, or solely in terms of possibilities in the future, is an error. History is a polarity of destiny and freedom, of actuality and possibility —and it must be interpreted theologically in accord with this its ontological structure.

Because of these elements of the unintended given and their effects, events in history seem to happen, as Hegel put it, "over our heads" and "behind our backs," unplanned either in Washington, Moscow or Peking—or even on Wall Street. All our purposes can do is at the most to direct, divert, slow down, accelerate or give a new push to the march of these unplanned processes and changes which set the stage for our action.[32] As I noted, many speculative philosophers of history, such as Hegel, Spengler and Marx (if he may be placed there), and most contemporary social scientists, have emphasized these seemingly overwhelming unintended factors in historical change as the real explanation of historical process. I have argued that while destiny is crucial, its necessitating power is always qualified by the need for human response. Only out of the union of these two does an historical event arise —for all these factors are mediated into event only by what men and women in fact do.[33]

If we grant these two categorial elements of historical movement, the given and our intentional response to it, it is clear that politics is essential to the life of history. Through its political activity, a group organizes its various powers into a unity capable of "government" and so achieves a centered organ of judgment, decision and action, a power over all the other powers in the community. It is through this unified center created politically, therefore, that the self-awareness of the group in the flux of contingent events in time is embodied, and it is here that its will for itself, its power of self-creation for its immediate future—its *humanity*—is brought to realization and enacted. In political life, in joint action for the future, the group as a group seeks to deal with the given of each new present, and so to direct its own destiny into its future. The freedom of mankind in history that is polar to destiny, and that makes history "history" and not merely determined occurrence, is incarnated in the corporate action of each community, i.e., in its political life. Politics is the category within which each group affirms its freedom and its responsibility for itself, deals with its destiny and enacts its will, as best it can, for its own future; it is the corporate realm of decision and responsibility essential to human "existence" in time. Politics is, as noted, correlated with the category of "public good." Thus communal good is basic, and not antithetical, to human freedom in *history*. When a society is constituted solely by considerations of individual good, by the pursuit of private economic gain alone, then the meaning both of the "political" and of the "public" or "common good" evaporates; and with their disappearance the ability of the community to direct in part its own life in time—its freedom in historical passage—recedes to nothingness. Thus in the political realm the central concerns are the unity and the security of the group, both necessary for its continuing being and for the power, authority and capacity to make the basic decisions relevant to its existence in the future, to its drive beyond its negative destiny in the present toward a more secure and more creative communal state in the future.

As the instrument of communal unity and so of political decision in the movement of time, government occupies a role in all communities very close both to the being and to the historicity of the community, to its sense of its own power to be and to control through decision its own destiny. Thus does government represent the central form of power in all communal life. Through its government each community sustains, fosters and directs its own being and in doing so rises to the level of freedom and responsible enactment of its own life for the future. This is the ontological basis for the puzzling fact that the organs of government and the persons associated with them always participate in ultimacy and sacrality. For rulers share the sacred attributes of both being and freedom; they are media to the life of history of permanence and stability and of decisive power for the future, conquerors and shapers of time.[34] Economic activity and economic organization are of course also essential for many of the same reasons, namely, sustenance in the present and in the future. But even those who regard economic activity as primal both for the being of the community and for the future quality of its life know they must act politically and through the government if they would defend the old or effect the new in economic affairs. Since it is in political life that a group achieves freedom for the future, i.e., becomes human and historical, politics has a sacrality that the more "secular" realms of economics have never achieved.

Central as they are, however, politics and economics are not all there are in a community's common life and its corporate drive into the future. As with individual men and women, so with communities, cultural life forms a whole, expressing fundamental social meanings and values, ideas and goals in its significant symbols. This system of symbolic meanings is incarnated throughout the community's life: not only in its reflective thought, its creative arts, its social institutions, its courts and legislatures, but also in the lowliest of its vocations and its most private and individual patterns of behavior.[35] Thus each community participates in history and interacts with other groups in expansion, defense or alliance not only in terms of its political and economic power but also in terms of the total "way of life" which its common life represents.

Sacral Dimensions of Historical Being

Most of the above and a good deal of our analysis in the first chapter would be seconded, as we have seen in our notes, by many commentators on social history, though some might emphasize more the collective or the individualistic, the determined or the intended, the materialist or the "spiritual" poles of our description. Our question is: Is there anything relevant to religion or to theological reflection here? Why, in order to understand the processes and meaning of change in history so described, do we need theological as well as the natural and human categories we have already used? Why is not a secular or humanistic understanding of history and of politics sufficient to elucidate our experience of historical life?

The fundamental reason such further, theological thematization is necessary is, as I shall now try to show, that our historical horizon as we experience it in communal life is not as "secular" as our age (and the analysis to date) has supposed. Ingredient in our experience of history and of politics is a dimension of ultimacy and of sacrality. This dimension of ultimacy, I believe, provides the real environment within which human beings live in historical experience, calling there as in individual experience for religious symbols if that horizon is to be comprehended and creatively dealt with.[36] The ontological structure of history, therefore, if this analysis be correct, includes not only the polarity of destiny and freedom constitutive of finite being in time, but also a transcendent ground of that destiny and that freedom, uniting actuality and possibility and giving to the experience of both destiny and possibility the dimension of ultimacy which we are here seeking to uncover. Where, then, in concrete political experience, in our communal experience of historical passage into the future and our communal (i.e., political) efforts to direct, control or influence that social passage, does the dimension of ultimacy, this transcendent dimension to our experience of destiny and freedom in history, appear for us (as well as for Durkheim) and so require symbolic thematization of a religious or a theological sort?

Humans are historical beings, beings in temporal passage through and through. Thus we experience our own passage into the future, and that of our social world —and we experience the two together—on every level of our complex being, that is, respectively, with regard to our being, our activity, our thinking and our valuing. On each one of these levels, in our communal as in our individual experience, a dimension of ultimacy and of sacrality appears and is central to that social experience.

POLITICS AND BEING

We experience as individuals the deepest ontological level of our life in our awareness of our own reality, our existence. This experience is an awareness from within of our being, of its vitality and its powers.[37] Even when, as with our health, we are not consciously aware of this gift of being—when we are "forgetful of our own being"—it is there as the ground of our most important self-affirmation. Perhaps the most fundamental level of neurosis is the lack of this awareness of one's own being or reality, a lack which results in the sense that I alone am weightless, substanceless, and so totally vulnerable, passive, weak (and persecuted) in a world of weighty, self-directing and powerful other people. Correspondingly, the joy in this awareness of our being and activity, of our reality and our powers, is the deepest of our joys, the basis of most of our experiencing of values, of "goods" in life and of the goodness of life.

This awareness of our being, and the joy and the vitality that accompany it, may not be "conscious," i.e., an object of conscious awareness or reflection. But whether we are conscious of it or not, it is *felt*. It is an apprehended inner tone to our own existence, an awareness that we exist, are real, and possess energy and vitality; it is one that emanates outward to others, who also feel it, as self-affirmation, a sense of reality and identity, and so of power, confidence and vitality. No persons, one may hazard, can be creative, morally, culturally or politically, who are not blessed with this fundamental self-affirmation and joy or exuberance in being, this sense of the reality of their own being, and so this basic vitality and activity. It is the ground of all creative self-determination, independence and originality of spirit, of physical, moral and intellectual courage, and of the capacity genuinely to love another person. Alienation from self at *this* level only cripples our powers of life for ourselves, in relation to others, and surely in all political activity—as the great political figures, both conservative and revolutionary, amply illustrate.[38] But we also can experience both in felt awareness and in explicit consciousness the potential negation of this vitality of our being. We can experience our own radical contingency, that we may *not* be at all. And as the joy in our being is the most fundamental of our joys, so the anxiety about our being or our not-being is the most fundamental of our anxieties[39]—and of immense political importance.

The reason this experience is politically important is that we *are*, and continue to be, communally. Thus not only are we in the modality of our personal identity and self-affirmation social beings formed by our community; even more our identity and security, our being and its continuance, are socially secured through the power and the strength, the "being" of the community to which we belong, and through our participation in that being. As a direct result of this correlation of individual security and communal security, quite naturally, in fact without any conscious thought about it, humans "work" in and for their communities. Thus a great deal of the imaginative, rational and practical creativity of human existence has understandably gone into the creation of common social and cultural structures, ways of organizing effectively the community's economic and political life through which the community can protect, sustain and increase its being.[40] We do exist through our communities, and so through the political and economic ways of life which they embody. Those of us who are tempted to scorn the activities that create and maintain these structures of economic and political order—and so the being and existence of the community—merely show that we have never ourselves been hungry or faced an anarchical situation. To be and to continue to be is good, and thus are these social structures crucial to all human life as human. Nevertheless our anxieties about our being and its continuance can become demonic; and this concern for our being generates the peculiar intensity of political and economic conflict, as well as the dominance of these areas over other values of life.

As a consequence of this social grounding of our individual security, our own personal self-affirmation is strangely and frighteningly strengthened when the community in which we participate, our nation, race or class, waxes strong and seems secure. Correspondingly, a vast anxiety appears among the individual members of a group when their community is threatened; with that threat their own security is endangered. Perhaps the deepest level of our political experience, generating its most significant passions, is this experience of the *contingency* of the social group, with its common way of life, that secures us. Frightening indeed is the awareness that the group on which we depend—in contemporary history, this will domestically be a class or a race, internationally a nation—is *itself* historical, that it too is subject to changes in history, that it too is relative, that it too can weaken and even die—and so be subject to fate. Our discussion of power in the last chapter revealed how crucial the power of a given group is to every member of that community. Now we have found the reason: on the power of the group, its power to be, to continue to be and to direct its own future, its power to escape subjection to fate, depends the power to be of each member. Thus is politics, the joint action of a group for its own security and well-being, a matter of the deepest level of ultimate concern for each of its members.

In understanding politics and historical experience in the light of the question of our being and our not-being, the destiny we have uncovered in our analysis as polar to freedom must be distinguished phenomenologically from fate.[41] Put more accurately, the destiny which is polar to freedom in temporal passage can *become* fate in an estranged history. As freedom becomes sin in human experience, so destiny becomes fate in historical experience. It is this distinction, this "fall" of destiny into fate that we here wish to explicate phenomenologically. Only with this category can political experience be understood.

Destiny as we have used the word points to one aspect of the fundamental ontological structure of temporal being, to the presence in historical experience of a "given" in personal and especially in social life. On the one hand, this given from the immediate past includes the constellation of trends, social structures, past actions of ourselves, and contemporary or recent actions of others that make up our "situation," what is given to us in this moment to deal with. On the other hand, it includes the identity, character, powers, abilities, goals and norms of our own past self or community which we in the present inherit as "ourselves." Destiny refers to the entire inheritence of this moment from its immediate past; it is therefore referent *both* to the "world" with which we have to deal *and* to the "self" formed by the past which deals with that world. In a temporalistic account of being, destiny temporalizes the polarity of self and world into an inheritance to be balanced by present freedom; union of the two creates the "event" in the present which then becomes "world" and "self," or destiny, for the next present, for the future. Because process and freedom are basic ontologically, the primary ontological structure is for us constituted by destiny and freedom, actuality and possibility, not by world and self.[42]

Destiny in its essential character is a given which, to be sure, we cannot remove even if we would. It is there; it was in part formed by us or by our predecessors, and it has certainly been formative of us. Nevertheless, when we call it destiny we refer to it as a given on which our present freedom, our judgment, decisions and actions, can work and so in some measure shape and control toward our own ends; though of course never as completely as we might wish.[43]

As malleable to freedom, this destiny in turn becomes *fate* for us when we experience the given and the ongoing changes it represents as overwhelming and oppressive, as destructive of our powers and so of our freedom. Then the situation into which we are "thrown" appears as one which our judgments, decisions and actions cannot at all shape, as that over which we have no control. Those who are conquered or enslaved, those who are oppressed or exploited, those who are on the lower ranks of a class or a class structure, those who are weak and totally dependent, and those who are lost in a social mass of "others," experience no freedom to shape their life; they experience destiny as fate. Here we have no freedom, no power of relevant projection or enaction of possibilities, and so here the given is experienced as the ultimate principle of our helplessness, vulnerability and so of our non-being. As a given which our freedom and intentions cannot in any way divert or determine, and so as a given essentially alien to our potentialities and aims, fate is that in our experience of history which is the ultimate threat to our personal and communal being in the future. Destiny on the other hand is the historical materials out of the immediate past on which our creative powers of being can work for our future. The connection between social and political history—social structures and their changes —and "existence" is made in the relation between destiny and fate on the one hand and the possibilities of our freedom on the other. Although it is, moreover, part of essential finitude to possess a destiny, the capacity to determine in part the given, it is not a possibility for finitude, however "free," to be free of destiny entirely. Correspondingly, it is the promise of finitude as "good"—and this is in large part what that category implies vis-à-vis history—that everything finite can be freed from fate.

It is, moreover, evident that the central aim of politics and of most historical activity is to achieve freedom from fate, to restore or retain our "lot" as destiny. No understanding of the concern of political activity for power, and so the ultimate seriousness and the potential fanaticism of politics, is possible unless we understand politics at this deep ontological level: concerned in its feeling tones and its most fundamental drives with the issues of the possibility of control or of ultimate helplessness, of destiny as opposed to fate, and so with the issue of our being and our non-being in the impinging future. For example, the patriot becomes a blind and cruel patriot in a given political situation because his own individual security and autonomy in a changing historical world are bound up with the power and security of the nation he defends. When his nation is strong, he knows he *is* more, he is bigger and safer in history, more able to deal with the given and so with all future threats. And when because of its strength his nation is autonomous, apparent master of its own destiny, he too feels relative freedom and autonomy on the plane of history and in the face of its changes. Then as an individual he participates in and profits from the apparent control of destiny through the power the group gives its members.[44] Correspondingly, he is weaker and more anxious when through internal disunity or outward weakness his nation seems incapable of exerting that control, when the destiny of his nation threatens to become fate. Politically, there- fore, he smothers internal dissent and piles up weapons because of his deep fear of becoming fated. His overwhelming interest or concern for his own being as it is supported by the power of his national group is the force that drives him to act as a member of that group in the grasping, proud, cruel and vindictive ways to which national groups are prone. To understand the ultimate concern and so the fanaticism latent in patriotism we must understand the deep sense of being and of autonomy latent in national strength and the deep fear of fate implicit in national weakness.

Thus also are privileged classes fanatical and cruel in defense of *their* order, because they are rendered secure and protected by that order; it gives them a means of freedom and control in relation to their economic and political future, and thus makes fate for them into destiny. And they will use every available form of power to defend that order that protects them and gives them autonomy in the face of change and its terrors. Also the most basic drive or élan of oppressed groups, dispossessed of political or economic power—though perhaps not of the intellectuals who support them—is for the security they have never enjoyed. Revolutionary movements are directed to the acquisition of power, power over what has been for them only fate, namely, the inexorable "given" that each moment brings. What they seek is the sense of freedom and autonomy in history which such power brings with it, freedom to exorcise fate and so to deal with their own destiny.

Hobbes and Marx were right: the vital ground of politics is neither primarily intellectual nor moral but is *interest,* the overriding interest in security, in being, in the power and so the autonomy through one's group to control change. Political action seeks basically to evade fate, to transform the given in all historical life into a destiny which our freedom can in some measure control and direct. Actual history is by no means comprehensible only in terms of its ontological structure. For it is not necessarily compounded solely of destiny and freedom. It can become fate and the loss of freedom. Thus the creation of an open history is a political and historical achievement, and the preservation of it a continuing political task. Politics, therefore, seeks to open history, to establish the effectiveness—if not the rule—of our own freedom; to maintain history as destiny and to banish history as fate. Social justice, moreover, is a genuine moral concern because material security, the social power that accrues to security, and the sense of reality and self-determination that come from security and power, are essential needs of human beings. Each is based on a person's deepest interest and need to continue in being, and, as an autonomous, self-directing *human* being, to have some measure of control of its own movement into the future. Consequently, when in any society power and security are radically unequal, there is a manifest injustice, a moral wrong, a deep deprivation of a central facet of humanity, that some men and women are subjected to fate, helpless before the given and unfree to shape their own future, while others are free in some measure to direct their own destiny. No human can become fully human, self-creative and self-determining, if he or she is ultimately insecure and finally helpless.[45] Nor can they feel human, with some measure of autonomy, dignity and responsibility, if they are aware of this their ultimate helplessness. They are then, and they feel themselves to be, "things" or "objects" in time, because all the events that determine their life are fated. Like sin and death, fate has been and is one of the major enemies of human self-realization. It represents the experience of history as demonic, as an ultimate threat to all we are and hope to be. To be fated is to be stripped of one's humanity, and so anxiety about being fated is a fundamental human anxiety—and central to all politics.

We all experience the future politically under the threat of fate, the menace that the future may hold for us only ultimate vulnerability and helplessness. More than anything else each group fears a future in which the forces of history or of other powers totally control the events in which each participates, in which it has neither destiny nor freedom. Each group fears the situation of finding itself powerless, unable to guarantee its continuing being; above all, it fears fate. As we saw, the future *can* be a menace. The new that betokens fate as well as the new that is creative possibility come to us from the future. Political action as centered communal action for the future is fundamentally directed against fate, at gaining or keeping control over the forces that shape our security and so at giving or keeping *self-direction* in time. Thus again, unless a government be radically ineffective or radically unjust (and then it is barely able to survive), does government in every situation manifest a mysterious aura of majesty, of sacral power and glory. This is not merely because governments *are* just, for most in fact are not. The majesty of government, we have suggested, is based on its fundamental ontological role. This role is as we noted that of maintaining the being and of expressing the freedom and self-determination of the group in time. Now we have added the further point that in so doing the government seeks through its power and the freedom its power brings to "contend with" fate in the name of the group. As that which is commissioned for and by the group to represent *its* freedom in guiding and shaping the community's common destiny in the future, government is granted inevitably a numinous character and a sacral role. As most traditional religions have recognized, government is in a strange, ambiguous way a major representative or medium of the divine in social time, that which expresses, preserves and continues the being and the self-determination of the group as it moves in time, that which on the level of concrete, embodied historical life defends the group against fate. Thus also is power the fundamental political reality and goal: the power, as in established groups, to maintain themselves and their life, and through that maintenance to preserve their precarious control over destiny; or, as in revolutionary groups, the power to grasp that control, the power therefore to establish their own mode of existence and thus at last to be secure and autonomous.[46]

Power, like the politics that seeks it, has a future reference: the power to exorcise a future characterized by fate, and so the power to make that future into a destiny we can control. Past and present in human life point to the future: an unknown that is ambiguous and unclear and yet freighted with the ultimate questions of being and of non-being, of destiny and of fate. Because of this interrelation of political experience with the future as promise and as menace, and so this character of ultimate seriousness, politics and through it history have their infinite, demonic drives, their ultimate violence, their final cruelty, their capacity for murder and destruction, and their ideal, their mythical character.

With the specter of fate, the power of a changing history over our contingency, the power that can render powerless our powers to guarantee our being, we arrive at a transcendent, an ultimate category. Man's experience of history as fate has always been religious. In fate he experiences history as an objective power over against his own enfeebled powers; as a power against which he, his group, and even the finite gods have no power, no freedom and so no security. For destiny and fate alike represent the historical sea out of which human beings and each group have arisen; it is by destiny that every human power is *constituted* and so it can be by fate, when destiny becomes fate, that every human power can be submerged. The historical given out of which we come literally founds and establishes our creative powers as destiny. Thus history can also as fate overwhelm our powers completely, destroy our autonomy and so render us helpless. The history in which we are immersed is thus experienced by us as creative or as demonic, as either destiny or as fate; we can hardly be objective to it since it is the direct source of our being and of our powers.[47] Phenomenologically our past, present and future together impinge on us as ultimate menace or as ultimate promise, as an ultimate sovereignty with which we must come to terms or lose our being.

Politics is the human effort to deal with this ambiguous but quite ultimate sovereignty in history over which we have little control. Only if the given *is* destiny, do we have any control at all, any autonomy or any communal freedom. Thus groups have little power or freedom to make fate into destiny; their freedom, their political effectiveness, already presupposes that gift. Freedom in history is always a gift of fortune, of the gods or of providence; it is never humanly achieved without the unbidden help of historical forces far beyond the control of individuals or of groups. Thus is history so terrifying and the future always so essentially mystery: our control is itself quite beyond our control. We are creatures, not lords of time and of passage. We control history only if history so chooses; if it does not, we can hardly control anything. And thus is humanism, a viewpoint based on confidence in human control, capable of historical and social concern only when "destiny" is kind and cultures are on the rise. When history is experienced as fate, humanism, by the logic of its own position, must, as illustrated in the Stoics and existentialism alike, drive inward to the only citadel still apparently undetermined by fate.

The fear of fate, therefore, is the fundamental anxiety of a creature whose very being is in process.[48] It is the anxiety concerning process as process, the anxiety of being immersed in a march of events which founds our powers and possibilities and yet which marches inexorably into an unknown that may no longer support our being and our powers at all. The *question*, therefore, of the shape and direction of the uncontrollable march of historical events is inescapable and ultimate for each group as for each person. What seems a foolish and unreasonable question reflectively in present philosophies of history, the question of the ultimate sovereignty in history, turns out to be the most unavoidable of concerns in the political enactment of historical being. For there is a fundamental terror as well as an open possibility to historical being, to any finite being that has been "thrown" into a situation that it did not create, that maintains its precarious being over time and so projects that contingent being into an unknown and uncontrollable future.

Such *care* about our being in time, and its correlate, care about the ultimate shape of the temporal passage we are in, is expressed in all religions aware of history. Hellenistic religious speech about Tyche or Fortuna, the control of fate over even the gods, and Hebrew speech about the divine sovereignty over all principalities and powers, were, therefore, not irrelevant and empty words but exceedingly meaningful forms of speech about the deepest problem of history and the most crucial concern of politics. Progress and the Marxist dialectic were merely the latest religious myths —in this case, overly optimistic ones—which saw the development of history to be the gradual transformation of fatedness into destiny for all of mankind. That these "myths" concerning history, collective philosophies or theologies of history, appear is no accident. As we have tried to show, they function as essential answers to the deepest, desperate questions of historical being, to human being in passage, and so they provide the grounds for the possibility of human freedom in that passage, i.e., the grounds for political existence itself. If humans will at all to live actively in time —and some cultures have not—then they cannot escape coming to terms in reflection and action alike with the massive sovereignty that rules history and with the question of fate.

The question of the nature of ultimate sovereignty in history, a religious question by definition, is the fundamental question of all concrete political life, existential or reflective. Thus no political movement, party or theory fails to embody in reflective form some answer to that question. For this reason the issue of legitimacy, so puzzling to modern republican ears, is basic to politics, monarchical, democratic or socialist. At its heart the claim of legitimacy is the claim that *this* political order, or person within it (and not others), participates in the ultimate sovereignty or order of historical being. Because of this participation, the "legitimate rulers" can exorcise the terror, the chaos and the ambiguity, the non-being, of fate—whether that participation be through divine ordination, through family and blood, popular mandate, or through obedience to a program or a philosophy. In every case, whether it be based on status or contract, legitimacy is established by relating governmental power to what is conceived to be the ultimate sovereignty of history, to the grain and texture of the movement of historical time. We may laugh at other forms of legitimacy as "mythical"; we do not laugh at our own.

Fate is a religious category, then, because it represents or reveals an ultimate sovereignty which founds, overwhelms and threatens us; it is, so to speak, the negative face of God, his left hand, his alien work. With fate the ultimate sovereignty is apparently demonic, and that is utterly terrifying to any finite, temporal creature. Fate is also a religious category because in our experience of it it manifests dislocation, alienation, estrangement; it is the radically "fishy" side of history, history gone awry, become unnatural, out of joint, rotten. When historical consciousness has once appeared, no one experiences concretely a fated situation as "natural." Always there is "something wrong here"; it is as it should *not* be. To be fated is no neutral necessity of inexorable economic laws; it is "exploitation," oppression, racism. If oppressors appeal to the inexorable laws of economics or of distribution, the oppressed know well that that is all ideology, and that what *they* suffer from are the sins of the mighty. Thus the moral category, as we shall see, appears so inevitably in historical experience. What is given to us as our concrete destiny in history is thus never wholly innocent or natural at all; in it are elements of fatedness that should not be there. Historical experience is always tinged with moral decay and greeted with moral disapproval. If these elements predominate, and destiny becomes fate, then the whole world is saturated with evil, with moral fault, with sin. Along with the moral category intrinsic to history appears then universally the hurling of accusation and of blame. If all this is not natural, then someone is at fault—and if the real culprit cannot be located (and often, of course, he cannot), then a substitute must be. A historical situation that is experienced as fated, or as threatening to be fated, produces inevitably scapegoats as demonic instruments of that fatedness. The essential or ontological reason for these characteristics of historical experience we have intimated: fate *is* "fishy," it is not natural, and there are culprits; these deep and universal political intuitions of mankind are quite accurate. It is unnatural and culpable because fate represents the fall of freedom in sin; fate is a destiny which has been corrupted by fallen freedom. Historical actuality represents the corruption of its ontological structure of destiny and freedom; the ultimate sovereignty of history represented by destiny and the freedom ingredient in history both become demonic—and fate represents this strange union. This is, we suggest, the way history *feels* in experience and in politics, and why people are so fanatical and cruel in political life. The academic pictures of change as determined by impersonal social or psychological laws or, alternatively, as creatively shaped by informed intellectual judgments and moral intentions are true in part, but not wholly true. A naturalistic or an "essentialist" understanding of history strips it of its qualitative characteristics, its demonic character, its unnaturalness, its guilt. Concretely we apprehend an ultimate dimension to history and a fallen character to it. Both appear in the struggle between destiny and fate that constitutes and drives politics. fate and sin, the ultimate and the demonic, are categories ingredient in our primordial awareness of history.

The fear of fate, or anxiety about it, and the awareness of dislocation, are as ever present in modern politics as in ancient, though this anxiety surfaces into consciousness only at times of real crisis and upheaval, and so times of great anxiety. In such periods political existence becomes therefore itself explicitly "religious" and so demonic. The nation, race or class, the government which unifies a group and directs its life, and the leaders of class, race or government, become unconditioned and sacred authorities and powers, in effect, *lord*, that which can rule the fates that threaten to rule over us. And our competitors become demons, hostile, guilty, and blessed with transnatural powers and aims. At such times even our "scientific" modern political and historical ideologies, and even nonideological pragmatic liberalism, alike partake of explicit myth. For only a story with divine institutions and sacred actors can now give a saving answer to the question of radical change, that is, can challenge the unconditioned power of fate over change and the power of the demons over us. Were history merely destiny, that on which freedom could "naturally" work, and were freedom in truth uncorrupted—as most social theory assumes —the undoubted religious and mythical aspects of even contemporary politics would be simply incredible. It is the fact that destiny can become fate, that humans are well aware of this and fear it desperately, and that this transformation is in part the effect of sin and guilt, that gives to politics its fanatical and its mythical character. In turn all hope in history, and so all creative political action, are based on some faith in things unseen, that is, on the promise of destiny, that man's freedom and autonomy will subdue fate for all and achieve its authentic and promised creativity. This hope for a permanent destiny represents an ultimate resolution to the primary *political* problem of history. Such hope—that the future can become destiny and not fate—is the necessary presupposition for all action for the future and so for all creative politics. It is in turn itself grounded on a confidence, utterly unestablished by any sequence of past facts or events, that the ultimate sovereignty of history is such that it will not crush our political actions but may be participated in by them.

The deepest question of ordinary political experience has, then, a religious dimension. It is religious because on the one hand it points to the religious fear of fate and to the religious promise of a universal destiny, to a sovereignty that can conquer fate and to the hope for an authentic history. On the other hand, it is religious because it apprehends a "fall," a warping of what is natural and normal in time—and so a need for redemption. Thus does every example, however banal, of political speech and every form of political action pose questions and proffer answers concerning the character of the whole of history: it appeals to a sacral order of legitimate rule and it promises successfully to contend with demons. For the driving concern of ordinary politics is the question of the shape of that determining sovereignty that rules over historical process and so over our historical human being. More concretely, the political question is the question of the way *our* group as a contingent entity —by continuing or reestablishing this legitimate sovereign government, by embodying this or that pattern of social existence, or by taking this or that common action —may participate in that sovereignty, may eradicate threatening demonic forces, and so become secure and autonomous. No established government and no political class or group, conservative or radical, nationalistic or imperial, fails to answer these religious questions through its political speech and its political action alike. Each in principle portrays the whole of history in such a way that its control is legitimate, possible and even guaranteed—whether it appeal to an established order of traditional "authority," to a Marxist historical dialectic, or to a democratic and capitalistic "natural" and so "rational" base of political and economic life.[49] Only by relating its own rule to the sovereignty of history generally—which each of these "myths" does—can a group or party claim legitimacy, can it make good its promise to overcome the demons, and so can it offer hope against fate and confidence in the future.

Political speech is not "really" pragmatic and only "hypocritically" mythical and symbolic; religion is not a public relations addendum to practical politics. The pragmatism itself depends on destiny and is rendered helpless by fate. Thus any pragmatic political sentence itself presupposes a sovereignty in history that makes that pragmatism possible and credible—and it is to portray that ultimate sovereignty that the essential mythical aspects of political speech are there. Thus no claim to power by a political group, no spokesman of established government, and no political ideology expressive of that claim, fails to share in this claim to ultimacy. This is a religious dimension appearing in all government and in all political activity, and a theological dimension appearing in all political ideology. Politics as concerned with fate, with the ultimate character of historical process, and thus with the questions of autonomy, security and of being itself, is inevitably mythical. For the Christian community—and for all men and women too, we believe—the final answer to this political question of ultimate sovereignty in history, providing real grounds for security and necessary guards against the demonic, is expressed most fully in terms of Christian symbols, pointing to the power, activity, intentions and promises of God. In any case, in part at least it is *this* experience of the ultimate dimension within which history moves in our daily political and communal life, and so this experience of the wonder and yet the terror of history, that the biblical symbols of God's sovereign action in history mean or have reference to in our ordinary experience.

POLITICS AND MEANING

Politics, however, is not concerned just with the question of the security of our being and the autonomy of our control over destiny, though these are fundamental. Political activity also involves the question of *meaning,* of purpose or of worth. Every life must for the person who leads it embody some worth or meaning; it must incarnate some eros towards value in the future. Our activities are unavoidably teleological or intentional in that sense, directed at a value or what is for us a value, be it our family and its well-being, our art, our career—or the creation of a better world for ourselves and others. The realization through our activity of these values for our life involves us inevitably in community, and in most cases within the cultural world around us, in participating in that world and either in preserving its established order and so worth or in helping to shape it in a new and to us a better direction. Thus, in part, we do what we do in the world: not only to eat and be secure, though these are crucial, but also to participate creatively in the legal, commercial, economic, educational, scientific, artistic, or the social and familial structures of our common world.[50] Human reason, imagination and action have created and shaped these structures; human eros, intentionality and purpose send us into them and energize us to be active and creative within them. A "vocation"—be it being a mother, reformer, scientist or theologian, in the wider culture or in a separated community—involves an experiencing of value and so of commitment to some communal structure, its goals, its norms and its joys. If we find the wider cultural community's activities and goals meaningless, as some in our day have, then quickly we shall find ourselves—if we are lucky—living within and working for some separated, withdrawn, or counter-community, be it a sect, an ashram, a commune with crafts, or whatever.

One of the most fundamental needs and therefore rights of a human being, as basic as the rights to security, to privacy or to free speech, is this right to participate in the creation of meaning for ourselves and for the social world of which we are a part—a right systematically denied to our racial minorities and to women. One of the most fundamental forms of personal and historical disintegration occurs when this eros towards participation ceases. When to great numbers of potentially creative people the community's life seems barren of value, excitement and creativity, then many of them become simply indifferent to the rewards of participation, and, experiencing the community's life as void of meaning, they cease to will to be part of its creative work. Then the community loses its creative individuals, and the individuals lose their "world"—and, unless the individuals find separated communities of their own to become their "world," both disintegrate. For the ordinary person working daily within society, unless some one of these communal or social modes of activity has or is creative of meaning or worth, he or she cannot know why they do what they do in the world. If the social structures within which we ply our trade contain no objective meaning for us, our own inward eros dies. In turn, without eros, our activity is pointless: meaningless motions on a treadmill leading nowhere and so utterly empty. We dry up inside; our vitality and our sense of reality slip away. The active power and so the ontological reality of human being is intentional, directed toward and dependent on the meanings latent within the objective structures of our social life. Without an object or goal of worth to us, to be represented, enhanced or achieved by our work, we despair, we become powerless, we cease to feel real, creativity stops—and, its objective meanings having dissolved, a community made up of others like ourselves can wither and die.[51]

This intentionality of our human being in the world, expressed in a sense of the value or worth for us of the communal way of life in which we participate, has tremendous political implications on every level. We cannot understand historical or political life without this category. Among oppressed groups meaningfulness of activity and work is almost as large an issue as is security. Excluded from the political, economic and social systems of their culture, where activities lead somewhere, have recognized worth, and are materially rewarded, they find their work unrelated to the objective meanings of their culture, their toil unrewarded, unable to provide either security or greater well-being, and unrecognized by others, and thus pointless, literally worthless, an object whose values belongs not to them and their worth but to others. This is an aspect of what Marx rightly called alienation, the separation of ourselves from our work, from its results and from its rewards; and it represents real social despair, a mortal threat to a person's identity and dignity. The poison of exploitation is not only the insecurity, the fatedness, it brings, but the pointlessness, the void it represents—and so the human indignity it produces.[52] Such an exploited life has no eros, and so no sense of inner power, freedom or dignity—it is less than human. It rightly breeds the political drive to overthrow a social order if that order cannot be fundamentally reformed in its mode of economic, political and social participation.

Strangely enough, privileged classes—if they are affluent—also can experience the alienation of meaninglessness. With material plenty, with a multitude of things, our activity can also be empty and pointless—for nothing any more can excite us. Things *in themselves* have no worth for us, and once they satisfy our needs, they provide our life and its work with no further significance or meaning. Modern industrial culture, by centering our life entirely around the private possession of an abundance of consumer goods, has thus moved the problem of emptiness and pointlessness, formerly confined to the aristocracy and the idle rich, down into the growing middle classes.[53] Success and still more affluence—a still larger car, two refrigerators, a raise in position—have been the usual bourgeois answers to this latent sense of insignificance. If individual well-being is the highest goal of society, there is not much more that such a consumer-oriented culture can offer. But the accumulation of things can never give significance to a self that finds no inherent worth in itself or its activities. Moreover, in the modern technological world of gigantic corporations, larger government, unified continents and ceaseless and accelerated mobility from community to community, every achievement is relativized into a trifle. Except in rare cases, achievements have little *meaning* without a community which evaluates, recognizes and affirms those achievements. In a mobile society "meaning" as achieved status disappears—a matter of telling and retelling how important we are to new faces who know and care little about these things; vital insignia of importance are always lost on strangers.[54] A unified consumer culture thus seems to provide nothing but the most insubstantial, external forms of achievement and meaning, and the most shifting of communities to confirm and acknowledge that meaning. Unless we are geniuses, "world historical individuals," or among the favored "famous," all we can do can seem trivial. Needless to say, such a culture is also infinitely vulnerable to the ecological crisis in which affluent standards of living must soon cease to rise and in fact must in the end be lowered. Then what meaning can life hold for us, if meaning is found solely in the goods we can accumulate, count and recount?

But even without the threat of future scarcity, such a culture is in danger of becoming seriously decadent, i.e., a culture where, even to those inside it, the eros toward worthful ends has vanished, and a sense of meaninglessness permeates the upper as well as the lower classes. Again the political implications of this characteristic of human life—its fundamental intentionality in relation to objective social meanings—are enormous. The visions of the oppressed are in part determined by it: the new world of which they dream is one imbued with participation in meaning through dignity of work and of life, as well as with material security. Correspondingly, if the upper and middle classes feel the despair of an emptiness in their life as well as an anxiety about their continuing security, then they will be even more ripe for a reactionary ideology. For one major function of ideologies—reactionary or liberal—is to provide a symbolic picture of a social world, be it of race, class, nation or humanity as a whole, in which each individual has place and role and so an infinite access to meaning and significance. Thus do political ideologies fill that vacuum with a sense of the meaning and purpose for what each individual does, at the same time that they provide a unified national (or racial or class) community that recognizes their worth.[55]

"Masses" are people whose activity contributes nothing to themselves or their society, who have therefore no role or place in their social world, and so have no sense of worth, of authenticity or even of reality. Above all, such a person, devoid of a meaningful present, a structured world and a sense of creative activity, lacks a future. Without a meaningful world and a creative self—and the two are mutually dependent—masses are passive, pushed about by arbitrary forces alien to and so uncontrollable by their individual and corporate freedom. Their lack of creative activity is balanced by a given that is sheer fate. "Displaced persons" in this sense can arise in all classes if the dissipation of objective meanings and the inner correlates of anxiety, of lostness and of emptiness, are acute enough; and in every case they breed terrible political results domestically and internationally. Such a social and personal void, and such an historical environment constituted by arbitrary fate, are unbearable. By giving role and place to each person and by structuring the historical environment in terms of destiny rather than of fate for their group, social and political ideologies can act as literal "saviors" from the terrors of this void. One cannot, I believe, understand at all the political experience of Germany in the 1920s and 1930s or the current problems of our own country, without a political analysis that reaches down, first of all, to the level of the ontological *interest* in security in the future, and, second, to the basic spiritual need for *eros* in relation to objective *meanings* in our social existence.

Even if most people, therefore, are not explicitly or reflectively conscious of this need, the activity of almost everyone must participate in some systematic network of wider social activities to which their work contributes and which as a whole, and through their participation, leads to recognized value, for themselves, and also for the community at large. These meaningful "worlds" can be the world of commerce and production, of government and law, of art, education, scholarship, healing, or the smaller but perhaps more important and satisfying worlds of family and town. Without this participation in an objective system of activities leading to value, our work has no meaning for us and we despair. As we have already seen, every cultural whole, as every tribe, has a "way of life" expressed in terms of significant social and religious symbols, which gives meaning and value, as well as form and structure, to all its activities. If that way of life is not so valued, then participation in it has no meaning, people within it die inwardly, and the community crumbles. As a society is constituted by its symbolic structure, so internally *eros* toward that shared system of meanings is a fundamental factor in all social and political affairs.[56]

Intellectuals especially exist and so are political on this intentional level. What is in others *felt*, the sense of worth, the need to exist and participate in a structured social world that provides meaning and value, becomes explicit and reflective with them. They have to *think* that felt participation in objective worth in terms of an explicit system of symbols; they must, in other words, be "ideological." Most intellectuals cannot be active, make cultural or historical assessments, arrive at important political judgments or participate actively in politics, unless they understand and approve the systematic meaning of the way of life, or the vision of a way of life, in which or toward which common action takes place. Intellectuals must set their own vocational participation and their political action in what is to them a *logos* or order of meaning, a wider pattern of society and of history in its movement into the future, and so an order that will hold good for the future, if their political eros is to be aroused—a fact which continually puzzles the proletariat, the commercial man or the man of power, for whom self-interest or the interests of their own community seem to be reason enough for hard political work.

Thus, as Reinhold Niebuhr used ironically to put it,[57] "wise men" (or in modern parlance, intellectuals or experts) always stand beside the men of power giving intellectual, systematic ideal reasons for the latter's acts in defense of a given social order, setting that established social order into reflective, conceptual form as the divinely ordained, the eternal or the most "natural" order of past and future history. Correspondingly, while, as I have noted, intellectuals do not generate the fundamental élan of revolutionary forces—interest does—they nevertheless do give symbolic and conceptual shape and so power to the visions which lure and direct those forces.[58] Further, they transform their visions into possible or alternative systems on whose basis the sufferings of the present may be coherently understood and criticized, and policies seeking a transformation of the political present may be devised. As Marx rightly said, intellectuals create the political self-consciousness that is the necessary basis for all political action, and so the necessary fuel for all political forces, conservative or radical alike.[59] Without political self-consciousness there is neither understanding of the intolerable and unjust character of our present situation nor are there alternative possibilities relevant to the future. And without this self-understanding as oppressed people with new and real possibilities, there can be no freedom, no autonomous judgment, no decision and so no political action in history. The slave must himself *know* he is a slave and that he *might* be something else for his political action to arise. A spiritual and intellectual transcendence of the immediate into the universal, the possible, the ideal and even the ultimate is necessary if politics is to arise and flourish as the human direction of history's events.

In the preceding chapter the crucial role of a system of symbols in cultural existence was uncovered, and the important but ambiguous role of social symbols in a situation of social change was emphasized. In this discussion social symbols, and systems of them, have reappeared, this time providing meaning and direction as well as form or shape to human activity, and thus of even more political importance. The loss of attractive power by a social system can spell its doom; and the lure of a new political and social possibility can seal that doom. Symbolic systems, therefore, do not have merely a static or conservative role in social history. Rather they may perform a creative, even radical, function as well.[60] The basic ground for this role of symbols is that human activity at home and in the world, and thus all political activity as well, must participate in an order of meaning and worth, a network of values to which work or action contributes. Thus the relation of a community to its symbolic system of meaning is crucial to its life, to its death and to its anxieties about its death; and it is crucial as well to all political action directed at new possibilities and so to its renewed confidence in its future.

Our present point is that with this intrinsic relation of social and cultural activity, including political activity, to a cultural way of life, a system of meanings leading to future value and so to significance, again an ultimate or sacred dimension makes its appearance in "secular" social life. Such systems of social meaning are invariably ultimate in character or claim such ultimacy. They are in that sense both "religious" and "ideological."[61] Each appears on the stage of history as the eternal, the natural or the final system of history, the system that will order into a *logos* or meaningful order the chaos, the potential fate, of the future. This ultimacy or sacrality appears whether we speak of established orders that therefore are conservative in their role, or "not yet" orders, utopian dreams that are correspondingly revolutionary. It is in the ultimacy represented by crucial social symbols that the question of *being* in politics and the question of *meaning* in politics meet and unite. As we saw, the question of our continuing being in social time drives political speech to the question of fate and so to that of the ultimate shape of the sovereignty that rules history. Here the question of the worth of activity in a community's life, the question of objective social meaning for our life activity, drives in the same direction, namely, to a set of symbols of ultimacy in which the entire course of history is symbolically shaped, its sovereignty, its norms and its goal portrayed. Being and *logos* are words intrinsic to political life; as enacted in political experience, they reach beyond themselves to an ultimate being and an ultimate *logos* that characterize the whole of historical passage.

This internal relation between the question of the being of a group and the meaning of its life is well illustrated in the deep ideological conflicts of our time. Each vast "bloc" in our present world struggles of course for its own power and security, for its control over fate and so directly for the continuance of its being. But each bloc is also vitally concerned about the way of life it embodies and defends. Each is deeply aware that its own *internal* commitment to that way of life is essential to its own strength. Thus follow the often abortive, often oppressive domestic efforts at total ideological unity by governments devoted to the continuing being of the group—and to their own continuing being in power. Each knows that the *external* defense and propagation of its way of life are necessary for the security of the group. As the ideological power of a group, the grasping force of its system of meanings for other groups, waxes strong, so does the being of the group, its security, wax strong. As its way of life loses its appeal, so the power of the group weakens. Above all, each feels—and claims—that its way of life is ultimate for history; in America it is regarded as the pattern of "natural" human community.[62] By means of these claims to ultimacy, the government's power over the group, and the exercise of that power in relation to other nations, are legitimatized. Through awareness of the fundamental accord of its way of life with the ultimate texture of history itself, the group feels its participation in the final sovereignty of history, and so enhances both its sense of its security in the present and confidence in the future, its sense of the "worth" of all it does, and its sense of rightness in being thus secure.

The fanaticism and cruelty of political experience have one root here. Each side, each nation, race or social class, regards and so defends its order as a "divine" order, that is, as *the* order or way of life natural to historical being—a status that was made explicit in traditional societies when every established order was founded by the gods of the tribe, city or nation, but has not diminished at all in the humanistic politics of a secular age. If these orders that give meaning to our work and a secure confidence for our future become in our eyes relative and transitory, and so insignificant, as are our own small acts within them, they contain neither power over fate nor objective meanings for daily life. In such a situation it is hard for men and women to feel human, for the community to survive and for political eros to arise.[63] In any case, insofar as the social way of life in which we participate and so which we defend, or which we envision for the future, parades before us as an *ultimate* order, ultimate for man and for history alike—and all in some measure do—we have reached a religious or a theological level in historical experience. This is a level that is related to *religiously* by human beings in terms of belief, commitment, surrender and obedience, and one which can be expressed and articulated only in religious, symbolic language, in stories that soon take on a mythical character. Here ordinary, political experience becomes relevant to a multitude of important Christian theological symbols: that of divine natural law, that of *die Ordnungen* (the orders of creation), of the logos or order of historical passage, of providence and especially of the eschatological vision of a new heaven and a new earth.

POLITICS AND THE MORAL DIMENSION

A third significant ingredient of political experience is its moral dimension. This dimension worries many (though not all) secular analysts of politics, conservative, liberal or radical, since moral considerations seem restrictive in the face of the hard, practical needs of political action; at the same time, they seem subjective, arbitrary, ideal and even "religious" in the rigors of objective historical or political analysis. This is, I shall argue, a mistake in analysis, the product of naturalistic and scientistic prejudices. One cannot understand our most secular political reactions and acts, our political concepts and visions or our human relation to history itself, without the moral dimension.

Human beings are inalienably free beings. However driven by interest and by ideology, they remain at least potentially autonomous, responsible for what they are and do. Human beings are never just *objects* of historical forces but also *subjects* of political action and so of centered responses, responses in judgment, decision and action; and these responses invariably have a moral component. Every politician, right or left, democratic or dictatorial, recognizes the significance of this latent autonomy in political life, the polarity of destiny and freedom in history, by arguing his case, by appealing for support among his followers and by worrying about consent. Propaganda ("public relations") is the demonic recognition of the latent autonomy of all men and women. However distortedly, it seeks to deal with the need in politics to know the truth, to consent to the truth, to be "in the right," and so it seeks to elicit autonomous assent—through the lie.

Human autonomy, furthermore, is itself inalienably moral, responsible in character, directed at what each of us, as selves or as a community, understand to be the good. The symbolic systems within which we all live and through which we decide and act embody and shape the forms of our moral commitments. No political support for this or that program is therefore possible unless in one way or another that program can appeal to our moral sense, a sense molded largely by these communal symbols and norms.[64] This is also recognized by every politician who, in appealing for support, argues that *his* view represents justice, order, peace and the general well-being while his opponent's view represents only injustice, self-interest, exploitation and aggression. The universal hypocrisy of political life—the claim of each side to be moral when in fact it is not—is the unquestioned sign that all politics is suffused with a moral category.[65] As propaganda seeks assent to truth through the lie, so propaganda also embodies the moral category in its hypocritical claims to virtue, and its castigations of the immorality of the opponent.

The moral dimension of political life is very apparent in every age of political crisis and so is evident on every side today. The moral health of a community is as crucial to its continuing life as are the viability of its economic and its political institutions, its technical mastery or its engines of defense—in fact, this dimension is basic to each of those institutions. Moral laxity within its institutional life, for example in its commercial, its legal, its governmental or even its military roles, will in the end render ineffective each of these roles and so dismantle the commercial, legal, judicial and defense systems they represent. The "majesty" of government—and in a subordinate way of all the institutions necessary for a community's life—is, as we have found, based partly on the coercive power supportive of these institutions, and above all on their creative role in maintaining and guaranteeing the being and the meaning of the community's life in the future, that is, on their effectiveness. But since that effectiveness vis-à-vis the being and the meaning of the whole community's life is itself in part dependent on their moral character, on their justice and their incorruption, an important element in political and social "majesty" is moral. No political or social institution can long function without moral respect; "consent" has a moral component. As that consent fades, coercion becomes inescapably the sole—and ultimately ineffective—ground of power. Correspondingly, moral injustice in economic distribution or oppressive force in the use of the legal and governmental power of the community will, if not corrected, in the long run erode the effectiveness of these institutions. Injustice and oppression will, moreover, also objectively destroy the community as a meaningful and creative unity, either by means of an internal conflict that splits the community or through an imposed tyranny that smothers it. Moral corruption is as virulent a disease threatening the existence of a community as can be the loss of its access to the raw materials necessary for its survival.[66] Both in its creative and its self-destructive phases, social history is incomprehensible without this moral dimension, and social developments are not to be understood without moral assessment.

Since the moral character of a community's life is essential to its continuing being, moral judgments and assessments are an intrinsic part of all political judgments—

judgments which, as we have seen, are concerned with the continuing being of the community. Moral judgment is intrinsic to all serious political speech, as it is to all political activity. If a speaker speaks of injustice and discrimination, exploitation or aggression without moral condemnation, he will be regarded as himself immoral, as having sold out to the "establishment" or the dominant powers that wish to suppress awareness or condemnation of these things. The same is true of conservative forces: they cannot but be moral in their defense of their system, and they demand a moral defense of it from all the leaders that satisfy them.

One can see the importance of this moral dimension to political judgment and political participation illustrated clearly in the sense of moral alienation from our culture's life that suffuses those groups excluded from that life, and that recently characterized the youth of our time. With the former, their alienation—for example, that of the Blacks in America—is articulated and felt largely in terms of the *injustice*, the moral wrong of the society. In this, of course, they are quite right. The same applies to the sense of alienation dominant in the Third World: they say with great justification that "we are *exploited* in the present system," and that is a moral term referent to a moral wrong. As we noted, the experience of fate is always also the experience of being sinned against; it is the experience at once of God and the devil, of a demonic absolute. With youth in the 1960s this moral alienation was the major ground for their vigorous political participation, for their refusal to support an unjust war and for the revolutionary zeal that characterized some of them. In the long run, this moral outrage, communicated largely through them to other sections of the population, was an effective element in the variety of forces that stopped the Viet Nam war. They did not find their own culture merely ineffective and unaesthetic, though it is both. They found it evil, unjust and cruel, and therefore worthy of death as well as in fact decaying. In all these cases there is a moral condemnation of social reality that can be, whenever it retains its strength, of immense political importance as a factor in historical change.[67] However "objective" or "scientific" the condemnation may claim to be—as, for example, with many orthodox Marxists and most of the New Left—its moral character is easily apparent both in the tone with which words such as "exploiters," "racists," and "aggressors" are used and in the fury of the response elicited. "Interest," and with it "pragmatic self-interest," are categories one can coolly analyze and even approve in reportorial or academic social analysis. But when naked self-interest appears incarnate politically—at least on the other side—or is embodied in an oppressive or exploitative social structure, it rouses in all of us our moral sense, and we condemn.

Such moral condemnation (or moral defense) of communal structures and behavior bespeaks at once a dimension of ultimacy in social experience. It presupposes a vision or a model of an authentic self and an authentic society in history if we are morally to condemn or seek to justify what is.[68] That model or vision of authenticity is clearly not incarnated "here," visible around us in community practices and behavior—for this is precisely what it is we condemn. It is therefore not an empirical datum to be discovered by inquiry. In some strange sense, that vision of authenticity is transcendent to what is given for immediate observation. If we were Greek, we might have called it the transcendent "idea" of man and of the community. If we are conservative, it will be an idealized picture of a past that was (or was it?); if we are radical or reformist we may call it the "not-yet possibility," the realization for which we hope in the future.[69]

However we understand this transcendent norm or model ontologically—and there are many lively possibilities, some philosophical and some theological (I shall suggest one subsequently)—let us note now that for us the model or norm by which we judge always functions for us as an *ultimate* norm. In our political judgments we do not think exploitation, racism or aggression (or alternatively, revolution and radicalism) *relatively* wrong, wrong only in our own eyes, the eyes of our culture or country; we do not hold to them *as* an ideology. To us they are *really* wrong. A phenomenological analysis of any actual condemnation or defense in social and political life—or even in social reflection—shows that that judgment inwardly reflects an experience of transcendence, of transcendence of all cultural relativity and ideology, and so implicitly of historical passage itself. It is based on a model of humanity and of an authentic world that is experienced by us as ultimate—else we are not moral in our reaction to the political evil we see around us.[70] To say it is "unwise" of the government to bomb a small land or to shoot dissenters is a relative statement; to say it is *wrong* to do this is to invoke an obligation on them as on ourselves that is not relative to circumstances, and that thus has for the speaker the character of ultimacy. Political conscience, for the person who experiences it, is never a relative judgment generated only by the special interests, the prejudices and the perspectives of one's own cultural locus—though one may feel that way about the political conscience of others! It is for him or for her the sacred, a call that cannot be refused. And its object, the old or the new social world that is the goal and standard, is taken as the ultimate goal of historical process itself.

Thus the political visions, the lost orders and the not-yet utopias, that generate political action are both moral and ultimate in character.[71] Again they picture not just an efficient or an aesthetic world; they primarily portray a just and a humane world, where all persons are secure, their life and work meaningful and creative, and their consciences untortured. And one of the fundamental reasons these visions lure us to action, if they do, is not only because we might hope in that world to be secure and satisfied (though we probably do), but because we also recognize this as the authentic human world, somehow ingredient to the fundamental character of historical being—even though we be as secular as the Enlightenment revolutionaries, as a modern liberal reformer, as the Marxist or the New Left. Thus the objects of our political hopes, as of our condemnations, are moral in character. Communities cannot accept themselves as actors in political history unless they feel justified morally in so acting. None of us can view social reality without moral expectation; nor can we hope politically without giving a moral coloring to our visions of the future. The ultimate we experience daily in political life thus has a sacred, a moral character. Even if our age does not believe in God, it experiences historical being morally, and in its political hopes it expects a moral issue to come out of the appearance of the future. As politics cannot function without an ultimate vision of the *structure* of historical communal life, so politics cannot and does not function without a corresponding vision of an ultimate *norm* for history's life.

Finally, and for this discussion of crucial importance, these ultimate norms—be they the transcendent norms of an established culture or the "possible" norms of a not-yet vision—that ground our moral judgments in politics do not only represent abstract "values," as the secular world is apt to name the sacred to which it finds itself related. Phenomenologically these norms or values also have for us a unique place within historical *reality* and so within being itself. For political action, if not for secular reflective theory, the norms of history are united with the ontological structure of history. No political action is possible unless what is regarded as ultimately authentic and good is also regarded as most real: as the traditional that always was and always was meant to be, or as the *not-yet that will be*—in both cases as the fundamental grain or texture of historical process itself. While the "good" which is the object of our political hope and so of our political action may be only a not-yet-actual possibility, that possible object must for us itself be grounded in what is or has been existent. Any effective political theory, therefore, grounds all its ultimate moral goals and norms in the actualities of past and present, that is, in the character and direction, the ineluctable trend or tendencies of historical process itself, in the shape of history's ultimate sovereignty and so of history's ultimate goal. Only in this way does the norm for which action is undertaken and life is risked hold out promise to become actual. The political strength of Marxism and the psychological certainty of its hopes have been based on its *ontological* affirmations, namely, that the moral norms of history coincided with that objective dialectic of economic history that had determined the movement of historical process itself—thus that there could be in the end a guarantee of the union of ideal possibility and real actuality. And every powerful political movement of conservation, of reform or of revolution, has felt itself to be so based in the real character of historical change.

If religion be characterized as affirming an ultimate identity of the *is* and the *ought*, of the real and the ideal, politics in its moral judgments is inescapably religious. For every moral norm by which we judge the present, and every moral hope by which we bear in anticipation the unknown future, is taken by us to be an aspect of the ultimate grain of history itself, to be ultimately real as well as ultimately good. This need for political hope to be grounded in the character of ultimate actuality does not *prove* the ultimate union of the ideal and the real, the existence of a "benevolent" tendency in things, nor, surely, does it establish the existence of God. Such hopes *might* be vain, and human aspirations unheeded and unsupported in a directionless and ultimately contingent historical process. But what this universal need does show is that political experience and political action have a religious ground in that they make the instinctive "wager," "hypothesis" or postulation of a dimension of ultimate value that is also a dimension of ultimate reality, that they presuppose some union somewhere of what is good with what is real.[72] For this reason, too, the political rulers and the priests, the political programs and the religious myths of traditional cultures were always in league, if not identical with one another. Finally, it is no accident that in modern secular experience, where few official gods are met with in either nature or history, it is primarily in political forms that "religious" commitment and faith appear, and so it is in the political arena that ideology and mythology are especially virulent. The gods of our time have largely been the nations, classes or social systems, the communities, in which modern people historically exist and on which the being, meaning and values of their life depend. And the language of myth has been most pervasive and powerful in modern life insofar as any of us become articulate about our political experience, our political fears and our political hopes.

Political experience is thus unavoidably religious and therefore theological. It exists within a horizon of ultimacy. Its actions are engendered by the ultimate concerns of being and meaning; its judgments are grounded in ultimate norms; and its élan is enlivened with an ultimate hope for the future. Politics is, however, also ambiguously religious. Religion is an inescapable element in historical life; but religion is infinitely risky. It injects the demonic as well as transformative grace into history. For the call to authentic action in each of us is only partial, and we corrupt it as we seek to embody it. The judgments we make on our world and on our political opponents are partial, stemming from our self-interest and fear as well as from the clear voice of conscience. And the vision we seek in history to realize, or to defend, is never as ultimate, as universal, as healing as we claim. As a consequence, if we understand this call on us, this condemnation of the other, and the old and the new world to come through us in *too* simply religious or eschatological terms, as themselves ultimate, final and good, then again the demonic has appeared—this time in *our* history. The deepest mystery of political history is not merely that it exhibits an ultimate or sacred dimension and so is inescapably religious and eschatological in character. The deepest mystery is that the demonic in history appears precisely for that reason, because of that transcendence and self-transcendence, and that it appears through *us.* In claiming too quickly that our preliminary political future embodies the ultimate future, we ourselves postpone that future, as have countless revolutionary and conservative forces before us.

A true theological politics, then, will not only point to the ultimate and eschatological dimensions of political life. It will also "demythologize" the claims of its own politics.[73] And it will, for that reason, effect a division between the preliminary and the ultimate relations of ultimacy to history, between, as I shall suggest in these chapters, providence and eschatology.[74] Because the call to us is fragmentary and the called partly unclean, the condemnation is on us and on the immediate future we will help to create as well as on the world and the world's past and present. We do and should act in response to that call and for that new world. But the real ground of our hope must, as I shall argue throughout this book, be the divine action that transcends our powers and our autonomy and completes them. Thus the demonic character of even the most moral political action leads to the transcendent as the only creative form of ultimacy in political and historical life. This raises the fundamental question of a political theology: How are we to understand the creative role of the transcendent in a politics directed at the future? How are we to understand the providence of God in historical change, in the crucial issues of justice and of injustice, of power and of powerlessness, since it is the real basis for our hopes for the future? And how are we to understand that present divine activity and our present action in response to it in relation to the final eschatological goal and meaning of historical passage?

Meanwhile, I have tried to show that at every level of historical and so of political life—at the levels of our being and security, of our meanings and our way of life, and of our moral judgments in and on history—a dimension of ultimacy appears as the real horizon of secular communal experience. It appears as the question of the ultimate sovereignty that rules historical time, in the sense of radical dislocation and "fault" in history, in the ultimate order or *logos* that gives meaning to our activities in time, and the ultimate norm that grounds our moral decisions—all together providing the most basic ingredients of political experience. Because of this dimension all politics has a religious and so an eschatological character. And because of this dimension of even secular political experience, Christian theological symbols have relevance and meaning in political existence—for it is *this* dimension of history and of political life which the biblical symbolism seeks to thematize and to which it seeks to give creative Christian form.

Let us note that if it is valid, this argument carries one further theological implication for our understanding of God. The continual presence of this dimension in political experience, qualifying all of our creative and destructive activities in history—in fact, our most fundamental existence, identity and activity as social beings—also implies that the divine activity is unquestionably "there" as the creative and threatening basis of the present as well as "coming" in future social history. In turn this means theologically that providence must qualify eschatology if we are coherently to interpret political experience in theological terms. In any case, like all other aspects of our human existence in time, politics and historical experience—dealing as each does with the creative yet cruel fact of change in time within a horizon of ultimacy—cannot be comprehended without religious symbolism and so without theological understanding.

3

CONTEMPORARY
SCIENTIFIC VIEWS OF HISTORY

In the following two chapters we shall consider several nontheological ways of dealing with our large subject: historical passage, the nature and prospects of social change, man's place and role in this process, and the future as terror or as creative possibility, as anxiety or as hope. The discussion will by no means be exhaustive. Many important analyses of social change are touched on only briefly, as in the case of the functionalist approach to sociology; and several novel and interesting contemporary philosophical interpretations of history are omitted, notably that of Herbert Marcuse and Norman O. Brown.[1] Clearly, the reasons that I have chosen as I have lie partly in the limited scope of my own learning and reflection, and partly in my special interest in those views which seem to advance my theme.

The group of views I wish to talk about in this chapter can be labeled "scientific views of the future." Within this wide field, however, it is well to distinguish three quite different approaches and so, in the end, three quite different views of history and of the future. We may name them the New Eon, the New Seers and the New Nightmare. The scientific community increasingly has said and does say a great deal about the future and so implicitly about the character of history, and what they say on these subjects is important, almost authoritative in our wider culture.

THE NEW EON

The first approach can be called "nonscientific" views of the future advanced by scientists and by the scientific community in general. We call them "nonscientific" because in many instances scientists have spoken rather informally of the future: of what sorts of changes new knowledge, new techniques, new means of control and so on could be expected to effect in our social future, and so what new opportunities and demands this scientific knowledge and technical power will bring with them. Without making the future itself an object of *scientific* inquiry they, in the name of the scientific community, have tried to tell us what our future may or will be like. These views thus represent a vision of the future as a large part of the recent

70

community of the physical, the life and even the social sciences has, until almost yesterday, felt and seen the future—and this is important.[2] Although, as will be evident subsequently, this vision of the future, rendered almost problemless by the future developments of science and technology, has in large part dissipated, it has until the early 1970s been dominant among the scientific community; still, it resonates, albeit in muted and possibly embattled tones, at every scientific gathering.

Perhaps the main theme of this vision has been its sense of the utterly new, open and promising situation of human life in history because of science: now men and women have learned how to know, and hence through this knowledge they have learned how to control.[3] What we do not yet know, said these voices, we will know soon enough; thus what we do not yet control, we will soon find out. This "exponential" acceleration of knowledge, and with it of the possibility of control through knowledge, opened up, they felt, a new era of history, unlike anything in the past. In the first place, they argued, unlimited possibilities are now open to us to refashion our world, our society and ourselves.[4] Secondly, our relation to destiny itself, to the determining forces that have heretofore controlled our life and so our communal passage through time is changed. Now human beings have through knowledge been made "free" to control those forces and thus, for really the first time, men and women are faced with crucial "choices" which will in turn determine the human future. Already an actuality in some spheres—and almost infinitely in potentiality (now that we know how to know)—this control means that men and women can direct for their own ends and purposes the natural, social and psychological factors that have in the past determined social history "blindly." They can even take the process of natural evolution, and surely that of "cultural evolution," into their own hands and make of themselves and their history what they will.[5] Through physical science and technology, men and women can make of their natural environment a place that serves them; through the biological and psychological sciences, they can remake themselves into more efficient instruments of their own ends;[6] and through the social sciences and their development, they can reshape their economic and political environments into ones illustrating a rational society. In this way, knowledge has at last given the human race freedom from fate and almost total control over its destiny—the most radical sort of change in the status of human beings within historical passage that could be imagined.

Of course, continues this viewpoint, this sudden introduction of almost total freedom into history through scientific knowledge and techniques (a strange contradiction in itself!)[7] does not entail that the future utopia that *could* thus become realized is by any means necessary or inevitable. Freedom always means choices, and choices mean real alternatives (as scientists writing about the *future* realize well, and also that the stark alternatives facing us are crucial indeed for the future[8]). Men and women may choose wrongly, or perhaps better, continue to choose wrongly.[9] They may be foolish or greedy, or they may ignore the challenges before them; they may refuse to refashion their economic and political institutions to keep pace with technological developments. At least, however, the future course of history is now entirely up to them. Knowledge has transformed destiny not into fate but into almost total freedom; a new historical era is upon us dominated by new problems and characterized by ultimate choices. In this situation the grounds of our hope—and they are surely secure and comforting ones in our modern age of science—lie in the continuing growth of knowledge,[10] the further developments of technology, and in the cultivation of those virtues of objectivity, tolerance, responsibility and integrity that characterize a scientific culture.[11]

This view of history and of the future expressed by most of the recent scientific community and by a lingering number of its present members is surely a contemporary version of the perfectionist optimism of the eighteenth century. It is history seen from the perspective of the scientific community, then fledgling and embattled, now established and dominant,[12] namely, history as guided and redeemed by human science and by technology. For this view, history progresses because of the undeniable accumulation of knowledge; because that accumulation leads to possibilities of control, knowledge frees humanity from what had heretofore blindly determined its life. Now that knowledge has and will continue to accumulate almost infinitely, history is "freed" through science to enter a new age of intelligent control over destiny. Two aspects immediately impress the more skeptical (or perhaps more Calvinistic) observer of these views of history and the future. (1) Human problems in history are understood here as predominantly problems in *knowledge*, in knowing enough to be able to control, with the consequence that radically more knowledge means a radically new and more creative history. This is, then, a modern form of gnosticism, and (in the perspective of the sociology of knowledge) typically academic in emphasis. (2) While it is recognized that a maximized freedom is not utterly dependable (we may choose wrongly), still the main issue with regard to what may be called the tragic component of history is, so to speak, that of "freeing freedom," of rescuing human knowledge and will from destiny and fate, from the forces that have controlled that freedom from the outside, from beyond itself. The awareness that the real problem of history may lie in the inability, or apparent inability, of men and women to control *themselves,* and thus that the tragic character of history stems not so much from our lack of knowledge and power, as from our misuse of them, does not appear in any of these views.

One of the dangers of such optimism about human intelligence and will is of course that it is continuously falsified by the actual facts of history, and thus is it always subject to rapid and deep disillusionment. When the waywardness of freedom, even a freedom formed by the most sophisticated knowledge, is deeply felt, then this "Pelagian" view faces real despair: having counted on informed intelligence alone, and then having found knowledge misused by greedy, insecure or ambitious men and women, it finds it has nothing at all to count on as it faces the unknown future. The anthropological myths of modern science are thus vulnerable to the facts of history, and provide a shaky foundation indeed for confidence and hope in the future. Currently, this "gloomy" issue of the Pelagian hope is manifest in those members of the scientific community who take the coming crisis of a technological culture and of natural resources with great seriousness; seeing the difficulty of benevolent decisions in a future world of dwindling resources, they sense the human future as nothing but a nightmare of tragic want and conflict.

In any case, it is interesting to note that when the vast majority of the scientific community has viewed history from the perspective of its *own* community, of its knowledge, its powers and its creative role in the future, it sees history as *not at all* essentially determined by blind, necessitating laws or factors—as it sees nature, and as it views society and the self in history in other contexts, and as it thinks historians (as we shall see in the next chapter) should view past history! Rather, in this case, scientists regard the historical future—i.e., the future now to be dominated by science—as a realm of almost unconditioned freedom, a realm itself free from exhaustive determination by "law" and so a realm of infinite possibilities of the new. They have taken their own real control over natural forces through technology as a clue or paradigm to their projected control over history, assuming somewhat simply that history is a field to be dominated by inquiry and technical control as easily as is nature. Here history has science as its creative *subject,* as its dynamic, dominating and controlling force, not science history as its *object.* Thus with science now dominating history, everything in the future can be different from the past, history is open to human control, and is utopian in prospect.

Here, I believe, is real myth, or more accurately, false myth. Mankind in history is here imaged as now embodied in one transcendent figure who has the capacity freely to "choose," and to choose in such a way as to determine almost completely what its destiny will be, rather than—as is evidently true of "ordinary history"— at best to direct or shape a destiny that is given to it. It is, moreover, an abstract or docetic figure that is here imaged, since the ordinary passions, greeds, prejudices, anxieties and hostilities that are still a part of all of the rest of us in the present seem to have disappeared with the donning of the sacral white coat, leaving only knowledge, technical intelligence, objectivity and benevolent if dominating humanitarian concerns. Veritably we have here before us a modern-day Indra standing above or astride the monster of historical passage and subduing with his new technical weapons the potential chaos of the unknown years to come.[13]

THE NEW SEERS

An interesting parallel development in scientific circles is the rise of the new discipline called "futurology," the deliberate effort to make the future an object of scientific scrutiny and, with many qualifications, of a kind of prediction.[14] Beleaguered clerics and theologians have long complained that science has "taken over" most of the functions in society that men of God used to fulfill. They hardly thought the scientists would claim one of the most ancient of these sacred roles—and one long since abandoned by the clergy—namely, prophecy! In any case, there are innumerable groups in Europe and in America now devoted to this effort to clarify "the last barrier of mystery," as one put it, the future.[15] *Daedalus* devoted a whole

issue in 1967[16] to a study of the year 2000 by a host of distinguished scholars; and
Herman Kahn and Albert Wiener have pioneered the method, the initial research,
and tabulated the early results of this inquiry in their work *The Year 2000.*

These men are well aware of the difficulties of any sort of "prediction" in history,
and consequently they reiterate that all extrapolations from the present, even scientific ones, are vastly tentative or hypothetical.[17] The problem of contingency, of the
unexpected, that makes prediction hazardous is, however, resolved by projecting one
main "standard future," that which is the most plausible (surprise-free) according
to all present signs, and also a number of "canonical variations," alternative futures
or scenarios of presumably less plausibility. It is evident, especially from the very
sober note on which the book ends,[18] that the authors are by no means utopian or
simply progressivist. In fact, they picture with impressive imaginative power several
"twenty-first century nightmares" as alternative scenarios for the future. Still, their
"standard future" and its closest alternatives present us with a future world in almost
undeviating continuity with our present world; and one in which clearly the more
benevolent possibilities (to the authors) of present technological, bourgeois, pragmatic, nonideological, affluent, sensate, diversified and relatively stable world society
are extended into more and more of the same. While, therefore, their immense
learning and striking insight make them aware of many of the darker possibilities
in the future that will emerge out of the present, still, on balance, this remains a
world in which, despite its many potential perils, pragmatic, scientific, humanistic
and bourgeois Americans will feel contentedly and securely at home—the aforemen-
tioned not surprisingly being the dominant characteristics of the intellectual class
to which these "seers" belong. Clearly the "scientific" value of their effort—that
which raises it above an imaginative literary excursus into the unknown—is not its
power to predict. Rather is it its power to assess the *relative probability* of imagined
alternatives: that their "standard future" is more plausible than its more frightening
alternatives. Needless to say also, the relatively serene tone or "meaning" of the book
is likewise dependent on this higher plausibility of their standard future.

There is no intent at this point to argue in favor of menace rather than in favor
of creative possibilities in the future—although it is ironic that the one thing they
did *not* predict was the ecological crisis that now dominates and darkens our present
views of the future. It is rather that the concept of probability or of improbability
in this context, on which the whole value of the effort and the character of its results
depend, seems to me to have little except purely subjective import: what we trust,
hope and therefore "feel" will be the case in the future on the basis of what we know
now.[19] In the end these "predictions" are like all others, purely intuitive, wise or
unwise guesses, and no more. The scientific trappings, lingo, graphs and other
apparati make no *logical* difference to this fact; the mystery of the future is still
mystery and is by all this not at all dispelled.

Obviously *everything* cannot be assumed to be contingent or "variable" if any sort
of projection of probability or of improbability is to be possible. Thus certain
"long-term trends" or continuities are assumed by the futurologist at the start to

hold for the future in some analogy to their present form and their present influence and effectiveness. I refer here to continuities in scientific and technical development, in economic growth (the continued rise universally of GNP, for example), in economic structure and development (modes of production, ownership, distribution, etc.), in political institutions, in social structures and habits, in the general tone of cultural values, norms and goals.[20] On the assumptions, therefore, (1) that these long-term trends will continue in a rationally extrapolatable form, (2) that they will expand across the globe, and (3) that their probable directions can thus be induced, the picture of these alternative futures, and their relative probability, is composed.

What, however, is the logical status of such large assumptions, not to mention the much lowered probability of these assumptions in the light of what we now know about the relationship of expanding production and natural resources? Are these assumptions themselves, despite the graphs and the references to all the relevant sciences, in any way "scientific"? That is to say, are these assumptions *themselves* based on any sort of empirical inquiry? But if the assumptions of a method are gratuitous and therefore questionable, how can even the most elegant statistical refinement henceforward transform the results of that method into science? Are these assumptions about continuities in the future in fact made because they are "self-evident" to any American social scientist—though surely not to a revolutionary in the Third World, a Marxist, or let us say, a Yogi? Is it relevant to point out how much more comfortable it is for an American to make *these* assumptions about the continuity of a "free" capitalistic, technological society than to entertain others— assuming he is *able* to entertain other possibilities!

In any case, it is obvious that if these relevant trends should *not* continue, then all the extrapolated graphs which assume their continuance are irrelevant, and without these assumed continuities, there is literally no dependable assessment of probability or improbability at all on their basis. Historical trends, as the authors recognize clearly in theory, however long-term, are not laws. Laws hold necessarily and universally *if* the conditions are met, and laws can be the basis of prediction under those conditions; trends, on the other hand, refer to existential realities—that such and such a pattern has been and is now the case.[21] There is no "law" that any given historical trend will continue. The continuation of a trend is dependent on the character of all the events that together constitute the trend, and *that* constellation is contingent, not necessary. No prediction on the basis of the trend is, therefore, logically possible at all unless it is already known that the conditions upholding the trend are or will in fact be present. Nor is any assessment of the probabilities resulting from a trend possible unless the probability of all these supporting conditions is also known—and these two matters, as the authors repeatedly admit, they simply do not know, nor do they have any way of knowing.

The dependable continuity of a long-term historical trend can be an optical illusion generated by the comfortable and warm (and ideological?) feeling of the stability of the culture supportive of that trend. But historical trends are radically culture-dependent as well as culture-creative, and of this the historian needs to remind the social scientist. As Karl Popper notes, with the collapse of the natural, historical or cultural conditions that support a given trend, the trend may disappear without a trace. Had Messrs. Kahn and Wiener been assessing probable or improbable futures on the "long-term trends" of an agrarian, plantation culture in the Richmond of 1856 or the "long-term trends" of the Hapsburg Empire (long-term enough for anyone!) in the Vienna or Berlin of 1914, their "probable scenarios" would have looked very different from the actualities that had emerged in the American South of 1870 or 1890 or in the Europe of 1920 or 1935–45. The assumption, as long-term as human history itself, of unlimited natural resources, on which most of their own "scientific" extrapolations of ascending Gross National Products into the year 2000 depend, has itself been rudely shattered since the book's publication. Consequently, as of now, it is crystal clear that not one of the book's economic graphs has the slightest relation to the real probabilities of economic production in the decades to come.

Predictions of the relative probability or improbability of alternative futures make sense for an abstracted and so restricted aspect of a total social scene. For example, it is possible to predict alternative futures and future moves in a war or in the shape of the developing market; in both cases supporting and surrounding conditions or trends *can* be assumed, and *must be* so assumed, in order that the assessment of probabilities be logically possible. But when one deals with the *whole* of historical life in the future, as these men do and must do in this context, the entire picture changes. Then, since everything depends on everything else, since by definition all is included, and since all is problematic in its continuities and in its changes (i.e., no one trend can be assumed to be stable except arbitrarily), radical contingency infects every trend, however long-term; probability or improbability become matters more of hoping or at best of feeling than they do of science.[22] Futurology is, therefore, more a helpful way to view the present and its priorities, the possibilities and the dangers latent in the alternatives facing the immediate present, than it is a way of viewing the extended future. Scientific prediction is a very helpful literary device or genre for arousing creative and imaginative thought about the latencies for good and for evil in our present. In no way does it part the veil of the opaque future.[23]

The logical confusion, well muted to be sure, in these efforts to peer into the murky future, arises, I believe, because of the deliberately pragmatic, "scientific" stance of these otherwise wise authors. Thus this confusion reflects a maze of issues that were never discussed or even raised.[24] As we shall see, these issues are largely philosophical in character, issues of the structure and dynamics of historical passage and so subjects within the general field of the philosophy of history. To these men, however, the suggestion that such philosophical issues be discussed would entail the abandonment of the security, the certainty, and as they modestly said, the "seriousness" of science. It would mean entrance into the realm of irresponsible "fancy."[25] Apparently, scientific assertions of probabilities about the future based on *philosophical* premises seem to these empiricists no better than oracle bones or Ezekiel! For are not all philosophical views infinitely debatable; are any of these issues verifiable or testable; is not this precisely the "ideology" from which pragmatic American academia has at last freed itself? Yet *not* to raise these logical and even ontological issues, at least in order to comprehend and elucidate the obvious presuppositions of the scientific predictors, leaves the whole enterprise of futurology haphazard, ungrounded and theoretically irrational—and in concrete fact, as our discussion of it has shown, itself based on debatable, unverifiable and obviously ideological assumptions. If the presuppositions of a scientific study are in fact infinitely debatable, parochial and ideological because unverifiable, it does not make that scientific study more secure or objective by refusing to discuss them. Not talking about an important presupposition does not render it any less problematic. It merely threatens the whole investigation with unexamined confusion, irrationality and prejudice.

The most obvious issue left undiscussed was the question of what in fact are the important "causative" factors in historical change. In order to project any picture at all, probable or improbable, of the future—as to produce any explanation of the factors causative of a particular past event—one has to have some view of what effects what in history, that is, a theory of historical causation. Such views of the dynamic factors in history are, as is well known, multiple, produced implicitly or explicitly by any working historian, and characteristic of any sociological view of social change. It is also true that any given view on this subject is not easily verifiable; in fact in systematic form such views are one aspect of what "speculative philosophies of history" have primarily formulated.[26] If one refuses to debate these difficult "ontological" issues, one merely accepts an unexamined viewpoint from what Kenneth Boulding has called with amusement the "folk science" of one's own time.[27] In this case, somewhat ironically, the "folk science" included the commonly held view among social scientists that developments in our technology, economic growth and, possibly, learning are the main and probably exclusively effective initiating factors in historical change.[28] This is not the place to debate this assumption. My purpose is only to point out (1) that it *is* an assumption, and a big one—one closely allied with the Marxist philosophy of history, which at least admits it represents a particular view of history—and (2) that if the methodology based on that assumption is to be rational, the assumption itself must be rationally grounded by careful discussion and, if possible, a look at the facts—in this case, the facts of history.

The influence of what we might call "spiritual" factors, i.e., nontechnical, noneconomic and even nonmilitary matters, in shaping the future was never really taken seriously. This was possibly because developments on these spiritual levels of cultural life seem even more contingent and unpredictable than economic and technical matters, and also because, as they admitted, the authors are "committed" (a strange, ideological, even "religious" choice of words) to the "dominant Sensate (or better Early Sensate) assumptions of our society."[29] In any case, fundamental alienation from the symbolic structures of the society, dissolution of commitment to the society's symbols, a revolutionary spirit against the society based on massive injustice and disaffection, basic changes of attitudes, values and conceptions of authentic community on the part of the population, or the loss of the "attractive power" of a given symbol system for other peoples—these are and have been important factors in the shaping of historical events, and so they too can warp or even break the easy continuities from our present cultural scene on which predictions are based.

Finally, the depth of the contingency in history was not plumbed—and could not be without discussion at this level—though it was frequently admitted. The contingent character of past events when and as they happened means that the future—especially as it moves farther away from the present given—is radically open to new possibilities, and open at places, in ways and on levels that it is for us now impossible to determine.[30] Everything is in principle open in the future, else everything be closed now. Thus while there will inexorably be some important continuities with the present—known with relative certainty when they are present, and known as apparently necessary when they are past—it is impossible for us now to determine which continuities and trends will in fact characterize the future. The farther one moves into the future, the less possible it is to determine with any precision which trends will be continuing there. Concretely, our culture as a free, technological, capitalistic, democratic, scientific society not only faces variations *within* its own basic cultural terms, so to speak, its own alternative futures. One among many other historical possibilities is the demise or dissolution of that culture, and thus of most, if not all, of its long-term trends and continuities[31]—as past contingent events helped bring about the demise of the agrarian, plantation society of the South and the structured society of pre-World War I Europe. The radically new is thus always a possibility in history, a "new" that is, to be sure, bred by conditions latent in past and present, but a new whose appearance in history is, before it comes, *ontologically contingent, epistemologically unexpected and historically transformative.* This sense of the generic openness of the future and so of the possibility of the radically new was, as I noted, the point seen all too clearly by those "scientific" views of the future which took science as the creative *subject* of history. But it is, despite Kahn's theoretical reiteration of its truth, a point that becomes inevitably obscured when scientists seek to make future history their *object,* and so to extrapolate probabilities from our present shaky continuities into the darkness ahead. It is difficult to face objectively and scientifically the fact that the future is *really* contingent and so *really* open, especially when you wish to be able to predict, and even more especially when American culture has so much to lose by radical change. Thus there is an almost irresistible pressure to emphasize continuities, to extrapolate laws into the unknown, and so to prophesy, as many have before, more on one's hopes than on one's knowledge.

What is manifestly lacking in these "scientific" views of the future is a sense of the depth and complexity of history, and the radical difficulties that history manifests as a subject matter for reflection, in comparison to the usual objects of the physical or the life sciences—or even in comparison to an abstracted and strictly delimited aspect of the larger social scene like a community, an institution, a market or a war. In history freedom is polar to destiny, a deep contingency to continuity; here too spiritual continuities and changes are as important as are technical and economic ones. Since these "ontological" matters were not considered, in each case an abstraction—incidentally quite antithetical versions or scenarios because each was based on one pole and not on the polarity—resulted: (1) emphasizing freedom and openness, one version portrayed the mythical and therefore noble engineer freely and purposefully determining the future flux in entirely new and benevolent directions, or (2) based on the pole of destiny, the second version pictured a stable continuity with moderate variations moving with discernible probability into a knowable future. What is missing in these scientific attempts to deal with a veritable mystery is reflection upon and so symbolic thematization of precisely those dimensions of ultimacy: destiny, fate, and their strange relation to human freedom and to historical contingency, which we uncovered in the last chapter. If history is as we experience it, reflection on the nature of historical passage, on human nature and its freedom and unfreedom, and on destiny and fate, must be carried on if there is to be a rational basis for scientific thought about the historical future. If science is to seek to understand history and to make the future less obscure, it must elicit the help of that very partner it had seen itself as displacing, philosophy of history.

THE NEW NIGHTMARE

A third view representing the scientific community has arisen in the last half decade. As new as it is radically different, this view is the result in general terms of the sudden realization among scientists that modern science and technology (or better, their misuse) have depleted and so almost emptied our environment of its natural resources. This realization about resources is then combined with the insights of social science and social theory about human behavior to provide for us a projective picture of what that exploding ecological crisis means socially and politically for the future. Many scientists have outlined the nature of the impending crisis in the earth's resources; few have seen as clearly as Robert Heilbroner the probable social effects of that crisis, and thus essayed realistically to assess the total character of our future. We shall comment on this latest scientific picture of history and our future in terms of Heilbroner's book, An Inquiry into the Human Prospect.[32]

In Heilbroner's book, the proximate future (two or three generations) is pictured neither as a new utopian day nor as a steady continuation of present culture. Though a new day, it is grim, bleak and filled with suffering, a day of darkness and not of light, of despair and not of hope. Heilbroner argues that not only will the future continue the travail and suffering of the past, but even more the future will multiply this suffering.[33] The hard-won and flickering values of our present—affluence and security, freedom of ideas and self-determination of lifestyle, and (one may add) hope of a better future—will be threatened and in all probability extinguished. Our movement into the future will be a descent into the bleak cave of bare and unrelieved survival, a survival characterized by overcrowding, material want, rigidly determined systems of life and authoritarian government. Unlike other "dark ages," it will have no prospect in history or in time of the alleviation of its bleakness. If supernatural religion and theology were for many in modernity made irrelevant by the brightness of yesterday's scientific view of the possibilities of the future, they are seemingly now made almost irresistible (if also almost incredible) by the grimness of today's scientific understanding and its own jaded prospect for our earthly future.[34]

This newest of scientific views of the future, then, not only signals a sharp end to the theory of historical progress ending in social utopia. Even more, if it is accurate, it signals an end to the Enlightenment culture that fathered that progressivist theory. Seldom has the end of an entire cultural or historical epoch been so dramatically foretold—and, ironically, by the same science that created that epoch. The era, Heilbroner says, of an emphasis on the conquest of nature and the comforts and security that conquest brings, of the celebration of technological and industrial expansion, and of the desire for more and more production, must now be all over. Correspondingly, the era of the domination of the culture by science and its modes of inquiry and of truth, of intellectual freedom, love of heresy and the thrill at novel ideas, is now too dangerous to be afforded. The era of individuality of lifestyle, privacy of life and of judgment, individual participation in public decisions, will be impossible in the probably authoritarian future that faces us. Above all, the era of confidence in man and in his future earthly blessedness, the sense that happiness here *is* possible, that human ingenuity and creativity, knowledge and know-how lead to human fulfillment, and that freedom is the key to human self-realization, is at an end. All of these beliefs in man and his vast potentialities in history that characterize the "modernity" created by the Enlightenment, have been proved to the hilt not to have established and secured human life on earth. Quite to the contrary, says Heilbroner, the hard facts and their implications (not, note, theological dogmas and *their* implications) tell us that these creative human powers encouraged by scientific modernity *threaten* human existence mortally.[35] Thus, his argument runs, will humanity be driven inexorably to the denial of this very set of notions and goals if humanity is to be saved. Whether Heilbroner realizes or not the transcendent meaning of his view, surely it is this: the dream of modern humanists —and many theologians too—that creative invention and the waxing power to manipulate, to transform and to produce will enrich, secure and bless future generations has evaporated, having like Frankenstein's monster begun to destroy the human being who created and lived by that dream. For Heilbroner, the only chance our race has to survive is to abandon this dream, to reverse this process of scientific, technological and industrial development, and to create another entire cultural Gestalt, as different from the goals and hopes of the Enlightenment as is conceivable.[36]

This impending demise, moreover, of the technological civilization and the Enlightenment culture which it fathered has, for Heilbroner, ironically been a case *not* of murder but of suicide, of *self*-destruction. The forces that have created these fatal problems for Enlightenment culture are the very forces creative of and created by the Enlightenment, namely, science, technology, industrialism and their wider cultural milieu that gives precisely these elements overriding (to Heilbroner, undue) prominence in its assumptions, its values and its goals.[37] In Heilbroner's vision, science here should understand itself as the ill-fated instrument not only of its own self-destruction but of the destruction of every cultural form it values, and even as a threat to life itself—as surely it once saw itself in the precisely opposite role. Thus Heilbroner agrees with our initial remarks: the age of progress through science, technology and industrial developments, of the expectation of an open and promising future, is gone. This is, he thinks, universally felt: on the level of feelings by all of us, and clearly, in reflection, by those who know. We all "share an awareness of an oppressive anticipation of the future."[38]

The causes of the present anxiety concerning the future that Heilbroner assumes, this unthematized certainty of fundamental breakdown, are, for Heilbroner, diverse but unfortunately utterly implacable and irremovable. Balancing an inner disintegration of technical, industrial culture, much like that we pictured in Chapter 1, are objective developments—"external challenges," he calls them—which in concert will surely destroy the liberal, dynamic forms of our present culture and, if the race is lucky enough to survive at all, bring in a new form of society. The first of these is the population problem created by medical science and exacerbated by the science of agronomy. Doubling the population of the earth's poorer regions every quarter of a century, it threatens, unless checked by mass starvation, to place here forty billion persons (as opposed to the present 3.5) in 100 years.[39] Such a growth in population seems to require an almost infinite agricultural and industrial expansion if the most tragic levels of starvation are to be averted. The social situation, Heilbroner notes, of such a crowded, unemployed, starving and hopeless mass of people jammed into immense urban centers is unimaginable; the only certainty is either massive unrest or iron discipline. The most probable political result, Heilbroner feels, will be revolutionary governments in the poorer, more crowded lands, possibly using nuclear weapons to force the rich nations into a redistribution of the world's goods.[40] Or, as I see it, the greater danger is that the powerful of the earth—now unified by détente—will see all this coming, will assert control over the underdeveloped world both to seize the earth's remaining resources and to prevent precisely this revolutionary redistributive action; thus, at the price of a tight, universal tyranny both at home and abroad, they will seek to retain for a brief time their present levels of affluence.[41] In either case, a situation of almost total and universal authority seems inevitable.

The second objective development—in collision course with the first—leads inevitably in the same social direction, namely, toward authority. It is (1) the depletion of the earth's resources, which seems certain surprisingly soon to demand a slow-down and then a halt to industrial expansion.[42] In league with that, (2) there is as well the danger of overreaching the thermal limit for the atmosphere, which long before the extinction limit is reached in a century and a half (three or four generations) will also require a slow-down and a halt to industrial growth.[43] The result, as inexorable to Heilbroner as the advent of winter, is "the inescapable need to limit industrial growth."[44] "Every sign points in the same direction: industrial growth must surely slacken and likely come to a halt, in all probability long before the climactic danger zone is reached."[45] The only alternative to such industrial contraction is, he believes, in the end death. The dilemma is that the industrial expansion on which our existence as a proliferating race depends, is in turn precisely that which threatens our existence as a race.

Because of this inexorable need to limit and then absolutely to prevent industrial expansion, a vast increase in the extension of control by government and so in the authority of government will be unavoidable. There are three reasons for this.

1. The expansion of technology in and of itself entails a growth in systematic and so total controls. In turn, the *control* of technological and industrial expansion, halting its free and unfettered development, limiting its rate of growth, and a fortiori effecting its diminution or reduction will require even more control over every form of research and technological development. Thus an expanding and finally a total scientific, economic and social planning carried on under increasingly authoritarian governments is apparently an unavoidable part of our future.

2. Halting the rates of economic growth, not to mention lowering all present affluent standards of living, will have immediate social repercussions, domestic and international. It has been the expansion of production that has kept order and peace in our contemporary world—among the unequal economic classes of capitalist countries, among the unequal political classes of socialist countries, and between the have and the have-not nations of the world. When standards of living level off and then go down, or even threaten to do so, Heilbroner argues, these inequalities will become suddenly intolerable, and every society will be threatened by lethal social conflict. Authoritarian governments will be needed to control this universal unrest, and then to implement whatever difficult political and social options face us in this situation of scarcity, anxiety, jealousy and unrest.[46]

3. Finally, as we noted, authoritarian governments will be called for whether men and women seek to redistribute food more evenly among nations, whether they seek to preserve and ration the world's rapidly decreasing supplies, or whether (heaven help us) those with power seek to retain with force the present radical inequalities between classes and peoples.

Despite the language of certainty that Heilbroner uses about the appearance and effect of these "challenges," and so about the demise of our experimental, industrial and technical culture, Heilbroner is not a total fatalist or determinist in his view of history. He recognizes throughout his "prophecy" that although there are unavoidable conditions for each age (or "challenges"), nonetheless these conditions arising objectively out of trends in nature and society do not determine with rigid necessity what actually occurs or will occur. Rather the events that in fact transpire are also dependent on the human responses to these challenges. "What in fact men *do*," as John Herman Randall puts it, or, as historian Gordon Leff insists, events depend on the human response to a given natural or social condition.[47] In other words, for Heilbroner as for us, past and future alike reflect a polarity of conditions *and* response, of destiny *and* of freedom. Moreover, it is clear to him that these conditions and problems—our future given "destiny"—are themselves not predetermined necessities of natural or social "law" but rather the results of the past use, or misuse, of our human "freedom," configurations, that is, of human response; or, as he puts it, they are *social* problems, originating in patterns of human behavior and so potentially capable of transformation.[48]

Nevertheless, despite his understanding of the ever-present reality of the freedom inherent in response and in policy, he has a very deep sense of the limitations of freedom in history—a sense the scientific optimists of a generation earlier did not share. First of all, the freedom of response, he argues, is radically limited by the conditions and possibilities given to it. In this future, if we are to survive, we *must* cloose to control technology and industry, and we *must* choose order rather than continual unrest. If, moreover, we are to have a just world, we *must* choose a forced redistribution; if, on the contrary, we are to have an affluent life for ourselves alone, we *must* cloose to seize the world's diminishing resources and to defend our affluence in a starving world. The fascinating point is that in all these areas the objective situation forces responding human freedom, whatever the virtue or the wisdom of the responders, to choose authoritarian government, frugality of lifestyle and corporate social existence. Despite the real choices that will remain, therefore, we seem to him nonetheless "fated" to accept, even to encourage, stronger and stronger patterns of social authority, and vast and fundamental changes in styles of life. This sense of an ineluctable fate on which our freedom must operate is, I take it, one ground of Heilbroner's gloom and the explanation for much of the objective force of his argument.

Finally, with regard to the limitations of freedom in history, Heilbroner recognizes that a just and relatively painless answer to these challenges is more than can be expected of concrete freedom in history. Such a creative answer would require a voluntary and so *political* reform of our social institutions that would provide a gradually increasing control and so make possible the necessary but painful redistribution of the world's shrinking goods. The similarity of his picture of the future with Hobbes' picture of the past, and the similarities of their two resolutions is striking. In each a chaotic human situation, unbearable and destructive, is to be resolved only by the imposition of an impregnable authority over everyone. But Heilbroner is less optimistic about man than was Hobbes, for he does not believe that such a radically self-limiting "social contract" is a historical possibility even if its future alternative, like Hobbes's past alternative, is a life "nasty, brutish and short." Such an act of social creativity, namely, the voluntary submission to authority in order to reduce living standards and redistribute goods—an act demanding incredible foresight, rare self-control, self-sacrifice, and a transcendent fellow feeling—can, he says, hardly be conceived as a possible *political* action. What politican, asks Heilbroner, who promised such a voluntary reduction in the standards of living of his people, would be able to survive, be he capitalist or socialist, leader of an undeveloped or of an affluent country?[49] Thus, concludes Heilbroner, the new future will be brought in by external forces not by social contract, "by changes forced upon us by external events rather than by conscious choice, by catastrophes rather than by calculations. . . . Nature will provide the checks, if foresight and morality do not."[50] Wars, preemptive seizure of raw materials, revolutions, crises in resources, mass starvation, etc., will do what politics, as the communal instrument of free response, *cannot* do. The new unfree world will not be willed by freedom but created by fate—even though a wise freedom, were it *really* free, would have willed its own unfreedom. Theology has never, even in the hands of Reinhold Niebuhr, produced more intriguing paradoxes!

Interestingly, whereas the older generation of scientists looked forward to a day when through technology free choice would increase in scope and influence throughout the range of historical existence, the present generation, conscious of the ineradicable limits of freedom in concrete history, finds the area of choices in the future strictly limited both by objective conditions or "destiny" and by the intellectual and moral weaknesses inherent in a self-concerned humanity. The dream that free will can create its own kind of future through its own creative powers has entirely faded. In this view, human freedom will be constrained in the future by a self-generated fate that will, whether it will or not, force freedom to contract itself and finally to abdicate and to submit to authority.[51] Soberly realistic about the way we are, about the real limits of our freedom in history, and about the self-destructive character of autonomous freedom, Heilbroner's analysis comes close to the orthodox theological interpretation of man's situation. He does not say it, but he portrays an estranged and warped freedom whose unlimited use, guided by its heedless concupiscence, in the end destroys itself and its world. Unintentionally, he has provided an empirical documentation of the symbol of a freedom in self-destructive bondage, of the taint of original sin.

Our theme that Heilbroner's future—and that of all who have taken the ecological crisis with seriousness—represents the end not only of the progressivist vision of the Enlightenment but of the Enlightenment as a total system of cultural values, priorities, beliefs and hopes, is confirmed when he portrays the kind of world which he believes alone can survive in this future.[52] That future world is a civilization and a culture at every point precisely opposite to that envisioned by developing modernity—and thus a world which, as he admits, the intellectual children of modernity will find utterly abhorrent. This will first of all be a *static* society, because expansion on every front, the incredible dynamism of modern civilization towards change and the new, has brought man to this pass, and only rigid control and so utter stability can prevent ruin. As a static society, it will, moreover, be *traditional.* Constrained by rigid patterns of behavior and presumably authoritarian myths which function to confirm these patterns, it will shun the new, the unorthodox, the innovative as a threat to its stability and as a renewed sign of the feared expansion. One can surely surmise that only that sort of strong priestly theocracy and mythic heteronomy despised by the Enlightenment could so enforce the norms and symbols of stability and of authority. It will, further, be rigidly *frugal,* and thus probably *ascetic,* not "pragmatically" for a better tomorrow as in early capitalism, but because, as in medieval or Eastern asceticism, all inner yearning for "more" will quickly spell personal and social doom. Finally, because of energy shortages life will cease to expand into larger and larger scale units, whether of urban complexes, offices, or factories; small units, simple machinery, reduced communities will be necessary.

In sum, we move back beyond the teeming Hellenic, medieval and early Renaissance towns into an almost prehistoric village situation with its crafts, its elders, its traditions, its holy men and its immense mythic sanctions, the world of Henri Bergson's "closed religion and morality."[53] Having abjured of necessity the conquest of the outward world, this postindustrial society will return to the inward: more varied and higher inner states of consciousness will, Heilbroner says, replace higher levels of material affluence and of external power as the goals of life.[54] Once again, therefore, as in the time before critical reflection and science appeared prominently in history, myth, ritual and spiritual techniques will again become dominant (and probably an authoritarian clergy to enforce them) over scientific hypothesis, laboratory process, innovative techniques, and the freedom to question and to invent. As in a tribe or a prehistoric polis, corporate values and aims will take clear precedence over individual ones; and individual conscience, intelligence and freedom of action will be smothered.[55] Thus almost everything the Enlightenment abhorred will be valued, almost everything the Enlightenment valued—and believed in—will be shunned as lethal to human good. As Heilbroner significantly remarks, such societies have lasted quietly for millennia *because* they lacked any dynamic, expansive thrust, any way of developing new and improved technologies, any mechanism of political protest, any mode of spiritual or moral transcendence over tradition. Here both the freedom and the individual creativity out of which the new and so the better arise are both banished in order that survival be possible—surely a non sequitur to a modernity that assumed that the freedom to invent and to develop the new was the very *secret* of human survival, and thus, in fact, precisely what is meant by "better". In this strange inversion of almost everything, society so pictured has stepped back quite out of the dynamic of history, or retreated from it. Human creativity is now seen to be essentially so destructive that it must be locked again in the chains of a traditional society if man is to continue to be at all. In truth, Prometheus has by his own daring brought upon *himself* his enchainment on the rocks.

Several remarks should be made about this new vision of history and the future. First of all, as I have tried through this example to show, a total vision of the future and so of history inescapably arises from the character of our human immersion in history. For, as previous scientists and now Heilbroner illustrate, despite their desire to escape "philosophical" and especially "theological" conclusions, even the most "empirical" and deliberately unphilosophical of humans are immersed in history in such a way that inexorably at the same time they transcend it, and transcend it with their minds as well as with their deeds. That is to say, they must raise questions about the course of events in which they are immersed, and so they must formulate views, coherent or incoherent, empirical or nonempirical, about that course of events. They must ask, as Heilbroner must, "What is going on in the historical process in which I find myself?", "Where are we going?", "Is there hope for us in history?", and so finally, "What is the general shape, direction and outcome of historical process as it interacts with human response?" If *they* do not ask these questions—as a positivist generation did not—it is because preceding scientists *did* ask them, and their positivist children are now living on their inheritance. Now in a new world, Heilbroner must re-ask and re-answer these same questions. This list of unavoidable questions forms the stuff of which philosophies and theologies of history are made. Thus, despite Heilbroner's own reiterated (and ineffective) distaste for philosophical accounts of human nature and the strictures of his fellow empiricists, his own example—and that of his Enlightenment and evolutionist progenitors—shows that the search for forms of conceptuality, for philosophical and theological notions and even myths with which to thematize these ultimate issues about history, is inescapable for humans. To be transcendent enough over history to seek to understand it through the social sciences and to manipulate it through technology and informed policy—enough, that is, to deal with it politically, and enough to organize with the help of even the most pragmatic theory useful social structures—necessitates "historical consciousness." Historical consciousness in turn entails a theory about history in its widest extent, that is, a view of objective conditions and their relation to freedom, of the patterns of historical process, and finally a vision of future destiny. Such historical consciousness, therefore, cannot avoid fundamental and so speculative social theory, philosophy of history, mythical speech and global beliefs about the whole. Whatever they *say* they do and wish to do, the scientific community in every age itself illustrates that human "historicity" involves inevitably the articulation of comprehensible and comprehensive visions of the whole of history, of its dynamic factors and its probable goals and meanings.

Secondly, as we have also indicated, the form of the social theory, the philosophy of history and the vision of destiny, to which Heilbroner is inescapably led by his understanding of present "facts," is in direct opposition to that to which preceding generations of modern scientists were led. Not only has their view of progress vanished; even more their essential values, that is, their ranking of the social and moral priorities of "civilization," has been fundamentally overturned. Gone are the Enlightenment values of disenchantment, skepticism, free inquiry, innovation and experiment leading to the expansion of useful control and production. Predominant again will be the values of stability, conformity, belief, acquiescence to authority and to tradition, and the heteronomous sanctions of a mythic horizon. Let us note in this connection how, contrary to humanist assumptions, moral values and priorities are not self-sufficient. Rather are they dependent on the more fundamental conceptuality of a vision of history, of process as a whole and of the relation of human beings to the character of that process, in sum, a "mythical" explanation of history. Within one vision of history the liberal values of the Enlightenment seemed utterly self-evident. With a radical shift in the understanding of history and its prospects, these same values become liabilities, harbingers of doom rather than of self-realization, and their precise opposites become "good," and so head the list of social priorities.

Most surprising of all, we are summoned to this *metanoia*, so directly antithetical to modern sensibility, not in the name of the forgotten and so angry gods, but in the name of earthly survival—the one lingering priority of earthy and naturalistic modernity! Here, therefore, this understanding of history takes on its peculiar irony and fascination. What Heilbroner is evidently saying—and surely the apparent facts bear him out—is that human creativity has led us to this doom—the intelligence, the inventiveness, the practical genius, the infinite curiosity, and the freedom to exercise that commitment and creative genius in inquiry and technology. Out of these have come increasing knowledge, even new techniques, expanding production, and the changing, reshaping and *use* of our world and of ourselves. All of this, which to an earlier generation was the recipe for survival and progress, turn out in the end not at *all* to be aids, even less necessities, for survival—perhaps that most beloved dogma of all—but precisely lethal threats to survival. Technological reason and the technological expertise it produces—the sacred instruments of modern culture—are here seen to possess built-in self-destructive elements that lead to their own inevitable break-down and abdication if survival is to be maintained. Correspondingly, those "primitive" mythic, inward, religious, unscientific, untechnical and so hopelessly impractical cultures, which were studied and scorned by modernity are now seen as having the best chance of "making it" in history. The relation of human creativity to historical process is reversed: creativity is seen now as ultimately alienated or estranged from social process and so from itself, since it leads in the end to self-destruction and not to security and self-realization. Strangely, critical and inventive intelligence and "the reality principle"—again as in the Prometheus myth but not in Freud!—are here viewed as violently opposed. Homo faber apparently cannot survive in history! Homo mythicus can and will. To be worldly is to move all too soon from this world to the next; to be otherworldly is to adapt successfully to the world. How strange an end to a scientific and secular culture when these parodoxes —not to say heresies—are uttered by one of its most perceptive antireligious savants!

Put this way, this historical vision of history runs counter not only to the scientific Enlightenment—though this is clearly its main dialectical opposite—but also to the magnificent transcendence that Hellenism achieved over its own mythic and nonreflective forebears, and to the biblical sense of human historicity and dynamic process against the surrounding nature and tribal religions. Only the Greek tragic sense of history—that the creative daring of Prometheus ends in chains or that a creative Socrates dies at the hands of the polis—and the biblical understanding—that the covenant people may culminate in exile or on Calvary—reflect in their own way this same sense of fundamental alienation of creativity from the iron laws of history. And let us recall that this is hardly for Heilbroner a myth *about* history; on the contrary, for him history *itself* incarnates and so manifests to empirical inquiry the lineaments of this tragic "myth." For the destruction, abdication, and final removal of human creativity and historicity are for Heilbroner "events," not within a reflective system or within a dramatic performance, but events that will characterize the structure of actual future time.

A word should be said about Heilbroner's use of myth, since it is so typical of the modern consciousness he otherwise rejects. He urges that the Prometheus myth extolling (Does it?) man's daring and creativity has been basic as an ideal for modern culture, but now is slightly dangerous as a model for us. It is that very creativity that has gotten us into all this trouble. Clearly Heilbroner understands myth as merely a moral ideal or example, an imaginative projection of those powers and virtues of man which we admire or should admire.[56] This is a typically naturalistic and humanistic view of myth as concerned exclusively with human capacities and moral inspiration in a cosmos to be known and interpreted by science. Traditional myth, however, had no such exhaustively anthropocentric or moral reference. Its purpose was not primarily moral inspiration—though that was part of its role—but *truth*, truth about the nature of things and so about the human role in the cosmic order and in history. Myth, to be sure, spoke in terms of a story, and it personified all its actors. But the point of the story or drama was to illuminate the underlying or divine structure of things and the human possibilities and obligations within that structure. Myth was a vehicle of religious and even ontological understanding, not of moral self-improvement, and on this score the Promethean myth seems to have been painfully accurate.

Despite his facile rejection of the present relevance of this myth, Heilbroner's own argument suggests that the Prometheus myth is in a strange way perfectly true about the real, objective history within which human creativity functions. Thus he seems to propose, at least implicitly, an entirely different interpretation of the myth. The titanic creativity of mankind, he tells us, has, by the logic of its own expansive dynamic in relation to the implacable character of the finite cosmos, inexorably resulted in condemning men and women to future chains. This "fate" is no chance accident, no arbitrary punishment or condemnation, the petty action of a projected father figure. Rather, the objective nature of our world is such that the scientific, technological and industrial experiment by its own intrinsic dynamic ends in tragedy, and thus we had better accustom ourselves to that grim fact and be quiet and patient, knowing now our fate.

In this utterly new self-understanding of our possibilities in the world, the role and character of Zeus—representing *now* the implacable objective order of things—totally changes. Instead of the symbol of our own neurotic subjectivity, Zeus is now an objective symbol referent to the way external reality has revealed itself to be in relation to us. Thus Zeus stands for a reality against which, as the Greeks understood but we did not, no legitimate or meaningful complaint can be lodged. Correspondingly, Prometheus's punishment is no longer the accidental and unjust result of a threatened tyrant's whim but the inevitable consequence of his transgression of grim, objective limits. I find no point at which Heilbroner's argument disputes the Promethean interpretation of human history, or its understanding of the tragic link between creativity and self-destruction.

Suddenly, therefore, our age has confronted in historical process a reality that is not only mysterious but in many respects terrifying, counter to our wishes and hopes and seemingly threatening to crush us *because* of our creativity. History appears here to be more like fate than like the promised malleable destiny it was for our scientific and inventive forefathers. Such a cold and even demonic mystery at the heart of historical reality our science never foretold, or could foretell. We wonder anew about how to comprehend the mystery in which we live and which we can never fully conquer because in the end that mystery has to do also with the ambiguity of *even* our creativity. This vision may lead us to greater self-understanding both of our own ambiguity and of the genuine enigma that surrounds us, and to greater appreciation for levels of understanding and of speech which our empiricist and positivist culture had scorned—levels which sought not only to tell us of our own attributes and ideals but also of the nature of the objective mystery in which we exist and toward which we move in the passage of time.

This vision of our future seems, finally, to vindicate the Christian tendency to see in Prometheus partly the figure of Lucifer and of a rebellious Adam—he who in being creative and daring *also* grasped power, rule and reward to himself and his own, and *thus* destroys himself. In this symbolic account it is not the creativity that is at fault, the transgression of limits set by old orders of things—for these acts of creativity are of the essence of the human which is good and one of the purposes of providence (as we shall see). It is rather the pride, the greed, and the lust for gain and security which accompany that creativity in historical life, that lead to enchainment on the rocks, the descent into the cave of bare survival and of authority. Surely this latter vision is the more accurate portrayal of our plight.[57] Our creativity in itself has not caused our present dilemma; it is rather our insatiable gluttony in our use of the earth, our unwillingness to share, our resistance to equitable distribution, our frantic use of power to grasp and to maintain security, that will in the end destroy us, if we are destroyed. But if the "fault" is a taint in our creativity, not the creativity itself—and here lies the difference in the symbolic accounts—then perhaps the punishment has a different character, the perpetuator of the punishment a different role, and the issue a different possibility.

Inevitably, therefore—and utterly surprisingly—the question of questions with regard to human destiny arises for us too—and from science! Does "Zeus, the sovereign power of history, represent providential creation and salvation as well as iron necessity and so inexorable punishment?—an ancient Greek and even more a biblical question now made vividly relevant as we look ahead through the eyes of science. Two things can initially be said, more of affirmation at this point than of theological analysis, but nonetheless important.

First, in a biblical world there is and there can be no fate—and it is an apparently fated future compounded of a finite nature, technical creativity and their implacable social consequences that we here face. But contingency is the name of history. There are continuities in history; developments in technology, in population growth and their relation to natural resources *do* have their consequences. Also pride and greed, injustice and domination do have their historical effects, and these must be undergone; new moments in time do portend new and terrible temptations to unwisdom and sin as well as new opportunities for creativity. Nevertheless, the future is open. No "force" or dynamic factor in history operates save *through* human beings and through their common behavior—and thus contingency and freedom enter into each interstice of historical life. Freedom, therefore, remains; and it is a freedom to create as well as to fall, in technology, in economic structures and in politics. Thus no sequence of determined events, benevolent *or* nightmarish, is fated for us in the unknown that is to come. This nightmare itself illustrates this: it was unguessed less than a decade ago, and so it is quite unexpected. Yesterday's vision did not see it; perhaps, all things being contingent, tomorrow's will see something quite different. In itself this nightmare is based only on what we can see now, in technical possibilities, in economic and political forms, in the general dynamic of historical process itself. This is not to say that Heilbroner's future is not possible, a resultant we must ponder and prepare for; it is to say that, like Kahn's "benevolent future," it is not a certainty, and thus we should not allow it to make us despair. A new constellation of all the significant factors in historical process is always possible. No determined future is the truth.

Secondly, both our experience of history and the biblical witness assure us that even within the most tragic situation of captivity, a new covenant in history is promised; in the darkest hour, new birth and new life in human affairs arise; damnation, either ultimate or historical (and we have gazed here at the latter), is never the final divine word, but that the providence of God offers continually new possibilities in each historical situation and ultimate restoration at the end. Thus is there meaning in each moment of time, and hope even for this future. I cannot see how a technological culture can view itself honestly, and not seek to understand itself and its future in the light of this or some similar word: as creative and yet as demonic, as threatened with self-destruction, and yet as always upheld by the divine power and the divine promise. Such faith in a nonfated future, in the continuity of open possibility and in the divine completion of our every abortive creation, is now more necessary than ever. Correspondingly, careful reflection on the structure, the dynamic forms and the possibilities of history in the light of all that we know becomes inescapable as all our familiar certainties about the future evaporate like exciting dreams in the cold ecological dawn.[58]

4

CONTEMPORARY
PHILOSOPHICAL VIEWS OF HISTORY

CRITICAL PHILOSOPHY OF HISTORY

History as a word has always had two quite distinguishable but interrelated meanings.[1] It can refer to the objective course of events in which humans live and about which they can inquire: the history historians write *about*. Or it can refer to that inquiry itself and its results, the human knowledge and understanding of that course of events, the history historians *write*. The two meanings are interconnected because history as the course of events is structured ontologically, as our developing discussion has shown, by the polarity of destiny and freedom. This ontological structure in turn entails that human beings are in history as entities aware or conscious of their immersion in temporal passage, remembering their past and projecting into their future. Human beings exist in time but also dialectically out of it, transcendent to it: their identity, consciousness and activity in the present are compounds of their memory of their own past and their anticipation of their future. This self-transcendence within temporal passage gives to history the complex character that it has. It also accounts for the possibility and the necessity of remembering events, recording them, and, in the end, investigating these remains, records and data from the past in order to reconstruct and "know" that past. The ontological roots both of history as the course of events and of history as a form of inquiry lie together in the character of human being in time.

The first meaning, namely history as the course of events reflected upon in philosophy, results in what is now usually called speculative philosophy of history, an attempt to understand the total course of events with regard to its ontological structure and its telos, i.e., its basic dynamic or causative factors, its fundamental patterns of development, if any, and its "goal" or "meaning" if there be such.[2] Here philosophical reflection is to history as scientific inquiry is to nature or social science is to society: an inquiry seeking to uncover the intelligible structure, the universal patterns of change, the most fundamental forms and the goals of its object, history.[3] Lessing, Herder, Kant, Hegel, Marx, Spencer, Spengler, Toynbee—and contemporary Marxists—are usually taken as illustrative of this kind of philosophy of history, as are the great theologians, for example, Augustine, Calvin and Ritschl, who propounded theologies of history.[4]

In the contemporary Anglo-Saxon world this sort of speculative approach to history, seeking to uncover its basic patterns and possibly its goal as a whole, has been out of fashion. Most philosophical reflection on history has therefore been *critical* in nature, that is, reflection concerned with human knowledge of history, with what sort of knowledge it is and especially with how it relates to the modes of inquiry of the natural and the social sciences. It is, in other words, to historical inquiry what the philosophy of science is to science.[5] Philosophy of science does not tell us what "nature" or "reality" are, but what *science* is. So in this case, philosophy of history does not tell us what history (in the first sense) is, but what historical knowledge is. Let us note that here philosophy—according to the general tendencies of contemporary analytic or linguistic philosophy—does not itself pose as a *knower*, in this case, a knower of history or of its essential character. Such philosophy accepts the pervasive empiricist canon that only the special sciences are cognitive or "know" anything; thus only on their basis (and that of common sense) can we make existential statements, i.e., assertions about what is or has been the case. Consequently, the sole role of philosophy on this view is to inquire into the logic, the epistemology and the language of the sciences. According to this view, therefore, what we know of history is what the historians say or (for many) what the social scientists say, and philosophy's role is to talk about their talk. Philosophy here is a second order, not a first order discipline.[6] All this does not mean that what the critical philosophy of history has talked about is at all trivial or uninteresting, either in itself or to us. Like the "scientific" views of the historical future dealt with in the preceding chapter, much of it seems (to me at least) to leave unexplored a vast number of essential issues. In any case, the main subjects of discussion in critical philosophy of history, of which I shall concentrate on two, are of great relevance to our theme.

The Nature of Historical Explanation

Perhaps the most interesting and lively debate has concerned the question of the nature of an historical explanation. What does it mean to explain an historical event; what is the logic and so the goal of historical understanding; what is the historian in his inquiry trying to do or to establish? On the one side are those who rightly stress that an historical explanation does not leave the event in question as "accidental," a mere product of irrational chance; they insist, however, that a complete historical explanation must, like an explanation in any science, be in terms of general laws.[7] For them, therefore, an historical event is *really* explained (scientifically explained) when the stated initial conditions of the event are connected with the event itself by means of the relevant set of universal and necessitating laws (of physical nature, of psychology, of the social sciences, etc.). As Carl Hempel, a leading exponent of this view, puts it: "A set of events [the initial conditions] can be said to have caused the event to be explained only if general laws can be indicated which connect 'causes' and 'effects'. . . ."[8] The fact that historians do not in fact make this sort of connection (via general laws) merely shows, to Hempel, that historians do not understand the logic of their own craft. Rather, he feels, they assume or leave implicit as part of general knowledge those general laws of sociology or of psychology on which their explanations in fact depend. Thus what they produce as explanations are radically incomplete: "Explanation sketches," "vague indicators" of laws which need "filling out" in terms of further specified conditions and further established universal laws in order to become genuine explanations.[9] Let us note that this view of historical explanation as constituted by appeal to necessitating laws bears ontological as well as epistemological implications. If understanding in historical inquiry comes via universal and necessary laws so that explanation and prediction represent the same causal relation looked at in two different directions, then clearly a necessitating historical continuum is assumed. Even if one of the factors explanatory of an event be human intentionality, that factor itself, as an explanation of the event, is in toto governed by the universal laws of sociology and psychology. There is, therefore, place neither for contingency nor for purpose in history, according to such a view.

Although Karl Popper represents much the same understanding of historical explanation, his own different "ontology" of history, if I may put it that way, gives to his view a quite different twist. Popper agrees thoroughly with Hempel that all scientific explanation, natural or social, has the same form, namely, the connection via general laws between initial conditions and event-to-be-explained, a connection that is testable by prediction and subsequent experimental "non-falsification."[10] All genuine *theory* in physical or social science thus involves the development and the experimental establishment of general laws. But, says Popper, such *theoretical* understanding (and here he radically differs from Hempel) is not possible with regard to history and its movements. For no general laws govern history's movements as a whole, and the effort to discover such general laws, and especially to "predict" on their basis, is one of the fatal confusions of our entire intellectual history. The historical "explanations" which historians produce are thus radically nontheoretical. Although, to be sure, they line up events in their proper sequence, such a series does not *explain* at all; and what explanation is available is usually in terms of general laws so obvious and so trivial that *their* establishment is of little theoretical interest. History informs us of the unique series of events that led to a given conclusion; although these questions of origin, Popper notes, are interesting to us, they are "of comparatively little theoretical interest," since no universal laws are thereby uncovered or established.[11] Thus it is a mistake to understand historical inquiry as a search for historical law, as a theoretical discipline. Rather, writing history is a mode of selective interpretation, viewing the series of events from an interesting but partial and ultimately arbitrary perspective, the one perspective being no "truer" than the other, since, none being testable, none are theories in that crucial sense.[12]

As can be seen, Popper has a very different over all view from Hempel. History's changes, while taking place according to a wide variety of laws, do not *themselves* obey any discoverable laws. Rather, such changes are the results of initial conditions, contingent trends, and rational or irrational responses and policies on the part of people. Thus since history is not determined by general laws in its movement, social scientists do not and cannot discover the "laws of history" which a wholistic political policy might seek to obey. All that social theory can do, according to Popper, is to tell us the unintended consequences of certain limited policies, and thus give the policymaker useful and pragmatic advice about means, but none about trends and structures which are universal and so permanent, and none about ends—as an engineer can tell us how to build a stable bridge, but not whether we should build it or when to build it.[13] Despite the fact that Popper's "world" is one of contingency and of relative rational autonomy, he leaves the historians in almost the same strange position as does Hempel with his implicitly determined sequence of events. For both thinkers, historians are inquirers in a nontheoretical discipline whose conclusions therefore have little truth content—since their theoretical base cannot be falsified —and so whose modes of inquiry hardly deserve to be ranked among the cognitive disciplines. One interesting conclusion of this discussion is that if the scientific concern for the establishment of general laws is taken as the *sole* theoretical concern of man, and if empirical verification and falsification is regarded as the *only* mode of arriving at judgments of truth and falsehood, then clearly it matters little what ontology one implicitly adopts with regard to the question of history, since in either case historical inquiry ceases to produce anything like historical *knowledge*.[14]

Another interesting conclusion of this debate between Hempel and Popper is that, if Popper be right, the "long-term trend" of sociology to seek for empirical and so testable "universal laws" of social continuity and so also of social change, is a logical error of the first magnitude, a misunderstanding of its own much more modest legitimate purposes and value. If concrete history, in truth, be infected both with contingency and with the possibility of autonomous choice, as Popper insists, then the search for general laws governing all social movement can only result in the creation of abstractions, abstract entities or systems, or institutions such as "the family," "the market," "transportation," "civilization," or "society. Such theoretical social "entities" *seem*, when abstracted, to be obedient to laws of continuity and change, but the price for this coherence is that these mental constructs are only tangentially related to the concrete and so contingent processes of actual history.[15]

This does not mean, of course, that the role of social science is a minimally important one. For humans to take creative action in society, they must understand the social world in which they act. Certainly they cannot transform that world for the better, i.e., introduce new and creative possibilities into it, unless they understand the structures and so the problems and the potentialities of the world in which they act. As we have noted, all politics depends on "political self-consciousness," an *understanding* in terms of theory of the given (of destiny) in our social environment. Such understanding is necessarily in terms of social theory: a theory concerning the structure, the continuities, the trends, the habits, the symbols and the goal of the social organism we seek to comprehend. Without this, action in the world is blind because a sense of real possibility proceeds in part from an understanding of actualities and their potentialities. This does not mean that the historical reality in which and on which we act *is* such a system. This is the fallacy of misplaced concretion, taking an abstraction for concrete reality. The historical reality is the union of destiny: trends, continuities, stresses and possibilities, which we must comprehend if we are to deal with them, and the response in the present of the humans immersed in that destiny. Social science, as does all objective inquiry, abstracts from the pole of freedom, of response, and thus falsifies the total reality; it presents only the objectified reality, the conditions for response and so for events, and thus only a continually "frozen" form of history. The possibility, however, of an intelligent freedom is dependent on the understanding through theory of that destiny as, correlatively, the possibility of creative freedom is dependent on the actual given in any social situation.

Returning to the debate about the status of history, we find, as can be imagined, that these blunt assertions of Hempel and Popper that historical inquiry is barely if at all cognitive in character have evoked a spate of counter-arguments from critical philosophers of history and from historians. Since these arguments are multiple and represent a wide variety of perspectives, I shall only try to summarize some of the major points that have been made in defense of the autonomy and integrity of historical inquiry.[16]

The first point made by these varied responses is that the logic of historical inquiry is significantly different from that of physical or even of social science. Thus historical explanation must be understood on its own terms—in terms of the presuppositions of historical inquiry and so in terms of what satisfies the community of historians as an explanation—and not in the terms of explanation, "scientific" or otherwise, derived from other modes of inquiry.[17] In history, as Popper recognized, interest is concentrated on the understanding of one unique case: the rise of the Renaissance, the origins of World War I, and so on, and not on developing, establishing or verifying general laws applicable to all cultural movements or all wars. In fact, general laws, even if discovered, are irrelevant to the central aims of historical explanation. If the law in question is too general, it does not explain *this* case (for example, do *all* generals linger with beautiful queens, as Antony did with Cleopatra?); if the law is made specific enough to explain the case in question, it is then applicable to that case alone, and thus does it lose its status as a law.[18] In any case, since it deals not only with unique but also past—and so unrepeatable—constellations of events, historical inquiry is such that its conclusions, i.e., its hypotheses about significant factors or effectuating causes, can never be experimentally tested.[19] Thus while it may use a multitude of what can be termed general laws or "truisms," as Scriven puts it, history is not concerned with their establishment, nor is its knowledge, and the certainty of that knowledge, even essentially dependent on those general laws that it does explicitly employ.[20]

Granted, then, that the historian wishes to make a past event intelligible, i.e., to reduce to a minimum by his explanation the sheer arbitrary, accidental, "chance" character of the event; and yet, granted, over against Hempel et al., that he does not do so by invoking some "whenever P, then Q" law, how does historical inquiry explain, or what does explanation mean here? First of all, argue the historians, in order that an event be made intelligible, its initial conditions, the "given" out of which it arose, what we have termed destiny, must be specified, organized and arranged into an intelligible sequence. The entire relevant (or what seems to the historian to be relevant) context of economic and political trends, of social habits, attitudes and ideas, of concrete events in nature or society, of personal dispositions and needs, etc., which gave rise to the event thus forms the initial condition of an historical explanation—as it did for the event itself. This potential infinity of ante-cedent factors—of all sorts—must be "graded" or "assessed" with regard to their significance for the event. Such a reconstruction on the part of the historian of the relevant context, while in large part dependent on the evidence, is also dependent on his imaginative reconstruction of the event, and so on his view of what are the *important* causes or, better, conditions of any historical occurrence.

Secondly, it is crucial for the nature of historical explanation that this initial context, now graded vis-à-vis its significance, is considered in the explanation itself to be an essential or necessary condition for the event, but not a *sufficient* condition. For the historian the event might not have happened, even given all these condi-tions, or it might have happened another way.[21] Thus is contingency interlaced into each "aperture" of history, and thus is there no predictive power in history's conclu-sions.

The most fundamental reason the conditions do not give a *total* explanation is that, as we have argued, history has an ontological structure of destiny and freedom, and so it is made up of human and so *centered* responses to these given conditions. If, as seems another inescapable ontological presupposition, the only finite agents in history are people, then the only actions that make up history (or social move-ments) are people's actions. Thus are historical events in part intended, the results of understanding, judgment, conviction, purpose and decision—however wayward, immoral, ignorant or deluded each of these may be. "Forces," economic or other-wise, "systems" of social behavior, "modes of production," etc., are ontologically abstractions from modes of human behavior in certain social roles and relations. Such worlds of behavior may be almost completely habitual and thus in large part determined; yet in none are the elements of understanding, judgment and decision totally absent. The pole of freedom is no more eradicable from any section of history than is the pole of destiny. As a consequence, the only *sufficient* causes in history lie in the actions of the actual persons within history, in the mystery of their feelings, their desires, their understanding, norms and goals, and their decisions and actions in response to the given that is presented to them.[22] Thus is the historian led inevitably beyond the initial conditions, the context or destiny, of an event to the actors, to considering dispositions and character, goals and desires, intentions and purposes, the understanding or the misunderstanding of a situation by its actors—the whole "inward," "human" side of history, as ingredient to his explanation. For the event would not have happened as it did without this centered, human response to conditions in action.[23] As is well known, the philosopher R. G. Collingwood made this uncovering of inner intention the ultimate goal, the final explicandum of historical inquiry, and most working historians agree that the response which is creative of the event is initiated inwardly through the *meaning* of a situation to the responders and through their subsequent judgments, decisions and actions.[24]

Nevertheless, even those who agree with Collingwood on the importance of the "inward" in historical explanation, insist that intentions, goals and meanings alone do not explain events as a historian wishes to do. In the first place, every interpretation of the given by an actor in history, every judgment about what is practiced, wise or good, every goal of action, and so on, is *itself* shaped fundamentally by the social structures and the social symbols, the "world," in which the historical agent lives.[25] To quote Leff again: "Historical facts are societal; they presume conventions and roles and values not given in the facts themselves. . . . [The historian] has to abstract the complex of attitudes, values, intentions, and conventions which belong to our actions in order to grasp their meaning. He must, therefore, look to norms before he can assess motives, causes, or any other form of individual response. This is the historian's supreme task."[26]

In the second place, whatever the intentions that inspired an action, its objective outcome, its social and temporal effects—which alone interest the historian—are always different from the initiating inward intention for a multitude of reasons.[27] Thus events are not to be understood merely in terms of intentions as if the resultant character of history had been planned or even willed. Events or outcomes are, therefore, the results of (1) the symbolic social world of a time, (2) the preceding conditions, trends, problems, tasks, (3) the inner response and intention, and (4) the contingent constellation of other contemporary acts and events. As Randall notes, history as a series of events is not a cause but an outcome, an outcome of all of these unique factors resulting in a unique sequence of events.[28] Historical events, we reiterate, result from the polarity of destiny and freedom, from the given and the new human response; it thus unites given and "necessary" actuality with possibility in creating new events. Actuality is in each case the new result of preceding actuality and possibilities presented to freedom. Being is temporal and comes to be as destiny is actualized ever anew by freedom.

A given event, and the series of which it is a part, is to be understood *historically*, therefore, only by the imaginative reconstruction of that singular "whole" compounded of destiny and freedom: symbols, conditions, trends, intentions and constellations of factors culminating in an action and its consequences for the future. In such an unfolding whole the event is made intelligible—though never necessary —as a part or perhaps the culminating part of that unfolding story.[29] Thus the historian does not understand through general laws applied to similar cases. He understands through reconstructing a developing particular and unique situation in all its relevant and significant characteristics, and the human responses to it as it develops, of which whole or series the event or events in question will find their places as resultant parts, so that the entire sequence "makes sense" as a self-explanatory story.[30]

Insofar as the historian uses general laws to reconstruct that explanatory story, the most important "laws" or "principles" are not those that the physical sciences, nor even the social sciences, formulate. Rather these "laws" or truisms are his own most basic ontological or philosophical principles of interpreting human nature and its place in history. First, there is what he regards as the general patterns of human behavior, its possibilities, its modes of response, its fundamental drives, ambitions, weaknesses, goals and limits.[31] Secondly, there is his view of the dynamic factors of history, what are the most significant causes that bring about the general shape of any historical situation. On that understanding of the structure and dynamic of historical process, which determines for him the relative significance of preceding factors, depends, needless to say, the whole shape of his reconstruction and so the mode of his explanation.[32] Thirdly, there is his understanding, derived from the social sciences, of how continuities and trends in social structure develop, and so how the conditions for the event, its given destiny, came to be and function during the period under study.

In any case, if this view of historical explanation be valid, it is clear that historical inquiry is not devoid of a crucial theoretical component, as Hempel and Popper maintained. Even if it refuses to explain through necessitating laws behind the events, nevertheless it does make events intelligible by moving through their apparent incoherence to a deeper level of understanding. Historical explanation consists in the creation of a vast and informed mental construct, an interpretation which—like the laws of science but in a different way—goes "beyond" the given data to set them into an intelligible pattern by creating the total world of the event: its conditions and their structural forms, its symbolic horizons, its motivating forces and intentions, its contingent interactions and its consequences. In this intelligible construct the event ceases to be incoherent and becomes understandable, and yet it is a construct appropriate to its subject matter, namely, one that is in accord with the basic ontology characteristic of history itself as compounded of destiny and freedom, actuality and possibility, and so as contingent, diverse, centered and creative of the new.

The Question of Objectivity

Our discussion of the nature of historical explanation leads inevitably to the next general subject of contemporary debate in the critical philosophy of history. Is historical inquiry in any meaningful sense "objective"? Are all historical conclusions so utterly dependent on the viewpoint, norms, stance—and so on the biography, social and psychological situation, metaphysical preferences and epoch—of the historian as to be merely subjective, a "personal interpretation"? In the end, does historical inquiry succeed merely in revealing more about the historian's own perspective, and that of his age, than it does of his object?

Certainly whatever objectivity and so knowledge and truth may be involved in historical inquiry, they are not identical with those of physical science.[33] The theoretical component of science, its general laws through which the given data are explained, can be tested, at least in the minimal sense of being falsified or not falsified, by repeatable experiments that reproduce the requisite conditions. Since, however, the theoretical component of history has reference, as we have just seen, to unique, and even more to past and so unrepeatable constellations of events (e.g., the "whole" out of which the event the American Revolution arose), the requisite conditions cannot be reconstituted and so the theoretical component can never be empirically tested.[34] There is no way to falsify by experiment an historical hypothesis that such and such factors brought about a given revolution in the past. Moreover, this nontestable hypothesis by which the historian explains, i.e., the reconstruction of the whole as a dynamic sequence, is inevitably the product of the historian's informed imagination. And in that imaginative reconstruction, the role of *interpretation* is crucial at every level of historical work, from that of the "hard facts" to be understood to his most general theories of explanation.

1. The historian begins with no given and solid "facts" or even "events," but only with present data: documents, records, reports, pictures, artefacts, etc. Out of these he must reconstruct whatever he regards as the "facts" or "events" in the past which he then wishes to explain. In turn his reconstruction of the events which become his facts (what actually happened on July 4, 1776) is determined by the way he interprets or uses the canons or rules of historical inquiry through which he reconstructs the event out of the present data, that is, the kinds of factors he believes to be significant in the appearance of an event.[35] Thus as Leff notes, "There is not a part of history which is objective—the facts—and another part—the historian's interpretation or judgment—which is subjective. Judgment and interpretation are equally inherent in deciding what are the facts, which are the relevant ones in a certain context, and how significant they are."[36] Paradoxically, the same interpretive principles that guide the formation of his conclusions direct his logically prior reconstruction of the facts which his conclusions seek to make intelligible.

2. The wholes by which the historian explains his reconstructed facts are themselves purely "mental" constructs, i.e., they do not and did not exist as empirical entities, and they are qualitative in their character, defined and determined by qualitative attributes. These "universals" (barbarian invasions, Norman conquest, colonial expansion, Industrial Revolution, French Revolution, etc.) are an essential part of the explanation. Yet as mental constructs and not given entities they are the creatures of the imaginative if informed interpretation of the historian himself. Naturally the widest scope is here possible for legitimate disagreement as to whether such wholes are plausibly implied by the data. Moreover, since anything in history is "situation-dependent," i.e., receives its particular shape and, in fact, its possibility from the cultural whole of which it is a part, no explanation is possible without taking that cultural milieu into account. Thus there are no useful *universal* generalizations or laws (*whenever* P, then Q) which arise as conclusions of historical studies. This importance of the context to all historical understanding means that *periodization*

is essential to all historical inquiry. A period or epoch must be conceived on the basis of the data, for only in the terms of its qualitative attributes can the data in turn be made into "facts" and the facts set within an intelligible whole.[37] But the formation of the period—while usually conventional and so to most of us obvious, as for example, "medieval" or "Renaissance"—is itself an act of historical and imaginative interpretation. Its formation is guided by the historian's most elusive yet crucial feelings of qualitative similarity and dissimilarity, of continuities and changes, by his or her assessments of attitudes, goals and norms, and by his judgments of what is or is not significant in historical change.

3. As is obvious from our discussion, there can be no choice of an event to be explained, no explanation of the event in terms of factors, nor any creation of a significant universal or period, a whole within which events make sense, without *selection* by the historian. The past has an infinity of particulars, and certain among them must be chosen—often merely because surviving and so available data point to them—in order for any coherence or intelligibility to appear. The "subjectivity" of selection is not, as, for example, Nagel and White say,[38] merely a matter of the "interest" of the historian selecting one portion or aspect of history rather than another. Selecting has far deeper epistemological roots and so far more important theoretical consequences than that. For her or his principles of selection determine how the historian approaches at the most fundamental level whatever portions of history she or he chooses to investigate. Selection is based on the criterion of importance: what event has significance for other events; what events are significant as illustrative of this movement or this period; what factors throughout the period are determinative for the shape of the process as a whole; and what sorts of intentions or actions, if any, on the part of people were significant in the development of events. The process of selection, in other words, is based on judgments of significance and importance, and these, in turn, are based on the historian's views, implicit or explicit, about what *are* the dynamic factors in historical change. Selection, like reconstruction, is grounded in the historian's "ontological beliefs," what Scriven calls "universal truisms," although such beliefs vary from age to age, from class to class and from historian to historian. These include views of what cultural factors are basic to social change and how they tend to develop; what drives, modes of psychological determination, desires or motives are fundamental in human action; and how impersonal and personal, outward and inward, unintended and intended factors are interrelated in human and social life—matters which heretofore have been the subject of speculative philosophical debate. Thus what we can only call the *ontological* perspective of the historian determines in part his use of his data and the shape and meaning of all of his explanations.

4. Finally, there are no important historical judgments without moral assessments. To perceive the significant factors in the "rise" of a community, a movement or an epoch presupposes judgments about such things as the growth, strength, health, vitality, and so on, of the community or movement. To speak of its decline is to presuppose judgments about what is for it ill-health, loss of strength, loss of vitality,

etc. Each of these sets of judgments is "moral" in the broadest sense, concerned with the health and the ill-health, with what is creative and what is destructive in a community's life. And these presuppose a view of health or authenticity in human affairs, veritably a norm for human community, in which these judgments essential to historical inquiry are grounded. Moreover—and more controversial—moral judgments in a narrower sense, the "rightness" of actions, the humanity of modes of behavior, the justice of a community's life, and so on, are intrinsic to historical inquiry. How can one understand the issues of the Civil War without moral assessment of slavery, explain the rise and fall of colonialism without the moral categories of oppression and of self-determination, make comprehensible the reforms in American economic life without the categories of justice and injustice, or speak meaningfully of Hitler and his significance without moral assessment of his acts of aggression, his tyranny, his genocide?[39] Just as any determination of the significant factors in history requires as its presupposition an *ontology* of man's role in social process, so any judgment of the health or decay of community life requires as its presupposition a view of authentic human community which functions in some way as a *norm* for community life and so can provide the basis for moral assessment of concrete illustrations of that life in history. If, as I argued, humans cannot act in history without moral judgments about events and their relations to them, in a parallel way historians cannot understand history without using their own moral norms for history's processes.

To sum up our discussion, it is evident that historical inquiry presupposes both for its construction of "facts" and "events," and for its construction of the wider contexts within which events are intelligible, a perspective on the part of the historian that can be called an implicit philosophy of history. That is to say, it presupposes a view of the significant factors in historical process and their interrelation, a view of the inward grounds and character of human action, a view of the relation of objective factors in social change to human intentions and actions, and an intellectual commitment to a moral norm for human action and for social community in history. Put in our own language, this "implicit philosophy" encompasses an implicit ontology of history as a union of destiny and freedom, a union in which destiny is constituted and dealt with not only by "causes" but also by "norms," and in which freedom is shaped not only by possibilities relevant to actuality, but also by intentions aiming at what is taken to be the ideal. Because of these "philosophical" presuppositions, history as an inquiry is radically "theory-laden," an interpretive exercise in imaginative reconstruction essentially guided by a particular way of looking at man and his world.[40] As a number of commentators have recognized, disputes over historical interpretation stem from disagreement not so much over matters of fact as over the philosophical perspectives which the historian brings to his inquiry and which, as we have seen, determine at every level his reconstruction of the past.[41]

One may go even further and argue that these perspectives through which history is reconstructed have an "existential" as well as a theoretical base. What is of greatest importance to us in our present as having possibilities for *our* future is generally made into *the* dynamic factor of our past: be it science, learning, democracy, an economic structure, a form of religion, a social mode of being, liberation or whatever. Correspondingly, what to us impedes that hoped-for future becomes for us the principle of stagnation or of resistance in the entire past.[42] Thus is the past interpreted through whatever is of ultimate concern to us in our present, as that present moves into our future.[43] Both philosophical views concerning the structure and norms of history, and existential (or possibly one could say "religious" or theological) presuppositions about history's potential meaning and fulfillment seem, therefore, to constitute essential presuppositions for any reconstruction and interpretation of the past. Like the history which it studies, historical inquiry and its conclusions are multi-dimensional. The content of inquiry is given by the data reconstructed into significant sequences of events through imaginative scholarship, and its form, in the sense of its most fundamental emphases, connections and tendencies, is provided by the views of men and women, their world and the meaning of the future which the historian holds.

If this analysis be correct, then the issue of "objectivity" is unavoidable: how can a discipline claim to offer objective and so universal knowledge if it is shaped by such subjective factors as a scholar's "metaphysical and moral beliefs," to quote Walsh. Certainly if we confine the term objectivity alone to those inquiries which are completely free *ab initio* of any presupposed theory—i.e., ones in which all relevant theory, implicit or explicit, is constituted by theories tested within and established by inquiries of the discipline itself—then history cannot be called objective. This is a definition which many philosophers of science advance, and thus, as we noted, they find history at best "non-theoretical" and at worst "merely interpretive," not yet a science and not even in its present forms cognitive. But possibly the fault lies with their understanding of inquiry in any form, and thus with their exclusivist and to many interpreters abstract definition of objectivity. It is dubious that actual experimental science is itself as free logically of significant implicit presuppositions as their own "logical" analysis of scientific method tries to assert—though this is not a subject into which the present discussion can go. And it is even more questionable that their view of science as a totally presuppositionless discipline is coherent either with the history of science, which manifests its clear embeddedness in diverse cultural epochs, or with any rigorous anthropological, sociological or philosophical analysis of human knowing per se.[44]

Men and women exist, and so know, as total selves within a wider social world. Before he or she can know or deal with that world—which we have here temporalized into destiny—it has been formed and shaped for them linguistically and symbolically (and so socially) into a definite structure on which his or her expectations of *all* sorts in relation to it depend. As a form of relation to that "world" (or destiny), *any* mode of knowing, therefore, presupposes that basic prior shaping. Behind any methodology thus lies a prior socially transmitted ontology, be it only the "pre-ontology" assumed within a given cultural whole and communicated through language and tradition. Thus knowing is multi-dimensional, as we noted: it involves, to be sure, the gathering, the arrangement, the manipulation of the data and the formulation and testing of hypotheses concerning the data. But also in order that any arrangement, manipulation and testing of any sort be possible, it involves the ordering and shaping of the whole manifold of relevant experiences through implicit symbolization—a shaping which, on reflection, becomes precisely those "metaphysical and moral beliefs" referred to above. It is within *this* situation of an already shaped world, or of a "pre-ontology," that the concepts of objectivity and of knowledge arise, not outside it; thus the objectivity of our knowledge is not threatened by the process of prior shaping so much as made possible by it.[45] As I have argued, historical theories or interpretations are not "testable" since the conclusions of historical study consist of existential propositions about singular, unrepeatable entities rather than universal and abstract laws subject to repeated confirmation. In history, moreover, the distance from hard data to reconstructed "facts" is greater, the dynamic factors more elusive and more complex, the modes of connection more controversial—and so the role of imaginative interpretation is at every level much greater than in experimental science. The logic of historical inquiry is, therefore, substantially different from that of physical science, and thus in the former the level of objectivity is different. But since *no* mode of knowing is free of personal and especially cultural interpretive presuppositions, the greater role played by interpretation in history does not destroy either its own form of objectivity or its cognitive status. Men and women know historically in a valid mode of their cognitive powers —though within that mode there is inescapably less precision, less definitiveness, less public verification, and so less communal assent, and consequently more possibility of continuing controversy, as every historian will happily admit.

Two conclusions that are relevant to our wider theme may be drawn from this discussion of objectivity in historical inquiry. In the first place, if there is, as seems evident, this philosophical component to historical inquiry, the widespread prejudice against all forms of what is somewhat disdainfully called "speculative philosophy of history" seems irrational if not downright silly. A careful investigation of critical philosophy of history—and we have here attempted one—shows that an analysis of historical knowing uncovers inevitably in that process of cognition inescapable ontological and normative presuppositions necessary for that process. In this sense, each historian in fact possesses a "philosophy of history" whether he or she has considered it reflectively and critically or not.[46] Certainly, therefore, if that be the case, historical inquiry will be more subjective and less objective if this implicit theoretical component is not discussed, evaluated, and rationally grounded—in whatever way this may be possible. Objectivity, in any realistic meaning of the word, will not be achieved by seeking to rid history of this philosophical component; then historical inquiry is forced into the form of a scientific method inappropriate to itself and of only dubious relevance to actual experimental science. Objectivity will arise only when rational criticism addresses itself to the questions raised by this theoretical component: questions of the dynamic factors in history, the relation of impersonal causes to intentions, the relation of symbols to social structures and to action, the role and status of norms in communal experience and in knowing, and the relation of "meaning" to historical process, i.e., some of the classic subjects of speculative philosophy of history.

Not only is such rational consideration of the presuppositions of historical inquiry necessary if its objectivity is to be increased and not diminished. It is also necessary in order to bring to more conceptual unity the other disciplines involved in the general subject of social process and historical change: psychology, anthropology, sociology, economics, political science and history, all heretofore isolated in their own abstractions with no clear (i.e., rational) way to think their way back to the unity of the historical process which each seeks from its own relatively abstracted perspective to study. Philosophy of history is not, as is often portrayed by a culture frightened of unverified thought but utterly dependent on it in order to verify, a matter of individual "fancy," of special pleading, of irrational belief, in short, an abdication of reason. It is rather the sole means of providing our common study of and reflection on historical process with rational and so objective grounds.[47]

This point leads to the second conclusion. Our analysis of the mode of knowing appropriate to historical process has led us beyond the surface level of events to the elaboration of fundamental structures and meanings expressed in and through those events, i.e., to a philosophy of history—if historical knowing is to be possible and rational. On the one hand, we have found historical events, as interpreted by historians, to be composed of a given constellation or complex of conditions and a response of human freedom, of assessment, understanding, judgment and decision, on the other. This fundamental ontological structure, combining as it does decided or determined actuality—now "necessary" as a condition for all that follows—with undecided possibility or real alternatives in the present, alone makes intelligible the epistemological questions and issues raised in critical philosophy of history, and alone makes possible resolutions to these issues effective in the practice of inquiry by historians. Since we have already found this ontological structure appearing in our analysis of change and of concrete historical and political experience, it seems to appear as the necessary and universal structure of temporal historical being; it will therefore be an ontological presupposition fundamental to all that follows in this volume.

As we have just noted, moreover, our prior analysis of the *experience* of historical process, both of social change and of politics, led us also to dimensions beyond the immediate surface of political life and its problems, ontological and theological dimensions which I argued must be thematized in terms of intelligible symbols if that historical experience is to be serenely borne and creatively directed. Thus on two interrelated but quite separate levels of the modern experience of historical change—the experiential level of passage itself uncovered by phenomenological analysis, and the reflective level of the interpretation and understanding of passage uncovered by critical analysis of historical inquiry—we have found ourselves at odds with the dominant empiricistic, positivistic, "secular" character of our cultural life, which denies the relevance and the possibility of philosophical and theological interpretation of temporal being. We have, therefore, also urged the reappropriation of that philosophical and theological heritage—though in *modern* terms—which affirmed the possibility, the rationality and the necessity of reflection about human, ontological and religious questions. Thus both because *historical experience* raises questions of destiny and fate and their strange relation to freedom and intention, to meaning and to morals, and because *inquiry into history* raises questions of the structure, the meanings and the norms of history, we now turn to those contemporary speculative philosophies of history that at least deal forthrightly with these unavoidable themes.

SPECULATIVE PHILOSOPHY OF HISTORY

Ernst Bloch

The most important form of speculative philosophy of history in our time is unequestionably Marxism. In this country, the intellectual élite on the whole has not quite regarded Marxism as blasphemous, unclean or evil. It has merely regarded it as obviously wrong, a mere ideology, an emotively held set of absolute and so almost "religious" principles that have no "scientific" (in the sense of social scientific) value—and so not worthy of serious discussion or debate.[48] This is owing, in part, to the fact that in the experience of this generation (i.e., the older one) Stalinism, as one centrally important interpretation of Marxism, seemed for several decades to represent Marxism's only possible form, both as a political and social embodiment and as a systematic social philosophy. But that identification of Marxism as a social philosophy with its Stalinist or even its Soviet forms is no longer excusable considering the innumerable varieties of Marxist social theory that have emanated from Western Europe, from Asia, and from South America. The insistence that Russian communism is the only social embodiment of Marxist theory reveals only a deliberate blindness to the realities of our age, which the various embodied forms of communism in China, in Viet Nam, in Rumania and Yugoslavia easily refute, not to mention innumerable forms of socialism dependent in the end on Marxist theory. Thus to continue to assume that identification of Marxism with Russian totalitarianism, as much of present American social and political theory seems to do, is at least as inaccurate as the opposite assumption that capitalism is identical with the America of the robber barons; both assumptions reveal that other grounds than those provided by intellectual analysis are at work. This is not only an ideological position parading as "science"; it is also foolish. One cannot understand European, South American or Asiatic social theory without being thoroughly familiar with the Marxist categories in terms of which the majority of their social scientists work. One could go further and say that no one can understand mature European intellectual life generally without Marxism and its intellectual descendants, any more than one can understand American intellectual life—its literature, its drama, its social theory, its theology—without Freud and the many psychoanalytic theories which his system spawned.

One of the most important Marxist philosophers in Europe has been Ernst Bloch. His influence on European theology, and now on recent American theology, has been immense. In this brief summary, I shall isolate only a few themes in Bloch which directly relate to our subject and to the theologies concerned with history and the future which he has influenced.[49]

1. The first theme is Bloch's vigorous and brilliant criticism of empiricism and verificationism as exclusive methods of arriving at valid thought, the notion that thinking, to be significant and true, must accommodate itself to the visible and so present "facts." Every hypothesis, argues Bloch, tested by available facts is confined to the present world expressed through those facts. If all thought that is relevant to what is, is restricted in this way to the present state of things, socially and humanly, thought in effect submits to the status quo as the test of its validity, and reason loses its true role of directing and shaping given reality into new possibilities. Empiricism as an exclusive canon of thought is, therefore, an ideological tool of established forces.[50] It may not have intended to be this, but this is, argues Bloch, what has happened and what in principle could be expected. As the claim to be "pragmatic" can hide a mass of ideological commitments, so the claim to be "objective" because purely empirical can be the modern academic mode of blessing the status quo.

On the contrary, argues Bloch, almost all important thought in human history— religious, philosophical, literary and social—has done precisely the opposite. Implicitly or explicitly, it has sought to present what are *not* the facts, the not-yet, what might be, the ideal that is not yet actual—utopia. These daydreams, visions of lost paradises, folktales, messianic theologies, and even the ontologies of true being, have for him been crucial to historical process.[51] Creative thought directs rather than is directed by the facts; it transforms the given rather than is conformed to it. Thus is the ideal possibility the most important object of thought since it is through it that the new forms in historical process become possible. Without thought's relation to the ideal that is not yet, thought is confined to the present, and process stagnates. As Bloch remarks, the proposition "a thousand years of injustice do not justify one hour of them" was an insight so little in accord with the facts that all it did was to bring about the English, the American, the French Revolutions![52] Of course, adds Bloch, empiricism has its provisional place, for creative thought directed at possibility must keep in touch with what *is*, lest it be totally irrelevant and futile. Thus empiricism plus "metaphysics," the study of present tendencies plus an intelligible vision of possibility, are the key constituents of human rationality in relation to a changing historical process—a process that not only *includes* human experiments, hypotheses, projections, but is *itself* an experiment and so for which projection beyond the present is a basic role for thinking.[53]

Bloch is also in part critical of Marx for being too materialistic, too scientistic, in effect, too bourgeois, for concentrating solely on technological and economic developments, and on the essential and political conditions of a new world—which are important—but leaving the human, the inward, the "soul" out.[54] In his struggle with religiosity and with idealism as instruments of conservatism, Marx, says Bloch, overlooked the important point that the purpose of social reconstruction is finally the development and liberation of human inwardness. The spirit or soul is the only locus of value in men and women: the new world as a gigantic workshop or factory without soul is no culmination for history. Thus, says Bloch, historic Marxism is a social and political philosophy in need of humanistic development and so, as will be evident, in need of supplement from religion and its concerns.

2. As is already obvious, for Bloch the essential nature of historical human being and of its world is *process*, the movement into what is not yet, what might be but is not: "World history is an experiment—a real experiment conducted in the world and aimed towards a possible just and proper world."[55] To understand reality, then, in terms of what is now, and therefore what are now the facts, is to miss the whole point— humanly, historically and ontologically—as if in an inquiry one drew one's conclusions in the midst of the experiment rather than at its end. If all is process, the essence of any given entity is only what it can and will be, its fulfillment, its telos. The essence, therefore, of human being, of society and of history is only what each can become.[56] To portray or envision this essence which is the telos and so the future completion of all things is the hidden aim and truth of all important thought: of religious myth and rational theology, of literature and philosophy, of folktales and fairy stories. It is by these "not yet" images that both the essence of things is known and the process of things realized.

3. If, moreover, all is, in this way, process toward a goal, then *the future*, in which moving reality is to be realized and in which essences will be manifest, is the most important ontological category. As Bloch reiterates, the future determines or masters the present. What a thing is to be is its own essential nature, shaping the process of its being into completion; thus is everything "determined by" that latent essence which will be realized and manifest in the future. In human history, moreover, all action and so the course of historical process itself that results from action, is molded, if not mastered by human intentions and aims, by the dreams and images of future possibility which action can bring to embodiment. Thus as the locus or "space" of possibility, of the goal of nature's latencies and of human history's dreams alike, the future determines or masters the present and gives shape to the developing process. What is, is rectified, even "saved" by what is not but will be, by utopia. Thought, therefore, can never, and should never, refute possibility by a falsification based on present facts.[57] Empiricism is the hidden ideology of conservatism and fascism, and thus the major ideological instrument for closing an open history.

4. The central creative factor in history for Bloch lies in human action, in human subjectivity embodied outwardly in historical activity.[58] Human dreams and utopias, man's hopes for the future, expressed first in artistic and reflective forms, become actualized in historical events. Thus do these imaged possibilities determine history,

for it is under their direction that political action takes place. It is through them that the new, the not-yet which is possible, is realized. Through imaged possibility enacted by human deeds the future determines the present.

5. There are, however, also objective, external, nonhuman factors active in the future realization of possibility in process. Bloch has not explicated with care the ontological status or the historical character of these objective factors as did, for example, Marx in his theory of the materialistic or economic dialectic. Nevertheless, it is clear that for him there is an immanent directing "tendency" in process, a "push," a drive in things that impels them toward the realization of their hidden essence.[59] Bloch refers to this in terms of "objective latencies," "trends," "real possibilities about to become actual," the "cosmic incognito": "In fact, everything that arises in this way demands an exploration of the being of the world itself as potential-being-on-the-ascent, as matter that objectively might allow itself to be, and could be, raised from its own alienation. . . . The history of being itself is the experimental attempt to identify its impulse and origin; the impulse and origin of that history which it is man's task to illumine."[60] The world process, then, has inherently a tendency or latency to find what is redeeming and whole, an instability to remain in its present desparate state. Hence, the future and human hope, and human action toward the future and on the grounds of hope, are utterly significant for humans and for process alike. Only with the union of the latencies of being with the creative activity of men and women can being in flux discover and realize its as yet unmanifested essence.

6. Bloch is a staunch atheist, though by no means in traditional Marxist terms. For him, as for Feuerbach, the gods, or the god, of religion are mistaken hypostatizations of the ideal. Nevertheless, this is Feuerbach with a difference. For the ideal that is by religion made into a real entity "up there" is here not an ideal of humanity from which men and women are alienated in a false consciousness. It is rather the ideal of the *future*, the not-yet possibility from which, to be sure, we are in a present evil world alienated, but which must be projected, imaged and conceived in order for that temporal alienation to be overcome. Thus, while for Bloch the religious hypostatization of the ideal into a real "being" is unfortunate, still the role of religion as holding before mankind the ideal which is future is absolutely essential. And against Marx, for him religion has a radical rather than a conservative role in history, and consequently, when perfected, a generally creative function in any valid society. Thus Bloch intends to purify religion on his own terms, or in his words to "humanize" religion, not to eradicate it—for the full eradication of religion, far from accomplishing or aiding the eradication of human alienation, as in Feuerbach and Marx, would increase and solidify that alienated confinement within the bounds of the sorry present.

The god of traditional religion, however, at least the god of classical theism, the omnipotent ordainer and ruler of all that is, is for Bloch both a superstition and a demon. For such a god, sovereign and lord of all, has obviously willed the evil character of the present; and as sole ordainer of all from eternity, he is also the enemy of freedom in mankind, openness in historical process and real possibility for the future.[61] What is needed for the conquest of alienation is to separate the messianic hope in a kingdom to come resident in all true religion from the concept of god, and to reinterpret the age-old religious hope for an ideal that is to come into a hope based on human rather than on divine action. The divine, a category which Bloch seeks to retain, must, therefore, be radically redefined. No longer does it refer to present, ultimate and sovereign reality. Rather, its legitimate reference is to possibility in the future (the "sacred space" of the not-yet) and to the final realization of that possibility in the messianic but eternally godless kingdom to come.[62] Divinity here is neither "real" nor "active," now or in the future; it represents no "reality," neither one creative of nor one created by the process. Nevertheless the sense of the transcendent, of sacrality, mystery, depth and wonder associated with traditional deities is in itself valid and of great human significance and it forms the essence of religion's creative role. For Bloch, a humanized religion is thus the source and ground of history's creativity and hope.

More specifically, Bloch believes that the sense of transcendence, i.e., of depth, mystery and sacrality, characteristic of religion has had two valid but heretofore hidden referents, each of which has had in the past and will have increasingly in the atheistic future a more creative role. The first referent of sacrality and transcendence is the future itself, that "space" on which the utopian possibilities of men are projected, the "field" where possibilities *are* as they lure men into action, and so as they lure history to its fulfillment.[63] As we have seen, without the temporal transcendence represented by possibility, no movement is possible. Thus in keeping possibility open, the religious sense of transcendent sacrality has been creative rather than destructive in process. Secondly, the religious sense of transcendence and sacrality has kept alive the awareness of the depth, value and, above all, the possibilities inherent in humanity's essence, i.e., in what men and women will be.[64] In mistakenly praising God, religion has really fueled and refueled the possibilities of *human* divinization, that mankind can be redeemed and whole. Religion is, therefore, essentially eschatological promise for a perfected humanity in an ideal kingdom: "The good news of Christian salvation is *Eritis sicut Deus* ('you will be like God')."[65] This is what the Christ figure means for Bloch as the final and culminating form of religion:[66] a humanizing of religion, the dissolving of transcendent deity into an identity of divinity with men to come and, above all, a promise of that realization in the future messianic kingdom.[67]

Bloch is an exciting and inspiring philosopher. His sense of the vast possibilities of process and of history, of its movement into the new, of the dominance of the future, of the mystery and spiritual depth of human being, and so of the real sacral character of the not-yet is very relevant to a revolutionary age, and self-consciously breathes an eschatological spirit. It is no wonder that he has had such immence influence on modern theology.

As his leading theological followers, Wolfhart Pannenberg, Jürgen Moltmann and Johannes Metz, point out, however, his atheism has been inconsistent and crippling to the genius of his own thought and the credibility of his hopes.[68] What, they ask, are his real grounds for hope? How can a blind, naturalistically interpreted process be the basis for our hopes in the realization of the *good*, in the final conquest of tragedy and alienation? Are mere "latencies" enough as grounds for these hopes; and how can the really new arise out of such immanently developing latencies? Further, if we are to count merely on human autonomy and action—and that is, as we have seen, what Bloch does mainly count on[69]—what valid basis can there be for hope? Can really alienated man alone so recreate himself and his world? Is it not clear that man can become so "forgetful" of his real nature and possibilities as to become happy and content in his misery and so to cease to strive?[70] Thus they argue that the sacred space of future possibility, the objective ground of the not-yet that will be in the future and that now "determines the present," must again become God —must be, we may say, *re*-theologized into a real and effective deity on whose power and goodness our hopes for the future can therefore rest. Whereas possibilities for Bloch were ideal and inactive, merely "luring" men and women, this eschatological God is both real and effective, actively determining the present from the future. Nevertheless, this future God, or God of the future, is for Bloch's followers and critics not the traditional God, the unconditioned and eternal being, the all-pervasive ruler of all times. His being, like the Blochian possibilities which he has now replaced, is future, and thus he brings in the new world not from an eternity above the present but from the future ahead of the present. The conception of God in contemporary eschatological theology finds its roots in Bloch's concepts and in a re-theologization of those concepts.[71]

Alfred North Whitehead

The last philosopher we shall briefly consider is Alfred North Whitehead.[72] Although he was not, as Bloch is, directly a philosopher of history or of politics, Whitehead dealt creatively with many of the same themes and is, as I shall argue later, an even better philosophical guide in thinking out a theology of history and of eschatology than is Bloch.

Reality for Whitehead, as for Bloch, is process, a flux of events rather than the endurance of substances which undergo changes.[73] Since new events continuously replace or follow each other, continuity of forms and the endurance of "things" constitute puzzles or problems for Whitehead's thought, as the possibility of change and of the new constituted a puzzle for traditional substance philosophy. For Whitehead, then, events in coming to be arise out of other events in their own past,[74] and in being generated out of that past, they repeat certain characteristics of it.[75] Thus are there the continuities and so the relatively stable societies of events, "enduring objects," which in ordinary speech we name things or persons. In arising, however, each event also is able to enact under the requisite conditions a new form, a new possibility—and thus out of the enaction by new events of new possibilities do our macrocosmic experiences of change and of novelty occur.[76]

For Whitehead as for Bloch, therefore, possibility, the form that has not yet been incarnated in the world, is central to the understanding of all that is actual—for each actuality has appeared as the child of both the given from the past and of possibilities for its future.[77] Order is also necessarily an aspect of reality: lest a world of flux, of events in becoming, be a total chaos; lest therefore there be no continuities between successions of events; and so lest there be no macrocosmic entities or "things" in our world. In a world of flux and process, where being is conceived temporally, order is the ontological *condition,* not the *result,* of "beings," of substances, of existing things and persons.[78] Correspondingly, without an order which organizes, shapes, and channels into formed intensities the infinite chaos of orderless events, there would and could be no intensity of experience and so no grades or levels of societies. But order as we experience it in the formed entities of our world is continually qualified by new possibilities ingredient in new events, and so by novelty.[79] Out of novelty, as out of order, arises the possibility of *higher* ranges of order, of vivid contrasts, of newer and richer harmonies. Without order no real entities, no novelties, and no intensity in a world of becoming would be possible; without novelty the flux of things would be warped and deadened into dull mediocrity by the mere repetition of what had originally been.[80] Thus, as for Bloch, possibility and the new are for Whitehead essential for creative being. But in Whitehead creative and redemptive novelty arise out of past and achieved order, and so in continuity as well as contrast with what has been rather than in opposition to it.[81] Or, perhaps better, novelty arises out of *established* order and harmony rather than out of a tendency that was only *hidden* or *latent* in the distorted past and present. In this sense, the mood of Whitehead is liberal, gradualist, progressivist and providential, rather than radical, even catastrophic and eschatological.

Events or occasions as they arise conform to their past and so in part repeat it or manifest its influence. Thus, as we noted, the categories of substance and causality are applicable to our experienced world, and thus we are able to perceive and know our world. Events are affected in this way by past events because they feel that past, and in feeling it reproduce it in their own being. These conformal feelings of the past, creative of the visible order of things and relations in our world, Whitehead calls physical prehensions and causal efficacy.[82] But events, we noted, also enact new possibilities, new forms both of being and of action not yet characteristic of the achieved actuality. Thus every occasion is also characterized, in more or less degree dependent on its depth and complexity (they in turn are dependent on the character of its society), by conceptual prehensions through which they can feel or experience novel possibilities or forms in coming to be. Each event, therefore, is in as direct relation to what is not yet the case as it is in relation to what has been the case. Possibility, change and novelty are as crucial to the understanding of existence as are objectified actualities.

Events in coming to be are also "free," self-determining: *how* they feel their past and so *how much* they conform to it, and *how* they feel new possibilities and so *how much* they enact them are finally determined by the entity for itself.[83] An event, says Whitehead, is *ultimately* determined by nothing outside itself, neither by the shape of its inheritance nor by the objective possibilities of its present. Self-determination and decision intervene before past conditions and new possibilities unite to become event. Autonomy and self-creation are, therefore, ingredient to all process; temporal being is, as we have argued, structured ontologically by the polarity of destiny and freedom—and Whitehead explicates this view elegantly. On the basis of this ontological structure, and on it alone, is the future radically and actually open, undecided. It is not merely that we do not *know* a future that has been or will be decided from beyond us. Rather, it is that ontologically *nothing* has determined or can determine the concrete shape of future actuality except the "decisions" of future actual entities—and these are yet to come. Thus possibilities for the future are real in our present only as *possibilities;* there are alternatives in every present and so in every future. In turn, these alternative possibilities will become events, decided, definite and actual, only through the self-creation of finite entities. Actuality is a decision among possibilities that takes place in time;[84] before actuality occurs there is, therefore, only possibility. Temporality, then, is the locus of the shaping of finite being, and the most fundamental ontological distinction is a *historical* distinction, that between achieved and definite actuality and undetermined possibility.

In this metaphysical situation, as Whitehead calls it, there are then three fundamental and universal factors: creativity—the ongoing flux of events in which and out of which events arise, the ontological "ultimate" in Whitehead's philosophy;[85] eternal objects or forms and possibilities for the flux;[86] and the freedom of each entity to create itself out of this its world. So far we have before us a more universal (i.e., metaphysical), subtle and intricate elaboration of Bloch's general scheme contrasting the actual, present world with the not-yet that will be. But, says Whitehead, there must be a further factor present to explain process as we experience it, a factor he calls God. His argument in this regard depends ultimately on his conviction that only through such a divine factor can the union of actuality and possibility that is our experience of temporal being be intelligently and coherently conceived; God is, in other words, ontologically the principle of the coherent unity of actuality and possibility in each passing duration.[87]

Whitehead argues that possibilities if in part explanatory of actuality, must *be* somewhere in actuality. "It is a contradiction in terms to assume that some explanatory fact can float into the actual world out of nonentity. Nonentity is nothingness."[88] Thus there must be some actual entity of universal scope and abiding permanence that envisions all of possibility, orders it, and so can relate possibility to the real ongoing flux of events.[89] The only "reasons" for things, insists Whitehead, must lie in actual entities, not in possibility—lest the ideal world determine this one.[90] Thus the "reason" for possibility, for its general and for its particular order, must lie in an actual entity that spans, unites and brings into reciprocal relations achieved actuality and infinite possibility.[91] Furthermore, we cannot explain the *particular* character of this process as a whole, that it is *this* process and not some other total sequence, without a primordial principle of concretion or "decision" (or, as Whitehead puts it in one place, the "primordial accident"),[92] uniting formless creativity with infinite possibilities to form a given definite world.[93] The only alternative, if one is to explain particularity, is to regard that particularity itself as necessary, and thus to freeze out all contingency, openness and novelty from ongoing concrete process. Finally, we cannot explain the continuing order within process, necessary if there are to be continuing things and persons, unless there is a permanent, changeless and objective order in the possibilities open to each entity. Unformed creativity, plus the infinity of possibility, plus an arbitrary freedom in each entity, could not altogether—unless there were some prior and permanent ordering of possibilities—form a world of social order, and especially a world where increasing value is created. Granted freedom, there must be some limiting of possibility, some ordering of it in relation to actuality, if chaos is not to result; the only alternative is to shut off openness.[94] Bloch's mere "latency" is not enough for Whitehead; it cannot explain the order we know or provide an objective ground for the hope in the not-yet that is good which Bloch himself envisions.

For these reasons there must be added to the "metaphysical situation," as a universal factor in process, an entity God. God is the metaphysical factor that unites actuality and possibility. Although, for Whitehead, not the ground of either actuality or possibility, of creativity or of eternal objects,[95] God is the "ground," so to speak, of the creative interrelations between them that make up our world: the ground in actuality of possibility and so the "reason" for possibility; the source of the particular shape of the world as a whole; and the continuing principle of order, of relevance within possibility and so of advance into novel possibilities in our world. As one actual event (or as a "route" of actual events), God is dipolar, as are all other entities. God's primordial nature is transcendent, unrelated and changeless, independent of all relations to the given world as the presupposition of that order. It is that ultimate conceptual prehension of all possibilities for all events in all of process that gives a changeless, consistent and permanent order to the realm of possibility, and which communicates that changeless order to each occasion as it comes to be.[96] Thus does each event in arising receive its own appropriate ideal from God, a novel possibility and yet a novelty which through God's transcendent ordering is in harmonious relation to actuality. God is then the continuing ground of both novelty and order, of those novel possibilities for the history of process which for Whitehead lead to the achievement of the creative new in life. The consequent nature of God is God's "physical" prehension of achieved actuality.[97] Each entity as it has become is prehended or felt by God, influences God's experience and so the divine life and the divine being themselves, and is thus brought into the everlasting unity and harmony of God's experience according to God's subjective aim. Thus is nothing of value lost, and the passingness and transience of becoming are rescued by the permanence and harmony of God's everlasting being.[98]

This is a magnificent vision of process as characterized by both actuality and possibility, destiny and freedom, permanence and change, order and novelty—and of immense theological relevance. Since Whitehead argues, as we shall, that these polarities are unintelligible without God, their divine ground, we shall refer to this philosophical scheme throughout this work. More than the thought of Bloch, I believe, it provides conceptual modes of ontological understanding useful in making intelligible in contemporary terms the nature of historical experience and some of the modern meanings of our most important biblical symbols. Two central problems remain for me with this vision as Whitehead explicated it.

For Whitehead the creativity out of which self-determining entities arise is *formed* by God,[99] not "created" or produced by Him. Ultimately neither the source of the flux nor of the forms themselves, God provides the existing flux with its possibilities and its relevant forms. Thus our experience of our own being is here only partly indebted to God. Both our existence as such and our freedom are elements God may at best mold or shape by luring them in their achievement of actuality; they are not his creatures. But as we saw, our contingent being and our freedom themselves each point to an ultimacy in which they are grounded, and so to their own dependence upon God. This is, I believe, also the clear biblical witness.

It is hard—though possibly not impossible—to comprehend the principle of the demonic, of a bound or fallen freedom, and so to explicate helpfully the tragic character of historical existence, in terms of Whitehead's conception of process as a creative and orderly advance into novelty.[100] Or to explicate how God so understood can act in radically new ways to redeem a lost world. Again these aspects of historical experience and of biblical symbolism seem to fit uneasily into this essentially progressivist ontology in which the redemptive activity of God is, as in most nineteenth-century liberal Christian thought, apparently identified with his creative providential activity.

Thus, as will become more evident as we proceed, we hold that Whitehead's thought, like that of Bloch, must be reinterpreted and in part refashioned, not adopted *en bloc*, by theology. A reflective examination of history on the grounds of ordinary experience alone, to which secular philosophy is confined, cannot provide the final vision elucidating our historical experience. For as nonspeculative, critical philosophy of history has emphasized, we do not yet stand at the end of history, and thus its most basic structures and principles are not yet quite clear to us. In uncovering the significant ontological structures of our present, and then elucidating for us in clarified form our own contemporary experience of history and its movement, philosophy can illumine those fundamental religious and theological symbols by which we may think out the wholeness of historical experience in all its creativity, its vast contradictions, and its hope. Thus as we were driven beyond science and even critical philosophies of history to ontology, so are we driven beyond speculative philosophy to embark on the theological question of history.

PART II

Entr'Acte

5

INTERLUDE ON METHOD

As in the entr'acte of a drama, our discussion is about to pause to give us time to see where we have come in the development of our theme, and by thus looking backward over the argument to date, to project at least formally our movement into the future. At the same time, since this book, at the very best, is an *illustration* of a coherent and intelligible method, not a book on method, it spends little of its time on the many problems of method. At some point, therefore, it is well to suspend the argument in order to look at its form and legitimacy.[1]

Most important, as in almost any drama of some length, there is a point where the action temporarily stops, where the story to date comes momentarily to an intrinsic halt, and where a *new* movement of the *same* story begins. This momentary halt at the end of one sequence, and resumption with the start of another, is also true, I believe, of theology. There is here too a break in argument because there is a corresponding change or transformation on the deeper level of our existence, our commitments and our self-understanding, a corresponding shift in the reflective interpretation of ourselves and our world that results, and so a separation or distinction of moments which the same form of argument cannot mediate. Something new is here added, a new stance, a new perspective, a new total view of things and so a new constellation of fundamental symbols which, while perhaps implied in the action of the first act, nevertheless is not clearly demonstrated as embedded within that action nor exhaustively supplied by it. The form of the present entr'act, set in its own part of the book as a whole, symbolizes as vividly as it can that break between prolegomenon and constructive or systematic theology.[2] On the other hand, the content of the interlude, looking back over the argument of the past and relating that argument to what is to come, attempts in all sorts of hopefully intelligible ways and with a variety of arguments to mediate between these two parts of the *same* story.[3] Our first question, then, is: What has been the theme of the story to date, and where has the development of that story brought us?

In the first chapter we explored the contemporary experience of social change and of the impingement of the future with respect both to the structure of change and to its "meaning." For in the experience of social change history impinges on us with immediacy, and we become aware of what it is "like" to be in history and to face an unknown future. With regard to the structure of change, the categories through which it may be understood, we distinguished five levels: cumulative changes or trends, intentional responses or policies, symbolic structures, the factor of power and the relationship to nature. All of these forms of structure had, as we noted, relevance to the "meaning" of change, i.e., to the character of the future as possible menace or as possible promise. And inevitably each of these levels or facets of change called not only for wise political responses, but also for serenity, courage, compassion and hope in relation to the uncertain future.

Change, we noted, raised *moral* and *religious* issues for men and women. Perennially, change touched the range of human ultimate concerns. In transforming our world, in threatening our security and power, in opening up new possibilities, it both tempts us to serious sin and yet challenges and lures us as well to new levels of grace. It is in temporal man's movement into the new future, not in some frozen eternal moment, that the "shock of non-being" largely occurs, and the questions of courage, wisdom and justice are posed. It is our temporality, and the contingency of our being which temporality and change uncover, which reveal to us the anxieties connected with our finitude and so tempt us to sin, and which call us to answer that anxiety in acts of courage and of justice. We *are*, as personal, ethical and religious beings, in our historical situations; this is the deepest meaning of our historicity. On the one hand this means that no understanding of change and of history's movement into the future can ignore these existential, ethical and religious dimensions of change; and on the other, that all religious and even philosophical symbols have a *meaning* in relation to their social and political implications, that praxis in part defines and surely enacts the meaning of any theological concept.[4] The main conclusion, therefore, from this analysis of our current experience of social change was to reinforce an argument often carried on on other grounds, namely, that the existence of men and women as beings in time who must face the future in responsible decision is a *social* and so *historical* existence. It is social change even more than personal change that forces these fundamental human issues upon us, and it is the coming of our historical future that poses our deepest concerns of religious commitment and moral praxis. It is in historical and social praxis that our religious commitments and values have meaning or are meaningless, can be real or of no healing effect. Thus no understanding of human beings as either historical or as existential is possible except in relation to the historical, social and political changes in which they participate. Religion—and philosophy—must be historical, social and political if they would speak of human existence in time and be creative in the enactment of that existence.

In the second chapter we sought to lay bare by a phenomenological analysis of political experience the ontological structure of that passage and the horizon within which social and political events were experienced.[5] Again a number of categories of understanding were uncovered and described: the centrality of community, the self-awareness of the community, the relevance of unity, government, political decision and issues of the common good in community, the role of the intended and the unintended in history, and consequently the wide variety of "causal" factors that were effective in historical change. The fundamental ontological structure of our existence as temporal and historical, we discovered, was expressed by the polarity of destiny and freedom, the given actualities from the past and the response to that given demanded of us in terms of new possibility.

To understand the quality of historical and political experience, however, it was found necessary to go beyond that analysis of factors and of fundamental ontological structure to a deeper ontological level. Political experience cannot, I urged, be understood unless it is set within an ultimate, a religious horizon, unless the dimension of ultimacy that infects and inspires all historical experience and all political action is itself uncovered. To the ontological structure of destiny and freedom was therefore added an ontological horizon, as yet unexplicated conceptually, of ultimacy and of sacrality. Through this phenomenological description an attempt was made to ground the unique character of political experience in this ontological structure of man and of his history as essentially religious, i.e., as existing within an ultimate and sacral horizon, as experiencing his life as set within a "world" of moving process whose dimensions are ultimate in character. It is because of this ontological character of man as religious that his movement into the future in his communal and in his individual life is experienced as ultimate threat and as ultimate promise, as blessed by destiny or menaced by fate. Consequently, it is because of this religious dimension to historical experience that his political life is at once filled with deep violence, cruelty and destruction, that it searches for ultimate meanings, that it is directed by ultimate moral judgments and buoyed up with ultimate hopes. The "subjective" tonalities in historical experience of the impinging future of ultimate concern and of ethical and religious challenge, uncovered in the first chapter, were, therefore, here balanced by the "objective" character of the world of historical experience as qualified by a dimension of ultimacy.[6] The burning existential questions of anxiety and terror or of confidence and hope vis-à-vis the social future form the inner side (the side of our responsive awareness and "tone") of a polarity of which the religious or philosophical questions of the ultimate sovereignty in history, of the ultimate meaning and norm of history, form the outer or objective side.

All politics, I argued, was dominated by the quest for continuance and expansion of *being*—and so by the religious question of fate and sovereignty; by the quest for *meaning*—and so by the religious question of a *logos* or system of ultimate meanings in history; and by the quest for an ultimate *norm* for man and community—and so by the religious quest for authentic community in history. These three fundamental characteristics of historical existence show that the ontological structure of destiny and freedom which structures history is set within a horizon that is religious; and it is in that ontological structure within that horizon that the passions of political action, the mythological character of political speech, and the ultimate ambiguity of all political enterprises find their ground. Since political experience in itself has this essentially religious dimension, religious commitment is relevant to secular political action in relation to the future, religious symbols are relevant to any creative existential and ethical stance toward the terrors and possibilities of the future, and theological understanding is relevant to a full comprehension of the character of social experience. Just as the ethical and "existential" analysis of the experience of social change in the preceding chapter led to religious issues of ultimate concern, so now a phenomenological analysis of political experience has led to a religious dimension of historical existence and so to a theological comprehension of human being in time.

In the third and fourth chapters we looked at current scientific reflection on historical change and the future and philosophical reflection on history. This represented, one may remark, a particularly crucial area in establishing the relevance and the necessity of religious or theological understanding. Modern men and women exist in a religious dimension, and this can be shown—in this case in relation to social and political experience. But their intellectual grasp of their experience, both on the prethematic level and on the level of explicit understanding and reflection, finds on the whole little reality to a deeper dimension and so little place for either philosophical or religious symbolism about history.[7] If such reductionist and "secular" attempts to understand and explain historical passage worked, if they were both self-consistent and explanatory of the experienced facts of historical life, then the case against the objective meaning and the relevance or usefulness of philosophical and theological symbolism—and of the religious consciousness theology expresses—would be a serious one. If, on the other hand, the efforts of the relevant academic disciplines to comprehend historical passage were discovered themselves to presuppose or, as in the case of Heilbroner, to call for levels of understanding or of preunderstanding that were speculative and religious in character, then the necessity of philosophical and theological symbols for reflection on historical life would be as clear as the necessity of religious commitment and religious symbols had been shown to be for human existence in time itself. Critical analysis of reflective procedures and their results in the study of history would corroborate a phenomenological analysis of political experience and an existential and ethical analysis of the experience of change—the former pointing to the necessity of a level of understanding transcendent to the manifold of facts as the latter two pointed to a religious dimension and an ultimate concern transcendent to the immediacies of political life and of current social changes. In our analysis of three widely varied scientific attempts to envision the future, presuppositions were uncovered about the general structure of historical movement, about its qualitative characteristics and about the norms by which it may be assessed. Above all, each was shown to be guided at even its most "scientific" levels of analysis by a vision of social process, its relation to freedom and its probable destiny which should be clarified by philosophical and possibly theological conceptuality if that vision was to become coherent and credible. The discussion was concluded by examining critical philosophy of history and then two contemporary speculative philosophies of history which sought precisely to make coherent in terms of the nature of reality as a whole the ontological, epistemological and normative presuppositions of the special disciplines.

As persons are led by the experience of change to face existential and ethical issues of ultimate concern; as communities are led by the exigencies of historical life to seek in their political action an ultimate sovereignty, and to embody an ultimate meaning and an ultimate norm; so evidently the disciplines concerned with history presuppose a deeper level of understanding that is initially philosophical and ultimately theological in character. The questions of an ultimate sovereignty in history, of the ultimate shape and quality of history's passage into the future are at once political, existential, religious and theoretical questions. The legitimacy, therefore, of speaking of historical and social change, of politics and so of our common human being in time in terms of philosophical and theological categories as well as "scientific" ones, was established by this critical analysis and the general ground prepared for the movement of our thought to an explicit treatment of these matters in a theological manner. For such categories have by this analysis been shown to be implicit within and so called for by the objective contours of the materials to be interpreted. History is multi-dimensional; human societies live, move and act in this multi-dimensional history. Thus, as we showed, social theory and the philosophy of history are as crucial aspects of understanding historical passage as are historical inquiry and social science—in fact, the latter two make no sense without the presuppositions clarified by the former. Further, one dimension of this multi-dimensional reality of history and of social change was found to be a dimension of ultimacy, a horizon of transcendence and of sacrality. This dimension gives to societies their cohesion and their self-transcendence into the new; it gives therefore to history and to the changes which characterize history their promise and their terror, and their creative and their demonic sides. Thus a theological as well as a philosophical understanding of history was shown to be essential if its experienced structures and tensions are to be understood.

We may, perhaps, sum up our conclusions in the following terms: To be human in time is to be immersed in temporal passage and so within its fundamental changes. This changing social world sets for us the "situation" in which the deepest personal, ethical and religious issues of our existence arise: it tempts us, challenges us and calls forth from us our political projects. And yet to be human in time is, by the same token, also to transcend that passage so as to be aware of it, to fear or rejoice in it, to seek to know and to understand it, to judge it and to act upon it for the future. Human history is thus qualified essentially by the ontological structure of destiny and freedom. To be human in history, to respond to its given and to act for its future, is to unite through interpretation, understanding, judgment and decision that given actuality and its own real possibilities into a present event. Human freedom does not create destiny; but it actualizes destiny in the light of its own not-yet possibilities ever anew into events. Further, both in apprehending and dealing with the *future* that impinges on us and in understanding and appropriating the *past* or the destiny that is our present inheritance, men and women find themselves driven inexorably beyond the surface level of observable "facts," trends and their immediate possibilities to the deeper levels of an underlying ontological structure, an authentic order and an authentic norm to history. Both human inquiry into our past, and political action for our future subsist in a history characterized by a depth, richness and complexity which only philosophical and theological categories—and in politics, mythical forms of speech—can articulate.

Human transcendence of history, to be "out" of it *as* one is "in" it and so to bring to awareness, understanding and acknowledgement its basic structure, is the condition for response to history, for judgment and action, for politics—for the actualization of the pole of freedom that makes history history and human beings human. Entailed, therefore, by the categorial structure of history as destiny united to freedom, such transcendence requires awareness ("political self-consciousness") of trends, dislocations, problems in the past and present, and, correspondingly, of possibilities, demands and threats in the future; it demands the rational penetration of history to its depths. Thus, in order to be human in time we are led to conceive of the history in which we swim, to set it into dominant symbols, to comprehend our destiny in terms of social theory, to comprehend the immediate future politically in terms of mythologizing and to comprehend history itself reflectively in terms of a philosophy or a theology of history. Finally, since this depth is characterized by an ultimate dimension or horizon and this complexity is characterized by the deep inner alienation of history from its essential structure (the actuality of sin and the fear of fate), such participation must be (and always is) religious and such understanding must be (and always is) theological. A "religious" relation to the passage of social time and so a mythical or theological understanding of that passage are intrinsic to human being in time. Thus does the most fundamental theological question arise inevitably out of being human in history. This question can be posed as follows: As human beings in passage "make" history by uniting a given actuality and future possibility, destiny and freedom, into *event,* is there such a principle or factor uniting past actuality and not-yet possibility, destiny and freedom in their widest scope, an ultimate creativity and sovereignty in history that makes intelligible the ultimate dimension or horizon of history and the quest for an ultimate order and a sacred norm? To this issue, the issue of theism, hopefully prepared by our prolegomenon, we now turn.

THE MYSTERY OF HISTORY AND ITS IMPLICATIONS

A vivid conclusion of our argument is that history is a great deal more difficult to make intelligible than the official forms of modern reflection have supposed.[8] One example is the wide variety of "scientific" views of history: as glowingly free through science, as predictable through science and as fated to doom through science. The basis for this strange, elusive unfathomable character to history lies in many aspects of history and of our relation to it: epistemological, ontological and theological, which our analysis has intimated but not yet clarified. One way to proceed in our analysis of these deeper ontological structures of history and to delineate more clearly what we might mean by its ultimate dimension, its ultimate principle of sovereignty and its ultimate norm, is to explore the character of its complexity and opaqueness, in short, the bases for the "mystery" that characterizes history.

The provisionally unfathomable character of history arises first of all from the evident fact that humans are apparently unable to view it "objectively," to separate themselves from it—as in modern times they have separated themselves from nature —and examine it not as it affects, engulfs or empowers the viewer but as its relations manifest themselves in and to themselves. Even the most rational of philosophers, when he views history reflectively, expresses in the coherence or the incoherence he finds there the feeling-tone of his own biography, of his class and of his time with regard to history, its optimism or its despair. Because humans are historical and exist as immersed in history, buoyed up or overwhelmed by the destiny history presents to them and menaced or excited by the future they face, men and women think about history "existentially," as involved in it. A *logos* of history, an understanding of its structure and meaning, is thus subject to the *kairos* of history, the qualitative character of its own time.[9] Thought, in this case, peculiarly follows the fortunes of being, and thus since the fortunes of history are infinitely various, and the coherence among them difficult to achieve, philosophical understanding of history is doubly elusive. In some ages, and to some classes and groups, the negative, destructive, irrational and evil side of history's opaqueness seems overwhelmingly evident; then "philosophies of history" present to us a gloomy, cyclical understanding of its objective structures. In other ages—and for other classes and groups—the creative, growing, meaning-laden, purposive side of history is predominant, and then meta-physical philosophies are rational, optimistic and progressive. It is no accident that the latter were more dominant in the eighteenth and nineteenth centuries, the former in our own age. With regard to history—because that is where we *are* as humans—existence and reflection are unusually correlated, making judgments about the objective structure of history seem partial, one-sided, parochial and ideological. The perspectives and convictions in terms of which we deal with our existence in history, as persons and as members of a group, impinge far more effectively on our reflections about history than they do on most other subjects. Thus, general agreement is absent, general criteria are elusive, and the pretense of a "philosophy of history" seems to dissolve into the actuality of a series of parochial and subjective mythologies.

The difficulty of philosophical and theological reflection on history, however, has even deeper roots than its undoubted existential character. As we have shown, there is a structure to history presupposed in our existential relation to change and the future, in all political actions in the present and in responsible reflection on the past. Such structural elements in history are, however, elusive and shifting, and, in our age, scorned as valid objects of intelligent inquiry and expression. The full reasons for this will be apparent only when we have completed our analysis of history, and seen the complexity and depth of that structure. We may, however, now outline formally some of these characteristics of history, and correlate with them the kinds of argument and exposition that seem relevant to such a complex subject.

1. The fundamental ontological structure of finite being in history is the polarity of destiny and freedom. This has already become partly evident in our analysis of social change and of reflection on social change; there gradual and unintended changes called for a political and intended response. It became clearly manifest in our analysis of historical inquiry, where to understand a historical event we found it necessary to uncover the given that conditioned the event and the response that precipitated it: both factors were evidently as necessary for the understanding of the event as they were for its actuality.

If finite being as historical, and so history as the process of historical being, is constituted by this structure of destiny and freedom, of a given and our response to it, then one reason for the difficulty of reflection about it becomes plain. Structure and freedom are uneasy bedfellows, even more than structure and contingency. For the essence of freedom is that while it has a structure (as the word "essence" implies), it can introduce novelty, and a novelty that is not predetermined and so not to be exhaustively comprehended by a continuous structure of events over time. For this reason, history, as composed of freedom in union with destiny, has no simple structure, either of law or of ontology[10]—as the arguments between Hempel and the historians amply illustrate. For this reason, we find that many historians, intent to defend contingency and the efficacy of intentions in history, and certain theologians, intent to preserve the reality of freedom, of responsibility, of the new and the unexpected in history, have tended to mistrust a "metaphysical" account of the structure of history.[11] To them metaphysics inevitably implied an ontological structure which predetermined historical events and thus compromised history's freedom and openness—though clearly what they were thereby rejecting vis-à-vis history was not an ontological structure as such but one that denied the polarity of destiny and freedom as constitutive of history. Part of the mystery of history to rational reflection, therefore, lies in its ontological structure of destiny and freedom.

Actually, the polarity of freedom and destiny, far from making an ontology of history impossible, possesses metaphysical implications relevant to a theological understanding of history. As the basic ontological structure of temporal passage, this polarity entails a further ontological polarity that contains very important consequences. This is the polarity of actuality and possibility within which destiny and freedom necessarily subsist, a polarity which Whitehead has used to construct a most intriguing argument for God.[12] Insofar as freedom is real, alternatives are open in the future, alternatives to be made actual by a concrete decision in the moving "now" of temporal passage. But alternatives imply possibilities as opposed to actuality. Actuality is decided, done, definite, limited, determined. The consequences and so the "meaning" of a past event can change, but not the fact that it has been as it was. Possibility, on the other hand, is open, indefinite, not yet decided, in principle infinite, waiting as a not-yet for realization. Actuality is thus a union in a moving present between the inheritance from the past and possibilities from the future. This distinction between actuality and possibility is ontologically fundamental, not only for the reality of freedom and of novelty but for that of temporal passage as well.

As many philosophers have recognized, the relation between actuality and possibility is a puzzling one, opening up a host of important metaphysical and ontological questions. Possibility can be taken to be the determining category, all actuality stemming from a realm of possibility transcendent to the given world of experience. But in this Platonic view, the actual world becomes shadowy and ineffective, its character determined by causes lying outside the realm of ordinary, natural experience. If, on the other hand, actuality is taken as the source of possibility or potentiality, as in Aristotle, then nothing novel in nature or in history can occur—a view contradicted by important elements of modern experience and conviction. Clearly, if there be novelty, possibility is a wider realm than actuality and is effective in the creation of actuality; and yet clearly, if our given world be determinative of its own changes and intelligible according to its own data, present actuality must provide the only "causes" for what transpires.

Two questions for Whitehead arise from these propositions: (a) if actuality provides the only "reasons" for things, how can possibility be a reason or be at all, if it is not related in some way to actuality? (b) If possibilities are wider than actuality, and if actuality is "free" in its determination of possibility, how is *order* in passage to be explained, and a creative relation of actuality to possibility, of past to future, to be made intelligible? The only way that this double dilemma can be resolved, says Whitehead, is to conceive of the possibilities open to actuality as, on the one hand, aspects of what is already actual if they are to be real and effective, and, on the other, as in some kind of orderly relation to what has been. If both actuality and possibility are to be real and effective in events and in an orderly relation and yet fruitful of novelty, some factor of universal scope must unite them. Thus there must be a factor "God" whose role it is to make coherent the relations of actuality and possibility to one another. If for Tillich the basic ontological structure of self and world implied a unity below both of them that made their polarity and reciprocity in life possible,[13] so for a more radically temporal understanding of finite being the ontological structure of destiny and freedom, of actuality and potentiality, similarly implies a ground uniting these two, an actuality that includes within its envisionment the infinite realm of potentiality. The ontological structure of destiny and freedom that helped to deepen the mystery of history for rational reflection is also the basis for a relevant "argument" for a metaphysical theistic interpretation of history's passage. We shall refer to this argument repeatedly, and even expand it,[14] although we do not wish—for reasons to be given in what follows—to base our theological interpretation of history *solely* on its cogency.

2. As we shall argue repeatedly in what follows—and as the evidence of history abundantly shows—the ontological structure of destiny and freedom which characterizes history is itself an abstraction, though a legitimate one. For actual history

reflects not only the structure of destiny and freedom but also an estrangement and alienation from that structure or a warping of it.[15] That is to say, freedom in actuality corrupts the possibilities which it seeks to enact; freedom is alienated from its essential nature and so from its own goals and intentions, and functions in actual events as much self-destructively as it does creatively. Thus is the destiny that freedom helps to create in the end also warped, corrupted, alienated and estranged; it becomes fate and tends to eradicate rather than to empower the freedom it brings into being. Nothing in history but illustrates its essential structure of a destiny potential of creative actualization and a freedom capable of that actualization; and yet nothing in history also fails to illustrate that destiny becomes warped and freedom corrupted. Thus arises the ambiguity in which the coherence of history is further obscured. Not only is that coherence subject to freedom and to novel possibility, to contingency and to the radically unexpected. Even more, history's essential structure is warped and obscured, its norms are defied and so made invisible, covered over with false norms, and its essential goals infinitely beguiled, seduced, ignored and desecrated.

The actuality of history is thus as much in partial contradiction to its essential structure as that actuality is revelatory of that essential structure. And thus speech about *concrete* history inevitably takes a paradoxical form. Both the structure of freedom and responsibility and the bondage consequent on the warping of that structure must be spoken of, since to obscure either side is to ignore real aspects of the concreteness of historical experience. For those who are primarily aware of this negative side of history, therefore, history appears as chaotic and incoherent, without rational or moral structure. If they are aware of history's concrete actuality, they feel unable to understand history's essence, and are conscious only of the fated, grim "given" of history and the wayward freedom that responds to it. They can only see history—as Heilbroner did—as meaningless. For those aware predominantly of the creative side of history, the structure of destiny and freedom is plain. But as in the present case of the optimistic scientist conscious only of the future possibilities of freedom in history, history itself will reveal soon enough how abstract and inaccurate was their grasp of history's actuality.

An empirical, "positivist" account of history, abjuring all philosophical conceptuality, seems fated to achieve no rational intelligibility—and becomes sheerly mythical (cf. modern progressivist interpretations) or despairingly empirical. A philosophical understanding of history in terms of its ontological structure, correspondingly, seems fated to obscure history's evil, its incoherence and its tragedy. Because of sin history cannot be understood solely "metaphysically," in terms of its ontological structure of destiny and freedom, without misunderstanding it and without, as Niebuhr used to say, overlooking the "facts" of history. A metaphysical understanding of the structure of history leads, mysteriously, to an abstraction from the concrete actuality of history; and thus, in large part, away from its object rather than toward it. An appeal to experience, to confession, to other modes of argument than those included in the construction of a metaphysical system is clearly called for.[16]

More categories than actuality and possibility, destiny and freedom are needed if history is to be comprehended, categories relative to the questions of fate, sin and grace, of estrangement, self-destruction and reconciliation, of the relationship of man and of God. For this reason, in understanding history we shall attempt to use the religious symbols not only of creation and of providence, relevant to the polarity of actuality and possibility, of destiny and freedom; but also those of sin, Christology, grace and eschatology, relevant to the problems of a warped freedom and an obscured destiny—categories not directly derivable from the given structure of ordinary experience, which being in self-contradiction calls for a rescue from beyond itself.

The confusing consequences for a theological understanding of history of these two points taken together are obvious. Seemingly, if we would establish the legitimacy of the theistic underpinning of a Christian interpretation of history, we must emphasize history's essential ontological structure of destiny and freedom and their interrelation—and, by the same token, overlook history's self-contradiction and its tragedy. If, on the other hand, we would establish the relevance and the legitimacy of the redemptive side of a Christian interpretation of history, we must emphasize the contradictions latent in history's actuality—and so obscure the reality and intelligibility of the God who purports to redeem. A natural theology seems to miss the actual character of history's life, and to make irrelevant the main message of the redemption it seeks to defend; a purely kerygmatic Christianity, aware of evil and centered on the saving gift of grace, seems to undermine its own ontological and theological foundations.

This dilemma, illustrated over and over in the conflict between the "proofs" of rational philosophical theology and the proclamation of kerygmatic theology, leads to the "break" in argument referred to at the start of this chapter. A Christian interpretation of history cannot be based on one sustained argument but only on a *series* of arguments, each of whose limits, whose types of evidence and whose modes of intelligibility are clearly discriminated. For, as noted, if we argue solely from our experience of the structure of history, we shall miss the self-contradiction of history; if we argue solely from our experience of the disruption of that structure and its resolution—i.e., existentially and kerygmatically—we shall be unable to comprehend conceptually—i.e., with coherence and adequacy—the nature either of the history that is so redeemed or of the God who redeems.

Thus, in this volume we distinguish as clearly as we can: (a) a prolegomenon in which the structure of history and its dimension of ultimacy are uncovered and explicated—and the legitimacy of philosophical and theological language in order to understand history established; (b) an attempt on the basis of that structure to show the intelligibility and so the reality of a theistic interpretation of that structure —though in the light of the following points we recognize the preliminary character of that argument; (c) a description of the paradoxical if not contradictory character of history's actuality as compounded ontologically of destiny and freedom (these interpreted in terms of providence) and yet as also characterized in the concrete by sin and fate, categories not derivable from the structure of history, and so not metaphysically "provable," but categories essential to the understanding of history's actuality. (d) Finally, in explicating in the light of the self-contradiction of history the meaning and hope in history of which we are nevertheless aware, we use categories also not derivable from the universal, given structure of history but given redemptively to it, namely, the categories of revelation, Christology, grace and the eschatological promises.[17]

Clearly, the categories illustrative in the last two points cannot be "proved," for they do not derive from the structures discoverable by empirical analysis of our general experience of history. However, they can be made intelligible and validated in two interrelated ways: by showing that alternative ways of understanding the mystery of concrete history are inadequate to interpret its ontological structure and to its manifest empirical reality; by showing that such a system of symbols provides both the basis for a creative existence in history and for an intelligible understanding of the many facets of history's mystery, i.e., by their coherence and by their "adequacy" to the full range of "facts" present in common human experience.[18] The remainder of the arguments in this volume will illustrate these fundamental forms of argument.

The criteria of theology are, as in philosophy, coherence among its fundamental concepts and adequacy to the facts of experience. The mystery of history here outlined, derivative from the reality and yet the hiddenness and obscurity of the structures of history's life, makes, however, theological argument, based not only on a belief in God but also—if that belief is to be itself credible and possible—on an apprehension of the radical need for grace and a belief in its reality, infinitely more complex and varied than most philosophical discussions would allow themselves to be. But so is history infinitely complex and varied; perhaps the secret of method is to make the variety of category, of symbol and of argument fit the complexity of the object of understanding. For all of these reasons, those who find the Christian interpretation of history credible and empowering are probably those for whose experience not only the open possibilities of history are real—and so have a "basic faith in the meaningfulness of life"—but even more those to whom the tragic ambiguity, self-contradiction, and potential if not actual meaninglessness of our human existence, and the reality of unexpected healing of that existence, have also manifested themselves.[19] Without that threefold apprehension of the "realities" of our common historical experience (of possibility, of destructive self-contradiction and of healing), the paradoxical affirmations of divine sovereignty, of an irrevocable freedom and responsibility, of destructive self-contradiction, of unmerited succor and of the beginnings of a new reality amidst the old, may well seem arbitrary, aimless and wishful. But to those who experience life thus, this interpretation represents both wisdom for a puzzled reflection and power for a difficult existence.

3. One further element in the ontological structure of history compounds the mystery of our object and the consequent difficulty of talking intelligibly about it.

As almost every argument in this volume in its own way makes clear, history is not just the career of finite being, a matter of human interaction with its material and social environment and destiny. Thus the structure of destiny and freedom, of the given from the past and our response to it, is not sufficient for a coherent and adequate interpretation of history, since it does not encompass the entire reality that is history. Rather, fundamental to the ontological structure of finite being and so of historical being is a transcendent ground of that being, and so nothing about history can be fully comprehended without relation to that transcendent ground. In this volume, this point is established—or such an argument is essayed—on three different levels. (a) An analysis of historical and political experience reveals that this experience occurs within a dimension of ultimacy, and that in all its other central characteristics historical experience reflects that ultimate, transcendent, and sacral dimension. (b) The relation of actuality to potentiality necessitates a ground of both, if the character of temporal and so historical passage as a movement characterized by continuity, by self-actualizing freedom and by novelty is to be made intelligible. (c) The complexity of the creative and the tragic, the moral and the immoral, the sinful and the healed, the despairing and the hopeful aspects of historical experience, cannot be comprehended unless history, i.e., human freedom and the destiny to which it responds, is understood as being enacted in continuous relation to the divine source of its being, of its possibilities, of its experiences of nemesis and judgment, and of its hope for reconciliation and renewal. Only in relation to this religious dimension, in relation to God, can the depths of the tragedy of history be comprehended and yet the possibilities for hope in history be affirmed. Without this dimension all else is an optimism that abstracts from the warped concreteness of existence or a pessimism that in the end enervates historical vitality. Without the category of the transcendent, of the ground and power of temporal being, of God, history remains an enigma that defies comprehension.

There is no question, however, that such a religious, theistic and Christological interpretation of history, necessary to the clarification of history, nevertheless immeasurably deepens the mystery of history. For now every interpretation has reference not only to factors available directly and indirectly within the manifold of experience but also to a transcendent reality, impinging on that manifold, but, in various ways, not a simple part of it. In a strange way, we are now understanding the seen in terms of the unseen, the visible in terms of the hidden, the contradictory facts implied in experience in terms of a reality that transcends and eludes that manifold of experience. The religious dimension involves inescapably, moreover, ultimacy and sacrality, and thus overleaps many of our empirical and rational canons of meaning and of testing, and it stretches language far beyond its "ordinary" usages. The trouble is, as we showed, history *also* involves this category, and so, difficult as it is, its use is inescapable if we are to understand.

In any case, such an interpretation is, on the one hand, forced on us by the phenomenological character of historical and political experience, by the implications of the ontological structure of history, and by the complexity of history's estranged and yet redeemable and redeemed character, and thus is warranted by rational argument. On the other hand, it involves us in all the added difficulties of metaphysical and especially of religious discourse and thus, in many obvious respects, transcends the recognized canons and order of usual rational argument. This is not the place to investigate exhaustively the problems of religious symbolism, its relation to ordinary language, to the language of the sciences and to the language of metaphysics—and so the rational grounds for its often seemingly "irrational" usages.[20] Suffice it to say that in presenting a theological interpretation of history in terms of Christian symbols we must bear in mind not only the rational grounds for such speech but also these problems, and so make as clear as possible why, empirically and logically, we are using religious symbolism: what forms of meaning it possesses; what limits there are on its precision and exactness of meaning; and how it may be validated or tested. In any case, as our argument to date has shown, a purely empirical account of history is unintelligible, a metaphysical view relatively abstract, and so only a religious or theological interpretation, itself related to transcendence, ultimacy, sacrality and so to essential mystery, can unify the empirical and the ontological and clarify the more proximate mysteries of our historical being. As grace must deal with an estranged freedom in history for meaning to result, so reflectively the transcendent must be introduced for the whole range of history's complex structures to become coherent. That entails a variety of arguments, an appeal to many different dimensions of being, and the use of several different forms of language.

EXPERIENCES OF MEANING IN HISTORY

Ours is an age in which experientially few threads of meaning in the events of history are easily evident. It is also an age which, possibly for that reason, discourages any rational attempt to uncover an intelligible structure to events. To most intellectuals the question of "the meaning" or "a meaning" to the sequence of historical events seems unintelligible and futile—though most subscribe on some level to a theory of progress or its opposite, a vision of despair. One may well ask, therefore, on what direct grounds in experience (i.e., *ontic* grounds)—as opposed to the complex phenomenological, ontological and symbolic arguments just rehearsed—the claim can be made that there might be a meaning to history, a meaning whose concrete shape is to be discovered by inquiry. In order for any inquiry intelligibly to get started, we must have some hope that there is some object or structure "there" for us to describe. To be sure, the efforts to understand and interpret history without a philosophical or theological structure can be shown to be inadequate—but why even make the effort? Does our ordinary experience, personal and social, provide any warrants for the search for a deeper meaning? Let us briefly try to answer this problem before we go on.[21]

The first experienced clue to such an order transcendent to human intentions and surface conditions within the events we experience can be called the experience of the creativity of the unwanted given in personal life and in history.[22] Often what we do not intend, what in fact no one has willed, least of all ourselves, turns out to be immensely creative, more creative than what we had or could have planned. In fact, in many cases those things which we did not under any circumstances want, what we in fact abhorred and in that deep sense could not have either willed or planned, were the source of whatever creativity our autonomy, our willing and our planning were later to possess. A negative destiny, what appears to us at the time as fate, as smothering our freedom, turns out to be a creative destiny that is instrumental in the long-term realization of our freedom and selfhood.[23] Many common experiences—private and public, personal and historical—manifest this.[24] In the author's own life, a war internment camp and a divorce, both of which he abhorred when they occurred and so neither, in fact, intended or could have intended, have changed from unwanted givens, seemingly a fate that had only destructive consequences, into a creative destiny that opened up new creative possibilities—possibilities literally impossible to the life which he had previously willed or intended to live. Thus can one look back at life—though not forward to any particularly "unpleasant given"—and honestly say that it would have been less creative had it enacted our own intentions, had it unfolded as we had planned it. Developments that happen, as Hegel put it, "behind our backs" have led to creative if undesired changes and so to new possibilities. What seemed a destructive fate has become a creative destiny. Here, possibly, is one ancient as well as contemporary "empirical" root for an intuition of an order of meaning that transcends both our intentions and our powers, and so, in Christian terms, for a conviction of the work of providence in the lives of men and women. There is often a creative purpose in the destiny or the given that our purposes reject or struggle against which, in fact, can rescue those purposes of ours and turn them in more creative directions.

The second intimation of meaning within the overwhelming contingency and destructiveness of events can be called the proximate intelligibility of much of the tragic. As is evident to any careful and full analysis of their roots, many of the most destructive and evil elements of personal and historical life are not totally irrational in character, an arbitrary nemesis with no coherent relations to ourselves or to other events, and so with no meaning. Rather—and this is especially true of events in the lives of communities and groups rather than events in individuals' lives—in many cases destruction arises in our present because of the past injustices that same group has committed: of race against race, class against class, national group against national group.[25] The author experienced this vividly many years ago in observing that the personal tragedies that overwhelmed the European communities of Asia, and sent them rootless wanderers around the globe after World War II, were not arbitrary. They were the result, rather, of the past history of imperial arrogance and greed, not necessarily of themselves but of their communities. As we shall see, many contemporary evils and potential tragedies in our present have the same intelligibility—if we are willing to recognize it. Insofar as past sins are thus recognizable and real causes of historical destruction, judgment is continually executed and experienced in historical life. Obviously, as with the case of the creativity of the unpleasant given, this cannot without both absurdity and rank injustice be made a general principle of explanation, especially of the evils that beset others. The Jews were also rootless wanderers, persecuted and well-nigh exterminated before and during World War II, but not from their own fault. Yet evidence seems to show —in accord with much of the "prejudice" against the mighty of the earth expressed in the scriptures[26]—that the sufferings of those communities which have had power, affluence and spiritual advantages are on the whole deserved, brought about by the past sins of their own community. From them much was asked, and for their misuse of what was given, because of the immensity of the effects of their betrayal, they and theirs will suffer much. In general, the mighty suffer for their own sins and those of "their own," the weak from the sins of others. There is therefore undeserved as well as (in *this* sense) deserved suffering in history, unintelligible as well as intelligible suffering in historical life, and it is very important to be able to discern the distinction. But the experience of the meaningfulness or justice of the tragic because it arises as the result of the deep and immoral misuse of power is surely an ancient, and a contemporary, clue to a meaning that in some mysterious way coheres seemingly unrelated, arbitrary and so meaningless contingencies.

Finally, there is the experience, deeply felt in all groups dedicated to social change, of the possibilities of the new in history despite the tragic character of the present. Such creative possibilities—as in the other two cases—are here hardly dependent on an assessment of human powers or even human intentions. This intuition of revolutionary possibility arises precisely when the overwhelming weight of political power and the explicit balance of sentiment, and so the apparent intentions of men and women, are on the other side. Creative possibilities, at best, in such situations are latent not manifest; and yet as the inner presuppositions of revolutionary movements, there is the clear confidence that within that which is at best latent and explicitly weak, there lies promise, a deep promise of future realization. Thus do all revolutionary forces both intuit and affirm, and in their important speech and reflection explicate, an order of meaning that is not yet clearly visible, an order of meaning which is both normative and redemptive, ideal *and* actual, not-yet and yet real, and which will in time work itself into realization through human intentions and human action. No one can understand the courage and confidence of the democratic and bourgeois revolutionaries of the eighteenth century, or of the nationalist and socialist revolutionaries of the nineteenth and twentieth, or of the revolutions and hoped-for revolutions of oppressed races and peoples (and women) today, without recognizing this intuition basic to their courage, and this "political self-consciousness" common to them all—an intuition of possibilities latent even in the most tragic actualities, and so a confidence in a hidden and yet real order of meaning that will in the future realize itself.

In each case, an empirical, realistic, practical (in the sense of praxis) sense of the course of history points to a thread of meaning, the hidden working of some principle of order within the ambiguity of time and change, that undergirds both our confidence and our autonomy. In each case, this power or order does not overwhelm or even replace our creative action—or our scientific study of history. Rather it provides the conditions for creative action, their context and their possibility, bringing to naught many old actualities that have lost their fruitfulness, forming unwanted constellations into creative possibilities, and presenting each apparently tragic situation with new possibilities leading into a novel order of things. It is this series of intuitions—perfectly possible (if not finally coherent) without Christian symbolism—within ordinary historical experience of a real and yet hidden order in events which the symbol of providence, in significant connection with the other relevant Christian symbols, will thematize into a Christian interpretation of history.

6

INTERLUDE ON METHOD (CONTINUED)

In the chapters that follow we shall attempt to give a Christian interpretation of the dimly experienced order or meaning described in the last chapter, and of the dimension or horizon of ultimacy uncovered earlier. Thus it is now appropriate to say briefly how we conceive Christian theology to proceed, what its peculiar problems are, what forms of meaning its language encompasses, and how its propositions may be tested or validated.

Christian theology is the enterprise of understanding the totality of contemporary experience—in the present discussion contemporary historical experience—through the forms of or in the terms of Christian symbols, as Christian faith is the effort to live one's life in the illumination and power of those symbols and the presence of deity they mediate.[1] Thus at once theology is driven critically to examine and constructively to reinterpret the traditional symbols of its faith in order to interpret experience in their terms. Immediately the question poses itself: How can we in our day understand our experience by means of these ancient and strange symbols?[2] And so at the very beginning we encounter the now famous hermeneutical problem. I resist *defining* theology as hermeneutics since that implies the theologian works only with texts (the enterprise of hermeneutics is officially defined as inquiry into the principles for interpreting texts with regard to their meaning[3]). The definition of theology as the interpretation of texts seems to me a sophisticated version of the older understanding of theology as exhaustively the interpretation of the word in scripture—a view of theology's task which is, I believe, woefully inadequate. For, as we shall see, there are many levels of meaning in theology: phenomenological, ontological and ethical as well as eidetic, and exploration of these levels of meaning requires a much wider scope of inquiry and reflection than can be afforded merely in the interpretation of given texts or of the *effect* of such texts in "word-events," however sacred these texts may be taken to be. Still, if theology is the interpretation of experience through traditional symbols, it must include hermeneutics in this sense, for the places those symbols are to be found are texts or their equivalents, and thus they, and the texts that bear them, must be interpreted and their relation to ourselves discovered and established. The problem of constructive, hermeneutical interpretation, the meaning of these symbols for us today, is a complex one; briefly, it seems to me, there are four levels to the problem that are crucial for our purposes.

1. The first level is the one universally discussed in recent European theology and familiar to us all: the scriptural texts come to us from another age with a different Weltanschauung, a different horizon.[4] How are we in this age to understand these texts and appropriate them to ourselves? Our modern historical consciousness—that we are people living in one cultural situation, and that they lived and understood themselves and so wrote in another—has led to our sharp consciousness of this distinction between two epochs or ages. And the same consciousness, that each age has its own horizons within which alone do symbols mean for that age, tells us apodictically that our theological understanding, to be relevant and creative for us, must be in terms of the thought forms and of the "world" characteristic of our age, lest what we say have no meaning for us or importance for our life and activity in our world. We all know Bultmann's important answer to this problem: though the biblical age was "mythological" and ours is not, there is one level of meaning in common, the important one, and that is the self-understanding of man, the mode of man's being in the world, the "anthropology" that can be appropriated from the text into our own modern existence.

The difficulties of this view have become manifest; Wolfhart Pannenberg, among others, has helped to point them out.[5] (a) The scriptures speak not only of man's self-understanding, what the possibilities of human authenticity are, but also of God, his acts in history and his promised actions. Thus for these texts self-understanding and Weltanschauung are not at all separable; men and women and their total world are to be understood together. Bultmann has here implicitly imported into theology a contemporary existentialist principle separating humans and their self-understanding, on the one hand, from their view of the cosmos and of the course of history, on the other; and thus Bultmann is led to misinterpret the scriptures in terms solely of a privatizing inwardness. (b) As a consequence, history and its meaning drop out entirely in this hermeneutical principle; we are left only with the individual and his existential inwardness as the substance of faith.[6] Again this misinterprets the scriptures which talk of God's work in and promises for the course of historical events as well as for the individuals along that course. For this reason post-Bultmannian hermeneutics, as especially represented by Gadamer,[7] has spoken not only of an appropriation of the human self-understanding of scripture, but also of the "fusion of horizons," the horizon or world-view of scripture and that of ourselves, as a clear requirement of a full hermeneutics. There is, however, an implication of this point which neither Pannenberg nor Gadamer has explicitly drawn, namely, that such a fusion of horizons means that the biblical ontology, i.e., its view of the structure of natural and historical process, and our ontology must be "fused" in relation to the biblical symbols; and *that* requires the mediation of modern philosophical ontologies and modern views of history if we are to appropriate the biblical word theologically.[8]

2. The second level of the problem of hermeneutics is implied in the first, an issue pointed out by von Rad and Pannenberg among others.[9] If the subject of theological affirmation in scripture and contemporary witness alike is God's action in history, then we are faced not only with two ages or epochs with *their* perspectives on history but derivatively with two histories. For scripture views history within the terms of its early "mythical" Weltanschauung, its ontology, and this is clearly not the way *we* see history as modern historians. Thus there are for us two histories relevant to theology: the history the text reveals in its witness, and the history which for us modern historians lies "back of that text" (what we think probably and so really happened). The difficulty is that *our* theological affirmations about history and God's role in relation to it cannot be based exclusively or unequivocally on that biblical interpretation of history, i.e., on the history the Bible reports, for that is not a view of history we ourselves can necessarily accept. Thus *our* theological affirmations concerning God's action in history (as opposed to our exegetical affirmations about what, say, "the Hebrews believed God did in history") must be theological interpretations in some regard based on and related to the modern historical consciousness and so the history that modern historiography reconstructs, and not just the "biblical history."[10] As von Rad puts this, the discipline of biblical theology and that of systematic theology in our day are inescapably different. To affirm, to interpret and to conceptualize in our day the work of God in history, and that is the task of constructive theology, we must "go behind the texts"—in relation to the history of Israel and of Jesus—and do our theological construction in the light of the way *we* regard history and the way *we* view their history. As Pannenberg puts it, for this reason hermeneutics can escape neither the historical task—the historical reconstruction of the history behind the text—nor the development of a general view of history as a whole.[11] Again, we are led by the implications of theological hermeneutic to the development of a theological and yet a contemporary ontology of historical process, an elucidation of how we understand history and God's relation to it.

3. The third facet of the hermeneutical problem is intellectually and theologically the deepest and creates one of the major crises that have beset theology in our period. This has to do not merely with the fact that we live in a different age than the age of scripture, but with the *character* of our age. For our age—at least those academic and scholarly portions of it which participate in scientific, historical and philosophical reflection and so within which the theologian, in large part, intellectually exists—is "secular," or better, secularistic. I do not refer here to the sociological fact that social institutions have become separated from ecclesiastical or even religious control, that the world is recognized as world, i.e., as relative, autonomous and as "good." I refer to a deeper characteristic of the Geist or spirit of our age, namely, that our prerational, prereflective mood or spirit, what gives our culture its tone and our lived experience its determining forms, represents a secularistic or naturalistic spirit, a spirit that finds that the world of finite things is all that there is.[12] The

ordinary experience of contemporary men and women, and so the world they inhabit, possesses for most of us no transcendent dimension; the horizon of that experience seems closed or cramped; the actuality in which we live is composed only of finite, creaturely factors and causes. What is real to most of us, and so alone effective in natural or historical change, are only those natural or human factors.[13] Correspondingly, what is knowable for us are only the interrelations of these factors, only what can be directly or even sensuously experienced and verified. Whether we look with science at nature and its workings, with historical inquiry at the events of history, or with social science at society and its changes—and even at the future with its promises and its threats—all we moderns seem to see there are these "secular" forces. This is true both of modern reflective life represented by the various disciplines of the university, and also of our everyday "existence" among the factors that seem to create our weal and our woe—all of which are for us creaturely and none of which are supernatural or divine.

It is because of this confinement of our world, of our Lebenswelt, to the parameters of the secular, to the immediate context of the creaturely world around us, that the two levels of the hermeneutical problem already discussed are so perplexing, difficult and sharp. The problem of translating theological texts and their meanings into the thought forms of such a secular age is vast indeed. Only our inner "self-understanding" seems potentially religious in dimension; and the problem of finding anything theologically relevant, i.e., any appearance of transcendent factor or event in a modern historical reconstruction of the biblical history is even vaster. The result of this secularity of our souls is that the biblical categories about God and his relations with history, his "acts" therein, central as they are to the Old Testament,[14] seem, however translated, not "to fit" anywhere in our own real world, or to touch that world at all. They are not symbols for us of *our* experience of history, but "above" it, floating and ghostly. Since our sense of what is real and effective in existence is formed for us in our daily life world, what has no relation to that life world has little meaning for us and little power to grasp us. Thus, while we may be able to proclaim biblically or doctrinally concerning the divine activity in history, neither we nor the people who hear us have an easy time knowing what we might mean.

The most crucial questions for hermeneutics thus combine personal and existential elements with reflective elements: how are we to find and explicate the experiential meanings for *us* in our secular age, in our life world, of the symbols traditional to our faith? For without a meaning in terms of our own sense of history and its passage into the future, these symbols will have no role or use and so no meaning for us; they will not cohere, illumine, direct or transform *our* experience, and thus will mean little.[15] To resolve this problem is the role of what we have chosen to call prolegomenon in theology, an effort illustrated in Chapter 2 of this volume. There we analyzed our historical and political experience and found that at its most significant points it called for religious symbolism. It is, then, these facets, or dimensions of ordinary secular experience which give experiential meaning to our theological words about history. Their effective presence in theology keeps a theological elaboration of these symbols from culminating in merely abstract and so formal notions unrelated to the contours of our concrete experience. Also required, and for the same reason, is the translation of these symbols into modern ontological terms, so that the theological concepts with which we try to think our experience of history will be capable of thematizing our contemporary experience of history.

4. The final facet of the hermeneutical problem is what may be called the ethical-political level. Part of the intrinsic meaning of any religious symbol, but especially of a biblical symbol, is its meaning for praxis; among others, three obvious reasons for this claim may be cited. (a) The symbols of any form of religion involve or seek to invoke action, since in defining man and his place in the world they set the fundamental norms for behavior and since they promise some form of redemption from the tragic elements of existence, a redemption that again implies a particular mode of existing and acting. (b) As we found in the first chapter, the meaning of religious commitment and so of its symbolic articulation is finally achieved and made real only in our response in embodiment and in action to the future that impinges on us. Religious symbols are meaningful or meaningless, creative or demonic in their use, in praxis. If they do not qualify the freedom with which we respond to our destiny, they are nothing; in a historical religion the meaning of religion is involved with praxis.

(c) Finally, however, biblical symbols—and so the religious traditions that stem from them—are in a special way intrinsically related to the character of our concrete existence and to the modalities of our action. To be sure, they promise illumination, a new understanding of our life; but even more, however, they challenge the way we concretely are, they call for a new way of being, a new attitude to ourselves and to others, new forms of our actual relations in community, and a new kind of action in the world. Each fundamental symbol has this teleological or dynamic-historical thrust toward the future, a thrust which, so to speak, moves what is at present the case on to become what it should or could be. God is not only the principle of present creation and value, but also judge and redeemer, rejecting what is at present the case, promising a further end and directing all to this end. Human existence also is incomplete and wayward, judged and called to become what it presently is not. And one can see the same dynamic themes in the symbols of the law and of grace, of faith resulting in love, of the promises of fulfillment, and of judgment and final redemption at the end. In sum, because for the Christian viewpoint existence as it is is warped, ambiguous and suffering, and calls out for transformation, and because the gospel answers this condition with the promise of a new existence for men and women, a new meaning and a new possibility, and drives toward the realization of that promise in praxis for the future, so every fundamental theological symbol means a critical stance toward past and present forms of existence and order in the social world, and the call to historical and social action on behalf of a new earth.[16]

Thus Christian reflection concerns praxis above all, a new understanding of our being in the world leading to creative action for the future. As Marxism and American pragmatism have alike emphasized, valid concepts resolve actual life problems and transform the conditions of existence; they affect changes in the reality of which they speak—else they are dead and in effect ideological.[17] So, correspondingly, theological assertions are distorted into an ideology for the status quo if their symbols do not have critical and transformative political meaning for future action. Thus one of the primary meanings of theological symbols is constituted by the attitudes and activities toward the world and the future which they bring about, activities leading to the overcoming of estrangement and the establishment of freedom. A valid hermeneutic requires an ethical and political as well as an ontological and experiential dimension.[18]

Such an ethical and political hermeneutic entails, moreover, the same sort of constructive translation of existential and ethical symbols as was required by the theological dimension. The new scientific world which we accept, the new understanding of human beings and their world, and so of the factors at work in historical process, have, we noted, required that the traditional theological symbols of God, of man, of history, of revelation and incarnation be reconceptualized and so reset in modern terms—in terms of our understanding of history and its movement. So it is with the ethical dimension: our conceptions of men and women, of their relations to community, of their fulfillment and so of their authenticity, their obligations and their possibilities have shifted. New perspectives have appeared for us in the status and requirements of the law, in the meaning of love, of the neighbor, and of our responsibility to him or to her, and of the fulfillment of humanity and of historical community, than were possible for past epochs of Christians even though they were challenged by many of the same ethical problems and guided by the same symbols. To write constructive theological ethics in our day entails, therefore, an interpretation of the classical symbols concerning Christian obligation in communal and historical as well as in transhistorical terms, and so in social and political as well as in individual categories—just as it requires new ontological forms for our reflective understanding of God, his world, ourselves and the historical process. There are no relevant contemporary theologians who do not in effect manifest such a transmutation of the *ethical* meaning of symbols in correlation with a transformation of their *theological* meaning, whatever their intention to be strictly "loyal" to the original biblical categories or to the traditional symbols of their communion.

Four Levels of Theological Meaning

To draw this discussion of method to a close, we can, on the basis of this analysis of the hermeneutical problem in theology, distinguish four different aspects of meaning ingredient in a fundamental religious symbol or system of symbols and so necessarily explicated by theological reflection.[19] This does not mean that these four aspects must be dealt with either singly, separately or in serial order; rather it means that any full theological understanding must be inclusive of all of them and must satisfy the particular requirements that each of these four aspects imposes.

1. First, there is what I have called the historical and the *eidetic* meaning of the traditional symbols: what they have meant, in all the ways that are relevant, in their original form in the biblical witness, and as they have been interpreted and reinterpreted in the life of the Christian community.[20] The two theological disciplines, biblical theology and historical theology, are devoted, as far as their roles in constructive or systematic theology are concerned, to the uncovering of these eidetic meanings. This enterprise is historical and objective in two senses: (a) the question of the meaning and the truth *for us* of these symbolic meanings should recede far into the background. The aim is to discover what these symbols meant for their age, for that community, for that writer—irrespective of how we view that meaning with regard to either its truth or its fidelity to the faith. In principle, our description, and our relation to it, should be the same, and follow the same principles, whether we are speaking of another form of faith or our own, of heresy or of orthodoxy—lest the way we depict the meanings of their affirmations be strained through the narrow confines of what we today in our community of faith regard as holy and true.

When we ponder a viewpoint or a system of thought *historically*, it is strangely and wonderfully abstracted from the passions and anxieties of our own persons and our own age, though the passions and the praxis that *it* embodied in its time are very much an intrinsic part of its eidetic meaning for us. We do not ask how these symbols or systems of symbols fit into the real world we know, what their relevance for our existence, for us and our life, may be, or even whether they may or may not be true. These are the questions for our own constructive theology, the theologies of our own time. To ask these questions—once dramatically raised in relation to these symbols in their own time—would be to relate them brutally to our world, to cramp them into our own narrow frame, to submit them to our own prejudices and criteria. We seek as historians to see them in their own terms, as they appeared to another time, as they *meant* to that time, unrelated to all else we know, value and hope to be true.[21] Only thus can this cluster of symbols come before us with its own intrinsic power and beauty, and can it challenge us as another, a new viewpoint.

Because we ask its meaning for them and not for us, an eidetic cluster of symbols appears on its own, a total world defined by itself alone and out of relation to the teeming world around *us*. It comes before us as an *eidos*, a unified picture of God, the world, mankind and its destiny shaped by crucial symbolic forms with their own intrinsic character, their own peculiar contours, their own particular "existential" problems, their own contradictions and probably fatal flaws. This unique picture is in its individual shape and as a unified whole the object of our study; it is also that which makes the religion which embodies it unique and particular. Thus we are concerned with the *intrinsic* meaning of the symbolic forms that constitute that total picture and their relations to one another as interlocking parts of that unified whole. Each symbol here *means* as a part of that special world, as shaping that world in the way it does. Hence it is defined not in terms of our experience, of its relation to other aspects of our world (i.e., to modern social science or science), or of its ethical and social use for us—but solely in terms of its *own* world, i.e., in relation to the other symbols with which it forms that unique unified world.

For example, "Yahweh" is in any adequate Biblical theology defined or described in terms of the other symbolic structures characteristic of the Old Testament tradition under consideration (be it J, D or Isaiah), the whole series of events, experiences, witness and symbols constitutive of that document and tradition. Thus, this understanding of Yahweh relates that symbol to *their* history (not to ours), to their view of the world (not to our scientific view of it), to their understanding of community (and so to covenant, people, etc., as they understood them), to their view of law and morals, etc.—and to their communal and "existential" issues (as we can understand them) and not to ours. These "objective" symbols are to be understood in relation to the symbolic world, the history and the existential meanings of their own time.[22] We must enter their historical and symbolic world—not our own—if we are to understand; in that sense, this study is "objective." These, then, are the intrinsic or eidetic meanings of religious (or philosophical) symbols, and understanding them is essential in comprehending and using creatively the Biblical and the historical sources of theology.

(b) The effort is objective in the second sense that not only the subjective or existential meanings, the meaning for their existence and their possibilities for action in that past world, are important in this eidetic study. Also the objective picture of God, of the world, of man's place therein—of man's distress and of God's answer to that distress—forms the central object of our study. It is not Israel's "faith," nor even "her mode of being in the world," that is central to biblical (and historical) theology; it is the symbolic picture of God, of his relation to the world, history and man, and man in *that* relation, *coram deo*, that is the referent of our study.[23] Thus, such eidetic meanings are inclusive of the experiential, the ethical, *and* the "mythical" and ontological levels of meaning of symbolic forms as these levels manifested themselves in that historical setting. To understand the symbol *historically* is to understand its objective mythical, ontological and social meanings as well as its experiential and existential meanings, how it pictures God, man's world and his historical destiny as well as the way in which it challenges him as man; and to understand them in the context of their own rather than of ours.

This historical enterprise can in turn be called *eidetic* (concerned with the *eidos* or idea) in two senses. In the first of these senses, the kind of historical interpretation of a theological symbol we have described is eidetic as an historical enterprise which defines the meaning of a symbol largely if not exclusively in terms of its own vision of the world and so in terms of the system of symbols, and the internal relations of the cluster of symbols, in which that symbol functions. Out of that essentially connotative analysis of each symbol, the intrinsic shape of the symbol and the shape of the faith it expresses are given to us.

Let me explain. For reflection the most concretely unique or individual aspect of a religion or a faith is, I believe, that vision or picture of ultimate reality, and, correspondingly, that mode of human being in the world, of personal and communal being in time and for the future, which that faith or "religion" involves. Because it is human and so multi-dimensional, the mode of concrete being of a form of religion includes many aspects or facets which therefore also participate in and manifest the uniqueness of that religious form; thus these facets are also valid, and perhaps more easily accessible "handles" with which to grasp that unique character. By these facets I refer among other things to the forms of experience, the modes and styles of ritual, the ethical norms and goals, the characteristic institutional structures and forms of community, and finally, the symbolic content. None of these is prior to the other or alone primary in the life of religion, which includes them all as being fully human includes them all. If the religion has integrity and unity, these different aspects of its wholeness will mutually shape, enforce and interpret each other. Since theology is *reflection* on the symbolic content of a religious tradition, uniqueness in the *theological* realm appears through the Gestalt, the particular shape or form, of its *symbolic* structure. What distinguishes one faith from another as a form of understanding of ultimate reality, of self and of its world is, therefore, the unique shape of its symbolic structure: the *way* it understands the universe in which it finds itself, the way it views humanity and its world, and the way it sees the problems and tragedies of life and their resolution, and the forms of being and of acting that it implies.

Clearly differences of fundamental symbolic structure are crucial, for each religion, for its self-understanding and its integrity—as anyone who cherishes a yoga tradition, Jewish existence or Christian existence knows well. These differences between "faiths" are, I believe, not ultimately crucial either for creative relations to God, to ourselves or to salvation—for relatedness to God, ourselves and salvation can, I think, be found through any form of religion, thanks to the universality of the divine presence and the promised width of divine grace. But surely these differences are crucial for the *way* the religion is, for what we are and can be within it; for what it communicates to us in grace and in truth; for the kinds of experiences, hopes and expectations we have within it; and so for the way we are in the world. Thus are some people helped, rescued or saved in terms of one religion and not of the other: for example, in yoga, in Zen, and not in Catholicism or Protestantism —although, I believe, the divine grace permeates them all. Thus does one and not the other communicate the divine to us; does one and not the other seem true to us. The symbolic structure, the *eidetic* structure of its system of symbols, defines for reflection the essence, the shape, the form of a given religious tradition.

If, therefore, a scheme of contemporary interpretation of God, history, self, world and destiny is to claim to express or re-express through reflective interpretation a form of Christian faith, to be a Christian *theology* in that sense, it must adhere with fidelity to the symbolic structure of its tradition and be shaped by its contours, its emphases, its basic assertions, and its hopes.[24] However much it *re*-interprets, revises or rethinks that structure—and it must—in its own contemporary terms, it must have the intentionality of re-expressing it, and not expressing some *other* structure of faith. This is, I think, what Tillich meant when he said that the symbols of a theologian's tradition must be matters of ultimate concern to him or to her, and to express them with integrity the theologian's central vocational passion.[25] Thus

Christian theology must begin with an eidetic study of the symbolic structure of Christian affirmation and show that its reformulation of those symbols is "appropriate" to their eidetic meaning[26] if it would claim to express a contemporary Christian perspective, to be a Christian theology.

This historical enterprise, for the purposes of systematic or constructive theology, is "eidetic" in a second sense. The plurality of the meanings, in the above sense, of any symbol in the Old and New Testaments, let alone in the history of theology that follows, is staggering, and it threatens to grow steadily as enthusiastic scholars uncover new shades of nuanced differences in the documents they study. Perforce, the theologian cannot seek to make contemporary sense of the faith as a whole if he accepts as equally relevant *all* its symbols; nor can he make sense of any one symbol if he gives equal authority to the vast plurality of the traditional forms of that symbol in the many documents that make up both scriptures. No christology can be written on the basis of *all* the possible views of Christ to be found in the different documents that constitute the New Testament. Before any Christian symbols can function creatively in contemporary theology, they must be "reduced" from the plurality of their historical variations to some unity and coherence of form —to some unified meaning that represents *one* perspective of God, human existence, the world and the divine activity therein, not a multitude of divergent perspectives on each of these subjects.[27] Thus an "eidetic" reduction of every crucial symbol takes place as a precondition of systematic theology,[28] a reduction that brings to the coherence and unity of one perspective the wide variety of viewpoints found by the modern historical scholar in the plurality of documents in scripture and in tradition. This reduction will no doubt horrify if not offend many historical colleagues of the theologian. But nothing can be said by any of us (even by them) *theologically*, i.e., concerning the meaning and value of these symbols *for us*, without that reduction. Needless to say, that reduction, done either by another historical scholar or by the theologian himself qua historian, is a creative task and so it is a "risk." It can represent an error; it will certainly be partial; and necessarily it represents and expresses the limitations of his or her own implicit theological perspective, of his place and of his epoch.

Nevertheless, for all the risk involved in their achievement, the eidetic meanings of symbols are essential for theology. It is these meanings that give "Christian" form to our understanding of God, of ourselves, our world, our history and our future. It is this symbolic structure witnessing to the Christian apprehension of God and his activity that mediates between the Christian fact, the revelation of God on which Christian faith is founded, and our present understanding of experience as a whole. If Christian theology is the explication of our general experience in terms of Christian symbols, then the careful, and insofar as possible, the objective delineation of the meanings of these symbols in their traditional forms is requisite for a sound theology. The chapters which follow on the historical meanings of the categories of providence and of eschatology, and the crucial use of biblical analysis in our own creative work, represent that eidetic element in our subsequent enterprise.

2. For theological symbols to mean for us, however, they must express more than this eidetic meaning, this meaning intrinsic to another age and so abstracted from the life world and the existence of our own age. Fundamentally a symbol, religious or otherwise, means to us only if it thematizes, shapes, illumines and directs our own actual experience, if it gives form to a definite region of our life world.[29] If it does not have this creative shaping relation to *our* experience, and so this *use* in our ongoing life, its meaning content slips away, its touch with reality vanishes, and it is for us empty and inert, an abstract philosophical or poetic form to be merely aesthetically viewed or intellectually pondered. It is then no longer a religious symbol for us, a thematization of the ultimate which challenges, judges and transforms us, which relates to the questions of our being and non-being, and is a determination of our ultimate concern. Christian symbols do not arise inductively out of our everyday Lebenswelt, and they often seem to run counter to much within it. But they must touch experience somewhere to be intelligible to us, and shape definite regions of our life world to be meaningful and true for us. They must have a use if they are to have a meaning, and thus they must qualify our understanding of the destiny given to us and the form of the response of our freedom.

Part of the task of theology is, therefore, to relate traditional symbols to life experiences, to manifest the experiential meaning of theological concepts in terms of our life world. This is the role of prolegomenon, not only as a preparation for constructive theology but also as an intrinsic part of it. Its role, so to speak, is that of uncovering by phenomenological analysis the experiential questions for which the symbol is taken existentially as a resolution or an answer. Analysis uncovers those aspects of experience as religious in character that are *illumined* by the symbol, given creative shape by it; its role is to disclose the "world" and the "self" which the Christian message is taken to illumine and to redeem, and so which gives experiential meaning to the symbolic structure of that message—in the case of this volume the world of historical experience. Prolegomenon, as I have used this term, represents the phenomenological analysis of concrete experience designed to lay bare the religious dimension latent within that experience and so both the fundamental depths and the most important questions ingredient in that experience. Prolegomenon, therefore, is essential to the manifestation of the contours of experience to which theological symbols refer, which they creatively shape, and so, in that sense, which they "mean." Our previous analysis of political existence in Chapters 1 and 2 as revealing a religious dimension in historical experience and raising religious questions about that experience attempted this task, and will be subsequently used in our constructive interpretation of the symbols of providence and of eschatology.

3. Theology is reflective activity, an attempt to understand in reflective categories that which is lived in religious commitment. Thus, since theological understanding relates traditional symbols to our concrete present experience of our life world, it must achieve that relation to contemporary experience *reflectively* in the categories and forms with which that experience is reflectively appropriated. Combined, there-

fore, with the second, experiential aspect of meaning (i.e., "meaningfulness") appears a third: the ontological aspect of theological meaning, or the interpretation of the symbol in terms of modern and so credible ontological categories.[30] For theological categories to mean for us, and to be true to us, they must make contact with our world as we experience it and reflectively apprehend it. We cannot in any way *think* the divine activity in our history unless the symbols expressive of that activity are coherently related to the way we can think history, that is, to the implicit or explicit ontology of historical process that is ours. The way we think out (as well as experience) natural and historical process, temporality, causality, substance and continuity, freedom and contingency, destiny and fate, the future as possibility and its relation to present actuality, these ways of thinking about the structure of finite being, provide the forms with which, in integrity, we can think out anything, including theology, that we ponder concerning history and our part in it.

At issue here are ontological answers to questions about the structure of finitude; such answers are not and cannot be revealed in scripture or dogmatic tradition. The perspectives relevant to these questions that are to be found in scripture or tradition by eidetic study represent in part an *older* ontology, a Weltanschauung which we no longer share because it is a product of their cultural world and not of ours. Thus we cannot merely "lift" the views of substance, causality, time and space (to name a few ontological categories) out of scripture or tradition and without *critical* transformation insert them into a relevant contemporary theology. But as any perusal of contemporary theology will reveal, positions on these ontological issues are ingredient in every dogmatic formulation of theology, whether the theologian admits this fact and takes account of it or not. Thus, a critical revision of the doctrinal interpretations of the past and translation into some mode of *modern* ontology is requisite for—and found in—every relevant "biblical" or dogmatic theology. If this is so, then the recognition methodologically of its necessity, and so an explicit and so controlled procedure for its accomplishment are both necessary. A critical and constructive ontological explication of a theological symbol, therefore, is an intrinsic part of its systematic or constructive, i.e., of its *present,* theological meaning.

To be meaningful reflectively to us and so to articulate what is true for us, a theological concept must be systematized and related to all else that we hold to be true and so to the shape reality as a whole has for us. Unlike biblical and historical theology, then, systematic or constructive theology inevitably relates, in some coherent fashion, theological symbols to our reflective interpretation of our entire present world, and so to the disciplines that articulate that world—else we who live in that world, whether we will or no, be unable to think these symbols. Since this potential coherence with science, social science and contemporary ontology is mediated only through ontological and epistemological elaboration,[31] part of the meaning of a theological symbol is its ontological component, as part of the meaning of the category of revelation is its coherence with a modern understanding of epistemology. In the present work, two elements of our analysis to date will contribute to this ontological aspect of theological construction: the uncovering of the categories relevant to and necessary for the interpretation of history in Chapters 1, 2, 3 and 4, and the explicit delineation of exemplary contemporary ontologies in Chapter 4. All of these will be used in expressing the *ontological* meaning of the symbols of God, of providence and of eschatology.

4. Little further comment is, I believe, necessary with regard to the fourth level of theological meaning, the ethical and political level. This aspect of religious and theological meaning has appeared throughout the development of our theme, especially in the first chapter when the ethical and social issues of present society as it moves into the immediate future were delineated and, thereby, the moral and so religious challenges of the future were uncovered. Ultimacy manifests itself to us continously in historical experience through moral categories, as was noted in Chapter 2, and thus our response to ultimacy, our religious commitment and affirmation, has moral and political content and relevance. Our subsequent understanding of providence and eschatology, therefore, should not only reflect that ethical and political dimension. Even more, the adequacy of our interpretation should be assessed, not only by its fidelity to the eidetic forms of tradition, its relevance for our experience of our life world, and its ontological coherence, but also by its power to evoke, direct and sustain creative Christian action for the future.[32]

TWO LEVELS OF TRUTH IN THEOLOGICAL REFLECTION

Religious symbols are true for us in two interrelated ways—and correspondingly, the arguments of this book aim to show the truth of our symbolic understanding of history in these two modes: (1) A symbolic account can claim to be "true" because it brings to coherent, systematic understanding the wide variety of relevant experiences, of "facts" constitutive of that experience, in this case, our experience of historical passage. This adequacy to experience in its widest extent can be demonstrated by revealing the inadequacy to the facts and resultant incoherence of other views, and by showing how the central elements of relevant experience achieve intelligibility, coherence, and illumination within this set of symbols.[33] To show the adequacy and intelligibility of the Christian interpretation of history in this double sense is the aim of every sentence of this book.

(2) Because as rational beings we must assent autonomously to whatever is to be of ultimate concern to us, we must hold to be *true* whatever it is to which we commit ourselves. Thus, such adequacy and intelligibility, and their demonstration, are important for the life of faith as well as for the integrity and coherence of theological reflection. Nevertheless, to establish the adequacy of a symbol structure to the "facts" of a complex and controversial subject matter such as history is itself hardly a completely objective enterprise. Our sense of what the facts in fact are is in turn determined, in large part, by the way we look at things, i.e., by the symbolic structure through which we interpret experience. In turn, the way we look at things is itself more often than not a function of the status and prospects of our own being, and

so of our class, sex, national or cultural origin. In the end, our apprehension of the truth of a *fundamental* symbol system, that system through which we view all facts, all tests and all purposes, reality, truth and value, depends on more than "adequacy" in its usual sense, an objective fitting of facts to theory.[34] With regard to the fundamental symbolic systems through which we view and live within the world, the question of truth leads us to the deeper level of self-evidence, of the irresistible manifestation of truth to us and the healing transformation of us and of our world by truth. Many times in experience facts once adequately "controlled," i.e., explained or made intelligible, by one symbolic system, suddenly erupt and break that small symbolic world into pieces. What was once a rationally adequate truth can become for us inadequate by a turn of events. Alternatively, a quite unexpected coherence, despite a treasured interpretation of our world as fatally incoherent, may sneak its way in and form a renewed and clarified world around us. Truth, and the knowledge of truth at the level of ultimate concern and so of fundamental (i.e., metaphysical) symbolism, has as much the character of an "event" in our existence, a manifestation *to* us, a sudden uncovering or disclosure, as its does the character of a logical or verified conclusion.

Strange as it may seem, therefore, a metaphysical, a phenomenological—or both in unison—argument seeking to establish "objectively" the coherence and adequacy of Christian symbolism—and this book is an example of such argument—is a necessary but not a sufficient condition for the establishment of the "validity" of that system. Nor is such an argument, even if reflectively assented to, sufficient for an awareness that here truth is expressed—if, again, we are dealing with fundamental matters and thus matters not only of our existence and so of our ultimate concern but also matters that determine the deepest level of our interpretation of everything else. For one thing, a symbol that may seem reflectively adequate to "explain" experience, to cohere all its facets adequately, may yet seem unreal, to possess no referent beyond itself, to communicate no sense of reality to us. For many people Christian symbols make excellent sense as intellectual interpretations of an experience in which there is in reality no God at all. Truth at this level, we must understand, is deeply a matter of *self*-evidence, that reality really is *this* way and really manifests *these* contours, as expressed in *these* fundamental symbolic forms.[35] The experience of adequation, of correlation, of congruence with "reality" as it manifests itself to us must be there—in whatever appropriate form that experience of adequation takes. Put more appropriately for the categories of religion and theology, we may say that religious symbols finally become *true* when the reality with which we have to do in life and in thought is experienced to communicate itself to us through these symbols. Such an experience of symbols as *media* of communication with reality is, I believe, fundamental to any sense of truth at this level, whatever the form of the "philosophy" or "theology" articulated. Only if the basic symbols with which we think out all else serve for us to shape given reality, the reality we encounter in our real existence and our life world, do we know them to be true. Truth is a relation not only of propositions or notions to "facts"; it is at its deepest level a relation of ourselves to reality. This means that if theology is taken to be true, ultimately it is because its symbols are experienced to communicate a real encounter with God, because through them the divine presence, the divine activity and the divine promises are communicated to our existence.

If our understanding of the truth of symbols is confined to the relation of the symbol to the facts that it coheres—if, so to speak, the *symbol* is that which ultimately coheres, illumines and heals—we shall not understand the relation of religion to its truth. Nor will we accurately explicate the character of religion itself: the power of religious symbols, the danger of religious symbols, the transrational character (i.e., the limit-character) of religious symbols, the ambiguity of their relation to experience and of thought alike. There is something else in this relation that is crucial: the impinging—threatening and healing—presence of the ultimate and the sacred which is mediated and expressed by the symbol, the mediation by the symbol of the transcendent ground to which it points and which it communicates. Such an apprehension of symbols as media of the divine self-manifestation is necessary in order that symbols function as religious speech and witness, and so it is necessary if they are to have theological meaning and validity for us. Without this they are human projections and by no means of ultimate concern. Our intellectual sense of their coherence and their adequacy to common human experience can, to be sure, help us immensely to experience them religiously; the illuminative and cohering power of symbols can force us to return to them again and again for clarification and illumination, and consciousness of their interpretive power can hold us fast to them in situations of doubt. Finally, however, they will be true for us only if they so communicate the divine presence and activity, not merely because they "make sense" of our experienced world: though the two forms of experience, the one existential and the other rational, are strangely interlocked and inseparable in much of our experience. But as we all have discovered, no argument, however clear, novel and incisive, that demonstrates the adequacy of symbols to facts can establish by itself the *reality* of the divine presence to which these symbols refer. A theological interpretation of history may help with many of the problems of faith and even help to show the adequacy and the truth of faith. However illuminating the intelligibility it achieves, however, as a human work it cannot bring that faith into being.

THE ROLE OF MYTH IN THE COMPREHENSION OF HISTORY

Finally we must speak, however briefly, of the logical and linguistic status of the theology of history here presented. In that effort, first of all, it must be emphasized that theological symbols—even as "adequate and coherent," and even as media of our own deep participation—remain "symbols," referent to, communicative of a *mystery* that they neither encompass nor exhaust. As the sea may be a symbol of and communicate an experience of infinite power and eternity—and yet as finite be neither—so our verbal symbols in theology, however "appropriate," are human words, partial, rooted in historical usage, referent in that usage to mundane things, and thus neither precise nor univocal predications of the mystery which they com-municate.[36] We have spoken of the complexity and depth of history itself and also of the even deeper mystery of God. Theological symbols are modes in which the interrelation of these two mysteries, experienced and lived in time, is mirrored in verbal or linguistic-symbolic reflection. They illumine both history and God—so we shall argue—but, at the same time, they disclose, through that illumination, the continuing and inexhaustible depth of the mystery in each. Thus a Christian theol-ogy of history provides for us neither a blueprint of the structure of history nor an itinerary of its career. Such is not possible for any human thought, scientific, philosophical or theological; we are *in* history, and our language, our symbols and even our reflection on them are embedded there, and thus through them we cannot be taken out of history to survey it and then produce our report.

Such symbols express, for me, a *relation* of us who are actors in history—and thus partially effective there—with the deepest ground of history's order and continuity, its novelty and possibilities, from which the creativity, the disruption and the renewal of history stem. Theological symbols relate the dynamic structures of histori-cal passage, its "trends and chances," its continuities and novelties, its fundamental structure of destiny and freedom, to the ground of those ontological structures; they do not replace those structures nor does their illuminative power remove explana-tions in terms of those structures. They add that other dimension which history itself illustrates in all its movements, that men and women live, think and act *coram deo*, and which, therefore, repeatedly provides the basis for an existential "comprehen-sion" of history, a reflective interpretation of it and our active participation in it—as we have sought to demonstrate. To experience, to reflect upon and to understand these fundamental relations characteristic of history—"the work of God in history" and "the response of men and women to their temporality"—is to understand anew much about history's structure, the source of its terrors and the grounds of its hope —but is not enough for a full and coherent understanding of either God or of time. To live within that relation is to come much closer than reflection to its reality; in fact, it is sufficiently close to provide the basis for a fully human life before God in time. Thus is the partiality and inadequacy of our reflection continually secured, validated, tested and transcended by its fruits in our existence in time—inwardly by the assurance and commitment of faith and outwardly by a new reality of love and of creative action. A theology of history is validated by the illumination it gives for our temporal existence and the praxis it engenders in the world—it is never adequate to its subject nor more than a glimpse of the truth for which it seeks.

When, moreover, theological symbols are referent to historical passage and are clustered together so as to form a theological interpretation of history, then inescapa-bly they take a "story" form: they describe the "mighty acts of God" or the "divine economy." All theological symbols in our tradition, I believe, relate to our life in time and seek to explicate a divine activity which transcends in some sense that temporal-ity, and yet is in relation to that temporal life. Thus all theological symbols take this story form—be they the symbols of creation, of providence, of revelation or of eschatology. They express the relation of God to temporal passage and so speak of God as an "actor" in temporal affairs. In short, they take a "mythical" form, a form which is unavoidable in a theology centered in history and in what it knows of God in and through history, whose God, therefore, transcends history and yet is *known* because he is in continual and diverse relations to historical life.

Myth, as a form of language, uses a story form, phenomenal or ontic language descriptive of events in space and time and of actors in those events, to describe or illumine structures and relations that transcend that phenomenal and that ontic manifold.[37] In mythical discourse itself, therefore, there is a tension between form and content, between the language or form that keeps it related to phenomenal and temporal experience, and the referent or content that points beyond that plane of experienced life to its transcendent ground and principle of completion. In traditional myth these two levels; phenomenal or ontic events and transcendent referent, were inextricably entangled, such is the "mythical consciousness" that makes no division between the divine and the natural, the divine and the historical. Slowly in the history of reflection, and especially in the history of *theological* reflection, these two dimensions have been disentangled. As a result, a distinction has appeared between "primitive myth," where phenomena and transcendence are intertwined in one story, and "permanent myth" or "broken myth," where myth has the character of symbol qua symbol, and does not *on its own authority* legitimate or validate (though it may refer to) any empirical, natural or historical fact. Such "myths" seek to relate the events and sequences of historical passage to their own deepest source, to the ultimate norm that impinges upon their estranged actuality, and to their possibilities and grounds for hope, i.e., to God.[38] They *shape* into Christian form (or whatever tradition they may represent) the dimension of ultimacy and sacrality characteristic of the total stuff of history, instead of pointing to specific factual events that "explain" events in history. When in connection with a theological interpretation of history—or any modern interpretation of history, for that matter—we speak of "myths," it is to the second permanent or broken form of myth that we refer, not to the first. As we have emphasized, a Christian interpretation of history does not replace a historical, economic, social interpretation—nor does it add its own "facts" to their interpretation. It provides symbols for a unifying interpretation of some of the data with which all modes of inquiry into history must deal.

Any view of history as a whole—be it Christian, progressivist (New Eon), Marxist or New Nightmare—has in this sense a mythical character; it is a dramatic description of the whole of passage, and thus mythical in form. (1) It tells a story about fundamental forces and/or divine actions in relation to human freedom that unifies the entire scope of history into an intelligible and comprehensible whole; (2) it concerns our questions about meaning in life, i.e., about the careers of good and evil in historical passage, and so about the prospects we face in the proximate and the ultimate future; and (3) it provides norms for our common existence and standards and guidelines for social structures (politics, as we saw) and for education. In this sense, as we have here argued at length, modern societies, scientific and secular, liberal or communistic, in comprehending and dealing with their historical existence depend as much as did traditional religious societies upon a fundamental mythical structure symbolically expressing the relation of historical passage, as they are immersed in it, to ultimacy and the sacred. If this be true, the word "myth" bears no connotation at all of untruth or of illusion; to term a viewpoint mythical is *not* to say it is untrue. Rather, this term specifies the form of language with which any community objectifies for reflection the ultimate historical horizon in which it lives. Thus, myth represents the symbols through which the "religious substance" of a culture or a community's life in historical passage expresses itself. Since forms of rationality (how intelligibility and truth are to be gained) as well as views of what is real (what *are* the facts) stem from and are dependent on such a fundamental mythical structure, it is not at all easy to test myths or to determine their validity or their value rationally. Fundamental viewpoints, as we have noted, set the terms for argument and so are only with difficulty "provable," and all myths are validated finally by participation and self-evidence, not by demonstration. Nevertheless, it is possible, as we have seen, to argue in this realm in terms of adequacy and coherence —and that we shall seek to do.

When we ask why the form of language we have called myths is not only appropriate to the interpretation of history but inevitably basic to all interpretations of history, cultural or theological, we encounter the dialectic of mystery and meaning in historical existence. The basic presupposition at work in our answer to this question is, as Niebuhr was wont to put it, that meaning is present in and so related to our experience of history, and yet not identical with that experience.[39] History is experienced as both menace and promise, as incoherent and coherent, as meaningless and meaningful, as condemned and as redeemable—and the problem of understanding history is in the end the problem of sorting out and interrelating in dialectical form these tangents of both mystery and meaning that suffuse historical experience. Because of this dialectic, to search for an undialectical account of meaning in history is, therefore, either to regard meaning as undialectically *transcendent* to historical passage and so to deny the meaning and the possibilities of that passage, or to find that meaning and coherence *in* the passage itself and so to overlook both the transcendent and mysterious grounds of all meaning and the mystery of history's self-contradiction and estrangement. Basic to the argument of this book is the affirmation that our experience of history uncovers a *dialectical* relation of mystery and meaning in history, neither a simple disjunction nor a simple conjunction of mystery and meaning; that this dialectical interrelation is the essence of the biblical and Christian views of history as expressed in their major relevant symbols; and finally, that this dialectic, found thus in both experience and tradition, is formally most adequately expressed reflectively in the form of symbolic myth,[40] and materially in the cluster of symbols that constitute the Christian mythos.

Specifically, four characteristics of our human experience of history point to this dialectical presence of mystery and of meaning in that experience and so to the usefulness and adequacy of a mythical mode of historical interpretation. (1) Both to live in history communally and politically and to reflect upon it in the relevant disciplines humans must conceive of history as a whole, of its dynamic factors and of its meaning. Yet, as immersed in history, and so viewing its passage from a particular vantage point, they are incapable of viewing the whole with adequacy, coherence and objectivity. Thus is their inescapable "comprehension" of history, its coherence and its meaning, symbolic at best and affirmed and adhered to more by means of faith and participation than by demonstration. (2) Historical events are essentially characterized not only by coherent continuities and trends, but also by the intervention of radical contingency and of centered and so free responses. Thus, while an ontological analysis of these immanent structures of destiny and freedom, actuality and possibility and their interrelations, are possible (here we disagree with Niebuhr), nevertheless the shape of the whole of history, and so the form of its meaning—necessary again for communal existence, for politics and for reflection on history—is unknowable and unformulatable from any vantage point within history. Only an interpretation that locates both mystery and meaning within a field characterized by contingency and within the career of freedom can adequately express whatever meaning as well as structure history may contain—and such an interpretation must, therefore, ultimately be in terms of a story or drama and not in terms of necessary, albeit coherent structures.

(3) History is in strange contradiction to itself; it manifests "estrangement" and thus essential ambiguity; its structure and the possibilities that emerge from that structure thus are no final or reliable clues to its meaning. The relation between the structures of history (its ontology) and its possibilities thus participate in both mystery—the mystery of the self and its self-contradiction—and meaning. A "rational" account of history as a whole in terms of its structure, if it affirms the meaning latent in history, thus tends to overlook the estrangement that is part of history's concreteness and so is abstractive; or, in uncovering its contradictions, such a view overlooks the real possibilities of meaning latent in historical existence. Consequently, the principle of interpretation of history adequate to its facets of meaning and its mystery, must appeal to a principle of unity and of meaning that is transcendent to its observable interrelations and its ontological structures and so capable of dealing with the distortions of that structure and the tragic character of those interrelations. (4) As a result, the dialectic of mystery and meaning in history points to a transcendent source of both, a source which, moreover, is itself in dialectical relation to the events and sequences of history. It is not purely immanent within them as history's estrangement shows, nor is it completely transcendent to them as history's possibilities of meaning reveal.[41] Such a transcendent principle of being and of meaning is present in all historical experience as the ground of the immanent structures of historical life; but also, if it be the source of history's meaning, it is also present in *variant* and in *new* ways to redeem that structure from its own distortion. However far an ontological interpretation of history's structures may be pushed— and we shall push it a good way—it is in the end completed and overarched by

symbols expressive of a wider horizon of meaning: symbols of judgment, redemption, and the end as well as the structural symbols of destiny and freedom, and of divine creation and providence. The unity of historical existence can be known only by faith in more than the coherent structures of historical life, and expressed in a mythical use of symbols that unites an apprehension of those structures with a confidence in their redemption. Human existence in time, both individually and communally, cannot escape the question of the unity and meaning, the interpretation, of historical passage. To seek to bring such unity to historical existence on any other basis than that of a global myth is to be tempted to overlook its possibilities of meaning, to abstract from its evident contradictions and tragedy and, above all, to impose on historical life a principle of interpretation reflective of a partial, and so idolatrous, vantage point.[42] A theological interpretation of history as "mythical" is, therefore, not at all dogmatically or arbitrarily enforced on history's materials. Rather, those materials themselves, in their dialectic of continuity and change, destiny and freedom, structure and estrangement, mystery and meaning, continually call—both existentially and reflectively—for such an interpretation. For this reason, the historical course of human culture continually manifests similar, if less adequate, forms of "myths about history."

A Christian interpretation of history is thus one based on a theologically formulated myth: a cluster of religious symbols concerned with the evident mystery—both transcendent and immanent, both of God and of man's freedom—in historical life in relation to its elusive and yet real meanings. These symbols, together forming a myth or story concerning history's career, are "objectified" by theological interpretation into conceptual form: as creation, anthropology, providence, revelation, incarnation, redemption (justification, sanctification and ecclesia) and eschatology. Thus are they made capable of reflective application to the generic traits of concrete historical experience on the one hand and to historical praxis on the other, and correspondingly, to the disciplines or forms of inquiry relevant to the understanding of history and of action within history. It is in this application—as providing principles of interpretation—that such a mythical scheme, and the symbols that compose it, is validated—as the most coherent and adequate mode of interpreting our common experience of historical passage, and as the most coherent and adequate horizon within which the reflective disciplines concerned with history can find their ground and their unity. Thus, a *theological* interpretation of history constituted by these symbols, and so by the myths which they together form, finds its origin, and the test of the appropriateness of its interpretation of these symbols, in the biblical tradition and in subsequent Christian interpretations of these symbols in relation to history. It establishes its meaningfulness as the principle of interpretation of our common experience of history, as expressive of the relation to ultimacy and sacrality that, as we saw, dominates all historical experience. Ultimately every myth about history is validated in relation to the experience of history.[43] And this myth, and so the different symbols that constitute it, is itself interpreted (retrieved or revised) in relation to the modern historical consciousness, as that consciousness is reflectively expressed in contemporary ontologies. Thus is a myth capable on the one hand of becoming a principle of interpretation of *our* experience of history, and on the other, of providing a unifying center of interpretation for contemporary reflection on historical passage. Let us note that as the content of the myth portrays the dialectical relation of God to historical life as the principle of its meaning, so the *form* of the myth incorporates in principle and in fact the dialectical interpenetration of symbol with experience and with reflection on experience—the symbol providing ultimate shape and unity to that experience and to the disciplines concerned with that experience.

Some of the symbols which together constitute the myth and so the Christian interpretation of history derivative from it by reflection are here understood to portray in symbolic form the "invariant structures" of man's being in historical passage, and thus the synchronic structures of history itself. These are the symbols of man's creatureliness and his self-transcendence (i.e., finite freedom), of God as creator and providential preserver and ruler and of the estrangement of man from himself and from God. These are here regarded as universal structures of man's being and the universal distortion of that structure, expressed at their most fundamental level in the symbols of creation, providence and anthropology. In a theological interpretation of *history*, therefore, these symbols of man's being in relation to God provide the *ultimate* horizon: in terms of this horizon the ontological structures of finite, historical being discoverable by an analysis of history—destiny and freedom, actuality and possibility, self and world, individual and community—and the norms of historical communal life—justice, equality, order and freedom—are to be interpreted, understood and united for both reflection and praxis. Thus a preliminary ontological explication of these symbols is both possible and necessary—as illustrated in Chapter 12, where an effort is made to interpret ontologically the immanent and so ontological (synchronic) structure of creative providence in relation to destiny and freedom, and to past actuality and future possibility. However, because the *meaning* of history (its diachronic aspect) transcends its structure, since that structure evidences estrangement, the total myth transcends the limits of its own ontological explication (as it transcends the symbols of creation and providence), and so is completed only in such further symbols as those of judgment, revelation, incarnation, atonement, justification, new life and eschatology. Thus it is a theological myth as well as a philosophical vision; it is expressed not only by ontological elaboration but also by religious symbols; it is grounded not only in reflected experience but also in religious faith; and it is known as meaningful and true not only by its adequacy and coherence but also by participation in its power both to renew our existence and to refashion our praxis.[44]

The Christian interpretation of history here proposed has, therefore, the following characteristics and aims: (1) it is a reflective interpretation of a cluster of relevant Christian symbols (especially those of providence and of eschatology) concerning human historical being and its relation to God, gathered together into a story or a myth that illumines both the invariant structures—and their distortion—and the "meaning" of history as a whole. Insofar as it illumines the structure and the meaning of history, and empowers us creatively to be and to act in history, it is received as "true"—though it remains a symbolic and so partial medium of such truth rather than a final statement of it. (2) This is an interpretation in part derived from and in toto applied to the "facts" and "characteristics" of common historical experience, providing thereby their "ultimate" (though not exclusive) principle of interpretation, as in turn these facts of common experience provide the basis for testing and partially validating this interpretation. (3) The interpretation is explicated ontologically (as far as is possible) in terms of the modern historical consciousness so that it can become an aspect of our own thinking about ourselves and our history, and a principle of unity for contemporary disciplines concerned with history. The total aim is to provide an appropriate (true to the sources), coherent (in itself and in relation to the categories of other disciplines) and adequate (interpretive of all historical experience) set of categories and symbols with which (a) our experience of history can be understood and creatively dealt with, (b) reflective interpretations of historical experience (historical, psychological, sociological and political) can be usefully grounded and unified and (c) political praxis and cultural life can be creatively grounded and guided.

PART III

The Christian View of History: A Reinterpretation

7

TRADITIONAL VIEWS OF PROVIDENCE: AUGUSTINE AND CALVIN

Our subject in this final part of the volume is the Christian interpretation of history. Our aim is to reinterpret or "revise" that understanding in the light of the modern historical consciousness and, in the process, to show that such a reinterpretation provides the most intelligible and adequate set of symbols with which to understand the strange and unlikely course of history. Such a reinterpretation in the light of the modern historical consciousness, while in many respects "unorthodox," is, as we have argued, a necessity for us; also it is by no means arbitrary, for the relations of the Christian interpretation of history to the modern historical consciousness are close indeed. As we shall try to show, it was in large part on the basis of the Christian interpretation, as formed largely by Augustine and later developed by Calvin, that the modern consciousness of history arose—although, ironically, when it arose in the seventeenth and eighteenth centuries, that latter consciousness understood itself as the direct antithesis of the orthodox Christian interpretation that preceded it and made it possible.

There is little question that the new conception of time and so the Christian understanding of history, implicit in the scriptures and expressed in preliminary form in the earliest theologies of the church, reached its first complete and explicit statement in Augustine.[1] With Augustine the sequences of time ceased to be made up of a cyclical or even a random series of moments. Rather, each moment is unrepeatable and so unique; above all, each can bear an eternal content and significance, i.e., each can become a moment in which a relation to eternity and so to human fulfillment is possible. The ontological ground for this confidence in the potential meaningfulness of time was given by the doctrine of creation and of divine sovereignty over time, and the linear conception of time that they imply; the ground for "meaning" of each moment of time was provided by the promise of eschatological fulfillment; and the seal, sign and proof of the eternal meaning of these finite moments was given by the experience of grace on the one hand and by the fact of the incarnation, on the other.[2] This basic Augustinian affirmation of time and so of history as creative and good under the lordship of God, despite their real tragedy and apparent aimlessness, was further enlarged by Calvin in his conception of the sovereignty of God, both providential and redemptive, as involved in the transformation of individuals and of communities alike into the divine image, into a new holiness. Out of this dynamic interpretation of the Christian view, the "biblical" view of time and of history prepared the way for the modern historical consciousness.

The Christian view of history arises out of a confluence of all the major "doctrines" or symbols intrinsic to Christian faith: creation, the nature of man, the work of providence, revelation and covenant, the incarnation, grace and renewal, the community or church, and eschatology. Traditionally, central to our subject, however, has been the concept of providence. For providence is that symbol which describes the activity or "rule" of God in the world as a whole over the entire course of time, "the lordship of God over all world occurrence," the relation of God to the "creature as such and in general," to use Barth's expressions.[3] Clearly, in the traditional view the symbol of providence presupposes on the one hand God's creation of the world, i.e., of nature and of man, for in creation both the goodness and the potentialities of nature and history and God's sovereignty in history are given their ontological basis. Providence presupposes on the other hand the purposes or intentions of that God as those intentions are revealed in the covenant and in Christ and as they are to be realized in the end—i.e., incarnation and eschatology. Nevertheless, it is through the symbol of providence that traditional theology has expressed the mode of the divine sovereignty over temporal process, i.e., over natural occurrence, over historical events, and so over the course of events everywhere and at every time which constitute "history." If there has been in traditional theology a Christian interpretation of social change and of the course of history's events, of God's relation to the natural order and to the freedom of men and women—and so to the continuities and changes in historic process—it has been expressed centrally through the symbol of providence as that symbol is related to creation and the fall on the one hand and revelation, incarnation and eschatology, on the other.

The purpose of this chapter is not to write a history of the concept of providence in Christian tradition. Rather, it is to describe the *meaning* of this symbol (in relation, again, to creation, fall, incarnation and eschatology) as it has appeared in two crucial, illuminating, and generally "classical" expressions of that meaning. Through such an analysis the shape of the eidetic meaning of the symbol, as central to the traditional Christian view of history, will become clearer and the way prepared to reinterpret that meaning in contemporary terms potentially relevant to our own sense of history. Although logically the various biblical interpretations of history, and so of providence, are prior to these meanings appearing in the history of Christian tradition, an analysis and use of these primary biblical forms of this symbol will be postponed until our own reinterpretation is broached.

St. Augustine

Providence is a symbol that appears frequently among the early postcanonic Christian writings. Depending largely on Stoic philosophy, the use of that symbol there, however, largely concerns itself with the order of nature, the justice of divine retribution and with the "economy" or administration of divine blessings to human life, rather than with the question of the meaning and direction of the sequence of historical events.[4] With Augustine, however, the question of the meaning of the sequence of history's events poses itself as a central theological problem, both with regard to events in an individual's life and with regard to the events that constitute history as a whole. Thus our analysis will begin with Augustine, whose delineation of the sovereignty of God in history not only establishes the view of time and of history characteristic of subsequent Western culture but also determines in large part—as in the case of so many other symbols—the subsequent meaning of the symbol of providence in traditional Western theology.

In Augustine's account of the symbol of God's providence—and so in his understanding of the course of history—certain general principles or meanings of this symbol of the divine activity appear which will characterize the symbol throughout the classical tradition. Our concern in this and the next two chapters is to see how these principles appear and reappear in different forms and with different emphases until the contemporary period. A preliminary summary of these "themes" of the symbol of providence is as follows: (1) providence expresses the sovereignty of God over historical (and natural) events and so a sovereign or ruling action fulfilling God's final purposes for his creation. Thus God's providential action is controlled and defined by his electing will on the one hand and by the eschatological or ultimate goal of God, on the other; providence and eschatology are not antithetical but polar or mutually implicatory symbols, the former providing some of the means in time for the fulfillment of the ultimate goal. (2) God's providential activity includes sovereignty over the "external" or objective historical actions and events, individual and social, in which all humans live as well as a sovereignty in various ways over the ordinary decisions of human beings. On the other hand, at least in "traditional theology," God's electing or predestinating activity (a more fundamental symbol), concerns his sovereign ruling over those internal events, responses and decisions in an individual's life which lead directly to that person's Christian faith and obedience and so to his or her ultimate individual salvation. Both equally are defined and controlled by God's eschatological goal, i.e., providence controls events *in order to* fulfill that goal, and God "elects" individuals *for* that goal and thus gives them faith. As we shall see, in both Augustine and Calvin God's election of individuals for eschotological glory directs the activities of his providence in history. (3) In his providence God does not "work" in history as one external cause among other causes (though for the tradition he may well so work in miracles), but always in and through the various dynamic factors, including freedom, effective in all historical change.[5] (4) Providence works through, not against, human freedom, through our voluntary willing, and so even through our sinful willing. Providence is not contradicted by the reality of sin but precisely made necessary by it—else the eschatological goal be quite impossible for human beings to attain and so remain utterly unfulfilled. Thus as the divine activity in a free and therefore sinful history, the work of providence is "hidden" rather than obvious since the purposes of God are obscured, although never defeated, by the dubious purposes and actions of men and women. (5) Because of providence, there is no fate in human historical existence. Despite the tragic character of much of history's course, no blind chance or *fortuna* ultimately destructive of human self-actualization appears. Rather, the course of events as governed by providence moves toward the increase of freedom and toward the realization of human potentiality. (6) Providence is active both in the course of an individual's life and in the course of history generally—and in both areas of activity what the divine providence is doing is directly related to the electing will and the eschatological goal of God's sovereign rule.

God's providential activity, as Augustine understands it, is controlled and so defined by God's eschatological goal for mankind and for history. It is, therefore, well to begin with Augustine's understanding of eschatology, for Augustine effects a fundamental reinterpretation of eschatological symbols that is to dominate the tradition until the modern period. Briefly put, Augustine transfigures the apocalyptic and eschatological symbols intrinsic to the tradition he inherited into ahistorical, supernatural symbols. A good deal of the previous tradition[6] had understood the promises of "the end to come"—the return of Christ, the universal resurrection of the dead, the last judgment, the final kingdom, the new heaven and the new earth —as happening in and to future *history,* as the direct culmination and endpoint of history's movement, as a new and perfected age soon to appear here on "earth" through divine action amidst a perfected nature.[7] On the contrary, Augustine understood them as events in a supernatural, ahistorical realm; not a new age in future time and space but in a higher realm of being, a participation in God's eternity beyond death, space, historical time, the physical body and the physical earth—though each who will be "there" will at the end recover back his own transfigured body in that supernatural realm.[8] The "rule of the saints for one thousand years"—a biblical symbol previously understood as referent to a new age to come in the future of historical process—is now understood not as an eschatological symbol descriptive of God's final goal but as a symbol depicting the present rule of the church, through providence and grace, during the remaining interim course of history before its end.[9] Thus the biblical promise of the realized kingdom contains for Augustine no promise for history as such.[10] It is a promise of a divine community —a community blessed by a perfect vision of God and love for Him—beyond history, beyond nature and beyond spatial dimensions in eternity, a transfigured, supernatural life with God—or eternal damnation."[11]

Despite the fact that in this way he moved the eschatological elements of the tradition out of time and history into the suprahistorical, there is no question that Augustine is also rightly credited with giving to time and so to historical process an intelligibility and a meaning which they had not possessed before. With Augustine the Western, and so the modern, sense of temporal passage comes to definitive and formative expression: historical time is a linear sequence, each of whose moments contains the possibility of ultimate significance, whose events form a pattern related to that ultimate significance, and so whose course as a whole possesses an intelligible and coherent unity relevant to the gaining of final salvation. Thus because for Augustine history "goes somewhere," possesses meaning for salvation and so intelligibility for reflection, with him begins the tradition of philosophy of history,[12] an interpretation of the entire course of history exhibiting the intelligibility of its larger patterns and the relation of those patterns to ultimate salvation or meaning. Because the ground of both that intelligibility and that final meaning is the sovereignty of God (as creator, providential ruler and redeemer), this interpretation is a "theology" of history.[13] The conviction expressed in the scriptures that history under God moves through God's mighty acts toward an ultimate culmination is, in Augustine, on the one hand given a quite new form and yet on the other, made fundamental and definitive for all subsequent Western views of history. Our questions then are: How is it that time and historical passage possess intelligibility and meaning if the eschatological goal of salvation transcends them, and so is "beyond" history? And, what form does the sovereignty of God, especially in his providential activity, take in providing this meaning to temporal passage?

Augustine possessed a "theonomous" understanding of temporal passage, as he did of creaturely and especially of human being.[14] For him human existence, intelligence and will are real, creative and good in participation in God, but relatively unreal, in error and warped when separated from God.[15] Consequently, shorn of their divine content the moments of experienced time are unreal, passing and empty, hardly "there" at all and leading nowhere.[16] On the other hand, these same creaturely and transient moments, undergirded by the divine power of being, guided by the divine providence, and centered on the incarnation and its promises of ultimate salvation, can become creative loci of ultimate meaning, moments in which our relation to final salvation is prepared (through providence and grace), established (through grace and faith) and preserved (through grace, obedience and love)—and thus moments that lead to salvation. Individual existence in time, therefore, becomes "good" and "intelligible" when through providence and grace it comes to faith, obedience and love, i.e., when its "natural" creaturely dependence on God is realized inwardly in faith and becomes the spiritual pattern as well as the ontological character of our being.[17] Correspondingly, history as a whole becomes meaningful when, again through the work of providence and grace, its sequences of events and its institutions foster, nurture and develop the temporal realm of grace, the *civitas dei*, where redemptive grace is located and where the life of faith, obedience and love is led. In both cases without that relation to providence and to grace, creaturely being and so with it temporal passage, becomes unreal, empty, distorted—and damned.[18]

The logical and ontological ground for this new understanding of time as linear, teleological and meaningful, bearing within itself an eternal content, was the doctrine of *creatio ex nihilo:* God had created time along with material and spiritual creation, and thus was it an instrument in his purposive hands rather than a blind "fate" eroding, crushing and annihilating human being.[19] Because time had an absolute beginning, its moments were unrepeatable; they could "go somewhere" and build toward something. And because all creatures and so even time itself possessed under the divine sovereignty a final goal, these unrepeatable moments could lead toward eternity. The rule of God, the creator of time, over temporal passage is the ontological presupposition for Augustine's assertion that time and with it human history possess essential meaning. It is, however, instructive that the direct and so most fundamental *theological* basis for Augustine's assertion that the moments of time are unrepeatable, teleological and so can be ultimately meaningful lay not in his belief in creation nor even in his hope for eschatological fulfillment but in his own immediate experience of redemption through grace on the one hand, and in the event of Christ on which that experience depended on the other.

The most fundamental challenge to a sense of meaningful history in the ancient world came from the cyclical view of time, the view that the moments of time are caught on an endless cycle and thus, infinitely repeating both joy and sorrow, were in themselves meaningless because in time nothing ultimate or final could occur. Against this view Augustine cites neither the doctrine of creation nor of eschatology but what were for him the two most fundamental Christian convictions: the unrepeatability of the event of Christ's sacrifice for our salvation, and the certainty of the salvation based on that sacrifice and experienced in his own life.[20] Because of these two absolute certainties, each representing a "moment" with an unrepeatable eternal and infinitely meaningful content, he knows that *no* moments are caught on a meaningless and futile cycle, and correspondingly, that all historical moments are unrepeatable and so can mediate ultimate salvation, that all the moments of time can be filled with a content *from* eternity and so lead *to* eternity. It was the experienced presence of eternity within *certain* qualitatively unique moments of time that gave to all of history's moments, and so to the history that together these moments constituted, their meaning. Thus while the symbols of creation, providence and the eschatological end provided for Augustine the ultimate theological (ie ontological) framework within which the potential meaning of history's moments became intelligibly expressed and grounded, it was the divine redemptive activity in time of incarnation and of grace that originally established his faith in and interpretation of those symbols, and so formed the ultimate basis for his philosophy of history. One can only wonder whether this historical ground of the Western sense of a meaningful time through the presence of eternity within its moments is not also an essential and not an accidental ground. In this sense, while Augustine's doctrine of the creating and ordaining sovereignty of God extends to the whole of finite being and of history, bringing history into a purposive unity for the first time, his understanding of that sovereignty and his confidence in it were founded on and shaped by his experience of grace and of Christ. Now let us examine in more detail what for Augustine God is about in history and how divine providence accomplishes these purposes.

God's work in history, in providence and in grace, we have said is preparatory to a supernatural and transhistorical goal. It does not, therefore, involve the transfiguration of history either developmentally (an idea probably inconceivable to Augustine) or apocalyptically in a new age to come; the divine providence is not seeking to transform and redeem *history*.[21] Rather, the divine activity consists only of the various ways that God leads men and women into eschatological fulfillment. Concretely, men and women are led to salvation by coming to faith and love within the community of the church which, as the body of Christ, mediates grace and so salvation into history. In a proleptic sense, therefore, the church can be said to be the kingdom as the divine-human locus of grace sufficient for eternal life. As a community of people, however, it is not at all the kingdom but full of "wheat and tares" to be itself judged and purified at the last.[22] Thus because it is directed towards the eschatological goal, the work of providence in general history is, first, centered on the creation and sustenance of the church and, secondly, concerned with leading individuals into its midst for their salvation. In this way as providence is defined and controlled by election and the eschatological goal, so in turn the realization of that goal in heaven depends on the providential work of God in time saving individuals for eternity. And because of this interrelation of eschatology and providence, predestination or election—which determines the relation of each individual to eternal salvation—directs the providential activity of God among men and women. As Augustine puts it: God's providence uses "vessels of wrath" to serve the advantage of "vessels of mercy."[23]

The basic principle governing all of Augustine's understanding of God's sovereignty in history is that providence works in and through, not against, the free activity of men and women. He may not, from our point of view, succeed in holding onto both divine sovereignty and human autonomy, but he should be given high marks for effort. The presupposition with which Augustine works is the dilemma, evidenced in his own experience, that man is on the one hand incurably free and cannot be compelled or coerced into salvation, and yet on the other, that his freedom is itself too bound in sin to reach the eschatological goal alone or by his own efforts. We are all far too self-interested, wayward and lost to embody the love essential to ultimate fulfillment. Thus unless each individual, and history with him, be cajoled, fooled, lured, enticed, coaxed, pushed and pulled into a new state of existence—and kept there—the eschatological goal is impossible for anyone. Hence, the providential sovereignty of God working through our freedom is made necessary by both the autonomy of men and women and by their sin, and is the sole means through which the eschatological promises are fulfilled. As Augustine confesses about his own life, "It was thou, O my God, who didst it, for the steps of a man are ordered by the Lord, and He shall dispose his way. Or how can we procure salvation but from Thy hand, remaking what it hath made?"[24]

This fundamental principle of divine creative activity in and through the creaturely "causes" that bring events to pass determines Augustine's understanding of the work of providence in the corporeal creation (in "nature" as we would say). In the first place it is God's power, as the source and ground of the being of things, through which all creatures continue to be in time and are active in all the ways that they are active: God gives to each "nature" its power to be and to be as it naturally is. This inward power is multi-dimensional, depending on the "nature" of the creature; in man, and so in history, the work of God in and on man includes the powers of man's body, the norms through which man makes his moral decisions, and the truths which man's mind perceives and knows.[25] Creatures work on each other from the outside, pushing, pulling, moving, coaxing, and so are genuinely proximate causes of events—but the *power* through which they do this and so effect their causality comes to them from God and not from themselves alone or from others.[26] Thus God works inwardly in every creature in its continuation in being and in all of its activities. It is this power that makes trees grow, that brings forth young, that grows wheat and grapes, that creates health—and so that grounds and establishes what we now term the "natural laws" characteristic of the ordinary behavior of creatures. Nature in all its diversity of kinds and the harmonies of their interactions manifests the power, the order and the will of the ordaining providence of God. Miracles, therefore, reflect for Augustine no new intervention of God into nature or history; they merely represent an unusual mode of His natural or ordinary active presence in the world in order to create a "sign" for men of that presence and that power.[27] Correspondingly, the appearance of new creations, new species and kinds of natures likewise reflects no new divine intervention into the order of things. Rather, God has planted "seeds" (the *rationes seminales*) in nature which, at the appropriate time and through the arrangement of providence, appear: "the world is pregnant with the causes of things yet unknown."[28]

The goal and the primary result of this work of divine providence in the world is the establishment and continuation of its natural order and so harmony. For Augustine things *are* because of order—the order natural to their being; consequently, things are *good* because of their enactment of that order natural to them.[29] God's work inwardly in each creature, giving it the power to be and to be itself in its own way, thus has as its goal the establishment and maintenance of that order creative of good in both nature and in history. This order, of course, is for Augustine, as it was for almost all classical thinkers, largely a static or permanent order. Few new kinds of things (and so new kinds of order) appear in a universe made up of permanent and changeless forms—except where such forms have been planted there in seeds from the beginning. Only free will, in men and in the angels, upsets this order through defection from it in sin. As in most classical thought, therefore, change and novelty (with the exception of the "new thing" referred to earlier) have a predominantly negative, even destructive character. This order is, furthermore, only reestablished in toto eschatologically at the end, and the work of providence in history is devoted largely to preparing in various ways for that final establishment or reestablishment.[30] Thus the work of providence is not understood as creative of *new* forms of order in nature and history leading to the final goal, as in most modern theologies. Consequently, it is a providence that saves fallen souls within history but does not—and does not intend to—redeem the fallen social structures that appear and reappear in history's process. Finally, the goodness of this order of cosmos and of process is not wholly visible to us because, as finite creatures able to view things only from this restricted *place*, we cannot see the wonder of the *whole* within which each nature finds its role.[31] Its hiddenness is thus not there—again as in present theologians—because being in time we cannot, from our own partial *temporal* viewpoint, see yet the final, culminating *end* of the process. As these remarks indicate, some if not all of the largest differences between a modern Christian view of history, secular or Christian, and its classical Christian forebears—evident the moment our discussion of Ernst Bloch or of Whitehead is recalled—concern the very different ways in which each interprets the relations of order to change, of forms to novelty, and so of "meaning" to the ongoing temporal process.

As is already evident, history, where free will is at work, is for Augustine a much more complex arena than is the corporeal creation, and so the work of providence there is less direct, more variegated and much more subtle. Nevertheless, here too God's sovereignty is maintained, but now by different, if analogical modes of activity. The principles of the divine respect for the natures God has created, of the divine inward working effective in all power and ability, and the principle of the divine goal to establish order and harmony reappear in new ways as dominant themes in the historical context.

As before, for Augustine God sustains and empowers natures which he has created good.[32] But now that free will has entered the scene, Augustine is clear that God does not directly ordain, will or cause, i.e., compel, *what* in fact these natures, in this case human nature, do with their freedom. For the essence of this human nature is that it voluntarily wills whatever it wills, and that there "is no efficient or further cause aside from that self-same willing, of what it wills."[33] As Augustine observes about his own behavior, when the will wills, it is done; when the will does not will, it is not done.[34] Thus Augustine is adamant in insisting that God neither wills nor ordains the evil that characterizes human history; the sole cause of this evil is the free will of creatures, i.e., of angels and of men and women.[35] We will our sins; they are voluntary, not necessary, because they spring from our willing and not of necessity from our good nature (which is what God creates and sustains) as the possibilities inherent in that nature as free. There is, then, no cause of evil either in God or in our created structure which is of God; insofar as it has a "cause" it is angelic and human pride, the voluntary deviation from the order established for man as a creature of God, a deviation which results in his evil acts and which maims his history and destroys his destiny.[36]

Although God in this way neither ordains nor causes evil, he does for Augustine *permit* it, and he *foreknows* it.[37] He foreknows *that* and *what* we will will. Since such free willing on our part, argues Augustine, will be one of the "real" causes of the future event, it is an object of the divine foreknowledge of all the various causes to come in time.[38] Thus is our willing, at one and the same time, a real cause and also a real object of the divine foreknowledge. We are free in these foreknown acts because there is, as noted, no other cause of them; and because we really will them. Thus, in doing them we do them truly voluntarily and not as compelled from either the outside or from our own bodily nature inside.[39]

In these arguments it is evident that Augustine reflects a different view of freedom or of autonomy and a different view of time than most of us find in ourselves. For him freedom consists in the lack of *external* compulsion working on the free will, either from our bodies, from ontological forces (a principle of evil in the world outside) or from God; freedom consists in *our* willing it, our wanting to will it and so our "voluntary" willing of it. Thus if we will an action, under no compulsion but voluntarily, it is for Augustine free, even if that willing and its consequences can be foreknown by God and even if in eternity God has willed that event which we also "will" voluntarily. For us, on the other hand, freedom is not so much that we *want* to will an event (i.e., psychologically) as that we are *creative* of the event, namely, that through our willing of it we help to originate an event and so an event unknown and unknowable before it happens—else we have not really participated in its creation. Whereas for us, therefore, God's foreknowledge and a fortiori his "foreor-dination" deny real freedom as creative of the genuinely new; for Augustine neither one poses any such threat to a freedom defined merely as a voluntary willing that is independent of external compulsion. Clearly, the notion that freedom is creative of history, that it remakes and reshapes what has been given to it, is by no means yet an essential ingredient either to the experience or the concept of freedom. With Augustine we are at the beginning of the experience and appreciation of freedom, where it is a voluntary willing and not yet creative of its own future.

Correspondingly, time for Augustine is conceived on the analogy of space, as "there," so to speak, in the future as in the past if we had but a vantage point from which to view it, a vantage point which God in eternity enjoys while we in time do not.[40] For much of modernity, on the contrary, time is unique and qualitatively different from space; consequently, the future is not an actuality hidden from us but visible to God. Rather, the future is at best and of necessity a realm of *possibility*, of what is by its essential nature not yet fully decided, enacted or actual—and thus knowable (if known truly) only as possibility but never as actuality. Time, in other words, as essential to being, when the latter is understood as process, makes in its passage a modal difference, the difference between actuality and possibility, as space does not. Thus, in modern theology the question of God's foreknowledge, as well as of his foreordination, assumes an ambiguity unknown to classical theology.

It is on the basis of this understanding of freedom as a voluntary willing of what God wills that one of the apparent contradictions in Augustine's view of the divine sovereignty may in part be understood, if not reconciled. When he discusses providence, Augustine, as we have noted, confines the divine sovereignty to the categories of foreknowledge, permission and use of what creatures freely will, and he insists that God does not will the evil that men do. However, there is also no doubt that at another level Augustine's doctrine of grace, and so the doctrine of the predestination or election that lies back of the gift of grace, finally seem to undermine this relative independence and so "freedom" of the creature. This subordination of the relative freedom under providence to an ultimate "determinism" by election appears at several points: (1) as we have seen, the work of providence among men and women is determined by God's eternal election, and thus in his electing will, not in human decisions of freedom in history, lies the ultimate determinant of events. (2) The original evil that angels and men and women did at the fall, while initially the result of their freedom, is also and decisively a result of the divine refusal of a plenitude of grace, necessary for their continuing integrity, to those who fell.[41] (3) Finally, as his later works make plain, the doctrine of double predestination implies that not only is the salvation or damnation of men and women determined from eternity by God's election, but also the events of the history in which they live, as an essential part of the story of their coming or not coming to faith, are determined by the eternal divine decree.[42]

As the eternal foreknower and now the eternal "decree-er" of the ultimate salvation of men and women, God is also necessarily the eternal ordainer of the history in which their salvation occurs. To Augustine this prior divine ordination from eternity does not compromise freedom because, as we have seen, freedom is constituted by our voluntary willing of what we will rather than by our origination of the event that our wills bring about.[43] Besides this view of freedom, now insufficient for us, three presuppositions of his theology seem to lead Augustine in the end, despite his efforts to escape it, very near to what was later to be Calvin's position, namely, that the course of history is finally determined by God's electing will: (1) the absolute priority of grace and so for him of the divine decree of election and salvation (in Augustine's own experience, freedom was established by this prior divine decree rather than threatened by such a decree); (2) the eternity and changelessness of the God who in ordaining salvation also ordains the events that contribute to salvation (thus is there "an eternal plan" in God's providence that is "prior" to the events in history that illustrate that plan in time); (3) the interrelations of inward to outward history forcing the eternal decree relevant to the first to be also determinative of the events constitutive of the second. In many respects these elements also created the conditions for the historical consciousness. When, however, they were worked out in orthodox form they ran counter to it. It is, we may say, because of the *absoluteness* of the divine sovereignty over grace and over history that the modern historical consciousness found itself in utter antagonism to this doctrine of providence and the conception of history that it entails.

To return to our discussion of providence, God's providential sovereignty over the world of history's events which he does not directly ordain is achieved through a combination of his foreknowledge on the one hand, and of his inward participation in the power and activity of his creatures, on the other.[44] Because he foreknows what is to be willed—though he does not himself will it—he can adjust the situation and so *use* for his own purposes (i.e., eschatological purposes) what men and women voluntarily will. And because he provides all humans (as he had done corporeal creatures) with the *power* and so the *ability* to do what they will, he has, so to speak, an inward "control" on the effects and the consequences of—the events that result from—their free willing.[45] The divine sovereignty, therefore, can shape and use whatever events and deeds issue from the voluntary and evil willings of men and women. Thus is God's permission of evil in the name of the freedom of the natures he created mitigated by a "secondary" sovereignty over what the creature does and actually effects through its power. This shaping and use of human action takes several forms: it can be directly a healing and saving activity in the life of some person or group; it can bring a good issue relevant to the reestablishment of order or to blessedness out of some historical situation; or it can effect the punishment of some evil intention and so its nemesis in historical time. In every case, in healing or in judgment, God's providential molding of human action is guided by his eschatological goal, and so by the principle of election, to save those whom he has chosen for blessedness. Men and women, therefore, may intend, consciously or unconsciously in their actions, to defy the divine sovereignty, but God's *use* of what they do (either as healing or as punishment) in the end makes them unable to accomplish this defiance which they have intended.[46]

As Augustine sees it, the great and utterly authoritative examples of this dialectic of permission of evil and subsequent use of that same evil for God's own eschatological purposes of salvation are the devil (permitted to sin freely but conquered through the divine reaction in the work of Christ) and Judas' betrayal of Christ (a free act of betrayal through which the work of salvation was accomplished). As we shall see, however, these paradigms of the divine sovereignty over evil are merely supreme illustrations of the way throughout history that God uses men's ordinary ambiguous acts to bring good out of intended evil, to bring salvation out of what by itself would only be self-destructive action. In all of these cases, let us note further, the divine sovereignty is maintained in history—as in the corporeal creation—*through* the action of creatures and *through* their willing, by an inward, hidden and yet purposeful power working within the natural unfolding of events out of their causative factors. It is not maintained by an external force entering the stream of history from the outside as a "cause" and transforming and so manipulating the creature against either its nature or even its voluntary willing. God uses our willing, be it good or bad; destruction and so the divine judgment in events (if God's eschatological purpose so wills it) arise out of the inevitable results of evil, for evil is a vice against natural order and so is inherently self-destructive. And blessedness and salvation for the creature arise also out of a free, voluntary natural willing of the person whom God has, through his providential shaping of that person's freely willed life and the inner persuasion of his grace, prepared for a now freely willed faith and obedience. In this sense, God's providence is not "a cause," one among the natural, external causes of things; he does not act "mythically" as an intervening finite factor in the system of natural and volitional factors causative of events.[47] Let us note that in a theology dominated by the sense of the divine activity within and so the divine sovereignty over temporal events, this is the reason Augustine says that God "does not act *temporally*," i.e., as *a* cause among the temporal sequence of causes.[48]

In order to understand what Augustine considers providence to be doing in history, as opposed to the principles or the "ontology" by which he interprets its actions, which we have just discussed, it is well to turn to the two distinguishable areas in which Augustine describes the work of providence in time: the life of the individual as led by providence to grace, and the course of general history as preparing, fostering, supporting and protecting the temporal manifestation of the kingdom, the growing *civitas dei*, the ecclesia, the body of Christ. Clearly, these two "areas" are interrelated: Augustine as an individual is led to grace within the ecclesia, and the purpose of the ecclesia in history is to be that historical community within which men and women encounter and receive salvation. Nevertheless, the way providence works in each to give the course of temporality its meaning is different, and so I shall discuss each in turn.

The first area, the work of providence in the life of the individual, is the central subject of the *Confessions*. In this work, as has often been noted, Augustine is not confessing his sins; rather is he confessing the awesome and loving work of providence in bringing him through his free willing out of the bondage of that freedom —and so a hopeless and self-destructive situation—into the true freedom of grace. It was obvious to Augustine, as he looked back on this pilgrimage, that his freedom had been so bound that by itself it could not have saved itself whatever it had freely willed. Yet also he realized that at each stage of his past he had freely willed that step and so, in effect, freely willed himself on to the next step of the way. This, he confesses, is the work of God, not just in giving him his saveable nature or even just in granting through grace that grace which he finally accepted. Rather, it was through the work of God's hidden providence that he was led, unbeknownst to himself, *through* his freedom to a growth in his freedom; and through that strengthened freedom to full freedom, i.e., the full freedom of willing at last what he had at the start not even wished to will, much less been able to will.[49]

The hidden work of providence was necessary in his case, and in all of history— and evident in any case of renewed life—because the human soul is so caught in its own sin that it cannot (because it will not) will itself to be free to do the good, and so it cannot save itself. If, therefore, it is to reach its own goal, the eschatological goal—and this *does* happen—it must be that it had been led (hiddenly, slyly, coaxingly, by a long circuitous path) *through* its freedom to a higher level of freedom in which faith and obedience—acts which can be only if they are freely willed— are possible. Providence was necessary because without that long path of hidden "training," the road to grace would either have been externally necessitating (i.e., purely the result of a heteronomous divine fiat) or merited (that he had himself intended and chosen that path). The goal is *eschatological;* the *means* by which it is reached by sinful men is providence working on and through a free will that is progressively led into its own full freedom. The turning point in the path is a union, when Augustine's freedom has been by providence made "ready" to will it, of grace with his free obedience. Thus the *Confessions* is the story of how providence led Augustine's sinful freedom, through its own ambiguous and yet gradually strengthened freedom, to grace, a story which illustrates the way God achieves in a sinful history his eschatological goal.

The account is filled with the sort of strange, wayward, misguided but wholly natural intentions which make up the ambiguity of our freedom, none of them directly intending the ultimate goal, and none of them by themselves, or even the whole sequence by itself, able to accomplish it. For example, after leaving the Manichaeans—not because of piety but because of his secular study of astronomy[50] —Augustine decides to go to Rome to find more orderly and tractable students. Further, in order to accomplish this purely careerist aim, he lies to his mother as he boards the ship because she in turn, longing for his salvation, would keep him in Carthage. Both intentions (his bad, hers good) were counter in one way or another to God's will for him, but God's providence used the acts of both for the accomplishment of that will.[51] After a successful sojourn he goes to Milan purely to foster his career; his sole concern now is fame. He listens to Ambrose merely to study his rhetoric: "to him was I *unknowingly* led to Thee, that by him might I *knowingly* be led to Thee."[52] Slowly, inexorably, through and yet against his freely willed acts directed at anything but his own salvation, Augustine is led stage by stage to the point where first in mind and then at last in will he is able *freely* to accept and live from grace. Providence thus worked "behind his back" and through his ambiguous and yet increasingly coherent and effective willings. God's forknowledge combined with his use of Augustine's actions, whose power and ability are from God, enabled a providence guided by eschatological election to achieve its goal and manifest— to Augustine's impressed and grateful eyes—its sovereignty even over events caused by a wayward and ignorant freedom.

In universal history as in individual existence providence enacts the divine sovereignty in order to achieve God's eschatological goal over an evil that is not divinely willed but is divinely permitted. In this case, what providence does is to foster the appearance, the nurture, the development and the preservation of the *civitas dei*, represented and made visible in the ecclesia. Again, there is no question but that God is sovereign, here as elsewhere: if God creates, orders and rules the least entrails of the humblest creature, does he not also order the empires of history and subject them to his will?[53] Thus history is not under fate: a blind determination from the stars or from other impersonal, purposeless forces antithetical to human freedom and blessedness.[54] And again, sin is not of God but willed by freedom. Its results are at once self-inflicted and disastrous, the natural consequences of the blindness, confusion and ill-directed loves of a creature in contradiction to itself, its natural order and its role, in bondage to self-love and to love of things, and so alienated from true community. These results are also the divine punishment, the reaction of the divine principle of order against that which vitiates that order.[55] Nevertheless, even these destructive and self-destructive actions are used by providence to establish and reestablish social order in God's world and so, despite the tragic effects of sin, to bring history to its eschatological goal.[56] Thus is the world's history on the one hand replete with both the creation and establishment of communities, civilizations and empires, and with their inevitable destruction and decay; and thus, on the other hand, however meaningless such cycles may seem, there runs through the course of history a deeper eschatological meaning under the control of the divine providence.

The warping of man's nature at the fall and the self-incurred bondage which resulted define the city of the world in its opposition to the city of God. The nature of man cannot be lost else he entirely cease to be. That nature is such that its order and so its perfection are determined by the character of man's love, the center of his being; if man loves God, therefore, harmony of life follows—if he does not, and loves self, everything goes awry.[57] In turn, this natural order which is man's good (and every good reflects the natural order) places the soul under God its creator and lord, and the body under the soul as its instrument. Correspondingly, the "natural" communal life of men and women, manifest in the *civitas dei,* is likewise centered on the love of God, and so reflects a creative order parallel to that of the soul and body in the individual: the rulers are responsible, moral and loving to their subjects (not coercive or domineering), caring for and serving their needs; in turn, the subjects are responsible, obedient and creative in their work, treating one another with equal justice and with working cooperation but fundamentally indifferent to their own selfish needs.[58] In the situation of sin, this nature remains, but having lost its center in God (which is the meaning of sin), the order of both individual and communal life is upset. The community is characterized now by a love of itself and through that love a love of the world rather than of God, and it is that shared self-love that binds this community together as the love of God bound the *civitas dei* together.[59] Such self-love creates a city or community, to be sure, but one now intent on domination, on its own well-being and security, on an accumulation of power and so of goods. Thus it establishes an order and a peace that is *its* peace, one favorable to its own interests and not the interests of others. The internal order of such a city is also no true order: the rulers rule in order to increase their power and security—and thus are unjust and domineering, and so coercion has entered to infect and poison the diverse social roles of community life. The citizens are obedient only from fear of punishment or lust for gain and work only for their own goals.[60] Disintegration, therefore, inevitably engulfs even the most creative culture and state: since the internal order established is coercive, domineering and unjust and the external peace achieved is again coercive and unequal, revolution or wars follow necessarily. Thus, the harmony and through it the being of every historical community is fragile, transient and mortal. City and state alike, however legitimate and just their rule from an earthly perspective, are, in effect, from the divine perspective merely large robber bands,[61] using force for their own ends, preying on their neighbors for land, plunder and slaves, and exploiting their own populations: "Then it is necessary that misery follow and ever increase."[62]

Still, nature is not eclipsed: a love binds the community together, it is structured by an order, and so there is peace. Thus God can use these real but warped achievements of the worldly city to foster and aid the development of the true city, the *civitas dei*—as he had used Augustine's own ignorant, misguided and self-centered acts to create the conditions for grace to enter his life. Even in its fallen state, then, the world has a relative order and grace based on love. Since it is, however, an order based on self-love, it is an unjust, coercive and so unstable, representive of a "relative" natural law rather than the absolute natural law of God's ultimate intentions. These remnants of nature—the self-love and the relative order of the community—make possible the institutions of historical life, and make possible *their* relatively creative—as well as destructive—effects. That is to say, each of these institutions is now a remedy and guard against the excesses of sin, and an instrument for the punishment of sin. Government establishes law and order, and thus is it possible for the weak to be protected; property secures the possessions of the weak from the strong, and so on. Each institution, governed by relative natural law and now based on dominence and coercion, is potentially and, in the end, actually capable of becoming a vehicle of sin and thus itself can contribute to destruction. But each, as the wounded vehicle of health, is also capable of making good (relatively) human existence in time and, above all, of fostering the growth of the kingdom.[63]

Thus is the earthly city, and social history with it, essentially ambiguous, partly evil and partly good, representative at once of relative divine law against sin and yet of the destructiveness of sin, at once under judgment by God and yet an instrument of his providence. There is, however, no principle of genuine health or of genuine healing within this earthly city. No salvation of *it* is possible, for, given the conditions of sin, no real peace, order or justice can be achieved, and no permanent transformation of its life is possible. The achievement of salvation is, as we shall see, at best only *indirectly* related to the worldly city, and to God's providential work there. Providence does not lead historical institutions to their culmination in grace and the kingdom, as it had led Augustine's own wayward self to his culmination in grace. The highest possibility for history's communities is a relative order based on self-love, one possibly softened and mitigated by Christian rulers and Christian subjects, [64] the goal of history is not a developing order of communal life that might in its own character approach the eschatological goal of real love and real order. For Augustine no earthly Kingdom stands at the end of history. In the end, Augustine is not even interested in the kind or the level of order and justice among social institutions—provided they establish benevolent modes of peace and justice and so provide the basis for an ecclesia where salvation can be accomplished.[65]

The central role of the worldly city—and so the work of providence within it—vis-à-vis salvation, then, is as the worldly basis for the ecclesia, the body of Christ within which truth and grace dwell. The relative order of the worldly city and the arts characteristic of its life make family and social life possible, and thus produce potential citizens of the heavenly city; its peace provides a social place for the institution of the church and so a historical locus for the grace resident in the body of Christ; its governmental authority and force can protect and foster true religion and encourage conversion and baptism—but that is all. The relation of human life to its own ultimate goal is channeled *through* the ecclesia; and it is a relation into which only individuals directly enter. The relation of human life to that goal is not achieved through the development in history of the worldly city to its own eschatological perfection.

In Augustine history and its institutions are conceived as manifestations of a static and changeless order now fallen permanently and unredeemably from its own perfection. Providence reestablishes and supports that fallen order in its fallenness. God's purpose, therefore, is not to bring the institutions of history through higher levels of order to completion, but only to give social existence sufficient health to point individuals beyond and outside themselves to a realm of grace found in the church. Thus, despite Augustine's tremendous sense of the sovereignty of the divine providence over historical events and institutions; despite the interrelation in his thought between providence and the eschatological goal; and despite the undoubted relation he saw between the this-worldly city and ultimate salvation, nevertheless, clearly the historical working-out of that eschatological goal of ultimate liberation and salvation does not include the transformation of historical institutions. The creative work of providence in leading to ultimate liberation and so to salvation is a work done in and for individuals in relation to the church. Since all else in history is at best instrumental to that work, history's institutions and so the course of history itself are left in the limbo of untransformed and unredeemed ambiguity—until they pass away when the end comes and all is transformed.

When we speak, as we should, of Augustine as the father of the historical consciousness we should speak with care. As we have seen, it is through his interpretation of the biblical vision of time and of history that a sense of time as a linear sequence constituted by unrepeatable and significant moments appears: history is ruled by a divine sovereign power and so has within it a transcendent purpose. Nevertheless, much here is lacking that is characteristic of the modern historical consciousness: the creativity of freedom in time and above all the sense that the course of history itself, the "destiny" of its institutional structures, can constitute an intrinsic part of the unfolding meaning of history. As we shall see, therefore, the consciousness of history, and of the lord whose power gives it meaning, must shift before this initial sense of history's meaning under God becomes the modern consciousness of history. Part of that shifting is expressed clearly in Calvin's interpretation of history and of providence.

JOHN CALVIN

There are for our purposes many significant similarities between Calvin's view of providence and that of Augustine. For both theologians the course of historical passage was under the rule of God and thus possessed an ultimate meaning; and for both that meaning was defined by the electing eschatological purpose of God to bring men and women to ultimate salvation beyond time and space. For Calvin as for Augustine, because of men's sin, the goal of ultimate salvation, of the realization of the fully human in relation to God, could be reached by human beings only because of a divine sovereignty over their lives and over the history in which they lived. Consequently, the work of providence in history is determined finally by God's election of some to salvation and some to damnation. In each case, therefore, providence is understood as an instrument of God's glory and sovereignty through which alone God's eschatological purpose of salvation could be realized in time. The *way* providence guides history, as well as its goal, is controlled by the more ultimate eschatological decree of election; providence works one way for the vessels of mercy and another for the vessels of wrath. Finally, both view the divine activity in time as working *through* creaturely activity; and especially through the free intentionality of human beings. To both the purpose of providence (as of redemption) is the "freeing of freedom" from its own bondage and so the realization of full humanity. Providence, as in Augustine, is here a pedagogy leading humanity to grace, to God, and so to its own fulfillment.

There are, however, a multitude of significant differences between these two theologies of history. Among many sources for these differences, two are worthy of mention. (1) For Calvin the knowledge of God, and so the theology that expresses that knowledge, is to be determined, as much as is possible, solely by the scriptural word.[66] As a consequence of this methodological principle, philosophical categories, and especially those of Greek philosophy, play a minor role in Calvin's theology and exert relatively little influence on the development of his main concepts. Thus, especially the two classical categories of order and of natures, so prominent in Augustine's understanding of the work of providence, had little determinative function; God's rule is neither limited by the parameters and powers of the natures he has created, nor is his purpose in history the establishment and protection of a given, eternal order. Rather, as in biblical thought generally, God is understood in directly personal categories. As a personal agent in history, he is, insofar as he is God, characterized primarily on the one hand by the *power* of his will to ordain and rule events and, on the other, by the *character* of his will as utterly righteous and supremely loving.[67] God is not so much the eternal source of being, of its order and so of the natures that characterize that order, as he is the ordaining sovereign agent whose dynamic will orders events towards his own goal, and through his effective sovereignty impels creatures in the direction of that goal. In Calvin the dynamic, process sense of history under the divine sovereignty begins to replace a formal and structural interpretation of history and of God.

Two results relevant to our theme follow from this first point: (a) in Calvin human freedom appears, and is, less "free" than in Augustine. To Augustine freedom was resident in the human nature God had created and continued to respect; our inner volitions were what we, and not God, did with the nature he had created. Thus, as our voluntary willing, freedom and its decisions somewhat slipped the net of the divine sovereignty, although the latter controlled our exercise of our freedom insofar as those decisions became effective in action. For Calvin, on the contrary, God as omnipotent will ordains and rules events, and therefore ordains and rules those events, inner and outer, which are constituted in part by the intentions and decisions, or free willing, of men and women. (b) The principle of order (as of natures) is here subordinate to the divine purpose for history which works its dynamic will through any given order. Hence, all established orders are relative, capable of transformation under the sovereign purposes of God. Consequently, a more dynamic view of history and of its possibilities makes its appearance—in fact, one of the first of such views to appear in the West.

(2) For Calvin the knowledge of God and so the theology that expresses it are primarily related to piety, not to speculation or to philosophical understanding. The point of knowing God is not so much to understand as to realize in one's self "true religion," and so to be enabled to live a Christian life of trust and obedience.[68] Calvin is, therefore, interested in doctrines solely insofar as they provide the grounds for piety, a symbolic framework for faithful obedience. Thus the theological under-standing of providence is controlled and limited by questions of Christian *praxis*, and speculation about it extends only so far as the needs of praxis require. Hence, the doctrine of providence in itself provides no overview of the structure and direction of the course of history as a whole, no speculative philosophy of history. Its reference is confined to the problems, the obligations and the grounds for hope of individual Christian existence and individual Christian communities in a threat-ening and often calamitous history. The existential and reflective question which faith in providence answers is: How do the things that happen to us in the world relate to our relation to God, to the issue of our destiny with God, and so to our own personal inward and outward response to them? It is through its work on the growth of piety in individuals that God's providence in history relates itself to the issue of ultimate salvation. The relation of providence to history as a whole has, therefore, a different root in Calvin than in Augustine. Calvin does not speculate about what providence is doing in history as a whole, nor does he center its work on the rise and maintenance of the church—though he is concerned in another way with the church. Rather, the relation of providence to secular history and its institutions appears in connection with praxis, i.e., as the result of the divine work of providence and of regeneration through regenerate individuals and their commu-nity, through whose activity God's will is transforming history.

To sum up, for Calvin providence expresses the rule of God over the external life of the Christian, over what happens to him or to her, and election represents the sovereignty of God over their inward life of faith, obedience and regeneration. With, so to speak, this outer and this inner armor, both based on the sovereign will of God as directing us to salvation, human beings so chosen can face anything with serenity, humility, courage and confidence; all that threatens them outside in the form of calamity and inside in the form of weakness is in the powerful and yet loving hands of God. Such a community of men and women, impelled by and obedient to the eternal will of God which rules all of history and intends it to image the divine glory, can transform history creatively into that divine image. The role of providence for social affairs, therefore, has vast, if indirect implications; but they take a very different form from that evident in the Augustinian viewpoint. Our discussion will begin with Calvin's explicit doctrine of providence, proceed to delineate its relation to piety and Christian life, and then view some of its results in practice with regard to community and so to social history as a whole.

Central to Calvin's notion of God is the conception of a sovereign, majestic, holy *will*, the dynamic power through which all events occur and the ruling intention that shapes all events. Calvin appeals to innumerable biblical sources as the basis for this conception; but in reading him one suspects that the final justification for this notion lies in the experience of unmerited grace. The favor which we have received and to which (and because of which) our faith responds is *all* of God, wholly resident in his will toward us and not in our merits. It is, therefore, totally dependent, for both its effect in us and for its initiation in us, on his sovereign will and not at all on our will. This experience of *sola gratia* was the most vivid experience, and the most consistent affirmation, of each of the reformers. It combined with their common, almost ferocious struggle against any form of human merit as the main expression of rebellious sin to center all pious concentration, all trust and all acknowledgement of power and virtue on the sovereign will of God. It is this notion of the prior, overruling and so unquestionably effective will of God in grace for our salvation on which all Reformation theology—and all Reformation religious confidence —was based, and which is expressed in the doctrines peculiar to the Reformation theology of justification, election and of providence.[69] For none of the reformers are the speculative or metaphysical grounds of these fundamental affirmations about the priority and sovereignty of the divine will at all of consequence. These are *religious* affirmations, transferred (perhaps ill advisedly) from the domain of grace as victory over unbelief, sin and a guilty conscience to the wider domain of God's relation to all temporal events. More consistently than any one of the others, Calvin reinterpreted all aspects of the Christian conception of God in the light of this principle.

As is well known, for Calvin God is the absolute creator of all that is, the source of every aspect of every creature. The presence of this absolute divine power, moreover, did not cease with the original creation.[70] Rather, this power continues throughout the course of time in the divine providential power through which creatures, now existent, are sustained in their being and empowered in all their motions.[71] Otherwise, since the motions of the things about us are random at best, our lives would be subject to a meaningless external fate and our salvation left up to the vagaries of our own wills. For Calvin, therefore, the *meaning* of the doctrine of creation lies in its correlate providence, since the work of God's providence in our present is the ground of that confidence in God's rule over our lives and so that hope of salvation which are a large part of a serene and an active piety.[72]

In the area of external events, then—the region controlled by the symbol of providence—Calvin distinguishes sharply between fate and chance on the one hand and divine providence, on the other. In a world governed by the former, all happens blindly, with no meaning at all; here there is promise of neither liberation nor salvation. Since we are in such a world subjected to utterly senseless forces, all the miseries that these forces bestow on us, i.e., of failure, disease, bereavement, death, have no meaning vis-à-vis our own hopes and thus insofar as they are victorious— and they frequently are—they represent an unrelieved despair. Here, therefore, there is the possibility of neither serenity nor consolation and no ground for courage in facing life's inevitable trials. At best, we can depend only on our own transient and fragile powers to elude the forces that menace us—and thus do we face the inner risk, if we succeed, of callous pride, and, if we fail, of utter despair.[73]

Faith in divine providence is thus for Calvin starkly different from the belief that either contingency, chance or necessitating fate rules events. For him all that happens to us and all that occurs in us is under God's control and directed by his purposes. However difficult or even calamitous events may *seem* to us to be, they have for faith an ultimate, if presently hidden meaning.[74] That is to say, despite their apparent chaos they lead in the end to our salvation, for that—if we do have faith and so are certain of our election—is God's will for us.[75]

We should note at this point that while most modern reflection associates together fate and ordaining providence as similar, if not identical concepts, Calvin definitely does not.[76] The reason is that to us the "horror" of fatedness has to do with the qualification it implies to our freedom, and the same qualification is clearly implied by providence. For Calvin the "horror" of being fated concerns our ultimate *destiny,* and here a blindly fated destiny implies no ultimate salvation or renewal of our free will at all, while a providentially determined destiny has that clear promise. To us the question of ultimate destiny is clearly secondary: leave us our freedom, we say, and our promised destiny will be well enough taken care of in history and eternity alike[77]—and anyway, we are not at all sure that God will deal fairly with us or can, even if he wills it, help us with the real issues! Calvin, probably wisely, had no such confidence in either the power or the virtue of our bound freedom, and had much more certainty than do we that God's will was directed primarily at our salvation. Thus he tended to associate together as correlative concepts chance, fate and a total but unredeemed and so self-destructive human freedom on the one hand, and to set them over against a freedom directed and controlled by providence and so a freedom impelled, guided and brought to fulfillment by grace, on the other.[78] If what we long for in being free of fate is to have our destiny placed in our own hands alone, what Calvin wished for on the same score was that his destiny be placed solely in the hands of God, who through grace would recreate his freedom to be able to will his own destiny. As with Augustine, Calvin has a "theonomous" understanding of a realized or authentic freedom that is relatively unintelligible to most modern views of autonomy.

For the same reasons, Calvin distinguishes within Christian theology between general or universal providence and what he calls particular or special providence.[79] General providence is the view that God creates natures and their laws and sustains and upholds both—hence the general order of things in our world. But what creatures do with the powers they possess in accord with these laws is determined by the creatures themselves; only the general laws—e.g., of physiology—are willed by God, not the growth of cancer cells in a particular body. Against this view Calvin argues that not only do the scriptures clearly teach the ordination and so control of God over each particular event; even more, it is particular events, not general laws, that harass us and subject us to fate: a particular drought, a plane crash, a virus, a weak tire or a slippery road. If such menacing events are truly contingent, even though they may obey divinely upheld laws, then our lives, determined as they are by such events, are still subjected to a blind fate. Such a doctrine obviously robs God of his sovereignty over the concrete occurrences that make up our history. As an inevitable correlate, it declares that since a meaningless contingency rules our lives, events in no way conspire to the realization of our freedom but to its destruction. Such a view, therefore, forfeits the serenity, confidence and sense of a meaningful existence headed toward the fulfillment of our hopes that is promised to and available for the Christian. For Calvin, on the contrary, God rules through a *particular* providence, i.e., by a special ordination, "a power constantly exerted on every distinct and particular movement."[80] It covers, therefore, everything from "each drop of rain" and "each wind that blows" to all the deliberations and volitions —and so actions—of men.[81] This particular ordination includes the inclinations, thoughts and plans even of the wicked. Did not God ordain the intentions and actions of Judas if he was through the crucifixion to accomplish our redemption; was the role of Judas in that crucial drama just "God's good luck"?[82]

As a consequence, Calvin dismissed the Augustinian doctrine of permission as an unscriptural and disastrous limitation on the divine sovereignty—although he constantly appeals to Augustine on other matters in connection with that sovereignty.[83] The freedom of mankind for Calvin is not that men and women will what they will as the *sole* cause of that willing—God "permitting" that intention—as Augustine had said, although the enactment of that willing in action is for Augustine under the divine sovereignty. Rather, the freedom of mankind lies in our really willing what we do; it is in that, so to speak, *willing* willing that the "voluntary" character of what we do resides, rather than in the sole causality of our wills—since for Calvin God has already ordained all that men and women will and do.[84] In Calvin, therefore, there are, so to speak, two levels of causation: God's prior ordination from eternity, and man's "voluntary" (not compelled but willed) willing of the deed.[85] Freedom lies in the fact that man voluntarily wills, willingly, happily wills, what has been ordained; he is not compelled to sin by God's decree, he *wills* to sin, though it is decreed that he do so. It is evident, moreover, that God's providential work is therefore hidden, hidden within the ambiguity of the evil intentions, the selfish and brutal actions that make up the course of events, none of which on the surface at least reveals the love and righteousness, the mercy and the justice which are the real character of the divine will. Only in Christ, and the promise of election and reprobation known through him, is this tangled and obscure mystery clarified: that for the elect God's providential sovereignty is a means for developing, testing and refining their faith and obedience; for the reprobate, a means of manifesting the divine justice in relation to their undoubted sin.[86] Any understanding of the work of providence in history—*what* it is doing, and *why*—is, therefore, only to be gained christologically and interpreted eschatologically, in the light of election and the eschatological goal. The hidden work has as its major purpose the realization of the eschatological purpose of God lovingly to redeem his chosen for eternity and justly to punish those who are not chosen.

But, Calvin's reader and so Calvin himself immediately ask, is not God then responsible for evil and so himself evil; is he thus just if he punishes men for what he himself has willed?[87] Calvin gives many arguments in defense, in relation both to God's providence and his predestinating activity, none of which carry much weight to modern minds: (1) we really love, will and enjoy the sins we do; thus we are responsible for them as an issue of our own freedom.[88] (2) While God wills the wicked deed out of goodness (i.e., righteousness or mercy) and so is innocent of evil, we will it out of selfishness and in conscious defiance of God's revealed will in the Word.[89] Thus our freedom, although conformed to God's hidden will, is for us opposed to God's revealed will; and so, consciously doing what we know to be wrong, we are again responsible and guilty of sin. (3) There are in both sin and grace two levels of causation: the divine decree and the human willing and acting. In each case, *which* level is religiously and theologically relevant to us is dictated by the needs of true piety: vis-à-vis sin, therefore, it is well to be conscious of *our* causation of sin so that we will repent (and anyway we don't know the divine reason for willing this); in the case of grace, it is well to emphasize the divine causality, and not our cooperation, lest we be proud and give ourselves rather than God the glory for our salvation.[90]

(4) Above all, Calvin regarded this doctrine of utter divine sovereignty as revealed and thus beyond question; it was "God's doctrine," so to speak, not man's, and thus beyond serious dispute.[91] It is not an idea originated by Calvin, an idea therefore to be affirmed or rejected as wise, rational, consistent, moral, helpful, etc. It is in itself true as God's Word about himself, and thus given to us authoritatively and to be respected whether it seems to us to be wise, rational, etc. Our task, then, is not to judge the idea by our criteria as if *our* judgment made it true; our task is to try as best we can to understand it—the job of theology—and where we cannot, to accept it as reflecting the self-revealed mystery of a will that far transcends ours. But since it is also intrinsic to faith that we *know* that will to be just and good, by the same token we *know* that what that will wills, even if it might *seem* unjust to us, is in essence just—else we, in trusting our own judgments of right and wrong, doubt either the goodness of God (and so Christ himself) or the truth of scripture.[92] Thus, the only appropriate response is to recognize the finitude and partiality of our judgments in these matters—as in faith we have already recognized our ignorance and sin in all matters vis-à-vis God and our salvation—and to trust that the hidden will of God with regard to evil is just even though we don't understand quite how it is just. Both Luther and Calvin question in other places whether it is prudent for us to demand that God be "moral" according to our own human law of just deserts, if according to *that* law we ourselves would long since have been hopelessly condemned. The transcendence of God's mercy over his law in undeserved justifying grace is not at all unrelated to the apparent transcendence of God's hidden will over the visible "human" law of justice.

The above are theological "doctrines," based on scripture, elaborated into concepts, interrelated with one another and defended against counter-arguments by
theological labors. However, for Calvin both election and providence receive their
real *meaning*, what they are "about," in relation to piety, the experiences and so
the needs of Christian existence in the world. Theology is a correlation of an
abstract, ideational (eidetic) conceptuality based on scripture with concrete Christian experience and existence, the former, the "belief" in question, providing the
symbolic framework for the latter, a Christianized horizon within which a coura-
geous, confident, serene, active and loving existence, i.e., true religion or obedience,
is possible.[93] Our question now concerns the "religious" meaning, the meaning for
Christian existence in the world, of the symbol of providence as it has been delineated by exegesis of scripture and by argument.

Calvin's view of Christian existence in the world is best summarized in the ringing
declaration of Book III, Chapter 7: "We are not our own, but the Lord's."[94] From
this, of course, derives the sense of utter self-surrender to a transcendent will, the
obligation to obedience and self-control and the drive to active service for the lord's
glory so characteristic of the Calvinistic ideal. It is, however, from the same root—
"We are not our own, but the Lord's"—that the *other* aspect of this ideal arises:
namely, its deep serenity, its courage in the face of calamity and its sense of selfless
service for God's glory, and thus its astounding sense of transcendent meaning in
life, whatever good or evil may befall us. It is in this connection that the concept
of providence for Calvin plays a central role in Christian existence. If in truth we
are *God's*, and if we belong to a God who orders and controls each event for his
glory and so for our salvation, *nothing* that happens to us can detain, divert or cancel
that destiny and so the meaning promised to us in Christ and ratified for us by our
own faith. Rather, it is precisely through whatever befalls us that God is preparing,
testing and strengthening our faith and obedience, and so knowledge of this is the
source of the greatest inward joy. Thus Calvin regards the doctrine of providence
as the ground—with election—of "the inestimable felicity of the pious mind,"[95] as
the source of true religion's serenity and courage, of Christian "victory over the
world."[96]

Human life, Calvin reminds us, is beset by calamities, some expected, some utterly
unexpected, and many of these are overwhelming in their effect on both the continuity and the meaning of our life. This is both the lesson of experience and the clear
promise of revelation where the cross with its suffering is given to us as the paradigm
of the life the Christian is to expect in the world.[97] How, Calvin asks frequently,
is man to exist in such a precarious world, facing such a potentially menacing future,
without fear, anxiety and despair, or without trusting entirely and selfishly in his own
powers to cope with all that threatens him? The only way to face such a precarious
existence is to understand "that his affairs are ordered by the Lord in such a manner
as is conducive to his salvation,"[98] i.e., in the light of particular providence. Then,
what *seems* to be adverse, debilitating, threatening and destructive can be understood to be the way God is dealing with us to test and increase our faith; providence

uses our adversity (as it used Christ's suffering) to bring us closer inwardly to God, to trust, obedience, humility and surrender. Perhaps we have trusted too much in worldly success and so in our own wit and capacities—then failure can bring us to a deeper sense of the relative meaninglessness of success and the fragmentariness of our own powers.[99] Or, adversity can become a challenge and a trial for us and so a means, a pedagogy, of strengthening our renunciation of self, our obedience and so our dependence on God.[100] Again, persecution provides us with opportunities for sacrifice of self not only for the gospel but for "any just cause"; adversity, sent us by providence, can draw us out of ourselves to the service of others.[101] Finally, but by no means unimportant, adversity can awaken in us the consciousness of our own past sins, since it may be that through adversity providence is chastizing us.[102] In all of this, what is on one level "misery," is for faith, because of its trust in providence, on a deeper level conducive to serenity, since faith sees that through adversity God is bringing us in a variety of appropriate ways closer to him and so to our salvation. Correspondingly, if through the mysterious beneficence of God our life is *not* one of adversity—though such is rare for the Christian—consciousness of the providential source of our blessings keeps us humble and is the basis of any creative use we may make of our powers and our goods. What we have is not primarily for *our* enjoyment but for the benefit of our neighbors; it is only by recalling in faith that these gifts are the work of providence and not our work, that we are made aware that as stewards we "possess them only for our brethren."[103] Thus, whether our life is set within adversity or comfort, a centering of our existence on the divine providence as the ground of the character of that life is the sole basis of that life's inner health: of humility, of appropriate repentance, of serenity, confidence, joy and outgoing, creative service. When viewed under the perspective of providence, instead of threatening, tempting and so ultimately damning the inner life of man, events lead men to deeper faith and obedience. As in Augustine, God's providence uses the events of history to bring his elect inwardly and so freely to their promised eschatological destiny.

Also as in Augustine, the eschatological telos of the divine providence, that through it we are led to a relation to a transcendent goal, is essential to the work of providence and so to our understanding of it. These calamities of life are, Calvin reminds us, *real* miseries; truly we suffer under them, and appropriately we are sorrowful, upset and distraught. It is no solution to "harden ourselves" in the face of them in a sort of superhuman indifference; such an answer only dehumanizes us into unfeeling monsters.[104] Humanism, Calvin argues, deals with its correlate fate and the tragedy that fate brings only by becoming inwardly inhuman. Rather, an eschatological solution alone is possible: calamity to ourselves and others can be creatively surmounted only if it is seen as within God's ordaining providence and thus as a means for bringing us—and others—to a more permanent, transcendent salvation.[105] It is the eschatological goal as our *true* aim in life that gives to life's fortunes and misfortunes alike their only possible creative meaning; providence makes a difficult life meaningful to us because, as we have seen, it directs that life, outwardly and inwardly as well, toward its own transcendent goal. For Calvin, therefore, providence is not to be understood—as in much later Calvinism—as the activity of God in the world benefiting his elect in *this* life and according to the values of *this* life: wealth, success, power, prestige.[106] So to understand providence is to subvert human goodness on the one hand—to create nothing but pride and self-concern; on the other hand, in the light of the universality of the experience of calamity, it is to make the concept of providence a monstrous blasphemy on God's goodness. Rather, to appreciate providence, as for Calvin to appreciate all Christian symbols, requires an eschatological transvaluation of our values: that earthly evils are really *not* ultimately evil, and earthly benefits are *not* for our final enjoyment. On the contrary, both are for us as for God providential *instruments* for the attainment of a transcendent goal.[107] In this sense, as Calvin reiterates, resurrection to eternal life is the principle according to which the bitterness of the cross must be understood and so the sole basis according to which that bitterness, while really felt, may nevertheless be borne with serenity, joy and love.[108]

Despite the transcendent, suprahistorical, eschatological goal that dominates all of Calvin's reflection—and separates him from most of modern theology—the work of providence is also concerned with the regeneration of history and even of the character of its social existence. God's will is both active and sovereign, a creative sovereignty that has the regeneration of life as its preliminary if not its ultimate purpose. As Calvin makes clear, election and justifying grace have as their purpose more than the reconciliation of men and women to God. On the contrary, election and justification are *teleological*, directed at the sanctification, the transformation, of human life. As with all the reformers, justification, reconciliation with God, is not for Calvin based on sanctification, on the achievement (through merit or through grace) of a transformed life; justification is based on Christ's work, on election, and sanctification flows from the acknowledgment of this in faith.[109] Thus the aim to achieve sanctification does not draw men from their activity in the ambiguous world; rather, secure in their justification through election, believers can remain in the world without qualifying their own ultimate status before God. The process of their sanctification, therefore, represents the transformation of their life *in* the world and through them of the character of the world. Moreover, since the divine will that establishes their reconciliation with God and empowers their new life is essentially active sovereignty, creative of events in history, correspondingly, the justified are *active* in the world, seeking in their life not only to reach higher levels of perfection —to reflect God's glory in their own life[110]—but also to bring the world itself into a new relation to God, so that it too may reflect God's glory. Thus Calvin creates a quite new understanding of the relation to the world of Christian faith and obedience, and, as a consequence, shapes a lifestyle in which under God's electing and providential will the Christian is sent into the world both to become personally holy and also to shape the world itself in the direction of holiness.[111] God's activity in history, redemptive and providential, is not therefore designed, as in Augustine, to renew, support and so to perpetuate a timeless order in human social relations.

On the contrary, it is an impelling, dynamic, transformative force in social history, recreating social roles, institutional forms and common customs toward holiness, to God's glory in the world.

The unique power of Calvinism as a religious force transformative of Western society lay in its dual emphasis on the individual and on the community, and on the dynamic possibility of creative change implicit—under the divine sovereignty —in each one. As has been widely noted, the individual in Calvinism is given an unprecedented strength, autonomy and creative role within the structures of the world; there are multiple roots in Calvinistic theology for this new emphasis. First, there is the Calvinist view of conscience as a relation directly to God, a relation that is clarified and made ultimately binding by God's Word.[112] Human laws, representing the legitimate power of social institutions over individuals, are thus here radically relativized; even if they "are good or just, though they are necessary to be observed, [they] are not on this account binding on the conscience." "For our consciences have to do not with men, but with God alone." Thus does the individual in relation to the divine Word tower above his social context and its obligations and through his conscience experience the obligation to judge that social matrix by a higher norm.

Secondly, the concept of individual election toward active service in the world transformed the relation of each individual to his vocation in the world. Because of his knowledge of his own election, each individual knew that the roots, so to speak, of his own individuality and its unique powers were grounded in God's eternal will, an astonishing base for particular individuality with its unique and idiosyncratic characteristics and powers. Moreover, because the meaning of historical life is thus channelled *through* his individual activity, so related to God's will, his vocation is a creative role given to *him*, subject to *his* creative interpretation, and so "open" for the determination by his own creative will. It is not a preordained social niche into which in obedience he fits, as in Catholic thought and in Luther, but a task, a "post" given to him for his own future determination. And what the task is is defined by his responsibility to the community and its holiness. Thus is the individual strengthened inwardly, given immense creative authority and sent into an "open" world to remold it to God's glory.[113] Finally, the sense of ultimate invulnerability and so serenity under providence, already referred to, again seemed to strengthen the individual and to imbue him with confidence in his "victory over the world." Whatever may befall him at his post, it posed no ultimate threat to the meaning of his life or the ultimate fruitfulness of his vocational task. Grounded in the eternal divine will, critical of the given forces of the world, empowered to transformative activity in that world and invulnerable to its hazards, these were individuals with immense inner authority, power and energy, subordinate to nothing on earth and threatened by no possible earthly calamity.

As is clear, however, they were not in Calvin—as later became the case in the bourgeois version of his vision—individuals isolated from or unconcerned with community, either secular or religious. Their own faith had come to them from the church community, "the mother of us all";[114] and it is in that community and through it, not alone, that God wills Christians to sustain their faith, to be directed in their life and so to transform their own wider community.[115] As the purpose of redemption in the individual is that he or she become holier—though in time never fully holy—so the point of the grace given to the church in Word and sacrament is that the Christian community also become holier.[116] Thus, among the tasks and "powers" of the church, resident in the consistory, is the "discipline of manners," the control over the moral and social behavior of its members so that the community which they together form may become more and more an image of the divine glory.[117]

Finally, this active effort to transform community was not confined merely to the structures of the church's life, or even to the habits of its covenanted members. It extended out into the entire secular community in which the church found itself: to its economic practices, its political injustices and its social mores.[118] In no early Calvinist community was it ever conceived that economic or political institutions were independent from the moral supervision of the church, governed by their own laws, e.g., the "laws of the free market"; rather were they continually and in the most minute details scrutinized, judged and corrected in the light of what was regarded as the requirements of a Christian moral community. Thus, as Troeltsch and Tawney rightly argue, it is true that Calvinism provided a spiritual ground for the individualism of capitalism, which in the decay of the Calvinist spirit used the strong affirmation of autonomy and its obligations to activity in the world to create an energetic, individualistic, materialistic, successful and success-oriented bourgeoisie who were supported externally no longer by a moral *providence* but by the soulless, amoral *preestablished harmony* of the free market. Still, it is also true that Calvinism was equally formative of a Christian socialism in which the rights of individual gain were rigidly subordinated to the requirements of justice, and to the needs of the community as a whole.[119]

In any case it is clear that in Calvin the given, traditional order of roles and institutions in society was radically relativized. A new task for the regenerate Christian community was proposed, namely, that of transforming the world's institutions and communities to God's glory. Thus Calvinism, paradoxically because of the deep determinist and eschatological roots of its strength, succeeded remarkably in "opening up" history's institutions to creative transformation. In Calvin's sense of the active sovereignty of God over individual and community alike, the dynamic, transformative sense of history, characteristic of later modernity, is deeply felt, expressed and clearly implemented. One may suggest that here for really the first time—the apocalyptic political movements were in another way also representative of this theme[120]—the biblical sense of a purposive transformable history is first articulated. In Calvinism the biblical sense of a *history* that is moving toward its completion is realized long prior to the Enlightenment concentration on the progressive possibilities of history. As Augustine established the basis for the modern sense of the creativity and meaning of the moments of history, Calvinism is the link between the long implicit biblical confidence in history as moving toward completion and the final appearance of that confidence in secular modernity. Ironically, both "founders" of the contemporary historical consciousness had to be almost forcibly removed by modern experience and thought in order for some of the implications of their theologies to bear their full fruit.

8

MODERN HISTORICAL CONSCIOUSNESS

Our age, it has frequently been said, is one dominated by a historical consciousness. Clearly, by this is not meant that other ages and peoples were unaware either
of history or of their immersion in history, for surely they were. What is meant,
therefore, by "historical consciousness" is a particular kind of awareness of history
and a particular sense of how we are immersed in it, an awareness and a sense that
are in important contrast to that of other times and other places. If this be so, if
we feel and conceive of history and our roles within it differently than have other
ages, then obviously—if what we have said about theology and its essential relatedness to its cultural context also be valid—such a fundamental change in sensibility
will, and should, affect the ways in which theologically we comprehend history, social
change and the future, i.e., the ways we conceive of providence, of eschatology and
even of the nature of God. The task of this chapter will, therefore, be to outline
the changes in the modern consciousness of history that bear on our theme. In this
way, the ground can be laid for our own interpretation of these symbols in the light
of the historical world that *we* inhabit.

The Relativity of the Forms of Historical Life

1. Perhaps the most important change characteristic of the modern consciousness
of history concerns the relation of the forms of life to the process of time and of
change. One of the major inheritances that Western culture received from the
Greeks was the concept of process as the coming to be and then the dissolution,
the growth and the decay, of a definite limited number of changeless forms. Change
was certainly seen to be pervasive in the natural, the human and the social worlds.
It was, however, a change only in the relation of individual entities: particular
animals, particular people and particular communities, to changeless forms. It was
the entities that changed (as *a* man changes), not the forms of the entities (as the
species man changes). It was, therefore, not a change *in* the forms or *of* the forms
of either organic, individual or social life. Thus, for the biological sciences the
number of species was limited and permanently fixed; for philosophers and ethicists

188

the forms of human creativity and excellence static; for students of history the variety of types of communal organization restricted to a few.[1] "Natural law" represented the normative requirements of these changeless forms, the requirements for becoming a fully human being and a fully human society; such "laws" were universal and changeless because the forms they represented were universal and changeless. This understanding of natural and social change as taking place within a static order of changeless form was subsequently incorporated into Christian understanding by means of the concepts of creation and of providence (not, unfortunately, of redemption and of eschatology). God has created these species and ordained these social forms, and thus the natural law implied by these permanent orders is the eternal and universal law of God for his creation. This understanding of creation and providence in terms of a set "order" for history was illustrated graphically in our discussion of Augustine.

The view of nature and of history as illustrating a limited number of permanent orders, made legitimate by divine ordination, dominated—with some notable exceptions[2]—the consciousness of process in the West until the modern period. Nature manifested regular changes in the cycle of the seasons and in the cycles of birth, youth, maturity and decay—but no changes of species; and apocalyptic aside, changes in the forms of the earth's surface were inconceivable. Likewise, history was filled with changing events, but the forms of its life were unalterably given. And, as any thirteenth-century mural or Renaissance painting of the biblical past in terms of contemporary dress and architecture shows clearly, the forms of life in ancient times were assumed to illustrate few fundamental changes from our own. Meaning in history qua history, as Augustine illustrated, thus was achieved by the preservation of those forms that structured change, and meaning in ordinary life was gained by creative work within that given structure—as even the Lutheran view of vocation shows.[3] As ordained by divine providence and as embodying that order which resisted chaos amidst change, the permanent forms of life were, therefore, in their own way sacred. Each social form was "legitimate" because it was divinely ordained, and thus revolution against them was blasphemy and intentional change of them infinitely risky.[4] Above all, they were "given" as the unalterable and divinely ordained structure of history, not created within history; and thus were the structures of history almost as absolute, eternal and changeless as their divine creator. To be in history is to live peaceably within these sacral forms, not to criticize and to remake them, for neither can contingency shake them nor freedom transform them.

We cannot trace in any detail the dissolution of this understanding of the relation of forms to change and to historical process. This dissolution surely had its initial rise in the unorthodox forces of medieval apocalyptic thought that regarded every form as relative and changeable by divine fiat, in Renaissance humanism with its criticism of inherited medieval structures, and in the Reformation challenge to the "ageless" forms of the medieval ecclesia—though the latter two epochs looked *back* to older classical or biblical forms.[5] It received a stronger impetus from Calvinism with its sense of the creative work of providence in history. It is evident in the new understanding of history by Giambattista Vico and of politics in Machiavelli, Hobbes and Locke, for each of whom human decision and action help shape political structures, motivate political action and thus in part create history.

As all historical commentators agree, however, the criticism of the inherited Greek view of change amid changeless forms finds its most important root in the development of the new science in the sixteenth and seventeenth centuries. With that development the consciousness of new knowledge, and so the possibility of new forms in society—even ones superior to the old—appear. Perhaps its first literary and philosophical appearance is with Francis Bacon, whose challenge of antique learning broke in principle from past ways of life, and whose call to *useful* knowledge, knowledge that would effect changes in man's life for his own welfare, first implied the new possibility, the possibility of new forms, latent in the new knowledge.[6] Certainly, however, it was with Descartes that the sense of the new as an outgrowth of knowledge takes definitive form: here authentic reason arises only when traditional authorities are deeply challenged, and here genuine knowledge according to the immutable laws of nature is possible through a *new* method.[7]

With this strong, even rebellious, challenge of ancient authority and of the forms of life it represented, a sense of new possibilities in every field of thought and life swept Europe: through new knowledge a new order in life as a whole is a possibility. Initially, with regard to the view of history, the most important result of this sense of new possibilities in scientific knowledge and through it of useful changes in the structures of life, which surfaced in the late seventeenth century,[8] was that history could now be seen as meaningful *because* it manifests a succession of relative and transient forms, rather than because it was the reiteration of permanent, changeless and so absolute forms, for the older forms had to be challenged if the new possibilities were to appear. The forms of individual and social life—its economic practices, its political structures, its social hierarchies—are now seen to be themselves part of the dynamic, transitory and changing aspect of history, rather than elements of its changeless structure. Whatever else in history is essential, universal and absolute, it is no longer the forms of life we see around us in our social world. With this new understanding of history, what has been is no longer representative of the ultimate structure of process, and thus is the future open for change and for novelty through intelligence and its careful application.

Three corollaries of this new relation of form to process became plain as its implications were gradually drawn; each is important for the developing "historical consciousness" whose anatomy we are seeking to describe. (a) As the first result of this new understanding, the forms of life—in this case, historical and social forms of life (the biological equivalents have not yet appeared)—are seen to be relative to their place and time and thus contingent and transitory. Cultures and epochs have their own character, relative to their spatial and temporal situation; nothing within them, therefore, is absolute or universally normative, for all forms arise in their time, are relative to that cultural whole out of which they arise and pass when that time is over. What is good for one time and place is not necessarily good for another;

what is true in one cultural world may not seem true in another. At this point, there appears in Western life, as an issue never again to disappear, the relativity of all aspects of a cultural whole: its political and economic forms, its truth, its morals, its art, its social customs and its religion. History is thus not an embodiment and then dissolution of changeless and so absolute and normative forms which are the locus of truth and goodness. Rather, history manifests continually changing, contingent, particular and evanescent forms. If, therefore, it has any meaning at all, any mode of transcendence of a patternless relativity, that meaning must lie in the *pattern* of the *sequence* of these contingent, evanescent, relative forms. This principle of the relativity of all cultural forms to historical process was first and most clearly expressed by Vico and Montaigne, and perhaps most vividly by Herder.[9] The attempt to reinterpret the rationality or the meaning of history despite this relativity, i.e., in terms of the *sequence* within the changing forms of history, was initiated by the progressivist thinkers of the eighteenth century, culminating in Condorcet and Kant,[10] and given definite form subsequent to them by Hegel, by Marx, by Comte and by Spencer. It is worthy of note that precisely this same fundamental shift in perspective from understanding in terms of permanent and so absolute forms of life to an understanding in terms of a sequence of relative and so contingent forms took place in biology a century later, with the work of Darwin. At that point, the seventeenth and eighteenth-century biology of Ray and Linnaeus, which held that there were a limited number of permanent species[11]—from which all others are deviations—shifted to the "evolutionary" view that the forms of natural life are relative and continually shifting, developing out of one another because of random mutations and the pressures of their particular environment.

(b) If the forms of individual and social existence are relative to their time and place, then humans are immersed in history in a quite new and radical way. For clearly, in that case, the modes of their creative thinking and acting, the perspectives from which they view the truth, the norms of their life, and the symbols with which they understand themselves and their world are no longer identical with the fundamental forms of thought, of action and of self-understanding of other cultural epochs but are likewise relative, characteristic of their own life and not necessarily applicable to other modes of life. Thus cultures, embodying relative and so different forms from one another, are in this way estranged from one another. Each must be understood in its own terms if it is to be understood at all, and how is such understanding possible? Part of the meaning of "historical consciousness," implicit in this new understanding of the relativity of cultural forms and their transformation over time, has been this sense of the embeddedness, even imprisonment, of the mind and spirit of men and women in their own cultural whole. And a good part of the efforts of philosophy of history and of social science since the Enlightenment have been devoted to the problem of finding a standpoint beyond cultural relativity by which other cultures may be understood and assessed and the whole of historical process made intelligible. As is evident and yet ironical, just as it was the sense of the relativity of cultural forms that called forth the great philosophies of history of the eighteenth and early nineteenth centuries, so it has been the sense of the embedded-ness of the mind in a particular historical epoch that has dealt an almost mortal blow to the same speculative philosophy of history at a later period.[12] It is also this problem that has now raised the "hermeneutical question," how someone in the present, bound as he or she is to the world-view and the self-understanding of the present, can understand what is said to us in the texts that come to us from the past. Not only has any understanding of the meaning of history as a total course of events been challenged by relativism, but also the possibility of history as objective inquiry has been put in question.

(c) The third corollary to this new view of the relativity of forms of life to historical change concerns the question of the *meaning* for human existence in time involved in these changing and so relative forms of life. If forms are the permanent, inaltera-ble and sacred structures of change, and as changeless are embodiments of what is good and true, then clearly to help to bring them again into more complete being and to sustain them against dissolution provides ample meaning or vocation to life —at least this life. But if these forms come and go in ceaseless change, if *nothing* permanent remains, of what use is our toil?[13] What is the meaning of the endless parade of relative forms that now seems to constitute history? As we have already indicated, the answer of most of the enlightened in the eighteenth and nineteenth centuries to this new problem was the theory of progress: the sequence of relative forms in historical life is not a random or meaningless sequence, but a teleological development, i.e., a development leading toward a goal, the goal of the fulfillment of the potentialities of humanity. The many "speculative philosophies of history" which appeared in this period, philosophies associated with the names of Leibniz, Condorcet, Kant, Herder, Hegel, Marx, Comte, Mill and Spencer, addressed them-selves to this problem and expressed this conviction that history manifests a series of forms leading to perfection.[14]

Clearly, with this shift in the relation of forms to meaning, a totally different social and political praxis in history is implied. If permanent forms are the basis of value and of truth, then change is on the whole negative and praxis is devoted to the perpetuation and re-enaction, possibly to the reformation or restoration of forms— but not to fundamental reform and certainly not to revolution. However, if it is in the developing sequence of forms that meaning resides, if truth and value are advanced rather than threatened by change, then the encouragement of fundamen-tal change through reform or through revolution clearly follows. It is no accident that the intellectual world which represented these new ideas of history (with the possible and ambiguous exception of Hegel[15]) also represents radical reformist and revolutionary views of social praxis; and correspondingly, that those who are conserv-ative with regard to social forces represent entirely different assessments of history. Again, biology took its cue from this prior understanding of history when half a century later Darwin, and especially the Darwinists, pictured the development of the changing forms of organic and animal life in a progressive series, culminating first in *Homo sapiens* and then among all the races of man in European men.[16]

Clearly, with regard to the view of the divine activity implied by these changes in historical consciousness, Providence will no longer be understood as ordaining and maintaining a limited set of unalterable forms or orders of creation, nor will the intention of the divine will be the perpetuation structurally of what has always been. The changeless structures of life are no longer a sign of divine ordination, nor symbols of the presence of God. On the contrary, what is changeless and static has now precisely the reverse connotation, namely, as a sign of irrelevant archaism unrelated to the needs of a changing world.[17] Thus most modern views of providence have seen the divine activity as the initiating force for changes in natural, social and historical forms, and the divine will as an intentionality leading the whole sequence to higher and higher forms, each relative to its place in time, but all together moving to the divinely ordained end. Implicit in these shifts in theology, as we shall see, was an entirely different view of the relation of the divine sovereignty to inherited forms and structures of life, and a quite new understanding of the relation of the present processes of social and historical change to eschatology.

New Views of Human Creativity and Freedom in History

2. The second major element in the new understanding of history concerns the role of men and women in history. Although the "historical consciousness" has, as we have seen, greatly increased the human sense of immersion in history, it has also engendered, paradoxically but understandably, the sense of the transcendence of human freedom and creative praxis over the forms of history. If, as was previously believed, history is structured by permanent forms given to it unalterably at creation or by divine ordination, then the role of men and women, and especially of human freedom, will be at best that of fostering, restoring, replenishing and sustaining already given forms of life. Humans may do this in many ways, in new ways and with new zeal, but their freedom can only re-create what has already been given in time, and their will can only confirm through their own volition what the divine will has willed. Again, such a view of freedom as in effect willing what God wills was evident in both Augustine and Calvin.

When, however, the absoluteness of these structures of life dissolved, and history is understood as a sequence of relative and shifting forms in which new possibilities unknown before appear, then the role of human autonomy enlarges, or may enlarge. As relative and transitory, social forms do not imply a direct divine foundation; rather, they now appear as themselves creaturely or "historical," formed by time, by natural forces and also—and this is our point here—by human intention and achievement. Man now has the possibility of seeing himself as a creator, not merely as a re-creator, of himself and of his world. He can himself help to determine the forms that will shape his own life and his society; he is enabled to initiate the new. As the "maker of history" he is the maker of these forms of life in which he himself arises; and so in a strange way, the maker of himself. Man is at once the creator and the creature of history.[18]

The modern paradox of the embeddedness of the human in history and yet the self-creativity of freedom, of its ability to bring to actuality what was never actual before, appeared only when history was seen as a sequence of relative and contingent rather than of absolute forms. In understanding the precise character of this new emphasis on freedom, moreover, we should recall that this insight into the relativity and successiveness of the forms characteristic of historical development—and so in the freedom latent in that relativity—arose because of the awareness of the new methods of scientific inquiry and so of the growth of knowledge in post-Renaissance Europe. It was the seventeenth and eighteenth-century consciousness of the new and fruitful role of an autonomous reason in history that brought to their awareness their difference from the ancient world, of useful changes in the forms of life that intelligence now could accomplish, and so the open possibilities of history as a whole. Because of their new inquiries, men had dared to challenge older dogmatisms and had insisted on freedom of opinion; hence had arisen with scientific inquiry freedom from past and present authorities, freedom of the mind to reach and adhere to its own autonomous conclusions and, as a result, freedom for the new. And finally, because of his new method of understanding his world, man was now for the first time capable autonomously of transforming it.[19] Through the disciplined use of his reason, therefore, as evidenced in the new science and its twin offspring, technology and industrialism, man saw himself in a new way as free in history: free to reject past authority and tradition; free to accumulate new knowledge of the laws of nature; free to control nature around him through that knowledge; free to transform social structures into new forms if he understood their laws; above all, free to think what his own mind determines as the truth and his own will affirms to be right.[20] At the initial stages of modernity, it was the sense of the power of autonomous reason that both stripped history of its absolutes and gave to man a new sense of his own role as a creator of history and of its forms. Thus the modern historical consciousness includes as one of its facets an affirmation of rational autonomy against the absolute structures of the past and also against the conception of an all-governing providence, both of which seemed with some legitimacy to prevent new knowledge and also any new and useful applications of that new knowledge.[21]

In the century and three-quarters since the close of the Enlightenment, the understanding of human freedom within history has widened and deepened beyond these concepts of a purely rational freedom. The Romantic movement emphasized the uniqueness of the individual, and so the autonomy involved in being one's own peculiar self with one's own unique history—an understanding of autonomy inconceivable to the Enlightenment. In emphasizing the importance of feeling and the will, Romanticism, in many cases, also deemphasized the rational structures of autonomy, and saw freedom as the capacity to will new structures of value and a new form of the self, of self-creativity in its deepest sense—as in Nietzsche. And in continuity with this tradition, modern existentialism has gone even further: to be human is to be *self*-creative in freedom, to be aware of one's responsibility for oneself and for willing to be oneself, and so to will, through resolute courage and self-awareness of one's inexorable limits, one's *own* possibilities into actuality. Here the self is the sole creative principle in the actualization of its own reality. If it is to be a self at all, only its *own* possibilities can shape it, and it must be *itself* alone that wills those possibilities into actuality—all other agencies of the character of the self, mere tradition, the "they" or entities in the world, only collapse the self into the loss of itself and so into fallenness.[22] The principle of absolute autonomy could hardly be more determinative of all creative human actuality.

Interestingly, the same principle of self-creation at the deepest ontological level appears, as we noted, in Whitehead's cosmology, only now made inclusive of all becoming everywhere: granting all the influences of the given on any entity, both from precedent actuality and in terms of relevant possibilities offered to it by God, each entity becomes what it becomes only because it actualizes itself in freedom. Thus everything that is, is ultimately *self*-creative; autonomy represents the point where possibility becomes actual and so represents the determinative creative principle of all becoming.[23] In each case, freedom is defined as that which is creative of new forms in the future: outside the self in world and society, "inside" in new forms of self-realization. The contrast of this view of freedom as sharing in the *origination* of world and of self in time with the older view of freedom as a willing not coerced by compulsion is evident. Freedom here is *temporally* interpreted as originating the *new* in the future, as both in time and yet creative of a new time. Although we have mentioned only a few important philosophical expressions of this theme, it is clear that since the Enlightenment autonomy, the self-creation of freedom and so by implication the self-creation by men and women of the history they inhabit, is a pervasive characteristic of the modern sense of humanity and of its role in history, and so is an aspect of our "world" of which any contemporary theology must take full account.

The modern sense of history, however, would be inadequately presented if human autonomy were its only theme. Concurrently with the growing sense of human freedom to determine itself and its historical existence, in fact dialectically related to that sense, has appeared an increasing sense of the rule of law over historical existence, i.e., of regularities within the sequences of events which are both universal in scope and necessary in character. As we have seen, the confidence in creative action and so in autonomy arose precisely because of a new confidence in our ability to understand the universal rule of law in things. Correspondingly, the hope that man could remake history was dependent on the assurance that history was determined by a rational structure of law which reason could understand and action manipulate.[24] A sense of necessitating law and of creative freedom may be logical opposites, but historically (as in Calvinism) they arose together as twin aspects of the paradox of science (a deeper paradox than the Calvinist one): through understanding of the necessitating laws that rule all, man may change everything for his own ends!

Moreover, that some vast, invisible "power," above and beyond human intentions, is at work in the processes of history has always seemed obvious, since what happens, both in the short term and even more clearly in the long, accords so little with what anyone intended. For the Greeks it was the "nature" of a social organism, for example, the nature of political community, that worked itself out in the ups and downs of history;[25] and then beyond that—especially in the Hellenistic world—it was *moira*, the Fates or the stars which determined all that happens. As we have noted, in classical Christianity these hidden powers "behind the backs of men," working through their wisdom and benevolence, their foolish and their wayward intentions, became the providence of God. In the Enlightenment this providence generally becomes "Nature," an all-encompassing though hidden power, impersonal but clearly intentional, directing in a "rational" way the cosmos, man and history to their fulfillment in rational autonomy and in social peace.[26] This conception of Nature is, as is well known, transformed in Hegel into Absolute Spirit, which works through the passions and self-interests of mankind dialectically to achieve its own self-realization in a unity of freedom and community (the state). History *is* this self-creation of Absolute Spirit. Its events, unbeknownst to the actors involved, manifest the hidden work, the "cunning," of Reason in its dialectical self-development. The goal of history is the self-awareness or the coming to itself of Spirit in the self-conscious unity of men with the social whole which Spirit has slowly created, i.e., to full freedom, the inward identity of each subjective spirit with the objective Spirit as it moves through historical time.[27]

Such "metaphysical" concepts as Providence, Nature or Absolute Spirit, however, were unacceptable to the more empirically oriented side of the Enlightenment,[28] and even more to the post-Hegelian world of the nineteenth century. In August Comte, J. S. Mill and Karl Marx, history is determined by laws discoverable by empirical reason, and, by discovering these laws, rational men may act in accord with them and so realize the hidden direction to which they are moving events.[29] This tradition of seeing social change and so history as a "natural history" subject to laws discoverable to the social scientist as the laws of nature are open to the physical scientist, has been, as Nisbet points out, the theoretical basis of most of social science: a study of the laws of change in social process through which the evolution of any aspect of society (social evolution) may become intelligible to human reason —and so, paradoxically, in part controllable by human praxis.[30] The culmination, though one surely predicted by Comte and by Mill, of this effort to understand and then control or direct history in terms of law has been reached in behaviorist psychology, whose aim is to discover empirically, and (paradoxically) to apply for human betterment, the psychological laws determinative of all human cognition and motivation.[31]

As in the case of the development of relativism in the modern consciousness of history, the growth of the sense of determinative law raises sharply the question of the meaning of historical process: If all we do is determined by inexorable laws, can there be any rescue in life from meaningless fate, a fate that blindly pushes us where it will? And again, this question has been answered in almost all cases: from Condorcet and Comte through Marx to Skinner, by the conviction that, however unconscious and unpurposive they may be, these determinative laws of human behavior and of social change lead us—provided we understand and apply them—toward human fulfillment. The theory of progress has in this sense "saved" modernity from the terrors of two of its most important notions, historical relativity and the reign of law. Hence, part of the ground of the widespread contemporary sense of the meaninglessness of life in history has arisen through the dissolution of that faith in progress. With that dissolution the relativity and transcience of social forms and the determination of events by blind law now connote a directionless historical process and so an entirely different human meaning.

On the other hand, the important role of the understanding of law in social affairs cannot at all be questioned for creative social praxis and for the responsible use of freedom—as each of the thinkers briefly reviewed here has emphasized. Without an understanding of the factors at work in a historical situation, freedom, however morally committed it may be, is left helpless to shape creatively that situation for the future. As Comte and Marx (and their present-day descendants, especially the neo-Marxists) rightly insisted, positive action is possible only if the underlying structure of social movements and so the tendencies of the present have been made explicit and visible by inquiry and rational formulation—only if those who suffer from a situation have achieved "political consciousness." Freedom can shape the future only if it does so by knowledge of the essential economic and social factors at work, and in terms of intelligible schemes based on such knowledge. An understanding of society through law is the way the destiny with which freedom must work is made intelligible and useful praxis is generated. The understanding of social history in terms of law is, therefore, crucial to the enactment of freedom in history. The problem, obviously, is the relation between these two factors: the institutions and trends, the destiny in terms of which freedom must work, and the rational and informed freedom which must deal with these trends. Thus destiny and freedom, law and rationally purposive actions, are polar terms in historical life, not antitheses, although most of the modern representatives of each pole have seen them in the latter and not in the former light.

In any case, it is clear that modern reflection on social change illustrates in its understanding of man and of his history an old dialectic between "hidden powers" and human freedom. What may be new in the modern self-understanding is, first, the clearly nonteleological character of these hidden forces. Instead of Providence, Nature or Spirit, with their hidden purposes, these are now only blind necessitating laws. As a consequence, there appears, secondly, the stark separation in modernity of these two polar elements of historical experience into an absolute autonomy almost entirely creative of itself over against an iron reign of impersonal law almost totally determinative of what we are and will do.[32] Any contemporary understanding of providence, its relation to human freedom and thus to the developments of social history, must take full account of this dialectical if not contradictory emphasis of modernity on autonomy and self-creativity on the one hand, and on the reign of law in human affairs on the other, and seek to understand them both in relation to one another and to God. How are the elements in historical process of both contingency and self-creative freedom to be conceived in their relation to the unquestioned presence of destiny and so of law, and how are both to be conceived in relation to the work of providence?

The Naturalistic Understanding of History

3. Out of these themes we have just discussed has arisen a new understanding of history, what we may tentatively call a "secular" or "naturalistic" understanding. Permanent and absolute structures of life have gone, leaving relative forms that come and go as circumstances and the human response to them dictate. Thus the dynamic factors at work are all seen as natural or creaturely: on the one hand, the continuities out of the past, the laws that govern these continuities and the changes that take place within them; and on the other, human intelligence and will adapting to given circumstances and the changes that continually occur. As we have noted, the mysterious "hidden" forces at work in history, bringing about outcomes as surprising as they were unintended, have slowly and gradually ceased to have a divine, a metaphysical or even a purposive character. Such forces that shape events beyond our intentions are now viewed as the forces of "natural law" to be studied and clarified empirically by the social sciences. Herder expressed this precisely at the end of the eighteenth century; Comte, Mill, Marx and most modern interpreters of history have repeated this same naturalistic theme:

> But as the modern Greeks have become what they are only by the course of time, through a given series of causes and effects, so do the ancients; and not less every other nation upon earth. The whole history of mankind is a pure natural history of human powers, actions, and propensities, modified by time and place. . . . This philosophy will first and most eminently guard us from attributing the facts that appear in history, to the particular hidden purposes of a scheme of invisible powers, which we would not venture to name in connection with natural phenomena.[33]

The creative results of this relativizing of the structures of history and this "naturalizing" of the dynamic factors of history into intelligible law and creative human response have been great. With this view, history is suddenly open to human reshaping, as nature on the same grounds has been open to technological transformation—and the combination has dominated revolutionary and reformist social scientists alike. As the desacralization of nature prepared the way for technology, so the comparable desacralization of history in the seventeenth and eighteenth centuries prepared the way for political action to transform the social structures that are now seen to be relative. Only when social structures were understood to be *historical,* products of relative, finite factors, could they be legitimately the objects of secular and moral criticism and could the hope of their historical transformation become a possibility. If history has been created by secular forces, it can—and should, insofar as it is evil—be changed by secular forces; if history is secular, man can change it; if it is secular, he alone can change it; and thus is his responsibility clear. What we call humanitarianism and reformism, as well as revolutionary commitment, as modes of human being in the world, are therefore directly dependent both historically and in principle on this new relativistic and "secular" view of history developed in the Enlightenment and the nineteenth century. Prior to that time, history was regarded by conservative forces as divinely ordained and so as static, and by radical forces who abhorred its forms, as malleable only to a divine apocalyptic action. For these reasons it is no accident that upon the heels of these new conceptions of a secular and so transformable history followed the American and French Revolutions, their many progeny, some successful, some aborted, in the nineteenth century, and that after them came the socialist revolutions of the present century. It is also no accident that these forces were on the whole anticlerical and even antireligious in character. As Marx and the other left-wing Hegelians said, religion is the medium of the sacralization of the forms of society and so is the real enemy of all social transformation. And, finally, it is no accident that in the same period for the first time Christian commitment finds itself concerned explicitly with social and political reform and that Christian reflection creates a self-conscious social ethic. It was now seen that God had not ordained what we see around us in society; thus, insofar as it appears "evil," we are now obligated to change it by historical means. In this way, in the nineteenth and twentieth centuries the dream of radical apocalyptic groups that God would through his saints transform the world came down to earth and became historical, a historical and social task for his church—even though, ironically, the immediate cause of this insight was the desacralizing and the "detheologizing" of history.

The problems for theology of such a secular understanding of history are, of course, mammoth. How can the activity of God in social process be understood if history as a whole and political action within it are viewed at the deepest level naturalistically? This entire volume is devoted to an explication of and answer to this question. But any theologian who seeks to dissolve entirely this secular understanding of history as a sequence of relative structures created by natural forces in combination with human action will do so at his own peril. For he will thereby dissolve as well the grounds for his own Christian social ethic. Likewise, the problems latent in the human hope to transform history through intellectual planning in relation to the laws of history has—like its technical counterpart—revealed to our century the deepest ambiguities: man seems to desecrate as much as he improves the nature and the society he seeks intentionally to refashion. But again, despite the risks and the ambiguity, neither effort can be abandoned; creative political action on a moral basis is as necessary as is its counterpart, creative technology. The two can neither be separated—technology in the hands of the leaders of misshapen and corrupted social structure is demonic—nor rejected. Despite their ambiguity, technology and political action are the social expressions of human creativity in history.

The Temporalizing of Being

4. Along with a new sense of history and the factors that shape it has come a new meaning to time, or, better, to temporal passage.[34] This new understanding is indebted more to the developing themes of historicity and autonomy than to that

of law in the modern historical consciousness, but it permeates, I believe, all our thought about time. For, as we have seen, even those who believe that history obeys ineluctable law paradoxically wish on that basis to create a new world tomorrow, to be creators and self-creators in history. If entities and the events in which they participate in time are *self*-creative, then temporal passage becomes the prime locus of being and the ground of creativity. Actuality is decision, a decision amidst possibilities relevant to the entity. If, moreover, the decision creative of actuality out of its given destiny is made autonomously, in *self*-determination, then that decision, and the actuality that flows from it, *is* not until the event occurs. Prior to the decision of freedom as to what we are to be and do, there is ahead of us *only* possibility; with that decision the new entity and the new event become formed, definite and actual. If, then, freedom is involved along with destiny in the formation of human and historical actuality, if in that fundamental sense events are self-created, then events become actual, formed, definite—what they are—only as and when they occur, and in no other way. The projection of possibility as crucially ingredient to actuality, and so the importance of the future, are, as Whitehead and Heidegger reiterate, immediately involved in this view of the self-determination of each actuality. Nevertheless, central to our present purposes is another implication: what is projected are only possibilities, not actualities, and only as the present happens out of self-creation, do actuality and so finite being in that sense occur. The movement of time is modal, the movement from possibility into actuality; time is the locus of the becoming of actuality and so the locus of being. As the polarity of destiny and freedom became the fundamental ontological structure for our historical being encompassing both the reign of law and of autonomy in history, so now the locus of being is uncovered in the union of actuality and possibility. The moving temporal present is the moving "place" where being comes to be. The historical consciousness has led to a new *temporalizing* of being and so to a new understanding of actuality in its relation to possibility.

Temporal passage, then, the movement of events from possibility to actuality, is fundamental to the becoming of being, and is thus itself in a sense creative. It represents the continual movement out of possibility into formed actuality. Time, therefore, is no longer subsidiary to any other realm beyond itself from which creation of the new arises, a moving image of an eternity already fashioned; nor can it be the unfolding of a prior, static divine plan. Time not eternity is the place where being and actuality happen; and thus the future is not "there" as actual in its definite and shaped form either in eternity or in the prescience of God. Rather, temporal passage as it moves forward is itself the arena, and the sole arena to our knowledge, where actuality comes to be in the particular form it is. Before they occur events are at best "possible"; only when they occur are events actual. The future, therefore, is *only* possibility, the present alone where actuality is. Temporality, therefore, is where being as actuality is and alone where it is; for it is in the self-actualization of events in time that possibilities are transformed into definite actualities. Thus does temporality become the most fundamental category of being, and the ontological locus of all creativity of the new.

Two important corollaries for philosophical and theological understanding follow from this radical temporalizing of being that has occurred in modernity. The first is that such a view of passage as creative of actuality, of being in that sense, is the ontological ground for the "openness of the future," so commonly cited as a crucial ingredient of the modern historical consciousness. If the future is already actual, either in eternal forms, in God's vision or even in "God's being as future," then it can hardly be open. For then our historical decisions do not in fact shape what is and is to be; freedom becomes the confirmation of something decided elsewhere, and not the actualizing of possibility, the deciding of what is still undecided. The phrase "an open future" is at base not an *epistemological* category referent to what we know or do not know about the future. It is an ontological category related to the reality and effectiveness of creative freedom in historical passage.

First, the openness of the future implies the requirement that freedom is a necessary though surely not a sufficient creative factor in the determination of relevant actuality, that, in that sense, self-determination as we experience it in ourselves and in our history is a reality. The other ontological requirement for an open future is that freedom confront not only destiny in its present but genuine alternatives and not-already-decided actualities in its future. It is not enough to say that the future is open because we do not yet *know* what it is to be. If ontologically it is already "actual," in causal determination or in God's determination, then its openness and the reality of our own freedom are fatally compromised. Only if it is through the decision of finite freedom, of *Dasein*, to choose among real alternatives and so to enact its own possibilities—to bring those possibilities through its own decision into actuality—is freedom, as understood in modernity, real. The ontological ground for an open future is that the future is constituted by as yet unrealized and unactual possibility, and that it is the self-creation of each entity that embodies projected possibilities into concrete actualities. In turn, this implies the radical temporalizing of being, the notion that being itself shares and includes the temporal distinction between what has become actual and what still remains possible, that being is being in process, that it grows and changes as temporal passage enacts new and as yet unrealized possibilities.

Secondly, such a notion of temporality as the locus of the creation and self-creation of actual being has immediate consequences for any theological understanding of God. It implies the most radical redefinition of God's being in relation to time and so of the divine eternity, and of God's knowledge in relation to the future. For if in this sense being is temporal, then the distinction of present and future is to be interpreted as representing a fundamental ontological or modal distinction between actuality and possibility, and in turn that distinction is now taken to characterize being at its most basic level.[35] As destiny and freedom are the fundamental ontological structure of finite being facing its past, so actuality and possibility are the fundamental ontological structure of finite being facing its future. Thus God's being itself must in that sense share in temporality, moving within destiny and freedom and from actuality into possibility as temporal passage itself moves—else again the future not be open and creative freedom not be real. Further, God's providence cannot be a "foresight" of future actuality as in both Augustine and Calvin; for the future contains possibility alone, and only with the self-creation of entities will actualities come to have being, does what will be come in fact to be. Nor, clearly, can the Calvinistic category of "foreordination" be applicable since in that case neither would finite freedom be *creative* of the new through its *own* decision,[36] nor would the events to be in the future have the status now of new possibilities. Thus, becoming and being in the divine life must be much more essentially intermixed than heretofore in the Christian tradition.

The New Meaning of History: Progress

5. Finally, as we have noted, history or temporal passage conceived as a sequence of relative forms continually actualizing novelty and thus continually dissolving older structures contains *meaning* in a quite new sense. Meaning is resident in history and time not through the preservation of given, absolute structures; on the contrary, for most of modernity meaning has been found in the creation of better structures, in the progressive sequence of forms leading to the ideal. Thus were the threatening questions of relativity and of determination by necessitating law appeased by the belief in historical progress, a view generally dominant in Western experience and thought from the Enlightenment until the early part of the twentieth century. This progress might be thought to be the result of the hidden powers of Nature, of Absolute Spirit or of ineluctable laws of development or, as in the latter nineteenth century, the result of a general law of evolution; or finally, in a more humanistic manner, of man's intelligent control and use of the laws of change and evolution. In any case, men and women could have confidence that history was meaningful because it led toward human perfection. Here the ideal has clearly the character neither of the beginning of things, of an eternity beyond time, nor merely of human subjectivity. It is, on the contrary, intimately related to reality, only the reality of the future. For on such a view, the ideal is to be the character of the future, and historical development over time, not an individual ascent out of history, is the means by which the ideal is to be realized.[37]

Clearly, this notion of history as redemptive through the unfolding of its own immanent process will have large implications for the conception of providence; to this we shall turn shortly. At the moment our concern is to point out the implications for eschatology of the new understanding of history as moving toward the ideal. What this understanding meant was a radical *historicizing* of the eschatological elements of Christianity (and of Judaism as well among Reformed circles). The final eschatological purposes of God which, as we have seen in the examples of both Augustine and Calvin, determine and guide the divine work within history, are now no longer transhistorical, intending a salvation for individuals beyond history in eternity. On the contrary, these eschatological purposes now concern the historical itself, the end of history in the literal sense, since that end is now conceived to be the perfection of the humanum, a concrete, historical community of justice, peace, freedom and communion. The symbol of the kingdom becomes a symbol for the character of future *social history*; and the divine activity in history—and so the major task of the church—is seen as an activity which prepares that culmination by working, not simply in the church and on individual souls, but in the social process itself in the development of democratic rights, economic justice, social equality and international peace. As the eschatological goal was thus moved into historical process itself, so God's work in the world, and a Christian's obligation toward the world, was likewise moved into "secular" historical process to transform that process creatively.[38] Neo-orthodox theology and much biblical study have been inclined to find this historicized eschatology with its historical kingdom incredible and naive on the one hand and unbiblical on the other. Both of them should recognize, however, that their own Christian concerns for "social values" find their historical roots and much of their theological foundation in this new union of eschatology and future social history. Correspondingly, wherever that union is substantially broken, then those social concerns have found themselves to have lost their theological rootage. If the final purposes of God have little or no relation to the betterment of the social order, it is difficult to know why God is at work in social history, or what he might be about if he is, and it is even more difficult to say why Christians should have a concern which apparently God does not. One of the most important questions for contemporary theology, therefore, has been, granted that the theory of progress is barely credible to us, how eschatology and future history are to be related so that creative political and social praxis may have sound theological bases.

In sum, we may say that from the seventeenth through the nineteenth centuries a quite new view of history and of the human role and prospects within it arose, a view which together makes up the major content of the phrase "historical consciousness." History is seen as a sequence of relative forms of social life, forms produced by finite factors and thus reshapable through human intelligence, commitment and action. Men and women and all they produce are immersed in this sequence as products of it, and transcendent to it as potential transformers of it; hence, history is intelligible in terms of laws governing social life, and malleable by freedom in terms of informed and creative praxis. While constituted by relative and transient structures and determined by finite factors, this sequence was regarded as by no means random or meaningless, for it manifests a steady, if often hidden, development toward the ideal. This new view of history has transformed the understanding of providence and so the Christian view of history during this same period. To this transformation and its aftermath in contemporary theology we shall subsequently turn after a brief look at a parallel development in the understanding of the history of nature.

SUBSEQUENT VIEWS OF NATURE'S PROCESS

Although, as we noted, the developmental view of nature is subsequent in time to the progressive understanding of history, nevertheless once the evolutionary hypothesis appeared it combined with the views of history we have rehearsed to give, so to speak, a cosmic setting to the developmental understanding of history. A familiar irony, repeated often in the history of theology, repeats itself here in relation to the symbol of providence. Like the conception of historical progress that appeared before it, the idea of evolution arose self-consciously against the dominant understanding of providence; but then, having vanquished the latter, evolution soon found itself the unintended basis for a quite new understanding of providence. Let us see briefly how this pattern unfolded itself first in geology and then in biology.

In the seventeenth and eighteenth centuries the conception of God's providence was by no means at war with the findings of natural science.[39] On the contrary, to many Newtonian physicists scientific inquiry uncovered an orderly cosmos which must, argued many, owe its harmony to a sublime creator;[40] and to early biologists the remarkable adaptation of the fixed species to their environment demanded a purposive intelligence as the common source of these forms of life as well as of their natural setting to which they were so admirably fitted.[41] How else, asked one author of the Bridgewater treatises, can one explain the "miraculous" ability of the eye of the codfish to see in salt water, if not by a purposive and wonderful adaptation of the structure of that eye to its aqueous world?[42] The proof of providence, therefore, lay not only in the cosmic reign of law, but even more in the minute and intricate adaptation of permanent species to the earth they inhabited: birds to air and trees, animals to grasses and woodlands, man to hills, valleys and fields. The more this harmonious order of adaptation was uncovered by scientific inquiry, the more the glory of the providential ruler of that order seemed to be established.

In the late eighteenth and in the nineteenth centuries, however, developments in geology and biology challenged this understanding both of nature's order and of the providential will that apparently had established it. Geology was the initial challenger in the figures of James Hutton and Charles Lyell. Hutton first argued and then Lyell subsequently established beyond doubt not only that, as all geologists were coming to believe, the earth's forms had dramatically changed since the earliest days, but even more that these changes had (a) taken place over countless eons of time (versus the "biblical" six thousand years),[43] and that (b) they had been caused not by divine creative intervention—which might have had an "adaptive" purpose—but by uniform laws of change utterly unrelated to animal or human adaptation. As Lyell phrased this important uniformitarian principle: "All former changes of the organic and inorganic creation are referable to one uninterrupted succession of physical events, governed by the laws now in operation . . ."[44] As Galileo's and Descartes's mechanical view of the external world stripped the *present* cosmos of teleology (though providence soon recovered from that), so the uniformitarian principle of interpretation of the earth's *history* stripped the earth's *past* of any teleological implications. Providence, the purposive hand of God in the development of nature, seemed utterly absent from the course of geological history. Lyell's belief that the special creation of man was the sole remaining place where providential activity could be seen in past time[45] seemed a prophecy of the total demise of the conception of God as an explanation of the developments of the past.

Fifty years later the same process repeated itself in biology with regard to the origins of species, and the remaining "mighty act" of providence, the special creation of man, was similarly dissolved into the apparent effect of uniform, mechanical laws. By applying Lyell's uniformitarian principle of the reign of law in the geological past to the question of the "creation" of man, Darwin not only challenged once again the biblical account of the past but even more raised the equally powerful question: is the hand of God *anywhere* manifest in the developments of our cosmos, of our earth and of our human existence?[46]

In fact, Darwin's theory seemed to make impossible any providential interpretation of the course of nature—and at best made God an infinitely remote creator of a cosmos he subsequently ignored—on two grounds. (1) Not only are the forms of life transitory and impermanent, children of time; even more they have arisen, according to this theory, precisely by chance. For any divine control or direction of the development of species was eliminated in principle by an explanation of that direction in terms of *random* mutations and subsequent *natural* selection of the fittest among those mutations—and Darwin affirmed unequivocally the implicitly antiteleological meanings in the words "random" and "natural."[47]

(2) The argument for providence from the "miracle" of adaptation was dissolved by a theory that viewed forms as arising and continuing in being "naturally" *through* adaptation to their environment. In effect, the codfish is *there* because among other things it can see in water; and the only sorts of eyes that can be explained in terms of this theory are those that fit the water in which the codfish lives. Thus it would now be a case of *non*-adaptation that would be the "miracle" to be explained by factors external to the situation, not an example of adaptation.[48] Adaptation has, therefore, become a part of the "natural" explanation of each species, not a mystery to be explained by appeal to providence. The developments of geology and biology, constructing a history of the world and its life which unfolded through the interworking of chance and mechanical law and yet which explained thereby not only the vast changes in the history of the earth, of the history of the forms of life but also the obvious and useful adaptation of those forms to their environment, seemed to shut off once and for all any religious interpretation of the origins of our existence in the world. If structures of the earth, the forms of its life, even the human species, arise and fall with no purpose as well as no permanence, if all that is meaningful to us is subject to such blind remorseless fates, can there be any meaning at all in the human story? The nineteenth century gazed briefly at this vision of a soulless, blind world of transitory forms, which *might* include a human destiny not unlike that granted to the dinosaurs—and, buoyed up by its faith in progress, turned away.[49] This vision has, however, reappeared in much stronger form in the twentieth century.

The evolutionary staying-power of a providential deity, his ability to adapt and so to survive in a changing cultural environment, is, however, remarkable. Soon a quite new view of the role of providence in natural history was developed: the "evolutionary providence" of later liberal theology. The basis of this new conception was that element of the new understanding of history which most of the nineteenth century, despite the chill air of mechanical causation, took for granted, namely, the view that history, however blind its secret mechanics, moved in a progressive direction. For even though the evolutionary theory may have in one sense "reduced" man's estimate of his status in the cosmos as a whole, one thing remained clear to the intellectual civilized West of 1860. This was that cosmic and historical progress were objectively real characteristics of process since man was unquestionably the highest form of natural and animal life, and European culture the highest form of human existence. For them, therefore, all of process, blind or not, seemed "bent" on producing modern Western man as the final result of all its immense labors! Thus, whether the nineteenth century witnessed *in fact* a reduction of the sense of man's status in the universe, as all secularists unthinkingly proclaim, is a very dubious point. And it was this unquestioned element of progress, implied in the theory of evolutionary forms, which provided the entry point for the theological interpretation of Darwin's theory, as it had for the theological interpretation of the Enlightenment view of history.

Although Darwin had, without the aid of providence, explained the origin of new species, still questions remained. Could chance variations plus the purposeless and essentially negative scythe of natural selection give a convincing explanation of why the forms of life exhibited a *progressive* sequence, especially one leading from inorganic life all the way "up" to the extraordinary creature man? Does not progress inevitably imply the functioning and control of an aim, somehow, somewhere in the process of change, either in the variations produced or the selecting of them? And can the necessities of mere survival explain the appearance of more perfect forms, perfect in some sense not directly connected with immediate survival?[50] Darwin's friend and coworker A. R. Wallace began to realize that in the development of man an "instrument (the mind) has been developed in advance of the needs of its possessor."[51] Thus he argued that natural selection, which can explain only those structures that are needed for immediate physical survival, cannot account for the subtle, nonutilitarian elements of man's higher nature. And the same point could be made about any improvement, the utility of which for survival (like that of the eye, of a coat of white fur or of a mind) only appears when the characteristic as a whole is fully developed. For these reasons, Wallace agreed with another early evolutionist, Asa Gray, that "some higher intelligence may have directed the process by which the human race was developed."[52] Thus, in the evolutionary theory itself appeared new "lacunae" where explanatory power failed—in this case, the force that drove nature through its processes of mutation and selection to higher, as well as newer, forms of existence. Progress as a concept seems to demand that valuation and purpose be at work, else it is itself left totally unexplained. Thus again, some form of providence was implied as a conclusion from the hypotheses of science.[53]

The resultant evolutionary interpretation of providence, however, was quite different from the predecessor based on adaptation which had suffered such stunning defeat at the hands of Darwin. Now the earlier orthodox concept of direct divine control was removed in favor of the idea of change in total accord with uniform law, as in Darwinian naturalism. Moreover, in the place of the adaptive teleology of Paley, was now put the concepts of "wider teleology" (Huxley's term) or "design by wholesale" (Henry Ward Beecher's). Instead of a purposive power that once and for all fitted each permanent form or organ to its special environment, has appeared a purposive "force" that over the whole course of time directs the slow and uniform change of forms in a given direction and toward certain definite goals.[54] It is evident how close the essential structure of this view is to the conception of providence derived from the new view of history as development.

According to this view, providence is again the direct implication of cosmology, i.e., of the world process scientifically investigated and philosophically pondered. For, says this new argument, dominant from the days of David Strauss to Henry Drummond, Samuel Alexander, F. R. Tennant, A. N. Whitehead, William Temple and now Teilhard de Chardin, the progressive development of the cosmos and especially of life, moving by natural laws of change through lower forms of life to the development of novel forms culminating in man with his mental, aesthetic and moral faculties, cannot be explained merely in terms of matter in random motion, however controlled that motion may be by impersonal law. If mind and moral personality arise out of nature, it is certainly probable (or, as Tennant likes to put it, "it is strongly suggested")[55] that nature in turn has its own ground in a greater mental and moral person, at the least. And if the process of natural development moves not just in any direction, but in this sort of purposive direction, it is reasonable to assume that it is a directed and not a chance development. Thus again, the "Book of Nature" reveals (or "suggests") to the inquiring eye the action of the wisdom and beneficence of God, now not as the adjuster of things to one another, but as the guiding force in the natural development of process toward its present fulfillment in humanity—all in cosmic preparation for the "completion of creation" in the perfection of men and women and their society.

New scientific views of nature, therefore, combined with the historical consciousness of the eighteenth and nineteenth centuries to create an entirely new understanding of historical process, much of which we inherit from them and share. It was this view of historical process which liberal theology itself imbibed, and in terms of which it reinterpreted the Christian understanding of history and in fact the Christian gospel itself—as the next chapter will show. Since that time much has changed; our own understanding of history is partly informed by this consciousness we have here traced and partly in reaction to it, as the following chapter will also evidence. A full sense of the depth of the rejection of this view of "progress" can be gained by comparing this same sense of inevitable progress through science, technology and the industrial arts with the gloom of a contemporary like Heilbroner that it is precisely those "powers" of humanity that threaten to doom rather than bless the human future. In general, the dilemma for contemporary thought about history, religious and secular alike, has arisen because on the one hand the *process* character of temporal passage has been accepted, and with it the contingency, the relativity and the transience of all the forms of history's life; on the other hand, the *progressive* character of that process has not been accepted—and thus has the problem of the *meaning* of history been so sharply posed for us. But before we explore this dilemma illustrated by the twentieth century, let us review what liberal theology did with this new view of history produced by the Enlightenment and by its descendants in the early nineteenth century.

9

HISTORY AND PROVIDENCE
IN MODERN THEOLOGY

As we have seen, a new view of history developed in the seventeenth and eighteenth centuries which entailed fundamental changes in the traditional theological conception of history and so in the doctrines of providence and eschatology. Our purpose in this chapter is, in preparation for our own response, briefly to survey the responses that theology has made to the new historical consciousness and the difficulties which each response has subsequently encountered. While, as we shall see, there has been the widest variety in the theological interpretations of history and so in the understanding of providence and eschatology from roughly 1800 to the present day, there is a common pattern that emerges. In brief, this pattern is that while each new "secular" view of history and of natural process begins by challenging the understanding of providence that precedes it, in the end theology adapts its understanding of the biblical symbols to the new view of history and so reinterprets the symbols of providence and of eschatology in its light. A historical survey certainly shows that men and women understand God's activity in time in the light of their changing experience of history; whether or not in turn they understand that experience of history in the light of their theology is a bit more difficult to document historically![1]

As we have noted, the new consciousness of history arose as a challenge not only to older conceptions of changeless, absolute and sacred structures of history, but also as a challenge to the notion of a divine providence determinative of the events of history.[2] The reasons for this conflict between the classical conception of providence and the new view of history are obvious: (1) Orthodox views of providence seemed to imply that those structures which history manifests, being willed by God, are not relative and transient, but eternal, absolute and sacred; so that history far from being progressive is static in character. (2) The older view implied that change is a result of either a continuous divine action or an intervening divine action both of which contradicted the new understanding of history as determined by inalterable natural laws available to rational inquiry. (3) The older view implied that in effect God made history, whereas it is now obvious that finite factors, plus natural and progressive human intervention, "made" history. Thus, as all the relevant documents evidence, the perpetuators of the new view sought to expel a conservative providential interpretation of history in order to make room for a progressive interpretation according to natural laws and to human creativity.[3]

The intellectual and social forces at work in the Enlightenment, of which we have here traced only a few, forced on theology a fundamental reinterpretation of itself, a reinterpretation from the ground up. Among the concepts that were radically reinterpreted was that of the notion of the divine activity within history, and so of the relation of providence and eschatology to developments in history. In the liberal theology that arose out of the Enlightenment, therefore, the new view of history was gradually incorporated into the theological corpus and in the end, as we shall see, dominated that corpus. We shall illustrate this pattern of incorporation and then dominance in terms of two of the leading Protestant theologians of the nineteenth century: Friedrich Schleiermacher and Albrecht Ritschl, though many others might be used to illustrate the same development.[4] In the first, the new understanding of history permeates the entire theological system but has not yet explicitly become the most dominant principle in that system, with the result that Schleiermacher is rarely interpreted from this point of view. In Ritschl, on the other hand, the new view of history, as we have explicated it, constitutes the most fundamental principle of his system—as it will for most of the liberal theologians who followed after Ritschl. In each case, we are concerned only with the way the new understanding of history as a progressive development according to the inner action of natural laws and a human freedom gradually being "redeemed" by that development permeates the structure of the theology in question.

NINETEENTH-CENTURY LIBERAL THEOLOGY

Schleiermacher begins his description of God's relation to the world with two dramatically new assertions. The first was that the conception of creation, what God did "at the beginning" in bringing the world into being "out of nothing," can for religion and so for theology be included in the conception of God's preservation of the world over time—an assertion diametrically opposed to the way deism had understood the divine activity in relation to natural law.[5] In this way, Schleiermacher reinterpreted creation as a process of divine causality *over* time, a temporal, developmental process. The second was that God's activity of creation and preservation within the temporal world realizes itself entirely and exclusively through the "interdependence of nature," i.e., through what for us and for our inquiries is the system of natural and historical laws in which we find ourselves.[6] Thus, for Schleiermacher God works neither in a "mythical" way by establishing unalterable forms at the beginning nor by intervening miraculously within history. Rather, he works in time solely in and through the natural processes of temporal development, and consequently in and through the laws of those processes. What the Enlightenment had seen as antithetical to creation and providence, namely, the developing changes of nature and history according to law, Schleiermacher sees as evidences of the absolute divine causality. In fact, as he says, the two points of view—that of causal law and that of providence—"entirely coincide," and "it can never be necessary in the interests of religion so to interpret a fact that its dependence on God also absolutely excludes its being conditioned by the system of Nature."[7] God is thus defined as the causal ground of the developing process of nature and of history, not as a being outside of or opposed to that process.[8] And God's providential work in time through the nature system is for Schleiermacher the key to all we can know either of his activity or of his nature.

This absolute divine causality, the *Ur*-cause, so to speak, of both the system of laws in nature and of our freedom, is, moreover, *progressive* in its fundamental character, a theme utterly fundamental to Schleiermacher's system but somewhat hidden within his classical theological symbolism. Schleiermacher distinguishes as basic to his view of humanity and of religion three different "grades" or levels of self-consciousness: the animal or corporeal level; the "sensible" self-consciousness (the experience of being a finite being passively and actively related to a world); and the consciousness of absolute dependence or "highest" self-consciousness.[9] These levels are not only qualitatively characteristic of the development of the individual; even more they represent developmental stages in the history of the race. It is, moreover, clear—though he never says so much explicitly—that this developmental progress through history of the levels of human self-consciousness provides for Schleiermacher the key to his interpretation of the efficacy and purpose of Christian salvation and so to the real purpose of God in history. For the fact is that Schleiermacher reinterprets every crucial theological symbol in the light of this theme of the creative and redemptive development over time of the levels of human (or "racial") self-consciousness. Let us review briefly Schleiermacher's understanding of certain central theological symbols to show that, however covertly (so to speak), nevertheless he does understand them developmentally, i.e., in terms of the new conception of time and of history as a sequence of progressive stages leading to an intrahistorical redemptive goal.

The original perfection of man and his world is for Schleiermacher not an original *state*, an actual past condition of humanity and of its environment, but a *potentiality*, the potentiality of becoming through time fully human, of realizing the highest levels of self-consciousness and of community of which mankind is capable.[10] Thus are sin and grace interpreted not in terms of an original degeneration and a miraculous restoration, but in terms of steady temporal development from possibility to actuality: i.e., redemption through grace is a process unfolding and ultimately realizing in the history of the race the original and latent possibilities of humanity.[11] Correspondingly, sin is the first or earliest stage of human self-consciousness, necessary for its further development but incomplete or truncated, a stage when the animal or "flesh" consciousness out of which men and women arose predominates and the God-consciousness is accordingly weak. In this situation the appearance of the higher level is resisted and the experience of this resistance is what we mean by the consciousness of sin.[12] In accordance with this interpretation of sin as the early imperfect stage of human self-consciousness, the coming of grace is seen as a new divine "act" lifting mankind to a higher stage in developing history.

As Schleiermacher puts this fundamental principle, what begins or appears as supernatural, as a new insertion into history, becomes natural, the immanent ground of history at this higher level.[13] Thus, in Jesus Christ the highest level of human self-consciousness, a perfect God-consciousness, appears—and this is his deity and his saving work.[14] This "new creation" is communicated to us historically through the community in which his influence works over time and which redeems us insofar as we participate through that influence in this highest level of self-consciousness.[15] Schleiermacher ascribes the appearance of this highest and complete level of human consciousness in Jesus and its continuity in the church redeeming future generations to "a divine creative act," and he insists that this divine creative act is that which "completes human nature,"[16] i.e., that due to the providential activity of God the potentialities latent in the original appearance of mankind are fulfilled and realized.

Thus, and here is perhaps the main evidence for our progressivist interpretation, Schleiermacher says that there is *one* creative divine decree and action spanning all of history. This one creative decree brings the race into being at a necessarily lower level, and gradually (through supernatural actions that become natural) lifts it to higher levels of self-consciousness, which, since man is a religious being, means the level of God-consciousness.[17] Since this world-forming decree, whose object is the development of the race and only through that of individuals, is that to which God's "election" refers, it represents the most fundamental purpose or will of God. Its goal is the establishment in history of the kingdom of Christ as a community of people existing at the highest human level.[18] Thus, for Schleiermacher the doctrine of an "external" second coming, a further supernatural intervention to judge and transform an as yet unredeemed history, is irrelevant and unnecessary, not a part of the real gospel.[19] On the contrary, the final and so eschatological goal of God's activity in creation, redemption and sanctification has been and gradually will be realized *historically* in the communication to men and women of God-consciousness through Christ and through the extension of this blessedness by means of the historical community of the church and its influence.[20] Eschatology, as well as creation and redemption, has become historical in character, the providential activity of God over time lifting mankind to its highest possible level of development.[21] Despite, therefore, the strength of the "vertical" dimension in Schleiermacher's analysis of human self-consciousness and of absolute dependence, it is undeniable that his interpretation of the gospel exhibits as well a "horizontal," temporal or progressivist dimension, an understanding of the Christian religion in the light of the modern historical consciousness and so as the culminating instrument of the divine providence in achieving the progress of the human race over time.

As Schleiermacher interpreted Christianity as the means through which God's providential activity in history raised mankind to a higher level of consciousness, so Albrecht Ritschl understood Christianity as the means through which God's providence was realizing in history man's full humanity as a moral personality. Thus, despite the obvious and significant differences between these two theologians, they exhibit the same fundamental structure of a divine redemption working through and within the natural forces of history to bring history, and with it the human race, to its own completion. Both had accepted, each in his own way, the new historical consciousness and reinterpreted Christianity in its terms.

Perhaps the best place to begin is with Ritschl's conception of man as a moral personality. By "moral" Ritschl, heavily under the influence of Kant, understood the determination of the human will not by any "natural" instincts or desires for self-preservation or personal happiness, or by such natural social drives as family or national loyalty. All of these are for him "nature" and "the world" and thus at a lower level than the moral or the spiritual. Consequently, to be moral was for Ritschl to be determined by the absolutely spiritual end of universal love and fellowship.[22] Thus the fulfillment of humanity means the realization of man's *ethical* nature in determination by the ideal of universal love of his fellows, or, in other words, by the achievement of a universal *moral* society based on love rather than on natural desires or parochial instincts. Such determination by absolute moral ideals in a totally moral society is the "ethical self-end" of man. This "self-end" is from the human point of view that which fulfills the deepest potentialities of humanity; the same end from the religious point of view is the kingdom of God. Ritschl continually refers to this moral goal of humanity as "victory over the world" or "supremacy to the world," meaning by this transcendence over the world not an *ontological* transcendence of the temporal world into eternity but an inward, moral transcendence over the natural and social pressures, desires and self-centered goals of the "world." The goal of humanity is *historical* in that it is embodied in a historical society of men and women in relation to one another; it is transhistorical or supermundane only in the sense that it is governed by universal love and not by natural desires and loyalties.[23]

The center of Ritschl's argument for the Christian religion, which like Schleiermacher he regards as the perfect and absolute culmination of the religions of history,[24] is that it is only through religion, and specifically through the Christian religion, that this human self-end, the realization of full humanity in history, is possible. The realization of human moral progress in history requires for him a religious foundation; the fulfillment of the moral requires the horizon of religious faith in God and of personal commitment to the end of God in Christ, the kingdom of God.[25] The significance of religion in life—and so its irreplaceable role—is for Ritschl that through the help of a supermundane spiritual power, man may elevate himself above the world and so be directed by the moral end of universal love.[26]

This elevation above the world so that moral self-direction and self-fulfillment are possible is accomplished in several different ways by means of religious faith. First, through faith in a personal, moral God man knows that the entire natural order, and with it the shifting orders of history, to both of which he is instinctively bound and on which he is dependent, are themselves only instruments for the spiritual life in which he as man shares. Thus, through faith in God as creator and ruler of these orders for the moral and religious ends of the kingdom, man is enabled to be victorious over them—to rise above their pressures on him and terrors for him— and thus realize himself morally.[27] Religious faith is, moreover, specifically faith in God's providence. It is trust that the world government of God will in the end bring about the kingdom as a union of the natural, historical and, above all, the moral aspects of creation.[28] For it is through this faith in providence, and so through commitment to the goal of providence, the kingdom of God, that men are united to the community of the kingdom, to Christ its founder and so to the end of God himself. Furthermore, it is through his own teleological commitment to God's end, through his experienced faith in providence and personal commitment to the kingdom of God that providence will bring about, that the Christian is subjectively assured of his own salvation.[29] Objectively, Ritschl argues, the Christian is accepted by God, reconciled and made a child of God through his commitment to God's own providential end.[30] God loves us as sharing with Christ in God's self-end, i.e., through our faith and trust in, commitment to, and life for his own providential goal, the kingdom. In the deepest sense, then, for Ritschl Christian faith is faith in God's providential work in general history progressively bringing about the kingdom; faith is trust that providence will achieve its goal and so faith is commitment to that goal, the kingdom of God.[31]

In the plan of providence, and equally in the development of human faith in providence, the role of Christ for Ritschl is, as it was for Schleiermacher, central. For Christ is the founder of the kingdom of God, that goal which, as we have seen, unites the self-end of God and the self-end of man.[32] In proclaiming this kingdom, in giving himself to it, in allowing this end to dominate his whole life and in establishing the community devoted to this moral and religious end, Christ is divine. He shares God's end as his own, and through his work we too share that end, and are united and reconciled to God.[33] It is through Jesus that the self-end of God in the kingdom of God is revealed and made available to men as *their* self-end, in faith and commitment to the unity of the kingdom. Through him, therefore, the final purpose of nature and of history under God's providence is made plain so that our spiritual supremacy over the world is made possible. Through Jesus men and women are reconciled to God. And through the religious faith in providence that their new understanding of God's work gives them, they are enabled to be free of anxiety and evil, to be transcendent to their own natural desires and thus to be capable of realizing their own ethical and religious humanity in "victory over the world." The kingdom is the center of Ritschl's theology; since the kingdom is the ultimate result of God's providential work in time, providence thus becomes the central mode of the divine activity.

As is plain, this is a theology with a thoroughly *historicized* eschatology. Every basic symbol from that of God's creative and providential work, through sin, Christ, redemption and the church is interpreted through the symbol of the future kingdom —through the future kingdom as a historical, social and moral reality. Despite its this-worldly historical character and the immanent mode of its development, the kingdom can be called "eschatological" in the sense that for Ritschl it is genuinely God's own self-end, his final purpose for which all else in all time and all space is done. Despite its inward, moral character and its supermundane transcendence to the world's desires and goals, it is historical in character. Ritschl is clear that it represents the culmination of social history, being that goal toward which all history's developments in the past, present and future point; moreover, it is a unity of the historical groups of mankind in a concrete society.[34] In a well-known "this-worldly" passage, Ritschl says:

> The truth here brought about is completed by the further observation that in order to fulfill its destined end, Christianity must win over the nations as wholes. That is, it can only really accomplish its universal human purpose when it brings under its influence all the social conditions under which the spiritual life of individuals exists. A Christianity which should remain anti-national in the minority of a people would destroy the necessary foundation upon which the spiritual existence of its adherents rests, and thus itself sink into a fruitless particularism.[35]

The historicizing and "progressivizing" of Christianity could hardly go further than this. God's providence has worked through the developments of morality, science, philosophy and religion, and behind them through the institutions of family, tribe, city, state and empire to prepare the way for their culmination in the final kingdom of God.[36] And it is also plain that this vision of a history developing under God's providence toward its own perfection included, for Ritschl, the assurance that among all the nations those with Western culture were the closest to the ideal.[37] Naive and chauvinistic as this interpretation of the kingdom may seem to us, it is, I believe, this identification of God's goal with the development of social history that inspired, as much as anything else theological, the liberal social gospel. For here in Ritschl is represented in germ the conviction that the Christian is called to break "the world" out of its social suffering in the "kingdom of sin"[38] into the greater perfection of the moral society of justice, peace and love which is the kingdom. Ritschl's historical understanding of the gospel is itself radically incomplete since he did not understand the necessity of changes in the social structures of the world if that world was to approximate the kingdom.[39] Nevertheless, it was Ritschl's fundamental theological understanding of history as the instrument of providence leading society to the moral and religious ideal of the kingdom that originally fathered the social concern of modern Christians—even those manifested in neo-orthodox and futurist eschatologists alike!

In Schleiermacher and in Ritschl, therefore, we have two quite diverse theologians who, each in his own way, structured his thought upon the basis of the new historical consciousness. That is to say, each interprets Christianity as centered on the providential activity of God in and through the natural, creaturely forces of history, an activity which becomes explicit and open in Christ and the church, but which has as its goal the development of humanity from its ambiguous beginnings in the past, through the progressive advance of modern cultural life, i.e., through the changing forms of social existence, to its own completion in the kingdom—though each defines that development and its goal in quite different ways. History is here unequivocally a sequence illustrating a progressive development; and God's work of salvation is unequivocally a work achieved in and through that development, as the fundamental cause of history's progress toward the realization of that humanity. As God could not complete his own goal without history's development, so the progress of mankind to self-realization could not be realized without God's providential work culminating in the redemptive efficacy of the Christian religion. Because a developing history is thus the arena of God's redemptive direction, providence—the activity of God in the changes of history leading it toward its goal—is the central theological category. A view of history that began as a challenge to providence found itself a century later the apparently firm basis of a quite new, and now thoroughly dominant, view of providence.

In the latter half of the nineteenth century the two sources of liberal theology we have discussed joined together: the providential interpretation of a progressive history and the providential interpretation of an evolutionary development of nature. This interpretation of time, natural evolution, and historical progress through the work of providence encompassed, dominated and shaped almost all theological categories from creation, through redemption, to eschatology.[40] As nature and history were to be understood according to the developmental hypothesis, so correspondingly theology was to be understood in terms of providence, God's creative work over time leading to his own far-off goal. In view of the fact that continuous and progressive development in history was thus the apparently all-encompassing model for secular scientific and historical understanding, and that providence was the reigning theological symbol, there was little warning either in academia or in church that only sixty years after the publication of Darwin's great work this synthesis of natural science, history and theology would be rudely shattered, and that the ideas of continual progress and of providence should themselves cease to "progress" and in fact suffer radical discontinuity and virtual extinction.

TWENTIETH-CENTURY KRISIS THEOLOGY

There is no more dramatic change in theological history than that which took place in the early twentieth century with regard to the relation of history to God's activity. Whereas in the preceding "liberal" theology the developing history of nature and of human society had been the locus of the redemptive divine action, and the future perfection of history the eschatological self-end of God, now suddenly in the new Krisis theology, the processes of nature and history are radically sundered from God's redeeming presence and the eschatological goal of God is thereby separated from the future of human society. Correspondingly, providence as the symbol explicative of the divine presence and activity in natural and historical change itself virtually disappears, and other theological symbols take the central places. Clearly, what happened was that the "link" between the new view of history and providence, and between the new evolutionary understanding of nature and providence, namely, the belief in progress—on whose basis the relation of general history and nature to human meaning had been grounded—disappeared. The contingency, relativity and transience of forms of life in history were still affirmed, but not the progress—and thus did history manifest an entirely different visage. With that evaporation of the sense of progress, the liberal theological synthesis built upon it fell to pieces, and history was left with almost no religious meaning or theological relevance.

In the theology which followed, therefore, two fundamental distinctions, or better, "sunderings," occurred which broke apart this synthesis of historical progress, evolutionary development and redemptive divine activity. (1) First, the general course of history, seen now as a directionless sequence of relative forms, was radically sundered from the redemptive activity of God, from the "meaning" for human life which the gospel offered, and theology concerned itself no longer with developments in general history. (2) History and with it the problems and the hopes of human existence generally were in turn radically sundered from nature—and correspondingly, theology no longer concerned itself with the scientific study of nature or with philosophical interpretations of that study.[41] Again, it is obvious that if natural and social history as such become irrelevant to the understanding of God's redemptive acts, then providence, as the symbol of God's activity in nature and social history, also would become at best a minor symbol and at the worst nonexistent in any explication of the gospel. We shall illustrate this development with brief reference to two central theologians of this period—1918 to roughly 1950–60—Karl Barth and Rudolph Bultmann, and then in the light of this analysis seek to explain why this change occurred.[42]

The new theology—the dialectical or *Krisis Theologie*—began with Karl Barth's *Epistle to the Romans* at the close of the First World War. An entirely new vision of history is here powerfully presented: history is "the display of the supposed advantages of power and intelligence which some men possess over others, of the struggle for existence hypocritically described by ideologists as the struggle for justice and freedom, each vying with the rest in solemnity and triviality."[43] Thus history is the realm of meaninglessness, sin and death, a realm totally divorced from any immanent principle of salvation; in fact, the essence of the meaninglessness and incomprehensibility of history appears when, as in the preceding age, men saw the immanent principles of history as divine and saving.[44] There is, therefore, the starkest contrast between the realm of history and the realm of God, between time and eternity; they are two utterly distinct worlds, and so as distinct they "touch" or "intersect" at only a point which is hidden to the world, "a tangent which touches the circle without touching it."[45] The relation of God to the world, then, aside from this "point," is negative: the judgment of the divine wrath on the world's sin and meaninglessness: "The whole world is the footprint of God; yes, but, insofar as we choose scandal rather than faith, the footprint in the vast riddle of the world is the footprint of His wrath."[46] Thus history is in Krisis: "an all-embracing dissolution of the world of time and things and men, before a penetrating and ultimate crisis, before the supremacy of a negation by which all existence is rolled up."[47] The modern sense of a totally "natural" or "creaturely" history containing no absolute, permanent or sacral elements is here utterly accepted. All here is exclusively temporal, relative, directionless and so in itself meaningless. Barth's view of history is the modern historical consciousness radically "secularized," i.e., stripped of every one of its elements of progressive meaning, and thus for him utterly separated from the redemptive activity of God.[48]

The appearance of redemption, of mercy, of hope—the gospel—is, therefore, not at all through the general processes of history; nor is it even an incarnation of the divine embedded substantively in a certain course of history. Rather, it appears as event (as a "tangent"). It is a moment in history in Jesus' death and resurrection that is not a moment in history and time, for it is hidden there; on the contrary, it is a moment in God's time and thus is it apprehended only by faith.[49] This redemptive event is the eschatological event, an event of eternity, transcending time and passage, and entering history vertically in order to manifest the ultimate future of God. The word "eschatology" here is thus by no means referent to an event in the temporal future, as in apocalyptic, in liberalism, or in the new "eschatological" theologies. Rather, centered in Christ, it breaks into every temporal moment "from above" and gives to each moment, and so to the history made up of such moments, their meaning.[50] Through a relation in faith to this event, through an understanding of the meaning of Christ alone, are the incomprehensible and tragic elements of history, the "nothingness" of the world, made comprehensible; only in Christ can the positive role of God in history in judging and in opening up possibilities of grace be seen. "We see sense in the nonsense of history."[51] But outside of Christ and his grace, all in nature and history, all in time, is only senselessness, evil and death, a world with no principle of redemption or of meaning within it, a world illumined but hardly transformed by the redemptive grace of God.

As is well known, Barth in his later *Dogmatics* modifies this antihistorical emphasis, if not the fundamental structure of his theology. God enters history in a much more decisive way,[52] and the gift of grace to mankind in history rather than the negation of history becomes the overriding theme. Thus in the *Church Dogmatics*, part 3, he proceeds to unfold an impressive doctrine of providence, God's sovereign lordship over the general course of history.[53]

Barth asserts in the strongest terms the sovereignty of God over all natural and historical events: a sovereign ordering that preserves, precedes, accompanies, follows and rules (i.e., directs toward God's goal the covenant community of grace) all creaturely occurrence.[54] Thus God's foreordination is the real basis for that order of natural events to which our scientific laws as human symbols point, and thus each free creature "can and does go only the same way as the free God."[55] On the other hand, Barth recognizes with his contemporaries the full autonomy and integrity of the creature of whatever level, and so he maintains that when God works with free creatures, he respects and does not suppress their freedom and autonomy. To sum up: "It [the creature] goes its own way, but in fact it always finds itself in a very definite sense on God's way"[56]—i.e., as the instrument of God's purpose of the covenant of grace. This divine ordering of the entire creaturely cosmos is, says Barth, essential since the covenant community appears within the general realms of nature and of history, is intertwined with those realms, dependent upon them and thus can be understood only as a part of those realms.[57] No creature has in itself, however, the capacity thus to be "an outward platform or theater" for the history of the covenant; nor can this capacity to participate in meaning be thought to stem from the creature's own use of its freedom. Thus, as in Augustine, the divine sovereign rule is necessary in order that the covenant of grace, and the Christian life within it, be possible in space and time: "It [creation] is not glorious in itself; it can become so only in the right hand of the living God. That He uses it in the service of His Kingdom; that He coordinates and integrates it with his work in this Kingdom; that He causes it to cooperate in the history of this Kingdom, this is the rule of His providence."[58]

Although, as is plain, the scope of this doctrine moves far beyond christology to God's relations with the whole universe, nevertheless in Barthian fashion it is christologically grounded and interpreted throughout. We believe in God's rule outside of the covenant because of Christ and we understand its goal in him. Further, God's rule in nature and history receives *its* meaning solely as establishing the "theatre" for Christ, for the covenant community devoted to him and for the salvation which arises from faith. Nature and history are given value only as they serve the eschatological event of salvation which is the Christ and as they make possible the faith of the covenant community.[59] Finally, when we seek to comprehend the character of this divine rule: in how far God is sovereign, in how far we are free, and even the "how" of God's causality, we use only the pattern of God's work in grace to answer these questions. Thus, while Barth uses very freely ontological and metaphysical terms, as he must, in his doctrine (power, cause, being, existence, etc.), he is careful always to define, understand and interpret them by analogy with the work of grace through Word and spirit, and thus in terms such as love, judgment, freedom, etc. "For the God who in Jesus Christ is active by His Word and Spirit reveals Himself as the One beside whom there is no other being or operation. And He Himself is the One who is and works only in the one way, who works always and everywhere as there revealed, and He does so even when He does not encounter us directly as in the history of the covenant of grace, in Jesus Christ, but is rather concealed and hidden."[60]

Barth's final picture of history is, therefore, that of a radically contingent, relativized and transient history preserved and ruled by God's will, and therefore a history that hiddenly and through its own "natural" processes accomplishes the divine eschatological purpose—as in all the theologians we have reviewed. This rule is effected in conjunction or cooperation with human freedom: together God and man freely will what comes to pass. The purpose of this sovereignty effective in nature and history is the creation and sustenance of the covenant community, the community where Christ is preached and faith is therefore born. In this sense, general history is subordinated to sacred history (if that is the best expression) and has no telos, no meaning or possibility of perfection or completion of its own. Set in biblical language and shaped by modern and not Hellenistic conceptions of history, Barth's view seems nevertheless to be remarkably parallel to Augustine's: the role of history as a conjunction of divine sovereignty and human freedom is to provide the theater for the *civitas dei,* now understood as the church of the Word.

Only in his view of evil does Barth substantively depart from Augustine. The evil with which redemption contends arises not, as in Augustine, from man's will and God's permission. Rather, its root lies in *das Nichtige* (as Augustine's view is—to me wrongly—often interpreted), in the "power" of nothingness.[61] This "nothingness" is neither created nor willed by God;[62] nor is it, as is sin in Augustine, produced by the creature, whom it has like a "usurper" and "tyrant" "assaulted, possessed and dominated."[63] This power of nothingness from which the unbelief, rebellion and death of history arise thus seems to emerge from nowhere, to be a queer kind of active non-being, almost a negative ontological principle, difficult either to conceptualize or even to set within the biblical framework. Most important for our purposes, *das Nichtige* is not conquered in time by history's movement into the future as in liberal theology or as in the political and liberationist theologies that have followed Barth. It is, rather, conquered by Christ in his incarnation, death and resurrection: for Barth says that the alien element of nothingness, though not part of the divine ordering, is "comprehended" in Christ by that ordering.[64] Thus is the creature in his eschatological existence freed from the nothingness that dominates him. History is, therefore, redeemed in Christ not in but beyond history, in and through the gospel proclaimed in the covenant community and obediently acknowledged in Christian faith. Thus it is the covenant community and the eschatological salvation it offers to faith that define the purpose of God's sovereignty and so constitute exhaustively the goal and inner, dynamic principles of history. As in Augustine, history has no meaning or principle of realization in itself; its meaning comes only from the eschatological covenant community it includes and manages through providence to preserve and foster.

Although he differs radically on many important theological issues from his contemporary Barth, Rudolf Bultmann's view of history and its relation to the gospel is in its fundamental shape similar to the one we have just described.[65] Like Barth Bultmann recognizes the relativity of history and the embeddedness of men and women in their own cultural epoch; this "historical consciousness," as he terms it, creates, of course, the problem of hermeneutics to the discussion of which Bultmann has so vastly contributed.[66] But historical consciousness so interpreted also means that we cannot possibly know the meaning of history as a whole. The meaning of any temporal existence is comprehended only at the end of that existence; with regard to history this entails that only at the end of history can its meaning be known. Thus, since we are embedded in time, the question of the meaning of history as a whole is a meaningless question for us.[67] Rather, meaning for humans in time concerns only the meaning of events for *their* existence, the meaning of the past for their own present and future. The specter of relativism is banished not by a totalistic progressive meaning of history generally, such as liberalism offered or Marxism offers, but only by the possibility that through responsible decision in the present each individual may integrate his retrieved past into an open and full future.[68] Again, the "ontology" of the modern historical consciousness is accepted. History is contingent, relative and transient; what is left out is the progressive character of history's process, with the result that history itself has no meaning and is again quite separated from redemption.

Following Heidegger, Bultmann holds that authentic human existence is constituted by decision, decision in relation to its own possibilities for the future and in the light of the limitations imposed by its own past. The future and the past are united in responsible freedom; thus does each moment potentially have "meaning," the meaning of an authenticity that brings past and future into the unity of a self-constitutive existence.[69] Such moments in which freedom enacts itself into existence provide the sole meaning and the sole unity which this history as a whole has. Thus the "subjects" of history are not groups, peoples or cultures, and the meaning of history is not resident in its general course. On the contrary, the true subjects of history are its individuals, not the race; the locus of the true meaning of history is in its individual lives;[70] and the fulfillment of history is accomplished for each when his or her inward freedom constitutes one's own existence in responsible decision for one's future.

For Bultmann Christianity addresses itself as an answer to this situation constituted by the historicity of man: that he must *be* in responsible and open decision for the future. The realization of such freedom, says Bultmann, is not a capacity of man in his present state; he is bound to his past by sin and thus unable to give himself up in freedom from that past. Thus this freedom to be itself, to be historical, must be given as a gift, a gift of grace that frees man from himself for his future. This gift is given in Jesus Christ, the eschatological event in and through which God speaks to us his Word of judgment and of grace, challenges us to decision and then sets us free to be human in history.[71] This event repeats itself in time whenever the gospel is preached and faith—and its new eschatological freedom—is born.[72] Redemption is an event that enters time "from above," redeeming and fulfilling each individual moment which encounters it and responds to it; redemption is not a process transforming or fulfilling history as a whole. The locus of this "meaning" is the covenant community where through preaching and responding faith this meaning is realized. As Bultmann sums up this view:

We have seen that man cannot answer this question as the question of the meaning of history in its totality. For man does not stand outside history. But now we can say: *The meaning of history lies always in the present,* and when the present is conceived as the eschatological present by Christian faith, the meaning of history is realized. . . . Do not look around yourself into universal history. You must look at your own personal history.

Always in your present lies the meaning of history, and you cannot see it as a spectator, but only in your responsible decisions. In every moment slumbers the possibility of being the eschatological moment. You must awaken it.[73]

With all its radical existentialism and its total lack of concern for God's providential rule over history, Bultmann's view is in many respects identical with that of Barth. History itself, as a story of social change among peoples, is meaningless, vacant of divine structures or of immanent divine purposes. Into this history has come the eschatological event freeing man from bondage to sin, meaninglessness and death through its offer of faith and obedient decision. The community in which that event is re-enacted through proclamation is the locus of "meaning" and "fulfilment" because it is the "place" in space and in time where eschatological faith is possible and salvation is given. It is this eschatological event that alone gives history meaning, for here alone is history related to God. In this sense, in comparison with the liberal theology that preceded, Christ and his Word have recaptured the central place from providence as symbols of the divine redemptive activity in history; the eternal now of faith has replaced temporal process as the locus in time of redemption; and "sacred history" has replaced general history as the realm in which God is primarily at work. God seems, moreover, to be effectively present only in his Word and so only in the church, and his eternal will seems only concerned with the growth of the latter. For the ultimate meaning of history, if any, is provided by the possibility within history of individuals becoming inwardly in personal decision members of the covenant community. Whereas in liberalism the covenant community (or as they called it, "the Christian religion") found its purpose and justification in providing the necessary grounds for the fulfillment of humanity and so of general history, here, in Barth and in Bultmann, this relation is just reversed. As in Augustine, history as a whole finds its meaning in the creation and sustenance (as a 'backdrop') of the covenant community. On this important issue vis-a-vis Christianity and history, contemporary eschatological theology, as we shall see, is firmly on the side of the liberals. Finally, in Krisis theology the only relevant relation to God comes not through the processes of social history but inwardly, individually, "privately." In comparison with the liberalism that preceded it or the political theologies that have followed it, the world to which dialectical theology is relevant—with all the transcendent grandeur and majesty of the views of deity here represented— seems to have shrunken immeasurably.

As is obvious, the view of the course of events in general history and its relation to God's activity represented by Barth and by Bultmann is in the sharpest contrast to that of the liberal theology that preceded it. Although both alike accept much from the modern historical consciousness, the presence of the theory of progress in the one and its total absence in the other makes all the difference. In dialectical theology, God works in history only inwardly through his Word of judgment and of grace in creating inner repentance, faith, decision and obedience; he does not work "outwardly" at all directing nature and social history to the fulfillment of their own intrinsic goal or goals.[74] What then are the causes for this sudden change in the theological assessment of history, for this sudden divine evacuation of the scene of history?

(1) Among the causes of this change, the first to appear historically was a radical change in the way the New Testament was understood with regard to the problem of history. Shortly after Ritschl constructed his theology on the conception of Jesus' kingdom as a future historical commonwealth to be built by the developing social, political, moral and religious forces of history, his son-in-law, Johannes Weiss, showed, quite to the contrary, that Jesus proclaimed a thoroughly eschatological kingdom which was to enter history suddenly through God's action, not to be built by and out of history.[75] A decade and a half later Albert Schweitzer continued this interpretation and established that the center of Jesus' teaching was the proclamation of an imminent end of history in the sudden appearance of the promised kingdom, a truly apocalyptic preaching which was not only incredible to modern ears but demonstrably false in its prophetic claims for the immediate future.[76] However certain the modern liberal churches might be about progress in history, it was now plain that a progressivist interpretation of the kingdom, finding its locus in the developments of general history, was *not* the message of the New Testament. As a result, from that point on an eschatological kingdom, interpreted in one way or another, rather than a developing kingdom would be central to theology. It is, however, significant that no fundamental shift in theology generally resulted from these changes in New Testament studies until after World War I in 1918—and so we are led to the second cause.

(2) The second, but to my mind the most important, change was the dissolution of the conception of historical progress due to the new and very deep consciousness of evil in twentieth-century historical life. In the First World War—despite the refinement of European culture and the moral idealism of that culture's self-understanding—Europe experienced the apparent self-destruction of this most modern and developed of societies in a prolonged and senseless bath of blood. In the Depression and its aftermath the West as a whole experienced the self-contradiction of its economic forms, and the consequent rise of fascist and communist totalitarianisms that dissolved the hard-won political freedoms of modernity. And in the Second World War, with its slavery, genocide and technology of ultimate destruction, the world experienced an eruption of technological and sophisticated evil: personal, political and social, unknown to history before. History seemed to manifest demonic regress not progress in the social, political and moral realms.

Ironically, it was precisely those areas where in fact there *was* cumulation in history, i.e., in knowledge, technology, industrial machinery and in the social unity they created—on which cumulative "model" the theory of progress has been built —that now appeared to be the instruments of destruction. Progress on some levels now seemed only to arm an intractable human evil more efficiently for the social, political and moral annihilation of humanity. It seemed the obvious lesson of current events that morals do *not* advance in history. Hence, a progress of technology may in fact augur a regress in social harmony and social justice; and thus all that is cumulative, instead of "saving" mankind, can threaten to become the demonic instrument of mankind's destruction. This permanent ambiguity of historical process, this continuation of sin even in an advancing culture, meant that if there be a kingdom, it could not be realized through a sociohistorical development leading to a perfect society in history. If God works in history at all, he cannot, therefore, work providentially through the developing social structures that have become self-destructive and so have produced *this* chaos. The dominant cause of the dialectical or Krisis theology was, therefore, the breakdown in the theory of progress, the loss of confidence in the development of civilization and the conviction that if there be meaning at all in historical life, it must be transcendent to history's developments in a God beyond immanence, and inward in existential appropriation where alone meaning could be found. When this sense of the moral and religious meaninglessness of the general course of history joined with the eschatological understanding of the New Testament referred to above, it produced the Krisis theology we have reviewed. In any case, it was the character of the experience of history of that generation that made the permanent ambiguity of history, the continuation of the reality of sin and so the transcendent character of any eschatological promises of the gospel central themes in almost every significant theology.

(3) Two other factors, inherited surprisingly from the new historical consciousness of the post-Enlightenment age and so from the liberals influenced by that consciousness, also contributed to the reticence or, perhaps, inability of the dialectical theologians to speak of God's providential work in general history. The first was the omnipresent (if unadmitted) "naturalism" of almost all neo-orthodox theologians, the respect for the sovereignty in their appropriate realms of the laws of nature as explanatory of all natural events. For most of them material events in nature (e.g., a flood, the presence of a fatal disease germ, the wind that directs a bomb) are caused by the material occasions that preceded them and by nothing else. They agreed that if we knew all these preceding natural influences, we would probably know all there is to know about why the event happened. Consequently, despite their more "orthodox" theologies, most reacted as negatively as did the liberals to the statement, made about an avalanche, a cancer or a plague: "It was God's will."[77] Because they recognized the relative autonomy of the casual nexus and because they wished to separate God's will from the "evils" of natural occurrence—both results of Enlightenment influence—these "neo-Reformation" theologians did *not* subscribe to the Reformation doctrine—illustrated classically in Calvin—that all that happens is the result of the inscrutable ordination of God's will. Consequently, any view of providence as active in natural history was as difficult for them as it seemed irrelevant to the way they interpreted the gospel.

The other main element of the new historical consciousness besides this respect for law was the emphasis on human autonomy, on man's freedom to be self-creative and so to be creative as "maker" of history. The existential philosophy which helped to inform dialectical theology represented, as we have noted, an extreme form of this emphasis on human autonomy. Thus, despite their insistence on the necessity of grace if freedom is to be free, the dialectical theologians as a whole also emphasized that man must respond to grace if he is personally to be transformed by it, that rather than overcoming or redirecting our freedom, grace calls us to personal decision for our own self-actualization in and through freedom.[78] Thus they gave to human autonomy an Arminian freedom over against God with regard to sin and to the reception of grace. Accordingly, they interpreted the events of history as the results of human not of divine decisions. Sin was a real rebellion against God that God did *not* will, and the evil events of history—for example, the events of Hitler's reign—arise, like destructive natural events, *against* the divine plan for history and not as aspects of it. Again, a proximate "dualism" between God and the history in which man lives appears.[79] This dualism preserved both the autonomy of creatures and the goodness of God, but it was one which made it difficult if not impossible for dialectical theology to explicate how God is sovereignly at work in and through the autonomy of mankind. Only in the inward, personal world of "existence," where God's Word meets the response and decision of faith, did it seem possible either imaginatively or conceptually to combine God's sovereign "action" with creaturely freedom.[80] Insofar as all twentieth-century theology shares this dual respect for the causal nexus and for human freedom, it has not been easy for any theology to understand how God *can* be involved in natural and social process.

(4) The last reason that theological discussion of God's providential relation to the general events of nature and of history virtually disappeared concerned theological method. The most important epistemological principle formative of dialectical or neo-orthodox theology was the principle of personal existential encounter. Revelation, it proposed, was not composed of facts about the world or facts about history set in propositional form; nor was it a matter merely of our own religious consciousness or feelings. Rather, revelation was the self-communication of God through his Word, a communication analogous to the communication of persons to one another in "personal encounter," and thus a communication received inwardly in repentance, faith and decision, a communication that transformed the self.[81] Or, as those theologians were inclined to put it, revelation knowledge is always, at once and at one and the same time, saving and transforming knowledge.[82] Thus, in this one existentialist principle were the problems of biblicism, of the conflict of science and theology and of the "subjectivism" of liberalism apparently dissolved. Consequently, in one way and another every dialectical theologian from Barth through Brunner and Bultmann, the Niebuhrs and Tillich, shared this position—though Barth, for a variety of reasons, sought to free himself from it.

One difficulty with this solution, however, was that it made it seemingly impossible to speak theologically about any relation of God beyond this personal encounter of faith without immediately "objectifying" theological discourse into either a deduction of a doctrine from biblical passages, as orthodoxy had done, or by using objectivist metaphysical categories. But God's relation to the processes of history—

and a fortiori to the processes of nature—are by definition outside these "personal" relations, whatever they may be, to the covenant community through his Word. Thus, if all that is known of God is not only known solely in faith but as a direct implication of the relation of faith, and consequently, if the only known presence of God in history is through his Word to the church, then nothing theological can be either known or affirmed of God's work in social process, and so of his providence —which, as Barth admitted, involves the relations of God to occurrences far beyond the covenant community.[83] Providence, and with it a theological account of social history, may be an article *of* faith; but except as an abstract affirmation,[84] it is not directly part of what is known through and in the personal encounter of faith.[85] Thus a theology confined in its explication to the inward relation to God of personal response to the Word inevitably found providence at best an abstract confession, a belief in a sovereignty that could hardly be made comprehensible, and at worst, a doctrine irrelevant to the inward, personal and so the "real" concerns of faith. The method, as well as the historical context, and as a consequence of both, the substance of much dialectical theology, therefore, led it inevitably to a private, inward domain unrelated to the processes of social history. This private, interiorizing, individualistic emphasis of neo-orthodoxy—despite that theology's concern for the covenant community—has provided the basis for the radical criticism this theology has suffered when a still "newer" view of history and its relation to theology appeared a decade or so ago.[86]

RECENT ESCHATOLOGICAL THEOLOGIES

The new theological consciousness that has dominated most constructive Christian thinking since 1960 was, in relation to both the liberalism and the neo-orthodoxy that preceded, utterly unexpected, a genuine "novum" as it would put it: a futurist eschatology that was oriented politically toward radical social change in the name of a historical kingdom to come! Thus it used the eschatological emphasis in the New Testament, which had been a factor in the destruction of liberalism by Krisis theology, in order to reinstate over against that same Krisis theology the liberal concern for history, for social change and for the reign of God in the future. As in liberalism, the kingdom was to come in the historical future, and this futurist eschatological promise is once more the center of the gospel—this was said against neo-orthodoxy. The coming kingdom, however, is not to appear developmentally, out of the past and present, but through God's action from the future—this was said in contradistinction to liberalism. Thus, while again history and its processes have reappeared as the center of the gospel, "the subject of the promise," it is (as in neo-orthodoxy) a history in crisis, in conflict and in revolution that is to be redeemed. God in his future will negate the sorry past and present and establish his new world. In a strange way, therefore, Weiss and Schweitzer are here united with Ritschl and the social gospel (an utterly improbable combination!) to dismantle the Krisis theology and to create an eschatological political theology that has done much to rejuvenate establishment theology in Europe and America, and even more to provide the one basis for the important liberationist and revolutionary theologies of the Third World, especially in South America.

While as always there were important theological and biblical reasons for the shift in theological consciousness represented by this movement,[87] most important, I believe, was once again the radical change in the historical situation within which this theology appeared. Neo-orthodoxy lost its faith in developments in history because it was evident that modern technology and liberal culture could produce out of itself "antibodies"—namely, the fascist and Stalinist communities that could destroy the liberal, democratic, humane world that had produced them. This potentiality of self-destruction, applied as a principle to universal history, meant that history did not in fact progress and thus had neither an intrinsic nor an extrinsic meaning. Nevertheless, since it was antibodies in the culture and not the liberal culture itself (which most of them defended against the antibodies) which represented history's "evil," they did not understand the gospel as directed precisely *against* contemporary liberal culture; thus both positively and negatively in relation to culture their theologies were *a*historical.

The postwar world, however, has experienced the problematic of modern culture even more radically. It became evident that the liberal technological culture of modernity not only could produce its own antibodies, but that it *itself*, in its essential structures, could become an antibody against humanization. No longer the embattled principle of liberation against totalitarianism, it had become itself the foe of liberation. For the dominant social problems of the 1950s, 60s and 70s were not caused by fascism and communism, nor were the victims the people and the institutions of liberal culture. On the contrary, it was the economically oppressive, the racist and the imperialistic character of liberal culture itself that created victims inside as well as outside that culture's borders: among the poor, among the Blacks, among the oppressed of the dependent "colonies" of economic neo-colonialism. Thus did much politics become revolutionary in its consciousness, and correspondingly theology became eschatological and even apocalyptic, both indicating a deep sense that established structures must no longer be so much defended and preserved as challenged, refashioned and, if necessary, overthrown. As is obvious in such a historical situation, history not the individual psyche becomes the central object of concern, the future not the sorry present the locus of meaning, and social hope rather than individual courage to be or "faith" the central description of Christian strength. Let us now look at the theological anatomy of this new interpretation of history as that anatomy appears in the theologies of its main leaders: Wolfhart Pannenberg, Jürgen Moltmann and Johannes Metz in Europe, Rubem Alves and Gustavo Gutierrez in South America, and Carl Braaten in America.[88]

1. The main negative critique shared by all of these men against their predecessors is their rejection of a privatized, individualistic theology of encounter, reconciliation and personal decision—to them a kind of existential "pietism" unconcerned with

social change in history.[89] Correspondingly, each theologian in this group emphasizes that the gospel concerns *history* and thus the social future of mankind. The
knowledge of God contained in Christian faith, the relation to God of which
Christianity speaks and the promises of God central to the gospel occur and are
realized neither inwardly in a private "epiphany" of faith and personal decision
unavailable to ordinary people, nor do they concern a special history transcendent
to ordinary, social history.[90] Rather, God manifests himself in and through the
public events of history, his promises concern the future of public history and so the
future of human society, and thus the primary relation of the Christian to God's
promises is not so much a personal, inward and existential faith in personal reconciliation as it is a steady hope in God's future that leads to outward political action
in the world. In this theology the concentration of the Christian is radically shifted
from one directed inward into one's own existence and upward to eternity, to a
concentration that looks outward into the world and forward into the future. Correspondingly, the gospel is conceived no longer as providing the adequate basis for a
renewed personal inner life, an individual courage to be in a senseless world; on the
contrary, it is now viewed as the sole sufficient ground for reforming and even
revolutionary public activity.[91] The telos of the gospel is not so much personal
decision and personal serenity as it is social praxis, not so much the inner transformation of the self as the outward transformation of the historical world. Clearly, there
is a very great deal in this reaction which is directly dependent on the modern
historical consciousness in its emphasis upon the potential goodness of historical life
and the possibility and the obligation of Christian concern to establish that goodness
through political and social action.

2. The objective social history which now constitutes the center of Christian
concern is understood *eschatologically.* By eschatological these men clearly do not
mean, as did the neo-orthodox, the event of the entrance of eternity or of transcendence vertically into time, to which faith and the personal decision of faith are the
response. Rather, to them eschatology has reference to the future of the world, as
in the apocalyptic and in the liberal traditions. Christianity is an eschatological
religion—and that is its absolute center[92]—because it proclaims the promises of
God for the human future and thus provides the hope for that future necessary for
creative worldly activity to help bring that future about. Thus, as in the apocalyptic
tradition, eschatology here refers to a future divine transformation of the world in
which the full rule of God will be manifest. Unlike the older apocalyptic, however,
this transformation is not extrinsic, sudden and at the end of time; rather it occurs
during the course of temporal history as the "divine future" acts on each successive
social present to make it more like the promised kingdom to come.

In effect, therefore, futurist apocalyptic eschatology has been redefined or "demythologized" in terms of the modern historical consciousness—much as in neo-
orthodoxy eschatology had been redefined or demythologized in modern existentialist terms. Instead of referring to a miraculous instant at the end of time, the

eschatological category has reference to the "moving horizon of the future";[93] that is, it refers to the continuing and determinating influence of the future on a history that is assumed to be—and to continue to be—proceeding into that future. Thus eschatology refers to and interprets *the continuing character of history;* it does not refer to and interpret the miraculous end of history. And the history that thus continues "eschatologically" is the history in large part as viewed by the modern historical consciousness: a unified, linear history in which human freedom and creativity are effective for the new, a history that is "open," and thus a history filled with hope for the future.

What differentiates these theologies from that modern consciousness, however, and the foundation for their claim to be biblical, is that for them these elements of the modern consciousness, namely, the unity, the freedom, the openness and the hope of history are possible and intelligible only within the biblical eschatological framework.[94] It is because of the ultimate or eschatological character of that future that impinges on and determines the moving present, that history is radically opened to the new and not imprisoned by necessities derivative from the past. And because the eschatological future is God's future, that social future is to be characterized by the divine promise of ultimate fulfillment. Thus the divine future impinges upon every present to "pull" it away from the old, into something radically new and so ultimately toward God's promised kingdom.

Or, as Pannenberg puts it, "In every event the infinite future separates itself from the finite event which until then had been hidden in the future but now released into existence. . . . Thus does the future determine the present."[95] The eschatological future impinges on every historical present, determining its possibilities and so its form, and thus is the course of history created ("mastered" or "determined") by its ultimate future and so by the God of that eschatological future.[96] Theology is, therefore, eschatological and futurist at its core, because the gospel is constituted by the promise of God for the future, and that promise is to be fulfilled by the God of the future—by the impact of the eschatological future on the moving course of history.

Consequently, this theology, as fundamentally eschatological, has pivoted the basic axis of Christian thought and concern from a *vertical* axis relating time and eternity, creatureliness and transcendence, into a *horizontal* axis relating present and future, a godless world of the now with a God whose "being is future." In this fundamental shift it resembles liberal theology, but the mood and the language are different because the relation to the present cultural world is so different. Thus every classic Christian symbol—theology being eschatological—is understood in terms of the dialectic of present and future, and thus faith as a relation to the transcendent God is replaced by hope as a relation to the promises of God for the future.[97] A second important characteristic of this futurist eschatology is its radical negation of the present order of the world, a negation that has, of course, very important political consequences. God is not the God of the present, he who created and upholds the present order of things. Rather, he is the God of the future kingdom when his rule will be effective and manifest. Thus his ultimate future is in radical opposition to the evil present; and thus that future impinges on the present to negate it, to transform it, to bring in something radically new and in opposition to the old. In stark contradiction to the Aristotelian tradition and in relative opposition even to Whitehead, the new does not arise out of the old as a possibility latent within it; the new comes, on the contrary, from the future and thus even as an "impossibility" for the present situation.[98]

As the future eschatological fulfillment is for this theology the center of the gospel, so the fundamental tension within that gospel is a *temporal* one between past and present on the one hand and God's future on the other—not the traditional *vertical* contrast between time and eternity, or immanence and transcendence. In praxis this means that to be committed to the eschatological future of God is to be against the present power structure of the world, to be for the oppressed, the suffering and the outcast and to be involved in the revolutionary struggle for liberation from all that in the present binds and shackles mankind.[99] Despite its liberationist emphasis on history and the future kingdom, therefore, contemporary eschatological theology is by no means developmental or progressivist, seeing the kingdom growing through the continuation and expansion of trends in past and present. This theology sees the advent of the kingdom coming through the negation of the present by its opposite, the future of God, and so proximately in political life through activity that is more revolutionary in character, or at least radically reformist, than gradualistic. In sum, history is here understood eschatologically in two important and modern senses: (a) God as the ultimate future determines and masters from the future every present toward the ultimate goal of history, his kingdom, and (b) that determination or mastery appears as the negation of the dominant structures of the present and thus implies a political stance of radical reform or possibly of revolution.

3. Human nature, its problems and their ultimate resolution are likewise understood on a temporal axis, in relation primarily to past and to future rather than, as in neo-orthodoxy, to transcendence. Men and women achieve fulfillment through their freedom, and realized freedom is here characterized as "openness to the future," a freedom from bondage to past structures, past securities, past loyalties and prejudices.[100] Correspondingly, sin is equivalent to bondage to our own past and its seeming certainties and stabilities. Sin is not so much what we do in anxiety with our open future as in, say, Reinhold Neibuhr's thought, as it is a bondage to the past that closes the future from all creativity and the new. Politically, this view of sin and of free self-realization implies "liberation," the freeing of men and women *from* the oppressive social structures inherited from the past and *for* self-determination.[101] In fact, the gradual rise and appearance of such self-determination is regarded as a major clue to the eschatological purposes of God in history,[102] as the creation and encouragement of self-determination is by implication the central mission of the church.[103] Thus, since essentially a "good" humanity is defined as freedom from

the past and for the future, the achievement of such freedom for the future is equivalent to the conquest of sin, is unambiguous in its results and can almost be equated with salvation. For this reason, in a good number of these theologies liberation from past forms of bondage on all essential levels of life—economic, political, racial, social and personal—is a major meaning of the salvation that is promised by the gospel.[104] Interestingly, much as in Ritschl, a liberated society is the goal both of humanity's search for self-realization and of the activity of God in history, and thus in Christian service for the kingdom we unite the vocation or calling of a fulfilled human with that of the committed Christian. As in liberalism, salvation here is *historical* in the sense that a perfected history, i.e., a liberated society, is regarded as one of the main elements of the promise of God for the future.

4. As is already evident, God is here interpreted *eschatologically*. This means, first of all, that as eschatological God is not the God of the present, the one who is "beneath" us or "above" us, the sovereign and unconditioned lord of the past and present and so one available to be known as God through his present works.[105] Such a "theistic" God of the present is, for all of these thinkers, that which calls forth the rightful atheistic protest against God. Such a sovereign lord of the present is on the one hand the cause, if he be sovereign, of the evils of the present; and on the other, as ordainer of all, he is the enemy of human freedom and of an open history.[106] The future being of God and the fact he acts from the future resolves, for these theologians, the powerful question of theodicy, of an almighty lord of this miserable historical present: God's full being and rule are for us promises to be hoped for in the future, not present realities, believed against all the facts, as essential, if hidden aspects of the present. Thus does the category of providence, God's sovereignty in the past and present as well as in the future, seemingly vanish from this theology even more than it did from neo-orthodoxy, although for vastly different theological reasons.

Secondly, the eschatological interpretation of God means that he is the "power of the future."[107] As the power of the future, God, as we noted, masters and determines each present by representing the ultimate future of that present, and so, since the future in history determines the present, giving to that present its form and shape. This "reverse causality" (i.e., that causes come in from the future) characteristic of this theology is not made clearer by Pannenberg's difficult language: "God in His powerful future separates something new from itself and affirms it as a separate entity; thus, at the same time relating it forward to Himself."[108] As the power of the future God masters the present, and through that mastery we can have confidence that God's future will in fact be realized in history.[109] And yet, as we are here assured, this mastery of the present necessary for our hope and confidence in the future, does not threaten either our freedom or the openness of that future; in fact, it is its sole guarantee and ground.[110]

Finally, the eschatological interpretation of God entails that "His being is future" or "the future is the mode of His being." By this is meant that God's being is intrinsically related to history, that therefore God's being and his manifest rule or actualized sovereignty in history are one, and so, thirdly, that only in the future eschaton when God's power and glory are manifest "on earth as in heaven" will God's being "be" or "be realized" in that fullest sense.[111] Thus God's being and the eschatological future of the world, the kingdom of God, are strictly identified: "God in His very being is the future of the world."[112] The rule of God, God's full self-realization, and the future of social history—a liberated society—will, therefore, coalesce in the eschatological future. A "perfectionist" view of history as culminating in the realized kingdom could hardly have clearer expression. Thus again, social and political liberation, the building of the kingdom in history, and eschatological salvation, the rule of God (and even the fullness of the being of God), are identified. On the deepest level eschatology here implies a *political* theology of social liberation as the way in which history will realize the essential nature of God. As God in this deep sense is eschatological, so history itself is eschatological: a process that is to be completed at its end when God's rule will be manifest. The meaning of history is thus the future achievement of this goal, and so that meaning is eschatological in that sense. Again, as in liberalism salvation is historical, the achievement of a perfect human society in time and space.

Like the liberalism of the nineteenth century, therefore, the new eschatological theologies are oriented essentially to the social future as the future of liberation and human self-realization, when through God's eschatological activity history and the kingdom will be united. Although, as in liberalism, all identify salvation with *more* than historical progress, i.e., as also the conquest of death, nevertheless, very much like Ritschl, the achievement of a liberated society (or the rule of God) is the immediate center of the promise of the gospel.[113] Among themselves the largest differences on the issue of the character and direction of history seem to lie in the different ways they understand christology and its relation to history. For Pannenberg and the Moltmann of *The Theology of Hope,* the revelation in Jesus is largely proleptic, a sign of the promise of God for the future.[114] Thus the divine activity which is to bring the kingdom and history together is not so much an active presence in Jesus and the church he established as it is the promise through Jesus of an activity in and for the future, namely, the eschatological activity of God from the future. In the Catholic theologians on the other hand, the historical activity of God centers in the incarnation as a creative presence of God accepting the world and in that acceptance forming the kingdom.[115] Correspondingly, there is an emphasis not only on the church as a community of people living and acting politically in hope for the promised future but also on the church as "the sacrament of history" making visible the presence of grace within history and so history's future and ultimate meaning.[116] Significantly, for none of them (except possibly for Alves[117]) is the category of the divine providence (God's purposive work in the world at large) at all important in their comprehension of the divine activity in history. That category seemed apparently too closely associated either with an orthodox ordination of all the evils of present history or with liberal developmentalism to be useful to these theologians reacting against both orthodoxy and liberal progressivism. Thus, with the exception of Alves, God seems to work in history either solely eschatologically from the future, or solely incarnationally through Christ and the church—and of course through the political good works of committed Christians. Whether this is or can be a sound basis for political theology and for an understanding of the meaning of historical process in an era in which Christian triumphalism has long since become untenable, is a question we must raise in subsequent chapters.

Meanwhile, it is through these eschatological theologians that the questions of history and so of political and social praxis have become central again to Christian reflection. Our world is in the process of radical change; many of the world's political and economic structures are desperately unjust and destructive. Consequently, the future that impinges on us is fraught both with promise and with menace; its character, its possibilities and its ultimate meaning are matters of "ultimate concern," of deep religious moment for all humans. To have recentered our theological concentration on history and the future, and on the divine participation in the task of liberation from the oppression and bondages of the present—in effect, to have sounded once again the call of the social gospel—has been of the greatest significance for theology and the church, and for this we are all in their debt.[118] There are, however, major problems with the theological framework within which this interest in liberation, in social change and in the character and destiny of history has been expressed. In their own way, these eschatological views of history and of God's relation to it are as one-sided as were the liberalism and the neo-orthodoxy that preceded them. This framework must, I believe, be transformed if a viable Christian understanding of history, its possibilities and its meaning, is to be achieved. I shall carry on this critique and reformulation in the chapters that follow; meanwhile here I shall mention two broad areas in which such problems arise: (1) the problem of the notion of God as future in his being, and (2) the problem of the identification, or near identification, of salvation with political and social liberation.[119]

1. As we have seen, central to the uniqueness of these theologies has been the interpretation of all theological symbols eschatologically, i.e., in relation to the ultimate future. This means that God, his relation to the world and his activity in it are also understood eschatologically, as future and "coming from the future." God, we are told, is not the God of the present, the ground of its being nor the source of its form or character, of its trends or continuities; rather, his being is future, his activity in history comes from the future, and thus he is in opposition, if not in contradiction, to our present rather than creative of it. Clearly, the grounds for this novel view of God (besides the fact it is, or purports to be, eschatological) are that such a view seems to resolve the objections which atheism has raised against Christian faith, namely, that if there be a God of the present, then he is responsible for evil, and, at the same time, there can be no reality to human freedom or openness to history. In mastering the present from the future a future God seems to provide

a basis for hope for the future without becoming either the author of present evil or a threat to man's freedom and possibility. My argument, however, is, first, that this movement of God out of the present into the future solves neither of these atheistic objections, and, secondly, that in fact it raises its own grave difficulties both for theology and for political theory.

(a) To move God quite out of the present into the future—as the God who "is not in us or over us but always before us"[120]—is to divest present experience of any relation at all to the divine, much as Barthian dialectical theology did, only now on a temporal axis into the future rather than on a vertical axis into the transcendent.[121] Thus the present in human experience (and that, after all, is the only human experience there is) is left totally "secular," a present devoid of any experience of the divine except for the continuing "questionableness" of the present and an unaccountable pull toward the future. Two serious objections arise in relation to this temporal version of a radical neo-orthodoxy. Theological language has meaning— even if its reference be to the future—only in relation to dimensions of present experience. Thus, if our experience be void of any experience of ultimacy, which is for Christian faith an experience of the presence of God in and to our being, then theological language (even eschatological language) has no experiential component to its meaning; there is no aspect of our experience which these symbols shape into creative form and thus these symbols are to us void of meaning.[122] Secondly, our analysis showed social and political experience to be characterized by a dimension of ultimacy and man as a social and political being to reveal himself to be in constant relation to that ultimacy. Again, if God be solely future, and not also the God of our present, this "religious" dimension of social and political experience fundamental to that experience—as well as the mythical and the demonic elements of politics itself—become unintelligible and irrelevant, and theological language loses its intrinsic touch with social and political reality.

(b) To move God from the present to the future does not resolve either the problem of the evil of the present (the theodicy question) nor that of freedom and the openness of history if—as here—God "acts from the future" and from the future "determines or masters the present." If we assume that causality runs from past through present to future—as in our ordinary conceptions—then, to be sure, a God of the future is neither responsible for the present nor does he determine what we do in history. But, according to the same view of causality, such a future God would be ineffective in a history determined by causality from the past; as future he would be the *product* of history's causality and not its lord (as, for example, in the conception of deity in Samuel Alexander or of the consequent nature of God in Whitehead). But if important causality runs, as here, from future to present, then it is precisely a God of the future that is responsible for the present, and it is precisely from the future that our freedom in the present is or can be threatened, especially if God's future is seen to "decide what becomes of the present."[123] The claim, therefore, of the eschatological theologicans to resolve the problem of God's relation to present evil and to preserve the freedom and openness of each future by means of a God of the future depends on precisely the older view of causality which eschatological theology has explicitly rejected. Furthermore, this theology affirmed God's effective causality from the future precisely in order, against Bloch, to provide a ground for our hopes for the future. Only, said they, if God masters the present from the future and thus determines the character of our future, can there be grounds for hope. But if God is to master every future, has he not also mastered *all* futures, even those of the past and the present, and thus been responsible, as was any "theistic" God, for all that has happened in history? Like many theologies that preceded it, eschatological theology too is in danger of resolving the problem of the meaning of history (God's mastery of the present from the future) at the expense of God's goodness and man's freedom—only it does all this "from the future" whereas the others did it from the divine eternity. The problems of theodicy, of human freedom and of the goodness of the future are not, therefore, matters of *tense* to be resolved by moving God into the future—*if* the future is said to master the present. These issues can be resolved only by rethinking ontologically the way the God of the present acts in relation to human freedom and to the possibilities of the future, i.e., by an explicitly ontological doctrine of the self-limitation in every present of the divine power in relation to the freedom of the creature.

(c) Political action of any sort, liberating or conservative, deals with the possibilities latent in the present historical and social situation, realizing those latent possibilities in effective action. Political action, in other words, subsists within and depends upon the fundamental ontological structure of temporal being, namely, the polarity of destiny and freedom, action toward the future based upon and projected from the given in structures, trends and symbols from the past. Freedom at best shapes the given into new patterns; it cannot create the latter out of whole cloth. Unless possibilities are "there" within the given, therefore, located as possible in the structures of that present—though they be latent and by no means dominant—then no *new* in history can be established or even begun by present political actions. The conditions for the new in time must be an inheritance from past and present if that novel reality is to be created by freedom. Both Marx and Bloch are clear on this point.[124] Thus, in any political understanding of history and even more in an effective revolutionary one, the relevant ideal for the future cannot be understood as *utterly* new, as a *creatio ex nihilo* out of the future, as totally unrelated to the latent forces or conditions of past and present. Even the most apocalyptic revolution can but appear out of the contradictions and problems, the frustrations and the possibilities of the present—as in Marx the communist ideal appears only out of the dialectical tensions and developments of the capitalistic past and present. If then the new political possibilities are to be *theologically* understood, and understood in relation to our political action, as in all these theologies, they must be understood in relation to the hidden work of God shaping the conditions of the past and the present, as well as his eschatological activity negating what has been and is. That is to say, they must be understood in relation to God's providential activity in continuing history as well as his eschatological activity from the future. A God of the future acting only from the future, and so negating the inheritance from the past, provides no theological ground for the creative union of destiny and of freedom which is the basis for human political action amidst the possibilities developing out of the past and so latent in the social situation of the present. If politically we must work with the possibilities of the present, yet if we conceive that God acts eschatologically "against" these possibilities, and solely from the future, then in no intelligible way can our political action be united with our theological understanding.[125] For these reasons, an exclusively eschatological view of God as God of the future and not of the past and present creates insoluble problems for both the theological and the political sides of a political theology.

2. The second major problem of the eschatological theologies is the apparent *identification* of liberation and especially of political and social liberation with the salvation promised in the gospel. This is expressed through the identification of the eschatological kingdom with a perfect historical society, a fully just political and social reality. Such an identification of salvation with the achievement of political and social self-determination, the liberation of men and women from the oppression of other wills, forgets that self-determination is the ground not only of the fullest humanity but also of sin—for it is in our use of our *freedom* that we each sin against our neighbor. The most fundamental problem of history is not only that some men oppress others—though that is a vast problem; it is that each of us in our use of our own freedom creates suffering for others and for ourselves. In the terms of our previous discussion (Chapter 2), the basic problem of historical existence is not fate —the loss by human beings of the possibility of self-determination; rather, it is sin, the corruption of their freedom—for fate as a category of historical being arises from sin, fate is the character of history enacted by sinful human beings. It is the *corruption* of freedom in ourselves, not the enslavement of our freedom to others, that represents the most basic issue of history.[126] Thus the "freeing of freedom" in human society, even if it were to be achieved, and however valid a political and a Christian goal it may be, would by no means represent the final redemption of mankind or of history: for it is in freedom that we all sin. The freeing of freedom, liberation, achieves the conquest of the *consequences* of human sin in history (i.e., fate) and so—let us repeat—is an essential aspect of Christian concern and action. Nevertheless, it does not represent the conquest of the sin itself out of which fate and fatedness continually arise. Only a new relation of mankind to God, to self and to the neighbor can achieve that goal, an achievement far beyond the range of political activity.

By the same token, no level of political achievement, no "freeing of freedom," could prevent the reappearance of the injustice, the domination and the oppression which follow from it, because the latter follow precisely from freedom, albeit a freedom misused. In the long run, warped social structures are *consequences* not causes of human greed, pride, insecurity and self-concern which in turn flow from the exercise of freedom, not its oppression. We all sin in history with our freedom, not without it; thus the freeing of freedom frees us for sin as well as for good works, for the creation of injustice as well as the creation of justice. Political action is of tremendous Christian importance because it can reduce the suffering that sin causes and it can free men and women to actualize their power—if we will. But as the history of democracy shows, greater self-determination does not guarantee greater freedom from sin. After all, present oppressors are precisely those who have in the past been "liberated."[127]

The qualitative opposition between sin and grace is more fundamental in the Christian interpretation of history than is the opposition between unliberated and liberated, oppressed and oppressors, and a fortiori more fundamental than the temporal opposition between past and future within history. The largest error of the eschatological theologies, therefore, is to overlook the ambiguity of actual freedom, to make the temporal opposition between past and future fundamental, and to see the future in terms solely of redeemed freedom and the past solely as sin.[128] Both individual and historical experience show that "where there is history at all there is freedom, and where there is freedom there is sin."[129] If then human freedom continues, and with it the possibility and actuality of sin, some other dimension of meaning in history is necessary besides that of the liberation of human freedom, for such liberation, important as it is, does not resolve history's most fundamental problem, the use we make of our freedom. A Christian understanding of history is, therefore, different from a secular one not only because of its affirmation that God supports the historical process of liberation; even more it is unique in its affirmation of the grace of forgiveness, reconciliation and of new possibility that God gives to the continuing waywardness of liberated humans.[130]

One final word on contemporary futurist eschatology is called for. Any theology, including our own, which takes history seriously as relevant to the promises of the gospel is going to have immense difficulties with the ecological crisis as we have portrayed that crisis. Seen as accurately as it can be seen from our present, the future in the light of that crisis seems at best bleak and at the worst catastrophic. At the least, it appears to entail greater want, overcrowding, vastly increased controls over every aspect of life and therefore more centralized authority with a great deal less self-determination. At best, such a society might incarnate more justice and equality than does our own. There could be impressive values latent here, as we shall later argue; but there is little question that the goal of liberation as presently formulated seems, in the light of this prospect, to be even more utopian vis-à-vis this necessarily controlled future than it does vis-à-vis the unequal past. And with the picture, seemingly inescapable, of a more difficult social situation in the future, more perilous with regard to values of any sort because more threatened by want, by crowding and by possible extinction, it is well nigh impossible honestly to view the future as the realm of light as opposed to the past as the realm of dark, and to understand God's rule and even his being solely in terms of the future unequivocal manifestation of his will on earth. Christian faith does, and must, provide a hopeful answer to this deep despair about future time latent in the ecological crisis. But surely in the light of that crisis our hope cannot be based *simply* on a theological answer to a historical problem, namely, that despite all the social evidence and because of the divine promise, the future will manifest a perfectly liberated society. A valid Christian hope for history cannot be a hope in a miracle, even an eschatological miracle. It must be grounded on God's action in and through history, in and through given destiny, its possibilities and the possibilities of our freedom. Since each of these will remain suffused with ambiguity, it must contain other dimensions of meaning than those represented by utopian expectations.

We have in this chapter surveyed three quite different responses of modern theology to the historical consciousness of the post-Enlightenment world, each one influenced by a different assessment of history and its movement into the future. We have found liberalism affirming the obvious developments of history as the work of the providence of God; the neo-orthodox ignoring history as in itself meaningless in favor of *Heilsgeschichte*, a sacred history peculiar to the covenant people, transcendent to the ordinary course of history and unconcerned with the goals or the outcome of that course; and the eschatological theologians again affirming the promised future perfection of history through the action of God from the future. In some essential aspect each has been found wanting; each finally let the mystery of history as a creative and yet ambiguous union of destiny and freedom escape from rather than inform its interpretation. Perhaps the reason is that each emphasized one theological symbol to the exclusion of others. For liberalism providence provided the sole clue to the meaning of history; for neo-orthodoxy it was christology; and for the contemporary political theologies it has been eschatology. Possibly, therefore, a union of all of these symbols—providence, christology and eschatology in combination—will provide a better theological clue to the mystery of history.

10

PROVIDENCE AND ESCHATOLOGY:
A REINTERPRETATION

We stand, I have said, in the midst of a rupture in history, a moment of vast change explicit and pending outside, implicit and necessary inside. We are driven by the radical change around us to historical consciousness, to consciousness of the future and to acting politically. We need symbols of ultimacy with which these intense reactions and perilous ventures into the unknown can be illumined, channelled, strengthened and tempered. We need credible grounds for repentance and hope, and guides for creative action.

Our age calls for a philosophy of history or a theology of history—just at the moment when its secularity combined with its felt (if not yet explicated) despair make either one difficult and rare. Further, none of the recent theological options, portrayed in the last chapter, seems to fit either our situation or our experience of history. The nineteenth-century view of God's action as exclusively providential, a progressive world government leading through the gradual development of modern society to the kingdom, had far too little sense of the catastrophic in history, and of the nemesis facing that culture itself—and so too little place for the radically new, be it menacing or promising. The neo-orthodox view that there is no meaning to the general course of history did not understand the historicity of man in its fullest extent[1] and had too little grounds for historical hope. The current eschatological theologies, which see God's action as solely from the future, gave God too little relation to the present worlds of history and of political life, and express too little appreciation of the continuities in history that make the appearance of the new, even a revolutionary new, possible.

Since none of these options taken exclusively fits the experience of history and of political life that has been ours, or encompasses what I take to be the full extent of the gospel, they must be redefined, and redefined in relation to each other. In this redefinition, we shall seek to view history in the light not only of providence, not only of christology and the covenant community, or not only of eschatology, but in terms of all three together, each taken as helping to define the others. We shall draw largely on several sources in part already explicated: our experience of ultimacy

239

in historical-political life; our contemporary and well-nigh unavoidable ways of viewing the history in which we are immersed, as expressed in the modern historical consciousness and especially in modern ontologies; and, most important, the eidetic meanings of the biblical and classical symbols themselves as we can understand and appropriate them in our situation. The warrants for the theological interpretation here presented are, I believe, three: (1) the implications of the ontological structure of history here derived which seem to call for a transcendent or divine reality in which process is grounded and through which possibility is related to given actuality; (2) the adequacy of the view here presented to the experienced character of history in its creativity, its tragedy and its ineradicable hope; and (3) the experiences within the ambiguity of history of ultimacy, of order, of creative possibility, of estrangement and of the reality of redemptive grace on which such an interpretation is in the end based.

In this chapter I shall be largely concerned with providence, God's continuing action in our common life, in the general history in which we live. In our study of the views of providence of Augustine and Calvin we found certain themes common to both men which serve to define this concept as it has appeared in the tradition. It is these themes, sharpened by a new look at the biblical understanding of God's action in history, that we shall seek here to redefine or reexpress in terms of the modern consciousness of history and the role of men and women within it.

These elements of the classical concept were: (1) representing the sovereignty of God over history, the activity of God's providence was controlled, directed and defined by God's eschatological goal. (2) The work of providence concerned itself with the external or "objective" events, both natural and historical, cosmological and social, amidst which men and women lived in time. (3) Because of providence there was no fate in historical experience; rather, the purpose of providence, and so the ultimate goal of history, was the establishment and so the freeing of freedom—the transformation for all men and women of fate into destiny. (4) God does not work in history as an external cause but in and through the creaturely forces and dynamic factors of history. (5) Thus providence works through not against human freedom; it is, therefore, not contradicted by man's sin but made necessary because of sin— if the eschatological goal is to be reached. Of course, as our analysis of Augustine and Calvin made plain, these themes in the classical doctrine were set within the framework of the absoluteness, changelessness and omnipotence of God, and of his consequent foreknowledge and foreordination of all events. And they were directed at an exclusively suprahistorical rather than also a historical interpretation of eschatology. Our effort will be to reinterpret them in the light of the modern historical consciousness which we share, and so to modify, if not dissolve entirely, these latter "orthodox" elements of the conception. Our success may in part be judged by the coherence with which these five traditional themes are expressed in terms congruent with the ontology of the modern consciousness of history: of temporality, of order, of freedom and of novel possibility. To do this with theological integrity, however, we must now turn directly to the biblical notions of God's action in history and seek to work our way onward from there.

The theologian concerned with providence receives very little help from modern New Testament studies. There providence is at best a waif and a stepchild.[2] Conceptions of God's rule in the world are by no means absent from either the teachings of Jesus or that of Paul.[3] Nevertheless, the symbol of providence has in our day been almost entirely eclipsed by concern with the eschatological elements of the New Testament, as realized, or beginning to be realized in Jesus, and as coming in the future, or a combination of the two.[4] The activity of God in present history is, however, an absolutely central theme of the Old Testament, as Gerhard von Rad has newly made plain to us in his great work on Old Testament theology.[5] Our argument with regard to this dilemma, within which providence, while central in the Old Testament, almost appears totally displaced by eschatology in the New, is that as New Testament proclamation presupposes the history, the covenant, the law, the prophetic word and the expectations of the Hebrew people, so the eschatology of the New Testament presupposes the creative and providential activity of God portrayed in the Old. Just as the New Testament does not displace but builds upon, completes and fulfills the Old, so eschatology does not replace but depends on and completes God's providential work in history.

As von Rad has indicated, the main object of witness and reflection in Hebrew faith was God's work in and through history, the political history, in fact, in which Israel was immersed,[6] a history which begins and culminates on a universal scale, as world history.[7] Of course, as has often been pointed out, the formal structure of this divine activity in and through Israel's history is constituted by the word of promise—or of judgment—and the fulfillment of that word; and the special subject of this history is Israel. In this sense, after the tower of Babel, the work of God thus concerns a special history, *Heilsgeschichte*, the history of God's relationships with Israel, and not ordinary social history, the history of all men everywhere.[8] Nevertheless, the necessary presupposition lying back of the divine promise—or word of warning—and its fulfillment was God's hidden work in Israel and among the nations, an activity which was essential in bringing the word of promise or of judgment to fulfillment.[9] Even more significant, it was plain that whenever Yahweh's hidden work in general history was *too* hidden, too paradoxical, too elusive for the ancient promise still to be believed and counted on—as for example, in the rise of Assyria and in the Babylonian Captivity[10]—then the deepest questions about the purposes of Yahweh, and the most creative new answers of the Old Testament about those purposes arose. The Old Testament, then, has as one of its central themes the purposive sovereignty of God in and through the baffling, changing, upsetting, threatening and creative events of historical and political life. It is, therefore, legitimate to look for clues to our own understanding of history and of providence there, for surely we too sense history as baffling, changing and upsetting, and yet as having some elusive thread of meaning. As we have seen in our analysis of political experience, we act politically because history is baffling, changing and upsetting, and we are enabled to act politically because we perceive and affirm a thread of meaning in history with which our political actions may make union. Insofar, however, as the other central theme of the Old Testament is the special relation of God to Israel and not to history generally, and in the Old Testament the divine concern is apparently with Israel's history alone, the Old Testament can provide us at best only with *analogical* symbols with which to understand, in our own terms, the general course of the history in which we live.[11]

MODERN HISTORICAL CONSCIOUSNESS AND THE SOVEREIGNTY OF GOD.

It is not so hard to assert the sovereignty of God in our own history—though even this is rare among modern theologians. But it *is* difficult to believe it, and even more difficult for us in our time to know and express reflectively what we might mean by it. What does it mean, or might it mean, in relation to our experience of history, to our politics?[12]

The traditional view of the divine providence spoke of God's sustaining and ordaining work in history: the preservation of the creatures God had brought into being; the sovereign ordination of the forms of life, economic, political and social; finally, the sovereign ordination of the intentions and acts that the creatures achieved and of the events which they underwent.[13] Here, let us note, is the model of the omnipotent ruler of past, present and future against which most of modernity has violently reacted. The names of these objectors are multiple and honored, honored, that is, by most of *us*. And this is because much of what they said against the model of an absolute divine sovereignty has formed the sensibilities and the fundamental viewpoints which we all, whether we will or no, share. This notion of the absolute determiner of all events, good and evil, is not, as some maintain,[14] the cause of the "death of God" in our time—our wider secular spirit is surely the cause of that cultural demise. But it is certainly true that this view more than any other is the cause of the *rejoicing* over that death which is also an aspect of our time. This concept of the all-determining sovereign of past and present events runs counter to almost every facet of the modern consciousness of history. Thus, even theologians struggle and evade in order to assert it, rather than straightforwardly propounding it as the classical theologians did; *or* they quietly refuse to deal with the issue of sovereignty in general history; or, as in the futurists, they roll God out of the present into the future. This latter move, however, does not help—as we remarked—if the future being of God "masters the present" and thus seems to cause from in front rather than from behind or from above whatever woes we now suffer from!

Specifically, the classical view in this absolutist form is hard for us because it defies our engrained sense of history and of ourselves, the modern historical consciousness as we have portrayed it. To sum up our discussion of this point: (1) The modern consciousness, and we ourselves, are saturated by the sense of the *contingency* of events; that they are not necessary or determined from eternity, that they may or may not be, depending on the other contingent events in their context. Thus are they to be understood and interpreted "naturalistically" in terms of their relations to the other finite factors surrounding them, which were also contingent. This naturalistic or contextual interpretation of events is compatible with an understanding of historical causality either in terms of immanent laws or trends, or of human intentions.[15] It is *not* compatible with an understanding of events as transcendently ordained or caused from eternity (or from the future). Only if events are in this sense contingent, dependent on their own immediate past and present context and their own contingent reaction to that context, is the future open and genuine freedom possible; an understanding of creaturely events as genuinely contingent is the sole base for the reality both of creaturely logos and of creaturely freedom. (2) We are also convinced of *the relativity* of all that appears on the surface of history and so of every form of historical life. We know that everything in process arises out of its context, its "destiny," and therefore that nothing here—a political institution, a church, a creed, a document, an idea (even a political viewpoint)—is absolute, unrelated to its context and so subject to no change. All arise in their place and time and are, in every aspect of their being, relative to that context. Thus none is absolute or sacred in itself, so none can be conceived, even by faith, as the clear result of a divine ordination. (3) We also sense the *transience* of all that is, the movement of everything from possibility to actuality, and to "having been." Thus does all pass away, even our most cherished institutions and ideas (and thus possibly even this theological model is transient!). Again, nothing in history is eternally ordained, direct choices of the divine will for history. Rather, to us all things in history are human creations, relative and passing. (4) All of us, as lovers, parents, teachers, citizens or believers, feel in ourselves and for others the reality and the value of *autonomy*, of self-determination and personal decision, of freedom in the widest sense as essential to the fullness of humanity. It is, Charles Hartshorne wisely says, part of our deepest self-feeling that we wish and require to share in the ultimate creativity of deciding the undecided.[16] To believe that what we have done, or will do, is in the end the result of God's decision and not of our own is to take away our deepest sense of our own being as self-determining, and so both our dignity and our responsibility, our freedom and our guilt. It is in effect to deny, not to affirm, God's creation and preservation of ourselves. (5) Few of us, finally, can ascribe to the will of God whose deepest intentions are manifested in the love of Jesus for us all, the evident and real "evil" of history's actions and events. To do so is either to qualify his love too drastically for the efficacy of faith or to question his concern for history and its people.[17]

This emphasis on contingency, relativity, transience and autonomy practically defines the modern historical consciousness within which we appropriate our faith and conceive it reflectively. For these reasons, we all see history as a fabric woven by human creativity, error and sin, not as a pattern laid out by God. This view of history was potently expressed in the contemporary ontologies and theologies we outlined, with their emphasis on the new, on possibility, on the open future, and on our freedom and decision as ingredient to process and to politics alike. Most of the things we would defend—in politics or theology—reflect these fundamental emphases and themes of the modern consciousness; we can hardly deny them and be ourselves. Taken unqualifiedly, this modern spirit is "secularistic," finds no place for God and, I have argued, is in the end unable to make intelligible the complexity of historical experience. Strangely, as our analysis has indicated, secular views culminate either in an overwhelming destiny of law that smothers freedom, a freedom that believes it can eradicate destiny, or an almost total despair under an all-determining fate. However, when more deeply examined, as I have tried to show here and elsewhere,[18] each of these elements of the modern consciousness reveals a dimension of ultimacy that points to God. My present suggestion is that as the Old Testament writers and prophets reinterpreted promise, covenant and fulfillment in the light of their changing history under God,[19] so we should try to reinterpret this traditional absolutist view of the divine sovereignty in the forms of our historical experience. For God, if he be at all, is there in present-day cultural life as fully as he was in that of the Hebrew people or in that of the church in the "sacred" fifth or sixteenth centuries.

What, then, can we mean—if we do not mean this classical model—by the action of God in our history? How can this symbol be relevant and true for us? Clearly, the problem of causality is basic. What do we mean by a cause when we speak of history, and how can God be for us an actor, let alone the definitive actor, among the causes of history? We have argued in a previous chapter that since human groups are the subjects of history and human beings consequently its sole creaturely agents or actors, the concept of causality should accord with the kinds of dynamic factors characteristic of human responses and actions. As Tillich remarked—and we have illustrated—all the categories change their characteristics as one moves up the dimensions of being from the inorganic, through the organic and the living, to the spiritual and the historical: space, time, causality and substance take on new forms and new dimensions.[20] In history, therefore, the conformation of effect to cause, of event to the factors that brought it about, is never totally determined. For, as we showed, no factor is a cause in history until it elicits a human response, and that invariably involves human interpretation, intentions, norms, judgments and decisions. Thus history is a process of *centered* decisions in which there is an unremovable "given," a destiny, but in which also freedom and spontaneity—and so contingency and purposes—are at work. This is also true for the entities of historical life: what is effected and affected, what in turn has effects, namely, groups, communities and cultural entities, are likewise multi-dimensional. Consequently, as our own analysis has shown, action in history takes place on many different levels on each of which there is causation, i.e., dynamic events or changes which help to effect fundamental historical transformations.

1. A community must exist and continue to be within its natural and social environment. Thus are communities subject to the physical causality referent to factors in its geography, food supply, disease and health, to growth in technologies and means of production, to loss or gain of land or population through war, conquest, etc.

2. A community also has a spiritual dimension represented and structured by the fundamental symbolic forms of its life. Correspondingly, the social forms of its life, its "civilization" or "relations of production" are structured by these symbolic forms

that constitute its "culture." These structures, social and symbolic, are, therefore, also a part of its being in the deeper sense. Events, persons and communities that influence or change these forms are significant causes on which the renewed life or the death of the historical subject depends: whether they do this directly through shaping the institution in question or indirectly through changing the symbolic base of the institution, creating thereby new forms and challenging old ones.

3. There is also a shared eros running through the community, what Augustine called the *love* that binds the community together,[21] or, as we put it, a sense of the value and meaning of the life that is lived there which provides the inward basis for participation in its objective meanings and for commitment to that community and its way of life. This inward participation in the community, a participation through commitment to its symbolic forms is, as we noted, a vast source of the power in history of the community inwardly and outwardly; its loss, a sense of alienation and so spiritual disintegration, is, correspondingly, a cause of the weakness and imminent mortality of the community. Thus changes in fundamental attitudes and values, in eros and so in inward participation in the community's life, are important causes in the history of groups.

4. Finally, there is the moral dimension, equally crucial to a community's life. Moral sickness, injustice and spiritual disintegration can destroy a community's existence as quickly as an epidemic or a shortage of food; and moral norms continually govern the solutions to its pressing problems which a community accepts or rejects. Whether it will or no, a community aims at what it sees to be the good, and can only be itself if it thus does aim.[22] The eros shared by a community has invariably a moral tone. Thus communal moral judgments of approval or disapproval, a massive moral alienation or a renewed awareness of obligation, are important causes of historical change.

At all of these levels—of our being, of the forms of social life, of our meanings and our moral judgments—destiny as the inheritance from the past and action in response to destiny are effective in historical change. Causes can subsist on all of these levels insofar as some aspect of the given, of destiny, presents a pressing problem which elicits a human response, be it on the level of food supply—as, for example, when a drought causes a *Völkerwanderung*—or on the level of a change in political, economic or religious structures—as, again for example, when a combination of proletarian misery and a new political self-consciousness helps to cause a revolution and so a basic shift in institutional forms. Temporality defines all of creaturely existence, and thus all of its activity; things, persons and communities come to be and *are* in time, in passage into the future. In individual and in human history every action is a drive toward the future to maintain the being of what is and to establish the new, to resolve what is pressing from the past and the present through a project for the future. The aim is to achieve in the future a new possibility that is in continuity with the old and yet less ambiguous: a new security of our common being, a new structure to our common life in politics or economics, a new and creative form to social and cultural existence.

On the individual level our daily actions, taken in the aggregate, result in slow, cumulative changes in institutions, customs and forms; deliberate historical action on the corporate level—politics—supplements, directs, redirects, stalls or seeks to impede those aggregate unintended changes. Whether minute and individual or large and corporate, each represents precisely this projection into the future of new possibility in response to a problem within the given present. Such projections on any one of these significant levels become *historically* effective (whether they be small changes in individual techniques or habits, or massive political programs) insofar as they present to the eros or appropriation of the community (or a section of it) a new possibility for its future, a resolution of the problems of its present. Historical causality, therefore, is a dialectical interrelation between destiny from the past, continuing structures of common life and continuing goals of people and societies, combined with new possibilities related to that given actuality, possibilities that are projected into the coming future and that are embodied into action through decision and intention, all aiming at a new and better situation.

The Sovereignty of God Reinterpreted: God as Being and as Logos

Is God then a cause within history so understood? Does he intervene in this process in which human creative projection, human eros and human hope seek communally to cope with destiny—the given in nature, social tradition and other communities—with which historical action must deal? Let us turn again to the Old Testament for clues for our answer. As von Rad makes plain, there were changes in the Old Testament conception of God's work in history. In the patriarchical, exodus and conquest narratives God did so intervene as a "cause" among other causes and thus did rule history through miraculous acts.[23] In the period of the monarchy, however, he ceases so to act as an independent cause among other causes; rather, he is seen as acting in and through the ordinary creative and destructive actions of men in history.[24] Moreover (and here is the main point), perhaps the most vivid aspect of the Old Testament experience of God's action in history was a double, dialectical action: not only does God establish or *constitute* the forms and so the meaning of Israel's life with him, but even more, continually, God creates new and unexpected, even incredible forms of his relation to men and women in their social existence. On the one hand, God establishes covenant, judges and then kingship as the fundamental forms of Israel's social life; thus is providence constitutive of the structures of Israel's communal existence.[25] But on the other hand, the essence of the role of the prophets was dialectically related to this role of establishment: they recalled and called back to the covenant; still, they also declared *new* acts to come because the old covenant and the older forms of life with their certainties, which no longer apply, were now invalid, abrogated by the sins of Israel's past and present.[26] And new forms, a new covenant, a new relation to Yahweh will, they said, be established on which alone Israel may count.[27] Both traditional structures and new possibilities for history seem, therefore, to be the major results of Yahweh's activity in Israel's history. It is not irrelevant to note that it was out of the prophetic experience of the deep pain and mystery of the *nemesis* of the divinely given and yet of new divinely offered *possibilities* for the future that not only did the Hebrew sense of history arise, but even more that the sense of human individuality, autonomy and creativity also appeared—two major elements in the traditional biblical view that clearly lie back of the modern historical consciousness.[28]

The point is that this dialectic of hidden work within history is the symbolic "model" in the Old Testament of God's work with Israel: of establishment, protection and sustenance on the one hand, and of the creation of new possibilities out of the nemesis of the old on the other. God institutes the new and thus constitutes both community and tradition, the possibilities of social and so human existence; he is thus the ground both of the sacral that is old, uniting past and present, and the sacral that is new, uniting present and future—and the deepest issue in his action in history is this relation between these two. The first task then in a modern conception of providence, based on the Old Testament model, is to seek to understand the relations of God to the unity of destiny and freedom, to the unity of the past which he upholds, to the freedom which he calls into being and the new possibilities which he offers to history.

By proceeding in this fashion—by seeing God's work according to this Old Testament model in the uniting of destiny and of freedom, of past and present actuality and of new possibility—we are seeking also to avoid a "supernaturalist" explanation of history and yet to find a valid and significant meaning for the conceptions of the divine providence as the ultimate ground of the constitution of social institutions, as the source of their meaning, significance and efficacy, as the basis for their important criteria, and as the resource for the possibilities that may redeem (or destroy) them. It is essential to our modern consciousness of history that all that occurs there occurs "naturalistically," through the immediate agency of second causes. This has been a primary aim and emphasis of the great views of providence, though one not refined and definite enough to satisfy most of us. In what follows we shall try to conceive of providence in all its facets in such a way that this "naturalistic" principle of historical explanation on the level of direct, historical causation is not abrogated, that God can be intelligibly said to "act" in and through the secondary "causes" of destiny and freedom (in the sense we have just outlined), and yet to have a constitutive, critical and renewing role in that process—as the Old Testament model indicates he does have.

We experience a dimension of ultimacy on every level of our being.[29] As Christians we apprehend, name and relate to that ultimacy, so experienced, as God, i.e., through the biblical symbols and especially through the mediation of Jesus Christ. As our analysis of that experience has shown, we experience ultimacy not as the all-powerful, extrinsic and necessitating ordainer of what we are and do, but precisely as the condition and possibility, the ground, of our contingent existence, our creativity, our eros and meaning, our intellectual judgments, our free moral decisions and our intentional actions. Thus the divine ultimacy, experienced in our historical life as providence—an ultimacy that establishes, grounds, limits, judges and rescues the present—is not "unconditional" or absolute in the sense that it determines human action and thus every last character of what is in time, any more than it determined Israel's response to the covenant and its obligations. Rather, it is that on which our real—and not apparent—contingency, our real relativity and that of all we do and create, our real freedom and so the real openness of history depend. God's providential presence, the ultimacy that undergirds our being, is experienced and found *through* these characteristics and powers of our finite being and thus is not capable of dissolving them else it would not be experienced and known at all. For ultimacy appears precisely *within* the exercise of our contingent being, the discovery of our relative meanings, the achievement of our relative truths and spiritual creations and the enacting of our free decisions as their possibility. It is the ground, the dimension, the context that makes our contingency, relativity, temporality and free human being possible.

The presence of the providence of God as the dimly apprehended source of our contingent and yet continuing being, the context of our meanings, the inspirer of our values, and the standards by which we experience and judge our world, does not mean that what we will, God also wills. Nor does it mean that all that is reflects his unalterable intentionality, so that God is responsible for all that is, and we and history are incapable of creating or producing anything genuinely new. In the sense of ground, limit and resource of our being and its powers—and in that alone—God is ultimate. God as creative and providential sovereign is thus not only *essentially* active, dynamic and related, present in all of changing time, sustaining and driving forward all that is, and creative of the new.[30] He is also, as creative ground of our being, essentially *self-limiting*, producing a free, contingent being that is not God or a part of God and whose actions are not God's actions, for finite actuality comes to be through its own actualization of its destiny.[31] This creature, nonetheless, is one who can neither be, be in time, value, know, create, judge, decide, nor have meaning and hope without this continuing relation to God's present being, intentions, meanings and love—which together form his providence.

How are we so to conceive of God as the source of our continuing being and the ground of our creative autonomy, if that be the implication of the Old Testament model: of our knowing, our valuing, our shaping of ourselves and of our world? The issue of our being involves the symbol of creation, separable only in analysis from providence since God creates, maintains and guides during the course of time. We shall make only such brief remarks as are necessary to our comprehension of providence, i.e., concerning the continuing creation and preservation of finite being as it occurs over time.[32] To us the bringing of finitude into being, its sustenance and its preservation are essential aspects of the divine power which gives being in all its aspects to each creature in the process of its becoming. To separate God from the origination of the totality of the being which is ours, and so in ontology from the creativity and the flux out of which we arise, is first of all to reduce God to *one* metaphysical factor balanced by others, and thus to qualify his supremacy and holiness and our own monotheism. Secondly, it is to relinquish the essential sacrality of existence, of life, of being—the dynamic vitality which is fully as sacred as is form itself. It is to return to the Greek error of identifying the divine merely with order, Apollo, and to regard the Dionysian, the dynamic in our being, as nondivine. This is as much a misinterpretation of the nature of our finite existence as the first was of the nature of God. "Creativity,"[33] existence, "being" are not ontologically "neutral" to be formed by deity. They are rather sacred or demonic, and thus as much as possibilities or forms are they the work of creative providence. This emphasis on God as the source of our *total* existence—of the creativity and flux out of which we arise as entities—is our own largest ontological difference with most forms of process thought. The genuine freedom of the creature to create and do what God has not willed or done is here guaranteed by the self-limitation of God in bringing freedom into being rather than, as in process thought, by the separation of God from the flux of creativity and by the consequent reduction of God to finitude, to being one metaphysical factor balanced by other equally permanent and equally real factors.

If the notion of God as the source of all aspects of being, the symbol of *creatio ex nihilo*, is interpreted in terms of the fundamental polarities of destiny and freedom, of achieved actuality and of future possibility—i.e., in *process* terms—then that symbol means that it is God as the power of being that carries forward the total destiny of the past into the present where it is actualized by freedom. Creativity, the flux or élan of existence out of which in process thought each new occasion arises becomes, in other words, the power of being of God, the providential creativity of God that originates and sustains our continuing existence.[34] God has not ordained the shape of the destiny that comes to effectiveness as the given from the past: the freedom involved in past events has done that in relation to the possibilities then presented by providence. But the efficacy and so the continuing being of that achieved actuality, its power after having actualized itself to continue in being in order to become the presented destiny (the "data") effective within the next event, and so a living aspect of that present actuality, this is the work of a power that transcends contingency and passage. This conquest of passingness that makes the process of becoming possible, and so the continuation of order and all causation and cognition possible; this conquest of time which makes process as becoming possible —all of this is the work of God who is in dynamic process but not subject to process. For process, if taken seriously, means the passing out of existence of what has been. Thus there must be a power of being transcendent to finite temporality if destiny or facticity is to be effective and real. The moments of time are filled with non-being as well as being; they are passing away and so unreal as well as present and real, and thus do they vanish—to be held epistemologically only in the self-transcending power of memory and ontologically only in a power of being that transcends passage.[35] But they are real as bearing whatever finite reality there is, as giving finitude a "place" in which to become. And process depends upon transition, the continuing effect of what has been on what now is and is to be. The continuing effectiveness of finite events, themselves passing away, that makes all continuity and all becoming possible is itself dependent on that which does not pass, on a power of being which bears every achieved and objectified event beyond itself to become the destiny of the next event. It is the divine that mediates the continuation of being as well as the relevance of possibility between achieved actuality and novel possibility to make present becoming possible. Thus the being of God transcends and conquers the transience, the mortality and the contingency of passage, while at the same time being deeply immersed in passage as the ever-creative ground of its continuing reality.

This conception of God as the principle of being through which moment follows moment, occasion arises out of occasion and becoming takes place over time is an ancient doctrine formulated in many ways by Augustine, as we have seen.[36] Not only is the process of temporality made possible by the being which only eternity can bequeath to it; but the *power* of freedom to become event, and so to have effects on the next moment—and so on its world—is, said Augustine, of God. In this sense, he argued that God does not determine what freedom does with its possibilities; but God's being is the basis for the continuing being of each event and for the power with which each event effects what it has willed.[37] Our suggestion is that because of the the obscurity, the difficulties and even the incoherence of Whitehead's concept of creativity as the principle of transition from occasion to occasion—a principle which he radically separates from the divine principle—that "creativity" be included under the providential activity of God and thus made coherent with the notion of God as transcendent to the continuation of passage as well as immersed within it. Transition can be effected neither by the finite itself as now past (the subject-superject of Whitehead's categories), nor by a principle alien to God, the relative abstraction "creativity," but by the creative providence of God that effects the preservation of the completed past within the present, that brings destiny forward, so to speak, to come to union with freedom into event, and that is the ever-creative ground for the self-actualization and so the "reality" of the creature. Thus the first principle of providence is the conquest of the passingness of time and the continual creation and recreation of each creature through the creative power of God: or, as it was put in the classical tradition, the first element of providence is the preservation of the creature over time.[38]

Our greater interest at the moment, however, is in the second aspect of providence, namely, providence as the ground of possibility and so of human autonomous creativity in history: artistic and cultural creativity, cognitive creativity and the creativity of social and political actions seeking new resolutions to present problems. In this connection orthodoxy spoke of God effecting our intentions and ideas and through them of ordaining the forms that history produces.[39] Against this modernity has cried out for the autonomy of the finite and the natural, for our creativity and genuine possibility—not determined by God but by us. We have argued that both are right. Against the orthodox view, possibility in history must be real as possibility, as not yet decided even by God; history must be open; and the results in history of human creative action must be relative, transient and partial, i.e., human, if there is to be for us history at all. On the other hand, against secularist naturalism, as Whitehead has argued against Bloch, real possibility must be *some-*

where. Possibility must be in creative relation to actuality if it is to be effective, relevant and so really possible. Thus even the most creative, autonomous action requires a universal, systematic order of possibilities that spans past, present and future and so can relate real possibility as possibility creatively to what has been. Possibility must be related to an eternal, everlasting and encompassing actuality, some being that orders possibility for the whole process: to God's providence. Thus the very possibility of openness and of the new in the future, far from denying the presence of God, requires it.

God's providence represents, therefore, not only the necessary and permanent source of our continuing existence in all its aspects, the movement of past actuality, of "tradition," into our present and the recreation of self-actualizing actuality. It also points in the opposite direction, in the direction of the future: it relates unrealized possibility, the "new," to achieved and achieving actuality. For providence is also the ground or context of the possible, the not-yet forms which our intentionality creates. That "space" where future possibilities now are, and are in some structural or intentional relation to actuality, is located in the envisioning power of the divine providence. Thus does providence as the envisionment, grading and evaluation of possibility, determine and direct the relation of possibility to the actual present as process, and so historical process moves through the power of being of providence into the future. Our acts of creativity in history, our projections into the future, like all else in our being, are in relation to a context of ultimate possibility. Thus are there the possibilities of meaning, order and commitment in our creative and yet temporal life. Here we are related to God's ordaining and ordering providence, as in our continuing being we are related to providence as the creative and continuing power of being and as the principle of traditional continuity.

As our own analysis of social change—and most modern social philosophies—has emphasized, a vastly important aspect of historical and political life is the impingement on our present of possibility, of what is not yet real but what is possible, of the new form or structure more relevant and creative than the old. It is out of this vision of the new, of the more creative possibility related to given actuality, that creative traditions may be *retrieved* in new and more relevant forms, that thus the dynamic changes of history arise and receive their meaning, that history takes creative shape, and that hope and so creative action—political eros—are possible. Destiny can be reshaped by freedom only in relation to novel possibilities, new interpretations of our symbolic past; the creative actualizations of freedom are a union of the given from the past with new, as yet unrealized possibilities. Creative political life depends, therefore, upon a grasp of and a vision and commitment toward a new possibility[40]—not frozen devotion to an old form. This sense of ever-new possibilities, of creative change from what has been, has been the genius of our liberal culture. Its present waning strength among us, and our petrified worship of the old are thus the most serious signs of the loss of historical creativity.[41] It is, then, in terms of the relation of possibility to historical creativity, and thus to meaningful movements into the open future, that I seek especially in what follows to reinterpret the work of providence in history. For as we have seen, essential to Yahweh's action with Israel is not merely the sustenance of sacred tradition but even more the creation of the new in Israel's life.[42]

One of the most revered and ancient symbols in our tradition of God's activity in relation to the world has been the logos: the divine reason or order in and through which God creates the world. With an assist from Bloch and Whitehead, I would like to refashion and so to retrieve this concept in modern historical terms in understanding providence. One of the creative roles of God—distinct from but related to that of his being and his continuing creation and recreation of our being over time—is that he gives to each occasion, and so to each person and community, an ordered vision of possibility, a leap beyond the present actuality yet one in relation to it. Thus is our creativity possible. The logos of God through and in which process develops is, therefore, not a static rational structure timelessly determining the shape of things. It is God's envisionment and ordering of the vast and infinite realm of possibility *as possible.* Through participation in this envisionment we, in coming to be and in living in the divine presence, come in turn to apprehend the possibilities relevant to our situation.[43] But it is our autonomy that actualizes these given possibilities according to our will and so in freedom. Thus providence as logos is the ground of human creativity and autonomy, of human intelligence and praxis, the source of the not-yet forms that make novelty and so historical development possible, and so the divine structure within which the autonomy of the world moves into the future. Providence does not determine historical creativity; it makes it possible, gives it relevance and so limits and guides it.

In what has preceded this discussion we have interpreted the "given" from the past, impinging with effect on our present and providing it with the ground, the continuities, the materials on which the present can "be" and with which it can work, as an aspect of the work of providence in history. This provides an *ontological* basis or explanation for the continuing "causality" of being and of tradition in historical experience. Now we have sought to interpret the appearance of relevant possibility, also essential for historical passage in its creative aspects, as the work of the divine providence. In turn, this interpretation provides an ontological basis or explanation for the normative, the "ought" characteristic of relevant and new possibility as it impinges on our present. As we have noted, new possibilities do not appear in historical existence as merely neutral; they appear, as Tillich noted, as "demands" on our conscience, as an ought which our actions must seek to embody and realize. Possibility enters history with a moral tone, as a claim on our integrity and responsibility. The kairos of our present appears as a demanding possibility that calls forth the decision and commitment of those who see its presence among them. This is true of all political possibilities, obvious in all revolutionary and reformist movements; sacrality enters historical passage not only as the conservation and repetition of the past, but also as the obligation of novel possibilities. Thus are there grounds in historical experience, as well as in the biblical model, for interpreting the appearance of possibility as the work or "call" of divine providence.

God is being as the source and continuing ground of the flux and becoming, of the actuality that we are and that forms our destiny; God is logos as the ground of our possibilities and so the limit and ordering of our future. The essential structure of this gift of our creaturely being (what our authenticity *is* and so what our particular obligations are) and the goal and direction of that providential ordering of possibilities (what the "subjective aim" of God's primordial envisionment is)[44] are defined and known eschatologically in terms of the revealed end toward which all moves. Providence is the sustaining and creating work of God within the ambiguity of historical life that leads to the divine eschatological fulfillment as the latter's presupposition and ground.

THE ESTRANGEMENT OF HISTORY, NEMESIS AND JUDGMENT

History, however, manifests not only freedom and creativity in correlation with destiny. To understand the ontological structure of history is not yet to understand history in its concrete actuality. In the Old Testament account Israel lived within the covenant and the social institutions "established" by Yahweh; but Israel betrayed those "gifts" and so in the end abrogated that tradition. Freedom can and does also become sin; thus is divinely given possibility betrayed, and thus does destiny take the form of fate. To interpret, as liberal progressivism did, history solely in terms of its structure as "good," that is, in terms of novel possibilities, of freedom and so of a growing creativity, is to miss one of the essential aspects both of history's concreteness and of the Old Testament understanding. This aspect of its concreteness is the apparently ineradicable demonic element that equally characterizes all of history, permeates the Old Testament understanding of Israel's life, and that leads at the close of an epoch to nemesis: to destructive conflict, to universal suffering and to final tearing down. In such periods of experienced decay history seems devoid of its ontological structure of possibility. Human freedom seems overpowered by forces far beyond itself; and predatory violence being unleashed, only evil seems "free." So euphoric was the liberal apprehension of history, that while they recognized the reality of the demonic and the nemesis elements of history, they confined them to man's past and believed that through the process of cultural evolution, of an increase of knowledge or the growth of morals, these fated, self-destructive aspects of history would gradually disappear. Such an "essentialist" interpretation of history as basically and unambiguously creative and progressive is understandable enough in a period of waxing cultural growth and development when the sense of new possibility is widely felt, and where the power of those possibilities to resolve old problems seems continually to be validated by the facts of social experience.

It is, however, clear—from the Old Testament account, from history itself, and from our own present sense of it—that the experience of historical passage can present an entirely different face: when problems and dilemmas seem to multiply, when established institutions seem devoid of creative possibility, when future possibilities betoken menace rather than promise, and so when a sense of fated destruction rather than of creative possibility dominates the communal consciousness of men and women. If these elements of nemesis are taken not merely as aspects of the past but as ineradicable and so recurrent traits of history—as many speculative philosophies of history beginning with the Greeks and continuing in our day with Spengler and Toynbee have done—then history is seen not progressively but cyclically, as manifesting a recurrent rise of creativity and an equally recurrent fall into self-destruction. Such a cyclical process of rise and fall can be interpreted "naturalistically" as an inexorable law of the temporal and historical order, as if history repeated in its own life the life cycles of nature, as the Indian and early Greek mythology of the four ages, the Stoic views of history and Spengler were wont to do. Or it can be given a "spiritual" interpretation in terms of an inevitable *hubris* or "sin" as the tragic tradition, Toynbee and a number of Christian theologians of history have done.

It is safe to say that if this tragic element is taken seriously as recurrent, and therefore as a possibility for our future, whether in the form of a natural law of growth and decay or of a fatal fault in cultural life, it is only on theological grounds that hope can be brought back into history. For such a sense of history in which fate seems continually to engulf freedom, only a God transcendent to these now overwhelmed human powers can break the power of that inexorable fate.[45] This explains why while in optimistic eras the divine providence seems to constrict human freedom and to limit new possibilities, in more pessimistic epochs, when the power of the fated cycle over the futile exertions of an enfeebled human freedom is deeply felt, providence appears as a basis for hope in new possibilities and as providing a needed ground for an almost extinguished human creativity.[46] Thus, while over against progressivism Christian faith has seemed "gloomy," reminding liberal optimists of the recurrent realities of sin and fate and so of the tragic character of history, nevertheless, over against the cyclical view of history as a fated growth and an equally fated decay, Christian faith has been hopeful, proclaiming not only the reality of divine providence but also the promise of grace and renewal to historical life, and so in the end standing for the efficacy of a freed freedom to effect self-realization.

The question whether providence is seen as constricting or empowering creative possibilities, whether as numbing or supporting autonomy, turns, therefore, on the question whether one views self-realization as to be achieved autonomously by finite freedom or as possible only in relation to the divine power which grounds our freedom. If the former "autonomous" view of freedom is taken, then providence and fate will be viewed as identical concepts, for both challenge the independent, self-sufficient autonomy of man in his search for self-realization. If, however, freedom is experienced and reflectively regarded as caught in some self-generated form of bondage, then the possibility of self-realization is given rather than removed through providence and grace—and fate and providence seem *antithetical* rather than identical concepts. In any case, in providing a theological interpretation of the problem of historical nemesis, i.e., in disclosing a divine ground beyond the bondage within which freedom finds itself, Christian faith is capable of offering an answer to that problem rather than only capitulation to it. Thus the credibility and even more the sense of the validity of the Christian interpretation of history over against its alternatives depend more on an intuition into the permanent reality of ambiguity and nemesis in life, plus an apprehension of the effective answer of grace to them, than on any other aspects of human experience. As an understanding of human life and history, Christianity "makes sense" only to those who are dimly aware, not only of the dimension of ultimacy in human existence, but of the realities of sin and of grace there. All apologetic arguments, I believe, either seek to uncover and expose, or subsequently depend upon, these three foundations in experience of the meaning and validity of our fundamental Christian symbols (i.e., an awareness of ultimacy, of estrangement and of restitution).

Two factors are obviously involved in our awareness of the constriction and the helplessness of freedom and creativity in history. The first is the finitude of human freedom: the fact that our freedom is polar to destiny,[47] to a given which we do not create and cannot remove because it is the temporal presupposition of all our own being and so of our free activity. We arise out of a past, and so our powers and their efficacy are upheld and subject to that destiny. We can, therefore, only work, if we are to "work" at all, on a given from the past; we must retrieve, interpret and reinterpret our past if we are to have genuine possibilities at all.[48] Thus is all action governed by the shape of the actuality that it embodies and that it confronts. However much possibility is crucial for history, equally crucial is inherited and presented actuality. It is their union, as we have seen, that is central to the work of providence, and, as we have repeatedly maintained, that is central as well to our own historical being as selves and our creative action in the world. Now clearly this given ("destiny"), while an inescapable aspect of our finitude, is not *essentially* or in itself evil. On the contrary, it is the basis and so the possibility of all that is creative and good in life. However desirable the new may be, it is possible only on the basis of some relevant past, of the retrieval and reinterpretation of that past, and so on the grounds of some tradition. A free self which wills to be quite free of its destiny, of the given from its own past, has neither reality, being, structure nor power in itself and no materials which it can shape. Having no inherited actuality, it possesses no possibility. It becomes, therefore, mere ineffective and empty arbitrariness and thus loses itself in both an inner and an outer fate.[49] In history "liberation" arises out of actuality not out of nothing; and its aim is not a world without destiny, a world of total and uninhibited freedom; on the contrary, it can only mean a universal destiny for all.

The given, however, is not *merely* given, as if it had arrived straight from God's drawing board. The modern historical consciousness—and this is perhaps its greatest contribution—has seen that what we find surrounding us in the social world and what appears within ourselves as the given from our own past are themselves the result, in part but in important part, of human creativity. They too were once possibilities standing before a given actuality. Destiny itself is the child of freedom. What is in the historical world is in part the work of man, and what we are is in part the work of our own past decisions. For human creativity does create, and what it creates becomes objectified and remains at least for a time and has its effects. Individual actions build ourselves and others; our corporate actions build our world. These institutions we build through our actions, the social structures we rear, all these remain in time affecting the future. Thus every present receives a destiny from the past that its own past, individual or communal, has in part made. Even in this simple—and seemingly obvious—sense, historical freedom is as much bound by *itself*, by its own creations over time, as it is by events, powers and forces outside itself.[50]

Our freedom in history is of course also limited if not bound by another aspect of the given, namely, "others": other people, other communities, other groups with whom we share our present space. These others have, to be sure, shared in the creation of our own freedom. For finitude arises out of community, in encountering others, communicating with them and acting with, on or against them. Other persons make us persons: they are the primal destiny out of which freedom and human being arise.[51] They, too, therefore, are a "given" for us—though qualified of course by their own freedom—with which our freedom and creativity, in the light of our own destiny, must deal. The destiny which shapes us and with which our freedom in history must cope is, then, a compound of communal creativity from the past, now solidified in given structures and symbols, continuities and trends, and the other natural forces, creatures and humans with whom we share the duration of our present. This element of given destiny in history, as well as the ordered possibilities of providence, represent the truth in those speculative philosophies of history and of the social sciences which seek to understand historical change not in terms primarily of intentions and freedom but in terms of large historical, social and metaphysical factors or forces that work through and over men and women: economic as in Marx, cultural as in Spengler, spiritual as in Hegel. As I have indicated, I tend to see these forces, while always there, nevertheless to be more in continual correlation with and so expressive of the creations: economic, political, social and cultural, of human freedom, rather than all-determining powers over freedom. In any case, destiny is an aspect of our finitude, of our contingency, our relativity and our temporality. It is not in principle evil, for it is the creative condition of all finite freedom—but it is in history often experienced so.

It is experienced as evil because another factor has entered, and so far as our experience of history is concerned, universally and inevitably entered. I refer to what has been called in our tradition sin, the fallen, estranged state of mankind, however we may try to understand this symbol—and reality—in our own modern terms.[52] As many theologians and philosophers have recognized, because sin is an estrangement of our essential structure, an alienation from our nature, a misuse of freedom in which freedom is itself bound, it is not possible to describe it in ontological terms —for ontology knows only structure and not its misuse.[53] Among the most important things a Christian interpretation says of history is that that which is fated or evil in experience, while an undoubted part of the concrete actuality of history, is not the result of its ontological and so its "necessitating" structure. Rather, this strange, "fallen" aspect of concreteness is the creation of sin, of a warped human freedom, and not of God, of time, of the structure of our finitude or of inexorable natural and social forces.[54] Thus can fate be conquered and hope be possible. It is, as Tillich says, a universal destiny in which freedom itself is involved, a destiny *of* freedom created *by* freedom.[55] Thus, in the end, a liberated freedom is freed not so much from an objective fate nor from historical destiny as from itself and from the fate for itself *it* has created. Since fate arises from sin and not from the necessities of our existence, therefore, a creative destiny is always possible and life is never fated or evil. This awareness of continual possibility in life, in effect this "hope," constitutes the experiential meaning of the symbols of the good creation and of providence alike.[56]

With sin, however, destiny is always, though not necessarily, in danger of becoming fate: an objective historical situation whose given world is such that freedom can no longer seem to shape itself or its world. Freedom in history is always estranged and so ambiguous. Thus, on the one hand, the destiny which comes to us from the past is always ambiguous; and thus, on the other hand, what our freedom does with our own destiny is itself always ambiguous. Sin has warped the past that comes to us in our present; it also corrupts the future we create for our children. In certain historical situations this ambiguity accumulates, becomes hardened in social and historical forms, becomes unbearably oppressive—and fate appears. Fate is, so to speak, a negative or demonic kairos, destructive rather than creative of possibility. Fate is the situation where the accumulated sins of the past have built a social and historical structure or situation where freedom is historically bound: as in a war, in a structure of slavery, of radical political, social or economic injustice, of racial oppression, of economic and political exploitation. The consequences of sin are not only broken individual lives; they are also warped social structures and historical situations that break and bind large portions of mankind.[57] In these historical situations men and women are "fated" because they have no freedom; the given in their lives allows no room for their own determination of it.

These situations we have called fate arise ultimately from sin, and thus is Christian faith relevant to the social, political and economic problems of history. Since the problems at this level concern warped social structures, the *immediate* remedies lie in political and social action or praxis and not directly in inward religious salvation. Political, economic and social "liberation"—and this term should in theology be confined to this context of fate—is the eradication through political action of such a fated objective historical situation or structure. Because that situation is, as we have seen, not only the cause of immense suffering but also is a result of sin, liberation in that sense is an important aspect of the gospel. But because such liberation from a historical fate does not deal either with the sources of fated situations, with the deepest inward sources of sin, or with the present reality of sin, but only with the later outward social and historical consequences of sin, liberation from inherited social structures cannot encompass the full substance of the gospel nor can it deal with *our own* present and future sins. The political action that undertakes *legiti-mately* to liberate itself and others from fate must *itself* stand under a more final judgment for its own continuing ambiguity, and hope for a grace wherewith it can itself be cleansed.

Sin is the misuse which freedom makes both of the destiny which is given to it and of the possibilities relevant to that destiny. It is the misuse human freedom makes of the providential gifts of creative passage from the past (of tradition) and of new possibility (the not-yet) for the future. Thus, with the category of sin, necessary unfortunately for comprehending human history and its movement into the future, we move *beyond* ontological structure to warped actuality, and so corre-spondingly *beyond* the gifts of continuity and of new possibility that providence brings into the deeper need for redemption. In enacting new possibilities, as well as in hanging desperately onto old actualities, we seek to secure ourselves and our own. It is important to note—in understanding the relation of freedom and possibil-ity to sin, and so of all of these to politics—that sin is *not* merely undue attachment to the past and the closing off of an open future. Sin arises as well in the way we deal with an open future, in the warping use we make of even the most novel possibilities introduced into history. For it is precisely the "openness" of a future that is menace as well as possibility (as Chapter 1 indicated); that very openness thus breeds our deepest anxieties as well as our expectation of new possibilities, and leads both revolutionary and conservative forces to become infected by self-concern and the securing and defense of their worlds. It is the openness, the contingency, the risk and the demand, of the future that tempts us to sin as well as beckons us to new creative possibilities—and in *both* our freedom in union with new possibility is at work. The future is open because of our ontological situation of contingency, of temporality and of freedom; it is out of this that the temptation to sin arises. For those in power the anxiety of that openness is resolved by hanging onto the past; for those who seek power, that openness is secured by closing and dominating the future. Sin is neither merely the result of the structures of the past nor is it merely the obstinacy of conservative forces. It can infect the creators of the new as well —as bourgeois forces disclosed—for in freedom for the future as in bondage to the past we can and do sin. Because reformist and revolutionary action may be able to reshape a dominating fate from the past into a future destiny, they are, as we shall see, "preferred" by a Christian interpretation of history. But in so tipping the balance in their direction, a Christian interpretation should not be deluded into thinking that the creation of novelty in an open future is less prone to ambiguity than is the desperate preservation of a past structure of life.[58]

Thus even our most creative acts, cultural and political, individual and communal, end up more tarnished than we intend.[59] Instead of achieving the new resolution for which we aimed, the glowing possibilities we envisioned, our deeds and produc-tions arise in history warped and partial, reflecting more our own self-concern, our concern for security, position, power and prestige than they do the good or the new for which we had hoped. Such is our passion for our own security, being and value that we claim these productions of ourselves and our community—our well-being and sustenance, our way of life, our moral norms—to be ultimate, worthy therefore to be defended to the last against foes from without and reformers from within.[60] Thus is every community and culture in history partly the result of a union of providence with human creativity, but also partly the result of sin and consequent warping of those possibilities. And so the destiny we bequeath to those outside our communities, and the destiny we bequeath to our children can become fate. Through the demonic aspects of our creativity what we produce in the objective social world becomes itself demonic, full of evil consequences borne by the warped institutions that survive in time and breed more evil in their course.

This analysis gives us the basis for understanding what may be called the biblical —at least the "prophetic"—distrust of achieved power, of the mighty and the powerful of the earth, including the wise and the good.[61] Power is, as we have seen, essentially a good, for it connotes the power to be, to continue to be and to help shape one's destiny. Thus the total lack of power in life is an injustice and insupportable, as every revolutionary group knows. But power achieved is in our world power already corrupted; power as well as will and mind is tarnished by sin. Those who have power, the mighty and the wise, are not more sinful. Nonetheless, through their might their sin has more effect, and so creates the suffering—the fate—that over-shadows the lives of others. The weak create a fate only for those few who are in one way or another under their power: wives or husbands, children or relatives, servants and friends. Through their power, however, the mighty are enabled to create a fate for multitudes, since their actions shape not only their own destiny to their own ends but also that of others, and because through their power they shape the institutions and symbols that in turn structure the roles, the rights, the freedom and the rewards of their community. Thus it is that the mighty and the affluent are not loved or blessed but judged by the biblical word.[62] The responsibility of the mighty and the wise is, therefore, higher; more is asked of them; for them the way of salvation is consequently a very narrow gate, and nemesis based on their pride and greed always hovers in the future. A primary word of a biblical theology of history, therefore, after its celebration of the divine providence in the sustenance of our being, in the constitution of our social institutions, in the value of our freedom and the creation of the new, is the guilt of great power, the special responsibility of power, the danger of power to the peace of all and to the health of soul of the powerful—a word of judgment and warning to the mighty and the affluent.

There is no more tragic and ironic historical illustration of this theme of creativity, the achievement of power, and its ultimate destruction and self-destruction than the history of the liberal, democratic culture to which we belong. The creative achievements of this culture not only in science and technology but even more in politics, economics and social existence are so clear they need not be elaborated. They were so obvious to the classes creative of that culture that, as we have seen, they developed a theory of history as the story of the unlimited progress and gradual perfection of that same culture! Yet the destructive role of that same culture by its European creators in the entire colonial world and recently by its American inheritors in Southeast Asia, in South America and at home with regard to the Black community is visible to everyone in the second half of the twentieth century. The liberal heart has been doggedly idealistic and well intentioned; the liberal mind has deliberately sought to be open, tolerant and just. And yet such are the tragic dimensions of history that this culture has become, for those who suffer from it, as oppressive and demonic as were its historical predecessors. This same culture represented in its early days freedom for its bourgeois classes but domination for its workers; in its latter days it has represented freedom for most of its white Western protagonists but at the same time an unbearable fate to its Black and Third World victims. Ironically, it is precisely against *this* culture, which half-anxiously, half-complacently calls itself a "free society," that almost all the liberation movements of our present direct their action. Even the most open culture becomes tarnished in its achievement of freedom and openness, and through that tarnishing it spreads destruction into the lives of others and breeds self-destruction for itself.

The theme of creativity followed by demonic perversion and cruelty and culminating in destruction and self-destruction has, of course, been explicitly enacted in unparalleled fury in our time in the Holocaust. No culture regarded itself as close to the apex of "civilization" as did the nineteenth-century German culture. In the development of the arts, of science, of scholarship, of the conception of human freedom and of the forms of human excellence, it regarded itself as the final synthesis of the Hellenic, the Christian and the Enlightenment worlds. And yet it was this high German culture which produced an explosion of destructive evil, the attempted and in large part realized extinction of the Jewish people, unequalled in history for its deliberate ferocity, malice and cruelty—and it was precisely the height of the culture that made the perversion more deliberate and so depraved, more sophisticated and so infinitely more efficient. Though Anglo-Americans were rightly dubious about the political wisdom of German society, their own tendencies in the same directions show that while sound political institutions can help a community *guard* against the destructive evil in its own heart, they cannot prevent that evil from dismembering that community's life if the community so wills; and thus that evil is a principle in history that can use and then destroy the highest forms of cultural achievement.

As the Jews sadly and with pain—but frequently without bitterness—remind Christians, moreover, it was not merely a humanistic culture that was at fault here, though this was surely also true. For this was a "Christian" culture that became demonic, that had a long tradition of anti-Semitism deeply embedded in its own Christian heart, and countless Christians participated in, supported and affirmed the entire development of Nazism from beginning to end. To be sure, individual Christians and some notable Christian groups protested these attitudes and actions and suffered accordingly. But the church as a whole, both Protestant and Catholic, either approved them or stood aside. Not only, therefore, did Christianity "fail" in the face of this historical evil. It revealed that through the very medium of grace which it proclaimed, and in the midst of the people of God itself, the most extreme forms of evil can manifest themselves and make instruments of destruction of those institutions and persons so blessed. Though this point has been clearly manifested throughout church history, it has been unmistakably revealed to us all in our time; and any Christian attempt to understand the claims of Christian grace, of the church and of the Christian life must, if it can, take it fully into account. The redemptive creativity of Christian faith, like the creativity of the highest culture, is no "guarantee" of salvation—even when the religion in question understands doctrinally the depth of sin and the ambiguity of Christian holiness, and even when the culture understands the value and dignity of every human being and the signifi-cance of freedom. Neither the highest human culture nor the most profound and ultimate religion can complete and fulfill themselves in historical time, and thus does history continually bear the marks of ambiguity, of tragedy and the possibility of nemesis. Recent German history has been an extreme illustration of human es-trangement penetrating into the very heart of human and historical creativity; it is, however, no "sport," no deviant form of the human distinguishable on this issue from other national groups. As the American experience in Vietnam and South America and in her own racial conflicts shows, this history uncovers who we *all* are, and can be, when situations of extreme cultural anxiety and so of temptation occur; and as our first chapter pointed out, such situations are not going to be less frequent or less menacing in the impending future.

The same historical irony of creativity followed by nemesis is illustrated on an even vaster scale in the contemporary ecological crisis. That apparently most benevo-lent product of human intelligence and freedom, namely, applied science and technology, was believed capable in principle of bringing all the fates of human life: natural, social, genetic and psychological under the control of human purposes, and hence to betoken a new day of freedom and well-being for mankind. Along with the tolerance and humanitarianism of the Enlightenment, it was this aspect of moder-nity that established the sense of progress in history; of all the open possibilities of history, it was the most promising for a new future. And yet, as the ecological crisis makes plain, technology has today itself become a fate which threatens to effect the extinction and not the deliverance of mankind. Or better put, it is the use that human greed or concupiscence, the desire to take the whole world into itself, to consume a finite nature infinitely, that has made technology into this awesome fate.[63] Sin has made the most promising destiny of all into fate—such is its corrupt-ing power in history. Moreover, the self-destructive power of even human creativity, of man's openness to a new future and of his creation of the new, is nowhere more clearly spelled out than in this fatal misuse of his most celebrated instrument of creativity, his most dependable power over the future: his technology. For with technology the self-destructive dynamic of sin seems now at last capable of drawing into itself and its annihilating power both nature and history together and to threaten both in a way undreamed of before, except in the supernaturalist imagery of the terrible Judgment Day.

The Old Testament reflects a very powerful understanding of these social and temporal consequences of sin in historical communities—of the transformation by sin of destiny into fate—an understanding that developed in strange and fruitful ways. Very early it was seen that an evil deed had evil consequences as a part of its "essence," consequences not only for the doer but also for his community in the future—a point so obvious and valid empirically that it is hard to see why the liberal tradition found this social view of sin "primitive." Each sin had its "fate," an objective historical sequence of events that flowed inexorably from the deed. Thus was the community understandably fearful of wrongs in its midst. Yahweh's providence could, it was hoped, intervene in the fated sequence and rescue the community from this fate by an expiatory deed that was done before Yahweh.[64] Later, as the sense of the moral offense involved in sin grew and so the rebellion against Yahweh himself was more clearly seen, the evil consequences of sin became less the result of an impersonal fate inherent in the deed as the action of Yahweh himself, causing the evil that men set into historical motion to recoil on their own heads.[65] Then with the Prophets this fate *becomes* Yahweh. Yahweh is, says Hosea, the ulcer, the enemy, the raging lion with whom Israel in sin has to deal.[66] Finally, with Jeremiah and Ezekiel, the sin of Israel has become so great that the whole history of the old covenant has become warped, and Yahweh must even tear down the creative institutions that he has founded and built with Israel.[67] Because of Israel's sin the coming of God now signals judgment, and not only a judgment to be meted out at a last day but an historically located and historically mediated judgement through the destruction of the social institutions Yahweh has created.

Thus there is in the Old Testament model of the divine activity not only God's sustaining and creative work in history. There is also his judgment in and through history leading to the destruction of what had been created and preserved[68]—because that historical creation had through sin become a destructive fate. This double, dialectical theme gives a dramatic and ironical tone to the later prophetic portrayals of their history.[69] The story begins with the divine gift and promise, divine covenant, constitution and protection; it proceeds to Israel's deliberate rejection of covenant and promise; it moves then to catastrophe in which the very creativity of history is itself apparently overwhelmed. But then comes the striking and surprising prophetic note. A new act breaking the old cycle is to come—and it is on this and not on the older history that Israel must now count for the hope of its redemption.[70] This cycle of gift, sin and catastrophe is, let us note, never an inexorable necessity, as even Ernst Bloch admits.[71] There is always the possibility Israel will listen to the prophetic word of warning about this grim cycle, and in listening come to repent, to return, and be spared. Even more, there comes the promise of a new act even without that repentance in which a new history can begin with Yahweh.

This ironic drama between God and Israel as seen by the prophets is a most illuminating analogy for the strange course of general history itself and for the role of providence in history.[72] This model provides, I believe, the interpretative symbolic framework in terms of which alone the creativity, the sin, the tragedy and the renewal of hope, characteristic of historical experience can be comprehended. History does not manifest mere cumulative progress into the new, into novel possibilities of ever greater value—as the liberal nineteenth century felt and as the "essentialist" ontology of process philosophy implies. Rather, concrete history as we experience it has a dialectical, catastrophic, tragic character analogous to this biblical drama— as the present demonic issue of that same liberal culture shows. There is human creativity and autonomy (the gift of providential possibility analogous to the gifts of the promise, the covenant and of kingship to Israel), creative of new workable institutions, new modes of life, systems of meaning and of morals. But these creative institutions are always also corrupted by partiality and claims of ultimacy. And so they mete out during their time also oppression, injustice and violence to those around them and bequeath these same to their descendants. Through sin destiny slowly becomes a fate that mortally threatens the community that arose from creativity. Judgment is here felt and executed. American experience today amply verifies this drama of a new start, new creativity, corruption and potential disintegration and death. And beyond judgment and collapse there is, as revolutionary forces know deeply, the promise of the new, a new possibility initiating a new historical era.

We suffer today not from lack of intelligence or know-how. We are threatened not by our finitude, our ignorance, or by a nameless nemesis. What threatens us in the West and in America as fate—and through us our world—is the inheritance our own sins have created since we began our era: from the Asiatic, the African and the South American worlds, from the proletariat and the poor and Blacks and from women. And what threatens our entire race is neither technology and industrialism by themselves nor the ultimate insufficiencies of nature. What threatens us all as a terrifying fate is the consequence of human concupiscence, exacerbated by the genius, the superficialities and the lures of a technological and commercial culture into a demonic and hardly controllable force that has partly despoiled and now promises to devour the earth.[73] If catastrophe comes in the first arena, as it may, it will be our blind pride of power, our certainty of the ultimacy of our way of life and of our own virtue, that will destroy us. If catastrophe comes in the second arena, it will be our uncontrollable greed and self-concern that spell our doom. Repentance in both areas is possible, but unhappily it has not yet come. For Israel the divine word of warning opened up the possibility of repentance and so of renewal, and the divine promise pointed to a new act of creativity, a new kairos, beyond even the catastrophes to come. Such too can be the grounds of our faith in our history which faces the same apparent fate created by our own past sins.

Let us note that on this dialectical and ironical cycle the prophetic word is addressed to the particular situation on the cycle: it is a particular word of warning or of withdrawal or of comfort or of hope—and despite the proverbial vagueness of preaching, these are not the same! It is and cannot be—since it is related to a changing history—a general word addressed to all times and situations. It is a particular word for a particular constellation of history; it has its place in a particular kairos or moment, and little relevance elsewhere.[74] Correspondingly, when we ask what in our present we do politically as obedient to the divine Word, our answer is dependent on our situation in history. It is a Word related to its kairos, not a principle applicable to all situations. Insight into that relation depends on "discerning the signs of the times" with regard to the course of history in our time, to the situation on the dialectic in which we find ourselves. It may be that our culture has hope of renewal so that repentance and trust are the appropriate word; it may be worthy even of defense, and of the retrieval and renewal of its institutions and fundamental symbolic forms, because its creativity is still historically possible.[75] It may be, however, that nemesis has come, that what was once possibly creative has become now so hardened, petrified and partial that only antagonism and revolution can lead to the new in the future. To discern what this historical situation is, is an act of practical, historical judgment. On the one hand it is an act that must be informed and guided by critical inquiry and theory, by as much understanding of the forces at work in our present as social inquiry can produce. But on the other, it is an act that must discern the historical situation in all its particularity in order to determine what our kairos is, where on the cycle of creativity and destruction the forces at work in our present find themselves—and that is a judgment that no amount of social science can by itself produce, nor any sort of acquaintance with general ethical structures, important as both are to the making of that judgment. In this situation we are, therefore, in a new way "without the law" and thus called, each according to his or her capacity, to the difficult role of "prophet" in precisely this sense, namely, that of discerning what in our concrete situation, because of its place in the movement of our historical context, the Word of God has to say to us. Part of the task of theology, of ethical reflection and of creative proclamation is this prophetic vocation of determining the kairos of our time and what it requires of us in action.

We have discerned the work of providence in history as the universal divine activity of the preservation and continuity of creaturely being over time, as the ground of self-actualizing freedom and as the creative source of new possibilities in each situation. Providence is the ultimate source—though by no means the proximate, secondary source—of the social and cultural "worlds" within which humans dwell in time. We have described the further role of providence as the principle of judgment or of nemesis on the distorted elements of what has been created by freedom, the "hidden" or "alien" work of God in the destruction of what is itself destructive, the negation of the negative, the conquest of that in human history which is experienced as fate ("the footprint of His wrath," as Barth put it). This latter aspect of the historical activity of providence is so clear and visible in our own time (cf. Heilbroner) that the other, "creative" aspect of providence—the principle of new possibility—both in existence and in our own delineation, is apt to be forgotten or overlooked. In such a time, especially, it is important to reemphasize this creative, promising element—as in our analogy the promise of the new covenant was emphasized to those in exile. As Calvin so powerfully stated, to believe in providence is not only to discern the divine judgment implicit in what happens to us, but even more to have confidence that in *every* historical situation—even one of such judgment—the creative sovereignty of God is also a reality. Translating that into our present interpretation, it is to have confidence that in *any* historical situation new possibilities, new potentially creative "turns" of events and of the possibilities for our responses to those new events, will be present. Such a faith in new possibility—necessary for inward serenity and for outward "worldly" action alike—is by no means to be taken for granted in historical experience. Situations can seem to embody no promising issue, to hold only menace and further destruction. To have faith in providence is to *expect* a new kairos to come, new creative syntheses even of what is now given with what is to be possible, and so to be able to encounter the unknown future with courage and with hope—"in spite of" the evident judgment and tragedy which are often the human lot.

Redemptive Forces in History

For us as for the Hebrew prophets, then, history has a dialectical, catastrophic, revolutionary pattern, a convulsive movement toward the new, more like that of Marxism than that of liberalism. The problem with Marxism and with Bloch is that they relinquish at the end the deep insight of dialectical catastrophe and join the liberal perfectionists. One act of historical creativity, the achievement of the socialist society, will for them dispel the previously fated dialectic, the ironical drama of creation, corruption, rejection of the ideal and nemesis, and an ideal, seamless world beyond all catastrophe will be established. We seem faced with stark alternatives in understanding history. On the one hand, we may believe against history's evidence that one social act, one creative political construction, one new political reform will rid history of its estrangement and so of the grim cycle of destruction and decay. Put in the terms of our analysis of history, this is to say that the estrangement that besets history lies alone in the fate that threatens freedom, in the warped institutions of the past, and not in the corruption of freedom itself, in the human beings who, in our present and for our future, construct and defend those institutions. On the other hand, if this historical perfectionism seems to us naive, we are left with that grim cycle itself as the final clue to history and the final coup de grace of history's meaning. Once the problem of history has been driven into the heart of the human beings who make and remake history, as the evidence seems to indicate it should be, then apparently there is from within history no answer to the problem of history. Far better, therefore, is the view manifest in the variety of "views" in the Old and New Testaments that resolves this problem in a much more dialectical and so real manner.

The central theme of this interpretation of history, as I see it, is that while God's providence is, in the sense we have interpreted it, sovereign in history, providence —as the principle of the continuation of finite being, as the principle of new possibility and as the principle of judgment—does not constitute either the whole of the divine action within history or its culmination. Because of the ironical and tragic drama of providential possibility, human creativity, sin and then catastrophe —and beyond that a new historical creativity on a higher level—the divine work of providence as possibility, as the principle of creativity and the new in history, is *not enough*. Even with all its manifest creativity of the new, history remains ambiguous; however great and apparently cumulative the creativity of history—and what culture in history does not sense its own creativity?—that ambiguity itself accumulates and the potential nemesis grimly reappears. This is the real problem with much process theology and all forms of progressivist thought: they see no need and provide no apparent room for this "more" than providence. Providence must, therefore, be supplemented by incarnation and atonement, and ultimately by eschatology. As Augustine argued against Pelagius, because the freedom that enacts possibilities (the Law) is itself estranged, the principle of possibility and of judgment cannot be the sole or determining ground of salvation and so of hope. The autonomy which combines with providence in actualizing possibility must itself be transformed by grace if the possibilities of history are to be realized.[76]

Thus, into this one history—and it is no separate history but the "heart" or inner depth of general history[77]—redemptive and recreative forces enter, and with them a new and deeper relation of human life to the divine ultimacy in which humans live and create—and fall—becomes possible. This relation is on a more inward and more profound, illuminating and transforming level. For it is on that inward level that the nemesis of sin arises—and so arise history's catastrophes. Thus it is on that level alone that the ultimate issues of history can be resolved, healed, and history given grounds for hope. This new level, this new being or human reality in history,[78] this new beginning of God's end time,[79] forms no separate history. The inner life of men and women, where both creativity and sin gestate, is part and parcel of their objective social history. As we have argued throughout, the forms of that inner life arise according to the patterns of that social history, shaped by language, institutions and symbols; and in turn the patterns of social history are molded by the creative, inward life of spirit and by the demonic capacities of spirit.[80] The two most essential characteristics of objective history, the creative new, the enaction of possibility that gives to history its dynamic thrust and its ever-changing forms on the one hand, and the destructiveness or nemesis, that warping of institutions that leads in the end to communal suffering, violence and destruction on the other, find their roots ultimately in the inward freedom of man—as the continuities and trends of history find their roots in the finitude, the contingency, the relativity and the transience of man, thrown into an actuality that is inexorably given. If on the most fundamental ontological level the course of history is the compound of the objective given with the human response, and if temporal process on the deepest level of its being is the actualization of being out of the given as shaped by freedom, then inner and outer history are *one* history. And a new relation inwardly of men and women to the depths of their own being will effect a new character in the history that their creative, and self-destructive, being helps to make. Thus the new reconciling forces that appear, beginning the eschatological end to which they point, are a part of the one history of men and women under God.[81] They form a contrapuntal theme, running through, commenting on, interpreting, and hopefully luring and healing the one great history of humanity. Individual and social, inner and outer, personal and objective history are *one* story, each reflecting in its own way the relation of man's being, his creative freedom and his waywardness to the ultimacy that is God.

It is evident, moreover, that if in truth the deepest source of history's ambiguity is inward, in the inward relation of man's freedom to God, and if it is from that source that history's warped institutions and so history's violence, oppression and suffering come, then the problem of history is thereby moved to a new level. No longer is the reform of objective institutions, or even of patterns of social behavior, while *necessary*, sufficient finally to resolve the dilemma of history. If the problem lies within, then it will resurface within each new form—and nemesis will reappear. For this reason, even the achievement of "liberation," the establishment of a perfect society and the vindication of the righteous who are now oppressed against the unrighteous who are now oppressors—each of these goals, put forward during the course of the development of the relation of men to God, are found wanting.[82] And they are found wanting especially by the prophets who sense the divine judgment against all social forms, even Israel's, and against all rulers, even the righteous. Since the *root* of the problem lies not in the objective social structures of history—not in fate—but in the estrangement of men and women, the creators of history, so the ultimate resolution lies in the relation of man's inwardness to God, in faith, obedience and love, rather than directly in historical or political action. Thus is the New Testament in the end not a political document but a religious one. On the other hand, as we have emphasized, because of the unity of inner and outer in human history, the immediate implications and obligations of the religious judgment and the redemption it promises are political and historical, and praxis as the fruit in action of faith and commitment involves political action against the specific and oppressive forms of our fatedness.

This new theme of reconciliation and of new life in time begins in the biblical history with the word of promise and of covenant which guides and inspires Israel's history. It moves, as we have seen, to the prophetic word of warning and of judgment designed to mediate into repentance the fated dialectic of Israel's life amidst the nations. And it issues in the promise of renewal and of the new covenant as the fulfillment of Israel's destiny. In the New Testament, according to the Christian understanding of history, this same theme expands and deepens. Again it is not a separate history, a theme divorced from ordinary historical life, but the deeper illumination and interpretation of that life, and also the principle of its future healing.[83] This healing, reconciling work of God of the person, and so through him and her of history itself, is not, I believe, confined to the Jewish and the Christian dispensations. It appears to a more or less degree in all religions, and in many secular arts as well. For Christians, however, the criterion of this universal reconciling work of God is manifested in Jesus: *wherever* the judgment, the love and the promises of God *as* they are known and defined by him are evident elsewhere, there we know the universal redemptive activity of God to be at work.[84] For Christians the clarity and certainty of this as the ultimate purpose and will of God for mankind appears here: the forgiving love and the promise that are vague, obscured, hidden and ambiguous elsewhere are clearly manifest here, and on that clarity faith can rest. Thus while the sanctifying grace, as well as the creative and the judging providence of God are universal in historical life as the salvific will of God is universal, still the central *manifestation* of the reality and the character of that redemptive grace entered history in a particular tradition and in a particular person. Our knowledge of our salvation and our hope for fulfillment are alike founded here.

In the person of Jesus,[85] embodying in his life and history symbolic themes from his own tradition of new covenant, suffering servant, Messiah and above all the true *humanum*, the Son of Man to come,[86] the ultimate character and direction of history is illumined. For in him the deepest questions about history are answered: (a) the possibilities—what history might be and so what its norm for individual and for community is; (b) the problems—what is the real source and center of history's ambiguity, tragedy and suffering; (c) the resolution—how and in what form do rescue and healing come; (d) and the end—where is history going and in that sense what is its meaning. Even more important, in relation to the creative divine power he manifested and represented, a new life in history for men and women and so for cultures becomes possible. This is the center of history as the point of its illumination, the principle of its redemption and the proleptic seal or sign of its culmination. In sum, in Jesus the purposes and activities of God in history are made clear. Thus is history itself illumined since now the sovereign power on which human action depends, with whom it contends and by whom it is rescued and healed is known. In thus making itself known, that sovereign power achieves a new level of relation to men and women and so a new level of effectiveness in and with the human freedom it has created.

The three most fundamental questions that political existence and reflective thought alike raise about history are all here embodied and so answered and clarified: the question of the ultimate sovereignty in history, the question of the form of human personhood and so of human community, and the question of the norm for history.[87] With that answer both the fact that history has a goal and the character of that goal are known. The work of providence is by no means confined to the figure of Christ or to the community that followed him; nor is the goal of providence merely the redemption of that community. The church is for history, for the redemption and fulfillment of all men, not history for the church. The eschatological goal of God, like the creative work of God, extends far beyond the bounds of that community and its history. However the *character* and the *goal* of the universal work of providence, and so the quality of God's eschatological future, are revealed here. In him alone do we see the purpose of the whole, and thus is he unique and decisive, the center of human history.[88]

The *possibility* and so the *norm* for history is seen in Jesus and the kingdom he preached and foreshadowed. Since men and women have been and are infinitely creative, and their life is embodied historically in an infinite variety of styles, norms and goals, what authentic human being and authentic community are has by no means been clear. This self-understanding was manifest in principle in every creative culture but in actuality it was latent and obscured in the ambiguity of every culture's life. Facets of these possibilities were grasped and seen, but the depth of love and self-giving, of being for others, the need for repentance, humility and self-awareness, the joy in creation and in communion, the possibilities of truth, of confidence and of hope, the continuing self-surrender to God of one's past, present and future; and the basis of all of this *arete* in utter dependence upon God—all these essential characteristics of true humanity, and with them the characteristics of an authentic society, were not known or embodied. In him this is all there to be seen, participated in, shared and communicated, and a steady norm, pointing every actuality and every society to its own deepest possibilities of authenticity, is given to history.

The *problem* of our common history, of the nemesis to creativity which estrangement brings, is opened up and revealed in the contrast between his being and that shared by all of us. Above all it is manifested in the cross, which shows the character and depth of our alienation from our true selves. The cross points beyond the level of history's creativity and growth, beyond the acquisition of creative power and even beyond the question of the just distribution of power. In each creative social form and so in each embodiment of power sin also manifests itself. Each creative class becomes an oppressive ruling class. Each effort to defend against suffering involves further suffering. In embodying powerlessness rather than power;[89] in identifying with the outcast, the oppressed, and the guilty against the creative, the significant and the distinguished; in identifying himself with suffering and death rather than with the power that contends against suffering and death,[90] Jesus revealed the alienation of even the creative world from its true self, from the kingdom he preached. In his death at the hands of the government and the religious hierarchy, even the righteous powers of the world were revealed to be unrighteous. In a world of corrupted power, the divine must appear as powerlessness. Thus he uncovered the depths of the problem of sin as the universal corruption of that very creativity and acquisition of power on which history's accomplishments, as well as its sufferings, rest. In his own identity with the destructive consequences of sin, he embodied in a new and deeper form the judgment of God on the corruption of our freedom, and the estrangement of ourselves and our communities from their true norm—and thus drove mankind inward to itself, to a renewed and repentant self-understanding, if their outward history was to be understood and redeemed.[91]

The *resolution* of the ambiguity of history in reconciliation with rather than estrangement from God is manifested in the new humanity, the new being of Jesus, and his victory over estrangement and death alike. This resolution appears in him on a deeper level than merely that of historical and social creativity: on the level of ultimate faith, of complete love and self-surrender for others, and of acceptance of his own finitude and relativity, his own suffering and death. In all of this he manifested a new form of human reality, and yet the essential form of our reality. The presence of God, therefore, was realized in and to a human being in this man, a presence to be communicated to us through the inner dialectic of repentance and faith. Through this unmerited divine presence, i.e., through grace, a new relation to self, to world and to history is now possible for men and women. As in Jesus God identified himself with finitude, estrangement and suffering, and accepted them in love, so this identity or divine participation is now possible in each of us as well— and with that possibility the nemesis of history can be broken. For it is precisely to escape finitude, suffering, death and rejection that our creativity becomes warped and turns against itself and its world in destruction.[92] We can in a new way accept our finitude, the possibility of our suffering and the certainty of our death in sharing Jesus' identification with the divine presence, in sharing in the new being that was his. Thus is given the basis not merely for a new creation in history, but even more important, for the *renewal* of history's creativity and community. A new life in the spirit is possible that can in part escape the self-destructive nemesis of estrangement and sin.

Finally, the *goal* of history is manifested in the proclamation, the existence and the transcendence of Jesus over sin and death alike. He is the beginning of the end and in him the promise of God for history is manifest. As the true humanum, the servant of the kingdom, in him is unveiled the goal of God and so of history's processes. He is the embodied promise, the criterion and the first example of the future of God; here God's eschatological goal of authentic humanity and authentic community receive definitive form. Thus it is in him, and the eschatological goal of the kingdom he represents, that the goal of *providence*—hidden amidst the waywardness of human freedom—is revealed within the ambiguity of time. Correspondingly, the purpose and goal of our task in history of liberation from fate is given clear and luminous form. Now there is a visible center from which the past, the present and the future, in all the dark mystery of their cycles and the seemingly tragic pointlessness of their catastrophes, can be interpreted, and the direction of historical possibility, as the most real possibilities of history, seen. There are thus now criteria for praxis and grounds for hope in the new that is to come in the historical future, even amidst the continuing old that is our present destiny. For the intentions of God in his providential work are revealed to us in time.

11

ESCHATOLOGY AND PROVIDENCE:
THE FUTURE OF GOD

History as Cyclical and History as Progressive

We have spoken of history and providence as we have experienced history in our past and present, and as we can conceive of providence in relation to that experience of history, in relation to the biblical symbols and with the help of some notions from contemporary philosophy. We saw the work of God—his work as a whole in history —on three different levels. First, there was the work of divine creativity in the constitution, sustenance and preservation of our individual and communal being over time, and especially in the evocation in us and presentation to us of new possibilities for our historical creativity, cultural, intellectual and political, as history moves into the future. It is the providential activity of God which sets the continuing ontological conditions for the union of destiny and freedom in temporal events, for it is through God's power of being and transcendent vision of possibility alone that actuality is continually related to possibility so that creative process is possible. Secondly, we recognized that the inner life of human beings was estranged or fallen, even from their own intentionality as creators and actors in history. Our actualization of ourselves out of our destiny through acts of freedom, the events that result from that actualization, and so, finally, our creative actions and productions, all become in the end despoiled and warped. Thus the historical destiny of those who follow becomes a fate of unjust oppressive exploitative institutions, and in the end nemesis, conflict and tearing down ensue. This principle of intrinsic destruction and nemesis we recognize as a further "alien" or "hidden" work of God's providence as the principle of judgment in history.

Thirdly, following the Old Testament analogy, however, out of this process of judgment came new acts of creation, new possibilities. These appear on two levels: outer and historical, and inner and existential. Outwardly there are new cultural creations, some established by political action, some by cultural creativity, new social and cultural worlds arising from the older, sometimes retrievable, sometimes now demonic structures. Thus is the fate bequeathed to men by their warped institutions dealt with by providence and by political action in terms of new creations—though never finally, since the corruption of sin remains. Inwardly there is the beginning history of a new relation of humans to God to deal with the inner problem of estrangement and sin. This is the "covenant of inwardness"[1] and the covenant of the law, both leading to the new covenant of grace, the new being, the beginning of the end time in Jesus as the Christ.

These are one history not two; here the liberal and the liberationist theologians are right. For men and women are both outer, social beings and inner, self-determining beings. We are "historical" and "existential" at one and the same time. The forms of our personal, inner existence—our most fundamental anxieties, temptations and responsibilities—are in large part determined by the forms of our outer historical existence. And the objective structures of history, in their creativity and their ambiguity, are in turn shaped by the inner creativity and the inner estrangement of men and women. Self-actualization is the process in which destiny—the outer—unites with freedom—the inner; its results are historical event and cultural creation—the objective side of history. With each of these the estrangement as well as the creativity of our self-actualization is effective and so manifest.

As we have seen, just as for the Old Testament the outer history of Israel's life was determined by Israel's inner state of obedience or rejection of Yahweh, so the inner history of Israel's relation to God is illumined by and interpreted through the outer. In fact, these two principles together *are* the principles of the prophetic hermeneutic of history.[2] So in our history, too, the two are not separated. The historical destiny or the historical fate we fashion are compounds of the objective social institutions people create or mold and the historical acts they perform *with* our inner relation to, grasp of and action toward the ultimate, the divine, that is our historical horizon. On the character of our relation to the ultimacy in which we live depend the shape and strength of our cultural creativity, the depth of our estrangement and so the forms and the virulence of the fate we bequeath to our descendants.[3] The character of outer objective history is determined not only by destiny, by providence and by human creativity; it is also determined by sin and grace. The redemptive acts of God, directed at Israel's inner fidelity and loyalty, find their ground and their locus in the events of her objective history. Social institutions, political and cultural creativity, providence, sin and grace form one history.

So far as we have gone, history here pictured can be interpreted as representing a rather grim and pointless cycle of creativity and destruction. There is the presence of providence as the principle of new possibility and so of creativity, followed by judgment and the new cultural and individual possibilities beyond the judgment; in turn there is the response of human creativity to that destiny and so to these possibilities, a creativity accompanied by human pride, self-concern and concupiscence, resulting inexorably in historical destruction. And again, this cycle is followed by the hope of new historical chances, new creativity and then downfall. One feels this cycle in the Old Testament histories and in the seemingly endless repetition of "and Israel did what was wrong in the eyes of the Lord."[4] One feels it to some extent in Augustine, except of course for the supernatural destiny of man; and one felt it in most of the dialectical theologians. The latter took the continuing ambiguity of history with intense seriousness, and thus understood general history in terms exclusively of this cyclical drama of creation, sin, forgiveness and possible renewal, but the continuation of sin within that renewal. For them, therefore, the course of history never approaches the kingdom; or to put this point another way, the eschatological end is equidistant from every point in history. At best, despite the Hebraic character of their theological discourse, there is, therefore, much that is Greek in their view of history. Salvation comes only to the individual souls achieving authenticity within the Christian community at whatever moment of history they find themselves. Eternity hovers over each moment of time to be awakened, as Bultmann put it, by that moment. Or, as Barth put it, history is the stage for the covenant people—but in and for itself it has no real meaning; objective history contains no intrinsic significance and just carries on. Eschatology is a category referent to the appearance of eternity through the gospel and the proclamation of the Word in the community of the church, and the matter of ultimate salvation at the end beyond history. It does not, however, qualify the shape of history or our understanding of its course, except that these sacred events take place within history.[5] Thus, as the eschatological political theologies have said, theology turned inward and private, became a vertical relation to God in inner existence and in the church, and had only the briefest reference to objective history, to politics and to the social future impinging now upon us.

There are several objections to this neo-orthodox—at least continental neo-orthodox—view of eschatology which contemporary futurist theology has rightly pointed out. First, they have shown that the eschatological elements bulk large in both Old and New Testaments, that these in turn refer to promises of the new, and of the new for history and not just for the individual soul. And they have cogently argued that the kingdom—a category related to the covenant with Israel and so applicable to historical and social existence—is a basic category in the gospel, not just personal forgiveness and sanctification. Secondly, they make the point, as have I, that human beings are social, historical beings as well as individual, inward, private beings. The structures of their being as temporal include the social and historical dimensions of their existence as well as the personal—in fact, the two dimensions cannot be separated. Consequently, the basic human relation to the future, a relation constitutive of our humanity, is not merely to our individual but also to our social future —as we found so clearly in our analysis of social change and its vast influence on us as responsible persons. If, therefore, human beings as in this sense historical are to be fulfilled, this implies a historical fulfillment manifested in objective social history. Thus, while in the preceding chapters I have suggested that the exclusively futurist emphasis of these theologies be modified by a theological concern for the doctrine of providence and the issues of present, preliminary history, so now I suggest that a futurist and socially oriented eschatology modify the dialectical theologians' concentration on the present ambiguities of historical life and on the vertical impingement of the transcendent in personal existence. The Christian promise of a historical future that embodies the rule of God, and so a history guided by that goal, must modify the tendency of neo-orthodoxy to find the promise of salvation relevant only to the existential inner person and the small Christian community. How then are we to reinterpret providence *eschatologically,* as directed at a goal relevant to temporal process, as representing the culmination and not just the judgment of history? Can the kingdom, or even movement toward the kingdom, be for us as it was for the liberals a credible *historical* category, a category applicable to the historical future? How *does* the ultimate goal of God impinge upon and relate to the moments of historical passage; if it is not simply "above it," is it then simply its final end or terminus?

With these questions we encounter, of course, the theory of progress toward the perfect society so central to the modern historical consciousness as the sole principle of the meaning of history—if not of meaning in history—once history is conceived as constituted by relative and transient forms of life. It seems almost as if once such a dynamic, relativistic, naturalistic view appears, history is either void of significance as a succession or even a cycle of relative forms with no meaning to their sequence (one temptation of modern and of neo-orthodox theology), or history has significance as a cumulative and so progressive succession of relative forms of life leading to the achievement of perfection.[6] The debate between these two alternative forms of modern historical consciousness appeared in the arguments between nineteenth-century progressivism and twentieth-century existentialism and was paralleled in theology in the debate between liberals and neo-orthodox. The liberal position that history does have significance, that it will under God embody its own ideal goal, and, therefore, that a significant part of the gospel concerns the divine promise for the historical future has been brought back vividly to life by eschatological theology, albeit in Marxist dialectical and apocalyptic rather than in liberal progressivist form. Is a contemporary theology of history, then, really to rescind the negative judgment of existentialism and neo-orthodoxy—and seemingly of twentieth-century historical experience—on the liberal ideal of history as a progress (from the past *or* from the future) which finally achieves or embodies the kingdom? That would be a strange cycle indeed!

Problems in the Notion of a Progressive History

The idea of progress as it was fashioned in the eighteenth and nineteenth centuries and as it functioned in liberal theology reflected, to our jaundiced twentieth-century eyes, several confusions. In fact these were, one may say, confusions of just those ontological levels in history's drama that we have sought to discriminate. These centuries took their own experience of historical creativity, namely, the creation and development of the cultural, political, social, cognitive and moral forms of modernity in the West, of liberal even Protestant culture, as the clue to all of history. Thus it conceived that the autonomy and the power to create toward the ideal, which were so evident both as the dynamic factors in Enlightenment culture and as its own explicit goals, were themselves the underlying forces of history and the goal of history. History is the story of the achievement of freedom, realized by the slow and gradual freeing and so increasing exercise of intelligence and moral purpose. Moreover, the Enlightenment had experienced in its own history cumulative developments on almost all the significant levels of cultural life: cognitive, technical, sociopolitical, philosophical, moral and (to itself) religious. It's self-awareness of itself as an epoch was the self-awareness of an unprecedented cultural eminence achieved by progress in all relevant forms of cultural life.[7] Mankind had at last created through its autonomous reshaping of history a liberal, free and open society based on science, technology and humanitarian morals. What more could history want or achieve except the further progress of this autonomous society? If in this way the creative side of history—and it *is* a side of history—is taken as determinative of history as a whole, and if the creativity evident there is taken as being untainted and so free of intrinsically self-destructive elements, then one can understand how history as a whole can be viewed as a permanent development towards perfection.

As we have noted, however, history manifests estrangement as well as creativity. The very autonomy that creates is, as Marx was later to point out, tainted with class interests. And, as subsequent history itself would further point out, that tainting through class would be compounded by racial, national and even male chauvinistic elements. Thus do the most splendid historical creations become distorted and demonic in time, and destruction follows. Even this liberal culture, and especially the scientific technology on which much of its confidence in itself as progressive rested, have like all of history's creations become instruments of self-interest and of concupiscence. What were in the eighteenth and nineteenth centuries the clearest signs of the *progress* of freedom, namely, the development of liberal culture and of technology, have for the later twentieth century become signs of the mysterious *ambiguity* of history: to many the deepest obstacles to freedom, the clearest omens in our time of a fate that constricts our future possibilities.[8]

Even more, human autonomy and freedom in history are only misunderstood if they are at their deepest level understood developmentally. The technological and industrial instruments freedom uses for its purposes can develop; the self-awareness of freedom can increase in social and political self-consciousness; the objective social structures within which freedom is exercised can improve; the norms under which freedom operates can rise; ideals, social, political and personal, can mature in time. It was these developments, so to speak, *around* freedom and "freeing" freedom of which in its own history the Enlightenment was so deeply aware. But the relation of our freedom to these ascending norms does not *itself* develop, and so our use of these new instruments, this new self-consciousness and of these new social structures does not also itself progress. We can still defy these now higher norms in our every use and exercise of our freedom; and we do. Above all, as Reinhold Niebuhr tirelessly pointed out, the self can twist any norm or ideal for its own use.[9] Then a higher and a more universal norm, instead of saving us from ourselves, can become more dangerous than a lower, more exlusivist one.

The explanation for this aspect of the ambiguity of history can be found in the ontological polarity of destiny and freedom which we have here sought to develop. Every cultural development is an aspect of the "given" for each person and generation, an element in the destiny bequeathed to them and on which their freedom must work in response and in creative shaping. The destiny in each case may ascend, and has; thus the context, the scope and the materials of freedom can ascend. But destiny, as we have seen, does not alone create an historical event or a historical life. At every interstice of history, freedom responds, and *that* response does not so clearly or in the same mode ascend or progress. Ironically, the age that spoke most often of freedom and autonomy failed to see the fundamental ontological status of autonomy as polar to destiny in every historical moment. Rather, it included freedom within an ascending destiny, and thus conceived of history as a simple progress.[10] The same problem, as we will show, haunts the eschatological futurists. There is and can be, therefore, no steady, dependable progress of morality, of moral behavior and action, but only a progress of cultural and religious morals, of moral ideals.[11] The gap between "is" and "ought" remains fairly constant however lofty be the height of idealism to which the "ought" may rise. After all, Israel lived within the covenant and yet remained obstinate;[12] and, as Jacob Burkhardt once said, we must assume that the lakedwellers gave their lives for each other at least as frequently as we do!

The same point could be made that progressivists mistake a growing control over what is outside us—the technical instruments of freedom, the social structures within which freedom works, the goals of freedom, and so on; in other words, control by freedom over the natural and social environment—with *self*-control, freedom's control over itself. Our control over things in all its varied meanings may cumulatively increase. But within these ascending social wholes, men and women remain ambiguous, still haunted by the inward problems of self-love, still, therefore, unable to control themselves morally, to be just to their neighbor and to curb their own infinite concupiscence to consume the world—still determined, whatever their intentions, by their bondage to their own security, fulfillment and glory. And so when the ambiguity of freedom is given more effective instruments, freed from natural, genetic and social fates and thus accrues to itself vaster power, then the level of ambiguity in social history is raised along with its creative possibilities. What progresses—or may progress—in history is the destiny from past history with which in each moment freedom is confronted—though, let us recall, that destiny can through what freedom has done with it also in each moment become fate. What does not progress or develop cumulatively with time is the freedom which responds to this given from history, and so which is in part creative of the next historical moment. It is the ontological structure of destiny and freedom in history that clarifies the relation of the cyclical to the progressive in history, provided of course one adds the theological comprehension of the concrete actuality of freedom expressed in the category of sin. Thus the cumulative development of freedom toward perfection as the principle of meaning in history represents a fundamental confusion about the nature of history itself as a polarity of destiny and freedom.

Interestingly enough, the same dilemmas on the issue of the future perfection of history, of progress toward perfection as the meaning of history, confront the eschatological futurists as the liberals. Although they reject progressive development and speak only of God's eschatological activity from the future, nevertheless they too see the historical future as essentially different from the past, as the fit object of Christian hope since it is to embody a perfectly just and loving society, and therefore as manifesting unequivocally the divine will and rule. Clearly, this perfection at the end of history, this "realized eschatology in the future," is the principle of the meaning of history for them as it was for the liberals. Like the liberals and the neo-orthodox they have combined the modern historical consciousness with certain theological symbols—in this case, eschatological rather than providential or christological symbols. But of all these, the former combination is the least capable of becoming coherent, partly because eschatological symbols are at best at the edge of history and thus are the most difficult of all to historicize. If, as we have argued, eschatology cannot be historicized and retain its ultimacy without fanaticism, so eschatology cannot be fully historicized and retain its perfectionism without contradiction. The modern historical consciousness that has forced on them the historicizing of eschatology seems to make that very historicizing unintelligible. There are three reasons for this, each expressing a central aspect of the nature of history as we have analyzed it. To qualify any of these aspects of history is, I believe, to qualify history fatally, and so not to be speaking any longer of the concrete communal life of men and women in space and time. If valid, this argument means that a perfect society in history is inconceivable from the point of view both of reason and of faith, and therefore cannot provide the final Christian meaning of the historical story.

1. The ontological character of history as a union in each moment of destiny with freedom means that a perfect society is inconceivable. To be sure, history has almost infinite possibilities because ontologically history is a union of destiny and freedom; freedom is essentially creative of the new, and thus history is continually open to new possibilities.[13] However, this also means that no final society, in the sense of a permanent or stable one, is conceivable. Whatever the destiny of an enhanced social order given to that far-off generation, that destiny always unites with freedom to become historical; and the intervention of freedom always subjects the achieved order of history to the threat of dynamic change. There is too much vitality in any community; spirit always transcends any set form of social coherence; and thus every society—even an ideal one—is subject to the transformation and ultimately to the dissolution of its structures. Finally, if the ontological structure of history is thus permanent, the condition for history to be history, then the possibility of the "fall" —unless man is substantially altered—remains while history lasts, since both that possibility and the actuality of sin are derivative, though the latter not by necessity, from man's ontological structure. So long as freedom is finite, thrown into an ambiguous given and facing an unknown and anxious future, there is structurally the possibility of sin.

2. As we have analyzed history, estrangement (what we have just termed sin) is

an inescapable part of its actuality. There is little ground, either empirically, philo-sophically or theologically, for assuming that it will disappear. It stems from the ontological situation of man, though not with necessity, because it is an act of freedom; but if it thus arises from the permanent situation of freedom in relation to destiny and future possibility, then developments in time (of destiny) will not affect it—as if it arose by our being "close to our animal ancestors," or from particular social structures that might be transformed. If what is called sin could be eradicated by temporal development, then it would have arisen from accidental characteristics of man's environment, of his social order, of his amount of learning, and so on. It would not have arisen from his basic situation vis-á-vis himself, his neighbor, the future and God. If estrangement is to have *religious* implications and be of theological concern, then it is an aspect of man's universal actuality, if not of his essence, and so ipso facto permanent—unless of course it be solved by God's grace, but that raises, as we shall see, other issues. Thus, as the possibilities of history develop, the possibilities for the sinful misuse of these developments rise too. So long as man remains man, finite and self-transcendent, he will be tempted by anxiety at the impinging and frighteningly open future. So long as he lacks perfect trust in and love of God with which to bear securely that contingent future, he will fall.[14]

If, however, the permanence of the situation of man as estranged be assumed, no perfect society, no historical kingdom of love is conceivable. Since any social scheme of justice in any history we know anything about presupposes self-concern and so the claims and counterclaims of each person or group, the community must be formed according to general rules, to a universal system of law, and so be in some measure unfair to individual needs. The order of the community must be enforced by a governmental power capable of whatever effective coercion is required, and so a power whose potential misuse remains a possibility in all historical life.[15] At best, the community can equalize but never eradicate (and should never seek to do so) the special interests and groups abounding in any historical group, and so necessarily a potential instability of balance of power remains. Thus any historical society, however advanced in structure, is prone to the demonic possibilities latent within the permanent structures of history and to the reappearance of a fate in the given that freedom encounters: the government appropriating to itself too much power (tyranny and oppression), the dominance over the community of some special interest (oligarchy and aristocracy), or the unresolved conflict of groups in the wider community (anarchy).[16]

As history is always destiny and freedom, and thus freedom can and inevitably will become sin, so correspondingly it is always possible and therefore infinitely probable that destiny will become fate. Both poles of this permanent ontological structure, as long as the structure is there, have the possibility of "falling," the one into sin and the other into fate. Thus history qua history cannot be the unequivocal manifestation of the will and rule of God, identical with the being and the sove-reignty of God—unless freedom is redeemed by grace *(non posse peccare)* and with that the possibility of fate removed. Unless sin is assumed by some inexplicable principle to be eradicated by the passage of time, no social structure in history, however highly developed, can expect to reflect the solution to history's dilemma. A kingdom of love continues to be relevant as a judgment and as a lure to every historical approximation in terms of justice; but no historical order will perfectly incarnate such a society of love. And the more it claims to do so, or to represent the road to it, the more the special interests, and the governmental power that that social order actually represents and favors, will feel justified in their domination of the other vitalities of the community.

3. The final element of the ontological and so permanent structure of history is the relation of God to human freedom, expressed in our reinterpretation of providence. This relation, we have argued, is one of self-limitation. At no point does God overwhelm or determinatively direct our freedom; he does not ordain us to will what we will. Rather, it is we who actualize our own being in each present out of the destiny given us from the past combined with the possibilities and their demands granted us from the providential future. It is God's creative and providential power of being that carries our destiny into the present, that thus continues in being the conditions of our freedom in the present, our power of self-actualization; and it is providence as the envisionment of future possibility that presents us, challenges us and calls us with relevant possibilities. God as eternity spans and so unites past actuality and future possibility; he is inescapably an aspect of the ontological structure of process as its ground and possibility. God is alpha and omega in each instant of process, and thus is process as a union of past actuality and future possibility in the present event of freedom made intelligible.

It is, however, strictly as *self-limited* that God is ontologically and necessarily present as the condition of the union of destiny and freedom into event. It is we who effect and complete that self-actualization and so that active shaping of events. This self-limitation in God, and so the reality of our creative freedom, is, as we have seen, an almost inescapable implication of the modern historical consciousness. It is thus that future possibilities are genuinely possible, that freedom is real, and the future open, i.e., that history is history. But if this divine self-limitation be constitutive of history, as essential an ontological structure as the polarity of destiny and freedom, then God will have to act in the future as he has in the past, namely, *through* our freedom and *limited by* our freedom. History in the future, therefore, will remain open to the wayward as well as the creative possibilities of freedom; destructive conflict, exploitation and oppression as well as creative action will be possible; and divine grace, acting in and on our freedom, not an overwhelming divine mastery of freedom, is the only way God can act redemptively in our histories and so in history. A complete divine "determination from the future," eradicating the evil of the past and establishing a perfect future—as the language of the futurists implies—would thus also eradicate *history* as a union of destiny, freedom and the possibilities of God. An eschatological language that implies that God is the sole actor—as it always does—implies as well the end of concrete, human, open history, and so the end of the historical future.

If the future is to be history, it must be ontologically and theologically of a piece with the present. If future history is thus continuous with past and present, then a perfect society in history denies the ontological structure of history, the continuation of sin within that structure and the permanence of the self-limitation of God. Only an extreme theory of irresistible grace imparted universally into social history could make theologically intelligible the eschatological promise of a perfect historical society in the future—and no such theory has emerged from the futurists who speak so easily of just such a society. Eschatological perfectionism can be historicized only at the expense of the future as history.

If, then, as these criticisms of both liberal progressivism and eschatological futurism imply, no perfect and stable society of love is possible so long as history is history as the modern consciousness, and so the modern theological consciousness, understands history, then how is the meaning of history to be understood and how is the possibility of a better more hopeful future to be understood? Are we by these arguments sent back to the negation of history characteristic of dialectical theology? Are the only alternatives a perfectionist view of history's meaning, or a view in which history participates in no meaning at all? How does the eschatological category, the ultimate future of God, qualify the moments of historical passage?

Apparently the neo-orthodox were right that *tense*, the distinction between past and future, is not the most fundamental distinction in Christian faith, and that fate, sin and death cannot be equated with the historical past and redemption unequivocally identified with the historical future since this leads to historical, ontological and theological incoherence. On the other hand, the eschatologists were right that objective history participates in Christian meaning and in hope, and that whatever redemption is promised, it is promised for history as well as for individual life. The grace of God is not merely directed at individuals within a meaningless history, but into social history itself as well.[17] Our problem, then, is how to understand the truth in both these positions, how history as well as individuals can participate in the eschatological promises; how the ultimate future can qualify historical passage.

Power, Powerlessness and Meaning in History: The Workings of Grace

If ontologically history is characterized by the polarity of destiny and freedom and by the self-limitation of God's power and rule, and if the actuality of history is characterized by both creativity and corruption, then the meaning of history cannot reside in an unequivocal manifestation of the divine rule in history in and through human beings and human social structures. Divine power and human power are never in history so congruent as to be identical. This is one of the deeper aspects of the revelation—or the "hiddenness"—of God in Jesus, in the character of his person and destiny, and in the themes of the incarnation and the atonement. Jesus' person and destiny are proleptic to be sure: one may say that Jesus does embody the true humanity and true society, and thus the divine goal for both. It is, however, by no means accidental that in him as the historical manifestation of the divine will, it is also the case that powerlessness and not power, suffering and not dominion, were

central characteristics of his life and of his destiny. These are not temporal "accidents" of the relation either of true humanity or the divine will to history, as if they
applied to that piece of the past or even only to our present but not to the future
of history, as if the divine power is weak and suffers *now* but will rule in God's history
in the future. Rather, in remaining an arena of freedom, history remains an arena
of essential ambiguity and of divine self-limitation, and so of alienation from God
as well as participation in God. Thus on the deepest level what Jesus did and what
was done to him represent and disclose essential and permanent realities of human
history. As representative of God's will and purposes in history, the powerlessness
of the divine perfection within history, the suffering of the divine being within
history, the alienation from the structures and potencies of history—these aspects
of the story of Jesus, as they were of the prophetic word in relation to Israel—
disclosed the permanent relation of God to historical life, and so the meaning which
the divine power and love give to history.[18] Jesus Christ is the center of history not
only by what he promises for the future—though that is crucial—but even more by
what he discloses of God's relation to history in the continuing present. The central
disclosure is found in the character of his historical life and destiny through which
the relation of God to history's passage is revealed; and in that disclosure the
redemptive forces that give history its ultimate meaning are seen.

How is it, then, that powerlessness and suffering, clear signs of the antithesis of
history to the divine will and the apparent defeat of the latter, disclose and effect
a meaning to history—since meaning in history, as is evident in all we have argued,
is possible only if there be a realization of the divine sovereignty in history, and so
some fundamental accord between human freedom, destiny and the divine will?
This is no context for a full-scale discussion of the incarnation and the atonement
and the new possibilities that stem from them. But the reality to which these
symbols point is central to a Christian understanding of history that takes the
continuing dilemmas of history as seriously as it does the possibilities of the new.[19]

Power is a central category for historical life, as we have seen. It represents the
power to be and to continue to be in time, and thus is a good, a sign of the divine
creation and the divine providential sustenance, and an important analog to the
divine being.[20] Power, therefore, is the legitimate object of all communal and
political labors, and its total loss is devastating to any creature. However, as subject,
as are all things in history, to human freedom, power in history is not only creative
but also destructive. It is always in part an unrighteous power, alienated from the
divine will on which it depends and so from its own true exercise. It can be and is
in part demonic; and it becomes more demonic when it loses sight of its own
partiality and unrighteousness. All power to be is of God. All power in history,
however, is misused by men and women to secure themselves against suffering and
death. The possibility of or condition for this misuse is clearly the reality of finite
freedom and the correlative self-limitation of God that make freedom in history
possible. Thus, in relating himself to the powers of history, God not only upholds
each creaturely power and permits its exercise, but also contends with creaturely

powers in judgment. In the powerlessness, suffering and death of Jesus, God manifests his alienation from and judgment of these established powers of history who
control human destiny for their own use and so who create the fate that snuffs out
human freedom. The final manifestation of this strange or "alien" relation of God
to human power, universal in historical life, is therefore in terms of *total* self-
limitation, almost total non-being, and so total alienation: in terms of powerlessness.[21] So long as freedom remains as the principle of actuality and God remains
self-limited, God cannot reveal himself unequivocally within historical power, i.e.,
eschatologically, because all historical power participates also in the demonic. He can
only reveal himself in history "hiddenly" or providentially as creative ground, as
judgment and as new possibility on the one hand, and paradoxically, on the other,
as nothingness or powerlessness in Jesus' weakness, suffering and death, i.e., in Jesus'
total participation in the weak and vulnerable conditions, the non-being, of existence. God accepts our weakness as we did not, in order to show us as creatures how
really to live in him.[22]

In turn powerlessness means subjection to a fate we cannot control and so it
means suffering in history. For humans this suffering is especially the lot of the
oppressed, the rejected and the outcast, those who are under fate, who have no
destiny on which their freedom can work, who have only the freedom to die. In
seeking desperately to escape this lot, we all compel others to adopt it. In revealing
his judgment on all human power through his powerlessness, God in Christ shows
not only how the suffering and death of our brothers arise from our grasping for
power, but he also reveals his willingness to subject himself to fate, to suffer with
those who lack power, and to die with all those that die. In the participation of God
in powerlessness and suffering, sin, the basic problem of history, is revealed by God's
total alienation from it. The resolution of sin, participation in God again, is manifested in the new reality of Jesus' life. And the consequences of that problem, fate,
suffering and death, are now shared and so conquered by God.[23] For God's power
or rule to reveal itself as righteous *power,* as the unequivocal sovereign goodness that
will overwhelm the evil of the world—either then or in the future—would merely
eradicate history. None are righteous,[24] so none could be spared in a manifestation
of righteous power; and no redemptive principles for and on *freedom* would have
begun.[25] If God is to redeem history as history, and give it its own meaning, it must
be through our wayward freedom and not over against it, through participation in
the full human condition and not through the eradication of it. Thus it must begin
with judgment of what is evil in history, with identification with what is powerless
and so suffers from that evil, and finally, with participation in fate, alienation,
suffering and death, that they may be overcome from within.

If all are unrighteous, even those whose fate it is to have little freedom to molest
others—and this seems the clear lesson of history—then there can be redemption
in history, and so meaning to history, only if the unrighteous are not so much judged,
punished and eradicated as accepted, forgiven and healed. For this reason, the
meaning of history both within history and beyond it comes more from the princi-

ples of justification and grace than from the promise of eschatological fulfillment; or better, eschatology must be interpreted in the light of justifying and sanctifying grace. For grace works on freedom, forgiving, reconciling and healing it; it does not remove it in favor of God's ultimate action alone and so in favor of an absolute divine sovereignty. Thus grace is the appropriate category for understanding the meaning of God's redemptive action within a fallen history, as providence is the appropriate category for understanding God's creative and judging action within general political and cultural history. Both are, to be sure, defined and controlled by God's eschatological goal. They are, however, better symbols for the work of God with freedom, with sin, with destiny and with fate than are the eschatological symbols which leave aside both the ontological structure of history and the character of history's actuality.

Central to the work of grace is the forgiving acceptance of God despite our sin, and our believing acceptance of this divine mercy. As the Reformation understood, justification is primary because sin is never completely gone, so that both for the individual and for history as a whole, participation in God—the sole hope of meaning—is always dependent on God's mercy rather than on our own perfection and worthiness.[26] And clearly, this principle of the priority of justification, and so of faith in ultimate meaning rather than a possession of it, applies to history as a whole as it does to each individual life. The necessary if not the sufficient condition for meaning in history is, therefore, the grace of justification, that we are all of us saved by God's grace through faith and not by our own works. In the powerlessness and suffering of Jesus, and through him God's participation in our alienation and suffering, this grace of justification is revealed as the central characteristic of God's love for his creatures and so as the continuing basis for our participation in God in future history.[27]

All of creaturely life participates in God: in its being, its continuing being, its spontaneity, its freedom, its novel possibilities, its responsibilities. In human existence this participation in divine ultimacy takes all the forms we have described and is the basis of every human capacity. We are, we know, we love, we create in God who is, therefore, for us being, truth and love—and the ground of new possibility. However, in that participation an alienation or estrangement takes place. The power to be, to know and to create are misused; the possibilities given to us are warped; love turns to possession and hostility; and fate, suffering and death emerge. As a result of this alienation within creation and providence, the creative work of God in history is twisted and even destroyed—as the first covenant with Israel illustrated. Fate and nemesis appear and the relation to God becomes hidden. Life—though still upheld and made creative by the divine ultimacy—loses its security, its meaning, its hope and its love. The divine participation in these estranged conditions of existence, as Tillich calls them,[28] or in the suffering, oppression and death of sin, as Moltmann puts it,[29] is, therefore, the beginning of redemption: the beginning of a reawakening to the divine presence in all of creaturely life, an acceptance of our acceptance by that continuing presence, and so a return in the spirit to what has always been the case: our dependence ontologically and providentially on God.

Faith is the inward or spiritual adequation of our existence to our ontological condition as creatures of God. It is to be dependent spiritually, personally, in decision and awareness on God for our security, meaning and confidence in the future as our being is already dependent on God's creative and providential power. Redemption, or the beginning of redemption in repentance, faith and new life in the spirit, is not the return to God on *every* level; for no creature can be quite separate from God and be at all. It is a return in the spirit from what had been an alienation in the spirit, a bringing to awareness and decision of a relationship of dependence that has always been there.[30] It is a new self-understanding as dependent on God for one's being, creativity and confidence; a new being in explicit commitment, faith and hope. And this return in the spirit which is faith begins when our alienation in the spirit is disclosed, and repentance is born. It comes when the divine acceptance of us and participation in us is manifested and inwardly apprehended; and it flowers when confidence for the future is born: when we accept, apprehend and so receive the new being. This participation of God in all the conditions of human existence is manifested in the life of Jesus; in its freedom, its finitude, its anxiety, its powerlessness, its suffering and its death. Thus are we assured not only that we are accepted despite these conditions of our life, but also that within them we, and all who suffer, who are rejected and who die, are thus also made one with God. In God's participation in our powerlessness, suffering and death in Jesus, we know that these are to be redeemed by the divine power in and beyond history.

The principle of meaning in history, then, has several different but related levels: a level of creative providence, a level of redemptive grace and a level of eschatological fulfillment. These "multi-leveled" redemptive forces of history which give meaning to history despite its ambiguity leading to destruction are universal. But the character and goal of all three levels of the divine activity in history are known most fully in Jesus, and thus the possibility of our certainty about them and of our inward acceptance of and participation in them is fullest there.

Through these forces of acceptance and of new reality the inner life of mankind receives hope of renewal: through new assurance of the divine presence, through new apprehension of our own alienation and estrangement, through a new forgetfulness of our own imperialistic ego and so a hope of the power now to love, through confidence in and security concerning the future.[31] Sanctification and surely perfection are never complete—sin does continue in individual and historical life. But there is a growth in grace, for a new reality has entered history; it moves throughout the cultural and religious life of mankind; it is the principle of spiritual reformation and the ground of the hope of cultural renewals. The inner estrangement of sin is thus fragmentarily conquered; new possibilities for human existence are thereby available in history, whose sign is the new reality manifested in Jesus as the Christ.

Finally, there are under providence the assurance of new creative possibilities for cultural and historical life growing out of the older, now ambiguous if not demonic forms of the present. These new possibilities are "indeterminate" and can represent genuine advances in the destiny which each human receives. They do not and cannot eradicate sin, for freedom is continually polar to destiny; and thus they cannot remove the possibility of a given destiny becoming again fate. Like the inner life of mankind, man's outer life, his historical and social existence, remains incomplete and fragmentary in history. The kingdom is always "not yet" and points to a more ultimate resolution beyond history. And yet in history that kingdom is continually coming in the new possibilities for a fateless existence that are there. Faith in providence is confidence that even in a disintegrating or demonic historical situation, a new kairos, and a new possibility for history, will come.

POSSIBILITIES OF MEANING WITHIN HISTORY: ESCHATOLOGY AS LURE AND AS NORM

Granted, then, that despite these forces of meaning experienced both as providence and as grace, the actuality of sin continues and fate hangs as a dark possibility over the future as well as the past, can we speak of hope for the future, of the ultimate eschatological hope as relevant to general history and its course? Unless we can, are we not back with the neo-orthodox declaring history to have "meaning" only insofar as individuals accept and participate in the redemptive work of God through Christ and the covenant community? If sin and fate continue in the future as in the past, and this has been our argument to date, how are providence and eschatology *positively* related to one another so that the social future and the course of history as well as history's individuals participate in God's final eschatological meaning?

The most fundamental ontological structure of temporal being and so of history, we have found, is the polarity of destiny and freedom, the centered interrelation of achieved actuality and future possibility that creates the present as process moves forward into the future. In turn the relation between actuality and possibility, the synthesis of past, present and future into self-creative event, is the most fundamental role of providence, through its creative power moving each achieved actuality, each given, into the role of a destiny for self-actualizing freedom, and then presenting to each present, in the light of that destiny, novel but relevant possibilities for its future. Thus, in any historical situation, whatever the depth of estrangement it manifests and however bound by fate its future may seem, there are new creative possibilities for that situation. To believe in providence, as Tillich said, is to be confident that in every situation creative possibilities are real.[32] It is, in effect, to know that every given is in reality destiny, a given in which possibilities for freedom are latent; that, therefore, fate is as much a symbol of our alienation from God's providence as it is an objective characteristic of history. As political consciousness opens up possibilities of political change in the most hopeless situation, so the consciousness of providence can transform a seemingly fated situation into one full of latent possibilities. Thus there can be in history the development of new economic and political structures, of correspondingly new concepts and norms of social interaction. The new is possible in history, and despite the continuation of sin within each novel form of history—as sin continued within democratic and socialist forms—life can in many ways become better.

Because of these new possibilities for new social orders, history does ascend on one important level. The forms of historical life can progress—and have progressed —and can thus represent higher, more humane structures of human social existence. To be sure, the inner situation of man vis-à-vis ultimacy, himself and his neighbor, the character of human freedom, is not thus resolved by the progress of objective history, by a new and better destiny given to freedom. Thus the ambiguity of history remains, its cyclical patterns recur and nemesis always threatens. Nevertheless, the interpenetration of individual and community, of inner life and objective social patterns and of destiny and freedom, inevitably means that objective social betterment feeds back into *relative* inner transformation. Men and women in a cooperative society are more cooperative. Alternatively, in a society that is unjust because hierarchical and insecure, men and women encounter fate and are inwardly driven to greater anxiety and so to further estrangement from themselves and others. Thus in a more just system—more just conceptually, normatively and legally—there are more just objective patterns of behavior. Goods are distributed more evenly; humans are less able to use power arbitrarily over each other; fewer people are excluded from meaningful participation in society's work. Personal freedom and so self-development more frequently and universally take place. These are real possibilities for history and they do make history better, more like the eschatological goal, the utopian ideal, the kingdom. As redeemed and transformed men and women can have effects on the humane character of their social order—as all conservative Christianity has allowed—so a more humane objective structure of society can have effects on the inner life of men and women, on the shape of their freedom—though destiny never determines freedom, for good or for ill, lest history be transformed into necessity.

Secondly, it is clear, as Reinhold Niebuhr pointed out, that the consequences of sin in terms of injustice, exploitation, oppression and suffering—what he termed the "guilt" of sin[33]—are greater whenever an ego has power and its neighbors have none; or, in our terms, the consequences of their own sin are greater for the person or group blessed with destiny rather than for the person or group suffering from fate. The wealthy, the politically powerful, the distinguished, the wise, the good, are not more sinful than ordinary people, though they may in many ways be more tempted. Rather their power makes their sin more effective, gives it vaster range and potency, and so makes it more destructive of the destiny, the freedom and the character of life of others. Thus, at the end of each era the creative and so the powerful, those who have heretofore been symbols for their culture of excellence or virtue *(arete)*, are now taken as symbols of evil. "The prejudice against the mighty," referred to as characteristic of the biblical view of evil, joins itself in the Christian interpretation of history with the conviction of the unrighteousness of all into a quite new synthesis: a revolutionary theology against the mighty of the earth combined with a theology of the universality of sin, of the judgment of God on all, and so of justification by grace through repentance, faith and participation in God's creative presence in life. In any case, granted that the consequences that entail suffering arise from inequality or imbalance of power, it follows that if indeterminate advances in the economic, political and social spheres, and higher levels of legal and social justice can in fact reduce imbalances of power, then they will reduce exploitation, oppression and so suffering as well. In the equalization of power through social reform, fate can be vastly reduced, even if the sin that continually causes it to reappear is not thereby reduced. If there are differences in justice and injustice, and so in the effective scope of sin and the suffering it brings, between contemporary societies—and all the neo-orthodox recognized this vis-à-vis democracy and fascism—there is in principle no reason there cannot be indeterminate differences between successive societies. Although no society can be perfect, *the* kingdom, nevertheless fate and its immediate consequence, suffering, can be reduced in history.

This confidence in new and creative possibilities for the historical future is, we noted, the implication of the biblical analogy. Out of the decay and failure of the old covenant, spoiled by Israel's rejection, comes the promise of a new covenant, a new providential possibility for social life. This is, moreover, surely also the direct intuition of a revolutionary situation and the ground for all creative political action. Granted, we may say, that humans will still be sinful in a more just social order, still! —*if* we stand historically amidst radical injustice, a society ruled and oppressed by an outside power, as in much of Eastern Europe and South America; or *if* we stand in a racist society legally, economically and politically; or in an economically unjust society with maldistribution of goods, of social power and of social participation; or in a politically tyrannical society where none but the powerful have legal rights or political voice—*if* we stand historically in such a situation, calling for radical change, our deepest historical intuition, the "knowledge" that lies back of all political praxis, tells us that a new political, economic, social or legal possibility will make a real difference to life. Sin may continue and the promised land is not yet; but life can be more humane than it was though it remains in part and in fact inhuman. The new is possible, and it can be a new with more justice and more fulfillment within it. The direct intuition of the possibility of improvement in history through objective social change is the basis of all creative political action and of revolutions alike. It is essential to creative historical existence. Historically this view of politics and of history has found its roots in biblical eschatology, and in a view of providence which understands God's work as the development of new possibilities in history. Theologically we should understand the appearance of these new possibilities for history as the way in which providence prepares for and is the presupposition of eschatology. The lure of new possibility inspires that historical activity which shapes a recalcitrant history in the direction of the ultimate kingdom.

This lure of new possibility in history, essential for creative politics, is in turn defined eschatologically. As providence is the historical presupposition for eschatology, so is eschatology the defining and controlling symbol for providence. We see God's providence at work in the ambiguity of our present by keeping one eye on the eschatological goal, the kingdom, and the other on the social forces and possibilities of our present—and determine our freedom in the light of destiny, of providential possibility and of God's ultimate goal. The central eschatological goal is the kingdom proclaimed by Jesus as the ultimate goal of God for history and beyond history, a kingdom that appeared in part with him but that was to be fulfilled only at the last. This symbol represents the social or communal implications of the full humanity manifested in individual form in Jesus himself, the sociohistorical counterpart of the new being embodied in him and experienced there.[34] Thus the goal of providence, the character of God's hidden work within the ambiguity of social existence, is defined and so clarified both eschatologically and christologically. It is defined eschatologically because it is the promised kingdom as the community of humans that is in general history the purpose of God's providential work. And in turn the eschatological kingdom is defined christologically because the solitary and yet sublime figure of Jesus, alienated from history and yet sharing all of history's suffering and terror, is as the Christ transparent to the ultimate power, meaning and love of God and so gives in promise the character of the kingdom as a community of the fullness of being, meaning and love. In eschatology and christology, therefore, are unveiled for us the logos that lures history, and so the *norm* for history[35]—the purpose guiding God's creative and providential work (in Whitehead's terms, God's subjective aim). Thus there we find too the norm for our political activity. Here is presented to us in Christian form that vision of authentic man and authentic society implicit in all moral assertions in history and so in every political decision. The primary role of eschatology in history is to clarify the ambiguity of God's providential work and thus to provide norms for our creative praxis.

The characteristics of the kingdom as manifested to us in the teachings and existence of Jesus are life, community and love, or, to bring these closer to political norms: being, participation, and responsible concern.

1. The promise of eternal life, basic to the character of the kingdom, represents the eschatological fulfillment of the creative and providential work of God in granting us all being and vitality, the power to be and to determine our own being for the future. Wherever this power is lost, and where humans face the terrible anxieties of insecurity, hunger, want and violence, of helplessness and of powerlessness, of being an object of the power of others and so of fate, there their being at its deepest level and so their humanity are threatened, and the creative work of God is challenged. As we noted, this urge for being and the power of being represents the deepest drive of political life. If it is guided by the eschatological norm, it represents a coordination of the political will with the creative providential will of God who gives being. Thus, wherever men and women are called to political action to insure the security of others in society, to eradicate whatever in nature or the social order makes others insecure or in want, or threatens their life and their self-determination—a large part of the meaning of justice—there they are hearing a call to participate in God's providential work in giving new being through new possibilities for social life. Whatever natural and social forces tend to assure the

security of life for all, in them we know the hidden work of God as creative providence in time takes place.

2. Central to the kingdom is the concept of community, of the participation of all in the common life. This participation, as we saw, was basic for a consciousness of meaning or of worth in life, and it depends on an inward eros toward a communal activity that seems to us worthful and a social order in which for us such worth was embodied and possible. Without this subjective eros and this objective "place" for our work, our life dries up, becomes unreal, we lose our identity, we despair. Political life is suffused with this question of life's meanings and their relation to communal work, and through that to the general social principles of communal order. Wherever, therefore, social existence has in the present such a sense of worthful participation, and the social order makes that participation universally possible, there the creative power of providence is at work constituting the social, economic and political orders. Correspondingly, political action directed toward that goal, toward a new social order replete with more meaningful work for all, is correlated with providential possibility and directed eschatologically.

3. Finally, the kingdom is a community of responsible love, of the fulfillment of autonomous persons and responsible morality in concerned and respectful community. The moral dimension of life is fulfilled in the achievement of authentic identity; but the authentic identity of each of us is discovered and realized only when we are in creative relations with one another. Authenticity and community cannot be separated, and thus both are fulfilled in reuniting love. Thus, wherever communities of mutual respect, help and tolerance are evident, where men and women inwardly have autonomy and freedom and outwardly are bound with others in mutual respect and regard, wherever the common good is ingredient in the life and action of responsible individuals, there the further work of providence is present. Correspondingly, to work politically against social structures that encourage individual self-interest alone, that thus produce hostility, competition, isolation and loneliness, and toward possible structures that encourage mutuality, cooperation and respect is to work with God's providence.

In sum, we can discern the work of providence, and so the concrete political task, in the creation of social structures conducive to security, meaning, community and self-actualization, toward, that is to say, economic and social justice, communal participation, dignity and respect in work and relations, and freedom and self-direction in private and public life.[36] Security, meaning, community and self-actualization are, like their more abstract counterparts, justice, equality, freedom and order, political goals of the most general sort, norms for history's existence as a whole to be made concrete in each historical situation by political judgment and action. To me they imply for the immediate future, as we noted, a new synthesis of individual self-actualization with the common good, of socialist economic responsibility and universal participation with democratic self-determination and freedom. It is, we may note, possibilities in *these* directions, not necessarily possibilities for a more affluent or more secure life for ourselves, that are presented to us in all historical situations, however "fated" they may seem in themselves to be. Wherever we are, in whatever historical situation and at whatever level of material advancement, we can labor for greater security, meaning, community and self-actualization; under providence there is a "calling" for every present.[37] The possibilities which providence presents to us are defined by the ultimate goal of God. Through our understanding of the goal of providence as defined eschatologically, we can know what it is that we are in the immediate context called historically to do.

In the move from general norms, related to ultimate notions of human and social authenticity and so to the character, direction and goal of history itself—and all such sociocultural norms have such a relation—to more concrete norms suitable as basic to political policy, a dialectic between *retrieval* of traditional symbols and *reinterpretation* in the light of new possibilities inevitably appears. Historical action is, as is historical being, a union of destiny and freedom, of continuity and order, with novelty and change; and God's work is providential as well as eschatological. Creative action, therefore, retrieves what is given and reshapes it in a new form for the emerging situation. Every political action must deal with the continuities, structures, trends, problems and possibilities latent in the given that is that moment's destiny; but because temporality is change and process, it must deal with them in new ways. Thus, from within the given both the potentially creative structures and trends, and the potentially creative traditional symbols must be "retrieved," reinterpreted and reshaped for the new situation that is the present given to us. The symbols which judge our oppressive present, the symbols which shape a hoped-for future, are thus at once given from our own past and at the same time new possibilities for our future, part of a cultural tradition and yet possibilities for the new that is to come. This is as true of social and political symbols as of the more ultimate religious ones we have here traced. It was a new covenant, but still a "covenant," that was the new possibility toward which prophecy yearned; it was as Messiah, suffering servant and as second Adam and Lord that the new being in Jesus was interpreted and proclaimed. On the political level, therefore, the future must be dealt with creatively in terms of a refashioning of traditional symbols into new possibilities, a new synthesis of antitheses in our present—both of which, the socialist and the democratic, are also estranged from their *own* present. The ultimate Christian symbols of authentic humanity and society gained from a christological and eschatological interpretation of God's providential work in history are, therefore, not only possibilities for the future—though they are that—they are also aspects of historical traditions as well, the results of the continual work of providence within the responding creative and destructive life of men and women.

Correspondingly, it is important to note that this union of providence and of eschatology here offered sees religion as having both a constitutive and a critical role in social existence as the latter moves into the future. In our analysis of historical existence we have found, first, that human life in time is a social and in that sense "historical" existence, that its security, its meaning and its moral norms are given it by its community; and second, that this security, meaning and morality participate in ultimacy and thus have a religious dimension and ground, expressed in the sacrality of social structures and symbols. Thus is religion constitutive of society, its "substance," as Tillich puts it, and thus does society, and with it individual existence, disintegrate when that religious substance dissolves. Without question, this dissolution of the sacrality of cultural institutions, of communal meaning and the public good, and so of the meaning of the participation of individuals in that social world (except for their own self-interest) is one of the deepest sources of disintegration in modern society. To retrieve and so reconstitute the religious dimension of social existence—to encourage and enliven those structures and symbols conducive of security, meaning, community and self-actualization—is therefore one of the predominant—the "priestly"—roles of special religious groups—the churches—in society, a human response to the creative work of providence. But religion is a risk, and the religious dimension the ground of the demonic in history as well as of history's creative possibilities. Thus special religious groups have as their other task the criticism as well as the constitution of the structures of social order, and the obligation or calling to retrieve them in new ways closer to the norms of individual and social authenticity. This is the "prophetic" role of the church, a role of witness to the divine judgment and the call to new possibilities beyond the warped and desecrated traditions that have been given. We have found Yahweh's "providence" fulfilling both of these roles in Israel's history;[38] by the same token, the Christian community has, insofar as it is able, both a constitutive and a critical role in its own social world. The emphasis on one or the other is, as we noted, to be determined by the kairos of each present, the possibility that may be latent in that destiny of either active constitution and of retrieval, or of critical judgment and so of novel possibility. In either case, history moves through given destiny and creative human response—through communal judgment, decision and action embodied in politics —into the new. Such movement requires *interpretation* if it is to be conscious, purposeful and free, i.e., human, and not passive, irrational and blind; interpretation is the ground of creative praxis, of politics. And such interpretation in turn requires a symbolic apprehension of the fundamental sovereignty, the essential norms and the ultimate goal of historical process, as the courage, humility and confidence to enact the new requires participation in and commitment toward the work of the divine being in the movement of time.

The Role of Eschatology in the Continuing Present: The Immanence and Transcendence of the Kingdom

Hope for a new in history growing out of the old is, therefore, basic to political life and to Christian theology alike. To interpret history thus eschatologically, as moving through new possibilities toward the kingdom, although a practical and theoretical necessity, is, however, *also* a risk. It is a risk, first, because such political hopes in the new are easily disappointed—nemesis may appear—and then the theological framework, instead of supporting political confidence and courage, may dissolve when that confidence seems to have no historical grounds. The other risk is that a new and relevant possibility for *our* history can itself be taken to be ultimate, to be a resolution of the total problem of history, of the inner as well as the outer side. This is the utopian dream that has bewitched most revolutionary movements, in our present especially the Marxist, as it did Christian sectarians before them, and as it surely did ourselves the children of the liberal culture. Each believed that with new social structures a new human being would appear cleansed of his and her self-concern and so of their ideology, cruelty and will to power. And with this faith in our own eschatological role—the essence of all political idolatry—we can see our role in history as ultimate, our cultural achievements as absolute, and refuse to face, when their time comes, the fallibility, the injustice, the exploitation and the mortality of even that once new world. This is why eschatological symbols, especially that of the kingdom to come, must have a *double* reference. For the new in *our* history, even when it is manifestly creative, cannot be simply regarded "eschatologically," as the ultimate of God's future, lest a revolutionary fanaticism replace a conservative one, and the revolution in the end itself become a force for total repression.

The eschatological symbols of the kingdom and its glory, representing the *ultimate* goal of providence, must, we said, have a double reference.[39] First and foremost, the eschatological symbol of the kingdom has an *immediate* and *immanent* reference to the new possibilities of social betterment in the immediate future as defining those possibilities by indicating the ultimate goal of God's hidden providential work—namely, being, participation, community and self-actualization—and so guiding political action for the future. Thus does eschatology function as a lure, the lure of the utopian ideal, opening up a stable situation by presenting the stark contrast of an absolute ideal, by revealing the creative possibilities latent within that situation[40] and by indicating the direction that creative political action must take. Without the "not-yet," the vision of authentic humanity and authentic community that the present does not embody, political judgments, both critical and constructive, would have no grounded norm and the work of providence as new possibility would be quite obscured, undefined and to us meaningless, providing no guidance.

Secondly, however, the eschatological symbols must have as well a *transcendent* reference beyond every historical possibility, even the one that lures us now, and beyond even what providence and human freedom can together produce in history —lest our historical program and action claim to achieve and represent that ultimate goal. The judgment of God on what is alien to himself will be an essential part of the relation of the rule of God to *every* social achievement and so to *every* period of history. For no society in history *is* the kingdom, and realization of this is one essential part of every society's health. The very creative advance of history that inspires our hope depends on a vivid sense of the relativity and continuing ambiguity of what has been or is being achieved. Only if American culture realizes its own nonultimacy and fault can it help rather than impede progress in the immediate future. In this way in history the kingdom will remain transcendent to all of history's forms, however far they have progressed. The kingdom must be "eschatological" not only as future *in* history, but also as transcendent *to* history. Like providence, therefore, eschatology has a negative, judging role in history as well as a positive luring one.

The kingdom represents in symbolic form the impingement of God's ultimate goal on historical process: as the lure of new possibility, as judgment on what has been achieved and then as further lure of possibility beyond possibility. In conjunction with providence as destiny and as possibility, eschatology keeps history open for the new and so for the further realization of humanity within history. This correlative understanding of providence and eschatology is, as the dialectical history of Christianity shows, crucial. If history be understood providentially without eschatology, providence can be viewed statically, and the ambiguity of the present be seen as the final word of God for history. If history be defined eschatologically without providence, the new that each political movement seeks to achieve can be understood as itself God's ultimate intention—and in each case, religious symbolism becomes the instrument of a demonic politics, the one conservative and oppressive, the other initially revolutionary but in its own time brimming with reaction.

To understand history reflectively and to deal with it practically: theoria and praxis, are thus intimately associated. For history is event, a compound of destiny —of continuities, trends and latencies—with freedom, the envisagement of relevant possibility, the awareness of obligation toward these possibilities, and the enactment of one of them in decision and action. To *understand* such a compound of actuality and possibility, of given continuity and responsible decision, is inevitably to be involved in both comprehending history and participating in it, in both theoria and praxis—for history is compounded of an objective course and participatory decision. To act in history in terms of responsible freedom, it is necessary to understand it: its structure embodied in its ontology and its dynamic factors, its concrete latencies embodied in its actual major trends, and its relevant possibilities arising out of those trends in relation to our capacities and intentions. The pitfall of the interpretation of social change generated by social science is that the emphasis on theoria and so on continuity or law is so strong that the relation of freedom and of participation to history and so of new possibilities and of radical praxis, is given no theoretical grounding. The pitfall of purely political and moral interpretations is that they are so concerned with right decision that they ignore an understanding based on careful theory concerning history's structures and its dominant trends. We have tried to show how these two often disparate elements of our culture's life—represented by social and economic theory on the one hand and by political ethics and history on the other—can be brought to greater unity by an ontological and ultimately a theological analysis of history, and the unity of theoria and praxis rationally grounded in an understanding of history that involves as its essential motif human participation in history. To understand history without praxis is to portray it in theory as determined; i.e., to see history without human participation, and so to reject responsibility and to be unable to conceive as well as to be unwilling to will new possibilities. To view history solely in terms of praxis is to see history without determining continuities or structures—and so to envision possibilities unrelated to concrete actuality.[41] In each case freedom is rendered groundless and made ineffective. To unite destiny and freedom, or inwardly theoria and praxis, is of the essence of being historical; it is the ground of creative politics.

Our argument, however, has moved beyond this point. For we have claimed that both theoria and praxis in history necessitate a theological level of understanding. With regard to a reflective understanding of history, we have argued that: (1) the relation of destiny to freedom cannot be made intelligible or coherent without the divine activity of providence as being and as possibility; (2) the transformation of destiny into fate cannot be comprehended without the category of the warping or estrangement of freedom in sin; (3) the continuing presence of new possibilities within a fated situation cannot be comprehended without providence; and (4) the redemptive forces recreative of freedom are inexplicable without the category of grace—not to mention (5) the need for a theological understanding of the *meaning* of history: providence, christology and eschatology, if the continuation of sin is not to drain history in theory of its meaning and in practice of its hope. Only a theological understanding of history, structured in the categories of Christian faith, is, we have argued, adequate to the interpretation of the ambiguity that is history as we experience it, and as the modern consciousness has sought to understand and to interpret it.

In this chapter we have sought to complete this argument, such as it is, by indicating that creative praxis, as well as intelligible understanding, requires the same symbolic framework of providence, christology and eschatology. Praxis as creative action depends on the unity of destiny and possibility, and so of continuities and trends out of the past with novel but relevant possibilities for the future. Thus praxis expresses the human response to and creative enacting of the work of providence as constitutive being and as novel possibility in history. Creative politics is initially grounded in the work of providence and is unintelligible theologically without providence. However, as we have just argued—and here the eschatological thinkers are right—creative politics is also dependent on the impingement of the eschatological future on the political present lest the powerful promises of the immediate— of present destiny and of too relevant possibilities—lure a praxis solely hitched to providence into an enervating acceptance of the status quo. The pressure of the ultimate goal, politically of the kingdom, and the promise of fulfillment, of utopia, are crucial in the transcendence of the present into new possibilities—for it is, as we have said, eschatology that defines and clarifies the work of providence. Thus (1) the ultimate picture expressed in the kingdom, pressing upon the present, reveals the alienation and so the injustice of the present; (2) it thus defines and clarifies the judgment of providence upon the status quo through its illumination of this contrast. In this way, by expressing the ultimacy of God's future, eschatology opens the present to new possibilities in contrast to what is. (3) However, by its ultimate transcendence beyond all possibility, eschatology provides the only continuing ground for radical criticism. For in opening the present to new and relevant possibility, it also opens those possibilities to a sense of their own relativity. Only if the kingdom transcends those who seek to bring it in, will it come closer. Finally, (4) by its affirmation that the kingdom is the divine goal toward which the future points, eschatology grounds the eros of all political action and political hope in what is taken to be most real in history.

A noneschatological politics in the end either finds the kingdom latent in its own present reality; it finds the kingdom too unequivocally in the new reality that is being introduced; or it fails to maintain hope and so eros in the ambiguities of the present. This is not to say that only a politics explicitly grounded in Christian symbols is creative. It is to say that the presuppositions of creative political action—its sense of the unity of destiny and freedom, its sense of possibility and of judgment in relation to the present, and its sense of its own relativity as well as hope—that these presuppositions of praxis are made explicit, coherent and communicative of power for the future most adequately in terms of the symbols of providence, of christology and of eschatology explicated here. Theoria and praxis unite coherently and crea- tively in a theological interpretation of historical process—for history can be under- stood, born and creatively dealt with only in relation to God.

THE ULTIMATE FUTURE OF GOD

Eschatology so understood represents the impingement of the ultimate as future on the existential and political present. It tells us, therefore, more of our present dilemmas, possibilities and risks than it does of God's ultimate future. Our question now is, can nothing more of the meaning of the divine promise for our future—the eschatological promise—be known than this existential and political relevance to our *present?* Is this ambiguity, continuing in history despite the possibilities of progress already outlined, all we can know? What then is our eschatological hope in its ultimate shape? What is it that we ultimately hope *for* in the ambiguity of individual and historical life as they move into the future?

This question of the final goal of God, of the ultimate shape of the divine activity as it unites with human freedom in history, is the most difficult of theological questions. Here all theological reflection is vastly tentative and hypothetical in form, surely imaginative proposals and not doctrines.[42] But the ultimate shape of Chris- tian hope is in some measure symbolically definite, lest there be no such thing as *Christian* hope. Thus, as Tillich remarked, total silence is as impossible for us as is predictive certainty.[43] Methodologically the problem in this area is that two of the levels of theological meaning here drop away and abandon us. I refer to the experien- tial and the political dimensions of meaning. For we can have no direct, present experience of the future object of our ultimate hope, and, as we have just argued, these ultimate hopes in present political life mean only *indirectly,* as lure, as guide and norm, and as limiting judgment on the continuing present. Thus the intrinsic or referential meanings of eschatological symbols—what in the end we hope *for*— have for us in the present only eidetic and ontological form. Our *certainty* here is based on present Christian experience, the experience of God as power or being, as truth and as love.[44] We can, however, only deduce the meanings of these symbols for our ultimate hope from an interpretation of the biblical symbols and from the implications of our ontological understanding of God and his relation to history and to humanity. Hence these promises, however significant, feel so abstract and tentative, not defined by the relative sureties of present common experience or of immediate action.

Nevertheless, this much can be said in the way of argument from the character of present experience. If human experience is continually in relation to ultimacy, as we have sought to show; and if that relation is for us, as it is, intentional and historical in character, directed at the future both in our individual and our communal life, then the question of the ultimate future, the goal for history and for individuals alike, is inescapable. The blanket negation of such a goal represented by death, that death puts the term to this relation to ultimacy both for ourselves as individuals and for mankind in history, is a possibility never to be disproved in present experience. But if it were so, if death were the term, it would mean that our present relation to ultimacy was not in fact ultimate, that the sacral horizon in which we seem to live was not our real horizon, and thus that the presuppositions of most of our human individual and communal life, creative and destructive, were themselves illusions. Then the final, real environment of human being would be the physical world in which men and women die, and the final environment of history the physical universe which will almost certainly some day come to an end in its present form. Some sort of eschatological hope is thus implied in our direct experience of ultimacy in the present as well as entailed by the biblical symbols and the fact of the resurrection. But the form of that hope can be derived only from the eidetic shape of those religious symbols and from the ontological understanding of them we have gained—and this is very tentative indeed.

Is this ultimate future of God individual, and in another, suprahistorical realm, transcendent to history and to history's achievements and failures, as in traditional Christian eschatology? But then what can it mean as the goal of history? The answer would be: no more than it did for Augustine, and that was little enough. Or is the ultimate future of God social and historical, a "last time" in history that is in a simple sense the goal of history as in liberal Christianity, in secular progressivism and socialist thought, and seemingly in much liberation theology? But in that case, what can it mean for the individuals of history who died long before the end, and how does it square its perfectionism with the ontological structure of history: the polarity of destiny and freedom and the self-limitation of God, and with the character of the actuality of history as estrangement, alienation and ambiguity? Every theological symbol, Gustav Aulen once wisely said,[45] must be interpreted through our understanding of God and not just by and through itself alone. This is particularly true in eschatology for the reasons just given. Otherwise we are impaled hopelessly on the dilemma between an incredible final social goal of history without history's individuals, or an abstractive transhistorical haven for individuals without history's social achievements and without even the real ontological context for those individuals, a dilemma well illustrated in the opposition between conservative individualistic Christianity and collectivist Marxism.

In examining the notion of God's providence, I have said that God is experienced in our historical existence as the source of our continuing being, the ground of the possibilities which our freedom can actualize, and now most importantly as the initiator of our reconciliation with him, with our own authentic selves and with our fellows. God is being, logos and love, creating an autonomous, self-actualizing historical creature facing an open future of real possibility but in need continually of reconciliation, renewal and return. Perhaps the main theme of the gospel is the reality of that reconciliation and renewal, and the promise of that return.[46] This is the primary meaning of grace and the primary promise of our faith for the future. The divine life thus represents an ultimate being from which autonomous beings flow into process and continue in being, a creative logos in which autonomous beings are in turn creative under the divine guidance of new possibilities, and a divine love through which these creatures are brought back into relation with one another and into the divine life. This reunion of individuals with one another and of each with their divine ground begins here and is the basis of the new reality and quality of life experienced everywhere that the redemptive forces of history are experienced. It is not experienced in fullness here, but it points both in promise and in its own intentionality beyond this life to a final completion. This is a reconciliation and a reunion in which both the creaturely shares in the permanence and the harmony of the divine experience, and the divine experience in turn is added to, enriched and so made ever fuller by the creaturely that is reunited to it.[47]

Generally classical eschatology has stressed that it is individuals who are thus brought back into the permanence and harmony of the divine life.[48] But as we have seen, neither human individuals nor human creativity can be separated from the historical communities in which humans exist, and whose creations are the work in part of God's providence in history. If, then, God brings into himself, into his enlarging experience and life, what the creaturely world has achieved through his providence—a theme richly elaborated by Whitehead and Tillich[49] and fully in accord with the classical tradition—then the wayward but creative course of culture and so of history, as well as the wayward life of individual persons, finds everlasting fulfillment and completion in the experience of God. As his life is the source of our being and our possibilities, individual and social, so it is the completion of whatever his creatures have achieved in their freedom; and that is always a communal reality. The new that has been achieved in time finds its lodgment and so its eternal meaning in the eternity of God's experience.[50]

All that is of value in the course of time—all that has actual being, creativity, real communion and love—will be an *object* of the ultimate divine experience, transformed and elevated by the richness and compassion of that experience, and so itself a *subject* in that completed harmony. What each of us individually and collectively has done that is not of value—in being, activity and communion—will be known, but negated, itself unable to share in the divine experience, "dismissed," as Whitehead puts it, "to the triviality of merely individual fact."[51] This last represents a real and serious threat for most of us. What each of us has achieved in becoming authentic, in autonomous being, in loving and in creating, is little enough indeed. The basis for real hope, therefore, lies not in our own autonomously created value but (1) in the reality of reconciliation, participation and new life through the new covenant of forgiveness and of grace—the new being—which can accept, complete and even transform the paltry and distorted efforts we have made. (2) It is our humanity, our achieved humanity, that is the criterion for our participation in God, symbolized by the presence of Jesus, the true human, as our final judge. (3) The divine word of justifying mercy is such that it will complete our being with an "alien" righteousness, with the creative perfection of the divine love, and with the transforming harmony of the divine experience, despite the vast unrighteousness to be found in us all.

There can be no dual destiny in this hope, if there is to be hope at all. No ultimate division between persons who are sheep and persons who are goats, those who participate in God and those who are condemned to hell, is admissible if the divine power is to be ultimately sovereign and the divine love the ultimate quality of that power. Orthodox Calvinism was correct in its supralapsarian emphasis: God's will to redeem was made *not* in the light of either the fall or of our fallible individual efforts to regenerate or to fulfill ourselves.[52] The implication of this profound doctrine, however, for me at least as well as for that far more authentic Calvinist Karl Barth,[53] is that that eternal will of God for redemption had as its object not selected individuals but a lovingly created and gracefully accepted race in which, as this doctrine makes crystal clear, no ultimate division vis-à-vis redemption was for God's will possible.[54]

Experience and the gospel alike contradict such an ultimate division that has dominated our tradition.[55] Our experience tells us that God is related as creative ultimacy to all humans—and to all creatures alike—and that the differences between our responses to this relation—in our being, our loving and our creativity—are at best relative differences.[56] Whether we speak of faith or of works, commitment or love, we can never discover an ultimate division between ourselves and others. Even more, experientially, if we be honest, we know unequivocally that together we share tragically in the nonachievements and the waywardness that is characteristic of even the worst of us. Moreover, the gospel assures us from its side that all alike need mercy at the end if they are to be saved at all, that God's love reaches to the unworthy as well as to the worthy, and so in principle to all. It would be ironic indeed if the gospel preached a love that transcends all differences, divisions and faults, a mercy that was greater than all sin[57]—and then established a new and more ultimate division between faith and unfaith (unfaith being sin) which the divine love could not overcome. However we argue, so long as there is a dual destiny, faith is a merit that saves—unless God has inscrutably chosen us above others (or perhaps he has not!). In either case, the width, efficacy and supremacy of the divine love is abrogated in favor of an ultimate partiality that contradicts the glory of that love, and the divine agape has as its own background an arbitrariness that abrogates the essential meaning of agape.[58] The firm doctrines of the universality of sin and the nonexclusive character of the divine justifying grace mean, therefore, *either* that there is in God an arbitrary predestination that contradicts our deepest experience of our own autonomy and relativity and our certainty of his love, *or* that God intends as his ultimate goal the salvation through his many-colored grace of all that is of value or can be redeemed in each creaturely life. It is hard to speak of good news or of valid grounds for hope on any other terms.

We have come, then, to the end—an end, like the beginning, in God. The ways we have tried to conceive the divine beginning and especially this end, and the intervening work of God in our common history, as the infinite source of our continuing being, the creative ground of our new possibilities, and the loving source of our hopes for reunion and fulfillment, have been different from much in the classical tradition of Christian thought and witness—as is appropriate among humans whose commitment and understanding are historical in character. But we have also said that being, possibility and hope in the movement of time into the future depend on God's ultimate being, creative order and love alone. Further, we have said that the God on whom we depend is active in process, bringing the new out of the judged and decaying old, and leading history through the dialectic of creativity, sin and new fulfillment to its goal—this the Old Testament proclaims, and thus this Paul, Augustine and Calvin would have understood and possibly approved. Perhaps one day we shall know. What we do know now is the sovereignty of God in and through our wayward creation of new possibilities and the love of God which, knowing no limits, reaches to and includes his whole creation. This present knowledge, which is the substance of our gospel, shapes and grounds our hopes for creative political action, and our hopes for our own and for history's end.

12

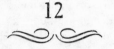

THE GOD OF PROCESS,
OF POSSIBILITY AND OF HOPE

The Temporality of Finite Being and the Actuality of God

The chapters that have preceded concerning the nature of historical passage have contained several strands of meaning: an ontological interpretation of historical passage, an appeal to our common experience of that passage as freighted with ultimate issues and a sacred dimension, an elucidation of the moral obligations, norms and possibilities involved in historical action, and finally, on the basis of crucial Christian symbols, an attempt to bring all of these strands together into a theological understanding of history. Our work has thus culminated in a Christian interpretation of the possibilities, problems, sources of resolution, prospects and grounds for hope in history. In this process of understanding history theologically, the symbol of God has, of course, assumed a central role—though our attention has been directed primarily at interpreting history rather than conceiving God. Because our theological reflection on history has sought to unite biblical and traditional symbols with the modern historical consciousness, the symbol of God in this account reflects important changes from the symbol as interpreted in traditional theology. It may, therefore, be useful in concluding this essay to center our concern directly on the notion of God herein implied and to begin to formulate a "doctrine" of God in the light of this interpretation of history. In these preliminary remarks on the doctrine of God our attention will be more directly concentrated on the ontological meaning of the symbol than at its existential meanings, i.e., on the conception itself rather than directly on its relevance for our questions of meaning and of salvation, and so of existence and of praxis. On the other hand, as our discussion of the relation of the structure of history to its meaning evidences, no clear and certainly no definitive separation can be made between ontology and ethics, ontology and meaning, between the nature of God, the responsibilities of faith and the promise of salvation.

The ontological interpretation of historical passage here presented[1] has been a "process" interpretation. Whether this ontology can be successfully applied to other areas of experience and other dimensions of reality than the historical is a question not broached here. However, the unity of experience and so of nature and of history as well as their difference—a theme we have emphasized—forces upon any interpreter of history the affirmation that ontological categories applicable to history must be applicable, in some analogical way, to all of experienced reality including what we term "nature."[2] By the process character of this interpretation are indicated three things. (1) Finite being is here viewed as fundamentally and essentially temporal, as in radical passage, as possessing as part of its essence the movement from an inherited and irremovable past into a future that is not yet. This movement from the actual into the possible, generating in that movement both finite being and time, forms the most essential character of being. Being is temporality, process; and our every experience of our own being (Chapter 1), and our reflections on our being (Chapters 1, 3 and 4) drive toward an ontology of temporal process. Thus, whatever continues in time, whatever forms the "substance" in this continuing passage, shares in the temporality, the relativity, the contingency and the ultimate mortality of things in time. The passage from moment to moment characterizes all of finite being, relativizes it to its context, illustrates its radical dependence—and opens up the possibility of its freedom and creativity.

(2) Events arise in time not merely because of inherited characteristics—as if some unchanging substance or unyielding route of causation continues uncontingently in passage. Events arise through self-actualization in each present. Because the achieved actuality "has been"—finite being being *temporal*—"room" is, so to speak, made in the present for self-actualization. Temporality is the ground for causality, the dependence of present on past; yet it is also the ground for self-realization, for the freedom of the present from the past that is now gone.[3] A response in the present occurs to the given that comes from the past, and it is out of that union of given with present response that the realities of historical passage arise, namely, events. Thus the fundamental ontological polarity of temporal being —of a personal existence, of communal existence and of the union of the two in history itself[4]—is the polarity of destiny and freedom: the inherited facticity of achieved actuality brought to a new synthesis by self-actualization in the present.

(3) While based on destiny and never free of it, freedom, moreover, also involves possibility. The essence of self-constitution is the retrieval of destiny in the projection of the self into possibility, into a new future. There is then no freedom, and by implication no temporality or genuine passage, unless the future is open; and openness means ontologically the reality of alternatives, the status of possibility as *possibility*. Temporality or process thus implies that the modal distinction of achieved actuality and undetermined possibility is as fundamental as inheritance and as freedom in passage: destiny, freedom and possibility together make event and constitute the ontological structure of history. Or, put another way, temporal passage is the locus of being, where finite being comes to actuality and is; for finite being is a union of destiny and possibility through self-actualization. Finite being achieves itself through decision, in uniting past actuality and future possibility in present event.

As we have noted, this ontological structure of destiny, freedom and possibility, of past, present and future, raises ontological questions about its ground, that is, in the symbolism of our religious tradition, about God: about God as necessary being and as providential possibility. Such an understanding of being as temporal seems to call for that which in some regard transcends passage in order that process, so understood, be intelligible. Whether such "questions," arising from our experience of our temporality and from our understanding of that experience, constitute a "proof";[5] whether the incompleteness of this ontological account of temporal becoming logically and demonstrably *entails* a further divine factor that in some measure transcends becoming, are methodological questions we shall not here fully investigate.

Suffice it to say that on this level of reflection questions merge smoothly into becoming answers; wonderings about whether a further factor is entailed easily become affirmations that there is one—*if* our deepest intuitions also manifest to us the coherence and rationality of all things.[6] The rationalist appeal to the relevance of "sufficient explanation" or to "the requirements of logic," the principles of sufficient reason and of noncontradiction, is at this level not a final or incontrovertable appeal, as the history of philosophy from Hume through Kant and Dewey to Ayer well illustrates. This appeal to the relevance of logic and of sufficient reason itself must be supported by the intuition—or the "faith"—that coherence is constitutive of reality as a whole and therefore that our desire to explain exhaustively and to understand coherently faithfully reflects the structure of the real. The validity of this intuition cannot by the nature of the case be demonstrated by rational argument, for the relevance of rational demonstration for that which undergirds experience is now the very question at issue. Probably both intuition and feeling on the one hand and rational argument on the other are, as in much of life, here interwoven. A deep intuition of being within emerging becoming, of a continuing structure of possibility within the changes of process, and of the continuing order and so rationality of proces—intuitions fundamental to religion, to knowing and to culture alike—are expressed or thematized in reflective arguments. Argument articulates, it does not create, the most fundamental intuitions or presuppositions with which we live—though arguments can open us to these intuitions and can hold our minds fast to their reality. Cut off from this basis in our existence, in these deepest levels of our awareness, these arguments as purely rational demonstrations become ineffective and irrational, and so vulnerable to a rationalistic criticism expressive of other modes of existence from which a sense of ultimate coherence has dissipated. In union with an apprehension of being within becoming, and of order within novelty and change, arguments can, however, add intellectual understanding and so intellectual assent to those affirmations through which a creative existence is possible. A "natural theology" is thus itself dependent on our deepest intuitions, which are in turn dependent on the manifestation of the divine ground and the divine logos within the experienced given. They do not take us to that ground so much as articulate its experienced presence and thus bring what is deeply felt to intellectual expression.

In any case, this ontological interpretation of historical process—like the phenomenological examination of historical experience—points to a principle of ultimacy within passage as the ground of its possibility. This is on three counts. All are involved in the phases of our temporal being on the one hand and in the fundamental ontological structure of actuality and possibility, and their relation to one another into present event on the other, a relation out of which finite being arises.

1. The first ponders the temporality of being in relation to the past: How is it that achieved actuality, if it is constituted by events and not by enduring and so determining substances or essences, presents itself in each moment as a given, a destiny over time from the now receding and so vanishing past? How can the past *be* in the present so as to affect the present, to be known by it and to be reshaped by present freedom and self-determination? If all is temporal and contingent, if all passes into a vanished and so ineffective past in coming to be, then how is the continuity of existence possible? Clearly, the possibility of being, of causing, of being caused, of experiencing and of knowing depend on this elusive unity between an immediate past that is now gone and the living present, between moments or durations of temporal passage. How can what is temporal *be*, how can becoming be and be known?

Some principle of necessary being or of "creativity" must be there as the principle of transition, as what Whitehead calls "the ultimate" in any philosophy. This is the élan or power of process by which each achieved moment is projected beyond its passing self to become the ground or the origin (the "initial data")[7] of the next moment. For finite being to be and to be contingent in passage, there must be a power of being transcendent to that contingency and to that continual passing away. The temporality and contingency of being itself requires that which essentially conquers or overcomes temporality and contingency. Such we have termed the creative "preserving" or "sustaining" providence of God[8] through which the continuation of finite being, the destiny with which each event begins and from which it takes its rise, is brought into effectiveness in present actuality. This is not to say that God is the *sole* "cause" of the given from the past, that primary causality replaces secondary causes. It is to say that the continuing divine power of being overcoming the non-being of temporality is the ground or condition of the *possibility* of secondary causality, i.e., of the continuation and effectiveness of the destined past in the living present.[9] God here is the power of actuality or being that constitutes or reconstitutes being from moment to moment, that brings achieved actuality out of the vanishing mortality of the past into the life of the present; that moves what is objectified and gone into the role of a determining factor in the living present. It is, therefore, that infinite power of being out of which and through which all aspects of our destiny continue to be in each present as active qualifications of that present and so as conditions for our existence, as conditions for the self-determination wherewith we come into actuality. God is temporal or in temporality, and not the negation of the temporal, in that his necessary being, threatened by no contingency, brings each past into its creative role in the succeeding present. On the other hand, he is eternal being in that his being is not lost by passage but is the continuing ground of passage present as is no other being to every moment as the ground of the arising of each moment out of its past.[10]

2. The *second* point where the question of God arises and seems implied is in the self-actualization of the present, a self-actualization *out of* its given past or destiny and *in the light of* the possibilities relevant to its future. Whatever emphasis we may place on the role of the past or of the future in becoming, there is little doubt that where being *is* and so where becoming *is*—if they are at all—is in the duration that marks and constitutes our present. It is here that the past is retrieved in the light of possibilities for the future; that these past determinations and relevant future possibilities are brought through self-actualization into present and therefore real actuality. Now, as we have emphasized, this present coming-to-be, effecting a union of past actuality and future possibility, is a *self*-actualizing or self-constituting process. All finite being is a becoming-to-be in itself and through itself, a projection of itself as a retrieval of its given destiny into new possibilities, and thus a constitution of itself through itself. It is not sheerly determined either by its past or by its future; rather it is a process of self-determination, a response of centered freedom to its given destiny in the light of real possibilities. Each present is a union of objectified actuality, alternative possibilities and integrating decision. As Whitehead puts it, "the world is 'self-creative' for in each occasion the universe actualizes itself anew."[11]

If this be so, then, on the one hand, the self-actualization that characterizes the present moment is itself in part an effect; it cannot bring itself to be out of nothing. All self-actualization presupposes the given "being" with which an occasion or entity actualizes itself, namely, the reality and power to be and to become oneself as freedom.[12] But, on the other hand, it cannot be *merely* an effect of its past, insofar as it is self-actualizing; then it would be sheerly determined. Thus it arises as in itself an example of being or becoming-to-be, in part over against its past as over against its future, qualified by both but in a sense, as *self*-determining, independent of both. If, therefore, it arises as an "act of self-creative being" neither from its past, from its self, nor clearly from its future—which is modally possibility and not actuality —the question of an ultimate source of its being beyond destiny, its own freedom and possibility alike (world and self) arises.[13] Its being, and so the being that characterizes all of finitude, thus cannot be merely passed on from occasion to occasion, from substance to substance, from cause to effect; it arises anew (out of "nothing" preceding it and no possibility ahead of it) in each self-actualizing event in order that the present be a *response* to the given, freedom in polar relation to destiny, or self-actualization out of what has been. Thus a power of being is called for beyond the "press" of the finite past or of the possibilities of the relevant future as the ground of each self-actualizing occasion, a ground for the present as a duration of free and intentional unification of its given past with its possible future.

This "ultimate," as the source and ground of each occasion in its self-actualization out of its past, is, as we have noted, what Whitehead calls "creativity," that which brings each occasion to be, i.e., in the sense that it is the élan or flux or principle of the ultimate that gives reality and so the power to become itself to each concrescent occasion. Thus the source of our freedom, and so, to me, of our deepest humanity, our "existing," is in process thought disassociated from God who is through his envisionment of relevant possibility only the shaper of that freedom given us by creativity. To us, as we noted, our freedom, like the destiny from our past and the possibilities given to our freedom, is also of God—and for this reason must it be related to him if it is to be itself. As a result, we call this ground or power of being, creative of the self-determining reality of each occasion through which it comes to be, the creative "accompanying" or "concurring" providence of God.[14] It is through his ever-present and so necessary power to be and to bring forth being that each contingent entity "becomes" as a self-determining unification of its past and the possibilities of its future. God thus not only *preserves* the past by bringing it effectively into the present as a determining factor for the present—and thus brings forth continuity and order into existence. He also brings into being the present as self-determining in each present. He is the principle of reality through which each new occasion, each becoming-to-be arises and becomes itself in and through itself. He is the ground of our freedom as he is the ground of our destiny —and as he is also the ground of our relevant possibilities.

3. The third point where the relation of achieved actuality to possibility raises the question of God concerns the relation of actuality to the future, to novelty and to change. For possibility must be related to actuality in order at all to be.[15] And yet as an infinite realm, full of possibilities not yet actualized, possibility cannot "be" solely by means of its relation to finite and so already achieved actuality—lest the future merely repeat the limited forms of the past. Thus possibility, which can be effective only in relation to actuality, must be in relation to an actuality of transcendent scope, an actuality that is capable of holding within its power of envisionment the entire and so open realm of possibility. Further, if actualization be genuinely *self*-determining, a genuine reshaping of presented destiny, then in a world characterized by order and so continuity, novel possibilities must be related to actuality in terms of relevance, in terms of an ordered structure of graded options in continuity with the past. Such a grading of relevance within possibility was, we found, implied as the condition of all change, and especially in all historical change however revolutionary—for only relevant or real possibility is historically and politically creative. Thus both the being and the order necessary for relevant possibility require some actuality that spans achieved actuality and infinite possibility alike, giving to infinite possibilities both their locus in actuality and also their relevance to that actuality—for every event arises out of given actuality in union with relevant possibility. Such a transtemporal actuality is God. On the one hand, he is transtemporal in the sense of transcendence over passage, a transcendence that reaches from its seat in present actuality infinitely into the unactualized future. On the other, he is "temporal" in the sense that the very movement of actuality into new possibilities and so into the future is an aspect of the role and so the being of that transcendence.

We have called this aspect of providence the graded and ordered envisionment of God of the infinite realm of possibility, and we have suggested that this ontological conception may be able to provide an interpretation in modern terms of the classical logos doctrine through which God was said to create and order the world. It is through this envisionment and its communication to each self-creative actuality that new possibilities in ordered relevance to destiny are presented to freedom—and thus that the movement of process into a new future is possible. As in the earliest patristic tradition, it is through the divine logos, in union with the divine power of being, that each finite creature comes to be in self-actualization. Again, that which transcends and yet works within the temporal appears to be a necessary condition for the openness of the temporal as it was a necessary condition for the continuation of the temporal: the becoming of reality calls for being, temporal passage calls for eternity, freedom and novelty for an ordered range of possibility, if a self-creative process is to be possible. Contingency, relativity, temporality and autonomy do not so much deny the creative presence of God to temporal passage as require it. As we experience our finite and contingent being as a continual unity through self-actualization of facticity or destiny from the past and possibility from the future, so the infinite and absolute being of God unites past and future into those self-actualizating "presences" which constitute process.

New Elements in the Conception of God

The conception of God presented here does not, however, arise primarily from philosophical reflection on the ontological structure of passage. Rather, it is from the character of concrete experience of historical passage, of human existence within time, in union with the symbolic structure of the Christian faith that this vague "ontological" intuition of being within becoming and of order within change has become "God."[16] Each Christian age has conceived of God in small part on the basis of its deepest but dim ontological intuitions, in greater part on the basis of its religious existence within the threatening structures of finitude, of sin and of the experience of grace, and in major part through the shaping power of the biblical witness. Traditional symbols, existence and reflection together in that order fuse into a theological conception of deity. The central forms of this concept in the tradition we have traced, and the difficulties that this concept has faced and the transformations it has undergone in modernity we have reviewed. In the last two chapters we have sought to conceive of history, and of God in his relation to history, in terms of a reappraisal of the biblical witness, in terms of our most important modern ontological notions, and finally, in terms of our own experience of the meaning and the meaninglessness, the order and the disorder, the tragedy and the hope of history. As is evident, such a rapprochement between the modern consciousness and the traditional symbol of God, while necessary if this symbol is to have any meaning and use for us, nevertheless has effected changes in our understanding of that symbol. These central changes, implicit in the notion we have here been seeking to develop, are three.

1. It is clear from our account of creation and providence that there is what may be called a basic principle of the *self-limitation of God* in relation to finite being. All that is, in all aspects of its being, in all facets of its ontological structure, arises from God. There is no final metaphysical principle "over against" God, balancing his power and will and so providing an ontological and thus necessitating limit to that power and will.[17] Rather, as we have understood this implication of *creatio ex nihilo*[18] in process terms, the entire destiny with which each event and so each actuality is presented and so out of which it comes to be—that which causes each event insofar as it is caused—and its freedom of self-actualization themselves arise and create into the present through the power of God's being. It is through God's power of continuing being, conquering the non-being of temporal passage, that moment follows moment, that cause impinges on effect, that objects become objects for subjects, that subjects remain in some sense identical over time—in sum, that the accumulated actuality of the past, now objectified and so gone, becomes the ground for the new present. God is the principle of creation of *every* aspect of finite being because his power of being upholds in time all of actuality; he is the ground of the creativity, the élan of process as it "flings itself" into the next moment. The being in its totality which each event actualizes arises from God, for the totality of its conditions are given from its actualized past to each succeeding moment by the power of God, and the freedom and self-creation with which it comes to be is also of God. Thus is God at once creator and preserver of his finite creation in all its aspects. He is not, however, thereby the ordainer of each present, and so the sole shaper of the character of historical process.

The basis for this last affirmation is the principle here under discussion, namely, the self-limitation of God as creator and preserver. For as we have emphasized, God alone does not create the present. The divine creativity out of which the present arises from its past establishes a *self-creative* process: God creates by giving each occasion the power of self-creation out of its destiny. Thus each event actualizes itself in freedom out of its destiny and out of the possibilities relevant to that destiny. We do not create ourselves in whole, *ex nihilo*, for freedom always is polar to a destiny we have not created; and clearly, we are not the cause of the power to be self-determinative. Our freedom does not arise from our freedom, and we are self-determinative through a power of self-determination given to us. But we do shape what is given to us into what we are. Thus do men and women help to shape historical process into what it is. The limitation on God's sovereignty in history is achieved, therefore, not through the notion of the finitude of God as one factor in the process balanced by other factors. Nor is God "in the grip" of a process which transcends and so makes him possible,[19] since as the power alike of being, of freedom and of possibility, he is the ground of process. The limitation on God's sovereignty is understood as the self-limitation of God in creating and preserving a finitude characterized by freedom and so by self-actualization.[20] The concrete character of actuality, then, is not wholly of God, though every aspect of its being arises from God and is preserved by God's power. For actuality is self-creative of the destiny given it by the divine power. As destiny and freedom unite to form event, divine creation and providence, as the possibilities or conditions of that union, unite with finite self-creation in the becoming of each creature. Thus again, the *character* of that destiny, which may be fate, arose from the work of finite freedom on its destiny. In past, in present and in future God's sovereignty is a self-limited sovereignty because it is the creative intention of God to create and re-create finite freedom. Creation, the coming to be of finite actuality, is the work of God in union with the freedom he creates. Only thus is history to be understood as self-creative and as open to novelty which our freedom may actualize. Only thus are the sin and so the tragedy that characterize history's life separated from the real intentions of God in creating and preserving history.

2. Besides the self-limitation of God in creation and preservation, such a process understanding of historical passage entails as well the *temporality* of God, the participation of the divine power of being in passage. As in the case of the self-limitation of God, this must be said with some care lest it be misunderstood as the finitizing of God, the setting of the divine within categories of finitude. As God is not finite by being balanced by other metaphysical factors of equal scope and reality —for all aspects of finite being arise out of the moving divine creativity—so God is not temporal as are his creatures by arising out of an actualizing process that precedes him and passing away into an ongoing process that comes after him. Nor is his action "temporal" in the sense that it enters process at a moment and then recedes as do all finite agents. Thus, in participating in every duration of temporal passage God is not contingent as are his temporal creations: he does not arise out of a process of which he is not the ground; he is not dependent for his being and so vulnerable to a process he does not found; nor does he pass away into a process which has given him birth. The moving process in all its structural aspects is his creation; it arises out of his own power of being; his own continuing being, therefore, is received from himself not from elsewhere. In this sense he is *a se*. The temporality of God does not render him a creature of process; it expresses his essential participation as the continuing and moving ground of process in the temporality of process. He is the ground of being of *all* process and thus as the condition for each moment, is present in each moment—and thus transcendent to its moving moments. As the power of being of each moment, he is in each moment and yet above it, not carried away by it into non-being but present and effective there out of the necessity of his own being. He is *a se* as the continuing, creative and so temporal ground of temporality.

It is, however, intrinsic to our understanding that the modal distinction between actuality and possibility is fundamental for finite being and thus also fundamental for God as the absolute ground of finite being.[21] Actuality *is* not as actuality until it actualizes itself in creativity. Before that act of self-creation out of its destiny and out of its relevant possibilities, actuality *is* only as possibility. Thus the future, even for God, is possibility and not actuality. God's relation to the future is thus a relation to possibility and not to actuality. God "foreknows" the future, and so guides the becoming of actuality, not through the knowledge of the future as an "already actuality" but through his envisionment of infinite possibility, and through his gradation of that infinity of possibility in relation to achieved actuality and in relation to his own ultimate intentions or aim in creation and preservation. God thus experiences temporal passage as constitutive and so essential to his own being: the past as achieved actuality, the present as self-achieving actuality, and the future as possibility. As the ground of being out of which all arises—in its completed facticity, its self-creative freedom and its wealth of possibility—he experiences these fundamental modal distinctions as essential to his own being. However, he experiences these modal distinctions inherent in process noncontingently. As the absolute ground of temporality and of finite creatures within temporality and as the locus of possibility and its ordering, he is threatened neither by any aspect of being (for all has arisen from him), nor by any aspect of possibility (for all possibilities are mediated to freedom through him). As the ground of process, he is not contingent within process, caught in what it has produced, imprisoned in one of its durations and overwhelmed in the end by its movement; rather is he necessary for it, ever-present within it and, in that sense, transcendent to it. As, however, the ground of a process that mediates possibility into actuality, he himself participates in that passage from possibility into actuality and so in that sense is temporal. Thus, since the temporal process or becoming of possibility into actuality is an aspect of the divine being *itself*, God is essentially dynamic, living and active. He may, as in the classical tradition, be said to be eternal, unconditioned and necessary as the continuing, creative ground of all of process; and yet as the moving ground of process, he is essentially, not "accidentally," in relation to the flux of becoming.

3. The third change from the classical conception of God, immediately entailed in the above, is that God, although necessary, *a se*, and so transcendent to mere becoming—as noncontingent—nevertheless, *himself "becomes"* or is subject to change.[22] The modal distinction between actuality and possibility is fundamental for the divine life. God's power of being creates actuality in union with the self-actualization of the creature by presenting each actuality in becoming with its destiny from its achieved past. Correspondingly, God's providential envisionment of possibility presents each actuality in becoming with the range of possibilities open to that entity. Thus, as creative power God is related to actuality *as* actuality and to possibility *as* possibility. Consequently, as possibility *becomes* actuality, as change and process occur, God's creative and providential relations to process themselves change, and God's "experience" and "knowledge" of his world change. God knows possibility, and so the future, in one way, namely, as as yet indeterminate possibility, and he knows actuality in another way, namely, as achieved and determinate actuality.[23] Or, put another way, it is self-creation, self-actualization, that mediates between possibility and actuality—though the divine creativity is necessary in order that destiny be an aspect of the self-creative present, and though the divine providential envisionment is necessary in order that future possibility be an aspect of the self-creative present. This self-actualization out of which an event emerges *is not*

until it occurs in the present, and it is this self-actualization that gives its determinate concrete and fixed form to each present actuality. Thus there is a crucial difference between possibility and actuality, a difference contributed by the creature and not by God. History, and with it finite being, is self-creative under God, not determined by God. As history changes, therefore, so inescapably God changes, for God is in essential relation to a world he does not in its final and determinative form ordain or make—although each aspect of its being comes to be through the power of his creative being and through the possibilities of his providential envisionment.

God is, therefore, self-limiting, temporal and changing. He "becomes" in process in relation to a world which as self-actualizing is neither identical to himself nor determined totally by him. And thus, as we noted, is it possible that the "world" is being brought by his love into his everlasting being. Nevertheless, as the transcendent and eternal power of being through which process continues in being and so through which each present has its destiny from the past and its power of creative self-actualization in the present, and as the transcendent and eternal envisionment of the infinite realm of possibilities through which each present is opened to new possibilities for the future, God's being is also necessary, eternal and *a se*. He is the God from whom all, even the passage of time, comes and so who is not dependent for his being upon anything beyond himself, nor is his being threatened by contingency and passingness. Yet he is the God who includes potentiality as well as actuality as they move with process in his own life; who is both beginning and end, and yet who can hardly be in all respects the same at the end as he was at the beginning.

GOD AS BEING, LOGOS AND LOVE

The view of God expressed here, while hardly traditional, can be best explicated —as can most views expressive of the Christian witness—in terms of the classic trinity of being, truth and love.[24] We can speak of God at best only in terms of our relations to him and so in terms of his activity in and on us and on our world. In turn, awareness of God, reflection on that awareness and so language about God arise when these relations stemming from that divine activity become aspects of our consciousness or experience and thence elements of our reflective understanding. Thus, as Calvin and Schleiermacher reiterate and Augustine exemplifies,[25] the knowledge of God which leads to religious and then theological speech about him is always correlated with our experience and knowledge of ourselves. In the present interpretation of history, then, the question of God has been raised and the dim but numinous presence of the divine has entered awareness at many different points of our consciousness of ourselves as historical. In the experiences of ultimate concern within historical change, in the dimension of ultimacy evident in and determinative of political and historical experience, and, above all, in the relation of providence to given destiny, to self-constituting freedom and to future possibility, and of both to present actuality, God appears whenever the relations of contingency, continuity, change and freedom to historical process are existentially experienced, deeply pondered or actively embodied in praxis. Further, as the analysis penetrates deeper into the mystery of historical passage, beyond its ontological structure to the ambiguity of its concrete actuality, the relevance of the symbol of God appears for awareness and reflection alike in the experiences of creativity, self-destruction, nemesis and the hope of renewal, of, that is, autonomy, sin, fate and the promise of new possibilities. It is solely in terms of a conception of God, structured in accord with classical symbols but interpreted in the light of the modern historical consciousness, that the structure as well as the ambiguity, the promise as well as the tragedy of history are to be reflectively understood and existentially borne. Process, history and hope alike find their ground, their unity and their intelligibility in terms of the overarching symbol of God: such is the most fundamental argument of this volume.

Basic to this conception of God, as to the experiences which give it meaning, relevance and communicative power, are the elements associated with the trinity of being, truth and love. This trinity has appeared and reappeared throughout our analysis as constitutive alike of man's experience of himself, individually and socially, of his experience of historical passage, and of his experience of God. The dimension of ultimacy appeared within the political question raised by the security of our being, the meaning of our common existence, and the normative character of our communal life. The philosophical question of God arose as the question of the power of being supportive of destiny and of freedom, the question of unrealized possibility and the problem of the "meaning" of history. Finally, the theological symbolism, expressive of a Christian encounter with God and from that encounter interpretative of history, emphasized God as the ground of our being, the source of our new possibilities, and the principle of our hope for reconciliation and reunion. Thus it is appropriate to conclude our discussion with this trinitarian framework as expressive not only of the central structure and the deepest problematic of historical passage but also of the divine activity which gives that passage its ontological possibility, its final intelligibility, and its redemptive meaning.

God as Being

The divine creativity is a continuous creativity in which temporal passage emerges, and so it is both over time and within time. It continually posits finite being into existence over against non-being as achieved and so objectified actuality is succeeded by living and self-creative events. And it posits that continuing finite being in all of its aspects: its spatial and temporal extension, its dynamic elements and its form or forms, its individuality, centeredness and freedom, and its participation in the communities that shape it, support it, and in which it realizes itself. Thus God creates, upholds and brings into present effectiveness and relevance that destiny or the total situation out of which each entity arises; and God creates the centered freedom with which each entity in turn actualizes itself out of its destiny and so shapes its given world. This is a continuous creativity, a process of the emergence of the new, and thus is the divine creativity the necessary, eternal, and yet moving ultimate ground—as self-actualizing finitude is the contingent and transient proxi-mate ground—of what is manifested to scientific understanding as the evolutionary process and as the movement of history. Continuous creativity, providence and eschatology unite with one another with finite freedom as the way in which God creates the moving process, sustains it in its temporal being and directs it through its own freedom to its fulfillment. God transcends time as the source of the move-ment of the process of finite being in the dynamic creative divine life; he is in time as illustrating in his own creative life the modal distinction between potentiality and actuality, the becoming of actuality out of possibility.

In manifesting temporality in his being and creating, God is never contingent in the passage of time nor subject to fate because subject to forces of destiny that are simply "given" to him. God is not in this like contingent creatures who receive their total being and its possibilities contingently in each moment from the constellations of beings in the preceding moment, and so in receiving their being and its possibility thus contingently, can lose their freedom and even their being. Rather, time and passage, that in which God has his continuing life, are present within his life without contingency and without fate since they are aspects of the infinite divine life itself. The God who is in passage is also, and necessarily so if he be God, *necessary* in his being, a status that can—as the seemingly insoluble problems of process thought on this issue show—only be understood ontologically if God also be the source of all ontological factors and so ultimately conditioned by none of them.

God as Logos

The divine creativity, however, not only grounds and sustains from the immediate past every aspect of the process in which we participate and the freedom with which that past is actualized in the present. It also shares in that process in directing, guiding and fulfilling it as it moves towards the impinging future. Thus, as we noted, if that natural and historical process is "open," if possibility is genuinely possible and not already actual, if finite freedom is itself creative of what will be in life and history, then genuine alternatives or possibilities confront every present, and thus is possibil-ity the real ontological character of the future. If, then, temporal passage be real and really open, the modal distinction between achieved actuality and unrealized possi-bility must be an ultimate distinction characteristic of process at its deepest level. Inescapably, therefore, life, process, movement into what is not yet, and the distinc-tion of actuality and possibility must characterize the divine life as well as ours. God must be the principle of open possibility as well as of continuing actuality. What is potential for us as possibility for our freedom must be only potential for him too, lest our experience of creative and decisive freedom—and the character of history as self-created—be an illusion. The divine life, in all its infinite power and reality, conditioned by nothing beyond itself except by the freedom which its own creativity produces, must itself move into an as yet unrealized set of possibilities, possibilities for which the divine power, logos and love, working through our freedom, will, we are confident, find fulfillment in the eschatological end. Thus potentiality is in God, in the divine life. A relative non-being must be part of that life, an openness to the new in the future, an openness or negativity—a potentiality of becoming something else, a something different that is to be made actual when future possibilities are self-realized by creative finitude.

Providence, therefore, is not a *pro-videre* of "already actual" events, seeable, so to speak, from the height of the divine eternity and willed into being by the divine power, as in Augustine's thought. Providence, I have suggested, is rather: (a) the creativity of the divine being sustaining or continuing our being through presenting and re-presenting in each successive moment our destiny as a living part of our present; (b) the creativity of the divine being as the ground of our self-actualization in the present, and so as the ground of our continuing life, our eros and our autonomy as our freedom incarnates new possibilities for that life; (3) and providence is God's creative vision and so evocation of novel possibilities, shaped and directed by his ultimate purposes, and thus made relevant to the flux of actuality. Past, present and future are held together in each actuality as the ground of that actuality by the power, envisionment and purpose of God.[26]

Possibilities are possibilities for the enactment of finite freedom, possibilities which offer the new, the unexpected, the novel contrast to or even the negation of the present, but which are nonetheless—because held in the unity of the divine vision—in creative relation to what has been and is. Out of the infinity of the living and creative divine being arise forms. As the classical doctrine of the logos states, becoming is at all because it participates in forms that give structure definiteness, identity and meaningful and intelligible relations to the flux of things. Such a logos within the world out of which we arise is also the presupposition or condition for our perception, our knowing and our intentional interaction with that world. The correlation of objective logos and subjective logos, the rational structure of reality and of our minds, is the ontological basis for common sense, for science and for action as it is for all philosophical and theological speech.[27] This rational structure which we experience in our being at all and in being over time has its roots in the divine ground of all, as does the dynamic flux which is formed and made definite. This divine logos, however, is not a static timeless order of endlessly repeated forms, the actualities or essences that give recurrent shape to the potentiality of matter, as it has been traditionally conceived. Rather, for a process view of being in which becoming is the self-actualization of novel events, the rational structure of experience represents the ingression of possibilities from the future—perhaps repeated, perhaps new—into the self-creative actualities or events of process. Thus the divine logos is a creative vision of future possibility, arising out of the infinite divine life, of forms not yet actualized and therefore merely potential as well as possible forms already resident in actuality. The logos points not to the endless recurrence of the past but to the future and to novelty, to unrealized potentiality, as the ordering divine vision which lures process: nature, social history and personal lives, into new forms of life, of society and of selves.

This view of providence as the creation, envisionment, and ordering of future possibility—as the action of God "from the future"—expresses at once the aseity, transcendence and eternity of God on the one hand, and the changeability and temporality of God on the other. For this envisionment is, like the divine power of being itself, the precondition of all subsequent becoming and so is not dependent beyond itself on any other factor or entity. As an envisionment of future possibility originating in God and not beyond him, and originative of all experienced reality, providence expresses God's creative aseity. Here he is in stark contrast to the originative capacities of the creature which depend not only on a given destiny but also on a prior order of relevance and so of possibility in order to create. As that single and so unifying envisionment of the whole of possibility which maintains and structures every finite event in process in its continuing relation to its past, its contemporaries and to possibility, God's providential relation to possibility infinitely transcends that of his finite creatures as the ground of their common relation to destiny, actuality and to possibility—and so as the principal of universal and persistent order among all things. Finally, as an envisionment of the totality of possibility for the entire past and the entire future and so which relates novel possibilities to all times, providence expresses the eternity of God. On the other hand, as the envisionment of *possibilities* that are not yet actual and yet that are to be actualized by finite freedom, providence expresses the changeability, the self-limitation and the temporality of God.

Finally, the providential vision of God encompassing new possibilities for the future has its own telos or goal which provides for that vision its ordering and grading principle. This is what Whitehead refers to as the "subjective aim" of God now rendered into specifically Christian form. For his aim or telos is eschatological, the ultimate goal of God in the new humanity within the kingdom. This eschatological goal has been manifested to us in Jesus who is the Christ, the embodiment in actuality of the goal or the future of God, he who heralded and promised the kingdom, the final community, within which a fulfilled humanity finds its ultimate locus and possibility. In the present case, then, providence is interpreted eschatologically, as the divine vision luring history toward the eschatological goal. To much of the classical tradition, on the contrary, the aim of providence was interpreted in terms of the order of creation or the "natural law" of creation, an interpretation which gave to the concept of providence its static character and its ideological temptations. The divine providence is engendered and directed by what is not yet, by the ultimate goal of God for the world, not by the structures of society and so of history available to our scrutiny in the ambiguous present. What God is doing in history is determined and directed, therefore, not by what has been or presently is, but by his eschatological promises—and here we are in accord with the most fundamental premise about providence in both scripture and tradition. Thus Christian commitment and action in their obedience to and enactment of God's providential activity are guided normatively not by the warped structures of the past and present but by the revealed promises for the future. A radical praxis of liberation has its theological roots not solely in revealed promise and in eschatological hope.

It has its central point of integration with God's work in relation to the providential divine activity in our world directing and luring every present on to a new liberated world.

God is creative being and creative logos, the ground of our total actuality and of the possibilities that lure our freedom into the future. These symbols of creation and of providence are central to our faith, and their interpretation to our understanding, since it is on their basis that the Christian community has been able to affirm and value the contingent beings that we are, their precarious continuance into the next moment, and the relative but creative possibilities of creaturely life for the unknown future despite our contingency, our relativity and our temporality. The meaning of historical passage, a precious but precarious basis or "substance" for our cultural life, finds its ground in the Judaeo-Christian belief in the creative providence of God leading history to the fulfillment of God's purpose.

God as Love

Human history, however, cannot be understood alone on the basis of a given destiny, of freedom and of freedom's enactment of novel possibilities presented to us by providence—as Pelagius would have wished us to do had he concerned himself with history. Freedom, to be sure, feeds on possibilities in history, and its creativity in historical life is immense, or, as Niebuhr used to say, indeterminate. Genuine improvements can take place: in knowledge, in techniques, in institutions, in modes of distribution of goods and of power, and so can result a more balanced distribution of protection, of self-determination and of meaningful participation in the common life. With these developments suffering can be reduced; unlimited possibilities of a fuller humanity are open in history that call for our own active commitment in political action.

Even within this new and potentially higher situation, however, freedom corrupts these possibilities in enactment. The demonic and the destructive enter history, and thus does history continually recede from the ideal to which it is continually and progressively lured. In the ambiguous enactment of the ideal the final perfection of that ideal which was sought by the enaction is inescapably postponed. Like the law of which it is a new form, providential possibility calls forth our response of commitment and of action. Commitment to the new and possible ideal is important since higher possibilities of human life can be achieved. But like the law, new possibilities, and so the work of providence in presenting them, are not enough in order that full possibility be fulfilled. For providence enters history through our freedom, and thus the character of our freedom must be further dealt with by grace. Through our corruption of its possibilities, destiny becomes fate; a nemesis of self-destruction which we bequeath to other people's children and to our own, a fate which limits and often overpowers our freedom and theirs because it seems to close future history to new creative possibilities. Because of the corruption of our freedom, sin and fate as well as creativity haunt our history, and people and cultures alike encounter death in meaninglessness and fear. Thus, for possibilities to be *really* possible in history, more than even creation and providence are necessary—whether we speak of our own personal lives or the social world in which we are selves. This "more" than creation and providence is the substance of the gospel; God is redeemer as well as creator and preserver and inspirer. He is love as well as being and logos. God appears and acts in new and varied ways to reconcile, reunite and heal a world sundered in spirit from his creative providence. This final aspect of God's activity within history is essential to an understanding of history and its meaning, as it is to our hope in its fulfillment.

The event in which for Christians this redemptive activity of God is centered communicates both disclosure and healing, both new logos and new being, both a new understanding of our life in history and a new reality to that life. It is disclosure as the revelation of God's love and through that the revelation both of his redemptive activity and of his goal for process. In that disclosure is provided the crucial principle of interpretation by means of which God's creative, providential and reconciling activity, otherwise obscured in the ambiguity of the history actualized through our own freedom, become clear. Thus, through the knowledge of God's love and of love's ultimate goal, the direction and so the character of God's providential and so hidden work in time are understood. We know what creation and providence are and so wherein they manifest themselves in the ambiguity of life—and so why despite this "hiddenness" we can have confidence in them—*through* this center to our faith which illumines both beginning and end and so the work of God in time. It is through our knowledge of God's love in Jesus as the Christ that the ever-vague, often threatening and always ambiguous ultimacy that permeates our life is named and on which our confidence is grounded that creative possibility is the character of history's future.

And it is new reality as well as disclosure as the communication of a new participation in and relation to the divine, a new center for our existence, and so a new awareness of our life in, with and through God. We not only *know* the reality of the divine power and love; we can and do become symbols, vehicles or media of both. Through participation in God in spirit as well as in being, there is a new balance, a new serenity, a new freedom and love, and a new hope. Thus is the Christ truth and grace, new logos and new reality—and both through the reunion he effects between our estranged lives and the source and ground of those lives. It is no accident that the tradition has been of two minds about the relation of Jesus to the principles of the divine manifestation and activity: he is, on the one hand, the logos incarnate as the illumination of the divine intention for history (God's "subjective aim") and so for the final direction of its structure. But on the other, his being is also the work of the spirit as the cause, paradigm and beginning of the reunion of creation with God.

God's love as the principle of reunion with God is then known fully and experienced in Jesus as the Christ. Thus to us God is being, logos, *and* love, the creative power in all, the creative possibility for all, and the reuniting principle of all. The divine life, which issues continually forth in all aspects of our being to be actualized by our freedom, which carries us forward in time to new possibilities through the creative destiny and the providential logos that have their source in God, comes to its own fulfillment—and ours—in the love which reunites us to God and through that reunion to one another. This recreative and reuniting power of the divine love is, like the divine being and the divine logos, manifested universally, appearing everywhere in history where redemptive forces are at work. It has, however, its central locus, its deepest reality and power, and its final criterion in the Christ and the community which lives in this spirit.

There are, I believe, three aspects or phases of this reuniting love as it is communicated to us and known by us in Jesus as the Christ. They are affirmed in the three major elements of this total event and expressed through the central symbols pointing to the meaning of this event: incarnation, atonement, and resurrection. Out of all three, and the works of teaching and witness that interpret them, arise our knowledge of the divine promise for the ultimate future and our certainty concerning it. Through this event there is disclosed to our understanding God's final aim so that the interpretation of creation, of providence and so the meaning of our human life becomes possible. And in and through all three symbolic interpretations of the event of Jesus the Christ is also expressed the new presence of the spirit, the new reality in which in faith and hope we live in a new way toward the future.

First, there is in the incarnation the entrance of the new reality into historical life: the reunion of the divine ground with human being and human freedom in a concrete person, from which reunion issues forth a new being, a new center, a new direction of the will, a new shape to the self. Grace unites with God's providential work in the *dynamics* of our freedom, giving us a new relation in will and in love to the possibilities presented by the divine logos. Such grace, creative of a unity with God that re-creates every aspect of our being, was, according to the witness of the earliest community, transparent and perfectly manifest in Jesus. It becomes the principle resources of the community that follows him, and is its primary gift to the world. And in him it exhibits the concrete shape of the divine promise for the future, the true human being in community toward which God's creative providence moves history.

Secondly, in the atoning death of Jesus as the Christ, the depth of our estrangement from God and the vast surprise of the divine response of mercy are seen. The divine love here is known as agape as well as reuniting grace, a love that comes to the sinful world and a sinful history despite their sin and so makes possible, against all expectations, the new possibilities for our common existence that sin had denied. On this forgiving love above all the hope of history rests, for recreation in grace is never full, possibilities remain and will remain only partially completed, and new work to come in the future will call for still further judgments, further recreation, still new possibilities. History, no more than our personal lives, achieves completion of its own potential meanings or the fulfillment of its potential promises, though it may well move to more just orders and so to less outright suffering. Thus forgiveness and reunion on the basis of forgiveness are the center of our hope for time.

Finally, in the resurrection—as in the words of promise—the final hope of reunion and of completion find their ground and first expression. Here the divine love is not only recreative of our present fragmentary existence and forgiving of our sins. It is also united with the divine power of being and with the divine goal for creation into a love that triumphs over the conditions of our finitude as well as over our sin, and brings us, as all love does, in reunion and communion again. Here in the final kingdom, which is not in history but which we believe is fashioned out of history's concrete achievements in the infinity of the consequent divine experience, is the culmination of history's processes, the fulfillment of the possibilities with which we started. The Christian understanding of history, its possibilities, its tragedy and its potentiality of meaning, I believe, includes the entire range of Christian symbolism. But above all, it involves the rethinking of that most fundamental affirmation of all, namely, that God is being, truth and love, and that on this threefold divine activity all our possibilities for the future depend.

THE THEOLOGICAL UNDERSTANDING
OF HUMANITY AND NATURE
IN A TECHNOLOGICAL ERA*

THE CHRISTIAN HOPE AND THE PROSPECTS FOR HUMANITY

A. The Promise

As Christians we share the promise of hope for the future with the people of God of all ages. This hope remains whatever our present situation and whatever the apparent prospects for our future. It is grounded in the presence of God in Jesus Christ and in the Spirit.

The promise to which our hope is attached is not for a kingdom "of this world" in the sense of an affluent, secure and contented life; we are not promised that we shall be given all that we want. On the contrary, the Gospel challenges our "natural" hopes for well-being and rearranges them into a new form, a form which is both more realistic and more lasting. Nor is there an immutable content to our hopes. This will change as Christian experience, knowledge and understanding change; but the object and ground of our hopes, and their certainty, remain unaltered.

There are two aspects to Christian hope for the future: (1) The hope for this life and for history: the hope that that "relative death" which because of sin characterizes all human creation and action in history will be overcome. We look for a new day in time, a new world in which human life and community will find a more complete realization. (2) There is hope for life beyond time and history in God, for a victory over the "ultimate death" that awaits us all and possibly our world. These two aspects are in fact *one* hope, two moments of one hope. They cannot be separated since the transcendent hope is the ground for the proximate historical hope. When our life and our expectations are grounded in the cross and the resurrection, the darkness of the future is dispelled and hope is possible; and if our lives are surrendered to what is beyond the promise of affluence and security, then new life and the prospect of a new society is possible. Hope for the future is a gift of grace, and the struggles for the new future a result of a faith that transcends all historical prospects. Our concern here is with the Christian hope for the historical future in the light of technology and science, not forgetting that such "temporal" hope is grounded in the transcendent.

*The original draft of this statement, published in *Anticipation* no. 19 (November 1974) by the Division of Church and Society of the World Council of Churches, represents the author's contribution to the Report of the 1974 Conference, held in Bucharest, on Science and Technology for Human Development: The Ambiguous Future and the Christian Hope.

B. Impediments to the Promise

The agonizing reality of poverty, exploitation and oppression, however, and the threat to the very survival of humanity overshadow all prospects for the immediate future. This future seems utterly devoid of promise, in fact one filled with great suffering and terror, a future marked with death. What has been most obviously creative in human history—the rational power and technical mastery, the ability intelligently to analyze and to organize experience and to shape and transform the reality which is encountered—has strangely become demonic, threatening not only humanity itself but the natural world on which human beings depend and in which they participate as creatures. This is the fault neither of science nor of technology but of humanity itself which begot and has misused them; like human reason, emotion and will, science and technology can become demonic in the hands of people, and like all human powers they must be transformed not rejected or suppressed.

The impediments to our Christian hopes for the future have been described in earlier sections of the report and are listed here briefly.

1. The immediate food crisis and the threat of widespread starvation, highlighting the extravagance of the affluent nations and the danger of further population increase.
2. The using up of the world's resources which will result in a general lowering of standards of living, with resultant suffering and social conflict.
3. The unequal distribution of economic and political power within societies and between societies.
4. The development of regimenting forms of authority to cope with the ecological crisis through control of all technology, and to cope with the resultant social crisis.
5. The personal emptiness, loss of inwardness and loneliness of a technological culture, oriented to material growth; and the corresponding loss of community, symbols and meanings in developing societies.
6. The total loss of a sense of control of human destiny; the sense of being fated, of being unable to act and so being bound for destruction.
7. The tendency of technology in the hand of concupiscent men and women to become a total process, perpetuating and spreading itself to all corners of life.
8. The crisis of faith, associated with the rise of a self-sufficient scientific and technological culture.

C. Hope for the New Life

What is there in the Gospel, and in the present Christian experience of the Spirit in Word, sacrament and life in the world that establishes the hope despite the present situation of despair?

1. We know that the temporal processes in which we live, the processes of nature and of social history alike, are the creations of God. History, as it arises out of, depends upon and also shapes nature, is ultimately purposive, grounded in God and under his sovereign care. There can be no ultimate meaninglessness in history, no determination by inexorable forces to destruction, despite our error and sin. Nor can we despair about the destiny of the life which God has given us. This confidence in the creative and directing power of God is based both (a) on our recreation in Jesus Christ in which finitude, contingency, historical being and human creativity were assumed by God and redeemed, revealing the purpose of God's originating and directing creativity; and (b) in our Christian experiences of the goodness and value of material, communal and historical life.

2. Because of our confidence in the providence of God, we know that despite our continuing freedom to defy God's will, history remains open, with ever new possibilities in every situation for creative transformation. For through his providence God presents to us new

possibilities even in the most desperate situations, though we may recognize that one of the conditions for creative action lies in our willingness to understand, to face and so to reshape the forces at work for destruction in our world. The providence in which we believe does not so much close off the possibility of the creative new as keep such possibilities open; God opens us to the new future by presenting us with new possibilities that can reshape our present. This communication of possibility to our freedom is universal, the work of God in all humanity and in all cultures. It far transcends, therefore, the life and the work of the churches and thus gives us hope even when we realize how ineffective our own work may be.

3. The incarnation represents the entrance of God in a new way into historical existence in order to conquer death in both its forms, to bring about a new quality of life and of history. Further, the cross represents the participation of God in the most radical suffering and estrangement of human life, and the resurrection the victory out of that suffering. Thus are the suffering and death evident in history overcome in Jesus Christ, and the basis for our hope for a new life is grounded. In Jesus Christ the power of God moved through finitude, estrangement and death to resurrection and newness of life. Herein lies our confidence that whatever the objective negative character of our present and our future, hope for the new remains. This confidence also finds its ground in the continual admonition of Jesus not to despair or be anxious—for he is with us and has overcome the world. These redemptive forces centered in Christ and receiving their criterion there are also universal; grace extends far beyond the Church though the gift and the responsibility center in her. Again our confidence in social process lies in God and his universal work, and not wholly in the success of our fragmentary works.

4. We look, therefore, for a new life and new age in the future; in ourselves as new creatures, in society as the New Jerusalem, and in history as the promised Kingdom. These future possibilities, structured for us by these central symbols of promise, are, we know, never totally or perfectly fulfilled. Finitude and freedom remain, and sin continues to distort both. Thus does the divine future appear as judgement as well as promise, as undoing and tearing down as well as recreation. But the promise based on incarnation, creation and providence holds fast; the future is a realm of hope and not of despair for those who know God. It is towards this eschatological goal that the creative and "luring" work of God is directed: the promise of the Gospel for a new day defines and names for us the hidden work of God in the world. It is this promise which justifies the spirit of celebration in the midst of struggle of many liberation groups. The new age promises hope for freedom from the oppressions of the old.

D. The Strategy of Hope

How is this promise of meaning in historical life, of a new reality of human existence, of a new day in the future, to be understood in relation to the impediments outlined above? It is evident that there must be change if the growing threats to human survival are to be countered. But many people fear change either because of their stake in the present or the uncertainties of the future. For others change is their only hope. Without pretending to know how God works in objective history through providence, or in ourselves through grace, some answers of the Gospel to these problems can be suggested.

1. The Christian confidence in the creative sovereignty of God over history—the final ground of our hopes—means that the ambiguous future, with all its manifold uncertainties, can be faced with serenity and courage. Because of our faith in providence, we have a confidence in the new that is to come. On this basis alone can the terror of facing the truth be borne, can new possibilities be creatively explored, and can risks to present securities be undertaken.

2. In the Christian experience of the oneness of God's creation, of the wonder and value of each of its parts, is latent the possibility of a new care for the earth and its creatures. This

will involve new attitudes towards our environment, new respect for its integrity and unity of interrelations, and new uses for our technological power to reshape it—as well as new prudence with regard to our own capacity to manipulate it.

3. In the oneness of humanity implicit in God's creation and redemption of us all, lies a new understanding of the community between nations and peoples. What happens to one happens to all—thus does present history reinforce the lesson of the Gospel, and thus does the Gospel in turn give grounds for dealing creatively with present history. In this new understanding of the community of humanity heightened by a growing comprehension of mutual obligation lies the hope for a redistribution of resources.

4. The sense of obligation to one another is the Christian ground for the reshaping of political and social institutions, and for preventing either the aim of private well-being or the need for highly centralized political control from destroying human life. History will enact that reshaping in any case, for the judgement of God is sure, but if such reshaping is qualified by obligation and a sense of community, necessary political change can shed much of its destructive cruelty and its self-righteous pride and so avoid the endless repetition of oppression and injustice.

5. The renewed sense of a Christian quality of life, of the call to perfection in a new form —a perfection of depth, creativity, and simplicity as well as of compassion and community —can enable men and women to accept restricted material well-being and so be open to those new obligations to others that will be the continual requirement in a world of scarcity. Only if the power of concupiscence is broken can the conflicts latent in scarcity be overcome, and the further destruction of the environment be prevented: a Christian quality of life is a ground for hope in a world of dwindling supplies.

6. The Christian sense of individuality within community, of freedom within obligation, makes possible creative life within a technologized and systematized society without loss of personal being in an empty collectivity—and yet without that personal depth being based on private well-being.

7. The renewed sense of ultimate confidence in God and in his promise of transformed life can encourage the sense that our being here is a pilgrimage not a vacation, that adversity is no threat if one knows a transcendent meaning. New life arises only if men and women are willing to accept the cross as the foundation of that life. A new and better world can arise out of the crises of the present only if we are not too much concerned with our personal well-being here. To seek to gain the world in goods and in power is, as the facts now show us, to die; to be willing to die to the world in that sense is the sole condition for being able creatively to live.

Our hope for the future is neither in the achievement of material abundance nor in the creation of a perfect society. Sin and injustice will remain in history, and so freedom and human creativity will continue to be ambiguous. Our hope lies first in God's providence at work in the social world around us; and further, that through our freedom, grace may remake both us and our world: that a new style of life will be gained, that new social structures will appear, that technology will be used and not misused, nature respected and loved, and real community will appear. Though this be a world of less affluence and possibly less freedom for those who are now privileged, it will still be a better world for more people and qualitatively closer to the promised Kingdom. This Kingdom is in its quality not at all a kingdom of this world; nevertheless as a historical order of fuller human realization for all, it is the legitimate object of a Christian worldly hope for the future.

NOTES

For bibliographical data on works mentioned in the Notes, confer Bibliography.

CHAPTER 1

1. The Greek world was sharply conscious of the universality in human experience of change, and, like modern thought, it identified the experience and the reality of change with temporality, with existence within time. (Cf. Aristotle, *Physics*, bk. IV, 11–12, 218b–222a.) They were also vividly aware of that aspect of change referred to in the text, namely the unpredicted and unpredictable, the new, that occurrence which could not be derived by demonstration from either the essential nature or definition of a being or from an analysis of the preceding causes. However, since intelligibility was to them defined on the one hand by those necessary characteristics entailed by an essence or form, and on the other by the effects of known causes, the new and the unexpected was in turn defined as the "contingent," or more directly as "chance," that for which no reason in necessity or in causality could be given and so that which was "irrational." (Aristotle, *Posterior Analytics*, bk. I, 5–6, 8, 30, 33; bk. II, 8, 11; *Physics*, bk. II, 3–4. Cf. also J. Chevalier, *La notion du nécessaire chez Aristote et chez son prédécesseurs.*) One of the continuing problems for a philosophical discussion of change, and especially of historical change, is how the contingent (the nonnecessary) and the new (the nonpredictable in terms of prior causes)—so pervasive in modern experience as an aspect of historical change—can be removed from chance and so irrationality. As we shall see, much modern philosophy and theology has concerned itself with this problem, that is, with the question of the relation of order to novelty. For examples of the biblical apprehension of the universality of change, temporality and so of transience in human life, cf. Psalms 38 and 49, and Isaiah 40:6–8.

2. That temporality is a central character of finite being is common to Hebrew, to classical and to modern philosophy alike. That, however, temporality defines "all the being we can experience and know" is, perhaps, what is unique to modern cultural experience and so to its philosophy. To document this proposition would be an endless task; possibly references to such diverse thinkers as John Dewey (cf. *Intelligence in the Modern World: John Dewey's Philosophy*, pp. 334–45), Martin Heidegger (*Being and Time*, div. II, esp. secs. 65 ff.), Ernst Bloch (cf. chap. 4 below) and A. N. Whitehead (cf. chap. 4 below) will suffice. In each of these thinkers—and in many more that might be cited—known and knowable reality is in process and so characterized by change and by temporality.

3. Most interpretations of Heidegger (especially of the "early Heidegger" of *Being and*

Time) emphasize the individualistic character of his analysis of human temporality and historicity, and surely the text of *Being and Time* seems to bear out this interpretation as concerned with individual historicity rather than with social process and so with the wider movements of history (cf. especially *Being and Time*, sec. 75). However, it is also clear that the entire Heideggerian corpus, and so *Being and Time* "retrieved," so to speak, from the perspective of that corpus, can be given a more "social" and "historical" interpretation. Such is the explicit aim of the work of Gibson Winter (*Elements for a Social Ethic*, esp. chaps. 3, 6 and 7) and, to a markedly lesser extent, of the present volume.

4. The *I-Ching* expresses this intuition of an order within nature's changes as the clue to human and so historical actions: "So too in the course of the year a combat takes place between the forces of light and the forces of darkness, eventuating in the revolution of the seasons. Men master these changes in nature by noting their regularity and marking off the passage of time accordingly. In this way order and clarity appear in the apparently chaotic changes of the seasons, and man is able to adjust himself in advance to the demands of the different times" (The *I-Ching*, sec. 49, character *Ko*, p. 190).

5. The basis of this remark—namely that the intuition of an intelligible order of change or development lies in back of social as well as of natural science—will be explicated more fully below. At the moment reference may be made to Robert Nisbet's fundamental division between perspectives on social change that are "historical" and those that are "developmental" in character, the latter concerned not with events and occurences but with gradual, necessary and cumulative processes of change which a scientific inquiry can bring to intelligible expression. Cf. Nisbet, *Social Change and History*, pp. 30 f., 112–13, 117–19, and chap. 5.

6. The growth of the apprehension in modern cultural experience of social change and so of historical process will be a subject dealt with specifically in chap. 8. At present, since our view is that the awareness of social change has *grown* in modern experience, it is well to comment on Wilbert E. Moore's thesis (*Social Change*, chap. 1) that social change is normal in human society and thus that the modern emphasis on change is no valid indication of a new situation in modern life. Of course Professor Moore is right that social change of some sort has characterized every society, and that in that sense change is normal in human affairs. However, two points should be added, which he seems also to admit: (1) the rate and the depth of change can increase, and (2) the awareness of change can increase. Both of these seem to have occurred in modernity: the first has occurred largely through science, technology and industrialism, i.e., through techniques introducing planned change. The second has occurred through (a) realization of an increased rate of change (cf. Toffler's elaboration of this point in *Future Shock*); (b) changing views of human life in relation to history and its changes, the growth in the awareness of "historicity"; and (c) the occurrence of certain events that seemed to introduce radical change into social existence and so effected a new awareness of the reality and pervasiveness of change in social life. One thinks especially of the French, the American and the Russian revolutions in this connection. On the effects of the French Revolution on European sensibility and its understanding of social existence, cf. Robert Nisbet, *The Sociological Tradition*, pp. 31–32, and George Steiner's remark: "Those who lived through the 1790's and the first decade and a half of the nineteenth century, and who could recall the tenor of life under the old dispensation, felt that time itself and the whole enterprise of consciousness had accelerated" (Steiner, *In Bluebeard's Castle*, pp. 11–12). For a powerful expression of this consciousness of history as a continuing change of forms, cf. the following from Karl Marx: "History is thorough, and it goes through many stages when it conducts an ancient formation to its grave. The last stage of a world historical formation is comedy. . . . Why should history proceed this way? So that mankind shall separate itself *gladly* from its past" ("The Critique of Hegel's Philosophy of Right," in *Karl Marx: Early Writings*, p. 48).

7. The risk of the loss of individuality through massive social change, so commonly cited vis-à-vis an advanced technological civilization, was already seen clearly in the nineteenth century by many pioneering sociologists, only there as a result of a development characterized by egalitarianism, contract and rationalizing cultural forms, e.g., by Tocqueville, Durkheim, Weber, Tonnies and Simmel (cf. Nisbet, *Sociological Tradition*, pp. 75–76, 90, 155, 305).

8. The exception in modern social theory is classical functionalist sociology, but this "unawareness" of dynamic change as characteristic of social systems is also the basis for most criticisms of functionalism and apparently for some of its newer emphases, e.g., Moore, pp. 7–11; Alvin Gouldner, *The Coming Crisis of Western Sociology*, esp. pp. 352–53; and Nisbet, *Social Change and History*, pp. 226–39.

9. Pertinent examples of such slow, cumulative changes in social groups and institutions, and the way sociology uncovers and "explains" them, are found in W. Moore and Robert Cook, *Readings in Social Change*, as well as in Moore, *Social Change*. Nisbet gives an excellent summary of the characteristics such social analysis has found in these sorts of social changes (i.e., "natural, directional, immanent, continuous, necessary, and proceeding from uniform causes") in *Social Change and History*, pp. 166–68. For Marx, these slow, cumulative changes (in the forms of the means of production) are the fundamental dynamic factors of historical process from which flow its changes in the forms of "relations of production" and then in the forms of consciousness: "In acquiring new forms of production, men change their mode of production, their way of earning their living; they change all their social relations. . . . The same men who establish social relations in conformity with their material powers of production, also produce principles, laws, and categories in conformity with their social relations. Thus, these ideas and categories are no more eternal than the relations which they express. They are historical and transient products" (*Karl Marx: Selected Writings in Sociology and Social Philosophy*, p. 95).

10. Cf. Nisbet's remark about Comte: ". . . By history he meant 'abstract history,' history divorced from all particularity of the events, actions, personages, places, and periods that was the very substance of what the historians were concerned with" (*Social Change and History*, p. 165).

11. The search of modern sociology for "laws" of the social process, i.e., for universal and necessary patterns of change that make social process intelligible, is emphasized in all the sociological literature about change, e.g., Moore, pp. 11 and 70; Nisbet, *Sociological Tradition*, pp. 146 and 293.

12. The relation of Marxism to modern sociology is of course obvious at many points. With regard to the common search for a necessary, continuous, immanent "law of development," Nisbet has this to say: "Each of them—Marx with capitalism, Morgan with polity, property and family, Comte with human knowledge, and so on—was but declaring that a given sequence of development was necessary *to the nature of the system or systems* he was studying. Free of the accidental and the merely casual, it was *necessary* that a given institution have developed through time as comparative researchers showed that it had in fact developed" (*Social Change and History*, p. 178). For this sense in Karl Marx of laws in history and so the potential unity of natural and historical inquiry, cf. the following: "History itself is a *real* part of *natural history*, of the development of capital and nature into man. Natural science will one day incorporate the science of man, just as the science of man will incorporate natural science; there will be a single science" (*Selected Writings*, p. 70).

13. A more detailed discussion of "futurology" as exemplified in the work of Herman Kahn and Albert Weiner will occupy us in chap. 3. For examples of the assumption of regular and so intelligible patterns of change as the basis on which predictions of probability may be made —and so as the basis on which futurology is possible—cf. Herman Kahn and Albert Weiner, *The Year 2000*, pp. 2–6, 118.

14. Stephen Toulmin, "Contemporary Scientific Mythology."

15. The historian Gordon Leff, to which this work is vastly indebted, insists that both contingency and freedom (initiating human responses) are essential factors in historical happening, and that the task of the historian is to make intelligible a subject matter laced with the contingent and the unpredictable: "But in the main, historical events are in response to circumstances which although not of men's own choosing are largely of their own making. . . . For any epoch, we can posit a norm of behavior within which men tend to act. This, however, does not reduce the contingency of how they will act, but merely the area of likely action. . . . Whatever the regularities of their life, men have still to respond intelligently each day to its exigencies. . . . However often the same actions have been performed before, there has to be a new volition each time habit is translated into act. . . . For the historian, uncertainty is the principle of history . . . as Raymond Aron has said, to consider something as an event historically is to admit the possibility that it need not have occurred—at least at the time it did" (Gordon Leff, *History and Social Theory*, pp. 44–45).

16. For the "idealistic" philosopher of history R. G. Collingwood, human decision is the key initiating factor in historical events, and thus an understanding of the intentions or thoughts that are embodied in decision is the central goal of historiography: "For history, the object to be discovered is not the mere event, but the thought expressed in it. To discover that thought is already to understand it. . . . The cause of the event, for him [the historian], means the thought in the mind of the person by whose agency the event came about. . . . They [processes of history] are not processes of mere events but processes of actions, which have an inner side, consisting of processes of thought. . . . All history is the history of thought" (Collingwood, *The Idea of History*, pp. 214–15). That many of the creative minds of the sociological tradition also emphasized the role of ideas in historical change should not be overlooked; cf. Nisbet's remarks on Weber, *Sociological Tradition*, pp. 257–58.

17. Leff qualifies in favor of "contingency" Collingwood's emphasis on explicit thought and decision as *the* causes of historical events: "On the one hand most situations are the results of a series of intersecting actions which as we have said are the products of a number of wills acting independently of and often in opposition to each other; hence their outcome is neither willed nor foreseen by their agents" (Leff, pp. 61–62).

18. "As Ranke observed long ago, 'Freedom and necessity exist side by side. Necessity inheres in all that has already been formed and that cannot be undone, which is the basis of all new emerging activity. What developed in the past constitutes the connection with what is emerging in the present. For this reason free will and necessity, far from being absolute, exist only in relation to one another. An act is free only because it consists in deciding to do one thing rather than another; and the very act of choosing eliminates the alternatives in which its freedom consisted. Those that next arise will be in the new context determined by the previous action. Contingency is therefore not synonymous with the rule of chance" (Leff, p. 62).

19. Cf. the quotation from Leff above, note 15. Karl Popper goes even further, and insists that a wise social science will be in this sense "nominalist," i.e., view historical processes in terms of the actions of individuals and not of "social entities," and thus subject both to contingency and to the responses of decision: "And it destroys them [the doctrines of methodological essentialism] because the task of social theory is to construct and to analyze our sociological models carefully in descriptive or nominalist terms, that is to say, in terms of *individuals*, of their attitudes, expectancies, relations, etc." (Popper, *The Poverty of Historicism*, p. 136).

20. The classic modern theological expression of this view of history as characterized by contingency and freedom rather than by law is, of course, in the work of Reinhold Niebuhr (for example, "Coherence, Incoherence, and Christian Faith," in *Christian Realism and Political Problems*, pp. 175–185, and *Faith and History*, pp. 18, 20 and 56). Agreement on this issue comes, surprisingly, from Karl Popper, pp. 115 ff., in a sharp distinction between

historical trends, which social science studies, and *laws,* which are not applicable directly to processes in history; and from Leff, pp. viii–xi. However, as the sociological tradition has abundantly shown, a discussion of important trends in social process is both important for an understanding of change and "humanly relevant" for the clarification of the stresses, problems and tragedies as well as the possibilities of human existence in a particular society, as the studies of Toqueville, Marx, Weber, Durkheim, Tonnies and Simmel evidence.

21. For a description of the transformation in modern conceptions of history of the model of growth leading to decay to one of growth leading to ever enlarging perfection, cf. Nisbet, *Social Change and History,* chap. 3, pp. 104–125; also for a more complete history of the rise of the idea of progress, cf. J. B. Bury, *The Idea of Progress.*

22. As an example, the following from Robert Heilbroner may serve: "For the question asks whether we can imagine that future other than as a continuation of the darkness, cruelty, and disorder of the past; worse, whether we do not foresee in the human prospect a deterioration of things, even an impending catastrophe of fearful dimensions.

"That such a question is in the air . . . is a proposition that I shall not defend . . . I will rest my case on the reader's own response. . . . Thus I shall simply start by assuming that the reader shares with me an awareness of an oppressive anticipation of the future" (Heilbroner, *An Inquiry into the Human Prospect,* pp. 13–14).

23. As noted in note 20, the sociological tradition is particularly helpful in supplementing the "historical" causes (mentioned in the text) of our present anxieties about the future of society with analyses showing the trends in the development of that society that have led to deep problems that are seemingly insoluble: problems of community, of authority, of status, of individuality, of anomie, of meaninglessness and alienation. For a brilliant survey of this negative reaction to modernity in classical sociology, cf. Nisbet, *Sociological Tradition.*

24. For the character of the sociology of knowledge, cf. Karl Mannheim's classic *Ideology and Utopia,* chap. 5; and Peter L. Berger and Thomas Luckmann, *The Social Construction of Reality,* esp. 3 ff.

25. "The slaves, the wretched of the earth, those who are not in but under the private forms of good created by man's will to power, these are those who can have the vision and passion for and are able to understand the language of hope, freedom, and liberation. . . . Because his present is the suffering of futureness, the slave is made free for the risk of a new future that promises life" (Rubem Alves, *A Theology of Human Hope,* pp. 114–15).

26. "Political self-consciousness," as used by the Marxist tradition, refers to an understanding of the social structures and dynamics of one's present social context so as to be able to see that the present is unjust and to see the causes or roots of that injustice, and consequently to be capable of creative *praxis,* a creative political role in the future. We agree that an understanding through such an analysis of one's fundamental "world" is necessary for creative action—and thus is social theory essential for politics. Our point will be, however, that the symbol "social world around us" must be supplemented by the symbol "history in which we live," if that context is to be fully understood. Thus does political self-consciousness (which entails a developed social theory) involve also historical self-consciousness, and so in the end a philosophy or theology of history.

27. These remarks about modern technological society are based not only on personal experience of modern urban and corporate life, and on many interpretations of that life in film, drama and literature—though these are important—but also on a number of careful analyses of modern culture as technological: e.g., Jacques Ellul, *The Technological Society;* Erich Fromm, *The Revolution of Hope,* esp. chap. 3; Herbert Marcuse, *One-Dimensional Man,* esp. chap. 6; Karl Mannheim, chap. 4; Gibson Winter, *Being Free,* esp. chaps. 1 and 2; Alvin Toffler, *Future Shock;* see also Alves, chap. 1.

28. Toffler's descriptions of the transcience and superficiality of any community of persons in most of transcontinental corporate society, and of the effect of that transience on the real

relations that help to create real persons, is one of the most potent, and dismal, aspects of his book. Cf. Toffler, chaps. 5 and 6. On a profounder level, a recurrent theme of nineteenth-century sociology in its critique of modern egalitarian and technological society was the impending destruction of community, of real or internal relations within community and so of genuine individuality. Cf. Alexis de Tocqueville, *Democracy in America*, pp. 15, 57, 96, 192, 254–56, 259–60; Nisbet, *Sociological Tradition*, chaps. 3, 4 and 7.

29. Cf. Alves' profound remark that in a technological world, where each person functions as a part of a rational, coordinated "system," there is no room for either freedom or the new. Thus is freedom moved "inside," "domesticated" into leisure time. And thus is free time the time of impotence, of play, not of creation; only the technological elite has the "monopoly of power" to create the future (Alves, p. 27).

30. For the inner emptiness of a materially surfeited culture, cf. Heilbroner's analysis of "the spiritual malaise" of our time (Heilbroner, pp. 20–21, 70, 76–78). For the relation of egalitarianism and materialism to increased desire for goods, to envy, and to inner disappointment, cf. Tocqueville, pp. 198 and chap. 7. The relation of these psychological factors of envy, competition, the lust for material goods and the loss of inner norms to the ecology crisis, to the ravishment of the earth for more and more goods, is all too obvious.

31. One may say that an advanced technological culture, thoroughly organized in its life, material in its goals and consumption-oriented in its pleasure, has made apparent, i.e., brought to universal consciousness, what the nineteenth-century sociological tradition saw intuitively as implicit in modern social existence.

32. Two contemporary philosophers who have reflected on history point to the interweaving of the unplanned and the planned, the unfolding of a predictable series and the intermixture of unpredictable human response:

"The past has left us a deposit of materials and resources, setting the limits and conditions within which a choice of means is possible. That means, once chosen, further determines what the future will be when it has become a present. God—or the future—proposes, but man disposes; he forces God to propose something else. And what God—or the future—proposes is always problems and issues. Man responds and answers" (John Herman Randall, Jr., *Nature and Historical Experience*, p. 55).

"I doubt whether it is possible to describe the adjustments which take place as though they were simply due to social institutions working as if they were automatic mechanisms, without supplementing the analysis in functional terms with a study of how some effect of conscious policymaking, guided by notions of desirable change, may give a new direction to social life: in other words, recognizing that some of the things which are happening will need to be described in terms not of function but of purpose" (Dorothy Emmett, *Function, Purpose and Powers*, p. 75).

33. Marx distinguishes three levels of historical process: (1) changes in means of production, i.e., in the technology of production, (2) resulting changes in "social relations," modes of participation in work and in human interrelations and roles of work, and (3) conceptual changes in "consciousness" or "ideology," ideas about reality, truth and value: "This conception of history, therefore, rests on the exposition of the real process of production, starting out from the material production of life, and on the comprehension of the forms of intercourse connected with and created by this mode of production, i.e., of civil society in its various stages. . . . From this starting point, it explains all the different theoretical productions and forms of consciousness, religion, philosophy, ethics, etc." (*Selected Writings*, p. 54; cf. also pp. 74–75). Our discrimination of "levels" somewhat parallels and yet diverges from this: (1) cumulative changes in technology in modes of production, in social forms of interrelation and in modes of communal existence (cities, etc.); (2) policy and political decisions in response to the problems generated in no. 1; (3) symbolic structures which reflect and also guide and direct both no. 1 (cf. the relation of science to the developments of technology), and no. 2.

We agree that the level of cumulative technical, economic and social changes is basic; but we emphasize more than Marx (in theory as well as in existence) the effective role of policy and the role of symbol (the productions of consciousness) as dynamic factors in historical change. As many sociologists and historians have emphasized, history is an interaction of these three levels, none of them being therefore *the* cause and the others *the* effects—as both "materialists" and "idealists" have maintained.

34. We refer again to the paradox, disclosed by the great nineteenth-century sociologists and of special relevance to a technical society, that an egalitarian, individualist, autonomous culture in which each individual is given multiple and so "free" choices is itself a threat to real individuality, i.e., one guided by its own norms, reasons and aims. For here the individual receives little objective support from those social forces that *create* individuality: shared communal beliefs and standards, genuine community, a hierarchy of norms and of excellence, a sense of the common good and a communal meaning of individual work, legitimate authority, and so on. Cf. Simmel's remarks: "The deepest problems of modern life derived from the claims of the individual to preserve the autonomy and individuality of his existence in the face of overwhelming social forces, of historical heritage, of external culture and of the techniques of life. The fight with nature which primitive man has to wage for his *bodily* existence obtains in this modern form its latest transformation" (quoted in Nisbet, *Sociological Tradition*, p. 305).

35. Studies descriptive of the devastating aspects of modern Western culture on, say, the social organism and its members in an African culture find their earlier parallel in the sociological results of European society under the impact of the effects of the French Revolution, of growing industrialism and increasing technology.

36. Perhaps the most powerful, as well as one of the earliest (after Herder and Hegel) formulations of this understanding of society as constituted by a symbolic world was of course that of Durkheim. For him not only did these symbols have a "religious" character, as we here argue; rather the reverse was true: religion derived from the power of the community and the symbolic forms that constituted and expressed that community. Cf. Emile Durkheim, *The Elementary Forms of the Religious Life*, and the chapter on the sacred in Nisbet, *Sociological Tradition*, pp. 221–63. For one modern example of an understanding of society as constituted by symbolic structures—structures which have a religious character—cf. Clifford Geertz, *The Interpretation of Cultures*, Pt. II, chaps. 4 and 5.

37. Peter Winch, *The Idea of a Social Science and Its Relation to Philosophy*, p. 23. For other contemporary expressions of this point, cf. Alfred Schutz, *On Phenomenology and Social Relations*, pp. 245–52; Talcott Parsons, "Culture and Social System Revisited," pp. 34–36; Berger and Luckmann, pp. 50–52, 95–104; Leff, pp. x and 104–5; Emmett, pp. 22 and 141; and Winter, *Elements for a Social Ethic*, pp. 104 ff.

38. Leff, p. 141.

39. A symbolic world, the social and historical "reality" within which each person exists and finds identity, role, and so security and meaning, forms a unity of interrelated symbols in which even the most seemingly insignificant "minor symbol" can have a significant role. Thus a shift in habits of dress or of hairstyles—as well as more fundamental changes of sensibility and value—can signal the change, or the breakup, of a certain symbolic world, and so all of the insecurities such a breakup might entail. Only thus can one understand the intense emotional and absurdly repressive reaction of school boards several years ago to the appearance of long hair on high school youths. Such a shift in hairstyles clearly indicated an almost geological shift in fundamental social consciousness. A new age, i.e., a new symbolic world, seemed to those anxious school boards to be appearing with each new long-haired student—and possibly they were right.

40. Cf. Alfred Schutz's profound analysis of the experience of the "stranger" who seeks to live within a new social order in which he has no place, is familiar with no expectancies,

and recognizes no common norms, and so finds himself in a state of disbelief in relation to the "realities" commonly accepted there (Schutz, pp. 87–95).

41. "When this confidence in patterns of behavior that can be taken for granted breaks down on a wide scale, a society will tend to the state of affairs which Durkheim calls *anomie*. . . . It describes a state of rootlessness, a lack of any assured moral framework on which the individual can count" (Emmett, p. 146).

"Masses arise when men come to be without an authentic world, without provenance or root, disposable and exchangeable" (Karl Jaspers, *The Origin and Goal of History*, p. 128). As we shall see, an "authentic world" is one structured by social and religious symbols which give the world in which men and women live and their place in it a comprehensible and meaningful form. Such a world is "given" and cannot be intentionally created; it is, we shall argue, one of the major gifts of providence. The loss of such a world by the destruction of important symbols concerning man, society and history is, as noted here, often a result of social changes (Jaspers speaks specifically of technological developments), and this in turn leads, through the creation of anomie and the formation of masses, to deeper and more serious political changes.

42. Perhaps most basic of all to "political self-consciousness" is, as Hegel reiterated, the awareness of freedom, or the possibility of freedom in history, that man is a *subject* in history, not merely a passive object, and can remake in part the history in which he lives: This is "historical consciousness" in its broadest sense. For Marx ("history is *nothing* but the activity of men in pursuit of their ends" and "circumstances are changed by men" [*Early Writings*, pp. 63 and 67]) and present political theologies that stem from him, this general consciousness of freedom in history is given a more specific form in the understanding of the structures and dynamics of a historical situation, the injustices of its present, the causes of those injustices and the dynamic factors at work in and out of the present—and thus is intelligent action on the part of freedom, praxis, possible. Cf., for example, Gustavo Gutierrez, *A Theology of Liberation*, pp. 29–30, 46–47, 91–92.

43. Again we note the strange and unexpected parallel between the dominant classes in an affluent and powerful culture, who fear historical change as the loss of their familiar world, of their authenticity and security and thus also of their own dominant role in that world, with the tribal "elders" of an undeveloped or at least less powerful civilization, fearful of the impact of a new, potent culture borne by both foreigners and their own youth.

44. As Edmund Burke was perhaps the first to point out (cf. Nisbet, *Sociological Tradition*, pp. 117–18), the disruptive, revolutionary role of ideology (of new symbolic systems) was the work primarily of the intellectual elite—though the political forces effecting the social change, e.g., in the French Revolution, had their sources in the interests of oppressed classes. In any case, the point is the ideologies expressed and borne primarily by the intelligentsia have a dual role of conserving a society and its symbolic worlds and of radically remaking that society and its symbolic worlds. In this sense, (a) the word *ideology* applies to revolutionary classes as much as to conservative ones, and (b) symbolic worlds have a radical as well as a conservative role, a point which Berger recognizes but does not emphasize sufficiently (cf. Berger and Luckmann, pp. 79–128).

45. Reinhold Niebuhr frequently terms it the work of "providential grace" when out of fundamental *self*-interest on the part of the agents (e.g., self-interested nations), an unintended result ensues which has benevolent social results for all. Cf. Niebuhr, *Faith and History*, pp. 174–75, and *Man's Nature and His Communities*, pp. 106 ff. Cf. also June Bingham, *Courage to Change*, p. 126, and the discussion of the relation of "common grace" to providence in Niebuhr's thought in Keith Keeling's excellent thesis (unpublished), "The Transcendence of Grace: A Study of the Theology of Reinhold Niebuhr," University of Chicago, 1974.

46. It should be emphasized, as it will be in the text, that the author does *not* regard these

changes (loss of relative power on the part of the West) as bad. There are immense possibilities for good—for liberation and for self-determination and self-development—in that loss of power by the West. What is important to note, however, is that deep anxiety and its political results, fanaticism, on the part of those losing power is also a real historical possibility—and it is this about which we wish to speak. The apparent helplessness of the industrialized nations, primarily Western, in the face of Arab demands for higher prices for oil is merely one indication of this shift of power. A hundred years ago a Western nation so "defied" would merely have stepped in and commandeered the oil—a policy which, unfortunately, is still contemplated by some American leaders.

47. Again a stark contrast is evident. In the late eighteenth, throughout the nineteenth and in the early twentieth centuries, democratic, liberal and even capitalist ideals—the social symbols of the young America—provided the inspiration and the symbolic categories for innumerable non-Western groups coming to new social and political birth: in South America, Europe, Africa and perhaps most ironically China (the revolution of 1911). America represented a "revolutionary" force throughout the established orders of the world, a force whose symbols expressed and secured the hopes, not of the mighty and secure of the earth, but of the oppressed. The total shift of the role of our "ideology," now supportive of every possible form of ancient and modern privilege and most if not all forms of tyranny, is a sad destiny indeed for these ideals. Symbols which once promised the liberation of man now seem to many, and with good reason, to seal his and her enslavement.

48. As with most significant but misguided political actions, "the defense of democracy" in Vietnam and in Chile was the compound of two serious faults: (1) ignorance and foolishness (referred to in the text) in the application of "democracy" to a social situation into which it could not fit (for Tocqueville's wise understanding of the dependence of democratic societies on a *particular* social and cultural history, cf. *Democracy in America*, pp. 164–65, 199–200, 208); (2) hypocrisy—many genuinely were concerned with democracy (e.g., the "free ballot") and so were merely ignorant, but many others were hypocritical. The latter is seen by the fact that, having fought the communists in Vietnam and unseated a Marxist in Chile "to save democracy," American policy is then utterly unconcerned with the destruction of democracy in precisely the same sense by the forces in both places that we have supported and continued to support. In these cases, the lack of free ballots, of opposition parties, of a free press and so on—which brought forth weapons against the communists—now merely elicit pained assurances that the State Department "deplores" these errors.

49. As Paul Tillich rightly makes plain, power is at base an ontological category, signifying the capacity or power to be of an entity, and thus its capacity to continue to be, to preserve its identity and to function "authentically" in terms of its own creative powers. Cf. Tillich, *Love, Power and Justice*, chap. 3. Or, in Reinhold Niebuhr's terms, power represents the unity of vitality and form, vitality and reason, body and soul—clearly the condition of existence, of the self and of community alike, but also clearly the condition, as he points out, of the demonic as well as the creative power of self and of community. Cf. Niebuhr, *The Nature and Destiny of Man*, 2:258–59.

In the sociological discussion of power, a distinction is made between *authority* and *power*, the former representing an inward, recognized or "legitimate" authority in society, the latter an external, unified and so heteronomous power over individuals in society. Cf. Nisbet, *Sociological Tradition*, pp. 112–16, 121–25.

With the loss of organic, recognized authorities of family, community, class, guild and religion, power based only on contract and force enters as the sole socially unifying force—and with devastating results. As our discussion will indicate, we are not using the category *power* in this sense, but rather in one that seeks to include what this tradition means by authority, namely, the internal authority of tradition, of a symbolic world that "persuades" the individual as much as one that coerces him or her. In other words, our attempt is to begin or propose an ontological analysis of authority in terms of a wider concept of power in order to answer the question why "legitimate authority" persuades persons inwardly towards conformity to the community, i.e., why it is for them "sacral" and thus nonheteronomous. That internal and so legitimate authority can itself become demonic and oppressive, the whole revolutionary tradition from the French *philosophes* through Marx witnesses. For this point cf. Reinhold Niebuhr's strictures on the demonic possibilities of all spiritual, moral and religious power (*Nature and Destiny*, vol. 1, chap. 7, vol. 2, pp. 260 ff).

50. "All communities are more or less stable or precarious harmonies of human vital capacities. They are governed by power. The power which determines the quality and harmony is not merely the coercive and organizing power of government. This is only one of the two aspects of social power. The other is the balance of vitalities and forces in any given social situation. These two elements of communal life—the central organizing principle and power and the equilibrium of power—are essential and perennial aspects of community organization" (Niebuhr, *Nature and Destiny*, 2:257–58).

51. Since real anarchy among diverse social forces is intolerable, central power is not in and of itself an evil, except when (as the sociologists referred to in footnote 49 argue) it is the sole form of power in the community, possesses no internal legitimacy and thus is dependent for its unifying role only on its coercive capacities, i.e., when it is heteronomous.

52. "I notice we have destroyed those individual powers which were able single-handed to cope with tyranny, but I see that it is the government alone which has inherited all the prerogatives snatched from families, corporations and individuals; so the sometimes oppressive but often conservative strength of a small number of citizens has been succeeded by the weakness of all" (Tocqueville, p. 15; cf. also pp. 57, 96, 192, 251–60).

53. Cf. Niebuhr, *Nature and Destiny*, 2:267 ff., 284.

54. Ibid. This ideal of a balance of power, not only between competing subordinate forces in the community but also between those forces and the unifying power of the community expressed in government, is the way the valid insight of the conservative tradition in sociology (cf. references to authority versus power above) is given its due. Thus the ideals of the French Revolution (to dismantle subordinate forms of oppressive power in the name of individual freedom) and that of conservative reaction (to support subordinate forms of communal power in the name of the same freedom) are in principle united by recognizing the importance in any community of its unifying power, requiring justice against privilege, and its plural vitalities and communities, retaining a balance of forces against each other and against the power of the whole. In this sense a healthy democracy, as Tocqueville reiterated, must protect the minority from the majority as well as the reverse.

55. This internal acquiescence to power is, of course, what is referred to by "authority" and by "legitimate power" as opposed to mere coercieve power. No community can be governed, as every analyst agrees, sheerly by coercive force; there must be some consent or "silent acknowledgment" (Tillich) on the part of the governed. It is this inner consent that gives sacrality to the unifying and protective power of government and to the established order of a hierarchical community. As we shall see in chap. 2, one of the main "ontological" origins of this consent, and so of "sacrality," is the role of government in preserving and fostering the being of the members of the community against the threats of nonbeing implicit in the open future. On this point cf. Reinhold Niebuhr, *Reflections on the End of an Era*, pp. 58–59, 144, 152–53; and Tillich, *Love, Power and Justice*, chap. 6.

56. The ambiguity of power, in both its forms as coercive and as legitimate authority, is also necessarily a part of an analysis of power. To the conservative defenders of authority, internalized hierarchical power prevents sheer coercion. But to the radicals, and surely to those on the lower ranks of the hierarchy, such legitimatized hierarchical structure represents oppression, and so they appeal to the power of force and to "political self-consciousness" together to overturn the stable, internalized hierarchical forms of authority that cause oppression.

57. That power is the necessary condition and goal of liberation politics, and thus for them at least a good, is clear from the following representation of liberation theology: "The creation of history, however, is possible only through power. Only through the historical exercise of power is the inhuman today negated and the way to a more human future made open. It is because man is present in his act that the new day which it creates can be more friendly. His use of power is, therefore, the first historical form which his freedom, his transcendence over the given fact takes. But the use of power is politics" (Alves, p. 16; cf. also pp. 10 and 12, and Gutierrez, pp. 46–49).

58. There are many reasons why the picture of social history ("social development" or "social evolution") presented by many social scientists as a process of gradual, cumulative, necessary and immanent changes seems abstract and inaccurate (note Nisbet's critique of this picture in *Social Theory and History*, chaps. 5, 7 and 8). One of them surely is the omission, referred to in the text, of the effects of such change on the distribution of power, and so the explosive political reactions of men and women to these changes and their attempts to resist, direct, control or encourage them. That such unintended and even inevitable, and insofar "natural," changes are present is undeniable, as Marx rightly saw. But that they are merely conditioning factors in the total social and political situation, and thus subject to all manner of human response and so to political contingencies, is also true.

59. Popper recognizes this with his usual clarity. There are no general and necessary *laws* of development in history, he insists, but only partial and temporal "trends," trends which depend on conditions which may or may not continue to hold. Since these conditions in turn depend on innumerable historical contingencies of economics, of politics, or the power of symbols, etc., the persistence of a given trend can never achieve the status of a law, and predictions are impossible. Cf. Popper, pp. 128–29. Reference can also be made to Tillich's agreement on this point, i.e., that historical continuities are constituted by trends, which, however seemingly inexorable and necessary, are always balanced by what he calls "chances," "occasions for changing the determining power of the trend" (Tillich, *Systematic Theology*, 3:327; hereafter referred to as *ST*).

60. Consider, as examples of the impact of a war on the continuity of a trend and on the rate of economic change, (1) the difference the loss of the Civil War meant to the "trends" of the agrarian plantation culture of the South, and (b) the acceleration of economic development brought on in Israel as the result of its victory in the War of Independence.

61. The best, if not the most cheerful, description, and prophecy, of this problem is *The Limits to Growth* by Donella H. Meadows et al. There have been many penetrating critiques of the methods employed by the authors, but that some such crisis of industrial expansion in relation to resources is developing in our future seems beyond doubt. Whatever the precise character of that coming crisis, or its date of arrival, it is, I am sure, certain to become a major factor in our common future and thus, even now, an essential subject of social, political, moral and theological reflection—and action.

62. Cf. the author's description of the intense difficulty of sharing, of being honest, of "virtue" in a hungry internment camp (*Shantung Compound*, chaps. 5–8).

63. It is not irrelevant that in connection with the recent oil shortage several national spokesmen, including Secretary of State Kissinger, appealed to our "right of self-defense" to commandeer, "if ever it should be necessary," those resources essential for the continuance of our "present levels of well-being." One can well imagine what international robbery in the future, and so vicious conflicts, might be justified by those doctrines!

64. "Historical causation involves both sets of factors: the formal pair, material and formal causes and their relations; and the functional pair, efficient and final causes and their relations. The second set is usually neglected: 'historical causation' is then treated as though it were identical with 'historical determinism,' and exhausted by it. . . . When decision is overlooked, the 'limits' set to human action are taken as what brings those histories to pass. . . . All the various historical determinisms: geographical, climatic, racial, psychological, economic, and

the rest, treat a 'limit' as though it were an efficient cause or 'dynamic.' That is, they are all non-functional, and as such metaphysically unsound.

"Historical causation includes *historical decision,* operating within the limits of *historical determinism.* It is the 'decision' that actually brings about the eventuation, and thus the history itself" (Randall, *Nature and Historical Experience,* pp. 94–95).

65. Social scientist Robert Heilbroner agrees: "All the dangers we have examined—population growth, war, environmental damage, scientific technology—are *social* problems, originating in human behavior and capable of amelioration by the alteration of that behavior" (Heilbroner, p. 61).

66. Many humanists, philosophical and literary, have recently ceased berating religion, and especially Judaism and Christianity, for preventing scientific and technological development, and (now that the latter is out of favor) begun to blame these religious traditions for grounding and encouraging the scientific/technological misuse of the earth. Surely it is ironically true that a good number of us who once argued for the connection of our religious traditions with the developments of science (cf. the author's *Maker of Heaven and Earth,* chap. 4) now find ourselves de-emphasizing that connection! In reply it could be pointed out that post-Renaissance humanism has more than acceded to the negative implications of the biblical view of man as separate from, higher than, and so rightfully lord of nature—at worst the misuser of nature, at best the steward of it. Humanism, as fathered by Francis Bacon and the technological tradition that has echoed his views, has sought to center culture and man's hope for progress on scientific knowledge of nature and the control of and use of nature that such knowledge brings, and has always regarded Christianity as an impediment to that goal. It was antitheistic not because theism gave man control of nature, but because it seemed to discourage that control.

For this reason, modern naturalism has, despite its frequent claims in that regard, represented by no means a view of man as a "subordinate part of nature and its orders" (as, say, did Buddhism). Philosophically naturalism found man a mere part of nature and congratulated itself for its "humility" before nature; but *existentially* in social and historical actuality, it has enacted a quite different self-understanding of man in relation to nature, namely that of man the knower of nature and so its controller and user, dominant over it in ways inconceivable to an early Hebrew. Nature is no longer a realm with relative independence, integrity and value; it is purely "matter," material for man's use (and misuse). John Dewey perfectly expresses this "official" doctrine of subordination to nature, but this existential doctrine of separation, control, use and so subordination of and dominion over nature: "Greek and medieval science formed an art of accepting things as they are enjoyed and suffered. Modern experimental science is an art of control. . . . Nature as it already exists ceases to be something which must be accepted and submitted to, endured or enjoyed, just as it is. It is now something to be modified, to be intentionally controlled. It is material to act upon so as to transform it into new objects which better answer our needs. Nature as it exists at any particular time is a challenge, rather than a completion; it provides possible starting points and opportunities rather than final ends" (Dewey, p. 327).

It may be added that this "official" view of man as a product of nature and so in continuity with it, combined with an "existential" understanding of man as dominant over nature through technology, and then of nature as merely an instrument for man's purposes, is as evident in Marx's "naturalism" as it is in Dewey's, and correspondingly, as much a problem in technology-centered Marxist culture as in our own capitalist culture. For both traditions thought (consciousness) is primarily instrumental for human survival and well-being; for both history is precisely the history of the development of technology, of instruments for the domination of nature (means of production); and finally, for both nature is conceived as that which man uses for his own purposes: "The universality of man appears in practice in the universality which moves the whole of nature into his own organic body: (1) as a direct means of life; and equally, (2) as the material object and instrument of his life activity" (Marx, *Early Writings*, p. 126).

The ecological crisis reveals not only the depths of human greed but also the massive misuse of intelligence as the instrument of that greed, and it reveals as well the despoliation of nature through our application of technological skills, consequences of technological intelligence of which neither Bacon, Marx nor Dewey ever dreamed. It also poses ultimate questions to humanism, both liberal and Marxist. If it emphasizes, as its metaphysics implies, man's continuity with nature and so his subordination to it as a part of nature, humanism loses its sole principle and ground for confidence and hope, namely man's separation from nature in knowledge, dominion over it in control, and so man's capacity to fashion his existence towards his own ends. The grounds for hope in humanism involve, therefore, inevitably a separation from nature, a radical distinction between the realm of nature and that of culture, a distinction that has increased rather than decreased with the rise of science and technology—despite their metaphysical doctrine of man as "natural." Humanism is thus caught in a contradiction between its ground of being (nature) and its ground of hope (man as dominant over nature). It is no surprise (all "religions" being soteriological) that the latter theme has been dominant, and that a scientific age, proclaiming man to be "merely an animal" has felt man to be the new lord of all the earth—and so acted. In contrast, despite the variety of their views of nature, religious traditions, relating human existence and nature to a principle beyond both, have the capacity both to affirm the transcendence of human being over nature and yet its deep unity with and dependence on the natural order; for both proceed from a common source, both environment and self are "given"—gifts of a power beyond self—and both, being dependent beyond themselves, can feel, express and embody their dependence on one another.

67. Presumably theologians could produce a new exegesis, in this case of the promise of a "new heaven and a new earth," as a theological answer to the problems of depleted natural resources. No one, however, to my knowledge, has ever interpreted that promise as involving an intrahistorical divine replenishment of the waters, the fish, the fossil fuels, the uranium and so on of the earth; to employ such an exegesis in that usage would certainly indicate that the deus ex machina, "the god of the gaps," had returned with a vengeance.

68. Cf. Paul Tillich's discrimination between philosophy and theology: philosophy is directed at a reflective understanding of the *structure* of being with special concern for the character of that structure; theology is directed at a reflective understanding of the *meaning* of being, i.e., its meaning for us, its relation to our ultimate concerns, a meaning which is reflectively interpreted by means of that structure (*ST,* 1:22).

69. Cf. Heilbroner's query: "Is there hope for man in the future?" and his attempts to answer this basic query, raised by the effects of science, technology and industrialism, with a view of history that can bring confidence and courage to an almost despairing race (Heilbroner, pp. 13–17, 136–44).

CHAPTER 2

1. Reference here in the Anglo-American world is primarily to the writings of Reinhold and H. Richard Niebuhr, the seminal writings of Paul Tillich in the 1920s and 1930s (*The Interpretation of History; The Religious Situation,* pts. 1 and 2; *The Protestant Era,* chaps. 1, 2, 3 and 14; *Political Expectation,* chaps. 1, 3 and 4), Roger Shinn, *Christianity and the Problem of History,* Eric Rust, *Christian Understanding of History;* and in Europe, Nicolas Berdyaev, *The Meaning of History,* Karl Löwith, *Meaning in History,* and Rudolf Bultmann, *History and Eschatology.* One should also mention the great interest among theologians in the philosophies of Spengler, Collingwood and Toynbee, as well as the concentration of most

biblical interpreters on "the biblical view of history" as perhaps the central theme of the Scriptures.

2. Qualifications must be made to this general picture, though, I believe, its main lines are accurate. In the twenties and early thirties most discussions of history did regard the "problem of history" to be the conflicts, injustices and disintegration characteristic of Western capitalist culture: cf., e.g., Reinhold Niebuhr, *Reflections* (1934), chaps. 1 and 2; Paul Tillich, *The Religious Situation* (1926), and "Christianity and Modern Society" (1928), "Religious Social-ism" (1930), and "Basic Principles of Religious Socialism" (1923), in *Political Expectation;* also Tillich, "The World Situation," in *The Christian Answer.* It was with the rise of the even greater threats—and I believe they were just that—of totalitarian fascism and of Stalinist communism that the focus shifted from the problems of liberal culture to the threats to that culture. In this sense present political theology has returned to the mood of the twenties concerning history rather than that of the late thirties and forties.

3. A good deal more will be said of these differences in chap. 7.

4. There has been a tendency in some recent theology to feel that history is by nature "theological," so to speak, while nature is "secular," and thus that to move theological language from the categories of a philosophy of nature (natural theology) to historical inter-pretation is to move easily and naturally into theological speech. (For examples, cf. the writings of the late Carl Michalson, *Hinge of History* and *Rationality of Faith;* and more recently the near identification of historical and theological speech in Jürgen Moltmann, *Theology of Hope,* and Wolfhart Pannenberg, *Revelation as History,* introduction and chap. 3, and *Basic Questions in Theology,* vol. I, chaps. 2 and 5.) This is, I believe, an optical illusion. Although to be sure the categories appropriate to historical discourse include those of human freedom, namely, judgment, decision and intended action, nonetheless it remains just as large and as qualitative a "jump" from these humanistic categories natural to historical inquiry and to the interpretation of history to theological categories as it is from the categories of natural science. And probably for most of us who accept an historical explanation of events, the possibility of divine activity within historical events is as difficult, not to say incredible, a conception as is that of the divine activity within the forces of nature. Finally, a secular interpretation of history is as normative for contemporary social science and for historians as a secular interpretation of nature is for physical scientists. Which of the two "Books," the Book of History or the Book of Nature, is more immediately and directly revelatory of the divine is for our age, I think, a toss-up.

5. In this sentence the subject "history" has two interrelated but separable meanings: as (1) the inquiry or study of the course of events, and as (2) that ontic course of events itself. Some of the tricky issues arising from this double usage and meaning of the word *history* will be discussed in chap. 4; for the moment I shall proceed as if these two meanings were both recognized and clear.

6. Cf. the historian Gordon Leff: "History is by common consent the study of man's past; and more specifically man as a social being rather than as a species. Unlike psychology or sociology its concern is not with the individual or society as distinct types, but with diverse men as they have lived in diverse cultures. History deals with the worlds men have fashioned for themselves" (Leff, p. 3). The theologians Reinhold Niebuhr and Paul Tillich agree on this point. The first was concerned in his moral and theological interpretation of history with the creativity and sins of *communities,* similar and yet different from the lifestyles of individuals (cf., for an extreme statement, *Moral Man and Immoral Society* and, for his own later qualification, *Nature and Destiny,* 1:210–11). Tillich specifically denominated communities, not individuals, as the "bearers of history" (*ST,* 3:308, 324). For an entirely different view, namely, of "history" as the realm in which only individuals as individuals may find authentic-ity, cf. Rudolf Bultmann, *History and Eschatology,* pp. 139, 146, and 155.

7. This point—that individual persons alone are the "substances" or "entities" and so alone

act in history—has in recent debates been an important point not against idealist philosophy à la Hegel but against certain social scientists and social evolutionists who, according to their critics, speak of abstractions—"civilization," "society," "classes," "technology," "family," "transportation," and so on—as if they were ontic entities that change, develop or decline, and so follow their *own* laws, so to speak, as an organism or a substance might do. Thus critics of this sociological fallacy of "misplaced concretion" tend to insist that all ontological reality in history and so all action there—and so finally all explanations—must be located in individuals. And since the recurrent habits and the interpretations and meanings of people are constitutive of their social acts, all "explanations in society are finally psychological explanations." For example, cf. such diverse thinkers as Karl Marx: "It is above all necessary to avoid postulating 'society' once more as an abstraction confronting the individual. The individual is a *social being*" (*Selected Writings*, p. 77); John Herman Randall, Jr.: "All historical determination is *psychological*" (*Nature and Historical Experience*, pp. 87 ff.); and Karl Popper: "The task of social theory is to construct and to analyze our sociological models carefully in descriptive or nominalist terms, i.e., *in terms of individuals*, of their attitudes, expectations, relations, etc.—a postulate which may be called 'methodological individualism'" (Popper, p. 136). For Robert Nisbet's similar criticism, cf. *Social Change and History*, chap. 8. As Leff indicates, however, the concern of the student of history and so of social history (as opposed to that of the biographer), while to be sure confined to "people," is for people in their social relations and with regard to their social impact and effects (cf. the following note).

8. "The historian is interested neither in the rebel nor the conformist in isolation, but for his impact on other men. Hence he has to call in other men to enable him to understand both in their reciprocity. . . . He is concerned with his actions in their historical role: the 'inner' upon which he must focus is relevant only insofar as it is significant outside him" (Leff, pp. 29 and 33).

9. This point has been, of course, basic to the sociological tradition and has led it to "reify" in its own way the social entities within which men and women live and which enlarge or form them. Cf. Nisbet, *Sociological Tradition*, chaps. 3 and 4.

10. The becoming of a person in his or her social matrix received its most powerful philosophical expression in Hegel and in Feuerbach; it was further developed in Marx and later in the thought of G. H. Mead, and is currently explicated very clearly by Berger and Luckmann, pp. 131 ff., Alfred Schutz, esp. pp. 73–76, 119–20, and Gibson Winter, *Elements for a Social Ethic*. For an early theological understanding of this point, cf. Friedrich Schleiermacher, *The Christian Faith*, secs. 60, 71, 87. For Pannenberg's argument from individual through social matrix to universal history, cf. *Basic Questions*, 1:170.

11. Nevertheless, the assertion of the "independent" and "prior" reality of society, if not its capacity for experience, over against its individual members—philosophically a legacy surely of Hegel and represented in the nineteenth-century Hegelians Bosanquet and F. H. Bradley—is clearly the presupposition which for Durkheim at least makes sociology possible and an intelligible science: "Sociological method, as we practice it, rests solely on the basic principle that social facts must be studied as things; that is, as realities external to the individual. . . . It is not realized that there can be no sociology unless societies exist; and that societies cannot exist if there are only individuals" (quoted in Nisbet, *Sociological Tradition*, pp. 92–93). For a modern form of this position, cf. Maurice Mandelbaum, "Societal Facts," in Patrick Gardiner, *Theories of History*, pp. 476–88; and for a careful review of the problem, Ernest Gellner, "Holism versus Individualism in the History of Sociology," ibid., pp. 488–503.

12. As noted, this internal relatedness of individual to the social group and its structural forms, rather than the prior ontological reality of the social whole, is the basis of an independent sociology. Because of this system of internal relations, individual patterns of feeling and

of behavior are to be understood, in part, in terms of the character of the social structure, the form of its changes, the direction and implications of its major trends and so on. Thus is there a social (structural) explanation as well as a psychological explanation of human behavior—in fact, the two cannot be separated. As Marx says: "Consciousness is therefore from the very beginning a social product, and remains so as long as men exist at all" (*Early Writings*, p. 71, cf. also p. 77).

13. "Social order exists *only* as a product of human activity. No other ontological status may be ascribed to it without hopelessly obfuscating its empirical manifestations. Both in its genesis (social order is the result of particular human activity) and its existence at any time (social order exists only and insofar as human activity continues to produce it), it is a human product" (Berger and Luckmann, p. 52).

14. Thus Tillich said that the dimension of history—the life of groups—is the culminating, the most all-embracing dimension of life, bringing together the physical, the organic, the spiritual and the human dimensions into a new and more complete but analogous form (*ST*, 3:297). The discussion that follows of the "analogy" of individual and group life is vastly indebted to Tillich's ingenious description of the parallel but changing functions and meanings of categories as one moves from the inorganic through the organic and the spiritual to the historical dimension (*ST*, 3:313–27). Similarly, Reinhold Niebuhr analyzed the political and historical life of groups—their creativity, limits, pride, conflicts, nemesis and possibilities of renewal—on analogy with the categories and symbols applicable to and, in the concrete, applied only to individual men and women: sin, anxiety, idolatry, insecurity, pride, faith, greed and so on. This is clearly the Old Testament presupposition where Israel as a community or a people is the "subject" of her own history, and the object of Yahweh's historical activity of love, creation, preservation, judgment and renewal. Cf. especially Gerhard von Rad, *Old Testament Theology*, 1:118ff.

15. We shall discuss further in chap. 4 the problems of understanding history through the concepts of "natural laws," or laws of development, i.e., on the model of either the laws of physical or of biological science. For the moment reference may be made to Nisbet's critique, *Social Change and History*, chap. 8. For an exuberant, brilliant, perceptive and yet fundamentally fallacious case of the "organic" model for integrating history, cf. Oswald Spengler, *The Decline of the West*.

16. By this "nominalist" statement we do not, of course, mean to exclude either (1) the reality or effectiveness in history of a "divine entity" (if such language be appropriate): this whole volume is devoted to an intelligible explication of this theme; or (2) the reality of what Whitehead calls a "nexus" of actual occasion (cf. *Process and Reality*, pp. 35–51). On the latter point, as Whitehead insists, metaphysically the only concrete realities are actual entities (ibid., pp. 33 and 37), and finally the only "reasons" stem from actual entities (ibid., pp. 36 f.); nevertheless nexus or societies of actual entities are effective on the actual entities of which they are composed because each actual entity comes to be through its internal relations to the society within which it arises. Only such a notion of internal relations can, it seems to me, resolve this argument between the individualists and the societal realists.

17. It is important to note, however, that (1) sociology illuminates the character of concrete, individual existence by uncovering the ways in which trends and developments in social structure affect individual existence (e.g., how egalitarianism creates individual experiences of envy and of dissatisfaction—Tocqueville); and that (2) ideas and meanings are frequently effective in structural sociological changes, as Weber showed in his classic analysis of the influence of Calvinism on the rise of capitalism (cf. *The Protestant Ethic and the Spirit of Capitalism* and the commentary on Weber's thesis and its importance in Michael Hill, *A Sociology of Religion*, chaps. 5 and 6, and in Nisbet, *Sociological Tradition*, pp. 257 ff.; cf. also Reinhard Bendix, *Max Weber: An Intellectual Portrait*). Thus, although it deals with relative abstractions, sociology can illuminate concrete human existence; nor are its abstrac-

tions by any means necessarily devoid of "human elements," i.e., aspects related to, influenced by and important to the inward realms of meanings, ideas and intentions.

18. Insofar as the possibilities for creative action in politics are dependent upon the possibilities of a given social situation, the social sciences are intrinsic to political action. For it is only when the structure, the dynamics and the possibilities of a situation are understood that realistic and creative new possibilities can be projected and enacted. Thus Marxist thought has been right in making an intelligible sociology one component of "the political self-consciousness" necessary for historical action. For this reason Popper's definition of the role of social science in politics is too restrictive: "The task [of the theoretical social sciences] is to trace the unintended social repercussions of intentional human actions" (Popper, "Predictions and Prophecy in the Social Sciences," in Gardiner, p. 28). Social science can also reveal to us where we are, what major trends dominate our situation and so what "chances," as Tillich would say, lie before us to "change the determining power of a trend" (*ST*, 3:327).

19. If an understanding of social man (social science) is dependent on a prior understanding of human being as concrete man and woman, then one can understand the present importance of the use of phenomenology in the social sciences. As Schutz put this, it is important to understand the conditions for the possibility of sociality, if a scientific study of society is to have rational foundations, and thus the basis of social science is seen to lie in a phenomenological (and in the end an ontological) understanding of man, of his temporality, inner subjectivity, modes of communication and of interrelation and so on. Cf. Schutz, pp. 55 ff.; and for an attempt further to elaborate this important thesis, Gibson Winter, *Elements for a Social Ethic*, chap. 4.

20. For Tillich's important discussion of the *limits* of the analogy of community to "organism," cf. *Love, Power and Justice*, pp. 92–95; for Niebuhr's discussion of the same limits, cf. the differences between individual persons and communities in *Faith and History*, pp. 216 ff.

21. As many sociologists, preeminently of course Durkheim but also Tocqueville, Weber and Simmel, have emphasized, society itself has a sacral character, and without that religious dimension society itself loses its reality, its power, its norms and sanctions, its integration and directive efficacy—and correspondingly the individual himself disappears. Thus social symbols, constitutive and representative of this sacral entity, are intrinsically sacral, of ultimate authority and value, insofar as they are functioning socially; and thus is the sacred a social category, in part explanatory of the nature or being of a social group (cf. Nisbet, *Sociological Tradition*, chap. 6). In this sense, the argument of this chapter that social and political experience are inherently *religious* in character and so reflect a dimension of ultimacy in human experience parallels a good deal of sociological understanding. The difference here is that we are seeking to give first an ontological interpretation to this undoubted social fact —as they do not—and then on its basis to proceed to a theological interpretation. Marx vigorously denied that social institutions are essentially sacral; rather, he insisted that they be understood and interpreted in a "human and a secular form" if they are to be valid and real social institutions; for example, as he argued, if it is still viewed as "sacred," e.g., as Christian, the state is not yet realized as a state, as a secular institution (cf. Marx, "Bruno Bauer, die Judenfrage," in *Early Writings*, pp. 16–17).

22. This sense of self-awareness—of a group's identity, relatedness, possibilities, tasks, purposes and so on—is obvious among both developed and developing nations in the present, though for each it would not have been as obvious in the "racial" or "tribal" groups out of which they developed as nations. As noted, such self-awareness by a community is a condition for its political action, as Marx realized: unless the proletariat becomes self-conscious of itself *as a proletariat*, it is helpless and passive; not being aware of itself, its situation or the possibilities of that situation, it has no autonomy, no self-direction, no hope of control over its own destiny, no "existence" as a group. The same need for self-awareness in order to act

with autonomy and power in history is evident in the struggle of every oppressed group; the first requirement is self-consciousness of itself as a group, whether we speak of the communities fighting against colonialism in South America, Blacks in the United States, women and so on. As in individual existence, self-awareness and identity within essential relatedness are the necessary conditions for autonomy and creative action.

23. Tillich terms this total sense of itself and its destiny on the part of a group (the aim towards which the group strives) its "vocational consciousness." Since the German equivalent of the word *vocation (Dienst)* implies a moral vocation, service to the nation and the world, which the English word *vocation* in its ordinary usage lacks, I have used the American phrase "way of life," which in popular usage includes moral and ideal elements as well as concrete social, economic and political habits of behavior—though one must admit that to most of us now that way of life is more characterized by the dimension of economic abundance and comfort than it is by the ideals of freedom, equality and self-realization that once dominated its usage. Cf. Tillich, *ST,* 3:310–11.

24. The philosopher W. H. Walsh emphasizes the complex multiplicity of "causes" in history and concludes that this entire multiplicity forms less causes than "necessary conditions" for the event in question to transpire: "What caused relations between the main European powers to deteriorate sharply in the closing years of the nineteenth century? Now it is obvious that causes so understood cannot operate in isolation: a cause on this reading is only one of a number of necessary conditions of what is said to be its effect, and can produce the latter only in conjunction with the others" (Walsh, *Philosophy of History,* p. 190).

"Their relation to one another [the causes of the Third Crusade] can only be one of enumeration not causality, since they represent different kinds of factors operating in different ways—some (Barbarossa's death) on a direct temporal sequence; some (attitudes to Saladin and the holy places) by time lag; some by hypostatization (religious zeal, desires for prestige and aggrandizement); some as long-term, some as short-term. Hence to call them causes is to speak metaphorically, not in any exact scientific sense of the term" (Leff, p. 64).

"Historical causality is the embracing form of causality because of the fact that in historical events all dimensions of life are actively participant. It is dependent on the freedom of creative causality, but it is equally dependent on the inorganic and organic developments which have made historical man possible and which remain as the frame or substructure of his whole history. And this is not all; since the bearers of history are historical groups, the nature of these groups represents the decisive interpenetration of determining and free causality in the historical process. In a historical group a double causation can be observed; the causation from a given sociological structure to the creation of cultural content and the causation from the content towards a transformed sociological structure" (Tillich, *ST,* 3:324–25).

25. Collingwood, pp. 214–15.

26. "In what follows immediately I shall be taking it for granted that much history is an attempt to present the facts from the point of view of the agents concerned, and asking what sort of cause or types of causal question are involved in the clearing out of this task. First and most obvious, if it is true that the historian presents the persons he writes about as 'conscious and responsible agents,' to use Collingwood's phrase, the sense of 'cause' to which Collingwood drew attention will certainly be appropriate to history" (Walsh, p. 197).

"I now want to make a further modification: even given a set of initial conditions, one will still not be able to predict any determinate action to a historical trend because the continuation or breaking up of that trend involves human decisions which are not determined by their antecedent conditions in the context of which the sense of calling them "decisions" lies. . . . The point is that such trends are in part the outcome of intentions and decisions of their participants" (Winch, pp. 92–93).

"As Raymond Aron has said, to consider something as an event historically is to admit the possibility that it need not have occurred—at least at the time when it did. . . . We must therefore resort to individuals as the irreducible units of history and accept them as the agents of their own actions even if not of the circumstances which occasioned them. It is precisely at this level of individual achievement that sufficient cause can only be sought in the individuals. . . . Only if we keep comprehension distinct from causation can we be in a position to do justice to the new" (Leff, pp. 45, 48 and 49). For Leff's sharp criticism of Collingwood, despite the agreement evident here, cf. Leff, pp. 24–36.

"And though men's materials, the fruits of the past, *determine* or limit what men *can* do, they do not *decide* what men *will* do with them, nor do they decide what new and altered limits will be imposed by what men will do. This unique and particular 'decision'—the human action itself—depends, in addition, on the problems men see, on how clearly they see them, and on their ability and skill in bringing their materials and resources to bear on meeting the new problems" (Randall, *Nature and Historical Experience*, p. 90).

"The horizontal encounter under the dimensions of the spirit has the character of intention and purpose. In historical event, human purposes are the decisive, though not the exclusive, factor. Given institutions and natural conditions are other factors, but only the presence of actions with a purpose makes an event historical. . . . Man, insofar as he sets and promises purposes, is free. He transcends the given situation, leaving the real for the sake of the possible. He is not bound to the situation in which he finds himself, and it is just this self-transcendence that is the first and basic quality of freedom. Therefore, no historical situation determines any other historical situation completely. The transition from one situation to another is in part determined by man's centered reaction, by his freedom" (Tillich, *ST*, 3:302–3). For Winter's explication of the relation of sociality, intersubjectivity and freedom, cf. *Elements for a Social Ethic*, pp. 106 ff.

27. As a candid example from a scientist of the presuppositions of his method, cf. the following from cultural evolutionist J. H. Steward: "I emphasize causality because any assumptions that teleological or orthogenetic principles, divine intervention or free will, are at work would nullify scientific explanation. To those who disagree I can only say that science must proceed *as if* natural laws operate consistently and without exceptions, as if all cultures and all aspects of human behavior had determinants—no matter how difficult the task of unraveling the intricately interrelated phenomena" (Steward, "Cultural Evolution Today," in K. Hazeldon and P. Hefner, *Changing Man*, pp. 50–51).

28. Cf. Walsh, pp. 203–4. "These institutionalized behavior patterns are not themselves 'active powers' or 'dynamic factors.' The active powers in history are not 'habitual ways of believing,' but what men actually do; and such concrete human action is determined not only by social habits, but also by conscious and reflective attempts to deal with the problems forced upon men, with those generated by the unforeseen consequences of their dealing with the problems they have tried to solve" (Randall, *Nature and Historical Experience*, p. 82).

29. "History is concerned with the contingent; its criteria are qualitative. It must take account not merely of what happened, but how it happened and need not have happened. . . . History accordingly consists in the reconstruction of events, not inherently necessary in themselves, in the light of their achievement" (Leff, ix).

30. "On the other hand . . . men act in response to their own interpretations of a situation which, when it is not unthinking or under duress, is as much a product of their attitudes as of a clear assessment of the implications of a particular course of action" (Leff, p. 62).

31. Cf. Heidegger, pp. 172–79, 270–73, 329–35, 396–400, and esp. 425–39.

32. "Accordingly, individual actions are not explicable in their own terms, whether from their effects or their causes, but in relation to all the events in which they were a part; for history the context forms the indispensable whole without which the individual's role remains unintelligible. Thirdly, it follows that an individual's conduct is almost invariably in response to circumstances which are not of his own choosing. A man may begin as a reformer and end as a tyrant, or intend to be a man of peace and devote most of his life to war because of the

pressure of circumstances. Even at their most ideal and isolated it is seldom that our hands are not forced by events because any one situation is the result of the interplay of numerous factors under the control of no one" (Leff, p. 27).

33. Although he did not distinguish in analysis between "the necessities of nature" and the "destiny of history" that conditions, limits and controls human response, Reinhold Niebuhr had an acute sense of the importance of destiny and freedom in history, of the interweaving of unintended and intended factors, of the determination and yet the freedom characteristic of history: "Man's ability to transcend the flux of nature gives him the capacity to make history. Human history is rooted in the natural process but it is something more than either the determined sequences of natural causation or the capricious variations and occurrences of the natural world. It is compounded of natural necessity and human freedom. Man's freedom to transcend the natural flux gives him the possibility of grasping a span of time in his consciousness and thereby of knowing history. It also enables him to change, reorder and transmute the causal sequences of nature and thereby to *make* history" (*Nature and Destiny*, 2:1; see also Tillich's illuminating discussion of trends and chances and their interrelations in *ST*, 3:327).

34. "History-bearing groups are characterized by their ability to act in a centered way. They must have a centered power which is able to keep the individuals who belong to it united and which is able to preserve its power in the encounter with similar power groups. In order to fulfill the first condition, a history-bearing group must have a central, law-giving, administering and enforcing authority" (Tillich, *ST*, 3:308–9); cf. also Niebuhr, *Nature and Destiny*, 2:257 ff.). Thus is "authority" in society sacred because it is constitutive of the being, the continuing being and the freedom of the group, and so of the members of the group. By conceiving of the "majesty" of authority (and so the constitutive role of authority) as related to the being and the freedom of the group in history, we have sought to explain the sacral elements. Since on this view the sacral elements of authority have their relation to being and freedom—i.e., to "power" in the fundamental ontological sense of the power of the group to be and to act—we have sought to legitimatize the concept of power as more fundamental sociologically than that of authority, though we understand why on a different use of these categories "power" in much sociology is subordinate to "authority" (cf. Nisbet, *Sociological Tradition*, pp. 108–21). In this light we are in turn puzzled by Heilbroner's admitted "perplexity" at the sacred authority granted in all societies to rulers (Heilbroner, pp. 106 ff.) and regard it as incoherent, in fact, as an abdication on the part of a social analyst, to give, as he does, a psychological/familial explanation for this social and political reality (ibid., pp. 103 ff.).

35. The influence of the objective social world of symbols, norms and meanings on personal, individual behavior is well illustrated in Durkheim's analysis of suicide as a "social fact" dependent on the "state" of the objective social environment (cf. Nisbet, *Sociological Tradition*, pp. 92 ff).

36. Any reader familiar with the author's *Naming the Whirlwind* will note that the argument of this chapter is projected as a supplement to the argument of pt. 2, chaps. 2 and 3 of that work. Whereas there an analysis of individual experience showed the dimension of ultimacy or the sacred to be ingredient in individual life, here my attempt is to show its presence in social and political experience. Clearly while our analysis is related to sociological analyses of society as sacred, it seeks to provide an ontological and ultimately a theological explanation or ground for that characteristic of society, described and analyzed by them. Such explanations are, of course, not part of sociological theory, though that theory seems to call for some further explication (as, for example, the impoverished psychology in Heilbroner, fn. 34). Insofar, however, as the sociological theory moves into philosophy of history, some ontological status, whether naturalistic as implied in Durkheim or ontological-theological, must be provided.

37. "For we both are, and know that we are, and delight in our being, our knowledge of

it" Augustine, *The City of God,* bk. XI, chap. XXVI, vol. 2, p. 168).

38. Cf. in contrast Jürgen Moltmann's view that man finds himself only through alienation from himself in the present, and through harmony with himself in the future (*Theology of Hope,* p. 91). Though the contexts, and so the meaning of central categories, of these two discussions are very different, nevertheless this contrast is important for the view of man and of God. For us, as for Tillich, alienation from one's present being and its possibilities at the most fundamental level of the self, of its unity, reality and power is fatal to the self's creativity for the future; thus does God have a present role in selfhood and not only a future role.

39. Clearly this discussion is based on more than merely personal experience and reflection, though it has been for me continually validated there. It is in its reflective form indebted largely, as will be recognized, to Tillich. "Finitude in awareness is anxiety. . . . Anxiety is an ontological concept because it expresses finitude from 'inside'. . . . Anxiety is the self-awareness of the finite self as finite" (Tillich, *ST,* 1:191–92; cf. also *The Courage to Be,* chaps. 2 and 3, and for the relation of the anxiety about individual "being" to the "being" of the group, cf. especially chap. 4, pp. 87–90).

40. The author experienced the immense importance of the creation of these economic and political structures of common life in an internment camp in World War II. There it was daily evident not only that these structures support existence and make it possible but also that vast ingenuity and rational capacity, as well as dogged strength of will and courage, were necessary for their construction and maintenance. The vividness of this "appreciative" experience was partly due, to be sure, to the fact that without them we could not eat; but it was also due to the humbling realization that many of us are only very meagerly blessed with these forms of imagination and of intelligence that are relevant to such creative labors. Perhaps most important—and the point made in the text—is that such common work for a community is not so much consciously "merely utilitarian" or "for payment," though it can become such in certain situations. The essential and unconscious correlation of individual and communal security makes such work wholly "natural" and certainly not easily specified as either "self-interested" or "altruistic."

For Marx, also, work for the community is "natural" to us as humans, and any analysis that makes such activity into a means for individual life is an *alienated* analysis. For example: "Productive life is, however, species life. It is life creating life. In the type of life activity resides the whole character of a species . . . and free, conscious activity is the species character of human beings. Life itself appears only as a *means of life!*" (*Early Writings,* p. 127). "The first historical act is, therefore, the production of material life itself," and this is itself a disclosure of the creative faculties of reason, will and imagination: "Every day *material industry* . . . shows us in the form of *sensible external and useful objects,* in an alienated form, *the essential human faculties* transformed into *objects*" (*Selected Writings,* pp. 60 and 72).

41. The ontological (and so in our discussion the historical) polarity of destiny and freedom, which will play so large a role in this volume, owes its immediate origin, of course, to the thought of Tillich. That our own category "Fate" as an *estranged* destiny is not precisely Tillich's use of that category is evident from the following passages: "Destiny is not a strange power which determines what shall happen to me. It is myself as given, formed by nature, history, and myself. My destiny is the basis of my freedom; my freedom participates in shaping my destiny. . . . It points not to the opposite of freedom but rather to its condition and limits. *Fatum* ("that which is foreseen") or *Schicksal* ("that which is sent") and their English correlate "Fate" designate a simple contradiction to freedom rather than a polar correlation, and therefore they can hardly be used in connection with the ontological polarity under discussion" (*ST,* 1:185). On the other hand: "To lose one's destiny is to lose the meaning of one's being. Destiny is not a meaningless fate. It is necessity united with meaning. The threat of possible meaninglessness is a social as well as an individual reality. There are periods in social life, as well as in personal life, during which this threat is especially acute" (*ST* 1:201).

And cf. *Courage to Be,* pp. 42 ff., where the anxiety about Fate is made a central anxiety in historical existence, and is defined as the anxiety about a "total rule of contingency in our historical life." Clearly our own usage of Fate is a further interpretation of these passages. In contrast, Heidegger uses Fate *(Schicksal)* not as we here do, but as Tillich and we are using "destiny," as the facticity of our being in terms of which our possibilities and so our authenticity are to be gained; and he identifies destiny with the historicity of a people (cf. Heidegger, pp. 435 ff., 463 ff).

42. For Tillich the basic ontological structure is self and world *(ST,* 1:168–71); and one of the elements of that fundamental structure is the polarity of destiny and freedom (ibid., pp. 182–86). Because this interpretation seems to me (1) to be the ground of the "static" misinterpretation of Tillich's ontology, and (2) in order to enlarge and clarify the *process* character of our own ontology, and finally (3) in order to give a firmer ontological ground for the interpretation of history, we are here suggesting, with now great dependence on Whitehead, that destiny and freedom be considered the basic ontological structures of finite temporality, and self and world a discrimination within that basic structure.

43. Cf. Winter's helpful phenomenological and sociological discussion of the polarity of destiny and freedom as "project and conditions" *(Elements for a Social Ethic,* pp. 141–56, esp. 155).

44. The relation of the being and expansion of the group to the being and glory of the individual is very clearly pointed out by Niebuhr: "Collective egoism does indeed offer the individual an opportunity to lose himself in a larger whole; but it also offers him possibilities of self-aggrandizement besides which mere individual pretensions are implausible and incredible. Individuals 'joined to set up a god whom they then severally and tacitly identify with themselves, to swell the chorus of praise which each then severally and tacitly arrogates to himself . . . '. Collective pride is thus man's last, and in some respects, most pathetic, effort to deny the determinate and contingent character of his existence. The very essence of human sin is in it" *(Nature and Destiny,* 1:212–13; cf. *Moral Man and Immoral Society,* pp. 18 ff., 48, 91–95; also Tillich, *Courage to Be,* chap. 4).

45. "When man is alienated from power over his own destiny, even when he is alienated by the most benevolent system imaginable, he rebels and fights to have a voice in his affairs. Man is, among other things, an agent who seeks to shape his future, and make decisions on matters affecting his life" (Winter, *Being Free,* p. 43).

46. Winter, following Schutz, expresses well this relation between finite being, security, anxiety and the drive towards power: "Schutz postulates a fundamental anxiety over death and contingency which presses the organism towards control of the world in its projects and activities. The principle is, so to speak, the driving force of the 'interests' that dominate man's pragmatic orientation to the every-day world" *(Elements for a Social Ethic,* p. 73). Niebuhr adds depth and finesse to this analysis in his distinction of the organism's will to live from the human will to power, a distinction made possible by the intervention of "spirit": "But when the impulses of self-preservation are mixed with reason and the form of life grows more self-conscious, the will to live develops into the will to power. Its higher degree of self-consciousness increases the fear of death and extinction" *(Reflections,* p. 8).

47. Luther had a vivid experience of historical passage as "demonic," as ruled by an inscrutable and even ruthless divine will, the *deus absconditus* who in our present eyes is directly opposite to the loving God of the Word: "But God hidden in majesty neither deplores nor takes away death, but works life, and death, and all in all; nor has He set bounds to Himself by His Word, but has kept Himself free over all things. . . . God does many things which He does not show us in His Word, and He wills many things which He does not in His Word show us that He wills" *(Bondage of the Will,* p. 170).

48. It might be noted that our discussion is an attempt not only to comprehend, i.e., to explain in ontologically prior and so in universal terms, the experience of the social environ-

ment as "sacred" but also to understand that characteristic of society in fundamentally temporalistic rather than static terms, i.e., as a result of the temporality as well as the fundamental sociality of our being.

49. Our analysis seeks here to devise categories explanatory of the political and social concepts of legitimacy, sacrality and authority, and by so doing to illuminate the sacral character of politics, both conservative and radical or revolutionary. The tradition of sociology has generally emphasized the sacred character of established orders (e.g., Durkheim, Berger and Luckmann) and to regard democratic and socialist transformation of established orders as dismantling the sacred on a purely "rational" or "secular" basis. Though this be the self-image of such forces in many cases (e.g., the French and American revolutions and the Marxist revolution), it is, we suggest, a false one. The sacrality of the political, and of the power used to protect or establish it, appears in *both* cases and ultimately for the same essential reasons.

50. Again, the concept of "vocation" with which we are here concerned may have a conservative or a transformative connotation, depending on the view of social process, the view of the relation of social process to the sacred and finally the view of the relation of the sacred to time within which that idea of vocation finds its place. Vocation may be a "Dienst" in an established order of sacral worth and authority; here our activity participates in ultimate meaning by enacting a given role in the social order imbued with meaning and worth for all. By doing this task, we provide service to all and to the order that nurtures all. On the other hand, in a *progressive* culture, oriented to the manifestation of the sacred in the future, vocation represents a creative refashioning of the world for the better, as, for example, in recent liberal American life or in a different form in Marxist cultures.

51. Cf. the author's *Shantung Compound*, chap. 11. It was evident in that experience of life in an internment camp that without meaning in their work, the vitality that made hard work possible evaporated, and with this loss of a sense of "vocation" among its members, the community itself was, as a self-supporting social entity, deeply threatened.

52. As is well known, Marx's view of alienation is complex and covers a good number of distinguishable aspects: (1) that the worker is separated from the results of his labors so that the product "stands opposed to it (the labor) as an alien object, as a power independent of the producer" (*Early Writings*, p. 122). In certain relations of production this separated object is "expropriated," under the control of others for their interests; consequently the worker (under the dominion of this alien "object," his product) is himself rendered into a commodity, and thus himself subject to what we have called "Fate," the determination of his existence by forces beyond his control: "The more the worker produces, the less he has to consume; the more value he creates, the more worthless he becomes" (ibid., p. 123). This domination of his existence is both by economic and social forces beyond his own control and by alien hostile persons who govern those objects and so the laborer's life (ibid., p. 130). (2) "However, alienation appears not merely in the result but also in the process of production, within productive activity itself. . . . Consequently he does not fulfill himself in his work, but denies himself, has a feeling of misery rather than well-being, does not develop freely his mental and physical labors, but is physically exhausted and mentally debased" (ibid., pp. 124–25). This is the element referred to in the text, namely, the loss of intrinsic "meaning" in labor or activity, the denial of the fulfilment of the person and his identity in work, the separation in this sense of the process from the person, because (a) the product "is work for someone else," and (b) because it is "forced and not spontaneous, a matter of need rather than of self-expression," and (c) therefore "a means for satisfying other needs" rather than "the satisfaction of a need" or, in another place, "his *being* (as activity) is only a means for his *existence*" (ibid., p. 127). Finally, (3) alienation is alienation of man from man, from community (a point to be dealt with by the text later). Thus, "species life," communal activity and labor, becomes a means for the mere subsistence of his own individual life: "Forced to

be a commodity, labor inverts community into a form of egotism, and thus sets class against class, and, worse, worker against worker" (ibid., pp. 126–29). Thus to sum up, the miseries of alienation (as domination by Fate, as the Void of meaningless work, as a break in community and so as a triple loss of "being"), "the abstract existence of man as a mere *working* man, who, therefore, plunges every day from his fulfilled nothingness into absolute nothingness, into social, and thus real, non-existence" (ibid., p. 139). As is evident on many issues, while our text neither follows nor conforms to this analysis by Marx, it is in agreement with it at many crucial points. Cf. on the general subject of alienation, the study by Richard Schacht, *Alienation,* esp. chap. 3.

53. Toqueville identifies the prominence of the goal of success, the universality of envy and the consequent anxiety about status with the effects of egalitarian democracy, not with those of industrialism and of an affluent economy. Probably both are conditions of this undoubted character of modern Western and especially American society. Cf. Toqueville, 1:198; 2:566ff.

54. Cf. Schutz's explanation of this in his analysis of the Stranger (Schutz, pp. 85–95).

55. One may note that in reaction to this "anomie," the loss of meaning and so the loss of individuality and identity characteristic of egalitarianism, communal cultures, modern totalitarian states (especially fascist ones who do this explicitly) reestablish and so represent a hierarchical structure of common goals, norms and loyalties, i.e., of "authority," that make possible again communities both large and small in which the individual can find place, vocation and so identity. Thus a totalitarian structure mirrors a "traditional" class structure, only now in a radically centered way, in which each rank is sanctioned and ruled directly by the supreme power. Associations *over against* the central power, that serve in a traditional society to protect the individual against that power (Toqueville, 1:13–16), are ruthlessly eradicated, but not lower and ranked "associations" as such. These are now multiplied; thus does the individual now find his or her identity and role in a sacrally authorized structure of commune, bund, party group, town, workers' group and so on. Equality and individual freedom are gone, but identity and meaning are reestablished. It is a traditional society "retooled" into a transcendent authoritarian unity and power that reaches from top to bottom; totalitarian states thus combine in a devastating form "authority" and "power" as analyzed in nineteenth-century sociology.

56. "Intentionality is man's living toward the structure of his world in the unity of caring, hoping, conceiving, feeling, and meaning. Its subjective dimensions are the constituting intentionalities of embodied consciousness. Its objective dimensions are the forms in which the world appears for this consciousness. These forms take relatively permanent shape in the typified meanings of the everyday world—the sedimentation of social experience" (Winter, *Elements for a Social Ethic,* p. 198). This interdependence of objective forms and roles and internal intentionality and meaning have as their consequence that with the loss of "world" in this sense, individuality dies, and as individual meanings in life and work disintegrate, then community dies *as a community.* It is *eros* towards the meanings embodied in the life and work of a people that creates and sustains a community. This interpretation by no means exhausts the richness of Augustine's definition of a community or society, yet it is certainly one way to view that definition: "A people is an assemblage of reasonable beings bound together by common agreement as to the objects of their love" (*City of God,* bk. XIX, chap. XXIV).

57. Reinhold Niebuhr, *Reflections,* chap. 3; *Moral Man and Immoral Society,* p. 97 ff.; *Nature and Destiny,* 1:194–98.

58. On the role of intellectual elites in the French and American revolutions, cf. Nisbet, *Sociological Tradition,* pp. 117–18. Although Karl Marx had deemphasized the importance of "ideas" in previous historical change in his own analysis of it (cf. *Selected Writings,* p. 56), he also appreciated the role of *revolutionary* ideas and so of elites who bore them: "Theory itself becomes a material force when it has seized the masses" (*Early Writings,* p. 52). And

on the importance of utopian visions as conditions for social transformation, cf. the following from Gutierrez: "Faith and political action will not enter into a correct and fruitful relationship except through the effort to create a new type of person in a different society, i.e., except through utopia. . . . Political liberation appears as the path towards the freer, more human man, the protagonist of his own history. . . . Utopia so understood, far from making the political struggler a dreamer, radicalizes his commitment and helps his work from betraying his purpose" (Gutierrez, pp. 236–37). Cf. our analysis of Ernst Bloch on the same theme, chap. 4 below; and for much the same view of the creative role of utopia, cf. Mannheim, chap. 4. For a more dialectical appreciation of the role of utopias as crucial and yet as "risky" in political life, cf. Tillich, "The Political Meaning of Utopia," in *Political Expectation*, esp. pp. 169–70; Reinhold Niebuhr, "The Relevance of an Impossible Ethical Ideal," in *An Interpretation of Christian Ethics*, chap. 4.

59. "By means of an unalienating and liberating 'cultural action,' which links theory with praxis, the oppressed person perceives—and modifies—his relationship with the world and with other people. He thus makes the transformation from a 'naive awareness'—which does not deal with problems, gives too much value to the past, tends to accept mythical explanations, and tends towards death—to a 'critical awareness'—which delves into problems, is open to new ideas, replaces magical explanations with real causes, and tends to dialog. In this process, which Freire calls 'conscientization,' the oppressed person rejects the oppressive consciousness which dwells in him, becomes aware of his situation, and finds his own language" (Gutierrez, p. 91). It is thus, Gutierrez argues, appealing of course to Hegel, that freedom becomes aware of itself as freedom, self-conscious as freedom, and thus that "man gradually takes hold of the reins of his own destiny" (ibid., p. 29).

60. Cf., as noted, the implication of this predominantly conservative role of sacral social symbols in Berger and Luckmann, pp. 95–104; such symbols constitute and so legitimate through reification the already present and functioning social structure. That this is one of the important roles of such symbolic structures, there is of course no doubt. Symbols are constitutive of a society, and thus are significant elements in its preservation. But this role of the legitimization of the status quo is not the only role of symbolic structures in social history. As our argument has made plain, symbolic systems and the intellectuals who formulate them also have a radical, transformative role in history and for this transformative role novel "social" symbolic structures, "not yet possibilities," as Bloch terms them, are central. Both in terms of gradual and unintended changes in social forms, as in Weber's interpretation of the effects of religious idea systems on Western economic patterns of life, and in terms of purposive, political transformation, as in revolutionary action, symbols systems initiate social change as well as serve to retard or prevent it. Possibly, as Gouldner candidly and pointedly argues, "the sociology of knowledge" may help to explain the emphasis of many social scientists on social stability and so on the conserving side of idea systems; as the history of theologians and priests also witnesses, few professionals wish to upset the social order which gives them ample support and important prestige (Gouldner, pp. 35–43; Winter, *Elements for a Social Ethic*, pp. 182–91). Possibly also the anthropological background of such functional sociology, in which primarily primitive societies were studied, helps to explain also the accent on stability rather than on process and change.

61. This was, of course, the great thesis of Durkheim in *Elementary Forms of the Religious Life*, represented at present powerfully in Berger and Luckmann, pp. 95–104, in Berger, *The Sacred Canopy*, and in Luckmann, *Invisible Religions;* cf. Hill, chap. 12. Cf. also Reinhold Niebuhr, for whom the religious pretensions of every culture are the key to the interpretation of both its rise and its fall; as an example, cf. "The Tower of Babel" in *Beyond Tragedy*, chap. 2; and *Nature and Destiny*, vol. 1, chap. 8; also Paul Tillich, *The Theology of Culture*, esp. chaps. 1 and 4, and his powerful argument that the "conditioned" and "preliminary" meanings of ordinary cultural activity which produce human vitality are generated and sustained

by participation in and reference to an unconditioned, ultimate meaning (*Courage to Be,* chap. 3, pp. 78 ff).

62. The American sense that our liberal, democratic, capitalistic, consumer, individualistic culture was "the goal" of providence or (in a "secular" form) of a progressive history has somewhat diminished in the twentieth century. It has, however, been replaced, I believe, by the equally pretentious conviction that the American way of life is in one way or another the "natural" form of humanity, i.e., were history to remove all those historical accidents that have led to "deviant" forms—the reference is, of course, to other cultural traditions—another people, whoever or wherever they are, will "naturally" revert to the American way of life, i.e., espouse democracy, free enterprise, monogamy, suburbia, hamburgers and cokes. Thus by "building fences against alien aggressors" and providing "tools and opportunities for self-development," we have confidently expected that the people so aided will, whether they be South East Asians or South Americans, naturally become variants of our human type. That we regard our "free society" as normal and natural for humanity also may explain the strange conceit of many American intellectuals that while others (especially Marxists) have "dogmatic ideologies," the intellectual representatives of our American matrix do not, but rather represent, in their social scientific conclusions, positions based only on objective scientific inquiry.

63. The sacrality of both actual and potential symbolic social systems grounds, needless to say, the relevance of a *theological* basis for politics; but it also raises the central problem for a theological, and especially an eschatological, foundation for political action. By the explicit transcendence, ultimacy and sacrality of its own theological terms, a theological and/or eschatological politics either tends to endanger by its transcendence the value of any historical social system or revolutionary vision by "desacralizing" it entirely and so emptying it of important and vital meaning, or it tends to inject that religious ultimacy directly and un-equivocally into the social system, actual or potential, with which it associates itself.

64. The embeddedness of our political moral judgments in the fundamental systems of symbols and norms constitutive of our culture's existence accounts not only for the "religious" character of fundamental political positions (e.g., their tendency towards sacred sources, traditions, dogmatic formulations and categories such as "orthodoxy," "heresy," and "revisionism") but also for the "religious" character of basic political arguments, i.e., arguments about the most fundamental norms and goals. For there symbols expressive of fundamental norms and goals (possibly using the same language: "freedom," "democracy," "identity," "equality") subsist within a system of symbols that may not be shared by the opponent though the language seems to be in common. Thus is mutual understanding difficult, a negotiated resolution of the argument almost impossible, and neither arguer is apt to be considered "moral" by the other (despite his appeal to moral criteria and norms). Like the missionary who found all "pagan" Chinese blasphemous (not religious in a different way) because they failed to worship the true God; or the tradesmen who found the Chinese immoral (not moral in a different way) because they lived by a different system of values; so the political arguer often finds his opponent devoid of values and humane goals and so "amoral," almost beyond the human pale. When in traditional religious cultures this religious ultimacy in political argument was *explicit,* the clearest cases of fanaticism against the opponent as "demonic" arose; nevertheless in a secular politics virulent fanaticism can also arise because the symbolic systems by which moral judgments are made themselves inevitably appropriate the ultimacy once claimed by the now vanished gods.

65. "Perhaps the most significant moral characteristic of a nation is its hypocrisy. We have noted that self-deception and hypocrisy is an unvarying element in the moral life of all human beings. It is the tribute morality pays to immorality; or rather the device by which the lesser self gains the consent of the larger self to indulge in impulses and ventures which the rational self can approve only when they are disguised" (Niebuhr, *Moral Man and Immoral Society,* p. 95).

66. This was the unforgettable lesson for the author of two and a half years in a civilian internment camp during World War II: the continuing life of the community was more endangered by our moral failings in stealing from one another and from the temptation to injustice towards one another than by any "external" threats that short supplies from the Japanese created, or from Japanese power (cf. *Shantung Compound*, chaps. 6 and 8). It need hardly be stressed that this view of the fundamental role of immorality in social breakdown is part of the "prophetic" interpretation of history that informs much of the Old Testament, as we shall see. Meanwhile let us note that many classic interpretations of political life agree with this analysis: Plato (*The Georgeas* and *The Republic*) and Augustine (*City of God*, bk. XV, chap. IV); and it is of course the heart of Reinhold Niebuhr's interpretation of the "decay and doom" of civilizations (e.g., *Reflections*, pp. 6, 18, 31, 34, 87, 139; *Nature and Destiny of Man*, 2:304–307).

67. Moral condemnation will not effect important social change by itself, as Marx well understood: "It is clear that arms of criticism cannot replace the criticism of arms. Material force can only be overthrown by material force" (*Early Writings*, p. 52; cf. also Niebuhr, *Interpretation of Christian Ethics*, chap. 6). But important social change, and above all nonviolent change, is almost inconceivable without it. Not only must those oppressed by a corrupt or unjust social order be morally aroused against it, "politicized," in order to overthrow it. Even more, those who support the system have to lose their inherited and "ideological" certainty of its absolute moral superiority if they are peaceably to be dispossessed of their inordinate power by more direct (i.e., political or economic) forms of pressure—as Martin Luther King well knew. That is to say, if they implicitly (and perhaps even unconsciously) share aspects of the moral condemnation of the system under attack, they cannot retain their *eros* to defend it with "all available means of power" and to the end. The clearest cases in recent history of this weakening by a qualifiedly acknowledged moral criticism of the will to defend an old order have been Britain's moral uncertainty about her empire prior to its dissolution, France's moral uncertainty about Algeria, the uncertainty of the white middle South about the moral legitimacy of white supremacy and the moral uncertainty in America about the legitimacy of its role in Vietnam. In each case had the ruling group or class still believed it was absolutely right for it to rule as it did, it would probably never have allowed other factors (incipient or actual rebellion, economic pressure, military frustrations and so on) to force it to relinquish that rule, and it would have fought to the bitter end.

68. The presence of such a vision of authenticity in political moral judgments (of condemnation or approval) is fairly obvious. Its presence in reflective social judgments, and even more in reflective social descriptions, is less obvious but nevertheless significant. Cf. Nisbet's assertion of the importance of *moral* assessment and the dependence on a vision of authentic communal and personal existence in the founders of the sociological tradition (*Sociological Tradition*, pp. 18, 23, 34, 78, 304).

69. The implications for political and social theory, and for philosophy, of this undoubted fact—that the model of authenticity presupposed in political judgment is in some manner transcendent—are of course innumerable. One is Bloch's, namely, that sheer empiricism in social science is thus a conservative ideology confining intelligent inquiry to what is and so in effect blessing the status quo (cf. below, chap. 4). Another is Plato's, that any real analysis of human community must be (a) moral and so (b) must have as its ultimate object the transcendent *idea* of justice and of the polis. A third is the traditional theological conclusion that here we deal with the divine natural law for community, or as in Tillich with the structure of essential manhood as opposed to man in existence (cf. *Political Expectation*, pp. 134–35, 168), or as in Moltmann that they stem from the eschatological promise. A fourth is our present conclusion that political judgments being moral involve a relation to ultimacy (however that ultimacy may be understood ontologically or theologically), namely, to an ultimate norm and so an ultimate model related to but underived from the seamy relativity that is

before us. Probably the only certain implication to be drawn is that social science, insofar as it necessarily presupposes a more fundamental social theory, simply misses or abstracts away from its real object, i.e., the political and social process if it leaves out the moral category and confines itself to a quantitative, objective or deterministic analysis.

70. As is evident, this is a use, and certainly an extension, of Kant's analysis of genuinely moral experience as a relation of the mind to a noumenal reality, specifically to the apodictic laws of pure practical reason. Phenomenologically, as I am here arguing, he is right at least insofar as the experience of moral duty, of "ought," and so of moral judgment essentially transcends relativity and the pressures of self-interest ("desire" in Kant's terms) and bases itself explicitly on a norm taken to be ultimate and so obligatory. That the political judgment is in fact more "relative" and "self-interested" than in making the judgment it takes itself to be is also true. But that does not remove the experience of something transcendent and so ultimate as the source and root of judgments in moral life.

71. Reference here is to Ernst Bloch's interesting study of utopias in *Das Prinzip Hoffnung*. For a more detailed study of Bloch, cf. chap. 4 below.

72. It is thus significant that while traditional religious cultures, which looked "backward" to ultimacy, identified the union of the real and the ideal with an originating divine creation, modern secular cultures, which look "forward" to ultimacy, make the *same* identification at the end of history when what "ought to be" will finally be and be real.

73. It is significant to note the provisional accord or alliance between a self-consciously secular relativizing of "absolute" and "a priori," of "fixed" moral ends, ideals and principles, as for example in John Dewey (cf. Dewey, chap. 14, esp. pp. 775–78, 783–93), and of religious faith related to transcendence, and on that basis finding every specific moral ideal, especially those incarnated in the values of a given society or a political movement, relative, as for example in the theological ethics of Reinhold Niebuhr: "Religion, declares the modern man, is consciousness of our highest social values. Nothing could be further from the truth. True religion is a profound uneasiness about our highest social values" (*Beyond Tragedy*, p. 28). The naturalistic, pragmatic mode of relativization seeks to accomplish its demythologization of political life by banishing all ultimacy and sacrality from intelligent existence—an impossible and a dangerous enterprise, since the very claim to have done so and to be thus "objective" can itself mask a host of absolute presuppositions and norms. The second seeks to relativize partial values by grasping, or being grasped by, a genuine, authentic and so "transcendent" sacrality.

74. Jürgen Moltmann, whose earlier eschatological writings often seemed to give ultimate blessing, or to be in danger of doing so, to revolutionary forces seeking to "bring in God's future," has in his later works clearly preserved the "demythologizing" role of Christian theology in relation to political religions (cf. *The Crucified God*, pp. 321–29).

CHAPTER 3

1. Norman O. Brown, *Life Against Death* and *Love's Body;* Herbert Marcuse, *Eros and Civilization* and *One-Dimensional Man*. As we noted, the latter work supplied many helpful clues to the problem of a technolognical civilization discussed in chap. 1. For an extremely clarifying discussion of Norman O. Brown, cf. Don S. Browning, *Generative Man*.

2. Examples of such discourse by scientists about the present and the future are legion. Among the best known are Julian Huxley, *Religion without Revelation;* Theodosius Dobzhansky, *Mankind Evolving;* idem, *Evolution, Genetics and Man;* George Gaylord Simpson, *The Meaning of Evolution;* Victor Ferkiss, *Technological Man, The Myth and the Reality*. Among a variety of social scientists, perhaps the one who best fits the group now under discussion is Kenneth E. Boulding, *The Meaning of the Twentieth Century*.

3. The sense of a new era or eon is clearly sounded by Boulding: "The twentieth century

marks the middle period of a great transition in the state of the human race. It may properly be called the second great transition in the history of mankind.

"The first transition was that from pre-civilized to civilized society which began to take place about five (or ten) thousand years ago" (Boulding, p. 1).

These transitions are in turn based on accumulated knowledge: "The great transitions in the state of mankind, both the first and the second, may be identified primarily with changes in the state of human knowledge, involving therefore a learning process. . . . Nevertheless, the long, continuous and irreversible process which we all call the great transition is concerned primarily with human learning and the processes by which it is acquired" (ibid., p. 27). "The instability of all civilized societies and the fact that each one rarely lasted for more than a few hundred years is evidence of the fact that the base of the knowledge on which they were founded was inadequate and frequently harmful" (ibid., p. 35).

4. The almost infinitely "open" character of these new possibilities through scientific knowledge is made very clear by Ferkiss: "But what could take place in the realm of cultures so fundamental as to alter the basic nature of the human animal? . . . Simply by giving man almost infinite power to change his world and to change himself . . . for these new powers are not merely extensions of the old. The whole is greater than the sum of its parts, and absolute power over himself and his environment puts man in a radically new moral position" (Ferkiss, pp. 20–21). For a fuller discussion of this subject, cf. the author's *Religion and the Scientific Future*, chap. 3.

5. "Evolution need no longer be a destiny posed from without; it may conceivably be controlled by man, in accordance with his wisdom and his values" (Dobzhansky, *Mankind Evolving*, p. 347). "The old evolution was and is essentially amoral. The new evolution involves knowledge, including the knowledge of good and evil. The most essential factor in the new evolution seems to be this: knowledge, together, necessarily, with its spread and inheritance" (Simpson, p. 156). And from Ferkiss, first quoting Dr. John Heller: " 'The logical climax of evolution can be said to have occurred when, as is now immanent, a sentient species deliberately and directly assumes control of its evolution' is the way a leading medical researcher describes man's new status in the cosmos. . . . Together these changes constitute an existential revolution that gives new challenges for mankind" (Ferkiss, p. 111).

6. The theory that we can "remake" human nature is loaded with puzzles, possibly even contradictions, one of which is apparent in the following: "Men remake themselves so as better to achieve their own ends." To ease the clear contradictions (men both remake *themselves*, and yet preserve their best ends), the sentence must be refashioned: "Some men (scientists), who know humanity's proper ends, remake other persons (probably embryos) so that the latter become better instruments of the ends and values espoused by the former." When put this way the logical contradictions are smoothed out, but in their place appears an impressive set of political and moral problems.

7. The contradiction in this case lies between science as a method which assumes that the object of its inquiry exhibits a determined sequence (cf. Steward quote in chap. 2 above, n. 27) or "necessary connection" (Boulding, p. 69), and science as a creative human activity capable of transforming through knowledge, deliberation and decision (i.e., free will) man's natural and social environment and man himself. On the basis of his knowledge of himself and his world as *determined*, man will "freely" transform both. As the quotation given indicates, much of the scientific community holds onto both sides of this contradiction, and apparently feels no intellectual need of mediation between them. Two explanations of this contradiction within scientific thinking are perhaps relevant. (1) The two sides stem from two quite different aspects of scientific experience: (a) the experience of knowing an object as determined by "necessary connections" and (b) the *self*-experience of the subject which knows that object, a self-experience of a purposive or teleological method, of manipulating its data, of projecting hypotheses, of commitment to the truth, of verification, and of using

that knowledge for wide purposes—all of which give tremendous sense of autonomy, freedom and transcendence over "conditioning" and "determination" and over the temporal sequence. The mediation of these two aspects of scientific experience is a philosophical problem, and thus felt to be neither a real problem nor a resolvable problem. (2) For various reasons scientists do not take temporality as a human "existentiale" seriously. Thus they fall naturally into the logical trap of confusing the historical necessity characteristic of a past event (as irrevocable, done, actual and so on) with the ontological necessity of a determined sequence. In history all in the past is necessary in the first meaning, but that does *not* mean that all is necessary in the second, ontological meaning of determining necessity. When we look about us at our world, we see what has just been, and it presents us with a seemingly determined sequence of interrelations; but when we look forward into what is to be, and above all ponder what we should do in that approaching future, there is no system of determined sequences and there are alternatives that call for our responsible decisions. Every scientist quoted reflects this sense of his own future as open, as characterized by alternatives and as calling for decision —though when he speaks about "man and his world," or about "sequences of events," he speaks only about each as past, actual, settled and in that sense "necessary." Again a philosophical mediation is called for, a modal-temporal mediation between the past as actual and the future as possible, between what we shall here call destiny and freedom. For a historian's discussion of the temporal dialectic of necessity and freedom, cf. Leff, pp. 61 and 62; cf. chap. 6 below for a further elaboration of Whitehead's helpful clarification of this problem.

8. For this sense of absolute, and crucial, *choices* facing us in the future, cf. the following: "I have identified at least three ways which may either delay or prevent the accomplishment of this transition and may even lead to irretrievable disaster and to a total setback to the evolutionary process in this part of the universe. The three traps may be labeled briefly war, population, and entropy. Any one of them could be fatal. Not one of them has to be fatal. And the more self-consciously aware we are as a human race of the nature of the traps that lie before us, the better are the chances of avoiding them" (Boulding, p. 75).

"It is this 'critical mass' that presently threatens to explode the civilization created by industrialism so that humanity is left with the choice of creating a new civilization or else living—or perhaps dying—in chaos" (Ferkiss, p. 35). As these indicate, the categories of "freedom" dominate scientific discourse on the future, even though they continue to assume, to talk about, and in a strange way to count on the extension of "determining processes" into that future.

9. Both Ferkiss and Boulding recognize realistically that up to now "society" has made "the wrong choices" and has used its technical powers and its knowledge as much in misguided as in wise ways. Cf. Ferkiss, p. 149; Boulding, pp. 75–79. Nevertheless each denies by implication (a) that this is an "inevitable" characteristic of man that will characterize future as well as past history (*why* is not clear) and (b) assigns the blame to "our outmoded social institutions," i.e., the cultural lag view of evil. Cf. Ferkiss, pp. 155 ff., 195–96, 307 ff., and Boulding, pp. 75–79.

10. Part of the confusion of these scientific accounts of history is that the crucial word "learning" is used, apparently, in a univocal sense (as that which can be passed on and can accumulate), and yet is clearly referent to two quite different modes of learning. When they are describing the category and giving it scientific status, such arts as writing, counting, classifying and so on are mentioned, all clearly sorts of objective techniques or knowledge that can be passed on and so can accumulate (Boulding, chap. 2). When the category is applied, however, to social problems—and such application is, as noted, the ground for optimism in history—another sort of "learning" appears, namely, as Boulding puts it (p. 92), "The process by which man learns to manage his *conflicts*" (italics added). On any perspective the knowledge that leads to self-control and control over a conflict situation is vastly different from the knowledge of techniques, of objective facts, and of objective structures in any given situation.

Whether this latter sort of knowledge can be "passed on" and so can accumulate is an entirely different issue than whether the former can. It is, of course, on the basis of the identification (without discussion) of these two very different sorts of learning "processes" that the category of social evolution is derived. That is to say, the processes of objective learning, its appearance, transmission and accumulation are assumed without argument to be similar or analogous to those of organic evolution, and thus the process of social evolution (involving both objective and moral learning) is also equated with or made analogous to organic evolution. The result —utterly undefended—is a fusion of organic evolution with objective learning processes in human history and of both with moral and existential learning processes. Cf., for example, Herbert F. Blum, "On the Origin and Evolution of Human Culture," and C. Ledyard Stebbins, "Pitfalls and Guideposts in Comparing Organic and Social Evolution," in Moore and Cook, esp. pp. 213, 216–17, 230 ff. For a devastating (to this amazed reader) critique of this series of dubious identifications, cf. Robert Nisbet, "The Irreducibility of Social Change," in Moore and Cook.

11. Although a veneer of optimism remains in most of the writers under discussion, through it frequently an undercoating of despair about the future manifests itself: "For what emerges as the pattern of the future is not technological man so much as neo-primitive man trapped in a technological environment" (Ferkiss, p. 209). "It is very hard to avoid a certain pessimism in this area. . . . All existing solutions to this problem are either disagreeable or unstable, and yet solutions must be found if post-civilized society is not to end in disaster, and if our great technological accomplishments are not to result in an enormous increase in the total sum of human misery. There is need to devote a substantial intellectual resource to this problem, and this we are not doing" (Boulding, p. 125; cf. also p. 142).

The optimism is based on the category of "development," given scientific status by those aspects of culture that do accumulate, and so regarded as "inevitable and irreversible" (Boulding, p. 119). This category, like that of learning, has, in its habitual usage, been polysemic, implying not only the accumulation of knowledge and techniques but also moral development, i.e., development in wisdom and virtue. The pessimism arises, then, from the unavoidable introduction of the category of freedom (made inescapable now by the obvious misuse of the accumulated factors) which effects a disjunction between the two meanings of development illustrated in the quotations: i.e., an accumulated and so "developing" technological structure can be misused, can lead to disaster, and so to the precise opposite of cultural, if not of technological, "development." Once this disjunction between a *cumulated* learning and its *usage* is made, then the optimism based on a determined development of knowledge and techniques quickly evaporates. See below for a full-blown elaboration of this "pessimistic" side of the modern scientific vision in the study of Robert Heilbroner.

12. Many works of American, and European, social science reflect not only the contradictions of a "scientific" analysis of history outlined above; they also reflect the ideology of a commercial, affluent and powerful society. For example, Boulding has little sense of the moral ambiguity of what he calls the "institutions of civilized society," meaning those of the developed nations. Ours is, he says, a middle class culture and "has learned that military adventures do not pay" (Boulding p. 95); it therefore abhors bravado and violence, even hatred. Thus the "developed nations" are "more mature, polite and nonaggressive" and— by implication—the hope of the world—provided the "underdeveloped" also gain maturity (ibid. pp. 95–98). I am sure this view of American civilization would hardly be shared by citizens—or social scientists—of South East Asia or South America. The hypocrisy of a commercial civilization vis-à-vis power and violence, and of powerful nations vis-à-vis their "love of peace" (i.e., of *their* order), had long ago been uncovered, not only by Marx but also by Reinhold Niebuhr; cf. Niebuhr's *Reflections*, pp. 10–11, 16 ff.

13. For example, "Man has risen, not fallen. He can choose to develop his capacities as the highest animal and to try to rise farther, or he can choose otherwise. The choice is his

responsibility, and his alone. There is no automatism that will carry him upward without choice or effort, and there is no trend solely in the right direction" (Simpson, p. 155).

14. Cf. Daniel Bell's careful statement of the aim of "futurology" in the Introduction to Kahn and Weiner, p. xxvi.

15. A list of such groups, as of 1967, is given in Kahn and Weiner, p. xxv.

16. *Daedalus*, vol. 96, no. 3 (Summer 1967): "Toward the Year 2000: Work in Progress."

17. In fact this reader noted these disclaimers so frequently in Kahn's work that he began to wonder on what basis any statement about the future can be made, or credited, at all. E.g., Kahn and Weiner, pp. 13, 198, 264; and on special subjects, pp. 87, 95, 114, 118, 137, 194, etc.

18. For example, ibid., pp. 412–13. "But if we cannot learn not only to take full advantage of our increasing technological success, but also to cope with its dangerous responsibilities, we may only have thrown off one set of chains—nature-imposed—for another, ostensibly man-made, but in a deeper sense, as Faust learned, also imposed by nature" (ibid., p. 412).

19. For example, "How many will want fewer children is such a complex question of economic, social and cultural factors that we doubt whether it can be adequately predicted. We have the feeling, however . . ." (ibid., p. 114).

20. It need hardly be pointed out that to assume the continuity of present "long-term trends" across the whole spectrum of contemporary life is to assume in effect the continuity of the cultural whole which we in the West have inherited and helped to fashion—a fairly comforting assumption! It is thus to beg the main question people—whether "at home" in the present or alienated from it—ask about the uncertain future, namely, will it or will it not perpetuate the dominance of the present cultural life: tools, habits, social structures and symbols, norms and values?

21. Cf. Karl Popper: "Trends exist . . . but trends are not laws. A statement asserting the existence of a trend is existential, not universal. (A universal law, on the other hand, does not assert existence; on the contrary; . . . it asserts the impossibility of something or other.) And a statement asserting the existence of a trend at a certain time and place would be a singular historical statement, not a universal law. . . . A trend (we may again take population growth as an example) which has persisted for hundreds or even thousands of years may change within a decade, or even more rapidly than that" (Popper, p. 115). That Kahn, Weiner and Daniel Bell recognize this status of statements about trends is clear from Bell's Introduction: "The existence of a trend is no necessary guarantee that it will continue" (in Kahn and Weiner, p. xxvi).

22. Cf., e.g., the remark of Donald A. Schon, "We see forecasts as tools and aids for decision rather than assertions about the future," in *Daedalus*, 96:769; and the view of Andrew Schonfield that prediction is a modern form of the literary art of "utopia-building" in which more is revealed about what the authors think our present social priorities should be than about the shape of the actual future" (Andrew Schonfield, "Thinking about the Future," pp. 15–26).

23. Kahn and Wiener frequently seem to regard *this* value of their work as its central contribution. In stating their "objectives," they clearly concentrate on the creation of imaginative and open approaches to current policy decisions as the main point, e.g., pp. Kahn and Weiner, 398–407. Nevertheless, despite these modest disclaimers, the form of the enterprise as a whole, and the main impact of the book, lead the reader inexorably to conclude that this research has provided him with a sophisticated and "serious" vision of alternative futures, and of their relative probability or improbability.

24. One notes, for example, the total lack of any discussion of the usual issues associated with philosophy of history in the *Daedalus* volume.

25. Cf. Bell's characterization of Spengler, Toynbee, and Sorokin as "fancy" (Kahn and Weiner, p. xxv). And Kahn and Wiener's hardly modest claim that theirs is a "matter of fact" study, free of the "portentiousness" of metaphysical or speculative philosophy of history,

and thus unencumbered by any advocacy of a "point of view" (ibid., p. 28). In fact one of the deepest weaknesses of the book, infecting its content as well as its logic, was its assumption of the dogma that modern American culture—and so the authors themselves—is "nonideological" (note the remark that fascism and communism are "aberrant ideologies," ibid., p. 15). Thus throughout the discussion of the probable position and action of the U.S. in the future, America was portrayed as a nonideological national force, often coerced (to be sure) by events into strange actions, making mistakes (to be sure), but never subject to ideological passions, "irrationality," "megalomania," racism, etc. Other nations may well have these problems (cf. ibid., pp. 238, 272), as the canonical variations make clear. But none are envisioned as real possibilities for America (cf. the list of canonical variations, ibid., pp. 9 and 249)—*even* when we may be "forced" to take over Europe "for its own defense" (ibid., p. 224) or "asked" to take over South America (!) (ibid., p. 292). Here is surely the same empiricist "ideology" of the nation free from ideology that sent us into Viet Nam, kept us "righteously" *because* pragmatically there—and so able to function virtuously (a disinterested policeman) in a world of irrational and competing ideologies. This picture of the U.S. as "rational," "pragmatic," and of her actions as based primarily on a pragmatic assessment of "political realities and needs" rather than on deep ideological commitment is clearly (a) a projection of the self-image of the social scientist himself, and (b) an obviously hypocritical assessment of our national self. It is "a scientific myth" designed to hide our national self-interest, a comforting and necessary example of self-deception, and like most such national myths has little foundation in social fact and is surely not shared by most of the rest of the world. One hopes that among all the "long-term trends" in American academic life that do *not* continue, this mythical assessment of ourselves as "pragmatic," "nonideological," and so of our age as especially through us the "end of ideology," this one will be among the first to go! It is time America joined the human race and was able to see itself as it is—and as others certainly see it.

26. Cf. Charles Frankel's remarks on such "speculative" philosophies of history, their limits and their values to just such a study as this ("Explanation and Interpretation in History," in Gardiner, pp. 419–20).

27. Boulding, p. 63.

28. That technological developments, economic growth and the wise (or lucky) use of military power constitute the *main* factors in initiating and shaping significant historical changes, and so are the "dynamic factors" shaping the future, is clearly the underlying assumption of Kahn and Wiener's entire methodology—and so the assumption that guides their use of data to project alternative futures and their relative probability. Thus although the authors recognize the other factors mentioned in the text as potentially important, in the formation of the standard future and its canonical variations these other factors are given very little more than an epiphenomenonal role. In this case a "speculative interpretation of history" (cf. Frankel's definition) does inform their work as a guiding but unexamined and undefended presupposition.

29. Kahn and Weiner, p. 44; for a definition of "sensate," see ibid., p. 43. This one (unintended?) statement of their "point of view," after all their words about "pragmatic," "reductive," and "matter-of-factness," provides insight into the character of the working presuppositions referred to in the preceding note.

30. "Thus the complex of events which constitute history represent a bewildering confusion of destiny and freedom, which conform to the pattern of neither logic nor natural coherence. They are comprehended as a unity by memory but not by logic" (Reinhold Niebuhr, *Faith and History*, p. 20).

31. This is, of course, precisely what Robert Heilbroner now "predicts," namely, the dissolution of our particular democratic, liberal, scientific, technological, bourgeois and affluent culture. See the immediately following discussion.

32. Robert L. Heilbroner, pp. 13 and 22.

33. "For our question [Is there hope for man?] asks whether we can imagine that future other than as a continuation of the darkness, cruelty, and disorder of the past; worse, whether we do not foresee in the human prospect a deterioration of things, even an impending catastrophe of fearful dimensions" (ibid., p. 13).

34. Liberal religionists, Protestant or Catholic—and the author is surely one—may well ponder the irony of this new relation of science to religion. In our recent past, by promising to make "nature" into a garden for affluent, contented and self-fulfilled humans, the creative triumvirate of science, technology and industrialism progressively dismantled the supernatural religion of orthodox Catholicism and Protestantism with their grace from beyond nature and their goals beyond time and history (cf. chap. 8 below). Now, by threatening to transform nature into at best a prison and at worst a tomb, the same triumvirate will, according to Heilbroner, probably revive the very supernatural religion they once destroyed—or some surrogate therefor. Cf. ibid., p. 140. And there is no doubt that such a supernatural form of faith would, if his description is correct, provide the only possibility of meaning in the hopeless stretches of future time.

35. Ibid., pp. 56–57, 77, 134, 138.

36. For Heilbroner's description of "post-industrial" society as the total opposite of the values and ideals of the Enlightenment, namely, as a traditional, authoritarian, ritualistic, corporate, frugal, nonexpansive, unfree, inward, "religious" and static society, cf. ibid., pp. 138 ff. One may remark that this sort of society was one of the few that did not appear, even as a possibility, in Kahn's "alternative scenarios"; nor could it have been remotely regarded as probable by the older, more optimistic generation of scientists for whom, as we have seen, the future would not only be increasingly characterized by the domination of science, but would be one in which that increasing domination would only serve to augment the values of our present liberal, democratic, free and continually comfortable, i.e., sensate, culture.

37. Ibid., pp. 19, 21, 56ff.

38. Ibid., p. 141.

39. Ibid., pp. 31–40.

40. Ibid., pp. 42–45.

41. Heilbroner (p. 43), recognizes this danger, and the probability of rigid control of all nuclear forces (which would mean the same authoritarian structure in the end). But for some reason, possibly because he counts too heavily on our own benevolence and wisdom, he thinks blackmail by the revolutionary governments of the presently disinherited to be more probable than oppression by the affluent and the powerful.

42. As Heilbroner notes, in fifty years production at a 7 percent increase per annum will be doubled five times, and thus extracting and using thirty-two times the present amount of natural resources (ibid., pp. 47–48). Under no circumstances, he argues, could the earth's resources, however wisely used and reused, stand such a pillaging.

43. Ibid., pp. 50–55.

44. Ibid., p. 47.

45. Ibid., pp. 54–55.

46. Ibid., pp. 82–90, 90–94.

47. Ibid., pp. 24, 31, 61, 100, and esp. 138.

48. Ibid., p. 61.

49. Ibid., pp. 132–33, 135–36.

50. Ibid., p. 132.

51. Ibid., pp. 26–27, 140–41.

52. The description of postindustrial society is found ibid., pp. 138–42.

53. Henri Bergson, *The Two Sources of Morality and Religion.*

54. The beginnings of this return to the inward are already widely apparent with the present intriguing concentration of young and old, Jewish, Christian and humanist alike, on altered

states of consciousness, forms of meditation, yoga and associated techniques for raising spiritual consciousness. Although in its religious, philosophical, psychological and political history the West has opened up the individual's sense of the reality and value of the *inward,* creative and self-creative aspect of being human (of what has been called "soul"), it seems that this consciousness of the inward, both as real and as of value, has receded and almost evaporated. The concomitant and even more powerful conquest of the outside world, in knowledge and in transformative activity, especially the technologizing of both world and of our life within it, has apparently rendered this relation to the reality of the inward ever more precarious. Thus has the East in recent years been enabled to help the West begin to regain this "soul" through its many effective and healing modes of entering the reality of the inward self and thereby finding not only the self at a higher, freer, and more secure and creative level, but of finding thereby a reality and a value beyond the self. A generation ago—and decades before that—one could have said that the West had "rescued" the East through the former's conquest of nature, disease, poverty, caste, tyranny, and so on; science, humanitarian reforms, universal rights, democracy and socialism all were "Western" and once exported eastward, have transformed in new directions the life of Asia. If Heilbroner be right—and in this it looks as if he is—the flow will have to become even more sharply the other way than it is at present. For much of the traditional, ritual-and technique-centered culture of the East with its rich understanding of and effective touch with the realities of the inward life will be needed in the days to come to give substance to the culture he here portrays.

55. Before, let us note, the crucial "axis of history" described by Jaspers, 800–200 B.C., and especially around 500, when the isolation, creativity, individuality, depth, value and so freedom of the *person* was discovered ("as contrasted inwardly with the whole world"), Jaspers, pp. 1–21, esp. 2–4.

56. "Myths have their magic powers because they cast on the screen of our imagination, like the figures of the heavenly constellations, immense projections of our own hopes and capabilities" (ibid., p. 144).

57. Note Heilbroner's recognition of this influence of self-concern on the rise of our problems when (a) he says that each of the most fundamental of the "challenges" is a social issue, created by warped patterns of human behavior (Heilbroner, p. 61); and (b) when he ruefully concludes we are too self-interested to be able reasonably and effectively to control our own productive capacities (ibid., pp. 131–33).

58. The weakest portion of Heilbroner's analysis is his reduction of political theory to psychology. Seeing rightly that he must introduce the political dimension into any discussion of the future, he searches for a way to understand "human nature" as an entrance to political understanding. As a modern social scientist he decides that a philosophical (and of course a theological) understanding of man is useless because unempirical, and opts for psychology as disclosing to us "those origins of our later natures in our early childhood" (ibid., pp. 103 ff., 110 ff.). Thus two "puzzling" characteristics of political behavior, (a) its love of authority and its tendency to give rulers "majesty" on the one hand, and (b) its identification with the "we-group" on the other, are explained as carryovers of our dependence on parents and on our families in childhood and our desire to recreate those periods of security. Are adults also not insecure and anxious, dependent on their group and its leaders—as children are on their families? Certainly psychology can illumine much of politics, as political theory can and has, illumined psychology. But both depend in the end on a general interpretation of human being that can only be called philosophical—and Heilbroner's own "philosophical" understanding of man as by nature creative, individual, independent and autonomous, shines through this whole discussion. More fundamentally, neither childhood nor adulthood can provide a fundamental explanation of the other. Rather, both illustrate in various ways the situation of human beings in community and in time, and thus both are equally valid and instructive entrances into the mystery of "human nature." In any case, as we are seeking to show, an ontological

or theological understanding of mankind is far more illuminative of the reasons why governments are granted "majesty," and why we identify with our own we-group—both as children and as adults—than is the attempt to explain *fundamental* adult characteristics (essential characteristics of man as man) as "hangovers" from habits or training in childhood.

CHAPTER 4

1. Cf. Bernard Lonergan, *Method in Theology*, p. 175. The entire subsequent discussion of issues in critical philosophy of history is indebted to Father Lonergan's clarifying examination of history, historical inquiry, and historians (ibid., chap. 8 and 9). Cf. also for the same distinction Reinhold Niebuhr, *Faith and History*, pp. 18–19; Walsh, pp. 16–17; Randall, Jr., *Nature*, pp. 29–32; and Tillich, *ST* 3:300.

2. Walsh, pp. 26–28; Frankel (in Gardiner, pp. 419–20); Randall, Jr., *Nature*, pp. 32–33; and W. H. Dray, *Philosophy of History*, chaps. 1 and 5, for descriptions of the subject matter and so characteristics of speculative philosophies of history.

3. This attempt to uncover the basic intelligible structure of social and historical change, and so to formulate invariable patterns or "mechanisms" (to use Dray's term) explanatory of changes is what, as was noted in chap. 1, makes surprising allies of speculative philosophies of history and of much social science; cf. Nisbet, *Social Change and History*, pp. 255 ff., and 280.

4. Whether those writers who produced "natural histories," e.g., Adam Smith, David Hume, J.-J. Rousseau, J. S. Mill and Auguste Comte, are to be included here is largely a matter of definition. Certainly they did not compose histories in the usual sense; but also none saw himself as a "speculative" philosopher of history—though neither did Herder, Kant, Marx, Spengler and Toynbee, who are almost always included in that group. On this point, cf. Nisbet, *Social Change and History*, chap. 4. The leading modern continental example of this sort of philosophical reflection on history, its structures and possible goal, is Karl Jaspers, *The Origin and Goal of History*.

5. Cf. Walsh, pp. 16–17; for his description of the subjective matter of critical philosophy of history, cf. ibid., pp. 17–25.

6. Two notable exceptions to this general description, of which ample and grateful use has already been made, are Randall, Jr.'s *Nature* and Dorothy Emmett's *Function, Purpose and Powers*. Neither volume represents a speculative philosophy of history in the usual sense, i.e., one seeking to uncover the fundamental patterns of history or its goal and ultimate meaning. And yet they do much more than talk about historical knowledge or "historians' talk." Each seeks, largely empirically, to uncover the dynamic factors in the history of anything, the kinds of structures, entities, "powers," and activities that are visible and operative in social and historical events, and so to set down the kinds of categories that are demanded for an understanding of history. In this sense, if I can put it so, they are creating a preliminary or limited "ontology" of history, an empirical description of structures and operations much as Tillich in his own way did in volume 3, and, much more informally, Reinhold Niebuhr did throughout his writings. The first part of this volume attempts to illustrate the same enterprise.

7. Cf. Carl Hempel's classic statement of this position in "The Function of General Laws in History," in Gardiner, pp. 344–56, esp. 346–48.

8. Ibid., p. 347.

9. Ibid., p. 351.

10. Popper, pp. 130ff.

11. Ibid., pp. 143–44.

12. Ibid., pp. 150–51.

13. Ibid., pp. 58–70; cf. also Popper, "Prediction and Prophecy in the Social Sciences," in Gardiner, pp. 381–83.

14. In this connection it is instructive to note that those philosophers largely concerned with the philosophy of science and so inclined to take the methods and aims of physical science as paradigmatic for all inquiry, agree with Hempel and Popper about the relevance of general laws to historical inquiry, and so about the dubious cognitive status of what historians seem actually to do, e.g., Morton White, "Historical Explanation," and Ernst Nagel, "Some Issues in the Logic of Historical Analysis," in Gardiner, pp. 359–73 and 373–85 respectively.

15. Besides Popper's sharp critique (Popper, pp. 115ff., 129, 136–37), the reader is also referred to Nisbet's massive and learned critique of the search for "laws of social change" (*Social Change and History*, chaps. 7 and 8). Nisbet concludes his volume with the view, surely deviant from much of social science, that the only real understanding of social change is historical in character (ibid., pp. 280–81, 302).

16. The best and most comprehensive statement of the counter-position is historian Gordon Leff's; but cf. also Walsh; Peter Winch (although his work's theoretical basis in language philosophy makes it difficult to incorporate its main ideas in this summary); William H. Dray; and Allan and Barbara Donegan, *Philosophy of History*, Introduction. A number of the articles arising out of this debate have been published in Gardiner, pt. 2.

17. "The contingency of historical events—that they need not have happened as they did —and the uniqueness of the individuals and situations which made them up, render Hempel's search for regularities unattainable. The logic of any discipline must start from its presuppositions, and those of contingency and difference are central to history, as we have tried to show" (Leff, pp. 74).

18. Frankel, in Gardiner, pp. 415–16; see also Scriven, "Truisms as the Grounds for Historical Explanations," in Gardiner, pp. 451–58.

19. "History is distinguished from all other branches of knowledge in being concerned with what is exclusively past and can never be re-enacted; even the contemporary historian has only the record and the memories of living men, not their living actions, as his material. This irrevocability of historical knowledge means that its propositions can never be tested experimentally. . . . He [the historian] is in the paradoxical position of lacking empirical verification for knowledge that is empirically founded" (Leff, p. 11).

20. Cf. Scriven, in Gardiner, pp. 455–59; and Leff, p. 78.

21. Cf. Frankel, in Gardiner, pp. 411–12; Leff, chaps. 3 and 4.

22. "We must, therefore, revert to individuals as the irreducible units of history, and accept them as the agents of their own creations even if not of the circumstances which occasioned them. It is precisely at this level of individual achievement that sufficient cause can only be sought in the individual. The meaning that can be elicited from a work of thought or art enables us, as Dilthey said, to understand it, not to explain it casually. Only if we keep comprehension distinct from causation can we be in a position to do justice to the new" (Leff, pp. 48–49). Cf. also Popper's "methodological individualism" (Popper, p. 136) and J. W. N. Watkins, "Historical Explanation in the Social Sciences," in Gardiner, pp. 505–6.

23. "*Historical causation* includes *historical decision* operating within the limits of historical *determinism*. It is the 'decision' that actually brings about the eventuation, and thus the history itself" (italics in the original, Randall, Jr., *Nature*, pp. 94–95). "All historical determinism is thus psychological" (ibid., pp. 87); cf. also ibid., pp. 87–92. Cf. also Emmett, pp. 106–7.

24. "He [the historian] has rather to begin from the dialectic between what happens in men's minds and what happens outside them, between what was the case and what men took it to be, and hence the recognition that human actions are as much in response to the attitudes of their agents as to events themselves" (Leff, p. 49).

25. "From this it follows that individual intentions do not provide the intelligibility for historical action; on the contrary, they frequently only become intelligible when the apparent

senselessness of human conduct is related to a context which the individual cannot alone provide" (ibid., p. 26).

26. Ibid., pp. 104–5. "The problem of ideology is central to historical—as to all social—understanding. If men govern the rest of nature in virtue of their reason and technical power, they are themselves governed by their beliefs. All human action, as we have agreed, belongs to a frame of reference, however unconsciously formulated. It is this framework of assumptions and intentions, habits and ends, interests and ideals, values and knowledge, which constitutes an ideology—or, to use a less rebarbative term—an outlook" (ibid., p. 141). One can note how much more complex, and accurate, *this* view of the influence of cultural inheritance on action is than, say, that of merely "accumulated" learning referred to by cultural evolutionists (cf. chap. 3 of this book; cf. also Walsh, pp. 52–58).

27. Cf. Leff, p. 33.

28. Randall, Jr., *Nature*, p. 46.

29. ". . . What we want from historians is never a mere chronicle or catalogue . . . but an account which brings out their connections and bearing on one another. And when historians are in a position to give such an account it may be said that they have succeeded in 'making sense of' or 'understanding' their material" (W. H. Walsh, "Meaning in History," in Gardiner, p. 299). As Leff notes, historical explanations apply to *unique* wholes and unique *series*, made up of a multiplicity of unique and contingent factors, and thus is it utterly impossible to formulate them in terms of general laws. Rather, they "explain" by setting the intelligible but not necessary event into its total temporal and cultural context (Leff, pp. 66–67, 82–84).

30. Leff, p. 106.

31. "Now if there is anything in this contention, it follows that, in addition to the specific generalizations which historians assume, each for his particular purposes, there is also for each a fundamental set of judgments on which all his thinking rests. These judgments concern human nature: they are judgments about the characteristic responses human beings make to the various challenges set them in the course of their lives, whether by the natural conditions in which they live or by their fellow human beings . . . but that the body of propositions as a whole is extremely important is shown by the reflection that it is in the light of his conception of human nature that the historian must finally decide both what to accept as fact and how to understand what he does accept. What he takes to be credible depends on what he conceives to be humanly possible, and it is with this that the judgments here in question are concerned. The science of human nature is thus the discipline which is basic for every branch of history" (Walsh, pp. 64–65). We would only add to this that an implicit view or "philosophy" of history, of its dynamic factors, is presupposed along with a view of human nature as basic to all important decisions in historical inquiry.

32. "Yes, however metaphysical and unreal such questions may appear, they are inseparable from an inquiry into human history. Explanation of historical events depends on how they are conceived, which means precisely whether they are regarded as determined, or random, or whatever" (Leff, p. 60).

33. Some recent forms of philosophy of science, however, have challenged the total "objectivity" of physical science, through pointing out by means of historical and epistemological analysis the dependence of scientific inquiry, and its results, on important *non*demonstrable principles, norms, purposes, "paradigms" and levels of cognition that are not to be themselves established by objective inquiry but form its bases. Cf. especially Michael Polanyi, *Personal Knowledge;* Thomas S. Kuhn, *The Structure of Scientific Revolutions;* Bernard Lonergan, *Insight;* and the author's *Religion and the Scientific Future,* chap. 2—not to mention A. N. Whitehead, *Science and the Modern World.* If this view of scientific inquiry itself be valid, then the same problems concerning "total objectivity" appear in scientific inquiry itself as are apparent in a different form in historical inquiry.

34. It is cheering for a theologian to find such a respectable discipline as history also challenging the verification or falsification definition not only of meaning but also of validity by admitting that it too is involved in the "paradoxical position of lacking empirical verification for knowledge that is empirically gained" (Leff, p. 11).

35. Cf. Leff, p. 108; Lonergan, *Method*, pp. 201-3. The issue of the "canons of historical inquiry" has been crucial to recent theological discussion about the resurrection. Are the canons of homogeneity and analogy (nothing can be taken as characteristic of an historical event or explanatory of it which does not enter into the character of present events in ordinary experience, or as Becker put it: "no amount of testimony can establish about the past what is not found in the present"—quoted in Lonergan, *Method*, p. 222) inevitable and unavoidable to "historical inquiry" or not? Is such inquiry thus incurably confined within the "naturalistic" horizon of modern experience? If, says one group, we agree that these canons are unavoidable, then it is hard to posit *on historical grounds* the possibility of the resurrection. If, argues another, we agree that they are *not*—since they are the results of naturalistic prejudices—then can we not "on historical grounds" (i.e., the apostolic witness) posit the resurrection as an event assertable by *historical reason?* (Cf. Moltmann, *Theology of Hope*, pp. 172-90; Pannenberg, *Basic Questions*, vol. 1, chap. 2.) As the discussion in the text makes plain, I regard these canons as unavoidable for historical inquiry, as its basis; thus they are not subject to challenge "by the unique character of the event of the resurrection" insofar as the judgment about the event's uniqueness is taken to be a judgment based on historical inquiry *alone*. The reason is that, as historians, we do not yet "have" that event prior to the application of the canons; if we *did*, it might challenge their use by its uniqueness. Rather, qua historians, we only "have" an event historically *by means of* the canon since all we "have" are present data pointing to an as yet unreconstructed event, data which must be critically sifted by means of the canons. To become an "event" the data must be reconstructed by the historian, and that can be done only by using the canons—or others of a similar nature. In such a case, as the basis for the reconstructed event, they are hardly "rejectable" by the uniqueness of the event so reconstructed. Only if the apostolic reports are accepted as veridical on *other* grounds than are similar reports of other religious events, and if the historical events or influence of the event is judged on other grounds to be quite unique, can the event be "there" for the historian so that its uniqueness can challenge the canons. This is, I believe, what both Moltmann and Pannenberg in fact do; and it is precisely what the neo-orthodox meant when they insisted that only some form of a "faith judgment" could be the basis for the affirmation of the resurrection as a possibility.

36. Leff, p. 111; cf. also pp. 12-14.

37. Ibid., pp. 53-54, 119.

38. Cf. Ernest Nagel, in Gardiner, p. 377. John Dewey, however, despite his own agreement with Nagel on many "naturalist" assumptions, characteristically regards the "selection" operative in historical writing on a much deeper level. Not only, says he, is it a selection of an area for concentration (a matter, one may say, of taste), but more important, "there is no history except in terms of movement towards some outcome, something taken as an issue" (i.e., as a *problem* in the present); and this "existential" issue of the present—the outcome of the history to be reconstructed—is the moving principle of selection. Thus "the past is of logical necessity the past-of-the-present, and the present is the past-of-a-future-living-present." In this case both the "world" of the historian and his "interest" in issues in that world shape historical concerns and historical writing—though, of course, Dewey would and did apply the same analysis to all other forms of inquiry. See John Dewey, "Historical Judgments," in Hans Meyerhoff, ed., *The Philosophy of History in Our Time*, pp. 166-72.

39. In the text I have tried to avoid the complex issue of the relation of the *historian's* moral judgment (based on his own present norms) to the moral judgments, norms and actions of persons in the period under his consideration. We judge figures of the past (e.g., Nero or

Attila) to be cruel; and we find that judgment, perhaps, to be relevant to our historical assessment of the health and so the permanence of their communities; "Injustice does (or may) breed social unrest," etc. But how is that judgment of *ours* (necessary to historical assessment) related to their *own* views of cruelty or injustice, and those of their group and time, to *their* moral norms? Are they thereby "bad"? My own view is that the historian must, and cannot avoid, making moral assessments of communal life and so of actions in relation to that life, if he is to understand its health and ill-health, and so its rise and fall; and such judgments are guided by his own present norms. He should, however, recognize that since that community had its own norms which may be different from his own, he should be wary of classifying the cast of his drama as "good" and "bad" guys except on *their own* terms. How will future historians regard the nationalistic patriotism of most recent historians—and theologians? On this point cf. Isaiah Berlin, *Historical Inevitability* (and an excerpt from the same in Meyerhoff, pp. 249–71); and Herbert Butterfield, "Moral Judgments in History," in Meyerhoff, pp. 228–49; Leff, pp. 94–102.

40. Cf. Tillich, *ST* 3:348; Pannenberg, *Basic Questions*, 1:70, 98.

41. Walsh, pp. 103 and 107; Leff, p. 91.

42. Cf. Dewey's view that history is written from the viewpoint of its *present* "outcome" and our concern with that outcome (in Meyerhoff, pp. 166–72). An excellent example of this was Kenneth Boulding's "history" of the great transition in which accumulated learning and science, so clearly the keys to him of a brighter future, were made into *the* dynamic factors of important historical change. Cf. above, chap. 3, nn. 3, 8–11.

43. "We discover a 'future' in our present, and we then understand our past—the past of our present—as aiming at that predicted future" Randall, Jr., *Nature*, p. 43. This view, characteristic of Dewey and Randall's pragmatism, is not dissimilar to the view of Tillich and Niebuhr that history is always interpreted according to some fundamental principle of "meaning," of the meaning of the historical process as a whole—though both Dewey and Randall would like (if they could!) to confine themselves to "little meanings." Cf. Tillich: "Through the interpretative element of all history, the answer to the question of the meaning of history has an indirect, mediated impact on a historical presentation. One cannot escape the destiny of belonging to a tradition in which the answer to the question of the meaning of life in all its dimensions, including the historical, is given in symbols which influence every encounter with reality" (*ST* 3:302). And thus for Niebuhr are all interpretations of history—in our existence, in historical writings, and in each philosophy—ultimately dependent on "myth," a total scheme transcendent to purely rational comprehension (because of the dynamic, dramatic and distorted character of history) and yet expressive of an interpretation of history's meaning held by some form of "faith." Cf. his *Reflections*, chap. 10; *Faith and History*, pp. 103, 118–19, 126ff., 214ff.; *Nature and Destiny*, vol. 1, chap. 5 and 2:2–6; and "Coherence, Incoherence and Christian Faith," in *Christian Realism*.

44. Cf. the author's *Religion and the Scientific Future*, chap. 2.

45. Language philosophers and logicians have long berated the idealistic tradition for raising doubts about the certainty and objectivity of all of our knowledge since *all* of it, said the idealists, was shown by philosophical analysis to be "subjective." What other standard —if all is subjective—do you propose, the idealists were asked; do you not realize that the very distinction between subjective and objective, error and truth—and so all our words on these matters—arises *within* the context of the so-called egocentric predicament? Thus to argue, as the idealists did, from the "fact" of the egocentric predicament is meaningless since there is in human experience no available possibility of the kind of "objective" (i.e., *non*-ego-centered) knowledge which you hold up as a standard. As is evident, I have tried in the text to turn this familiar argument back on the scientific objectivists and say that *their* standard of objectivity, with which they raise questions about history, is nonexistent and irrelevant; and thus that the critique of history as noncognitive because "theory-laden" is at

least as meaningless as is the idealistic critique of scientific knowledge as "subjective" because egocentric.

46. The same conclusion, I believe, applies to hermeneutical as to historical studies, namely, that inquiry into the meaning of a text involves the same sort of general view of history as does historical inquiry proper. Such a view of history presupposed in hermeneutics must include an understanding of the relation of epochs to one another, to continuities and discontinuities between them, and the relations of human intentions and meaning to the rest of natural and historical process. As Pannenberg has persuasively argued, if, as Gadamer says (*Wahrheit und Methode*, pp. 286–90), hermeneutic requires a "fusion" of the horizon of the text with our horizon, this operation likewise implies a view of general history, of the relation of horizons (cultural epochs) to one another. Cf. Pannenberg, *Basic Questions*, vol. 1, chaps. 4 and 5, esp. pp. 115–36.

47. A number of philosophers who recognize this theoretical component in historical inquiry hope to resolve the problem of subjectivity latent there in terms of "universal agreement" on these metaphysical presuppositions; for with such agreement, then history will become "objective." One example, Frankel, seems logically confused when he proposes that these varying perspectives and varying norms involve "matters of fact" and thus disagreement about them can be adjudicated by a careful and objective "appeal to the evidence" (in Gardiner, pp. 425–27). Walsh is surely correct when he points out that appeal to the evidence concerning the very principles by which evidence is to be gathered and tested is circular and so futile (Walsh, pp. 114–15). But, as Walsh ruefully admits, his own solution, namely, that through philosophical discussion agreement be reached, is at best utopian. My own view is that while the *search* for agreement is legitimate and essential, the definition of objectivity in terms of the *establishment* of "universal agreement" on such presuppositions is delusive and destructive. It is this definition of objectivity, excluding a priori all matters where agreement is difficult if not impossible, that almost eliminated philosophy itself from the academic court; it is this definition that actively prevents most disciplines from considering their own philosophical foundations—on which agreement is difficult, if not impossible; and it is this definition that has driven every discipline more and more in a positivistic and so ultimately superficial and self-contradictory direction—if our analysis is correct. The definition of "objectivity" as being constituted by universal agreement or its possibility has arisen through a cultural optical illusion. The illusion was generated by a culture that so devoutly accepted and dogmatically assumed the debatable (at least in principle) presuppositions of its experimental science that it thought itself to be free of all debatable presuppositions. Consequently, it failed to take with any intellectual seriousness other cultural alternatives that might have challenged those presuppositions, calling them either "primitive," "pre-modern" or "ideological." It was the dogmatism of modern Western culture, not its objectivity, that led to the association of objectivity with an established universal agreement. Such agreement and so such objectivity never appear in final form in human affairs, for the men and women who think are neither universal nor timeless; it can appear only in fragmentary form (it is, so to speak, "eschatological"), and only when reason critically investigates and critically defines—as is appropriate for each level—every sort of assumption throughout the intelligent life of a culture. Objectivity, like all human values, is more realized in the *search* for universality through critical discussion of ultimate issues than it is realized in the *achievement* of universality.

48. Cf., for example, the comment of a wise sociologist, W. E. Moore, on Marxist theory in relation to "developing" cultures: "The rigidity of communist formulas is an ideological and political rigidity, not a scientific one, and other models for development are not only available in the abstract but also in actual diversity of historical and contemporary development programs" (Moore, p. 90). While I believe that in fact communism has been "more rigid" than ourselves in many developing areas, e.g., Portugal, nevertheless his sharp black-

and-white distinction is more comforting to ourselves than it is credible. On fundamental issues and in important areas (e.g., South America and Viet Nam), we also have impressed the world, and many among ourselves, with an ideological rigidity—or better put, we are infinitely flexible with a "rightist" ally and almost as sternly inflexible with a leftist one. Was our judgment upon and our action toward Allende either "scientific" or "flexible"? Moore mentions some of the faults (lack of commitment, etc.) in our relation to Africa, South East Asia, and South America; but he seems to think that our political and economic efforts there are essentially "ideology-free," as presumably he thinks our social sciences are purely "scientific" on these matters. It seems obvious (at least in South America!) that *both* our actual impact through our political and economic programs *and* our "social science" are as theory-laden by the presuppositions of our capitalistic, democratic society as those of Marxism, and that it is only to us that the sharp difference between our science and their ideology appears or is credible. On the whole, most social scientists in these regions would for better or for worse reverse his judgment. Also no mention is made of the important, subtle and pragmatic forms of Marxist thought represented, for example, by the Frankfurter Schule, where praxis as opposed to abstract dogmatic theory is the very quality of creative social thought. The obvious conclusion seems to be the by no means new observation that those (in this case both the Marxists and ourselves) who think themselves most free of ideology (i.e., "scientific") are in danger of exhibiting it most clearly. In any case, it is ironic that the social scientific communities in the two great power blocs of our time, supported by the two great ideological systems, should each be convinced that they, and they alone, represent "science" in the study of society.

49. A good number of these same themes are to be found also in the social philosophies associated with the Frankfurter Schule, especially Herbert Marcuse and Jürgen Habermas. These points of similarity will be noted as we proceed. On the general position of the Frankfurter Schule and the genesis of critical theory, cf. Martin Jay, *The Dialectical Imagination*, esp. chaps. 2 and 8.

50. Ernst Bloch, *A Philosophy of the Future*, pp. 109–12. This critique of empiricism as the ideology of the status quo (and therefore the need for utopian thought if social change is to be possible) appears throughout the Frankfurter Schule's thought, cf. Jay, pp. 62 and 82, Jürgen Habermas, *Theorie und Praxis*, pp. 204, 212. The same theme, that the function of reason is to *negate* what is, is predominant in Marcuse's work, especially *Reason and Revolution*, in which he argues persuasively that Hegel is on this account to be considered revolutionary and not conservative. Cf. also Karl Mannheim, *Ideology and Utopia*.

51. The vast text, *Das Princip Hoffnung*, is a study of this whole range of human expression —myths, folk tales, dramas, ontologies, etc.—to show how they express the "not-yet," the utopian future that is to be.

52. The full passage is: "There is a maxim of verification which involves so little correspondence to the facts that it brought about the English, American and French Revolutions: 'A thousand years of injustice do not justify one hour of them.' This basic proposition arising from a consideration of the *humanum* intimately connected with morality, as presented by classical natural law, was wholly opposed to 'verification' as the basis of nothing other than the political status quo, i.e., of injustice as it had come to be, as it was. Hence the difference between this and an accommodation of thought to facts is particularly clear; the illuminating *direction* of the human postulate would direct rather than be directed by nothing-but-fact —all the worse for the facts" (Bloch, *Philosophy of the Future*, p. 109).

53. "It need never capitulate before empirical method when the latter degenerates into a reified empiricism of facts; and of course it must never lose contact with *process*-empiricism, if its aspiration is not to become abstract eccentricity, and its ascent a descent. . . . *Empiricism*, if not statically reified, and *metaphysics*, if not rising with a valedictory gesture to the world into the lifeless seclusion of the idea, are both inseparable from the shield, spear and eye of

Minerva. . . . For not only thought can be experimental, but *world history itself is an experiment*—a real experiment conducted in the world and aimed towards the possible just and proper world" (ibid., pp. 110–12, italics in the original). It is important, especially in relation to the eschatological theologians, to note Bloch's strong emphasis on latent trends and so on an empirical study of actuality as a necessary complement—not the antithesis—of relevant possibility. A possibility in total disjunction with actuality is for him "abstract eccentricity." History for him, as for us, is a union of actuality and possibility, destiny and freedom, and a relation of connection and relevance, of retrieval and reinterpretation, rather than of total disjunction, must characterize the passage of actuality into new possibilities.

54. Cf. Ernst Bloch, *Man on His Own*, pp. 39–41. This critique is similar to the one the Frankfurter Schule has directed at both the later Marx and at "orthodox" Marxism for its objectivist, scientific and materialistic views of valid knowledge and of man. Cf. Jay, p. 42, and Jürgen Habermas, where, as in Bloch, a scientific, objectivist understanding of society must be supplemented by what Habermas calls "hermeneutical understanding," an understanding of man through his awareness of himself as an affective, thinking and active being. For Bloch's discussion of this, cf. *Man on His Own*, pp. 42 and 44ff.; for Habermas, cf. *Erkenntniss und Interesse*, chap. 3.

55. Bloch, *Philosophy of the Future*, p. 112.

56. "Hence the universal formula that applies at the *beginning* of philosophy: S is not yet P; no subject already has its adequate predicate" (Bloch, *Man on His Own*, p. 90).

57. Ibid., p. 91.

58. Ibid., pp. 37, 204–7, 224. It is clear that there is for Bloch no all-determining "fate," cosmic, divine or social, that shapes history in a certain direction; because of possibility as the true object of human thought and aspiration, and so as continually ingredient in history's becoming, and because the process is largely determined by human action, there is for Bloch "an open subject and it's open world" (ibid., p. 210).

59. "The aura of the continually threatened and precarious attempt to find what is redeeming and whole is inherent in the tendency and latency of the world process, as long as the process of the world endures and can endure" (ibid., p. 91; cf. also pp. 81, 114).

60. Ibid., p. 90.

61. Ibid., pp. 161–62, 67.

62. Ibid., pp. 160–65, 208, 215. "What atheism does, rather, is to remove from the world's beginning and process what had been conceived as God, that is, as an *ens perfectissimum*, and to redefine it as not a fact but the one thing it can be: the supreme utopian problem, the problem of the end" (ibid., p. 160). "Not-yet-being, the mode of reality of concrete ideals, is of course never a not-yet-being of God; the world is not a machine for manufacturing such a supreme person, such a 'gaseous vertebrate' (as Haeckel rightly called it)" (ibid., p. 164). The similarity with the view of God and of religion of John Dewey *(A Common Faith)* is here striking; as is the paternal relation of these "humanistic" concepts of Bloch with the God of the future of the current eschatologists. It should be noted, however, that since for Bloch there is (and will be) no real, active divine agent "from the future," there is for him no *efficient* (but only a final) causality "from the future." The notion of an "efficient" agent causality from the future is thus one not found in Bloch, and so is a new note introduced by the re-reification of God in current eschatological theology.

63. Bloch, *Man on His Own*, p. 222.

64. Ibid., pp. 154–56, 213–14.

65. Ibid., p. 114.

66. Ibid., pp. 152, 179–202.

67. "The existence of God—indeed God as such, as a distinct being—is superstition; faith is solely the belief in a Messianic kingdom of God, without God. Therefore, far from being the enemy of religious utopianism, atheism is its premise: without atheism, there is no room

for Messianism" (ibid., p. 162). Cf. also ibid., pp. 184, 190–91.

68. Cf. the essays in honor of Bloch by Pannenberg, Moltmann and Metz in Siegfried Unseld, ed., *Ernst Bloch Zu Ehren;* Pannenberg's essay appears in translation in *Basic Questions,* vol. 2, chap. 8.

69. For example: "Nothing and all, chaos and kingdom, hang in the balance in the one-time field of religious projection, and it is human achievement in history that will weight down the scale of nothingness or that of all" (Bloch, *Man on His Own,* p. 224).

70. Cf. Pannenberg, *Basic Questions,* 2:239. For the same point, namely, that alienated man can become "happy" and so cease to dream at all of a new world and of new possibilities, cf. Marcuse, *One-Dimensional Man,* chap. 3.

71. Cf. chap. 7 below for a fuller discussion of this "eschatological" conception of God.

72. This description, and it is barely that, of Whitehead's thought, does not pretend to represent either a thorough or an adequately documented analysis. Nor are the brief criticisms at the end sufficiently argued or established. They are mentioned solely in order to distinguish the view presented in this volume—which, as will be obvious, is very much influenced and shaped by Whitehead—from his own expressed view. A more thorough and adequate treatment of Whitehead is found in the author's doctoral thesis (unpublished) at Columbia University: "Maker of Heaven and Earth: A Comparative Study of the Concept of Creation in the Metaphysics of A. N. Whitehead, F. H. Bradley, and in the Christian Tradition."

73. Alfred North Whitehead, *Process and Reality,* Category of Explanation i, p. 33 (henceforth PR). Cf. also PR, pp. 44, 136, 335.

74. PR, pp. 79–80, 174–75.

75. Cf. Alfred North Whitehead, *Adventures of Ideas,* p. 235 (hereafter AI).

76. AI, pp. 247–49.

77. PR, pp. 366–67.

78. Alfred North Whitehead, *Religion in the Making* (hereafter RM). "Apart from God, the remaining formative elements would fail in their function. There would be no creatures, since, apart from harmonious order, the perceptive fusion would be a confusion neutralizing achieved feeling. Here, 'feeling' is used as a synonym for actuality.

"The adjustment is the reason for the world. It is not the case that there is an actual world which accidentally happens to exhibit an order of nature. There is an actual world because there is an order of nature. If there were no order, there would be no world, Also, since there is a world, we know that there is an order. The ordering entity is a necessary element in the metaphysical situation presented by the actual world" (RM, p. 104).

79. PR, pp. 131, 248–29, 380–81.

80. "Order is not sufficient. What is required is something much more complex. It is order entering upon novelty; so that the massiveness of order does not degenerate into mere repetition; and so that the novelty is always reflected upon a background of system" (PR, p. 515).

The dialectical relation of order and novelty and of both to God is also well illustrated in the following: "This is the conception of God, according to which He is considered as the creature of creativity, the foundation of order, and as the goal towards novelty. 'Order' and 'novelty' are but the instruments of his subjective aim, which is the intensification of 'formal immediacy' " (PR, p. 135). Cf. also PR, p. 377.

81. "There is secondary origination of conceptual feelings with data which are partially identified with, and partially diverse from, the eternal objects forming the data of the primary phase. . . . It is the category by which novelty enters the world; so that even amid stability there is never undifferentiated endurance. But, as the category states, reversion is always limited by the necessary medium of elements identical with elements and feelings of the antecedent phase. . . . Then in synthesis there must always be a *ground of identity* and an aim at contrast" (PR, pp. 380–81).

"The mental pole originates as the conceptual counterpart of operations in the physical pole. The two poles are inseparable in their origin" (PR, p. 379).

82. PR, pp. 28–30, 35, 361ff.; for causal efficacy, cf. PR, pp. 125–26, 176–77, 184, etc.

83. PR, pp. 34–41 (Categories of Explanation vi, xxi, xxii, xxiii, and categorial obligation viii and ix), 75, 130–31, and 339.

84. " 'Actuality' is decision amid 'potentiality.' It represents stubborn fact which cannot be evaded. The real internal constitution of an actual entity progressively constitutes a decision conditioning the creativity which transcends the actuality" (PR, pp. 68–69).

85. " 'Creativity' is the universal of universals characterizing ultimate matter of fact. It is that ultimate principle by which the many, which are the universe disjunctively, become the one actual occasion which is the universe conjunctively. It lies in the nature of things that the many enter into complex unity" (PR, p. 31).

"The creativity of the world is the throbbing emotion of the past hurling itself into a new transcendent fact. It is the flying dart, of which Lucretius speaks, hurled beyond the bounds of the world" (AI, p. 227). Cf. also, for an earlier view of creativity, Whitehead, *Science and the Modern World,* p. 248 (hereafter SMW).

"Creativity is the principle of novelty . . . the 'creative advance' is the application of this ultimate principle of creativity to each novel situation which it orginates" (PR, pp. 31–32; cf. also p. 11).

86. Cf. PR, pp. 34 (Category of Explanation vii), 70, 72, 366–7, 445; SMW, p. 121.

87. This argument is repeated in many different nuances and with different applications throughout the development of Whitehead's total view. A good summary is the following: "The things which are temporal arise by our participation in the things that are eternal [eternal objects]. The two sets are mediated by a thing which embraces the actuality of what is temporal with the timelessness of what is potential. This final entity is the divine element in the world, by which the barren inefficient disjunction of abstract potentialities obtains primordially the efficient conjunction of ideal realization. This ideal realization of potentialities in a primordial actual entity constitutes the metaphysical stability whereby the actual process exemplifies general principles of metaphysics and attains the end proper to specific types of emergent order. By reason of the actuality of this primordial valuation of pure potentials, each eternal object has a definite effective relevance to each concrescent process. Apart from such ordering, there would be a complete disjunction of eternal objects unrealized in the temporal world. Novelty would be meaningless, and inconceivable" (PR, pp. 63–64). Cf. also PR, pp. 46–48, 248–49; RM, pp. 90, 119–20; SMW, p. 249.

88. PR, p. 73.

89. Cf. PR, pp. 46–48, 134–35, 522–24; SMW, pp. 249–50.

90. This is a restatement of Whitehead's important (and "novel," PR, p. 27) "ontological principle of explanation" (or "naturalistic principle of explanation" that the only *reasons* lie in actual entities) formulated as Category of Explanation xviii in PR, pp. 36–37, 73. As is evident in the text, Whitehead ingeniously uses this "naturalistic" principle as the fulcrum for his derivation of "the non-temporal entity" which he termed God. (For God as a "non-temporal entity," cf. PR, pp. 11, 47, 73, 343–44, 524, 529.)

91. PR, pp. 46, 248–49, 522.

92. "In the philosophy of organism this ultimate is termed 'creativity'; and God is its primordial, non-temporal accident" (PR, p. 11).

93. SMW, pp. 243, 249–50.

94. Cf. for example, PR, p. 248; RM, p. 104; and the categorial explication of this "ordering" influence of God as each concrescence comes to be, i.e., God provides for each its "initial" subjective aim: cf. PR, pp. 343, 373–74, 522.

95. Whitehead speaks of God as the primordial *creature* of creativity, not as creator, i.e., the primordial particularization of creativity in *this* form (PR, pp. 46, 522), and as has been

noted, creativity, although it is clearly not God, is the ultimate category, the "reason" things *are* at all and the principle of their coming to be. Creativity and not God represent "force" or "power" (power of being); see PR, pp. 525–26. Correspondingly, God does not "create" eternal objects but rather conceptually prehends them into an order and a relevant order; thus he "depends" on them as much as they do on him, illustrating Whitehead's metaphysical requirement of coherence as the mutual interdependence of fundamental concepts. For that mutual dependence, cf. PR, pp. 392, 528–29; for the definition of the requirement of coherence, cf. PR, pp. 5, 9–10.

96. For descriptions of the primordial nature, cf. PR, pp. 521–22. Also, pp. 46–48, 73, 248, 392; and SMW, pp. 248–49.

97. For descriptions of God's Consequent Nature, cf. esp. PR, pp. 523–33.

98. Whitehead had a keen sense of the tragic character of becoming as "perishing," and, as is evident, much of the religious dimensions of his thought were devoted to proposing an intellectual and coherent answer to the question of transience: "The ultimate evil in the temporal world is deeper than any specific evil. It lies in the fact that the past fades, that time is a perpetual 'perishing.' Objectification involves elimination. The present fact has not the past fact with it in any full immediacy" (PR, p. 517). For his further, more detailed analysis of the "perishing" aspect of the becoming of things, that "they never really are," cf. PR, pp. 44, 129, 305; AI, p. 305.

99. Or, more accurately, God (as PN) is creativity's primordial, blind, and "accidental" formation or principle of particularization; cf. n. 95 above. Our own active mode of the verb is based on the ontology we have outlined, namely, that God's primordial aim "lures" each occasion to achieve itself through novel and yet orderly possibilities; on God as "lure," and not as "creator" in the sense of efficient cause of being, cf. esp. PR, pp. 525–26.

100. For example: "The 'creative advance' is the application of this ultimate principle of creativity to each novel situation which it originates" (PR, p. 32). "God and the World are contrasted opposites in terms of which Creativity achieves its supreme task of transforming disjoined multiplicities, with its diversities in opposition, into concrescent unity, with its diversities in contrast" (PR, p. 528). "Creation achieves the reconciliation of permanence and flux when it has reached its final form which is everlastingness—the Apotheosis of the World" (PR, p. 529).

In this view the principles of "evil" are, apparently, on the one hand mediocrity and triviality, the absence of vivid contrasts supplied by novelty against a large background of order, and on the other, perishing, the loss of subjectivity within the temporal process of becoming. There does not to my knowledge appear, at least in Whitehead's own formulation, any emphasis on or elaboration of the *distortion* of subjective aim, the *estrangement* of finite actuality, or the *demonic* possibilities involved in "creative" advance in intensity and effectiveness. This is, as noted in the text, of course not to say that a reinterpretation of Whitehead's thought on these latter terms is impossible.

CHAPTER 5

1. As the text indicates, these two short chapters will be involved, among other things, with issues of method. It should be stated as clearly as possible that the discussion here is not exhaustive, complete or even well documented. In fact, this is at best a concise statement of the method presented here, not an adequate defense or justification of it. For a more thorough treatment of the view implicit in these remarks, cf. the author's *Naming the Whirlwind* and the further elaboration of many of its positions on theological method in *Catholicism Confronts Modernity*, chaps. 2–5. The most completely argued, learned and original statement on theological method with which I am familiar—and with which I am in substantial if not total agreement—has just appeared from David Tracy, *Blessed Rage for*

Order. References to this remarkable work will therefore abound in the following notes.

2. In *Naming the Whirlwind* the same "break" between prolegomena and systematic or constructive theology was enunciated as clearly as prose might allow, although it was formally symbolized only by the movement from one chapter to another. As a consequence, many reviews interpreted the argument in that book as simply cumulative, leading from the prolegomenon in chaps. 1–8 directly into systematic theology in chap. 9, so that in effect prolegomenon established the sufficient as well as the necessary conditions for systematic theology. Since I believe the situation to be more complex than this, that other resources, stances, modes of argument and so on are essential to systematic theology than are available by means of prolegomenon, I wish here to symbolize the "break" between the two—as well as the continuity—by the formal device of an "entr-acte," a part 2 explanatory of method and of the interrelationship of prolegomenon and systematic theology, between parts 1 and 3.

3. In a sense, this discussion of method—and so the relation of prolegomenon (pt. 1) to constructive theology (pt. 3)—is a "junior" and so incomplete fundamental theology in the sense David Tracy enunciates that category (cf. *Tracy*, p. 15), i.e., a discrimination of "the basic criteria and methods for theological argument," and of the position that must be established prior to the enterprise of constructive theology. Despite many differences in these two approaches to theological construction, many of the same essential elements are here: phenomenological analysis of ordinary experience, critique of alternative positions, ontological elaboration, hermeneutics, existential application and praxis.

4. Praxis is a crucial word in current discussions of social theory and political theology, and also in the formation of this volume. As developed out of Marxism and critical social theory, it has come to entail the essential interrelatedness of two polarities: (1) the polarity of theory with action (the purpose of thinking is to change reality not merely to comprehend it) and of action with theory (no responsible and effective action is possible without social understanding of the structure, trends and possibilities in social actuality). (2) the polarity of actuality and possibility: present actualities are to be negated by future-oriented theory and practice, a negation by unified theory and practice of the negativities of actual theory and practice so that new possibilities may appear (cf. Tracy's excellent description of praxis, pp. 213ff.). Obviously Bloch's thought, as described in chap. 4, illustrates this concept in both its polarities of theory and practice, actuality and possibility, as does the work of Habermas; cf. esp. Habermas, *Theory and Practice*, Introduction, chaps. 2, 3, 6, and esp. 7; and Marcuse, *Reason and Revolution* and *One-Dimensional Man.* Cf. also Martin Jay. Our own emphasis in this volume on the interrelation of the symbolic apprehension of history to creative political action within history, and of the dialectic or critical relation of new possibilities to given actuality (providence) and to its distorted forms (fate), reflects a *theological* expansion of the notion of praxis so interpreted.

5. In a sense the analysis in this chapter parallels the analysis of predominantly individual experience in *Naming the Whirlwind*, pt. 2, chaps. 2 and 3; but in a sense it does not. As noted in the text, the analysis in this case attempts to reach the level of at least a preliminary ontology, namely, the discrimination of ontological categories or factors at work universally in temporal and historical being. The "ontic" analysis in *Naming the Whirlwind* had no such goal, but merely that of unveiling the dimension of ultimacy and the sacred that is constitutive of our experience of being human. The reason for this new plunge into ontology, difficult and precarious as it is, is twofold: (1) It is impossible, I believe, to talk intelligibly about history or to understand our experience of it unless the ontological structure of historical being is discriminated (i.e., as destiny and freedom). (2) We do intend to begin to establish and elaborate an ontological interpretation of the nature and the role of God in history—i.e., a "doctrine" of God—and for this enterprise the discrimination of ontological categories of historical finitude is essential. With regard, however, to the uncovering and establishment of the dimension of ultimacy in historical experience (the main purpose of chap. 2), a dimension

as noted in the text that is not yet conceptually elaborated (into ontological or metaphysical categories), this analysis of historical experience parallels the analysis of individual experience in *Naming the Whirlwind*.

6. In this description of historical experience as "qualified" by a dimension of ultimacy, one is reminded of Ian Ramsey's provocative and helpful description of religious language as an "odd" sort of language in which is present, as the essence of its "oddness," a peculiar qualifier, namely, one pointing to or indicating infinity. Corresponding to this characteristic of religious language, is the religious attitude of total involvement and universal significance which in turn this "peculiar" qualifier expresses. All that the present analysis has added to this excellent account is the notion that such involvement, such significance and such forms of language are there at all because in our personal and historical experience alike we are aware of existing within a dimension of the ultimate and the sacred to which these attitudinal and verbal responses have reference. Cf. Ian Ramsey, *Religious Language: An Empirical Placing of Theological Phrases*, idem, *Models and Mystery*.

7. It is ironical that a culture which experiences no ultimate structure of meaning as *given* or *securely established* in its history, and in consequence in much of its life seeks desperately to find one, should also make that search impossible or vain a priori by terming it useless and/or meaningless. Actually, as we noted, the answer to this obvious dilemma in our intellectual life is to smuggle in surreptitiously a structure of meaning, and so a basis for social hope, in terms of science and "myths" derived therefrom—and thus to lose both religious satisfaction and science at the same time.

8. "It is this mixture of freedom and necessity which gives the realm of history its peculiar character of meaning and obscurity, of partial but not complete intelligibility." "Thus the complex of events which constitute history represent a bewildering confusion of destiny and freedom, which conforms to the pattern neither of logical nor natural coherence" (Niebuhr, *Faith and History*, pp. 18 and 20, respectively).

9. Cf. Tillich's profound article on the dominance of the historical as kairos over the philosophical as logos, "Philosophy and Fate," in his *Protestant Era*. For a more radical extension of this idea into a more definitive relativism, cf. R. G. Collingwood, *An Essay on Metaphysics*.

10. Cf. the quotations from Niebuhr in n. 8 above.

11. Reinhold Niebuhr, despite his continuing efforts to relate Christian faith to "truths otherwise known," his perennial scorn of religious obscurantism and his apologetic élan, always denied that history can be comprehended in terms of an ontological or metaphysical "system." Cf. "Coherence, Incoherence and Christian Faith," in his *Christian Realism*, pp. 175–79.

12. Cf. the previous discussion of Whitehead in chap. 4. The arguments of Whitehead for the metaphysical necessity of the factor God, outlined in that chapter in the forms in which he presented them, are here summarized. For references in Whitehead to these arguments, cf. the notes of chap. 4.

13. Tillich continually reiterates that the self-world polarity points to and calls for a deeper ground of their unity, a unity presupposed by our reciprocal relations to the world, in perception and cognition, in experiencing our own being, and in cultural creativity. Cf. esp. *ST* 1: 79–81, 235ff. However, as readers of Tillich know, he denied that a "proof" of this uniting ground of our own being is possible (cf. ibid., pp. 204–10). We are here attempting two "moves" at variance with Tillich's formulation: (1) the "process" move from self-world to destiny-freedom as the fundamental ontological structure of being as historical, and (2) the move to recognize the relevance of an argument that shows how that structure entails its own deepest grounds. Thus (to my own surprise) a "natural theology" begins to appear as one moment in the preparation for a systematic theology. However, as the next section will attempt to make clear, the sufficiency, if not the validity, of such an argument in preparing

for "theism" is radically qualified by the evident distortion of the concrete actuality of that very structure that calls for theism.

14. In chaps. 10 and 12 this argument is expanded to cover the three relations of temporality, and the role of the divine ground in each of these: past to present, present to its own self-actualization, and future to present. Cf. Tillich's phrasing of this: "We may therefore combine our three questions and inquire after the eternal which presses out of the past, in and through the present, towards future actualization," in his *Religious Situation,* p. 36.

15. Cf. the powerful assertion of this aspect of "common human experience," in Tracy, pp. 211–14.

16. This is, I believe, the ground in concrete experience and so in the actuality of historical being, for insisting that "other resources" than those provided by metaphysical argument are essential for theology, since that metaphysical analysis seems to be confined to what Tillich calls "essential structures" and thus misses the concrete character of "existence." The God of theism is not only in himself a dipolar God with an abstract and a concrete character; even more that dipolar God *himself* has the character of an abstraction, i.e., an abstraction which, because derived from an analysis of only essential structures, abstracts away from the God related to our concrete actuality in judgment, grace and new promise. This is, I believe, the deepest reason why, as Tracy points out, theologians that "adopt" rather than "use" metaphysical systems, tend not only to ignore or minimize the depths of evil in history, but even more to miss the central if peculiar thematic structures of the Christian understanding of God as judgment and as love. Cf. *Tracy,* pp. 187–91.

17. The parallelism of this view with Tracy's admirable methodological outline of the moments of a fundamental theology: a phenomenological analysis of common human experience, a metaphysical explication and validation of the religious dimensions of experience as theistic, a hermeneutical analysis of Christian fact, and finally a systematic theological synthesis of the results of the union of these moments in christology and in praxis—cf. ibid., chaps. 3 and 8—the parallel between that view and mine is obvious, although each in its present form was arrived at in ignorance of the other. Mine too includes a phenomenological moment, an ontological explication and argument, a hermeneutic inquiry into the symbolic inheritance of Christian tradition, and an attempt to bring them to unity in a theology of history. Perhaps the main formal difference (the content of each moment is very different) is that for me each "moment" of prolegomenon or of fundamental theology, while rendered, hopefully, coherent, adequate and so "valid" by arguments, remains radically incomplete and even unfinished as an abstraction from both the richness and complexity of the concrete history to be understood and from the symbolic system that interprets that richness. Neither the common human experience phenomenologically analyzed, the "God" ontologically established, nor the eidetic analysis of tradition can remain as self-sufficient, in the role of an established "step," until the whole is complete. In this sense the whole is ultimately validated, as an entire scheme of interpretation, by participation in and through the *whole* scheme of symbols, not as a whole whose parts are established, clarified and validated one by one and on their own terms. Such "existential" verification appears only relevant for the last of Tracy's moments, not for the whole; cf. ibid., p. 221. Specifically, the "common human experience," I believe, that is to be analyzed phenomenologically and metaphysically does not in fact achieve full and accurate thematization until the further categories of alienation, sin and grace are added to it; and when these are added, let us admit, the theism established previously is suddenly rendered problematic in a quite new and radical way. That which finally, at this *new* stage, makes them again possible, the gift of grace, of new being and of promise, is not to be known merely by a phenomenological and metaphysical unpacking of common experience to find its essential structures, nor do they even form a set of implications to be built up out of universally human and so inescapable "beliefs" in relation to those structures.

18. Cf. Reinhold Niebuhr's discussion of the possibility and limits of "negative" and

"positive" validation of the Christian interpretation of history (*Faith in History*, chap. 10); and Tracy's recognition of this methodology vis-à-vis the issues of sin, of christology and of praxis (Tracy, pp. 213–14, 220–21.)

19. Our point in this distinction is that theism cannot, I believe, be firmly established on the grounds alone of creation and providence, i.e., through our response of "basic faith" and trust to the universal presence and work of God—as, I believe, Ogden and Tracy seek to do (cf. Tracy, pp. 14, 153ff., 187). The fact of evil, I think, intervenes both existentially and epistemologically, and renders the structure of existence distorted, the meaning of that structure ambiguous, and so the God creative of both that structure and its meaning infinitely problematic, as, *absconditus*. The full validity of the theistic interpretation of life only comes when the God implied in the structures, and our trustful response to them—but endangered if not eclipsed by the distortion of those structures and the threat of the loss of their meaning —is manifest as overcoming that alienation. Thus the God present in creation and in providence is finally known and finally trusted as redeemer, and life as meaningful, only when that God is known as redemptive love—though, to be sure, as we have argued, he can be provisionally, hopefully and hypothetically known and trusted in all the ways we have previously outlined. If this be sound, then the description of revelation as a "re-presentation" of that basic faith (ibid., chap. 9) is both true and untrue, appropriate and inappropriate. Revelation and grace make possible and so re-establish (re-present) "nature," but only after nature's fall, and thus is this not merely a re-presentation; there is the "new" here as well overcoming the broken character of our primordial relation to God, and the promise of ever-newer fulfillments. As our discussion will clarify, all this is said without qualifying the strong and forthright emphasis on the inclusiveness of grace as opposed to its exclusiveness in both Ogden and Tracy (Tracy, pp. 206–7).

20. The subject of religious discourse, its grounds, characteristics, uses, limits, meanings and problems, has been more extensively (if not more adequately) dealt with by the author in other works: *Maker of Heaven and Earth*, chaps. 2, 5, and 10; *Naming the Whirlwind*, pt.1, chaps. 3 and 6, pt. 2, chaps. 1, 2, and 5; *Religion and the Scientific Future*, chaps. 1 and 4; and *Catholicism Confronts Modernity*, chaps. 3, 4, 6. Obviously in the very brief summary in the text, a great number of important issues vis-à-vis religious language and philosophical language will be omitted; for fuller elaboration of our own position and documentation of its relation to other issues and views, cf. the above references.

21. Obviously the following are at best only suggested clues within experience that have functioned for the author as clues. They have only pointed to meanings, been intuitions of it. And they clearly appear only in the experience of some people, not of all; others likely have other clues and so other suggestions; and many have no such experiences at all. Thus these suggestions cannot be regarded as either exhaustive of all of experience, nor than as more than potentially universal. They are, therefore, not to be regarded as constituting a "natural theology": (1) even if in principle they were universal, they are too vague to bear that title; they are "rumors" of a meaning within experienced historical reality, not clear indicators of the ontological or moral characteristics of deity; (2) they are, as noted, by no means claimed to be universal in "common human experience." The role they play in our argument is, therefore, a suggestive and so a minor one, not that of an indispensable or indestructible link in any chain of proof.

22. The unintended that becomes a creative destiny for new possibilities is in fact Niebuhr's definition for "common grace" or "the grace of providence," a phrase he frequently uses for what we shall call one of the works of providence (e.g., *Faith and History*, p. 222; *Love and Justice*, pp. 294–95, 185–86).

23. Thus Tillich insists that the affirmation of providence is, and must be, "in spite of": "In spite of the darkness of Fate and the meaninglessness of existence" (*ST* 1:264, 267–68).

24. As we shall see (in chap. 7), it was this experience more than any other that led Augustine to speak of providence in his *Confessions*.

25. For a fuller analysis of the relation of sin to catastrophe and nemesis in history, cf. chap. 10 below. Needless to say, this understanding of historical catastrophe in terms of the effects of sin is basic, as we shall see, to the "prophetic" interpretation of history in the Old Testament, and in latter days the essence of Niebuhr's interpretation (e.g., his *Reflections*, pp. 6, 18, 31, 34, 87, 139).

26. From among many examples: Isa. 2:5–22; 14:10–21; Ez. 28:1–19; 31:10; Luke 1:46–55.

CHAPTER 6

1. As is evident, this definition is both similar and dissimilar to the definition of fundamental theology so persuasively advocated by Tracy: "A contemporary fundamental Christian theology can best be described as philosophical reflection upon the meanings present in common human experience and language, and upon the meanings present in the Christian fact." The similarities are fairly obvious: (1) The philosophical analysis of our common experience of history (Tracy, chaps. 1, 2, 3 and 4) to reach (a) an ontological interpretation of the experience of history and (b) an uncovering of the religious and then the theistic dimension of that experience, and (2) the critical and hermeneutical interpretation of the tradition of Christian symbolism in order to achieve meaningful symbolic forms that are both Christian and modern with which to interpret that common experience. The difference— perhaps because the present enterprise is a beginning into a constructive or dogmatic theology —is that whereas with Tracy the two analyses are relatively independent endeavors, phenomenological on the one hand and hermeneutical on the other, the results being correlated in transcendental or in his case metaphysical analysis (cf. ibid., chap. 3, theses 3–5), ours stipulates (1) that "common human experience" is not to be understood except in abstracto until it is comprehended by means of the symbols derivative from the Christian fact, nor (2) are these symbols appropriable by modern minds until they have been reinterpreted in the light of "common modern experience." Thus is our "method" relatively jumbled, our analyses more intertwined, and the "correlation" with regard to both meaning and truth achieved—if at all—at the level not either of prolegomena nor of fundamental theology, but only at the level of constructive theology when the entire spectrum of Christian symbols is applied interpretatively to the entire width of "common human experience." On the issue of the criteria of coherence, adequacy and "appropriateness" as tests of meaning, meaningfulness and validity, there is, I believe, full agreement in the two positions.

2. Obviously the prior question is: *Why* should we in our day (try to) understand our experience by means of these ancient and strange symbols? The answer—as opposed to the *how* of theological method—is the aim of the rest of this volume (both pt. 1 and 3). The answer is: Because these symbols—so it is affirmed—provide the most coherent and adequate means for interpreting the entire range of common human experience.

3. Cf. Richard Palmer, *Hermeneutics: Interpretative Theory in Schleiermacher, Dilthey, Heidegger and Gadamer*. There are, of course, other meanings to the now rich word hermeneutics. For instance there is that one usually associated with Heidegger: the interpretation of ordinary experience (the Lebenswelt) to discover its hidden structure and meaning. Theology also includes hermeneutic in that sense as one aspect of its total work, as illustrated in chap. 2 of this volume where we conducted a "hermeneutic" of political experience to uncover the "forgotten dimension of ultimacy" ingredient there. For further discussion of hermeneutics in this sense and its relation to theology, cf. *Naming the Whirlwind*, pt. 1, chap. 6, pt. 2, chap. 2. There is also hermeneutics as interpretation of every form of human *expression*, gestures, rites, art, etc. However, the definition of hermeneutic cited in the text, namely, the general theory of textual interpretation, is the original and still the standard and universal understanding of the term, and is that one to which reference is generally made when theology is *defined* as hermeneutical.

4. Cf. Tracy, pp. 73–74.

5. Cf. Pannenberg, *Basic Questions*, 1:109ff., 147ff.

6. Cf. for a fuller discussion of Bultmann's understanding of this relation of faith to the individual and of both to history, chap. 9 below.

7. Gadamer, *Wahrheit und Methode*, esp. pp. 286–90.

8. In fairness to Pannenberg, it should be said that recently (November 1975) Pannenberg has forthrightly stated in conversation that such a modern ontology is a necessary implication for any theology such as his own that is based on a conception of universal history and of God's relation to it, that has its sources in the biblical tradition but that seeks to reinterpret that tradition in modern terms; and even more to the point, that he intends soon to attempt its elaboration.

9. Gerhard von Rad, *Old Testament Theology*, 1:3–4, 106–7, 114; Pannenberg, *Basic Questions*, 1:6ff., 88ff., 113, 139ff.

10. This sentence must be carefully qualified. As has been repeatedly stated, a Christian interpretation of history is formed through the interpretive use of Christian symbols. This clearly implies that that interpretive use transforms in some measure "the modern consciousness of history." In this sense such an interpretation is not simply or merely "based upon" that modern consciousness. However, since that consciousness is in fact ours, and since, as noted, it differs significantly from, say, that of the author of the J Document or of Luke, what biblical study finds to be the consciousness of history in the biblical authors—or in past Christian theologians—must in turn be transformed in some measure by the characteristics of the modern historical consciousness. How the two may be brought together into an interpretation that can claim to be both modern and Christian is the enterprise to which the following chapters are devoted.

11. Von Rad, 1:106–15; Pannenberg, *Basic Questions*, vol. 1, chap. 4.

12. It seems to be an illusion of much of contemporary futurist eschatology to believe that for our age only the *present* is "Godless," and thus that if we move the referent of theological discourse out of the secular present—where God obviously is not—into the future, he will somehow become suddenly real, his existence as future credible, and theological language thus redeemed from the clear threat of secularity. This is an illusion: for a secular age, past, present and future, the whole stretch of time, is equally secular or naturalistic. Thus when the men and women for whom the present is devoid of religious dimensions or of deity look into the future, they find it equally devoid of deity and surely not to be "determined" or "redeemed" by any transcendent being. Only if the naturalism of the present is in the present challenged and broken, can there be any theology at all, even a theology the referent of whose God-talk is future! In this sense, as I shall argue later, any theological language in the present about the eschatological future depends on the *present* working of God's providence in and on our contemporary experience. To be the God whose "being is future," God must also be God of the present; for epistemologically, as well as ontologically and theologically, eschatology implies, I believe, the symbol of providence.

13. A much more complete description of this spiritual condition of a secular culture, its effects on theology, and the beginning of an answer to these problems, is found in *Naming the Whirlwind*, especially pt. 1, chaps. 1, 2 and 6.

A personal incident may illustrate this innate cultural secularity of even those of us who seek to "believe." On a plane to Kennedy one cold March day the pilot announced (in his Texas drawl) that it was snowing in New York, that no planes were able to land, but that we were going to go down and "try it." I turned to the man next to me and remarked nervously that I did not like the pilot's choice of words. Noting that my seatmate was a priest who (also nervously) was reading his breviary, I asked him whether "that" (pointing to the black book) was "doing him any good." He looked at me with intense hostility until I said, "Don't be offended; I'm in the same business; I want to know whether it helps you. I know *I'm* only thinking of creaturely factors as we descend through these dark clouds; for instance, ice on the wings, radar equipment, the state of the runway, the pilot's ability and so on. And, to be honest, I don't have any idea what I might mean by providence or how to fit it into this real world of creaturely powers and of nothing else which I seem ineluctably to inhabit whether I want to or not." The Irish priest looked at me with some gratitude, said he was thinking of much the same sorts of things—except also about a spot of warm stuff in the airport when we had landed—and we talked excitedly about the difficulty of believing in and conceiving providence in our age. By that time, we had landed, and I remarked as we sighed with great relief: "Well, at least one good thing about theology is, if you're in a tight spot, you can talk about theology, and before you know it the crisis is past!"

14. "The Old Testament writings confine themselves to representing Yahveh's relationship to Israel and to the world in one aspect only, namely as a continuing divine activity in history. This implies that in principle Israel's faith is grounded in a theology of history. It regards itself as based upon historical acts, as shaped and reshaped by factors in which it saw the hand of God at work" (von Rad, 1:106).

15. It is for this sound methodological reason that the futurist eschatologies must seek rationally to establish the relevance and the reality of a transcendent factor necessary for any comprehensive analysis of history, i.e., so that the "God of the future" makes some intelligible contact with our present secular experience of history. Cf. in this regard, the effort of Pannenberg to show that any analysis of history implies a transcendent, eschatological deity of the future as its principle of unity (*Basic Questions*, vol. 1, chaps. 2–5; vol. 2, chaps. 4, 7 and 8) and the effort of both Pannenberg and Moltmann to "prove" the resurrection as an *historical* event and so the necessity of the God who effects that event, cf. Wolfhart Pannenberg, *Jesus, God and Man*, pp. 66–107; J. M. Robinson and J. B. Cobb, Jr., eds., *Theology as History*, chap. 2; and Moltmann, *Theology of Hope*, chap. 3.

16. An earlier form of this same analysis of Christian symbols as intrinsically involving embodiment, action and praxis as essential to their meaning is found in the author's *Catholicism Confronts Modernity*, chap. 4.

17. "The philosophers have only *interpreted* the world in different ways; the point is to *change* it" (Marx, *Selected Writings*, p. 69).

"The function of reflective thought is, therefore, to transform a situation in which there is experienced obscurity, doubt, conflict, disturbance of some sort, into a situation that is clear, coherent, settled, harmonious" (Dewey, *Intelligence in the Modern World*, p. 851; cf. also pp. 308, 318–19, 330–31, 341).

"Einheit von Theorie und Praxis bezeichnet die Wahrheit, die herzustellen ist, und zugleich den obersten Massstab der Vernunft, soweit innerhalb der Entfremdung bereits alle die Anstrengungen vernünftig heissen dürfen, die auf die Herstellung der Wahrheit zugehen —Vernunft ist der Zugang zur künftigen Wahrheit.... Erst die kritischpraktische Tätigkeit, in der Philosophie sich aufhebt, um sich zu verwirklichen, wird den Baum der Ideologie als solchen brechen können" (Habermas, *Theorie und Praxis*, p. 316).

"The 'protestation against real affliction' is the unmythological kernel of religion" (Jürgen Moltmann, *Religion, Revolution and the Future*, p. 95).

18. "We must see the real agony behind man's search for himself.... Christian proclamation does not enter this quest only to make itself understandable, and to adjust its own tradition to the present. It enters it for the sake of liberation.... Hermeneutic is then not simply the 'art of understanding' written expressions of life, but of understanding all historical expressions of life within their political context" (Moltmann, *Religion, Revolution and the Future*, pp. 101–2). For recent examples of such a hermeneutic, cf. Ernst Käsemann, *Jesus Means Freedom;* Frederick Herzog, *Liberation Theology*.

One of the major criteria for Reinhold Niebuhr of a valid interpretation of the Christian religion, fully as determinative as its fidelity to the scriptures, was the fruitfulness of that interpretation for creative political action in the world. It was largely on this basis that

Niebuhr criticized orthodoxy and liberalism alike, not so much because either one was irrational, or incredible, nor even because they were unbiblical, though he felt them to be both. But because each one provided no useful or creative framework and incentive for creative Christian ethical and political action. Cf. esp. *Interpretation of Christian Ethics*, chaps. 5 and 6; *Reflections*, chaps. 15 and 16; *Nature and Destiny*, vol. 2, chaps. 7 and 8.

19. Earlier views of these four aspects of "meaning" in religious symbols and so in theological explication are expressed in *Naming the Whirlwind*, pt. 2, chap. 2 and 5, and in *Catholicism Confronts Modernity*, chaps. 2–4.

20. The discussion of the "eidetic" meaning of theological symbols corresponds roughly to that aspect of fundamental theology which Tracy terms a "historical and hermeneutical investigation of classical Christian texts" (Tracy, p. 49 and esp. p. 72ff. and chap. 5).

21. We are raising a controversial issue and adopting a controversial position. Of course, as noted, the "existentialist" meanings of symbols for people in the period under discussion (say the decades from A.D. 50 to 70 or those of the patristic period) are *very much* part of their "eidetic" and historical meaning for biblical and historical theology. Thus we are not proposing a "nonexistentialist" hermeneutic. What we are saying is that the existential meaning *for us* is not necessarily identical with that for them, and so to assume that identity and interpret them "existentially" in our terms is almost certainly to miss their historical and eidetic meanings—as much as to interpret those symbols in terms of our cosmology and ontology is to distort their historical meaning for past ages.

Now to be sure, we can only uncover and understand the existential or religious meaning of a symbol *for them* through our own participation in such meanings in our own existence: we must know what it is to be "religious" or religiously involved to understand Inca religions; but we do not and should not assume that the "existential" meanings of these symbols for them is identical with the meaning of similar (or even the same) symbols for us. Tillich was right, I believe, when he pointed out that the "norm" for hermeneutic—i.e., the "existential" problem governing symbolic meanings—shifts in different traditions and even in different epochs in the same tradition (*ST* 1:47–52. The existential meaning of symbols in the early church centered around the "liberation of finite men from death and error" (ibid., p. 48); in modern life the existential meaning of symbols is centered about the questions of meaning and authenticity (ibid., pp. 49–50). Thus again while an existential interpretation of *some* sort is a common presupposition of all hermeneutics of religious texts, it is not *our* existential meaning that should govern that hermeneutic lest the religious and eschatological issues of our age distort the possibly quite different religious and existential issues of another age. It seems to me that, as noted, Bultmann and much Bultmannian hermeneutic has too easily assumed the possibility of a similar Gestalt of self-understanding or mode of being in the world in common between ourselves and the New Testament period.

22. For example, von Rad makes clear that the *object* of "Biblical theology" is "Israel's picture of her own history," a history where "we encounter what appropriately is the most essential subject of a theology of the Old Testament, the living Word of Yahveh coming on and onto Israel forever, and this is the message uttered by His mighty acts" (von Rad, 1:112). To understand this Israelite "picture" of Yahweh in relation to her history, we must look as *she* looked ("through her testimonies," ibid., p. 112) at Yahweh in his activity; and to understand what she saw there, we must, argues von Rad, also understand (a) the events in her actual history which she underwent and (b) what those events, in relation to Yahweh, *meant* to her. In all this, as he makes clear, the way *we* understand history and its course of events is quite another matter ("another history," ibid., p. 107), and, as I am suggesting here, the existential meanings of our history to us cannot determine our understanding of those meanings to her. In any case, as the next section will argue, we agree with von Rad that the central "referent" of biblical hermeneutic is neither our mode of being in the world nor even theirs, but the God who makes through his presence and activity in history any creative being in the world possible.

23. "The subject [of a theology of the Old Testament] cannot be the systematically ordered 'world of the faith' of Israel or of the really overwhelming vitality and creative productivity of Yahvism, for the world of faith is not the subject of those testimonies which Israel raised to Yahveh's action in history. Never, in those testimonies about history, did Israel point to her own faith, but to Yahveh. Faith undoubtedly finds very clear expression in them; but as a subject it lies concealed, and can often only be grasped by means of a variety of inferences which are often psychological and on that account problematical. In a word, the faith is not the subject of Israel's confessional utterances, but only its vehicle, its mouthpiece" (ibid., p. 111). The same point, it seems to me, is relevant as well to New Testament theology: it is not the faith of the early church, nor even its "mode of being in the world," that is the central referent of its symbolic expressions, nor correspondingly of our interpretation of those expressions. Rather it is centrally God and his relation to history and to our existence. In this sense self-understanding ("the Christian mode of being in the world") is the subsidiary—though very important—"referent" of the biblical symbols; the primary referent is God, his activity and so his relation to possible modes of human being in the world. Thus is biblical theology primarily theology and not anthropology. This position seems to be in some disagreement with Tracy's emphasis on "Christian being in the world" as the primary referent of the hermeneutic of biblical symbols; cf. Tracy, pp. 51–52, 77–78, 124, 134–36, 214ff. The symbolism in both Old and New Testaments presents, I believe, first of all "God" in a new light and a new set of relations to us, our existence, and our history; thus and only because of this does it present a new possibility for our human being in the world. It is the task of biblical theology to explicate both of these referents as they are understood and affirmed in the scriptures, and of contemporary theology to retrieve or reinterpret ("revise") these symbols of both God and man in light of common, modern experience and categories. It is a misinterpretation of both of these tasks either to confine their concern to the second (human self-understanding) or even to regard the second as the primary referent—and so to leave the explication of the nature and activity of God as the task primarily of metaphysical analysis.

24. "It seems reasonable to state that the major specific differences of the theological as distinct from philosophical investigation of Christian language is the Christian theologian's responsibility to show how his or her present categories are appropriate understandings of the Christian understanding of existence" (Tracy, p. 72).

25. Tillich, ST 1:10–11, 22–24.

26. Cf. Tracy's helpful discussion of "criteria of appropriateness" in relation to a revision of the meanings of the Christian texts (pp. 72ff.).

27. When a contemporary systematic theologian approaches a biblical colleague with a request, reasonable but perhaps perfectionist, that the latter help him in his work in "christology," (or vis-à-vis providence or eschatology), he is apt to be met with the cheerful response: "Glad to help, friend. With which of the fifty-seven christologies in the New Testament can I help you?"

28. It should be clearly stated that this "reduction," which as noted is a precondition of systematic or constructive theology, is, while based on biblical theology, not to be interpreted as the task of biblical theology itself. The biblical theologian is quite right to insist that all that his discipline can do is to state the variant theologies of the Old and the New Testament, and not to perform this reduction as if it were, for example, the theology of the New Testament. What he can do, and should do, as biblical theologian, is to describe the theologies of Mark and Luke, of Paul and John, and not seek to unify them into one view. However, as noted, the constructive theologian cannot, in using biblical materials as he must do, leave it there. Some reduction of these "theologies" (these interpretations of fundamental symbolic forms) into a unified perspective must be achieved in order that these symbolic forms be "revised" or re-expressed into a coherent interpretation of modern experience.

29. It is this "meaning" in relation to our lived experience which Tracy helpfully denominates the "meaningfulness" of a theological symbol (Tracy, pp. 66, 69, 70, etc.).

30. "There is no ontological thought in Biblical religion; but there is no symbol or no theological concept in it which does not have ontological implications. Only artificial barriers can stop the searching mind from asking the question of the being of God, of the gap between man's essential and existential being, of the new being and the Christ" (Tillich, *ST*, 2:12; cf. also 1:21). For a more thorough, and to me convincing, analysis of biblical symbols as entailing in their "eidetic" meanings ontological conceptuality, cf. Tillich's *Biblical Religion and the Search for Ultimate Reality.*

31. Cf. Tillich, *ST*, 1:18ff. "The point of contact between scientific research and theology lies in the philosophical elements of both, the sciences and theology. Therefore, the question of the relation of theology to the special sciences merges into the question of the relation between theology and philosophy." While as is evident Tillich's main point (that the special sciences relate to constructive theology through the mediation of philosophy—as epistemology and ontology) is here accepted, a certain caveat is also necessary. (1) The special sciences have influenced theology in all sorts of ways, e.g., in the understanding of religious truth, of "creation," of eschatology, of miracle, etc. (cf. the author's *Religion and the Scientific Future*, chap. 1), and (2) historical inquiry (as opposed to the philosophy of history) has a multitude of relations directly to theology vis-à-vis the questions of the "historicity" of events witnessed to in the scriptures.

32. Cf. Tracy's reference to "an existential verification" of the "non-cognitive" uses of religious language (Tracy, pp. 211 and 221). This includes, apparently, both (1) an existential verification of the christologically manifested re-presentation of authentic possibility as the clue to the retrieval of *my* authentic existence (p. 221); and (2) an "existential verification" through creative praxis of the Christian faith and existence as providing through its "critical praxis" the way that these re-presented possibilities may become actually embodied in man's historical future. In other words, "existential verification" includes not only the establishment of the meaningfulness of Christian symbolism for my own existence, but also its fruitfulness in initiating, guiding and sustaining creative praxis in personal and political action.

33. Cf. Reinhold Niebuhr's discussion of the negative and positive validation of the Christian interpretation of history, *Faith and History*, chap. 10, and "Coherence, Incoherence and Christian Faith" in *Christian Realism.* Cf. also Tracy's description of the criteria of theory as inclusive of (1) "meaningfulness" as disclosive of an actual experience, (2) "coherence" as the internal intelligibility of fundamental concepts, and (3) "appropriateness" as faithful to the meanings of the Christian fact, and (4) "adequacy" as the establishment through a metaphysical analysis of the essential relatedness of a symbol or concept to the "conditions and possibilities of ordinary experience." In accepting that ontological or metaphysical requirement as an aspect not only of the meaning of a theological symbol but also as an aspect of its adequacy to experience, we agree with Tracy's criteria. Perhaps on this issue, the difference lies in the interrelation of ontological explication and argument and "existential verification." For him, as for Ogden, the ontological inquiry can establish on its own the truth of the religious symbol God. For us that inquiry only helps in that establishment as one of its moments. It is, as we noted, a necessary moment but not, we believe, a sufficient one. Because ontological significance can at best establish an "abstract" understanding of existence (i.e., of its essential structures), an understanding also threatened by the contrary implications of estrangement; and because religious symbols are "true" as *religious* symbols, finally by our participation as well as (i.e., not only by) our reflective process—therefore the final validation, even of theology's cognitive claims, must be an existential or participating verification of its primary symbols. Those who can establish by metaphysical analysis the truth of faith are almost universally those whose existence is qualified by participation in and through that faith. For Tillich's understanding of this point, with which I agree, cf. *ST*, 1:129, 240–41.

34. In these remarks we are explicating some of the implications to us of religious and ultimate ontological categories as "limit-concepts" (cf. Tracy, esp. 146–50). By that concept,

with which I agree, I refer to those concepts, categories or symbols which found or ground our modes of understanding and of inquiry, and so are not conclusions from their use; another term might be called "ultimate presuppositions." Such limit-questions, among others, will include questions of the relation of reality to concrete existence and so to any definition of "facts," and the relation of our thinking (and so of logic) to reality. They thus determine the modes of philosophical inquiry and analysis, as well as the modes of inquiry and analysis of all the special sciences. These ultimate presuppositions vary from culture to culture and epoch to epoch—and so is argument an adjudication of fundamental issues between cultures and epochs, as between religions, difficult. It is partly because limit-concepts in this sense as the ultimate presuppositions of cultural life are "religious" in character that Tillich speaks of religion as the "substance" (in this case the reflective substance) of culture in *Theology of Culture*, p. 42. And it is for this reason that I believe that participation in these presuppositions—a religious mode of relating to the truth—characterizes the final and culminating moment of validation—though, as I have argued, the rational exhibition of the "adequacy" of these ultimate symbols is also a necessary moment in the process of their validation.

35. On this issue, I find myself in agreement still with Whitehead: "Unless proof has produced self-evidence and thereby rendered itself unnecessary, it has issued in a second-rate state of mind, producing action devoid of understanding. Self-evidence is the basic fact on which all greatness supports itself. But 'proof' is one of the roots by which self-evidence is often attained.

". . . In philosophic writings proof should be at a minimum. The whole effort should be to display the self-evidence of basic truths, concerning the nature of things and their connection. It should be noted that logical proof starts from premises, and that premises are based on evidence. This evidence is presupposed by logic; at least it is presupposed by the assumption that logic has any importance.

"Philosophy is the attempt to make manifest the fundamental evidence as to the nature of things. Upon the presupposition of this evidence, all understanding rests. . . .

"It follows that philosophy, in any proper sense of the term, cannot be proved. For proof is based on abstraction. Philosophy is either self-evident or it is not philosophy. The attempt of any philosophic discourse should be to produce self-evidence. . . . The aim of philosophy is sheer disclosure" (*Modes of Thought*, pp. 66–67; cf. also AI, p. 379). For a more complete defense of this position, cf. *Naming the Whirlwind*, pt. 2, chap. 1.

36. The mystery of God beyond all our symbolism, however "appropriate" to the biblical witness, is emphasized (even) by Calvin in the following: "For who, even of the meanest capacity, understands not, that God lisps, as it were, with us, just as nurses are accustomed to speak to infants? Wherefor, such forms of expression do not clearly explain the nature of God, but accommodate the knowledge of Him to our narrow capacity; to accomplish which, the Scripture must necessarily descend far below the height of His majesty" (*Institutes of the Christian Religion*, bk. I, chap. XIII, sec. 1). For our own discussion of the linguistic character, appropriate "region," appropriate usage, meanings, possible validity and limits of religious symbols (religious language), cf. *Naming the Whirlwind*, esp. pt. 2, chaps. 1, 2 and 5.

37. The author has written more extensively on myths as a basic mode of theological expression in several places: *Maker of Heaven and Earth*, chap. 10; *Religion and the Scientific Future*, chaps. 1 and 4; *Catholicism Confronts Modernity*, chap. 3. The present discussion of myth in relation to the interpretation of history is a further extension of these previous discussions and an application of them to the particular problem of history.

38. Reinhold Niebuhr, "The Truth in Myths," in J. S. Bixler, ed., *The Nature of Religious Experience*, pp. 128ff.; "As Deceivers Yet True," in *Beyond Tragedy*; and *Faith and History*, pp. 103ff., 119ff., 214ff.

39. Niebuhr, *Faith and History*, pp. 103, 118–19.

40. Niebuhr, "The Truth in Myths."

41. Niebuhr, *Nature and Destiny,* 1:123ff.

42. Niebuhr, *Faith and History,* p. 119.

43. Niebuhr, "The Truth in Myths," p. 133.

44. Clearly the central source for these reflections on the role of myth in the interpretation of history has been the writings, cited continually here, of Reinhold Niebuhr. It is, however, also clear that the sense of the possibility, the relevance and the necessity of ontological explication of elements of the myth (i.e., of what we have termed "the invariant structures of historical passage") derives from Tillich. This writer is convinced that, despite their oft-noted disagreement on this point—i.e., on the relation of myth to ontology—Tillich would have agreed with Niebuhr that a Christian interpretation of *history* must be "mythical" at its final point, i.e., that mythical explication provides the ultimate principle of unity in the interpretation as a whole. Tillich argued that myth enters theology at the point of the "fall" of essence into existence, i.e., into history (*ST,* 2:29ff.). Thus his important category of the demonic is more mythical than ontological in its linguistic status. Correspondingly, the appearance of the new being, and so of each kairos, as reconstitutive of the relation of essence to existence, and of an estranged culture to its own theonomous possibilities, is likewise a "mythical" element intrinsic, in fact central, to his interpretation of history, as, obviously, is the important category of the kingdom as specifying the ultimate norm and goal of history's movement in the midst of existence. Finally, his insistence that kairos (a mythical and diachronic category) is sovereign over logos (an ontological or synchronic category) and thus that reason is to be understood through its *career* in concrete history rather than through its own innate or structural capacities alone (*Protestant Era,* chaps. 1 and 3) further validates this point. Although (like our own) it seeks as much ontological intelligibility as is possible, in the end Tillich's interpretation of history as a whole is mythical. The same is, I believe, true of Whitehead insofar as his philosophy represents a vision of the *career* of process and so of its meaning—insofar as it is a philosophy of history. The view that process represents an increment of value, a deeply held aspect of his total view, is to be sure an implication of his system of metaphysical categories; but as a vision it integrates these categorial structures in their *temporal* unfolding with regard to their meaning and so with regard to the meaning of the process as a whole. Thus does it become a "mythical" unification of those categories into a story. Put in more formal language, the synchronic analysis of relevant factors in process, which is ontology or metaphysics, merges into myth when it becomes diachronic, a philosophy of history.

Chapter 7

1. This summary statement can, of course, be almost infinitely contested. With the possible exception of those writers called the Apologists, the early interpreters of Christian faith— Irenaeus, Tertullian, Athanasius, St. Basil, Gregory of Nazianzus, etc.—understood time and history in a quite new way, namely, as characterized by the "economy" of the divine salvatory action. To them something *new* had happened with Adam; then, in order to resolve that, something *new* had happened in the preparation for and the coming of Christ and in the church which he founded; and, finally, to them all time and history will be completed and fulfilled in the final eschatological event. Only Origen among these formative figures qualified this view of linear time under the divine economy of salvation. Thus a "new" view of time and history, central to theological understanding, was clearly there. Our point is that in Augustine this "new" view becomes *itself* an explicit object of theological reflection, and so, rather than being the clear implication of other things that are said, is itself carefully and coherently formulated. Hence in our search for "classical" formulations of the Christian interpretation of history, we begin with Augustine.

2. For example, cf. *The City of God,* bk. XII, chap. XIII. Quotations from *The City of God* are taken from *Basic Writings of Saint Augustine.*

3. Karl Barth, *Church Dogmatics,* III/3, pp. 4–8. In this section of the *Church Dogmatics* Barth makes clear, as do all classical dogmatic theologians, that providence presupposes creation: the creature is now, says Barth, in existence through the power and purpose of God. The question, therefore, with which providence deals is the relation of the creature as existing and acting in time to the power and the will of God, a relation that covers the entire course of time. Moreover, the work of divine providence is not confined, as is the work of special revelation and redemptive grace, to the covenant community. Since providence concerns the relation of the creature "in general and as such," it is referent to the activity of God amidst *all* creatures of *all* sorts, and thus, to put it bluntly, "among the dinosaurs, the Sumerians, and the ancient Chinese, amid events taking place in Washington, Wall Street, Paris, Moscow, and the Third World."

4. For examples of the interpretation of divine providence as the ground of the order of nature, cf. for example, Clement's (of Rome) *First Letter,* sec. 20; *Letter to Diognetus,* 7:2; Origen, *De Principiis,* bk. I, chap. III, 10; chap. VI, 2; bk. II, chap. IX, 4, 5; Athanasius, *Contra Gentes,* secs. 35–44. It is interesting to note that in these early patristic works the work of providence is regarded as the work of the Word and not directly of the Father, a theme we will reinterpret in our own revision of the concept of providence. (Cf. esp. Athanasius, *Contra Gentes,* secs. 43–44; cf. also A. Harnack, *History of Dogma,* 2:206–14, 361–63.) For an excellent discussion of the patristic use of the concept of the divine "economy" as the dispensation of orderly rewards and blessings, cf. G. L. Prestige, *God in Patristic Thought,* chap. 3.

5. Cf. R. A. Markus's interesting point that for Augustine the difference between sacred and secular history is *not* a difference in the mode of the divine activity—since God rules all of history and yet all history is also the activity of man—but in the different modes of interpretation with which that history is viewed and understood, i.e., as a different way of "talking about" the events of the past. Thus except for an occasional miracle as a revelatory sign, God works *through* the ordinary dynamic factors present in historical change, and not alongside of them as a "second cause" (R. A. Markus, *Saeculum: History and Theology in the Theology of St. Augustine,* p. 14).

6. With the exception, of course, of Origen, for whom *all* eschatological references were to the "spiritual" consummation far beyond history, temporality and material being (cf. *De Principiis,* bk III, chap. VI).

7. E.g., Irenaeus, *Against Heresies,* bk V, Secs. XXXII–XXXVI.

8. *City of God,* bk. XX, chaps. VI, XV and XVI.

9. Ibid., bk XX, chaps. VII, VIII and IX. Cf. Markus, *Saeculum: History and Theology,* pp. 20–21. As Markus puts this point, with the "supernaturalising" of the eschatological element, the rest of history until its end becomes for Augustine not a part of sacred history in which there will be decisive turning points as in the past. It is an interim: "There is no sacred history *of* the last age; there is only a gap for it *in* the sacred history" (ibid., p. 23). Further implications of this "secularizing" of subsequent or future history will concern us later; right now it expresses clearly the "de-eschatologizing" of the future course of history.

10. It should be noted that Augustine denied the direct relation of history, and of history's institutions, to ultimate salvation in order to oppose both (1) the chiliast eschatologists who saw future history as the basis of a "literalistic" ultimate fulfillment, and (2) the Roman-Christian "establishment" (Eusebius, Theodosius and so on) who, along with the classical tradition, viewed the worldly polis and its ruler as an instrument of the purposes of God and so understood its security, power and success as correlative with the fulfillment of those purposes. Thus Augustine's "secularizing of history" was aimed in two opposing directions: against chiliastic eschatology and against its dialectical opposite, the identification of the

divine rule with present worldly power. It is, then, with his own necessarily dialectical answer to the resulting question of the relation of God to history that our discussion is concerned.

11. *City of God,* bk. XXII.

12. Cf. Walsh, p. 13; Dray, p. 60; Bultmann, *History and Eschatology,* pp. 56ff.

13. Cf. Löwith, *Meaning in History,* p. 166.

14. Theonomy, as Tillich uses that term, means a union of the creaturely with the divine ground of the creaturely such that the former can actualize its own powers according to its own structure and so in the light of its own norms. It is to be distinguished from "autonomy," in which a creature seeks to fulfill itself without the divine ground, i.e., autonomously, or on its own; according to both Augustine and Tillich such attempts at autonomous self-fulfillment in the end fail and culminate in the opposite, heteronomy, a dependence on the divine which is "over against" and so destructive of autonomous human capacities and goals. It must be admitted that much in Augustine's view would probably be viewed by us, as Tillich was well aware, as heteronomous rather than theonomous—nevertheless, I believe the fundamental positions are similar enough so that Tillich's category can be used to interpret Augustine. Cf. Tillich, *ST* 1:83ff., 147–150; *Protestant Era,* pp. 43ff., 56ff.

15. To document this assertion would involve a study of Augustine's complex anthropology. Suffice it to say that for him the reality of our temporal being, the truth of our minds, and the loving character of our wills are "theonomously" grounded and theonomously fulfilled. Only in relation to eternity *are* we, and so is transience overcome; only in relation to the divine truth is error overcome; and only in relation to divine grace is cupiditas transformed into caritas. Augustine sums up this theonomous understanding of human being as grounded in and so fulfilled by the divine being, truth and love in the following: " . . . The whole Trinity is revealed to us in the creation. In this too is the origin, the enlightenment, the blessedness of the holy city which is above among the holy angels. For if we inquire whence it is, God created it; or whence its wisdom, God illumined it; or whence its blessedness, God is its bliss. It has its form by subsisting in Him; its enlightenment by contemplating Him; its joy by abiding in Him. It is; it sees; it loves. In God's eternity is its life; in God's truth its light; in God's goodness its joy" (*City of God,* bk. XI, chap. XXIV). This Trinity of being, truth, and love, referent first to the Godhead and in analogy to ourselves, will be fundamental for our own interpretation of God in his relation to history (cf. chap. 12 below).

16. The non-being ingredient in temporality is expressed repeatedly with great power by Augustine: "Behold we speak and say, 'in this year,' and what have we got of this year, save the one day wherein we are? For the former days of this year are already gone by, and are not to be had; but the future days are not yet come, we are in one day, and we say in this year. Say rather, 'today,' if thou would speak of anything in the present . . . Thou speakest truth, henceforth I will say 'today.' Again, mark this also, how the morning hours are already past, the future hours are not yet come. This, too, therefore, amend, and say, 'in this hour.' And of this hour what hast thou got? Some moments thereof are already gone by, those that are future are not yet come. Say, 'in this moment.' In what moment? While I am uttering syllables, if I shall speak two syllables, the second does not sound until the first has gone by." From In Psalm LXXVI, 8, quoted in E. Przywara, S.J., *An Augustine Synthesis,* p. 92; cf. also pp. 90–96.

17. Cf. *City of God,* bk. XII, chap. I: where Augustine argues that "mutable things" (ontologically dependent upon God) can yet achieve "blessedness" by "adhering" (in the inward life of faith and obedience) to the immutable on which they are thus ontologically dependent.

18. For example, *City of God,* bk. XX, chaps. VI and IX, esp. the last paragraph, chap. IX.

19. Ibid., bk. XI, chaps. IV and VI; *Confessions,* bk. XI, chaps. XIII–XIV. Cf. the excellent discussions of the fear of "fate" in the classical world, and the corresponding

patristic use of the concept of creation and providence to counter that fear, J. Pelikan, *The Christian Tradition: Emergence of the Catholic Tradition*, 1:280–84; in Tillich, *Protestant Era*, chap. 1; and for the most complete study of the relation of Christianity to the classical "fate," cf. C. N. Cochrane, *Christianity and Classical Culture*, esp. chap. 12, entitled "Divine Necessity and Human History."

20. For the rejection of the cycles on the basis of the experience and the certainty of the grace of salvation: "For how can that [soul] be truly called blessed which has no assurance of being so eternally, and is either in ignorance of the truth, and blind to the misery that is approaching, or, knowing it, is in misery and fear?" (*City of God*, bk. XII, chap. XIII). "But if their idea is that the soul's misery has alternated with its bliss during the ages of the past eternity, but that now when once the soul has been set free, it will return henceforth no more to misery, they are nevertheless of opinion that it has never been truly blessed before, but begins at last to enjoy a new happiness; that is to say, they must acknowledge that some new thing, and that an important and signal thing, happens to the soul which never in a whole past eternity happened to it before" (ibid., bk. XI, chap. IV). And as the ground for this "new thing" occurring in moments of time that are unrepeatable and eternally significant, "for once Christ died for our sins; and rising from the dead, He dieth no more . . . and we ourselves after the Resurrection shall be ever with the Lord . . . " (ibid., bk. XII, chap. XIII).

21. Cf. Markus, *Saeculum: History and Theology*, pp. 82ff.

22. *City of God*, bk. XVIII, chap. XLIX; bk. XX, chap. IX; bk. XXI, chap. XXV; *Homilies on 1st John*, IIIrd Homily, 9; cf. also Przywara, pp. 257–65.

23. Cf. *City of God*, bk. XXI, chap. XXIV; *On the Predestination of the Saints*, chaps. XIV–XVI.

24. Augustine, *Confessions*, bk. V, chap. VII.

25. Cf. the interesting discussion of this distinction between God's providential work in nature and in history, Markus, *Saeculum: History and Theology*, pp. 86–92. For an explication of *how* God works through the "multi-dimensional" aspects of man's being, cf. *On the Trinity*, bk. III, chap. 3.

26. *On the Trinity*, bk. III, chaps. 6 and 8 (esp. sec. 14); *City of God*, bk. V, chap. VIII; bk. XII, chap. XXV.

27. *On the Trinity*, bk. III, chaps. 5, 6 and 9.

28. Ibid. bk. III, chaps. 8 and 9. It should be noted that this interpretation of the appearance of the "new" in nature is *not* identical with the nineteenth-century evolutionary hypothesis. In the latter, genuinely new kinds, not present as either latent or hidden in the previous order of things at all, arise from random mutations in relation to the law of selection (Darwin's two "vera causa"); for Augustine whatever appears to be new has always been there in the hidden form of seeds.

29. *On Free Will*, secs. 42–45; *Of True Religion*, secs. 36–40, 79–82; *On the Nature of the Good*, iii–x.

30. Both "establishment" and "re-establishment" are used because a real change—though not one involving the original, essential order of man's life—does take place at the eschatological end, namely, that now through grace freedom is at last fully freed to be itself and so to be good—to "take delight in not sinning rather than in sinning," i.e., *non posse peccare*, and so no longer able to upset the given order of its own life or that of God's creation; cf. *City of God*, bk. XXII, chap. XXX.

31. Cf. *Of True Religion*, 76; *City of God*, bk. XI, chap. XXII.

32. *Confessions*, bk. VII, chap. XI; *City of God*, bk. XI, chaps. XXII, XXIV–XXVII. (Cf. on this point, E. Gilson, *The Christian Philosophy of St. Augustine*, p. 147.)

33. *Confessions*, bk. VIII, chaps. VIII–X; *City of God*, bk. XII, chaps. VI–IX.

34. *Confessions*, bk. VIII, chaps. VIII–IX.

35. *On Free Will*, bk. I, i, 1; bk. II, 53–54; bk. III, 1–14; *On the Spirit and the Letter*,

chap. LIV; *City of God*, bk. V, chap. IX; bk. XI, chap. XVIIII; bk. XIII, chaps. XIV–XV; bk. XIV, chap. XIII; *On the Predestination of the Saints*, Chap. XIX; *Enchiridion*, chap. C; *On Grace and Free Will*, chap. XLIII; *On Nature and Grace*, chap. III. Augustine seems to qualify this blanket assertion evident throughout these writings that God does not ordain the evil men do—he only maintains and empowers that "nature" through which, by the free exercise of its freedom, men can do evil—in two instances: (1) grace, he says, was necessary for the angels in their freedom *not* to fall, and so apparently God gave those who did in fact fall, less grace (*City of God*, bk. XII, chap. XI); and (2) in his later writing he says that God "inclines and turns our wills in whatever they do" (but then adds in qualification of this "Calvinist" passage that this action is always because of and so in punishment for their prior sins, caused, presumably by their freedom). Cf. *Grace and Free Will*, chaps. XLI–XLIII. On his unquestioned earlier distinction from Calvin, cf. his remarks in *On the Spirit and the Letter*, chap. LIV, "Nowhere, however, in Holy Scripture do we find such an assertion as, There is no volition but comes from God." For very perceptive discussions of this change and the apparent tension and/or contradiction in Augustine's view on this matter, cf. Hans Jonas, *Augustin und das paulinische Freiheitsproblem;* Eugene TeSelle, *Augustine, The Theologian*, chaps. 4.5, 5.2, and 6; and R. A. Markus, ed., *Augustine*, for the essays by W. L. Rowe and J. M. Rist.

36. *Confessions*, bk. VII, chap. III. It is important to note that the well-known ascription by Augustine of evil to "deficient" rather than efficient causality (*City of God*, bk. XII, chap. VII) does *not* mean that the finitude and contingency of man's being (a "deficiency" of being) is the cause of his sin, as in neo-Platonism. Man's creaturely status is for Augustine merely the condition of the possibility of his sin; the actualizing cause, so to speak, is for him in man's will, in unbelief, pride, and the consequent turning away from the natural center of a dependent, creaturely being, namely, God. In fact, as is evident from all the above, Augustine is prepared to say that finally the only efficient causes of things in nature or history are free will, either that of God and his ministering angels in natural events, or of angels and of men in history's events: for God ordains all natural events as their primal (though not proximate) cause, and men will history's events as the sole efficient cause of what happens; cf. esp. *City of God*, bk. V, chap. XI.

37. On the category of foreknowledge, cf. *City of God*, bk. V, chaps. IX and X; *Predestination of Saints*, chaps. XVIII; *On Free Will*, bk. III, chaps. III–XI. On the divine permission, cf. *On Continence*, 15; *On the Trinity*, bk. III, chap. 9; *City of God*, bk. V, chaps. IX–XI.

38. *On Free Will, op. cit.*; *City of God*, op. cit.

39. "It is manifest that our wills by which we love uprightly or wickedly are not under such a necessity; for we do many things which, if we were not willing, we should certainly not do. This is primarily true of the act of willing itself—for if we will, it *is;* if we will not, it *is* not —for we should not will if we were not unwilling. . . . Our wills, therefore, *exist, as wills*, and do themselves whatever we do by willing, and which would not be true if we were unwilling" (*City of God*, bk. V, chap. X; cf. also *Confessions*, bk. VIII, chaps. VIII–XI). Cf. also *On Free Will*, bk. III, 7–8: "Because it is in our power, it is free. . . . My power is not taken from me by God's foreknowledge."

40. For example, Augustine remarks (*City of God*, bk. XI, chap. XXI) that just as we can look back in memory and see a past event "there," and in so doing not imply its necessity, so, because he is in eternity, God can "look forward" in time, and "see" our future acts spread out before him, and in so doing not imply *their* necessity. The understanding of time as a spatial extension spread out evenly like a plain filled with fields before the gaze of God from eternity—past, present *and* future—is obvious. Clearly Augustine seems to say, if we too were not immersed in time and so unable thereby to look over "time's wall" into the future, and so if we could ascend to the vantage point of eternity, we too could see the future "there" before our eyes.

41. *City of God,* bk. XII, chap. IX. Cf. Pelikan, pp. 288–89.

42. *Predestination of the Saints,* esp. Chaps. XVIII, XXXIII–XXXIV. Cf. Pelikan, pp. 296–99.

43. Cf. John M. Rist, "Augustine on Free Will and Predestination," in Markus, ed., *Augustine,* pp. 220ff.

44. That the principle of "inward action" of God on corporate creatures giving them the power to do what they "naturally" do is continued, albeit in analogous form, in the "free" willing of men—God gives the *power* or *ability* to do what men will—is made clear by Augustine in his argument with Pelagius: Men may *will* the good, says Augustine, but the "power" or "ability" to do it is only the result of divine grace (*On the Spirit and the Letter,* chap. LIV; *City of God,* bk. V, chap. IX). Thus in granting the power to do what men will, whether that willing be for good or for ill, God "controls" in the sense of shaping and so using whatever in history men really will to do.

45. Augustine makes an explicit distinction between God's *prohibition* (through his law and gospel) of an evil action and God's *permission* of that evil action—a permission that is "made up" or compensated for by the divine sovereignty here under consideration: cf. *On Continence,* 15–16.

46. On God's "control" of the evil will that is thus "contrary" to his declared will—though in accord with his "permissive" will—cf. *Enchiridion,* chap. C; *Predestination of the Saints,* chap. XXXIII. In Luther this same distinction appears between God's revealed will—in which he approves life and love and disapproves death and sin—and God's hidden will by which God wills death and "all in all"—with the difference that for both Luther and Calvin God clearly *ordains (wills)* the latter and does not merely "permit" them. Cf. Luther, *Bondage of the Will,* p. 170.

47. Our use of the word "mythically" in the text is Bultmann's, meaning that the divine activity is interpreted as *a* cause intervening into the world order—a viewpoint abhorrent—as we have seen—to Augustine. In that sense, Augustine is an ardent demythologizer.

48. Cf. TeSelle, pp. 220ff.

49. At the end of this road, when he has finally fully accepted grace, Augustine is vividly conscious that now he is able *freely* to will what he had been unable (because unwilling) to will before: "How sweet did it suddenly become to me to be without the delights of trifles," and "What at one time I feared to lose, it was now a joy to put away" (*Confessions,* bk. XI, chap. I).

50 Ibid., bk. V, chaps. III–VII.

51. Ibid., bk. V, chap. VIII.

52. Ibid., bk. V, chap. XIII.

53. *City of God,* bk. V, chap. XI.

54. Ibid., chap. I. Cf. also the following remarkable passage on man's freedom from fate through God's power directed by his love, a power and love illustrated by Christ's "powers to lay down His own life." The passage ends: "Let them, therefore, believe God when He says, 'I have power to lay down My life and to take it up again'; and let them inquire why it was said, 'Mine hour is not yet come'; and let them not, because of these words, be imposing Fate on the Maker of heaven, the Creator and Ruler of the stars. For even if Fate were from the stars, the Maker of the stars could not be subject to their destiny. Moreover, not only Christ had not what thou callest Fate, but not even hast thou, or I, or he there, or any other human being whatsoever" (*Homilies on the Gospel of St. John,* Tractate VIII, 10).

55. *City of God,* bk. XIV, chap. XV.

56. "The sins of men and angels do nothing to impede the great works of the Lord which accomplish His will, For He who by His providence and omnipotence distributes to everyone his own portion, is able to make good use not only of the good but also of the wicked" (ibid., bk. XIV, chap. XXVII).

57. On love as the determining center of man's being, cf. ibid., bk. XI, chap. XXVIII, and *Homilies on 1st John,* 2nd Homily. On the *right* directed love as the principle of good and the wrongly directed love as that of evil, cf. *City of God,* bk. XIV, chaps. V–VII; bk. XIX, chap. XIII; *On the Nature of the Good,* esp. I–XVIII.

58. *City of God,* bk. XIV, chap. XXVIII.

59. It is here that Augustine offers his justly famous definition of a community as an "assemblage of reasonable beings bound together by common agreement as to the objects of their love" (ibid., bk. XIX, chap. XXVI). Cf. Markus's discussion of the "two loves" that form the two cities in *Saeculum; History and Theology,* pp. 66ff.

60. Cf. *City of God,* bk. XV, chap. IV; bk. XIX, chaps. VII and XII. The major theme of Markus's perceptive book is that the fundamental perversion of the political—and individual—life of mankind separates the social and political arenas, and so history as the scene of political events, from the realm of salvation, from, i.e., the eschatological. No longer does political rule, therefore, represent the unambiguous will or purpose of God, nor can men achieve "blessedness" by means of political activity. Thus although, as we shall argue, society does have a relation to the *civitas dei* and so to the eschatological, and so concern for it is a Christian obligation, the "salvation" of society is not itself for Augustine capable of any realization. Cf. Markus, *Saeculum: History and Theology,* pp. 82–104.

61. *City of God,* bk. IV, chap. IV.

62. Ibid., bk. XV, chap. IV.

63. Cf., for example, ibid., bk. XIX, chaps. XII and XIV.

64. Ibid.

65. Cf., for example, ibid., bk. XIX, chap. XVII.

66. Cf. Calvin, *Institutes,* bk. I, chap. VI; bk. II, chap. XIII, secs. 3–5, 21. Cf. esp. the ingenious analogy of scripture as "spectacles" wherewith the faithful may now see and understand the ever-present work of God in the world: bk. I, chap. VI, sec. 1; chap. XIV, sec. 1. As the passages in bk. I, chap. III indicate, Calvin recognizes that theological language cannot be restricted to biblical language, and thus that nonbiblical terms and categories are essential to theology. However, the use of such "philosophical" language (self-existence, eternal, essence, person, etc.) should be determined, he said, solely by the function of expressing more clearly and precisely the biblical meanings. In most cases, Calvin believes, such legitimate use of extrabiblical terms has arisen to combat heresies (misinterpretation of biblical meanings) on issues not dealt with explicitly in biblical texts. For an excellent description of this position, cf. Edward A. Dowey, Jr., *The Knowledge of God in Calvin's Theology.*

67. Examples of this understanding of God in terms of *personal agency,* of *omnipotent will,* of *acts* in nature or history, and of *purposes or intentions* abound in Calvin. Four may be noted: *Institutes,* bk. I, chap. IV, sec. 1; chap. V, sec. 9; chap. X, sec. 2; chap. XIII, sec. 12. The same emphasis on the divine will and its intentions is manifested in the definition of faith: "For the apprehension of faith is not confined to our knowing that there is a God, but chiefly consists in our understanding what is His disposition towards us. For it is not of so much importance to us to know what He is in Himself, as what He is willing to be to us. We find, therefore, that faith is a knowledge of the Will of God respecting us, received from His Word" (ibid., bk. III, chap. II, secs. 6–7).

68. Ibid., bk. I, chap. II, sec. 2.

69. For perhaps the clearest expression of the sovereignty of God's will and effective action in the experience and reality of salvation, cf. ibid., bk. III, chap. XIV, secs. 15–21.

70. Ibid., bk. I, chap. XVI, secs. 1 and 4; chap. XVII, sec. 2.

71. This theme is clearly expressed not only in Calvin but in the Reformed tradition: "There is a single divine act by which God creates the world and determines its government. That is why Providence may be conceived as a continuous world creation . . . shown first of

all creatively and then as sustaining and governing. The government of the world is the proper purpose of creation" (Heinrich Heppe, *Reformed Dogmatics*, p. 251).

72. *Institutes*, bk. I, chap. XVI, secs. 1–3. For another example of the distinction for Calvin between "chance" and providence, cf. the commentary on Matt. 10:28–9 and on Luke 12:5, in John Calvin, *Calvin: Commentaries*, pp. 264ff.

73. Cf. the powerfully "existential" passage outlining the terrors of ordinary life, the despair if no hand controls these menacing events, and the consolation of the pious mind which knows by faith that these events are ruled and directed by providence. *Institutes*, bk. I, chap. XVII, secs. 10–11.

74. Faith, or our awareness of our own faith, is the inward *confirmation* of our election, though it is, of course, not the cause of election (ibid., bk. III, chap. XXIV, secs. 3–5). Also that the divine will and so the divine glory, are directed at *our* salvation is for Calvin the main theme of scripture (cf. the definition of faith, ibid., bk. III, chap. II, sec. 7, and its "purpose," chap. II, sec. 35). Thus an "external necessity" that is unpleasant but that is governed by God's will is no "fate" since it leads to our salvation; cf., for example, bk. III, chap. VIII, sec. 11. "God does not rule our lives except for our well-being" (commentary on John 11:9 in *Calvin: Commentaries*, p. 283).

75. "Now, we shall have a complete definition of faith, if we say, that it is a steady and certain knowledge of the divine *Benevolence* towards us" (italics added, *Institutes*, bk. III, chap. II, sec. 7), "But its [faith's] principal security consists in an expectation of the future life, which is placed beyond all doubt by the Word of God. For whatever miseries and calamities may on earth await those who are the objects of the love of God, they cannot prevent the Divine Benevolence from being a source of complete felicity" (ibid., bk. III, chap. II, sec. 28).

76. Ibid., bk. I, chap. XVI, sec. 2.

77. For the high assessment of freedom in recent modern culture as both capable of creating the new and of achieving the good, and so of fulfilling human destiny, however the latter be pictured, cf. pt. 1, chap. 3 of this volume and the following two chapters.

78. *Institutes*, bk. I, chap. XVI, secs. 2–9.

79. Cf. ibid.; cf. also *Calvin: Commentaries*, p. 268.

80. *Institutes*, bk. I, chap. XVI, sec. 3.

81. Cf. ibid., bk. I, chap. XVI, secs. 3, 4, 5 and 8; chap. XVII, sec. 6; chap. XVIII, secs. 1 and 2.

82. Ibid., bk. I, chap. XVIII, secs. 2, 3 and 4.

83. Ibid., bk. I, chap. XVIII, sec. 1. Cf. also commentary on Acts 2:20, in *Calvin: Commentaries*, pp. 267–68 and 273ff.

84. God's certain foreknowledge, not of what men and women will will (as in Augustine), but of the human acts he *ordains*, is clearly stated: "But since He foresees future events only in consequence of His decree that they shall happen, it is useless to contend about foreknowledge, while it is evident that all things come to pass rather by ordination and decree" (*Institutes*, bk. III, chap. XXIII, sec. 6). Cf. also *Calvin: Commentaries*, pp. 267ff. This relation of "fore-ordination" to foreknowing is continued in the Reformed tradition, cf. Heppe, pp. 269ff.

85. In discussing the Fall—and all subsequent sins—Calvin makes clear this "double level" causation: "Man falls, therefore, according to the appointment of divine Providence; but he falls by his own fault" (*Institutes*, bk. III, chap. XXIII, sec. 8).

86. Luther expressed much the same point but with a significant variation. For Luther God's purposes in history were even *more* hidden amidst the carnage—disease, war, death and devastation—which were the character of history and clearly, for Luther, the result of God's ordaining will for history. Thus is God in history the *Deus absconditus*. Only in glory, said Luther, will we see and understand how the "terrible" will of God, killing, maiming and

damning, is related to the loving will of God revealed in Jesus Christ. Meanwhile, unable to see how they are related (the theology of glory), we can only "hang on to the manger and the cross" (the theology of grace), where that love is revealed, and *believe* that this revealed will, not the providential will, is the true purpose of God. Calvin was more sanguine. In the light of the cross and of the knowledge of election, gained through scripture and ratified in the experience of justification by faith through grace alone, we can now *see* that the "hidden" will of God in historical events is either (a) God's righteous will punishing sinners, or (b) God's electing will testing and strengthening the faithful, and thus illustrating as does his election of some and retribution of others, the central two attributes of deity: righteousness and mercy. For these arguments in Calvin, cf. *Institutes,* bk. III, chaps. XXI–XXIV; for the corresponding arguments in Luther, cf. *Bondage of the Will,* pp. 169–77, 216–38, 314–18.

87. For Calvin's clear statement that *God* willed the Fall and all subsequent sins, and so all particular sins, cf. *Institutes,* bk. III, chap. XXIII, secs. 3, 7 and 13; Cf. also commentary on Rom. 11:7, *Calvin: Commentaries,* p. 298.

88. *Institutes,* bk. II, chap. XXIII, sec. 8; bk. I, chap. XVII, sec. 5; chap. XVIII, sec. 4.

89. Ibid., bk. I, chap. XVII, sec. 5.

90. Ibid., bk. I, chap. XVIII, sec. 1; bk. III, chap. XXIII, secs. 9 and 10.

91. Ibid., bk. I, chap. XVIII, sec. 3: " . . . This cavil is directed, not against me, but against the Holy Spirit, who dictated to the pious Job this confession. . . . " Cf. also ibid., sec. 4.

92. For further reference to the unquestioned confidence in the goodness of God's will, though it may seem *to us* not "good," and the consequent transcendence of that will beyond our ability to judge it, cf. ibid., bk. I, chap. XVIII, secs. 3 and 4; and bk. III, chap. XXIII. The situation for Calvin vis-à-vis scriptural doctrines of this sort is not unlike that which pertained between a loyal Catholic and the magisterium: "I may not *see* how my view is wrong, but if the magisterium, representing the divine truth as it does, says that it is wrong, then in obedience I must recognize it as wrong according to a valid judgment that transcends my own ability to understand."

93. For Calvin's concern for this sort of "meaning" of theological doctrines, cf. ibid., bk. III, chap. XXI, sec. 1, where, after enunciating the concept of election, Calvin immediately notes that only with a faith qualified by this doctrine will the Christian have the humility, the confidence and the assurance necessary for and promised in a Christian existence. Another example is ibid., bk. I, chap. XVII, secs. 10–11, where he shows how belief in providence conquers anxiety: "Must not man be most miserable [without this doctrine], who is half dead while he lives, and is dispirited and alarmed as though he had a sword perpetually applied to his neck?"

94. "We are not our own; therefore neither our reason nor our will should predominate in our deliberations and actions. We are not our own; therefore let us not propose it as our end, to seek what may be expedient for us according to the flesh. We are not our own; therefore let us, as far as possible, forget ourselves and all that are ours. On the contrary, we are God's; to Him, therefore, let us live and die. We are God's; therefore let His wisdom and Will preside in all our actions. We are God's; towards Him, therefore, as our only legitimate end, let every part of our lives be directed" (ibid., bk. III, chap. VIII, sec. 1). "God's care for those who are His own is like the solicitude of a shepherd for the sheep entrusted to him" (commentary on Ps. 23:1–4, 6, in *Calvin: Commentaries,* p. 260).

95. *Institutes,* bk. I, chap. XVII, sec. 10.

96. The phrase is, of course, Ritschl's. The concept of providence is in Ritschl very different, and so the way by which faith, through confidence in the divine providence, achieves a "victory over the world" is correspondingly different. Nevertheless in each case it is on God's purposive action in history that the inner serenity, confidence and creativity of the Christian are based. For a discussion of Ritschl, cf. below, chap. 9.

97. Cf. *Institutes,* bk. III, chaps. VI, VII and esp. VIII, secs. 1 and 2. For Calvin's

exceedingly realistic and pertinent descriptions of life's "everyday" calamities, cf. ibid., bk. I, chap. XVII, sec. 10; bk. III, chap. VII, secs. 9 and 10.

98. Ibid., bk. III, chap. VII, sec. 9. "Even though the obstacles on our way are so great that we could not overcome them in our own vehicle, we always find our way out with the wings which are given us, until we arrive at our destination; not because nothing adverse happens to believers, but because the very evils they meet are helps which bring them to salvation" (commentary on John 11:9, in *Calvin: Commentaries*, p. 284).

99. *Institutes*, bk. III, chap. VIII, secs. 2 and 5.

100. Ibid., bk. III, chap. VIII, sec. 4.

101. Ibid., bk. III, chap. VIII, secs. 4 and 7.

102. Ibid., bk. III, chap. VIII, sec. 6. In his commentary on John 9:2, Calvin states that while to be sure God visits sin with calamity, nevertheless we should *not* in the case of our neighbor conclude that his calamity implies a prior sin. "In passing judgment, a man ought to begin with himself . . . [for] God afflicts His own for various reasons" (*Calvin: Commentaries*, p. 282; cf. also pp. 280ff).

103. *Institutes*, bk. III, chap. VIII, secs. 5, 8–9.

104. Ibid., bk. III, chap. VIII, secs. 8–11.

105. Calvin's "eschatological transvaluation of values" is clearly seen in the following: "For if being innocent and conscious of our own integrity, we are stripped of our property by the villainy of the wicked, we are reduced to poverty indeed among men, but we thereby obtain an increase of true riches with God in heaven; if we are banished from our country, we are more intimately received into the family of God; if we meet with vexation and contempt, we are so much the more firmly rooted in Christ; if we are stigmatized with reproach and ignominy, we are so much the more exalted in the Kingdom of God; if we are massacred, it opens an entrance for us into a life of blessedness" (*Institutes*, bk. III, chap. VIII, sec. 7). For another example of this eschatological transvaluation of values, cf. commentary on James 1:9–10, in *Calvin: Commentaries*, p. 338.

106. *Institutes*, bk. III, chap. II, sec. 28.

107. It has been fashionable for theologians centered on the Protestant Reformation to castigate Augustine for his (Hellenistic) distinction between the *uti* of God (the enjoyment of God) and the *frui* of creatures (the *use* of creatures) as preparatory to that ultimate enjoyment. Such criticisms (cf. esp. Anders Nygren, *Agape and Eros*, pt. 2, chap. 2, sec. 3) should note that Augustine is there, in classical categories, saying much what Calvin in this connection is also saying, namely, that events and relations in history, and often our relations to other persons (e.g., to their failures, weakness and death), are instruments for our (and their) ultimate salvation, and are to be distinguished from that more ultimate salvation, *transvalued* in its light, and so *related* to only as they lead us (and them) beyond themselves.

108. *Institutes*, bk. III, chap. VIII, sec. 11; chap. IX, sec. 6. A most interesting contrast appears here between Calvin and modern eschatological political theologies. For both eschatology alone provides the true criterion for Christian valuation and so for Christian decisions in time—else the present be suffused with proud selfishness or abject despair. But for Calvin this transvaluation is in relation to a suprahistorical goal; thus are the events of history not ultimately evil, nor the goals of history ultimately good. Clearly such a view can lead, and has led, to reducing to a minimum the Christian valuation of social and historical goods (though not of personal goods!): fair distribution, justice, political and social equality, meaningful work, peace and so on. Thus most political reformist or revolutionary movements have rejected supernatural eschatology. Modern political eschatology moves the eschatological goal down *into* history and views it as a fulfillment of history's values: a "worldly" kingdom of justice and love is now the goal of history. Thus are Christians impelled to reduce and possibly to eradicate the evils of history's life. As we shall see, Calvin would agree to this task

—but he would speak of it differently, and ground it elsewhere symbolically and in different ethical and religious motivations.

109. Cf. *Institutes*, bk. III, chap. III, secs. 10–11, 19, 21. Despite his clear emphasis in these passages on regeneration as promised to each justified Christian, Calvin remains true to the Reformation emphasis on justification by insisting: (a) that sanctification is never perfect, and so (b) even the most saintly are continually dependent on the divine forgiveness, on justification by grace through faith alone, for their status before God.

110. Cf. T. F. Torrance, *Calvin's Doctrine of Man*, p. 32. The ceaseless activity and energy of the Christian in pursuit of greater and greater (though never complete) sanctification is well illustrated in *Institutes*, bk. III, chap. VI, sec. 5: "No man will be so unhappy, but that he may everyday make some progress, however small. Therefore, let us not cease to strive, that we may be incessantly advancing in the way of the Lord. . . . " Cf. also on the theme of ceaseless activity, commentary on Ps. 127:1–2, in *Calvin: Commentaries*, p. 340.

111. "The Calvinist knows that his calling and election are sure, and that therefore he is free to give all his attention to the effort to mould the world and society to the Will of God. He does not need to cling to God lest he should lose Him. . . . His duty, therefore, is not to preserve the 'new creation' and its intimacy with God, but to reveal it. . . . The individual was drawn irresistably into a wholehearted absorption in the tasks of service to the world and to society, to a life of unceasing, penetrating, and formative labor" (Ernst Troeltsch, *The Social Teachings of the Christian Churches*, 2:589).

112. *Institutes*, bk. IV, chap. X, secs. 3–5.

113. "The varied secular callings do not simply constitute the existing framework within which brotherly love is exercised and faith is preserved, but they are means to be handled with freedom, through whose thoughtful and wise use love alone becomes possible and faith a real thing. From this there results a freer conception of the system of callings, a far-reaching consideration of that which is practically possible and suitable, a deliberate increasing of the intensity of labor" (Troeltsch, 2:611).

114. *Institutes*, bk. IV, chap. I, secs. 1–3.

115. Ibid., bk. IV, chap. I, secs. 4–5.

116. Ibid., bk. IV, chap. I, sec. 17; chap. XII, secs. 5–7. Cf. Troeltsch, 2:601–7.

117. *Institutes*, bk. IV, chap. XI, secs. 3–4; chap. XII, secs. 1–4.

118. Evidences of this concern with the "discipline" and transformation of unjust and unfair economic, political, and social practices in the communities of early Calvinism, in order to make these communities as a whole "holy," are compiled by both Troeltsch and R. M. Tawney (*Religion and the Rise of Capitalism*, esp. chap. 2, pp. 102–32; chap. IV, pp. 193–227). "The organ of salvation (the church) ought rather at the same time to prove itself effective in the Christianizing of the community, by placing the whole range of life under the control of Christian regulations and Christian purposes" (Troeltsch, 2:591; cf. also p. 607, and for evidences referred to, pp. 901–10).

119. Troeltsch, 2:622, 649.

120. Undeniably the apocalyptic-political groups of the medieval and Reformation periods expressed long before Calvin the belief in the interrelation of the divine sovereignty to social transformation (cf. Norman Cohn, *The Pursuit of the Millenium*), and Joachim and his followers in the Franciscan tradition in still another way brought these themes together. My point is thus twofold: (1) Calvin represents the first important "main-line" Christian community so to conceive of the work of the divine sovereignty; and (2) it was conceived as a process brought about by the divine work of providence and of regeneration (i.e., by sanctification and the church) and thus, so to speak, *intra*-historical in its means (if not in its grounds)—rather than a "process" brought about solely by the divine eschatological or apocalyptic action.

CHAPTER 8

1. For the continuation into modern times in biology of the concepts of "fixed" species, cf. John C. Greene, *The Death of Adam,* chap. 5; for a description of the fixed types of political organization of the states in Greek thought, cf. Aristotle, *Politics,* bk. III, chaps. 6ff.; bk. IV, chaps. 1 and 2.

2. The exceptions, of course, were to be found within the apocalyptic tradition on the one hand (cf. Norman Cohn), and in the understanding of history by Joachim of Floris and his followers, for whom a new age of the Spirit, replete with new religious and social forms, will appear.

3. Cf. Troeltsch, 2:561ff., 602–12.

4. As we noted, except for the influence of Calvin, the Reformation made little difference to this static attitude to social history. In Lutheran circles the concept of the natural law was replaced by that of *Die Ordnungen,* the personal and social structures of human being established by God at creation. Their conservative role in the areas of politics, property, relations of men and women and so on are well-known, and, fortunately, are now under concerted attack by most Lutheran theologians. It was because an ultimate religious legitimization established, permeated, and defended the set, hierarchical social order of eighteenth and nineteenth-century Germany, uniting the "naturally" unequal social forms of an established society with the originating will of the transcendent God, that revolutionary and Reformist spirits (Ruge, Marx, B. Bauer and so on)—as in the eighteenth century in France —felt they must *first* attack religion if they were subsequently to criticize and then to transform society. ". . . And the criticism of religion is the premise of all criticism" (Marx, "Contribution to the Critique of Hegel's Philosophy of Right," in *Early Writings,* p. 43). Cf. the excellent study of James Massey, "The Hallischer Jahrbücher (1838-43): A Study in Radicalization" (Ph.D. diss., University of Chicago, 1973); as well as Karl Löwith, *Von Hegel zu Nietzsche,* pt. I, chap. II.

5. For the dependence of even the Enlightenment on classical ideals and forms, cf. Peter Gay, *The Enlightenment: An Interpretation,* vol. 1, *The Rise of Modern Paganism,* bk. 2, chap. 5.

6. Cf. Francis Bacon, *Novum Organum* (1620); for example, "For the sciences we now possess are mainly systems for the nice ordering and setting forth of things already invented; not methods of invention or directions for new works" (Aphorism VIII, in E. A. Burtt, ed., *The English Philosophers from Bacon to Mill,* p. 29). For his importance in the development of the concept of progress, cf. Bury, chap. 2.

7. René Descartes, *Discourse on Method* (1637), pt. 2; *Meditation* 1 (1641). For the importance of Cartesianism, cf. Bury, chap. 3. It should be noted, of course, that the particular character of Cartesian method, proceeding deductively from clear and distinct ideas, was not to provide the basis for science in its later, more creative forms; rather the union of experimental manipulation and observation with deductive mathematics was to open the door to new knowledge. Cf. J. H. Randall, Jr., *The Making of the Modern Mind,* bk. 2, chap. 10; bk. 3, chaps. 11, 12; and Ernst Cassirer, *The Philosophy of the Enlightenment,* chaps. 1 and 2. Nevertheless, Bury (chaps. 3 and 4) is, I believe, right that despite its "rationalism," Cartesianism introduced into European intellectual life a sense of the possibility of new methods leading to new knowledge.

8. Cf. Bury on the contest between the "ancients" and the "moderns" (chap. 4) and on the importance of Fontenelle (chap. 5). Also Nisbet, *Social Change and History,* chap. 3.

9. Cf. the following from J. G. Herder (1744–1803): "Finally from the whole region over which we have wandered we perceive how transitory all human structures are, nay, how oppressive the best institutions become in the course of a few generations. The plant blooms and fades; your fathers have died and mouldered into dust; your temples are fallen; your tabernacle, the tables of your law are no more; language itself, that bond of mankind, becomes

antiquated; and shall a political constitution, shall a system of government or religion, that can be erected solely on these, last for ever?" (from the *Ideen zur Philosophie der Geschichte der Menschheit,* in Gardiner, p. 38).

Cf. also the following from Hegel: "But as to what concerns the pervasive corruption and ruin of religious, ethical and moral purposes, and states of society generally, it must be affirmed that in their *essence* these are infinite and eternal; but that the forms they assume may be of a limited order, and consequently belong to the domain of mere nature, and be subject to the sway of chance. They are, therefore, perishable, and exposed to decay and corruption" (G. W. F. Hegel, *The Philosophy of History,* Introduction, pp. 36–37).

10. Cf. A. N. de Condorcet, *Sketch for a Historical Picture of the Progress of the Human Mind* (1793-94) and I. Kant, *Idea for a Universal History from A Cosmopolitan Point of View,* Theses I, II, III, and VIII.

11. Cf. Greene, pp. 4–10, 129–37.

12. Cf., for example, the repudiation by both Gadamer and Pannenberg—both exceedingly conscious of this embeddedness of man's mind in a changing history and so the depths of the "hermeneutical problem"—of Hegel's attempt to construct a speculative philosophical interpretation of the entire course of history. Gadamer, *Wahrheit und Methode,* pp. 335–44; Pannenberg, *Basic Questions* 1:121–22.

13. Again Herder, perhaps more than anyone in the eighteenth century, sensed the depth of the question of the meaning of life and of work implicit in the new sense of the *historical,* the new understanding of historical forms as relative and transient: "Thus everything in history is transient; the inscription on her temple is, evanescence and decay. We tread on the ashes of our forefathers, and stalk over the entombed ruins of human institutions and kingdoms. Egypt, Persia, Greece, Rome, flit before us like shadows: like ghosts they rise from the grave and appear to us in the field of history. . . . Thus we hew out blocks of ice; thus we write on the waves of the sea; the wave glides by, the ice melts; our palaces, and our thoughts, are both no more" (*Ideen,* in Gardiner, pp. 42–43).

14. It is plain that not every member of the intelligentsia in the eighteenth and early nineteenth centuries accepted this progressivist view, since many did not regard contemporary European civilization as representing clear progress over previous cultures. Cf. Nisbet's discussion of these dissident views (among them the ambiguous—on this issue—Rousseau), *Social Change and History,* chap. 3, and such important nineteenth-century figures as Søren Kierkegaard, Jacob Burkhardt, and Friedrich Nietzsche.

15. For good reason Hegel is usually taken, at least at the close of his life, as a "conservative" with regard to fundamental political change. After all, if what is, is ultimately rational and so "right"—as he reiterates in his *Philosophy of History*—and if the aim of history is the reconciliation of Christianity, developing human freedom, and the present German culture/state, then "what is" is not to be fundamentally and so radically challenged (Hegel, Introduction, pp. 9, 15, 17–18, 36, 38–39, and Karl Löwith, *Von Hegel zu Nietzsche,* pt. I, chaps. I and II). For a more "radical" interpretation of the implications of Hegel for social and political philosophy, cf. Marcuse, *Reason and Revolution,* esp. chap. 5, The Science of Logic.

16. For discussion of this homocentrism and "Eurocentrism" of nineteenth-century evolutionists and anthropologists, cf. Nisbet, *Social Change and History,* chaps. 5 and 6; and Greene, chaps. 6, 7 and 8.

17. To this observer the main philosophical and theological issue involved in the current crisis of Catholic ecclesiology, the center of the wider crisis within contemporary Catholicism, concerns the tension or conflict between the two views of the relation of the divine to history explicated in the text. The older view, representative of a conservative ecclesiology, holds that the divine manifests itself in absolute and so changeless forms of ecclesiastical life which must, if the ecclesia is to survive, remain changeless. The alternative view, clearly itself a result of precisely the new understanding of history in relation to changing forms we have here

examined, holds that the divine manifests itself in a *sequence* of changing historical forms so that reformation and change of these forms are necessary as historical life itself changes. To *this* view, therefore, older forms (e.g., of doctrine and so on), expressive of another ethos, are ipso facto archaic, irrelevant, empty and potentially demonic. For a fuller treatment of this issue, cf. the author's *Catholicism Confronts Modernity*, esp. chap. 1.

18. Despite his firm conviction that providence is at work in history, Vico (1668–1744) also insisted that man is the creator of history and thus can know history as he cannot know nature, which God alone made—for only the maker of something knows it truly. Cf. *The New Science*. Again Herder expresses this new view of man's "powers" in remaking history: "Let man be man; let him mold his condition according as to himself shall seem best. . . . God made man a deity upon earth; he implanted in him the principle of self-activity, and set this principle in motion from the beginning, by reason of the internal and external wants of his nature. . . . Everywhere man is what he was capable of rendering himself, what he had the will or the power to become. . . . The deity assists us only by means of our own industry, our own understanding, our own powers" (*Ideen*, in Gardiner, pp. 45–47). Cf. for the agreement of Kant (among all their differences) on this issue, *Idea for a Universal History*, Theses II–VI.

19. Francis Bacon, prior to Marx and Dewey, gave the paradigmatic statement of this relation between new understanding and knowledge on the one hand and new control over the world on the other: "Lastly, I would address one general admonition to all: that they consider what are the true ends of knowledge, and that they seek it not either for pleasure of the mind, or for contention . . . but for the benefit and use of life; and that they perfect and govern it in charity" (*The Great Instauration*, Preface, in Burtt, pp. 13. "Human knowledge and power meet in one; for where the cause is not known, the effect cannot be produced. Nature to be commanded must be obeyed; and that which in contemplation is the cause is in operation as the rule" (*Novum Organum*, Aphorism III in Burtt, p. 28).

20. The whole burden of Kant's philosophy, as a summation of the Enlightenment, is contained in this new sense of the autonomy of the rational self over all traditional and external conditioning: the cognitive self shapes its experienced world; the practical reason legislates its own moral decisions, and above all the mature self dares to think as rationality inquires. Cf. Kant's famous definition of "enlightenment" as "Man's release from his self-incurred tutelage. Tutelage is man's inability to make use of his understanding without direction from another . . . Sapere audi! 'Have courage to use your own reason!'—that is the motto of enlightenment" (I. Kant, "What Is Enlightenment?" in *Kant, On History*, pp. 3–10). As Condorcet's title indicates (*Progress of the Human Mind*), he shares with Kant the identification of an autonomous reason with freedom, and of both with progress: "In other words, will men approach a condition in which everyone will have the knowledge necessary to conduct himself in the ordinary affairs of life, according to the light of his own reason, to preserve his mind free of prejudices, to understand his rights and to exercise them in accordance with his conscience and his creed . . . and in which at last misery and folly will be the exception and no longer the habitual lot of a section of society?" (in Gardiner, pp. 57–58).

21. Cf. Bury's rhapsodic (but accurate) description of the struggle of the principle of rational autonomy (paradoxically based on knowledge of immutable laws) against authority, tradition, and divine providence: "Cartesianism affirmed the two positive axioms of the supremacy of reason and the invariability of the laws of nature; and its instrument was a new rigorous analytical method, which was applicable to history as well as to physical knowledge. . . . The immutability of the processes of nature collided with the theory of an active providence. The supremacy of reason shook the thrones from which authority and tradition had tyrannized over the brains of men. Cartesianism was equivalent to a declaration of the independence of men" (Bury, p. 65). One may note that Descartes's dualism of extension and thought prevented a contradiction between these two "positive axioms" and the demise

of the supremacy of reason in the face of immutable laws of nature; recent naturalistic philosophy has likewise sought to understand all events in terms of what Nagel calls "the executive primacy of material causes," and yet to retain emotionally and existentially the original theme of the "supremacy of reason."

22. Cf. Heidegger, *Being and Time*, for example, sec. 74, pp. 434–39.

23. While Heidegger confines this theme of autonomy to Dasein (to the human world), Whitehead expands it to the whole of the relevant cosmos, to every event everywhere; it is a categorial characteristic of all becoming and so universal and necessary. By the same token, while such self-creativity necessarily characterizes all of human existence for Whitehead as part of its categorial—and therefore "actual" or "concrete"—structure, for Heidegger it is rare, an accomplishment demanding immense courage, self-awareness, and anticipatory resoluteness, a characteristic of our authentic being that is a *task* set for men and women, a possibility to be sure but by no means universally achieved among a race "fallen" into inauthenticity and so loss of self-creation. In neither one is the presence of the Other directly crucial for the possibility of both self-creativity and of "world," as for example in Emmanuel Levinas, *Totalité et Infinité*, or (surprisingly) in Tillich, *ST* 3:40.

24. Cf. n. 21 above; and cf. Nisbet's interesting discussion of the history of this linkage of "natural" necessity in history with man's capacity to transform history, *Social Change and History*, chap. 4.

25. Ibid., chap. 1.

26. Perhaps the best illustration of this use of "Nature" in the place of providence to explain humanly unintended developments in history is Kant's; note in the following how Nature works *through* human freedom to fulfill the final goal of freedom, much as providence did in Augustine and Calvin—though the tragic side of freedom is here much more muted: "Third Thesis: Nature has willed that man should, by himself, produce everything that goes beyond the mechanical ordering of his social existence, and that he should partake of no other happiness or perfection than that which he himself, independently of instinct, has created by his own reason." "Eighth Thesis: The history of mankind can be seen, in the large, as the realization of Nature's secret plan to bring forth a perfectly constituted state as the only condition in which the capacities of mankind can be fully developed. . . ." *Idea for a Universal History*, pp. 93–104. Cf. Collingwood's interesting discussion of Kant's use of the concept "purposes of nature," in *Idea of History*, pp. 93–104.

27. Hegel, *Philosophy of History*, Introduction, esp. pp. 29–37, 72–79 and pt. 4, "The German World, The Principle of Spiritual Freedom," pp. 341–47.

28. For example, Condorcet and Herder—and Hobbes, Hume and Holbach would be other examples—appeal only to "scientific" laws as the explanations of history's development, cf. Gardiner, p. 57. "In der Naturwelt gehört alles zusammen, was zusammen und ineinander wirkt; pflanzend, erhaltend oder zerstörend; in der Naturwelt der Geschichte nicht minder," and thus "Bei diesen Betrachtung verschwindet alle sinnlose Willkür aus der Geschichte" Herder, *Ideen.*, 14. Buch, VI, in *Johann Gottfried Herder, Schriften*, pp. 125–26. Already the paradox that will increasingly dominate the modern consciousness of history is here enunciated: Inexorable law rules human behavior and history alike, but the same laws are the grounds of the development and increasingly effective use of human rational and purposive action, of creative freedom.

29. The subjection of historical events to laws, and the paradoxical use of these for his own purposes by a mankind now rational and aware enough to know these laws, is perhaps best illustrated in Auguste Comte: "Generally speaking, when the individual appears to exert a great influence, it is not due to his own forces, since these are extremely small. Forces external to him act in his favor, according to laws over which he has no control. His whole power lies in the intelligent apprehension of these laws through observation, his forecast of their effects, and the power which he thus obtains of subordinating them to the desired end, provided he

employs them in accord with their nature" (in Gardiner, p. 81; cf. also pp. 75 and 79). For Marx's similar view of the relation of law to intelligent action, cf. his "A Contribution to the Critique of Political Economy," in Gardiner, p. 131, and the following from later "official" interpretation: "On the other hand, Marxism proved that people make their history not arbitrarily but on the basis of the objective material conditions they have inherited from past generations. This struck a mortal blow at voluntarism and subjectivism and paved the way for understanding history as a process governed by natural laws" (*Fundamentals of Marxism-Leninism*, Moscow, Foreign Languages Publishing House, 1963, pp. 116–25, in Moore and Cook, p. 17).

30. Nisbet, *Social Change and History*, chaps. 4, 5, 7 and 8. For two recent and impressive efforts to provide new and sounder foundations for the use of a "scientific understanding" of social change in relation to creative praxis, cf. (1) the works of Jürgen Habermas, in which he seeks to unite social science with hermeneutics, objective study of the forces at work in society with self-reflection on human interests and human fulfillment: *Theory and Practice, Knowledge and Human Interests*, and *Toward a Rational Society;* and (2) Gustavo Gutierrez, *Theology of Liberation*, in which social scientific understanding and religious commitment combine into creative praxis.

31. Cf. B. F. Skinner, *Beyond Freedom and Dignity.*

32. The paradox, not to say contradiction, latent in the modern scientific understanding of man as determined, and yet on the basis of his knowledge of that determination, capable of remaking his life in freedom, has been analyzed above in chap. 3, and more fully still in the author's *Religion and the Scientific Future*, chap. 3. A fascinating analysis of the genesis of this contrast between determinism and self-creation in the modern consciousness is in Karl Löwith, *Nature, History and Existentialism*, esp. chaps. 1, 2 and 3.

33. Herder, cited in Gardiner, p. 39. Cf. pp. 118–37 in *Johann Gottfried Herder, Schriften.*

34. The discussion that follows in the text reflects, as is evident, the ontological understanding of four great twentieth-century figures: primarily Whitehead, and in some degree Heidegger, Dewey and Tillich. Thus it hardly represents a view of temporal passage explicitly held by the entire modern period; nor is it held where what we have termed "historical consciousness" has not yet manifested itself. As I have tried to argue, however, such a temporalistic ontology seems to me to be implicit in the whole series of concepts concerning history, destiny, freedom and new possibilities which we have here briefly reviewed. In this sense twentieth-century temporalistic or process ontology has uncovered the deepest *ontological* base for many of the most important ideas of modern culture concerning history and human historicity.

35. Although this understanding of passage as "modal" is basic to Whitehead's philosophy —and from thence it has moved into our text—it is certainly also true that no one has formulated its implications more clearly than Charles Hartshorne. Cf. esp. *Creative Synthesis and Philosophic Method*, pp. 29, 62ff., 133ff.

36. It is at this point that the novel aspects of the modern conception of freedom and its relation to human personhood and integrity are so important. As we have seen, previously theologians had attempted as rigorously as do moderns to "defend" human freedom and so human integrity of being. However they understood freedom as a noncompelled willing, and thus as a willing that could reflect or parallel the "prior" divine willing so long as the latter did not compromise the "voluntary" character of that willing. In modern culture, the creation of novelty has become inextricably intertwined with the concept both of freedom and of the integrity of human being. If freedom is not itself creative of the new, if it merely reflects an issue already decided, it is no freedom for us; we have sought to trace the development of this new aspect of the concept of freedom in part. Thus the modern understanding of freedom —or better, the modern awareness of what historical freedom is and requires—has implications that in turn transform our understanding of finite being, of temporal passage, of the

relation of actuality and possibility, and finally of the relation of God to these other ontological
categories.

37. Perhaps the best description of this "modern" view of time and of history as a progress
or development to a more ideal state, as well as the sharpest critique of that view, is found
in Reinhold Niebuhr, cf. esp. *Faith and History*, chaps. 4, 5 and 6; *Nature and Destiny* vol.
1, chap. 4.

38. In the following chapter, in our discussion of the view of "providence" which dominated liberal theologies, and in our discussion of the "eschatological end" which currently
dominates eschatological theologies, we will illustrate this "historicizing" of the eschatological
goal. Suffice it now to refer to the interrelation in Walter Rauschenbush's thought between
the kingdom of God conceived as a sociohistorical concept and his impassioned advocacy of
a "social gospel." Cf. *A Theology for the Social Gospel*, esp. chaps. 10–13; and *Christianizing
the Social Order*, pt. 2.

39. Cf. the excellent discussion of the "harmony" of modern post-Galilean and post-
Newtonian science with a rationalized Protestant theology in Charles C. Gillespie, *Genesis
and Geology*, chap. 1. For example, Roger Cotes, professor of astronomy and editor of
Newton's Principia: "He must be blind who from the most useful and excellent contrivances
of things cannot see the infinite wisdom of their Almighty Creator, and he must be mad and
senseless who refuses to acknowledge them" (in Gillespie, p. 7).

40. Ibid., esp. pp. 10–17; cf. also the quotation from the chemist Joseph Priestley, pp.
34–35.

41. Greene, pp. 3–13.

42. Gillespie, p. 210.

43. Cf. the excellent description of the transformation of the sense of the *quantity* of time
lying back of the present that occurred through the early developments of geology (circa
1750–1830): Suddenly an "infinite expanse of past time opened out before men's gaze," in
Loren Eiseley, *Darwin's Century*, chaps. 1–3. The change of time scale can perhaps best be
grasped through the following (to us) incredible view of time: " 'Time we may comprehend'
—wrote Sir Thomas Browne in *Religio Medici*—'tis but five days elder than ourselves, and
hath the same Horoscope with the world' " (quoted in Eiseley, p. 2).

44. Charles Lyell, *Principles of Geology*, I, 144, quoted in Gillespie, p. 126. Cf. Greene,
pp. 77ff.

45. Cf. Lyell's belief in the special creation of species, conveniently found in Gillespie, pp.
130ff. and 218–21; and Lyell's theory that the characteristics of species now domesticated
were "given" in order that they might accompany and serve man, in Greene, pp. 253 and
314.

46. Cf. Greene, chap. 9; Gillespie, chap. 8.

47. Darwin saw the incompatibility between providence and his two "vera causa" (random
mutations and natural selection) very clearly, and, despite immense pressure from many
friends and most of society, he never allowed a "theological interpretation" of either mutations or of natural selection to enter his own thought. As Ernst Haeckel said, "The gist of
Darwin's theory is the simple idea: that the struggle for existence in nature evolves new species
without design as the will of man produces new varieties in cultivation *with* design" (*The
Evolution of Man*, p. 95, quoted in Eiseley, pp. 334).

When Asa Gray suggested that God had ordained each variation, Darwin objected that
that disposed of his theory: "If the right [i.e., preordained] variations occurred, and no others,
natural selection would be superfluous" (Darwin to Gray, May 8, 1868, *Life and Letters*, III,
p. 85, quoted in Gertrude Himmelfarb, *Darwin and the Darwinian Revolution*, p. 330).
Darwin was apparently troubled by the antiprovidential bent of his own theory, but he never
accepted any other "grounds" of or factors in the process he depicted than the interaction
of immutable laws and chance—though he *did* assume an "objective" progressive develop-

ment in that process. Cf. Greene, pp. 301–7; Gillespie, chap. 8; Himmelfarb, pp. 362–68.

48. Gillespie shows clearly the interrelated and yet the mutually exclusive character of "adaptation" *either* (1) as a problem calling for an explanation in terms of design, *or* (2) as an explanation of the origin of a species or type, but not as *both:* "In one sense Darwin is Paleyism inverted. The adaptation of a species to its environment and to the necessities of its existence may be considered either as an explanation of its development or as evidence of a creative purpose," and then he quotes Darwin himself: "We can no longer argue that, for instance, the beautiful hinge of a bivalve shell must have been made by an intelligent being, like the hinge of a door by man. There seems to be no more design in the variability of organic beings, and in the action of natural selection, than in the course which the wind blows" (Gillespie, p. 219). Cf. Greene, chap. 8.

49. Cf. the anguish of many leading English men of letters (the Arnolds, Tennyson, Ruskin, Mill, etc.) at what Carlyle called "the iron, ignoble circle of necessity" (Basil Willey, *Nineteenth Century Studies*). The same "chill" concerning mechanical necessity is reflected in the theology of Ritschl in which religion provides the sole basis for a "victory" for moral and spiritual man set over against amoral, purposeless nature; cf. A. Ritschl, *The Christian Doctrine of Justification and Reconciliation*, pp. 199, 219, 233.

50. See the discussion of this point in Himmelfarb, pp. 320–22. And for Lyell's point that behind the ascent to higher forms of life lay a "law of development" that defied and transcended scientific explanation, see Greene, pp. 314–15.

51. Greene, pp. 316ff.; Eiseley, chap. 11, esp. pp. 310ff.; Himmelfarb, p. 354.

52. Himmelfarb, p. 329; Eiseley, pp. 320–21; Greene, pp. 394ff.

53. Cf. Greene, pp. 304–7, for the outgrowth, not intended by Darwin's "naturalism," of "process" views of evolution which sought, as he did not, to integrate value and teleology with orderly causation into a new, nonmechanistic understanding of progressive development and thus one that made philosophical room for theism. The example of this understanding of process as a union of actuality with new possibility, of the given with freedom and with purpose, which we have outlined, is, of course, A. N. Whitehead.

54. Cf. Lyman Abbott's well-known summary of this pervasive, progressive force: "The history of the world, whether it be the history of creation, or Providence, or of redemption; whether the history of redemption in the race or of redemption in the individual soul, is a history of a growth in accordance with the great law interpreted and uttered in that one word evolution" (Lyman Abbott, *Theology of an Evolutionist*, p. 15). Here is clearly shown on the one hand the synthesis of all theological doctrines and symbols into the one symbol of providence, and on the other the interpretation of providence solely in the light of the "scientific" concept of evolution. The same synthesis of theological concepts into one providential activity of "growth," and the interpretation of that synthesis according to the categories and patterns of contemporary evolutionary theory is seen in Henry Drummond, *Natural Law in the Spiritual World*, esp. chaps. 3, 4 and 5.

55. F. R. Tennant, *Philosophical Thelogy*, vol. 2, chap. 4.

CHAPTER 9

1. One of the major implications of the sequence of theological interpretations of history which we shall here describe is, therefore, the deep interrelationship and so interdependence of cultural experience and reflection—in this case the *cultural* interpretation of history—and *theological* construction (as well as exegesis of scripture). Such interdependence is here shown to be an historical fact, whatever the form of theology; for this reason, as we have argued above, it must also be a recognized aspect of theological method upon which therefore reflection can explicitly and critically dwell.

2. "The undermining of the theory of Providence is very intimately connected with our

subject; for it was just the theory of an active Providence that the theory of progress was to replace; and it was not till men felt independent of Providence that they could organize a theory of progress" (Bury, p. 73).

3. Again it should be emphasized that the apocalyptic interpretation of history characteristic of certain sectarian groups in Germany, England and America was by no means always "conservative" in its social implications, as Norman Cohn has abundantly shown (The Pursuit of the Millenium). However there is little question that such apocalyptic views did not characterize the "established" theologies of Europe in the seventeenth, eighteenth and nineteenth centuries.

4. For example, F. C. Bauer, David Strauss, John Henry Newman, F. D. Maurice, etc.

5. Friederich Schleiermacher, Christian Faith, secs. 36, 38, 39.

6. Ibid., secs. 46, 47, 49.

7. Ibid., sec. 47.

8. Ibid., secs. 50–51. In correspondence to our own religious "feeling" of absolute dependence (as creatures within the nature system and yet as free over against it), God as the "whence" of that feeling is defined as Absolute Causality, and all theological predication proceeds on the basis of that Absolute Causality communicated to us through the natural and the historical process. See sec. 50.3

9. Ibid., sec. 5.1.

10. Ibid., secs. 59, 60.

11. Ibid., sec. 33.1.

12. Ibid., secs. 66.2, 67. As with the doctrine of creation, Schleiermacher refuses to identify the symbol of the Fall with a single event in past time (sec. 72). Rather it represents a stage in the development of mankind as a whole and of each individual. Thus does he reinterpret this symbol in the light of the new interpretation of history which on the one hand made scientifically incredible and (for him) symbolically mistaken the conception of an historical fall and on the other provided a conception of historical stages developing out of relative imperfection to higher levels of human existence. For this mode of interpretation of the Fall as a first stage, Schleiermacher had, of course, the models of both Kant (Religion within the Limits of Reason Alone, pp. 23–39), and of Hegel (cf. Philosophy of History, pt. 3, sec. 3, chap. 2, pp. 321–22) to work with.

13. Schleiermacher, sec. 14, Postscript. Cf. also sec. 87 (grace has a supernatural cause, but manifests itself "naturally" in the common historical life of the Christian community); and esp. sec. 88.4: "In this whole matter [redemption through Christ] we posit, on the one side, an initial divine activity which is supernatural [i.e., not arising or able to arise out of the prior conditions of sin] but at the same time a vital human receptivity [the potentiality of the original creation] in virtue of which alone that supernatural can become a natural fact of history." Thus does God's creative work enter history, so to speak, "substantively," raising history to a higher level of human realization. Cf., finally, sec. 108.5, where the influence of Christ on future Christians is consummated historically ("naturally") through the influences of the Christian community.

14. Ibid., sec. 94.

15. Ibid., sec. 100–1.

16. Ibid., secs. 93.3, 94.3, 95.3.

17. "There is only one eternal and universal decree justifying men for God's sake. This decree, moreover, is the same as that which sent Christ on his mission, for otherwise that mission would have been conceived and determined by God without its consequences. And once more, the decree that sent Christ forth is one with the decree creating the human race, for in Christ first human nature is brought to perfection. Indeed, since thought and will, will and action are not to be sundered in God, all this is one divine act designed to alter our relation to God, its temporal manifestation is seen in the incarnation of Christ from which the whole

new creation proceeds, and in which it has its starting point. Thenceforth the promulgation in time of this divine act is really a continuous one, but in its effects it appears to us at many points separated and (as it were) strung out from one another . . ." (ibid., sec. 109.3). Cf. also sec. 120.3. Thus is the basic doctrine of election, which in all Reformed dogmatics governs creation, fall and redemption alike—and so the work of providence—here radically reinterpreted in a developmental sense encompassing the realization of the potential perfection of the race in the course of history's process. One may say that whereas for Calvin the decree of election governs and interprets providence, here *providence*, as the work of God in developing history, governs and reinterprets election. The similarity and yet massive difference here with Barth's equally radical reinterpretation of election is instructive. Cf. also sec. 119.1 and .3 for the explicit identification of election and God's providential world-government.

18. Ibid., secs. 100.2, 119.1.

19. Ibid., Secs. 99.1, 160.

20. Ibid., Secs. 113, 122.3.

21. Ibid., Sec. 157. 1–2. Schleiermacher recognizes that the kingdom is never absolutely achieved in history since sin and its problems remain, and he does assent to the reality of the promise of eternal life—though the latter is for him neither a part of the central promise of the gospel nor that on which any other element in Christianity depends, cf. secs. 158–159, 161–163.

22. "Moral fellowship as such neutralizes natural distinctions, for it springs from the subjective motive of love, which differs from that natural hereditary friendliness of fellow countrymen to one another which is, as a rule, an accompaniment of civil society. Moral fellowship, viewed in those two characteristics of possessing the widest possible extension and being assisted by the most comprehensive motive, can only be conceived as the Kingdom of God" Ritschl, p. 252 (sec. 32); cf. also pp. 292–93 (sec. 36), 514 (sec. 53).

23. Ibid., pp. 610–11 (sec. 62).

24. Ibid., pp. 211 (sec. 28), 223 (sec. 29), 483 (sec. 50). For Schleiermacher's assertion of this, among others, cf. Schleiermacher, secs. 7.3, 8.4.

25. Ritschl, p. 294 (sec. 36).

26. "In every religion what is sought, with the help of the superhuman spiritual power reverenced by man, is a solution of the contradiction in which man finds himself, as both a part of the world of nature and a spiritual personality claiming to dominate nature. . . . In this juncture religion springs up as faith in superhuman spiritual powers, by whose help the power which man possesses of himself is in some way supplemented, and elevated into a unity of its own kind which is a match for the pressure of the natural world" (ibid., p. 99 [sec. 27]; cf. also p. 503 [sec. 52]). The relation of this view of religion to a *negative* assessment of the natural world, and so to the most dubious and harmful aspects of the "liberal" inheritance vis-à-vis its attitude towards nature, as well as its locus in nineteenth-century mechanistic interpretations of nature, are quite apparent in this passage. It is no surprise that such a religious horizon should lead not only to the dualism of nature versus morality that Ritschl intended but also to the "technological domination of the world" that he did not (at least explicitly) intend—but his culture did.

27. Ibid., pp. 279–80 (sec. 34), 457 (sec. 49), 502–4 (sec. 52), 615 (sec. 63).

28. Ibid., pp. 223 (sec. 29), 280 (sec. 33), 294 (sec. 36), 184 (sec. 26), 334 (sec. 40).

29. Ibid., pp. 167–68 (sec. 24), 174–77 (sec. 25), 191–92, 507 (sec. 52). Ritschl posits a most interesting relation of the personal assurance of "faith" in God's forgiveness and justification to trust in providence, the world government of God which works even through suffering to bring about the kingdom of God in history: ". . . Faith verifies the forgiveness of God experimentally when it reaches out to grasp God's care and Providence over the whole of life, and relies thereon even under those sufferings involved in the believer's situation in

the world. . . . Thus, too, this exercise of faith in Providence and of patience under divinely ordained suffering is the form in which the believer attains assurance of the salvation guaranteed to him through Christ alone. . . . Apart from these functions of trust and patience, we can find no place for assurance of our justification by faith" (ibid., pp. 174–75).

30. Ibid., pp. 319–20 (sec. 39), 543–44, 550–51 (sec. 56), 578 (sec. 59).

31. Ibid., p. 25 (sec. 4), secs. 35–36.

32. "The Kingdom of God, the realization of which forms the vocation of Christ, signifies not only the self-end of God, but also the goal that constitutes the highest destiny of man" [ibid., p. 452 (sec. 49)].

33. Ibid., pp. 452ff. (sec. 49).

34. Cf., for example, the way Ritschl relates the concept of the developing kingdom (under providence) to the development of social institutions in the course of general human history [ibid., pp. 303–18 (sec. 38)].

35. Ibid., p. 135 (sec. 22).

36. Ibid., secs. 38, 39.

37. Ibid., pp. 135–38 (sec. 22).

38. This phrase "Kingdom of sin" (used much more powerfully fifty years later by Walter Rauschenbush) appears in Ritschl as an essential aspect of his reinterpretation of the symbol of original sin, but with no connotation of the necessity for a social or institutional transformation. Cf. *ibid.*, p. 344 (sec. 41). For Rauschenbush's use of a similar symbol—"the kingdom of evil"—to connote the destructive character of inherited social institutions and thus the need for their transformation, cf. his *Theology for the Social Gospel*, chaps. 6, 7, 8, 9.

39. Cf., for example, Ritschl, pp. 516–22 (sec. 53).

40. Cf. the quotation from Lyman Abbott referred to in chap. 8, n. 54 above.

41. The separation of theological concern from general history and from developments in nature did not mean that the new theology rejected either historical inquiry, and the views of historical change associated with it, or scientific inquiry, and the evolutionary views of nature now dominant within science. On the contrary, all of these theologians, like their liberal forefathers, affirmed the legitimacy of such studies in their own areas. What they did say was that inquiry into history and nature were now irrelevant to the gospel which was to be derived and interpreted, not on the basis of our knowledge of history or of nature, but on the basis of revelation and of responding faith alone.

42. We have selected Barth and Bultmann as illustrative of this new view of the relation of reality to history for two reasons: (1) because they are both of such transcendent significance to the whole theological scene of their times, and (2) because they illustrate more clearly than any other contemporary theologian this new interpretation of history. While they can thus be taken as representative of the theological view of history of this period, it should also be said that a number of theologians representing many of the same emphases, continued to be concerned with an interpretation of history and its relation to Christian faith. Thus although the latter, as "neo-orthodox," reformulated radically the "liberal" understanding of history, they nevertheless did not reflect the Barthian or the Bultmannian position on this subject. I refer especially here to Paul Tillich and Reinhold Niebuhr, for whom the interpretation of history remained very close to the center of their theological concerns. No separate analyses of their interpretations are given in this volume, largely because the position advanced here is so heavily in their debt. The dedication of this volume to them both, therefore, can be taken as a symbol of the self-understanding of the position enunciated here as an attempt at a synthesis and a development of the views they enunciated.

43. Karl Barth, *The Epistle to the Romans*, p. 77.

44. Ibid., pp. 48–49, 107–108, 166–70.

45. Ibid., pp. 29–30.

46. Ibid., p. 43. While almost every sentence of *Romans* is in direct opposition to the

liberal progressivism that preceded, the sentence quoted discloses particularly clearly the change from that progressivism: nature and history *are* the footprints of deity; but not of God's benevolent purposes of completion, rather of his judgment and negation. Thus the divine purposes of redemption are revealed *trans*-historically in "unhistorical" events in history (incarnation, atonement, and especially resurrection) to a faith that is not a historical possibility; and they are fulfilled beyond the negation of history, and so beyond the triumph of death, in eternity.

47. Ibid., p. 91.

48. "This initial point of view involves the apprehension that the world and human history are moving in a secular and relative context, which is in itself utterly meaningless; but it involves also the apprehension that they have meaning as a parable of a wholly other world; that they bear witness to a wholly other history" (ibid., p. 107). Note the acknowledgement of what we have called the Enlightenment understanding of history, *without* the Enlightenment sense of progressive meaning, and that the locus of the meaning of history is in a "wholly other history."

49. The separation of the resurrection event as the center of eschatological meaning and the "historical facts" that, so to speak, surround it and are visible on the plane of history, is, for Barth, absolute; cf. ibid., p. 204: "If the Resurrection be brought within the context of history, it must share in its obscurity and error and essential questionableness." *Because* for Barth history is as the modern historical consciousness describes it: internally related, relative, transient and vacant of all absolutes, *therefore*, it cannot "contain" the divine redemptive activity without overwhelming the latter with meaninglessness. The *ontology* of the modern consciousness of history is thoroughly affirmed; the *meaning* that that consciousness had seen in history is radically denied. Here Barth is closer to the mood of twentieth-century secular existence than are the liberals who regard him as "merely orthodox"—for they accepted as presuppositions about the sequence of historical events the optimistic mood of nineteenth-century secular culture.

50. Cf. esp. ibid., pp. 331–32.

51. Ibid., p. 95; cf. also pp. 79–80.

52. Cf. the important book *The Humanity of God,* and the entire *Church Dogmatics.*

53. Barth's discussion of providence (*Church Dogmatics,* vol. III, pt. 3, chap. XI, secs. 48–51) is one of the few full treatments of this doctrine in recent theology. For a fuller commentary on this aspect of Barth, see my article "The Concept of Providence in Contemporary Theology."

54. *Church Dogmatics,* III/3, pp. 3, 18–19, and sec. 49:1, 2, 3. For Barth's understanding of providence in relation to the "natural laws" that are the object of scientific inquiry, cf. ibid., pp. 124–28.

55. Ibid., p. 94; cf. also pp. 112–13: "God 'concurs' with the creature, but the creature does not 'concur' with God. That is, the activity of the creature does not impose any condition upon the activity of God . . . as God cooperates with the activity of the creature, his own activity precedes, accompanies, and follows that activity, and nothing can be done except the will of God."

56. Ibid., p. 94. Barth, therefore, seems to me to represent the older Augustinian-Reformation view of human freedom in relation to the divine will, namely that freedom consists in the voluntary willing associated with the act, rather than with the capacity of an action to *originate,* to decide what has been undecided before.

57. Ibid., pp. 35–40.

58. Ibid., pp. 41–44, 48–52.

59. Ibid., pp. 35–57. "The covenant is not creation, but its internal basis. And creation is not the covenant, but its external basis" (p. 38).

60. Ibid., p. 143.

61. Unlike Augustine, Barth radically denies that the "nothingness" (in Augustine the non-being of the creature) arises from the finitude of the creature (ibid., pp. 296, 349). Because he does recognize relative non-being as an aspect of finitude, Augustine specifies it as the *condition* but not the *cause* of sin (i.e., the "causes" are pride and unbelief). Because he refuses to identify *das Nichtige* with finitude, Barth, on the contrary, identifies it with sin as the ground of sin's dominion over man (cf. ibid., p. 305).

62. Ibid. pp. 304, 351–54.

63. Ibid., pp. 292, 296, 349. One question that arises for this reader from Barth's discussion is, if all in history is dominated by evil and so by the presence of *das Nichtige*, and *das Nichtige* in its dominion over the creature's will is *contrary* to the divine will, then how can it also be true that all that the creature does is "in accord with the sovereign will of God," as Barth insists? In facing this question, Calvin gritted his teeth and insisted that God as sovereign *also* willed the sins the creature willed and thus in the end accomplished his own mysterious purposes. Barth (for all his courage less willing than Calvin to defy ordinary human sensibilities) refuses to do this and thus separates, as most other modern theologians do even more enthusiastically, the evil that is done by men from the "hidden" will of God (cf. ibid., pp. 289–94). By the same token, however, Barth compromises the strength, and the meaning, of his repeated affirmations of the divine sovereignty. The "comprehension" of *das Nichtige* is, in opposition to Calvin, achieved by the incarnation and not by the control or direction of evil *(das Nichtige)* through God's mysterious but omnipotent providence.

64. Ibid., pp. 289–305.

65. It is for this reason that Jürgen Moltmann and Wolfhart Pannenberg, in constructing their quite new view of history and its meaning, consistently debate with both Barth and Bultmann as equally representative of the view which they wish to counter. For example, cf. Moltmann, *Theology of Hope*, pp. 50–69, 182–90; and Pannenberg, ed., *Revelation as History*, Introduction and chap. 4.

66. Cf. Rudolf Bultmann, "New Testament and Mythology," in *Kerygma and Myth;* "The Problem of Hermeneutics," in *Essays Philosophical and Theological.*

67. Bultmann, *History and Eschatology*, p. 120.

68. Ibid., pp. 135–36. Cf. the radically "individualized" and so (admittedly) "de-historicized" interpretation Bultmann gives to Jesus' own proclamation of the kingdom as "the encounter" of God with individual persons "aloof from the history of nations," in Rudolf Bultmann, *Theology of the New Testament,* 1:25.

69. *History and Eschatology*, pp. 140–44.

70. Ibid., pp. 42–43, 138–39.

71. Ibid., pp. 149–52; Bultmann, *Theology:* 1:276, 289–90, 300–1, 322–23, 329–40, 378.

72. *History and Eschatology*, pp. 151–53; *Theology* 1:302, 306–8, 319–20.

73. *History and Eschatology*, pp. 154–55.

74. That the views of Barth and Bultmann vis-à-vis the subject of history, probably represent a fair picture of theology generally "between the wars" and shortly thereafter, is difficult to establish without massive reference to many works of many writers. Suffice it to take a few notable examples which illustrate a new sense of dualism between history and God's activity, and the sole locus of that activity in the incarnation, and in personal, "existential" individual life of men and women. Perhaps the most extreme case is that of Nicolas Berdyaev. Here, apparently, God's activity has no relation to the general course of history, and so there is no doctrine of providence: "God is not in the world, i.e, not in its given factuality and its necessity, but in its setting of a task and its freedom." "God is present and acts only in freedom. He is not present nor does He act in necessity." "This world into which we are thrown is not God's world, and in it divine order and divine harmony cannot hold sway. God's world only breaks through into this world, the light of it shines through in that which really exists, in living beings and in their existence. . . . There is nothing of God in the dull and

prosaic normality of the objective world." N. Berdyaev, *The Beginning and the End*, pp. 152–55.

A milder form is evident in the Swedish theologian Gustav Aulen: "God is present only where His love realizes itself as grace and judgment . . . All questions whether God is in the flower or the stones are immaterial to faith" (Gustav Aulen, *The Faith of the Christian Church*, pp. 151–52). And although Aulen speaks of providence and of God's rule, he seems to mean only the continual presence of God's grace, love and judgment in any historical situation (*ibid.*, pp. 190–206). Similarly, Emil Brunner, who wrote extensively on almost every other theological subject, devoted only one chapter to the question of providence, of God's relation to history generally. And there again, the *meaning* of the divine sovereignty that is affirmed is the lordship of God in the life of Christian faith. This is a lordship achieved through God's judgment and his love and responded to in the inner life of repentance, acknowledgement and obedience; and thus a "potential" rather than an "actual" sovereignty in present history, a *claim* to be sovereign, not an active, actual sovereignty. See Emil Brunner, *Dogmatics: The Christian Doctrine of Creation and Redemption*, vol. 3, chap. 6, and pp. 300ff. It is clear that on this issue under discussion modern "neo-Reformation" theology represents a very different position than does the Reformation, an interiorizing and privatizing of the Reformation vision that God rules in his mysterious way the entire course of events both "subjective" and "objective."

Finally, in one of the classical works on the subject of "meaning in history," Karl Löwith enunciates much the same position after a masterful survey of the history of the philosophy of history: "In Christianity the history of salvation is related to the salvation of each single soul, regardless of racial, social, and political status, and the contribution of the nations to the Kingdom of God is measured by the number of the elect, not by any corporate achievement or failure" (Löwith, *Meaning in History*, p. 195; cf. also pp. 184–207). The marked "deviance" of both Tillich and Niebuhr on this issue from the rest of their "neo-orthodox" contemporaries can thus be sensed when one considers that a major portion of the theological concern of both was to comprehend general history and its meaning by the use of the same theological and even Reformation categories which their contemporaries applied only to the private, inner life of men and women.

75. Cf. Norman Perrin, *The Kingdom of God in the Teaching of Jesus*, pp. 16–23.

76. Albert Schweitzer, *The Quest for the Historical Jesus*, esp. chaps. 19 and 20.

77. Cf. Brunner, *Dogmatics*, pp. 171ff., where Brunner clearly rejects the divine determination of events that we call "evil." Cf. Aulen, pp. 192 ff.: "Christian faith does not conceive of everything that happens as the direct expression of the divine will," "God's omnipresence is entirely the active presence of the divine love" (ibid., p. 151). Aulen here does *not* mean that the power and causality of God is characterized by love; he means that only in redemptive love is God omnipresent, a far cry from both Reformers and also from Schleiermacher, for whom omnipresence is the universality of the absolute causality of God (Schleiermacher, sec. 53).

78. Cf., for example, Brunner's rather impressive interpretation of the lordship of God as a lordship of love, i.e, one calling for and fulfilled in a full, acknowledging, committed response of personal decision, a lordship that is fellowship, a *personal encounter* (*Dogmatics*, pp. 299–305, and esp. *The Divine-Human Encounter*, pp. 55–63. "God wills to have a counterpart who in free decision says 'yes' to him . . . God is Lord, He is not causality" (ibid., p. 99).

79. Cf. Aulen, secs. 22 and 23. And from Brunner: "It is not as if God did not have power over sin. He *Himself* reserved this sphere of freedom for man. . . . Man alone is responsible for evil; man carries the full responsibility for sin" (*Divine-Human Encounter*, p. 135).

80. "Real obedience is fully willed obedience . . . for this reason only *the* Lord, who at the same time is voluntary, self-giving love, can find such obedience" (Brunner, *Divine-Human*

Encounter, p. 72). Thus only in the union of freedom in faith and acknowledgement with divine Lordship is the sovereignty of God made "actual."

81. Cf. esp. ibid., chaps. 1 and 2.

82. Ibid., pp. 64–65, 84–89.

83. Barth, III/3, pp. 37–38, 43–44.

84. For example, "Faith also speaks of God acting in His control of nature and history, as creator and ruler. Indeed, faith must so speak. . . . But this knowledge can be expressed only as confession and never as general truth such as a theory of natural science or a philosophy of history. . . . The statement of God's creatorship and dominion has its legitimate ground only in man's existential self-understanding," quoted in J. M. Robinson, "Revelation as Word and History," in Robinson and Cobb, p. 24. Cf. also Bultmann's interesting assertion that in the New Testament there is no *concept* of providence, but only the *belief* "that nothing happens apart from the Will of God," in *Essays Philosophical and Theological*, p. 76. Nevertheless, in his *Theology of the New Testament* Bultmann minimizes even the "Providence" that faith affirms: The world is ruled by demonic powers (1:230), and the trust or confidence in the Christian is wholly in the eschatological event of Christ, and not in the divine sovereignty over history (1:323).

85. Cf. Moltmann's penetrating critique of the inescapable subjectivity of this "personal-existential" concept of revelation and the consequent loss of the categories of promise and of future history, in *Theology of Hope*, p. 46. The same critique vis-à-vis the loss of the ability to speak of history and of providence appeared in the author's "The Concept of Providence in Contemporary Theology."

86. Mention should be made of an excellent "theology" that appeared in 1968, that was based in general terms on the dialectical theology that preceded, and yet expressed an original, stimulating and impressive interrelationship of Christian symbols with history, namely, Gordon D. Kaufman's *Systematic Theology: A Historicist Perspective*. Largely because it appeared in the wrong "kairos"—when concentration and concern was on the problem of the "death and/or the reality of God," and in Europe on the beginnings of the new eschatological theologies to be now discussed—this volume has not had the influence that in our opinion it deserves. Much that is said in that systematic theology about the Christian interpretation of history finds parallel expression in the constructive efforts that will follow this chapter, as our continual references to this book will show.

87. The best history to my knowledge of the context within which this "movement" took its rise is J. M. Robinson, in Robinson and Cobb.

88. Inevitably a description of the essential "anatomy" or fundamental principles of an entire movement of thought such as this will miss many important differences between potent and diverse thinkers, and will, therefore, despite what general accuracy it may have, seem to saddle each individual thinker with emphases he may not himself wish to make. It is hoped, therefore, that this general description is not too unfair and is accurate enough to prepare adequately for our own subsequent discussion.

It should, moreover, be said clearly at the outset that at least one of the major contributors to this movement, Jürgen Moltmann, has—so it seems—substantively altered the concentration on eschatology and the future that characterized his earlier understanding of history, represented in the following description of his part in the movement. In his latest book, which to me is by far his best, *The Crucified God*, a quite new interpretation of God's relation to history appears, one dominated not so much by God's promises concerning the future and by his ultimate eschatological activity *from* the future, but by the participation in continuing history and its suffering of the trinitarian God: the creative and loving Father, the suffering Son, and the regenerating Spirit. This sense of the trinitarian God's *present* participation in the processes of historical development towards history's goal provides, it seems to me, a much firmer base for the political theology with which Moltmann continually rightly is concerned.

We shall refer to it continually in our own reinterpretation of the relation of God to history, for in many respects this new work parallels our own efforts. Meanwhile we shall return to what we regard as the earlier, exclusively "eschatological" view of Moltmann as one powerful voice in the new political and liberationist theologies.

89. Cf. Moltmann, *Theology of Hope*, chap. 1 (esp. pp. 85ff.), chap. 2 (esp. pp. 102ff.); "Theology as Eschatology," in *The Future of Hope*, esp. pp. 42–43; *Religion, Revolution and the Future*, chap. 5; Wolfhart Pannenberg, *Theology and the Kingdom of God*, chap. 2; Rubem Alves, *A Theology of Human Hope*, chap. 1; J. B. Metz, *Theology of the World*, pp. 82ff. The primary target for Catholic negativity is not, of course, existential encounter theology (although Metz has voiced some criticisms of Karl Rahner on this point), but the traditional Catholic supernaturalist interpretation of the eschatological goal and the corresponding concentration of religious energies and action on the health and strength of the church rather than on the health and justice of the world. Cf. Metz, chaps. 1 and 5, and Gustavo Gutierrez, esp. chaps. 5 and 9.

90. The viewpoint that revelation, i.e., God's manifestation of himself, is *indirect*, in and through the events of ordinary history, and not direct, in "existential encounter," is peculiarly characteristic of Pannenberg; see esp. Pannenberg, ed., *Revelation as History*, Introduction and chap. 4. The affirmation that God's redemptive action and the course of general history form *one* history, and the denial of a second, special history unconnected with and irrelevant to ordinary events, a characteristic of much neo-orthodox Heilsgeschichte, appears throughout the school, but is especially emphasized by Gutierrez, chap. 9, and Metz, chap. 1.

91. The insistence that a knowledge of God contained in the gospel leads neither to contemplative union, nor to theoretical understanding of the world, nor yet to personal "self-understanding" but to the transformation of the *world*, runs throughout all these writers. For all of them theology provides the theoretical framework for praxis, for Christian political-social activity directed at a new world in the future: cf. Moltmann, *Theology of Hope*, pp. 84, 326–27; *Religion, Revolution and the Future*, pp. 92–93, 132, 138ff.; Gutierrez, chap. 1; Metz, pp. 94ff.; Alves, pp. 160ff. The relation, therefore, of this view of theology to the instrumentalist and transformative understanding of knowledge in Marx, Dewey and now in Habermas is one of the most interesting aspects of the new movement.

92. Cf. Moltmann, *Theology of Hope*, pp. 16, 41, 164–65; Metz, pp. 87ff.; Pannenberg, *Theology and the Kingdom of God*, pp. 52 ff.

93. For these redefinitions of eschatology as "the moving horizon" of the future, cf. Moltmann, *Theology of Hope*, pp. 106–7, 125, 130, 132, 260–61; for Pannenberg, *Theology and the Kingdom of God*, p. 59. Chap. 1 of this book is the best explanation of Pannenberg's redefinition of eschatology in terms of the consciousness of historical passage into the future, esp. pp. 53–64.

94. Cf. Pannenberg's arguments to this effect, in *Basic Questions*, vol. 1, chaps. 3, 4, and 5; vol. 2, chap. 7.

95. Pannenberg, *Theology and the Kingdom of God*, p. 59. As Pannenberg admits, this conception, crucial to the understanding of eschatology, of God as future effecting the present *from* the future, implies a "reversal of our ordinary understanding of causality" (ibid., pp. 54 and 70). To this interpreter this reversal stems ultimately from Heidegger and from Bloch, for whom possibility determines the character of each present. In these eschatological theologies, however, the possibility of the future has been hypostatized into the *God* of the future who *effects* or *causes* the present from the future, i.e., as an active agent cause—a view quite different from the Heideggerian or Blochian view with which these theologies began. For further examples of this insistence that the future determines or causes the present, cf. ibid., pp. 54, 58–59, 61, 64ff., 69–70. For Moltmann's statement of this theme, cf. *Theology of Hope*, pp. 16, 30, 165; and *Religion, Revolution and the Future*, p. 28.

96. For Pannenberg's language concerning the future "mastering" the present, cf. *Theol-*

ogy and the Kingdom of God, pp. 55–56, 70, 111–12, 134. For Moltmann, cf. *The Future of Hope*, "Theology as Eschatology," pp. 10, 14.

97. This temporal axis is expressed by all, but Moltmann's voice is the clearest: "The eschatological outlook is characteristic of all Christian proclamation, of every Christian existence, and of the whole church. There is, therefore, only one real problem in Christian theology, which its own object forces upon it and which it in turn forces on mankind and on human thought: the problem of the future." "Present and future, experience and hope, stand in contradiction to each other in Christian eschatology, with the result that man is not brought into harmony and agreement with the given situation, but is drawn into a conflict between hope and experience" (*Theology of Hope*, pp. 16 and 18).

98. For Moltmann the resurrection and beyond it *creatio ex nihilo* are the keys or clues to this action of God "from the future" in bringing in the radically new, as Calvary is the clue to the lost character of the present. As the new was not a *possibility* for that past history either in the case of creation or of resurrection, so the eschatological new that is the result of God's action in history is not a possibility for present history; in all of these cases God creates *ex nihilo*, out of nothing, out of the nothing of the past. Cf. *Theology of Hope*, pp. 179–80; also pp. 31, 200–201; *Religion, Revolution and the Future*, chap. 1; and also on this theme, Metz, pp. 91ff. In the "liberationist" theologies of South America, the theological implication of the radical distinction of the sinful present and the divinely promised future leads to the political conclusion (with which this author agrees) that creative political action in *their* context involves a rejection of developmentalism (dependence on the large capitalist powers in present international structures) and the creation of a new political and economic structure of self-reliance—since to develop along the present lines of dependence promises no liberation at all. Cf. Gutierrez, chap. 2, and Alves, chap. 5.

99. A horizontal, temporal tension between the "now" of the present and the "then" of the future clearly provides grounds both for hope and for political activity, as notably a vertical tension between the transcendent, holy God and the relativities of all history did not. However, the former axis carries the implication that the ambiguity of history, characteristic of our present, will vanish with tomorrow's "new"—and that raises the problems of fanaticism and disenchantment. Partly for this reason, Moltmann's present grounding of the identification with the oppressed of the present and work for the overcoming of their suffering in the prior identification of God with them in the suffering of the Crucifixion, seems to provide a sounder basis. Cf. *The Crucified God*, esp. chaps. 6 and 8.

100. Cf., for example, Moltmann, *Theology of Hope*, pp. 31–32, 196–97, 285–87; for Metz, pp. 28ff. and 35; Alves, chap. 1, esp. pp. 15–17.

101. Cf. Alves, chaps. 4 and 5, esp. pp. 107–8; Pannenberg, *Theology and the Kingdom of God*, p. 69. The political significance—and the theological weakness—of this definition of sin as bondage to the past is that there appears then to be no sin involved in the creation of the new in history. Thus are conservative forces alone "sinful" and revolutionary ones apparently "sanctified"—a position in politics and in theology which history hardly substantiates. The one real weakness of Alves' book is its apparent affirmation of this ultimate theological differentiation vis-à-vis sin and salvation between conservative and revolutionary forces, between masters and slaves. The frequent historical lesson that those who once were slaves can become the new masters, and the corresponding theological point that both oppressors and oppressed, conservators of the past and revolutionaries for the future, share the problems of and temptations to sin, are both here forgotten. For this reason Niebuhr wisely sought to distinguish with regard to "guilt" (effectiveness and so responsibility) those "sinners" with *power* (oppressors) and those "sinners" *without* power (oppressed); for the same reason we have sought to distinguish the sin common to us all from the *fatedness* of the oppressed, and the responsibility of powerful groups for that fatedness.

102. Cf. Gutierrez, pp. 28ff.; Alves, chaps. 1 and 4. The dependence of this understanding

of history as the achievement of freedom on Hegel and the other "progressivist" thinkers of the Enlightenment and post-Enlightenment, is clear in Metz, Gutierrez and Alves. Thus the linkage of present liberationist theology with the liberal theologies of the nineteenth century is obvious, even though the rejection of the category of development seems to deny that linkage.

103. Cf. Moltmann, *Theology of Hope*, chap. 5; Pannenberg, *Theology and the Kingdom of God*, chap. 2; Metz, chaps. 3, 5, and 6; Gutierrez, chaps. 7, 9 and 13; Alves, chaps. 5 and 6.

104. Cf. esp. Alves, chaps. 4 and 5. Significant members of the group qualified this identification of political and social liberation with salvation: (1) by affirming a transhistorical salvation in God's eternal life (cf. esp. Pannenberg, *Jesus, God and Man*), and (2) by recognizing the continuation of sin and ambiguity in all of history, however otherwise "liberated" (cf. Moltmann, *Religion, Revolution and the Future*, pp. 77–80, 121, 127). However the general thrust of these theologies is clear: eschatology refers to the historical future where God's reign will be fully manifest, and consequently a society will appear which is the kingdom really present in history. In this sense they represent a historical (as opposed to an individual) "perfectionism" in which the promise of the gospel implies the achievement in history of a sanctified society—although through what combination of human freedom and divine grace that sort of society is to be achieved in the future is not explicated. For the author's further criticism of this point, cf. "Reinhold Niebuhr's Theology of History."

105. Cf. Moltmann, *The Future of Hope*, pp. 2–11; *Theology of Hope*, pp. 28–32, 164–65.

106. Moltmann, ibid.; Pannenberg, *Basic Questions*, vol. 2, chap. 8.

107. Pannenberg, ibid., p. 242; Moltmann, *The Future of Hope*, p. 14; *Theology of Hope*, p. 16.

108. Pannenberg, *Theology and the Kingdom of God*, p. 70; cf. also p. 54.

109. Moltmann, *The Future of Hope*, pp. 2–6, 10; *Theology of Hope*, pp. 16, 28–30, 143; *Religion, Revolution and the Future*, pp. 208–9. For Pannenberg, cf. especially *Basic Questions*, vol. 2, chaps. 7 and 8.

110. Pannenberg, *Basic Questions*, 2:243; Moltmann, *Religion, Revolution and the Future*, chap. 8, "Hope and Confidence," a conversation with Ernst Bloch.

111. Cf. Pannenberg, *Theology and the Kingdom of God*, pp. 55–56, 111; *Basic Questions*, vol. 2, pp. 242–43.

112. Pannenberg, *Theology and the Kingdom of God*, pp. 61–63 and 134.

113. The similarity with Ritschl is both ironic and profound. It is ironic because the eschatological theologies are constructed on the work of Weiss and Schweitzer, who are generally credited with dissolving Ritschlian theology. The similarity is profound because, as in Ritschl, the self-end of God, the special vocation of Jesus (and for Pannenberg his deity as the chosen proclaimer and effector of God's "self-end") and the vocation of the Christian are all centered in the future Kingdom, cf. Pannenberg, *Jesus, God and Man*, pp. 186–97; *Theology and the Kingdom of God*, pp. 74–76.

114. Moltmann, *Theology of Hope*, pp. 85ff. and chap. 3, esp. 202ff.; Pannenberg, *Jesus, God and Man*, chap. 4, pp. 130ff., 183–86, 190–97.

115. Cf. Metz, pp. 21ff.

116. Gutierrez, pp. 251–62.

117. For Alves the history of the world is the history of the process of liberation; this history has been dominated by the divine activity directed at the divine future of full liberation (ibid., pp. 87ff). Since this activity is not alone "from the future," as in Pannenberg and Moltmann (note Alves' critique of this understanding as "unhistorical," ibid., pp. 55–68), but an activity at work in past and in present, we may assume that for him the natural symbol for this activity is that of a providence working in present political movements toward the eschatological end, a view in this respect quite similar to the one to be presented here. Distinguishing his view

from that of Moltmann, for whom "the present does not mediate the future," Alves says, ". . . The future is mediated into history through the present, that the present is where the future is being formed. History is thus the medium in and through which God creates for history, man and Himself, a future that does not yet exist, either actually or formally" (ibid., p. 97).

118. The personal indebtedness of the author to these emphases of the eschatological theologians is very great and should be here expressed. Although this volume is critical of much in their theology, and seeks to reestablish these emphases on other theological foundations, the book as a whole owes much of its inspiration, not only to the radically changing character of the present social situation, but also to the influence of liberation and eschatological theology.

119. For a more extended and so fuller criticism of eschatological theology as described above, cf. the author's articles on Jürgen Moltmann, "The Contribution of Culture to the Reign of God" and "The Universal and Immediate Presence of God"; and for a critique of Pannenberg, cf. the author's review article *"Pannenberg's Basic Questions in Theology."*

120. Moltmann, *Theology of Hope,* p. 16.

121. Cf. Alves' critique of Moltmann for divesting the present of God as thoroughly as had Barth (Alves, p. 61).

122. Cf. *Naming the Whirlwind* for an extended discussion of this point vis-à-vis neo-orthodoxy.

123. Cf. Moltmann, *Future of Hope,* p. 10; cf. also Pannenberg, *Theology and the Kingdom of God,* pp. 55–56, 70, 111–12, 134.

124. "No social order ever disappears before all the productive forces for which there is room in it have been developed, and new higher relations of production never appear before the material conditions of their existence have matured in the womb of the old society "(Karl Marx, "A Contribution to the Critique of Political Economy," in *Karl Marx: Selected Writings,* p. 52; cf. also p. 55). For Bloch, cf. *Philosophy of the Future,* pp. 86–92, 96, 110–11.

125. Cf. Moltmann's wise admission that Christian political action must be broached in relation to the real possibilities present in the present social situation, in *Religion, Revolution and the Future,* pp. 121, 135, 144.

126. The criticism here and in the following remarks directed at the liberation theologies which identify liberation of mankind from various forms of social bondage and oppression with "salvation," and in that sense the eschatological kingdom with a righteous society, is variously indebted, of course, to the running battle of Reinhold Niebuhr against all "liberal" social theory which saw evil as arising solely from unjust social structures and not from the sin latent deep in every human will. These arguments are scattered throughout his works, but esp. in *Nature and Destiny,* vol. 1, chap. 4, vol. 2, chap. 1; and *Faith and History,* chaps. 5 and 8. For a fuller discussion of his understanding of history in relation to contemporary eschatological views of history, cf. the author's "Reinhold Niebuhr's Theology of History."

127. Karl Popper's remark is not irrelevant in this connection: "Whatever classes they [the rulers] may have once belonged to, once they are rulers, they belong to the ruling class" ("Prediction and Prophecy in the Social Sciences," in Gardiner, p. 284).

128. The near identification of the salvation of both individuals in history from sin with freedom from historical oppression is well illustrated in the following: "A new subject emerges in history: the master and the happy slave are no longer the same. The man who was once the object of history, impotent, the suffering slave, becomes now a subject. He is made free to insert his freedom into history in order to build a new tomorrow according to his love and activity. But more than that: the face of the earth can now be changed. It is free to become a new earth, a site of recovery, no longer under the hold of the will to power that made it hostile to man" (Alves, p. 127). Here social freedom is identified exhaustively with uncorrupted "love and creativity," and not with the activity of or even the temptation to renewed sin; and thus when freedom is socially "freed," in effect salvation appears.

129. Niebuhr, *Nature and Destiny*, 2:80.

130. As will be increasingly evident, one aspect of the effort of this volume is to effect a "synthesis," if possible, between the emphasis of the liberation-eschatological theologies on social liberation in history and the neo-orthodox emphasis on the continuity of sin and so the need for justification and reconciliation, a "synthesis" parallel to that projected two and a half decades ago by Reinhold Niebuhr between the Renaissance and the Reformation. Whereas, however, he built his synthesis around the symbols of freedom *(imago Dei)*, sin and atonement, this volume is centered about the symbols of providence as qualified on the one hand by autonomy and on the other by justification. For Niebuhr's synthesis, cf. *Nature and Destiny*, 2:204–12.

CHAPTER 10

1. Cf. chap. 1 of this book for the argument that since men and women are *historical*, and their total being is involved in the social changes in which they are immersed, an authentic religion, and so an authentic theology, must be oriented to history, to the future and to political praxis. In these two chapters we shall defend an interpretation of the scriptures that views Christian faith as also historical in the same sense. Although this volume is not an attempt to trace out the history of "traditions" relevant to this correlation, it is nonetheless our view that the roots in cultural experience of this contemporary self-understanding of man lie in the biblical tradition and the understanding of human being found there.

2. For example, in Werner Georg Kümmel's *The Theology of the New Testament*, there is no mention of providence either in the index or in the text (so far as I could discover), and Bultmann denies that the New Testament has "any knowledge" of the concept of providence *(Essays Philosophical and Theological*, p. 76)—though he recognizes that the "belief" that "nothing happens apart from the will of God" is present in the New Testament.

3. Obvious examples of "sayings" concerning providence are Matt. 6:26–34; 7:10–11; 10:29–31; Luke 12:6–7, 22–36. For the earliest church's assumption of the rule of God over past and present events, cf. Acts, 4:27–30; 14:16–17; 17:24–31; the Magnificat, Luke 1:50–53; and perhaps most important, the continual use of the theme of prophetic promise and fulfillment, esp. in Matt., to interpret the person and role of Jesus, a theme that presupposes the divine rule in general history. (Cf. Norman Perrin, *The New Testament: An Introduction*, p. 173.) For Paul, cf. Rom. 1:19ff.; 8:28; 11:28–32; 13:1–6; 1 Cor. 1:28–29; 3:6–7; 7:17–24; 10:13;11:32;15:3–7; 2 Cor. 1:8–11; 6:18; 9:8–12; Phil. 2:27. And in Deutero-Pauline writings, 2 Thess. 2:11–12; 3:3; Hebrews 11:23–32, 12:7–11. Although the above represent a wide variety of passages dealing with a multitude of stories and subjects, each presupposes the divine rule of events and thus what would be (and in doctrine has been) conceptualized as "providence." One reason this is not a *major* theme in the New Testament is, of course, the widespread conviction that history (the "cosmos") is ruled by demonic powers, now being defeated or about to be defeated by the *new* (eschatological) act of God in Christ: cf. esp. in Paul: 1 Cor. 2:7–9; 2 Cor. 4:4; Gal. 1:4; 4:4, 8. (Also Eph. 6:10–13, Col. 2:8; 2 Thess. 2:5–10.) The ambiguity of the New Testament as a whole on the issue of divine *or* demonic rule of events (cf. Bultmann, *Theology*, 1:230) is well represented by Eph. 2:1–3, where the present is both ruled by "spiritual powers of the air" and *also* under the active judgment of God. For the clear difference with most of the Old Testament on this issue, cf. Josh. 2:11: "For the Lord your God is God in heaven above and on earth below." For a New Testament theology that, in contrast to most contemporary ones, emphasizes the universal (and so past and present as well as future) divine sovereignty over events as a presupposition of the New Testament, cf. Frederick C. Grant, *An Introduction to New Testament Thought*, chap. 6. (All quotations from the Old and New Testaments are drawn from *The New English Bible*.)

4. Thus Kümmel interprets the "providential" sayings of Jesus about God's care as *promises*

("will care") for the eschatological event now coming and to come rather than as statements about the character of God's rule over all time and all space (Kümmel, pp. 40–46). Correspondingly, Bultmann interprets the proclamation of the kingdom, and the "rule" of God so implied as "de-historical" in the sense of implying no relation of divine sovereignty to the external events of nature or of history, but only the "sovereignty" of God over man's inner response and inner authenticity (Bultmann, *Theology*, 1:22–26). For Perrin's agreement with Bultmann on this point, cf. *New Testament*, p. 290. In this emphasis, the modern interpretation of the New Testament is, I believe, right. The activity of God with which most of the New Testament is concerned is the saving, redemptive activity of God in and through Christ, in the church and to come in the future, an activity which enters a world lost in ignorance, sin, fate and death—whether the major weight of that kerygma is placed on the future completion of this "eschatological event" *or* on its past and present reality in Jesus, his death and his resurrection. Thus rightly, providence as the rule of God in history generally recedes much further into the background than in the Old Testament. Cf., for example, even Dan. (2:21–23), "He changes seasons and times; He disposes kings and sets them up; He gives wisdom to the wise and all their store of knowledge to the men who know." Our interpretation of providence, based therefore primarily on the Old Testament, will also seek to include principles by which the New Testament emphasis on demonic rule in the old age, and the eschatological events of the new age, can be interpreted, without denying or ignoring the role of providence (and so the Old Testament understanding of history), or without artificially separating, as Bultmann and Perrin tend to do, "the history of the individual and his experience of reality" (Perrin, ibid., p. 290) from the historical processes in which the individual and his experience of reality arise, occur and act. For Kaufman's agreement with this emphasis on the relation of providence to Heilsgeschichte and eschatology, see his *Systematic Theology:* God here is portrayed as the lord of history (p. 136), shaping and controlling history (p. 216), sustaining its order (p. 238), and through that work in general history preparing for and leading to the eschatological goal (pp. 258, 286).

5. Gerhard von Rad, *Old Testament Theology*, ". . . The Old Testament writings confine themselves to representing Yahveh's relation to Israel and the world in one aspect only, namely as a continuing divine activity in history" (1:106). Cf. also 1:95–96; 2:181–82. Of course this divine activity within Israel's history, witnessed to by Israel's faith, includes more than what is usually included in the symbol of providence, namely, Heilsgeschichte—God's *special* acts in relation to her history—and the "eschatological promises" for the future. But, as we shall seek to show, and as von Rad agrees, both of these latter presuppose and disclose the divine sovereign rule of history generally, namely, providence," i.e., "He governs all that men do" (1 Sam. 2:3).

6. The interpretation of the "how" of God's activity in the history in which Israel participates, as von Rad points out, varied greatly (cf. von Rad, 1:pp. 51–53, 171–75). Beginning with the personal calling, guidance and care of the patriarchical narratives (cf. Gen. 12:1–3; 19:18–22; 30:28–31; 39:2–6, 21–23; 50:18–19), the form changes to the miraculous interventions of the Exodus and the conquest (von Rad, 1:281ff., 301ff.; cf., for example, Ex. 7:20; Josh. 3:9–17; 6:19–21; 10:8–15 and so on). Then (although this pattern is also there in the patriarchal narratives) appears a reflective, nuanced interpretation of the divine rule *through* the "natural" intentions and actions of men and women—a "secular," or better, "theonomous" interpretation of providence in the "succession document" within 1 and 2 Sam. (von Rad, 1:308ff.). Cf. Saul's "sin" and its consequences, David's sin and its consequences, and above all the "natural" (i.e., historical) course of events leading to David and thence to Solomon. Finally, there is the use of other nations (and so explicitly of general history) to "prepare Israel's downfall and begin the new saving event in the future," as witnessed by the prophets and the later historians; cf. von Rad 2:154–55. In this whole varied sequence it is assumed that God is the sovereign lord of general, "secular" history using its movement of

events for his own purposes with Israel, clear and then baffling as they seem to be. And in *all* of this, from beginning to end, Israel's faith is precisely that a divine plan of promise, of judgment, and of merciful care lies behind and controls the central events of her social and political history (cf. ibid., 1:106, 171; 2:162–63). For an "early" example of this pattern of promise (covenant) and judgment followed by mercy and a new beginning, cf. Judges 3:4–10; 6:1–8. It is this theme of promise, covenant or constitution, sustenance, judgment, mercy and new beginning, appearing in various guises throughout the Old Testament, as the "form" of God's providence in Israel's life, that we shall here take to be central to our interpretation of providence. Eichrodt makes much the same point, although his understanding of the Old Testament tends not to emphasize history as much as does von Rad's; cf. Walter Eichrodt, *The Theology of the Old Testament,* 1:235, 286–88.

7. Von Rad, 1:162–65, 172–75. As von Rad intimates, the "sinful" character of general history after Babel necessitates the "hidden" providence of God in general history paralleled with a new form of special, *redemptive* action establishing families, traditions and people, i.e., the covenants with Abraham and with the people of Israel constituting their communal life in a new form. But from beginning to end, the interweaving of general history and special "sacred" history remains as the dominant presupposition—and the ultimate goal. For an example of this interweaving and ultimate unity of the two histories in the patriarchal narratives, cf. Gen. 45:5ff. and 50:20; for a later example, Isa. 42:6; 61:1–9; 66:22–24.

8. Von Rad, 1:164–65, 302; 2:163, 184.

9. Ibid., 2:73–74, 93–95, 152–55, 163ff., 181–82. "Everything stands or falls on the precondition that the prophet claims to know the divine plan which lies behind an actual political event of his time, in this case the Assyrian invasion of Palestine" (p. 163). And of course in the Old Testament itself, the explicit claim is frequently made that Yahweh uses other nations, and so the political events of a given time, to carry out his purposes with Israel, whether of judgment or of redemption: e.g., 2 Chron. 21:16–17; Isa. 5:26; 10:5–19; 13:4–22; 14:24–27, 45:1–7; 46; Ezek. 29; 38:14–39; 7.

10. Von Rad, 1:170–72, 212; 2:162–69, 249–50, 263.

11. Perhaps the universal application and scope of the promises, in both the Old Testament and the New Testament—that through the chosen people *all* peoples will be blessed—makes this analogical universalization of the theme of God's relation to Israel legitimate: Isa. 42:6; 61:1–9; 66:22–24; and Matt. 28:8–20; Mark 16:15–18; Luke 2:29–32; John 10:14–18; 12:32; Acts 11:18; 13:46–48; 15:10–12; Rom. 11:25–32; Gal. 3:26–29; Eph. 2:14–16. In any case, the principle of the analogical use of "special revelation" in order to understand general history—of incarnation, cross and resurrection to interpret "providence"—is a well-established principle. For example, cf. Calvin's use of the cross as an analogical symbol with which to comprehend the meaning of evil, of suffering, and of death in individual Christian life (*Institutes,* bk. III, chaps. 6–10), and Moltmann's use of cross and resurrection, and behind them of *ex nihilo,* in order to understand analogically the "eschatological" activity of God in history, in *Theology of Hope,* esp. pp. 179–94.

12. Von Rad recognizes clearly the problem for both the theologian of the Old Testament and the systematic or constructive theologian of the contemporary fact of "two histories," namely, the "history" in which Yahweh's activity is witnessed to by their faith, and the "history" that modern historical scholarship has reconstructed for the same period, i.e., a history manifesting the ontological elements characteristic of the modern historical consciousness as we have sought to describe that consciousness (von Rad, 1:106–15). One may say that as his task was to interpret and describe the first in relation to the second, so the task of the constructive theologian is to interpret the second in the light of the symbolic contours of the first.

13. For a clear description of this "traditional" view in its severest form, cf. Heppe, chap. 12, esp. pp. 264–80.

14. Cf. Moltmann, "Theology as Eschatology," in Moltmann, *The Future of Hope*, pp. 4ff.; Schubert M. Ogden, *The Reality of God*, chap. 1.

15. Although on the surface there appears to be no conflict or contradiction between an interpretation of events as transpiring because of universal laws and the contingency of those events—for the two concepts have arisen in the same tradition of modern scientific inquiry —nevertheless, as we noted, there is, especially in the dimension of history, at least a paradoxical relation between the two, insofar as contingency implies that the event, before it happened, was not necessary and might not have happened or happened in a different way.

16. Charles Hartshorne, *Reality as Social Process*, p. 96. Cf. also his *Beyond Humanism*, pp. 153ff.; *The Logic of Perfection*, pp. 164ff., 230ff. For the older definition of freedom, characteristic of much traditional theology from Augustine until the modern period, cf. the following from Heppe: "The conception of personally free determination does not require that man should be the first cause of it. It is enough that he is the "second" cause of it at all" (Heppe, pp. 271–72).

17. In the Old Testament there seems to be a bewildering dialectic of apparently opposing themes vis-à-vis the problem of God's ordaining will and man's initiation of evil; one must, therefore, sympathize with the theologian who is by his belief forced to accept propositions on either side as veridical (cf. Calvin's wrestling with this "dialectic," in *Institutes*, bk. II, chap. V). For example, throughout it is assumed that God is unconditionally offended, angry, and so in total *opposition* to man's evil; also he seems to change his mind with regard to how evil shall be dealt with, at first ordaining unrestricted punishment, and then dispensing mercy and rescue when he "hears Israel's distress": for example, Ex. 32:9–14; Judges 2:18 (God "relents"); 3:7–11, 6:1–9, etc.—hardly the action of one who had ordained the evil rebellion. On the other hand, passages asserting God's ordination of "evil" intentions and acts also abound: God repeatedly hardens Pharaoh's heart, Ex. 7:3; 9:12; 10:20, 27; 11:9–10; 14:15–18 (cf. von Rad, 2:152ff.). And when he does not *do* it, he "foreknows" it—clearly it is an instrument in his wider purposes, as Calvin would later argue. Cf. also on the ordination of evil, 1 Sam. 16:14; 19:9; 1 Kings 18:37; Isa. 10:45; 29:9–10; Ezek. 20:21–26; Amos 4:6–11. In each case the foreordination of evil is an aspect, a means to the fulfillment of the basic divine plan for history that has been both foreknown and foreordained, a plan that is the central thread of all the significant themes of biblical history: Gen. 12:1–13; 13:14–18; 2 Kings 19:25—all summed up in Isa. 46:9–11: "I am God, and there is no other like Me; I reveal the end from the beginning, from ancient times I reveal what is to be; I say, 'My purpose shall take effect, I will accomplish all that I please' " (cf. von Rad, 2:183–84). Clearly, rule over history in the light of the promise is the referent or object both of Abraham's faith and of all subsequent definitions of "faith." Therefore to separate it (faith in divine sovereignty over history) from the ordination of evil, either in biblical theology or in constructive theology, is a perilous venture, a separation that is hardly *either* simply "biblical" nor surely "traditional." Nevertheless, to ascribe to God's foreknowing or foreordaining providence the evil that men intend and do—be they Hebrews, Egyptians or Malachites—is, I believe, as impossible for us as to adore the "Yahweh" who commands that Israel's enemies be hewed to bits, and not "to leave alive anyone that draws breath" (Josh. 11:14). For examples of the latter, cf. Ex. 17:14; Deut. 7:1–2; Josh. 7:12; 8:25–28; 10:20–21, 28–31, 40–43; 1 Sam. 15:1–3, 28:18; 1 Kings, 19:15–18; 2 Kings 2:24; 10:20–25.

18. Cf. *Naming the Whirlwind*, pt. 2, chaps. 1, 2 and 3; *Religion and the Scientific Future*, chap. 2.

19. The reference is to the radical changes in the interpretation of the divine promise of the "land," and so of the meaning of the covenant, from its earliest patriarchal form (Gen. 12:1–3; 13:14–18, 15) through its "covenantal" Exodus-Deuteronomic form (Ex. 19–20; Deut. 4:15–24; 5; 6; 7; 26), and finally to the form as found in the prophets, esp. Isa., Jer., Ezek. and 2 Isa. For this interpretation of the *changing* covenant concepts in the Old

Testament, cf. von Rad, 1:168–70; 2:161ff., and on the major prophets, chaps. D–F.

20. Tillich, *ST* 3:17ff., 313 ff. Cf. above, chaps. 1 and 3.

21. Augustine, *City of God*, bk. XIX, chap. XXIV.

22. Cf. ibid., bk. XIX, chap. XII: ". . . There is no man who does not wish to be joyful, neither is there anyone who does not wish to have peace. For even they who make war desire nothing but victory—desire, that is to say, to obtain peace with glory. . . . It is, therefore, with the desire for peace that wars are waged, . . . and hence it is obvious that peace is the end sought for by man. . . . No man seeks war by making peace." For agreement in modern sociology on this point, cf. Parsons, "Culture and Social Systems Revisited," pp. 34–36.

23. Cf. von Rad, 1:51–53, 125–26, 314–16. E.g., Gen. 18:13–15, 21:1–3 (though as noted there are here two *non*-miraculous "works" of providence, Gen. 30:29–30); Ex. 13:20–22, 14; Josh. 6:20–21, 10:7–15, etc.

24. Cf. von Rad's discussion of the succession document (1 and 2 Sam.), 1:312–18.

25. As was noted in chap. 2, the social structures of the community, and the symbolic forms that shape them, have a "religious" or sacral dimension—a point recognized of course by the tradition of Durkheim, Bellah, Berger and so on, and elaborated by Tillich. That this is *also* found—in the form to be sure of a divine ordination or "setting up" of Israel's social and political structures—as a central work in history of Yahweh (as well as in all traditional religions) is evident not only from the divine origins of Israel as a people and of her laws and customs through the covenantal law, but even more for the strange history of the "judges" that Yahweh gave to Israel, and the stranger history of the kingship and of Yahweh's own "ambiguous" attitude to it (reflecting, of course, different attitudes and traditions towards kingship; cf. von Rad, 1:39–48 and chap. C)—but in the end he "set it up": cf. Judges 2:16; 1 Sam. 3:10–11; 8:7–10, 20–22; 9:15–18; 10:1–2; 2 Sam. 5:1–5, 7:5–16; 1 Kings 1:29–32; 3:10–15, 28. Thus is one aspect of the work of providence the "constitution" of social forms, of a social dwelling place for communal humanity, as well as of their judgment, renewal and replacement by other forms, a point echoed in the New Testament in Rom. 13:1.

26. Among innumerable examples, cf. esp. Micah 3:8–12; Jer. 4; 5; Ezek. 7:1–9; Joel 1:13–2:6.

27. Von Rad, 2:54–55, 112–19, 297–300. For this "look" toward the *future* saving acts of God, quite different from his past acts of redemption, cf. Isa. 2:1–11; 9:2–7; 14:1–2; 25:6–12; 29:18–21; 32:1–8; 35:1–10; Jer. 3:14–18, 30, 31 (esp. vv. 31–34), 32–33; Ezek. 11:17–21; 20:42–44; 34; 35; 36:22–36; Hosea 2:18–23; Joel 2:28–32; Isa. 40; 54:6–10; 55; 61–62; 65:16–25. However, as we noted, this theme of *new* possibility beyond the older covenant and its betrayal by Israel, is found in germ in the histories, e.g., Judges 2:10–16; 3:5–10; 6:1–10; and esp. 10:11–18, when Yahweh declares he will "deliver them no more"—and then proceeds to do so.

28. Ibid., 2:57–63, 76–79.

29. Cf. *Naming the Whirlwind*, pt. 2, chaps. 2 and 3; *Religion and the Scientific Future*, chap. 2.

30. The active relatedness of God to the changing events of history is, as every biblical and traditional reference we have given to date shows, perhaps the central characteristic of Yahweh, of the "biblical" conception of God. That this conception should have been rendered problematic (to put it mildly) by the philosophical definition of God as changeless being, is, therefore, one of the ironies of Christian theological history; and it is to the credit of the many forms of contemporary theology, in its dialectical, its process and its current eschatological forms, that this "attribute" of God, namely, his essential relatedness to the changing events of history, has now come to the fore.

31. Thus we associate our reflections unequivocally with the "Arminian" tradition of interpretation, holding that human creativity, both for good and for ill, does not reflect the foreordination of God but rather the centered response to events, in judgment, decision and

action, of human beings. This seems to me clearly what the Old Testament accounts of history assumed to be the case, especially when the *judgment* of God on sin (on sins, therefore, that he has not willed) and the "relenting" mercy of God despite the sins are spoken of. To combine this affirmation of creaturely freedom (in this sense) with the divine sovereignty in history is, of course, a massive task; and one on which most theologians have suffered shipwreck. An example of the view we reject is: "God controls the free acts of men as well as unconscious things; he completely determines man's will. . . . Free causes are related to God's Providence not only as being fore-known as future and destined to do this or that, but also as moved, roused and applied by God and ordained for their own acts and results" (Heppe, pp. 169–70; cf. also Luther, *Bondage of the Will*, p. 267). We prefer (1) to understand the divine sovereignty as working *through* a genuine freedom, as, so to speak, "playing it by ear" in history in the light of what men do (cf. God's "relenting," Judges 2:18), and (2) to understand that "space" given to creative creaturely freedom as arising not from the *finitude* of God, as in process thought (God is *not* there the "ground" of the existence or being of entities; on the contrary "creativity" is) but from the self-limitation of God as creative of the being of freedom. Cf. Kaufman's clear agreement with this position: *Systematic Theology*, p. 382.

32. For a fuller treatment of creation, in a different theological epoch, to be sure, but representing a position that I still wish to defend, cf. the author's *Maker of Heaven and Earth*. We here clearly agree with Schleiermacher's dictum that for modern theology the doctrines of creation and of providence can only be distinguished in analysis, not either in our experience or even in their own fullest meaning (Schleiermacher, *The Christian Faith*, sec. 38).

33. The use of the word "creativity" here is, of course, a reference to Whitehead's "category of the ultimate," that ultimate principle of becoming out of which entities arise and so the principle of their reality. As we noted in chap. 4., for Whitehead creativity is radically separated from God as "another factor in the metaphysical situation," God having the sole role of providing possibilities (relevant eternal objects) for the creative flux.

34. There are, in our opinion, severe difficulties in Whitehead's category of creativity unless it is reinterpreted as the divine power of being, as the activity of God as creator and preserver. These difficulties may be put in terms of four theses drawn from Whitehead: (1) Actual entities "are the final real things of which the world is made up" (PR, p. 27). (2) Actual entities lose their subjective immediacy (PR, p. 130), "perish" and become "data" (superjects) affecting the new entity. Thus, having perished, *they* cannot be the ground or "reason" for the rising or arising of the new entity out of themselves as "data." (3) Thus creativity, not actual entities (even as superjects) is the "principle of conjunction," or of "transition" (PR, p. 322); the principle "by which the many . . . become the one actual occasion," "creating a novel entity other than the entities given in disjunction" (PR, pp. 31–32). (4) But according to (1) above, creativity is an "abstraction," a "universal of universals" characteristic of actual entities. Thus according to the ontological principle (category of explanation, xviii, PR, p. 36), *it* cannot be a "reason," even a reason for "transition," for "actual entities are the only reasons." Therefore, only the "actual entity God" can be that reason, i.e., can be the "ground" for what Whitehead terms creativity.

35. As we noted in chap. 7, Augustine expressed very powerfully the awareness of the passingness of all things in time. Whitehead shares this intuition about becoming and so time as a "perpetual perishing": "Completion is the perishing of immediacy: it never really is" (PR, p. 130); consequently he identified *perishing*, "that the past fades," or, as we have put it, the non-being involved in process, as the "ultimate evil in the temporal world" and the major problem for religion (PR, p. 516).

36. Cf. chap. 7. "The power of the Creator and His omnipotent and all-swaying strength is for each and every creature the cause of its continuing existence" (*De Gen. ad Litt.*, in Przywara, p. 117). Cf. also Luther's view that God "works all in all," "hurrying each creature on to the next moment," in *Bondage of the Will*, p. 203.

37. Cf. *On the Trinity*, bk. III, chaps. IV–IX. References can also be made to Thomas's Third Argument for the Existence of God; i.e., as the necessary ground for the continuing of the contingent creature over time, as expressing the same theme of the necessity of the *transcendence* of the *ground* of passage over passage and perishing; see *Summa Theologica*, I, Q. 2, Article 3.

38. Cf. Heppe, pp. 256–57; Barth, *Church Dogmatics*, III/3, p. 58. In chap. 12 below, this understanding of God as the necessary ground of the actuality of the present in its inheritance from the past is further expanded into a view of God as also the necessary ground of the self-actualization of the present.

39. "From which it follows, by relentless logic, that all we do, however it may appear to us to be done mutably and contingently, is in reality done necessarily and immutably in respect of God's will" (Luther, p. 80). Cf. Heppe, pp. 269–74.

40. The important category of "political self-consciousness," like all important political categories, has a reference both backwards to the past and forward into the future. Its past referent is (1) an understanding, through theory, of the structures of the socially given, destiny, which oppress and alienate men and women, and the real status of those persons within that structure as oppressed. (2) The fundamental symbols expressive of human social authenticity which are denied or abrogated by present reality: freedom, equality, dignity, meaning, autonomy, or as we put it, being, meaning and community. But it also has reference on the basis of that given structure and those symbols to *new* interpretations of the fundamental symbols creative of social health into new forms of economic, political and social associations. And it is these new possibilities that generate political eros, political policy, and so in the end creative political action. For the importance of new possibilities in order that man *not* be merely subject to the "fate" of irrational events, cf. Karl Mannheim, chap. 4, esp. pp. 222–36. Cf. also Tillich, "The Political Meaning of Utopia," in *Political Expectation;* Guttierez, pp. 232–39; Habermas, *Toward a Rational Society*, chaps. 4–6. Thus, as we have noted, both the constitution of past and present reality and the reconstitution of new possibilities are characteristic (1) of creative social existence, and (2) by implication, therefore, of providence. We have already found that this in fact is the Old Testament view of what God has done in Israel's history.

41. Cf. Arnold Toynbee's interesting analysis of the "breakdown" of civilizations because of the tendency of dominant groups, once having creatively established new possibilities for their culture, to "rest on their oars" and thus merely preserve the privileges once earned by their creative dealing with destiny, in Arnold J. Toynbee, *A Study of History*, IV, C, III (c) "The Nemesis of Creativity," 2, pp. 261–512. It is also relevant to note that Toynbee's basic "structure" explanatory of the rise of civilization, namely, "challenge and response," is close to our own categories of "destiny and freedom"; cf, ibid., vol. I, pp. 211–339, and vol. II, pp. 1–385. Cf. also Mannheim's interesting analysis of the deadening loss of utopian transcendence in liberal culture, and Habermas, *Toward a Rational Society*.

42. The indebtedness of this view of history as at special moments characterized by new possibilities, growing out of and yet different from the old that is now self-destructive, is—as will become increasingly clear—deeply dependent on Tillich's interpretation of history in terms of the category of kairos as well as on Whitehead and Bloch. In Tillich's interpretation, historical time is *qualitative* in character, manifesting out of the given destiny of an epoch new possibilities for authentic social and individual existence, possibilities that arise out of that destiny, are situated in it and relevant to it, and yet "break it open" into new forms that contain a renewed "theonomous" relation to the creative ground of being. "Kairos is the fulfilled moment of time in which the present and the future, the holy that is given and the holy that is demanded meet, and from whose concrete tensions the new creation proceeds in which sacred import is realized in necessary form" (*Political Expectation*, p. 61). Tillich himself felt deeply in the Twenties that such a kairos for religious socialism was at hand, arising out of the nemesis of bourgeois culture; later he stated that such possibilities had not

in fact been there, and that therefore we lived in a period of "waiting" for an as yet hidden kairos. For this interpretation of history in terms of kairos, see *Interpretation of History*, pt. 2, chap. 2; *Protestant Era*, chaps. 1 and 3; *Religious Situation*, Introduction; *Political Expectation*, "Religious Socialism" and "Basic Principles of Religious Socialism"; and *ST* 3:369–74.

43. As will be noted, this interpretation represents a "temporalizing" or "processizing" of Augustine's conception that it is through participation in the divine Logos that all truth is known, cf. *On the Teacher*, chap. XI. Cf. also my *Religion and the Scientific Future*, chap. 2.

44. One of the deepest puzzles in Whitehead's thought for this observer is the basis for our knowledge, yes, even our certainty, that God's "subjective aim," as the primary determinant of the character and direction of the process as a whole, is toward value, toward an increase in intensity of experience. Whitehead clearly assumes that it is (cf. PR, pp. 160–61) and yet gives few reasons for holding it—except that "all entities" have such an essential aim (categorial obligation, viii, PR, p. 41), and that process empirically clearly seemed to him to move in that general progressive direction. One can only conjecture that this certainty that "process moves towards increasing value" was such an unquestioned presupposition of his age that he never worried about it. In our own quite different age, when the face of present and future events appears much more menacing, the direction of process much more ambiguous, and so "God" at best deeply veiled, this question, "Is there a purpose behind it all, and if so, is it toward *value?*" is a much more searing question, and one not easily answered by a survey of past and present historical events, which seem at best to "veil" God, to reveal death as well as life, sin as well as grace, meaninglessness as well as value.

45. "For even if fate were from the stars, the Maker of the stars could not be subject to their destiny. Moreover, not only Christ had not what thou callest fate, but not hast thou, or I, or he there, or any other human being whatsoever" (Augustine, *Tractates on the Gospel of St. John*, Tractate VIII, 10).

46. Most of modern reflection, confident that human freedom contained no inherently self-destructive elements, apprehended providence as "fate," i.e., as a *threat* to freedom in history, as our discussion in chap. 8 showed; contrariwise, both Augustine and Calvin (chap. 7), equally certain that freedom, however creative, contained a self-destructive principle within its exercise, distinguished radically fate as a threat to freedom from providence as the ground of a renewed freedom. For Kaufman's agreement that providence is the ground not the denial of confidence in freedom in history, and so in progress of any conceivable sort, cf. his *Systematic Theology*, p. 285.

47. Tillich, *ST* 1:182ff.

48. Cf. Heidegger, secs. 29, 58, 68. The same view, that possibility, and so authentic freedom, arise only from an appropriation of and union with one's destiny or past, is clearly expressed in Whitehead's doctrine that conceptual prehensions, and so all novelty and possibility, arise out of and in strict and close relation to, physical prehensions of the past (cf. categorial obligations, iv., v, vi, PR, pp. 39–40 and pt. 3, chap. 2).

49. Cf. Tillich's analysis of the loss of freedom in its separation from its destiny; then destiny becomes an externally necessitating fate, and freedom becomes the fatedness of arbitrariness: *ST* 2:62ff.

50. It is, of course, of the essence of the concept of karma that all destiny in existence—and all events are in that view *explained* by destiny—is in turn created by freedom, by the accumulated "free" acts of one's infinite past. Thus, paradoxically, in a system where almost all events are in any one moment determined by past destiny, by karma, the whole is, as in no other system, ultimately determined by freedom. That there is in existence a "given" *not* created by our own past acts of freedom—but by creation, by providence, and by all manner of other "secondary causes"—is one point where the Hebrew and Christian traditions differ markedly from those traditions in which karma is the guiding category of explanation of

historical events. It is this implication of karma—namely, that past acts of "my own" *freedom* in another existence rather than past "historical causes" ultimately account alike for the *events* and the *character* of present social and historical existence, and not so much that it is a "mythological" concept—that has rendered the category of karma problematic for many modern Buddhists.

51. Cf. Levinas, *Totalité et Infinité*, for an impressive contemporary expression of this view of "personness" as arising in relation to the "other"; and also Tillich, *ST* 3:39–41, for agreement that "personal life emerges in the encounter of person with person and in no other way."

52. The three most important (to my mind) modern interpretations of this category are: (1) Niebuhr's *Nature and Destiny*, vol. 1, chaps. 6, 7, and 8; (2) Tillich's *ST* 2:29–78; and (3) Paul Ricoeur's *The Symbolism of Evil*, pt. 1, chap. 2; pt. 2, chaps. 3 and 5. For the author's reflection on this symbol, cf. *Maker of Heaven and Earth*, chap. 8, and *Shantung Compound*, chaps. 5–8 and 14.

53. Niebuhr, *Nature and Destiny* vol. 1, chap. 6; Tillich, *ST* 2:29–44.

54. This is similar in words but not in content to the "orthodox" tradition. In the latter, all evil, even death, arose because of sin, i.e., because of the historical Fall: Calvin, *Institutes*, bk. II, chaps. I, II and III; Heppe, pp. 367ff.

55. Tillich, *ST* 2:38.

56. Schleiermacher, secs. 59 and 60 on "The Original Perfection of the World" and "The Original Perfection of Man"; Tillich, *ST* 1:266ff., on "The Meaning of Providence."

57. We are enunciating here, possibly in a new form, the "liberal" concepts that sin is historical in form and thus helps to shape, and so to distort, the social structures of history into oppressive and destructive structures, what Rauschenbusch called "the kingdom of sin" (*Theology for the Social Gospel*, chaps. 7–9). This concept of the relation of sin to the historical situation and so to the social structures in which men and women live was first expressed in theology (so far as I know) by Schleiermacher (sec. 71, p. 288, sec. 76), and became the presupposition of the social gospel's effort to deal with "sin" by dealing politically with warped social structures. This conception of the interrelation of sin with social structures continued in the great "neo-orthodox" interpretations of society by Niebuhr and Tillich, and in its own way reappears in the liberationist theologies of the present. Equally clearly this interrelation of sin with warped historical and social structures (what we have called destiny and fate) in turn depends on the modern historical consciousness insofar as the latter has understood the social structures of history to be created (in part) by human freedom (and so by sin) rather than "given" by God as "orders of creation." Thus does the call to eradicate unjust social orders depend in turn on the beliefs that men and women, and so in this case sinful men and women, and not God have created these social orders. For a similar view that the *imago Dei* implies—even "means"—the culture and so the history creating capacity of men and women, and thus that the "fall" into sin implies the warping of the social and historical institutions created by men and women, cf. Kaufman, *Systematic Theology*, pp. 33ff., 368ff.

58. For this interpretation of sin as a relation of our freedom to the "open" future and thus to new possibilities as well as to old actualities, cf. Niebuhr, *Nature and Destiny*, 1:181–86.

59. This theme of creativity under providence, and then endless betrayal, is, as noted, a recurrent one in the Old Testament. It dominates the stories in Judges: new institutions were "set up" (Judges 2:16), and then repeatedly, "the Israelites did what was wrong in the eyes of the Lord" (3:7; 6:1; 10:6, etc.); and it dominates—not in toto but largely—the stories of the kings in 2 Kings 11–16 and 2 Chron. 10–36 (cf. von Rad, 1:334–54).

60. Cf. Niebuhr's analysis of sin as idolatry, the pride of power, of wisdom and of goodness which elevate man's finite accomplishments to a sacred status: *Nature and Destiny* vol. 1,

chaps. 7, 8, and Tillich's description of *hubris* as the self-elevation of creative man into the sphere of the divine in *ST* 2:50ff.

61. For example, Isa. 2:12–17; 10:12–14; 13:11–14:21; 16:6–7; Ezek. 22:6–16; 28:1–10; 29:1–7; 31:10–18.

62. Luke 1:51–53; 6:20–26; 1 Cor. 1:18–31, 59. "Man's proud eyes shall be humbled, the loftiness of men brought low, and the Lord alone shall be exalted on that day. For the Lord has a day of doom waiting for all that is proud and lofty, for all that is high and lifted up, for all the cedars of Lebanon, lofty and high" (Isa. 2:11–13). Cf. Niebuhr's ingenious distinction between the "sin" common to all men and women, and the "guilt" (responsibility for dire consequences on others) which in the "mighty" is greater in *Nature and Destiny*, vol. 1, chap. 8.

63. For example, in the present ecological and food crises, it is the "weak" and the "powerless" that more than the affluent threaten to overpopulate the earth; and thus are they "blamed" for the impending shortages of food and resources. In actuality, however, it is the affluent who have overconsumed and whose greed has endangered our future by beginning to strip the earth. There is no question where the greater actual responsibility for the problem lies, and so the greatest grounds for judgment and repentance. Cf. the very powerful analysis of estrangement as concupiscence in Tillich, *ST* 2:51–62: concupiscence is the "unlimited desire to draw the whole of reality into oneself" (ibid., p. 52). This analysis provides, I believe, the most helpful framework for dealing theologically with the crisis of technology: it is concupiscence more even than pride that has brought about the "fated" character of technology in modern life and that threatens to destroy us all. Thus in a new (sociohistorical) form does the old centering of sin on concupiscence, long thought irrelevant by a sexually tolerant modernity, again achieve frightening relevance.

64. Von Rad, 1:263–70, 272–80. Cf., for example, Josh. 7:23–26; 22:16–19. On this issue of sin as "defilement" or "stain," cf. Ricoeur, chap. 1.

65. Von Rad, 2:73–74. Cf. in a later form Ezek. 18:1–20; 33:18–20.

66. Von Rad, 2:143–44. Cf. for example, Hosea 5:14; 13:4–8; Isa. 8:12–14; Ezek. 22:13–16.

67. Von Rad, 2:184–87. Cf. Isa. 3:1–5, Jer. 3:12–18, 7:4–11; 8:7–17; 11:1–14, 30–31; Ezek. 7:1–19; 9:4–11; 12:1–6; Micah 3:8–12.

68. The universality of this judgment, encompassing not only men and women but also the destruction of *all* that had been created and established, is well illustrated in Isa.: "Because, the Lord will empty the earth, split it open and turn it upside down, and scatter its inhabitants. Then it will be the same for priest and people, the same for master and slave, mistress and slavegirl, seller and buyer, borrower and lender, debtor and creditor" (24:1–3). Here is *real* nemesis, the breakdown of religion and culture alike, a destruction that uproots all social roles, all security, all ranks—and threatens all life. The sense of the universality and depth of warping and corruption—of "sin"—is the presupposition for the universality and completeness of this impending judgment. Cf. also Isa. 34 and Jer. 4:23–28, where judgment is seen as a return to primal chaos, a counter-move to God's creation.

69. Each of the prophets unfolds the tragic irony of the tender care of Yahweh's sustenance, responded to with ungrateful rebellion, until a sovereign judgment is evoked—and ultimately an act of grace. Cf. von Rad, 2:180–82. On sustenance and care, cf. Amos 4:6–11, Isa. 5:1–9; Hosea 11:1ff. This theme, often termed "the prophetic interpretation of history," also dominates the histories, cf. 1 Kings 13:1–5; 15:1–7; 17:18–23; 2 Chron. 21:12–20, etc.

70. Von Rad, 2:184–87. Cf. Isa. 60; 65; 66; Jer. 3:14–18; Jer. 31–32; Ezek. 11:17–21; 36:22–32; 37:21–28; Hosea 2:18–23; Joel 2:28–32. As has been noted, this theme of undeserved grace after sin and judgment is also found in "rudimentary" form in Judges 3:7–11; 6:1–9; 10:11–16. In other words, the "unmerited" character of the covenant with Abraham and at Sinai, and so the character of "God's grace" in restoring and fulfilling it (cf. Deut. 7–9), itself becomes a theme that is retrieved and reinterpreted in the light of Israel's

subsequent sins, as the basis for Yahweh's continuing care of her in new situations and finally for his promise for a completely new covenant.

71. Bloch, *Man on His Own,* pp. 206–07; Cf. von Rad, 2:199, and Jer. 18:1–12. As von Rad points out, the capacity of Yahweh to show mercy and so to refrain from judgment, if repentance is forthcoming—and often, as above, even if it is not—shows the "freedom" of Yahweh in dealing with the unexpected and the contingent in history, or, as we have suggested, that he "played history by ear," and not by prearranged foreordination.

72. As noted, there is a precedence in Calvin—and in others—for this use of "analogy" from God's special activity with Israel and with Christ in order to interpret life and historical events generally. For Calvin the character of the life, death and resurrection of Jesus is not a pattern illuminative only of the incarnation. It is also a pattern illuminative of God's wider intentions and activity in history generally. It is, therefore, a clue, *the* clue in fact, to the hidden work of providence. Through the analogy of the Christ, Calvin argues, we can understand the meaning of *our* history, of our destiny, our suffering and our hope (*Institutes,* bk. II, chap. XV; bk. III, chaps. VII, VIII, IX and X). And we may recall Markus's fascinating interpretation of Augustine's view of general or "secular" history in relation to "special" or sacred history. For Augustine (as we noted), the presence of God's power and intention is central to both histories, as is the activity of men and women; the difference lies in the revelatory power of the "sacred" history to uncover the mystery of the hidden work of God generally or in ordinary history. Thus does sacred history provide a hermeneutical principle with which to interpret the general character of events, Markus, *Saeculum: History and Theology,* pp. 11ff., 158.

73. The view that sin, the past and accumulated sins of a community, is the ultimate cause of destruction and nemesis in history is, as we have seen, fundamental to the Old Testament view of history. It also dominated Niebuhr's analysis of our own present and future troubles. From an early work: "Oligarchies and social systems are actuated by the will-to-survive in narrow and unimaginative terms. They cannot see that the will-to-survive, when it has grown fearful and frantic, is transmuted into a desperate and futile will-to-power, and that the will to power finally makes survival impossible because it arouses the antagonism of all who suffer from its injustice" (*Reflections* p. 34; cf. also pp. 6, 18, 87, 139).

74. Von Rad, 2:129–30.

75. It is the author's personal view that this represents our "situation" at the present: a vast social disarray, of the irrelevant because anachronistic character of many of our social institutions and the symbolic forms that structure them, and yet of the continuing possibility of the "retrieval" of those institutions and forms provided there is a genuinely *new* reinterpretation of them (cf. chap. 1). However, I recognize that this is not the situation everywhere, and that in other places (e.g., South America, Asia and Africa), a quite new set of forms and of institutions, radically new possibilities, may be what that situation (kairos) requires.

76. Augustine, *On the Grace of Christ and On Original Sin,* bk. II, Chaps. XXVIII–XXXI.

77. Gutierrez rightly emphasizes the unity of general history (as the search for freedom) with saving history represented by the biblical and the ecclesiastical witness: "Rather there is only one human destiny, universally assumed by Christ, the Lord of History. His redemptive work embraces all the dimensions of existence and brings them to their fullness. The history of salvation is the very heart of human history" (Gutierrez, p. 153). Cf. Kaufman's agreement that sacred and profane history make "one" history: (1) The providential ordering of general history is the preparation for *Heilsgeschichte* (Kaufman, pp. 282–85, and (2) the purpose and goal of "sacred" history is the transformation of general history (*ibid.,* pp. 402 and 457).

78. Much of what is said in the following, as the symbols of the New Being or the New Human Reality indicate, is owed to the christology of Tillich, *ST,* vol. 2, pt. 3, chap. 2. It is also indebted, as will be evident, to Moltmann's powerful interpretation of the incarnation, atonement and the trinity in *The Crucified God,* which emphasizes the same symbolic

structure, namely the "new reality" that appears in the Christ (ibid., pp. 274–79, and chaps. 7 and 8). Kaufman, in his own way, stresses that the central meaning of the incarnation is the appearance of a new reality which overcomes estrangement and thus, as representing a new "stage" in history and a "new force" there, makes possible the advancement of "freedom" in historical existence (ibid., pp. 383–84, 402–7.

79. This phrase affirms our qualified agreement with the contemporary emphasis on the eschatological element of the New Testament as defining "God's time": this new eschatological time "of God" appears with Jesus and his proclamation and will be fulfilled in the future kingdom. Thus is eschatology partly realized through the reality of Jesus' proclamation, and partly still to come, cf. Ernst Fuchs, "On the Task of Christian Theology," in R. W. Funk, ed., *Journal for Theology and the Church, #6: Apocalypticism*, pp. 83, 91–92; cf. also Ernst Käseman, in Funk, pp. 116–17. The same emphasis on "God's time" as appearing for the first time in Jesus is found also in Kümmel, pp. 32–54, 141–50, and in Perrin, *New Testament*, chaps. 7–9; *Kingdom of God*, chaps. 4, 5, 7, 10; Bultmann, *Theology*, 1:4–26, 37–53 and chap. 5. As we have indicated, we do not agree that "God's time" entirely *begins* with the appearance of Christ, with this "eschatological event," as if there had been no providential sovereignty of any sort in history nor any preparation in history for that event. Such would be a "temporalistic" Marcionism that would reject the entire Old Testament message about history, as we have tried to show, and by rejecting providence would subvert most of the other important symbols, including those of the incarnation and of eschatology. However, that a "new time"—or a new mode of the divine activity in time—is uncovered and manifested in the appearance of the Christ, I do agree, a new qualitative character to the relation of God to mankind and so a new age in history, an age that is preparatory to the end-time. (Cf. Kaufman, pp. 283ff., 383ff., 402ff., 457ff.)

80. Reference can be made to Augustine's interpretation of social history (not to mention Plato's in *The Republic*) as determined fundamentally by inner history. A community is characterized by the mode of its deepest "love," a love that in history is distorted by sin into self-love; and the warping of its institutions and so the events of its "outer" history are due to that *inner* disarrangement. Sin is inward, but it has objective, historical results. That this is also the Old Testament view we have amply documented. For Tillich's agreement that cultural creativity, as well as cultural estrangement and destruction, arise from the inward life of man, cf. his analysis of culture as the "self-creativity of life under the dimension of spirit" (*ST* 3:57 ff.).

81. It was to emphasize this unity of creation, providence and redemption that Schleiermacher spoke of the "one divine creative act," and the "single decree uniting creation, providence and redemption"; cf. Schleiermacher, secs. 43, 100, 109, 120. This theme reappears in Tillich's emphasis on Jesus as the Christ as essential manhood under the conditions of existence, the New Being which is therefore the fulfillment and realization of essential finite human being, not a totally new history but the completion and fulfillment of the old (*ST* 2:118–25; 3:138–62, 245–82, 362–74). We have already noted Kaufman's agreement that incarnation discloses and provisionally completes the creative and providential work of God in and through history, a work designed to realize the historicity of man as free within history. (Kaufman, pp. 382–407, 457ff.). Appeal for this tradition could be made, of course, also to Irenaeus' use of the symbol of recapitulation and so of the restoration of the likeness of God lost in Adam (Irenaeus, *Against Heresies*, bk. V, chaps. II, XIX–XX) and beyond that to the recurrent New Testament symbol of Christ as the second Adam or the true humanum (Rom. 5:12–21; 1 Cor. 15:45–58; Eph. 2:11–16).

82. Cf. Niebuhr's perceptive interpretation of the "impasse" of the Messianic and the prophetic interpretations of history, without the promise of the new inward covenant, in *Nature and Destiny*, vol. 2, chap. 1.

83. It is, I believe, from the vantage point of the "new reconciling forces": of promise,

covenant, new covenant and New Being, that the deeper structure of historical passage can be seen; in this sense a hermeneutic of history, as providential possibility, judgment and grace, is itself a "hermeneutic of grace": of covenant and of new covenant. To be sure, both creativity and nemesis as characteristic of history's movement can be understood as a result of any general survey of history. But their relation to providential possibility, to divine judgment and to new possibilities of grace, are there *not* seen, and the dimension of ultimacy involved inescapably in the experience of history either recedes into the experience of fate and so into despair, or to an idolatry that takes the parochial forms of tribal, communal and national life as exemplifying the ultimate. If, therefore, this interpretation of history seems to "make sense" of the apparent contradictions of historical experience and to encompass both the tragic and the hopeful elements of history, then that "wisdom" is due more to the illumination granted in and through these reconciling forces than to a survey of history generally.

84. Note that a *criterion* of the reconciling and healing work of God is *not* identical with nor does it imply an *exclusive locus* of such work, i.e., that only in Christ is God's redemptive grace at work. A criterion implies that a "hidden" redemption is at work universally, manifested in all religions and in all creative elements of culture, and that it is only with regard to the deeper character, intent and goal of that work that a uniqueness is claimed, not with regard to the universal presence of grace or to its efficacy. The radical self-negating character of such a criterion, to be a *valid* criterion, is illustrated in Tillich's interpretation of the incarnation and the atonement: it is in sacrificing himself as a medium of grace, that Jesus is the Christ, i.e., the final (criteriological) manifestation of the New Being. Thus is there here, despite the centering of religion's ultimate concern on one historical event, maintained an affirmation of the universality of grace and at the same time a critical principle (the Protestant principle) with regard to this special tradition itself; see his *ST* 1:132–47; 2:120–35.

85. The author must freely admit—what will be evident to many readers—that in these few pages no fully conceived, worked out, or adequately documented christology is presented. The present volume is on history and providence, and so its efforts both in research and in symbolic systematization—such as they are—have been concentrated on those two themes. Insofar as neither can be understood without christology, christology appears—but in markedly inadequate form. Many alternative views are here omitted; many problems not thought through; many difficulties not yet faced. Hopefully a more adequate presentation will appear in the future, and one enough in line with what is here sketched out so as not to be embarrassing!

86. That Jesus presents to us the true humanum, the New Being, the authentic possibilities of our universal humanity (cf. Tracy, pp. 204–11), and so the norm as well the possibility of being human, is both important and biblical. With regard to our issue, history, this role as "second Adam" illumines the possibilities, the problems and the goal of history, as we have noted. However, since the fundamental question of human existence, and that to which Christian faith addresses itself, concerns, I believe, the character of God and so of his relation to us, to our social world, to history and so to the future, concentration solely on the "authentic possibilities" of our human existence, as the content of "final revelation," seems to me too limited. The Augustinian theological tradition—not to mention that of Paul—was surely right that to know our own possibilities (the law) is not enough; we must be granted as well a new relationship to the divine favor—both as individuals and as a race—we must know "God in Christ" or that in him "God was reconciling the world to Himself" in order to begin to understand ourselves and our history as authentic, or to have hope for the partial realization of that authenticity through grace. (Cf. Calvin's definition of faith as "the knowledge of the will of God respecting us. . . ." in *Institutes*, bk. III, chap. II, secs. 6–7). Thus balancing the second Adam, the re-presentation of the authentic possibilities of our common

existence, is the role of Christ as "revealer" or perhaps better "medium," to use Tillich's word, presenting as Irenaeus said, not only man in a new light to us and to God, but God in a new light to us, or as Niebuhr puts it: "In this disclosure of the power and will which governs history, both life and history have found their previously partly hidden and partly revealed meaning..." (*Nature and Destiny*, 2:35). It should also be noted that the issue whether Christ reveals *God* decisively and uniquely need not be the same issue as the issue of the *exclusiveness* of salvation in and through Christ; in these pages we try clearly to separate these two issues, and to affirm the first and to deny the second.

87. Cf. chap. 2 for the discrimination in political experience of these three questions.

88. This position is, therefore, in substantial agreement with Tillich that while the New Being is wider than the Christian revelation and community, it is uniquely and decisively manifested there in an unambiguous form so that Christ is the "final" criterion of all other manifestations of the New Being. I also agree that Christ can be viewed as in this sense decisive for *human* history, and thus not necessarily as decisive for all other "possible" creatures on stars (or planets) in God's increasingly infinite cosmos—although of course the same ultimacy of being, truth and love will be incarnate in a different form in these vastly different situations. The possibility of life in other places (cf. Ritschl's surprising recognition of this possibility, p. 615), it seems to me, forces this systematic conclusion unless we are to deny God's equal care for them as he has shown for us—though, as C. S. Lewis suggested, this issue may be moot, since it may be that we alone have "fallen": cf. *Out of the Silent Planet*.

89. "The God who is both powerful and good by reason of being the source of all power, and not some particular power in history, cannot remain good if he becomes a particular power in human society. Perfect goodness in history can be symbolized only by the disavowal of power" (Niebuhr, *Nature and Destiny*, 2:22).

90. Moltmann, *The Crucified God*, pp. 171–87, 195–96, 274–78, 327–29.

91. For Jaspers the "disclosure" of the inward reality of men and women, and their "contrast inwardly with the entire universe" (Jaspers, p. 3) appears during the "Axial" period (ca. 500 B.C., or more generally, between 800–200 B.C.); see ibid., pp. 1–8. On this he is surely right. However, our point is that this "preparation" of a newly discovered inwardness becomes itself clarified and given decisive form in Jesus with regard both to the depths of the problems within ourselves and to the character of our truly human authenticity. Inwardness as the basic principle of the human appears universally before Jesus; there is, therefore, a more universal "covenant with the Greeks" than the Fathers ever guessed. But because of him the form of a repentant and self-transcendent inwardness, and an interpretation of history on this new self-understanding—both shown in Augustine's *Confessions* and in the *City of God*—does not appear.

92. Cf. Augustine for the "misplaced" concentration of humans on escaping their finitude rather than their "sin": "... because men strove more to shun that which they could not shun, viz., the death of the flesh, than the death of the spirit ... the Mediator of life, making it plain that death is not to be feared, which by the condition of necessity cannot be now escaped, but rather ungodliness, which can be guarded against through faith, meets us at the end by which we have come, but not by the way by which we came" (*On the Trinity*, bk. IV, chap. XII). Cf. also Tillich's profound analysis of the structure of despair, not as the presence of non-being in our finitude, as "having to die," but as struggling against this, and then experiencing the utter futility and failure of that struggle, (ST 2:68–70).

CHAPTER 11

1. Reference is here made to the development of inwardness in many philosophies and religions in what Jaspers has called "the Axial period," which, as already noted, (see chap.

10, n. 91) was the explicit beginning or disclosure of the New Being and the preparation for its complete manifestation in Jesus as the Christ.

2. The essence of this hermeneutic, and also of any Christian interpretation of history, is that the events of history, creative and destructive alike, are interpreted finally as correlated with the inner relation of human beings to Yahweh. In the prophetic hermeneutic, if Israel suffers, this is because of her sins; if she is fortunate, this is because of providence and ultimately of "grace," the unmerited care and love of God. As the Old Testament makes plain —and our discussion as well—this fundamental principle of interpretation in terms of the inner relation of the community to God, does not at all abrogate strict attention to "second" causes: to the reality of other communities' intentions and actions, to the presence and effectiveness of trends and continuities in social existence, to the importance of creative political response to particular situations, or to the presence of new possibilities for social existence. The emphasis on the unity of inner and outer in history—seen also in the Platonic interpretation—is thus directly contrary to a "privatizing" of history into individual pietisms; rather, it provides a clue to an interpretation of history that can guard against either total despair or the demonic in response to the otherwise chaotic, irrational and unintelligible characteristics of objective historical events.

3. Thus is "religion" the substance of cultural history, as Tillich would put it; or as Niebuhr stated the same fundamental principle of the interrelation of inner and outer reality and so of individual and community: "The religious dimension of sin is man's rebellion against God, his effort to usurp the place of God. The moral and social dimension of sin is injustice" (*Nature and Destiny*, 1:179). On this general point, we are inclined to be more "Tillichian" and to emphasize what remained only implicit in Niebuhr's thought, namely the role of the relation to ultimacy (to God as the providential presence of Being, Truth and Love), in the *creation* and *constitution* of cultural life, as the "substance of culture," as well as the role of the relation to ultimacy in the sin, injustice and judgment that lead to the nemesis of cultural life.

4. E.g., Judges 2:16–20; 3:7, 12; 4:1; 2 Kings 13:2, 11; 15:9, 18, etc.

5. Cf., for example, from Karl Löwith, "Christians are not an historical people. . . . In Christianity the history of salvation is related to the salvation of each single soul, regardless of racial, social and political status, and the contributions of the nations to the kingdom of God is measured by the number of the elect, not by any corporate achievement or failure. . . . Similarly, the message of the New Testament is not an appeal to historical action but to repentance" (*Meaning in History*, pp. 195–96).

6. The stark antithesis between a "meaningless" history and progress is the way most dialectical theologians posed the issue, and thus in opposition to modern conceptions of progress they defined eschatology as an event or events totally unrelated to objective historical events. And as Löwith admits, "If there is any point where the Greek and Biblical views of history agree with each other, it is in their common freedom from the illusion of progress" (ibid., p. 200). Our effort, therefore, parallels that of the eschatological-political theologies in seeking to find some other mode of interpretation than either this "cyclical" one or that of a cumulative and necessary progress.

7. In his masterly survey of the genesis of the modern mind, J. H. Randall, Jr. quotes the following "recently discovered," "in the steeple nob of the Church of St. Margaret in Gotha, Germany, 1784": "Our age occupies the happiest period of the eighteenth century. Emperors, kings and princes humanely descend from their dreaded heights, despise pomp and splendor, become the fathers, friends, and confidantes of their people. Religion rends its priestly garb and appears in its divine essence. Enlightenment makes great strides. . . . Sectarian hatred and persecution for conscience' sake are vanishing. Love of man and freedom of thought are gaining the supremacy . . . Here you have a faithful description of our times." See J. H. Randall, Jr., *Making of the Modern Mind*, p. 384.

8. Reference may again be made to Heilbroner's interpretation, namely, that it has been primarily science, technology and industrialism that have perpetuated that series of crises: in natural resources, in production, in food distribution, and finally in economic and political developments, that will in the end lead *away from* the "free society" envisioned by the Enlightenment into a new authoritarian one; cf. chap. III above.

9. Niebuhr, *Nature and Destiny*, 2; 155–56, 245–46, 256; *Faith in History*, pp. 94, 123–24, 232–34.

10. One may say that theories of moral progress in history precisely *reversed* the doctrine of original sin against which they revolted, namely, that whereas, as noted, that doctrine viewed freedom as under a "necessitating" or at least "inevitable" destiny towards depravity, progressivist theories saw freedom in history as under a destiny to improve, that as the "given" presented to human self-actualization rose, so did the responding decisions and action of freedom.

11. "There is no progress where individual decision is decisive. This implies that there is no progress in the moral act. . . . The ethical content of moral action has progressed from primitive to mature cultures in terms of refinement and breadth, although the moral act in which the person is created is the same whatever content is actualized. It is in the cultural element within the moral act that progress takes place, not in the moral act itself" (Tillich, *ST* 3:333).

12. Jer. 5:18–24; 6:27–30; 8:4–6; 9:26; Ezek. 2:3.

13. Despite his alleged "pessimism" about history, Reinhold Niebuhr was as fully aware of what he called the "indeterminate possibilities of history" as he was of the inevitable corruption of those possibilities: e.g., *Nature and Destiny*, 2:84–85, 155–56, 190–92, 206–7, 209, 245–46, 256, 284; *Faith and History*, pp. 2, 126, 195, 232.

14. "Where there is history at all there is freedom; where there is freedom there is sin" (Niebuhr, *Nature and Destiny*, 2:80). For much the same view, concerning the continuing "ambiguities of history," cf. Tillich, *ST* 3: 333 ff., 382 ff.

15. Cf. Niebuhr, *Nature and Destiny*, 2:258–58. We may recall here Markus's interesting point that for Augustine, sin introduces a radical "dislocation" into "natural" political life, namely, inordinate self-love on the part of *both* rulers and ruled, and thus the necessity and actuality of *coercion* in political structures. In such a situation, no earthly society, organized by political structures, can embody "love" or incarnate real peace, since coercion tempts to and so leads to injustice and cruelty on the one hand and dissatisfaction and conflict on the other. Thus are "politics of perfection," or any identification of the kingdom with the historical or worldly "city," quite impossible (Markus, *Saeculum: History and Theology*, pp. 92ff.).

16. Cf. Niebuhr, *Nature and Destiny*, 2:20ff., 284.

17. This is, as we have sought to show, the central burden of the Old Testament message about Yahweh. Only by giving to that message an entirely "spiritual," "personalistic" and individual interpretation, an interpretation read back *from* the New Testament, can this concern for history in the Old Testament be ignored—but then one confronts the implications of the coming reign of God and the symbol of the kingdom, which however ultimately transcendent in its character (as is the perfection of individual existence), has as a symbol facets of relevance to man's communal and so social and historical existence. After all the New Testament concept of the kingdom has lineal relation not only with the hope of the Messianic reign but also with the originating *covenant,* constituting and forming Israel's *social* existence. In this respect, Calvin, the liberals, Niebuhr and Tillich and the eschatological political theologians are, it seems to me, correct. Perhaps the most interesting thing about Niebuhr's theology was his attempt to use the heretofore largely personalistic and individualistic symbols of Christian faith, central to the Reformation, namely, those of sin, of atonement, of justification by faith and of the hope of renewal, as principles with which to interpret the

whole course of history; cf. for *Nature and Destiny,* 2:204–12; *Faith and History,* chaps. 9 and 13.

18. Cf. from Niebuhr, "The God who is both powerful and good by reason of being the source of all power, and not one particular power in history, cannot remain good if He becomes a particular power in human society. Perfect goodness in history can be symbolized only by the disavowal of power" (*Nature and Destiny,* 2:22; cf. also p. 72). This is also the implication of Tillich's view of God as not "a being" over against other beings; of his insistence that the demonic appears when some finite medium and so power claims to *be* the divine; thus that the final "medium" is that one which sacrifices itself in powerlessness; and finally that the "sign" of the New Being is its complete participation in our finitude, our weakness and our death: *ST* 1:132–37; 2:118–35. It is also clearly the central theme of Moltmann's extraordinary volume, *The Crucified God* (chap. 5 and esp. chap. 6) in which God the Son's total participation in our finite powerlessness, suffering and death, expressed in both incarnation and cross, is *the* central new element of Christian theology and the central principle of interpretation for all other Christian symbols. Thus in this work Moltmann interprets God's continuing relation to history in trinitarian terms (the suffering of God in the powerlessness of the Son) rather than primarily in eschatological terms, this present participation being seen rather as the *basis* for our eschatological hopes. This theme of the participation of God in Christ in our finitude, suffering and death—in radical powerlessness —is a major one in the Pauline and Deutero-Pauline understanding of the being and the work of Christ: Rom. 5:6, 8:31–39; 1 Cor. 1:18–29; 2 Cor. 5:20–21; Phil. 2:5–11; Heb. 2:14–18.

19. Cf. Moltmann's penetrating statement that an encounter with the problem of evil, and thus with the powerlessness and the negativities represented by the cross, can yield principles for the Christian interpretation of history—and in fact for any interpretation of evil in history in *The Crucified God,* pp. 4–5. As we shall note in the next chapter, it is at this point that the relation of Christian symbolism to the Buddhist symbols of "absolute nothingness" becomes especially fascinating, and also productive for new insights for a Christian theology.

20. Cf. Tillich, *Love, Power and Justice,* chap. 3.

21. We traced in the preceding chapter the theme in the Old Testament of the judgment of God on all forms of power—as well as the constitution by God of those forms of power (a theme continued in Rom. 13:1). Our point at present is that that Old Testament theme of the "alienation" of God from all human power reaches its culmination in the final manifestation of God as "powerless" in the finitude, weakness, suffering and death implicit in the incarnation (and the birth narratives) and explicit in the actuality of the cross. If, then, as John witnesses: "Anyone who has seen me has seen the Father" (John 14:10), the element of nothingness, of non-being as well as of being, must be present within the divine as interpreted by Christians—again an intersting parallel with major themes within Buddhism.

22. Augustine, *On the Trinity,* bk. IV, chap. III.

23. The dialectic of powerlessness, humility, suffering and death—all the traits of the apparent *negation* of identity, life, being and victory—as the mode of divine appearance within history, and correspondingly, as the mark of divine redemption of history, is a recurrent Pauline theme. As in Christ God participates in our weakness, sin, suffering and death, so through our participation in his weakness, humility, suffering and death both our pride, our suffering and our death are overcome. We are able to accept our finitude, and our sinful denial of it, because he participates in it and gives us the courage, the faith, the confidence and the power to be what we are: 1 Cor. 1:18–31; 2 Cor. 5:21; 12:8–10; 13:3–4; Rom. 6:5–11. Also, as we have noted, the theme of Jesus' participation in weakness, suffering, fate and death–in the non-being of finitude—in order to affirm the authentic or essential being of finitude, and in sin in order to overcome our sinful rejection of our finitude, is basic to Tillich's understanding; and now to Moltmann's reinterpretation of God as in Christ "crucified" and thus redemptive of suffering, oppression and mortality in men and women. Cf. for the same theme,

under the rubric, the "non-resistance of God" in Christ, Kaufman, pp. 219 ff.

24. Rom. 3:9–20; cf. also 2 Chron. 6:36; Isa. 59:9–15; Jer. 9:2–9; 17:5–11; Pss. 14, 38, 51, 53.

25. "This ultimate problem is given by the fact that human history stands in contradiction to the divine will on any level of its moral and religious achievements in such a way that in any 'final' judgment the righteous are proved not to be righteous. The final enigma of history is, therefore, not how the righteous will gain victory over the unrighteous, but how the evil in every good and the unrighteousness of the righteous is to be overcome" (Niebuhr, *Nature and Destiny,* 2:43). Cf. also pp. 30ff.

26. Cf. Calvin, *Institutes,* bk. III, chap. XI, secs. II, VI, X and esp. XI.

27. Rom. 5:6–11.

28. Tillich, *ST* 2:59–78.

29. Moltmann, *The Crucified God,* chap. 6. "If Christian belief thinks in trinitarian terms, it says that forsaken men are already taken up by Christ's forsakenness into the divine history and that we 'live in God' because we participate in the eschatological life of God by virtue of the death of Christ. God is, God is in us, God suffers in us, where love suffers. We participate in the trinitarian process of God's history" (ibid., p. 255; cf. also pp. 263–64, 274–78).

30. "Accordingly we say that there is no unchangeable good but the one, true, blessed God; that the things which He made are indeed good because from Him, yet mutable because made not out of Him, but out of nothing. Although, therefore, they are not the supreme good . . . yet these mutable things which can adhere to the immutable good, and so be blessed, are very good; for so completely is He their good that without Him they cannot but be wretched. . . . and since this is so, then in this nature which has been created so excellent, that though it be mutable itself, it can yet secure its blessedness by adhering to the immutable good, . . . and cannot thus be blessed save in God—in this nature, I say, not to adhere to God, is manifestly a fault" (Augustine, *City of God,* bk. XII, chap. I).

31. "Now, if it be true, as it certainly is, that the whole substance of the gospel is comprised in these two points, repentance and remission of sins—do we not perceive that the Lord freely justifies His children, that He may also restore them to true righteousness by the sanctification of His spirit?" (Calvin, *Institutes,* bk. III, chap. III, sec. XIX.

32. Tillich, *ST* 1:266–70.

33. Niebuhr, *Nature and Destiny,* 1: 219–227, esp. 222.

34. The meaning or sense of the symbol "kingdom of God," central to the proclamation of Jesus, is one of the most important issues in current New Testament debates. Two questions seem to be involved: (1) is it here or in the future, realized or "not yet"? and (2) does it concern only the inner, private, individual realm, the sovereignty of God in the heart of each believer taken, so to speak, one by one, or does it concern the "public realm," history, society, the character of a historical people, the ruling of God over history, and so on. Generally those influenced by Bultmann take the first alternative in each question: the kingdom as Jesus proclaimed it is (1) present in the eschatological deed of his preaching of forgiveness and the need for decision and has little formal or definite future reference at all (cf. Norman Perrin, *Rediscovering the Teaching of Jesus,* chap. 4, esp. pp. 203ff.), and (2) the kingdom concerns the inward situation of the individual in his or her existential relation to God, an inward, private, not an outward, social, "ruling" of God: Bultmann, *History and Eschatology,* pp. 67, 107; cf. also Perrin, *New Testament,* pp. 290, 300–301.

On the other side are the new eschatological interpretations of the kingdom, regarding it as (1) primarily future, and (2) as related to the public, communal realm of historical events rather than solely to the private individual realm: Pannenberg, *Theology and the Kingdom of God;* Moltmann, *Theology of Hope,* chaps. 1, 2, and 5; "Theology as Eschatology," in Moltmann, *The Future of Hope,* esp. pp. 34–50. While the former interpretation surely has relations with traditional pietism, the latter has similarities with the liberal social gospel understanding of the kingdom, and is echoed, as we noted, in both Niebuhr and Tillich, for whom the kingdom, as with us, is a category relevant to history (i.e., to community) and not just to individual existence (cf. also Kaufman, pp. 318ff., 382 and esp. 458). Certainly the concept in the New Testament changed the Old Testament Messianic promise of the "reign of God" very markedly: the reign is now inward, hidden, "spiritual," as we have argued. However, not *all* of the elements of the Old Testament emphasis on the people, the community and the reign of God in history are (I believe) here absent (the "criterion of dissimilarity"—Perrin, *Rediscovering*, pp. 39ff.—is apt a priori to strip off these elements of similarity with the Old Testament). And as noted, the symbol of the kingdom traces its lineage back not only to the concept of the Messianic reign but also to the covenent and its gift of law—both of these aspects related not only to the inward obedience of man and women but also to God's rule in social history. Moreover, the inward life of the individual is polar to his or her communal existence, as we have argued throughout. Thus the separation of individuals from the public realm, of person from community, characteristic of existentialism (and of much modern philosophical and theological thought generally) is a false separation —both on biblical and on anthropological grounds. For this reason in speaking of the symbol of the kingdom we affirm that it implies the fulfillment of the communal and the historical dimensions of human existence in polar relation to its inward, private, existential dimension signified by such a symbol as that of sanctification.

35. In chap. 2 were uncovered the three fundamental questions of historical life and of political action: the question of the sovereign power in history, the question of the norm for historical life and the question of the goal for history's movement.

36. The interpretation of history's developments as based most fundamentally on the achievement of security, meaning, community and self-realization as its primary norms and so goals, is to be contrasted with those views which see historical development as primarily constituted by the achievement of "learning," i.e., by the accumulation of information, understanding and skills concerning (a) the constitution of the objective world, and (b) practical rules for the manipulation of that world. We are in agreement with Augustine that the health of a community, and so its history, is more constituted by the character of its *loves,* and so by the authenticity of its institutions in achieving security, meaning, community and self-actualization, than it is by its "knowledge," since the latter (unless a deep form of "self-knowledge") can be demonically applied and so lead to injustice and in the end to nemesis.

37. Cf. *Shantung Compound,* pp. 40–42, for an example of the possibility of a "calling" in whatever situation destiny may thrust upon us.

38. The "religious" constitution of society mentioned in the text as a part of the work of divine providence and so as an aspect of the task of the church—a role seen from "the outside" by Durkheim and his contemporary followers—finds its Old Testament locus, as we have argued, in the giving of the covenant, in the establishment of the judges and then the kingship, and it is expressed in Paul's both famous and infamous word that "the powers that be are ordained of God" (Rom. 13:1)—an expression which, taken undialectically, like the constitutive role of providence and that of the church taken undialectically, can lead to demonic perversion. Taken, however, dialectically in relation to the *judgment* of God on the perverted institutions he established in Israel and so in history generally, and in relation to the recreation of *new* structures both in covenant and in social situations, this view of the constitutive role of providence can provide a balanced and creative interpretation of the work of providence in social history, and can be the basis for a creative politics both of retrieval and of the new. Thus does Tillich's basic ecclesiological insight concerning the role of "Catholic substance" and "Protestant principle" expand into a principle for the interpretation of culture and of the role of "religious" in culture—namely, as constitutive of its *substance* and critical of its *distortions.*

39. Again an analogy with the "biblical" interpretation of history related to God's "special"

activity of redemption appears as a clue to general history, this time in the double reference of the eschatological kingdom as "having come" and yet as "not yet," the debate between realized and future eschatology. For the substance of that debate, and the conclusion that *both* aspects of the kingdom are essential to its meaning in the proclamation of Jesus, cf. Perrin, *Kingdom of God*, chaps. 4 and 5.

40. For this role of the eschatological (the kingdom) in Reinhold Niebuhr, cf. *Interpretation of Christian Ethics*, chap. 4; *Nature and Destiny*, vol. 2, chap. 10; and in Tillich, *Political Expectation*, "The Political Meaning of Utopia," pp. 167–70; *ST* 3:373–92.

41. It is not irrelevant to note that in current conferences on the ecological or the food crises, it is not at all unusual for the social scientists from industrialized and affluent countries to portray the crisis in terms of massive tendencies obedient to determining economic and social laws, and for representatives of the *same* professions from "developing" countries to portray the crisis as predominantly political, i.e., brought about by unequal economic and political power relations, by exploitation, and by oppressive domination. The "affluent" social scientists thus accuse their critics of a "political ideology" irresponsibly ignoring the "economic facts of life" in a unified industrial world—and are in part right; the others accuse the affluent sociologists and economists of the reverse "ideology", i.e., of seeking, through a cover of social-scientific judgments about "laws," (1) to avoid responsibility for their countries' exploitative controls, and (2) to discourage rearrangement of the balance of power in the world, economic and political—and they are *also* right. Surprisingly, therefore, as a sense of anxiety seemed more characteristic of the affluent and of hope characteristic of the depressed, so a sense of the *fatedness* of events through economic laws seems more characteristic of those on top who wish to ignore their responsibility and the possibility of the new, and an awareness of political *possibilities* seems characteristic of those who, driven by an actual fatedness, will to effect a transformation of given reality. Social status seems to determine (1) the discipline that is taken to be an entrance into historical being (economic law or political action), and (2) the "mythology" of history that is taken to be true (one of the reign of social law or one of the efficacy of human political action).

42. Cf. Niebuhr's comments that all eschatological symbols of the end are mere "pointers" and that "it is unwise for Christians to claim any knowledge of the furniture of heaven or the temperature of hell; and to be too certain about any details of the kingdom of God in which history is consummated" (*Nature and Destiny*, 2:289 and 294. Cf. also Mark 13:32).

43. Tillich, *ST* 3:396.

44. "But about the resurrection of the dead, have you never read what God Himself said to you: 'I am the God of Abraham, the God of Isaac, and the God of Jacob'? He is not God of the dead but of the living" (Matt. 22:31–33).

45. Aulen, pp. 14–17, 60–61. Cf. Kaufman's powerful expression of this theme: Christian faith in a culmination of life at the end and after death depends directly and solely on its faith in God, a faith generated from and based upon the past and present activity of God in our historical experience (Kaufman, pp. 466–68).

46. Rom. 3:21–26; 5:6–21; 8:1–17, 26–30; 1 Cor. 15:20–28; 2 Cor. 1:19–22, 5:18–21; John 1:10–14, 3:16–17, 11:21–27; 17:20–26.

47. 1 Cor. 15:20–28; 2 Cor. 5:1–10; Eph. 1:8–10; Col. 1:13–20. "But the term 'essentialization' can also mean that the new which has been actualized in time and space adds something to essential being, uniting it with the positive which is created within existence, thus producing the ultimately new, the 'New Being,' not fragmentarily as in temporal life, but wholly as a contribution to the kingdom of God in its fulfillment . . . Participation in the eternal life depends on the creative synthesis of a being's essential nature with what it has made of it in its temporal existence" (Tillich, *ST* 3:400–401).

48. Heppe, pp. 695ff.

49. Cf. Whitehead, PR, pp. 524–33; Tillich, *ST* 3:394–423.

50. "Man's creativity and divine self–manifestation are one in the fulfilled Kingdom of God. Insofar as culture is an independent enterprise, it comes to an end in the end of history. It becomes eternal, divine self–manifestation through the finite bearers of the spirit" (Tillich, *ST* 3:403; cf. Niebuhr, *Nature and Destiny*, 2:312).

51. Whitehead, PR, p. 525, "The revolts of destructive evil, purely self-regarding, are dismissed into their triviality of merely individual facts; and yet the good they did achieve . . . is yet saved by its relevance to the completed whole. . . . It is a judgment of a tenderness which loses nothing that can be saved. It is also the judgment of a wisdom which uses what in the temporal world is mere wreckage."

52. Heppe, pp. 146–48. Here the primary, initiating "decree" is neither to create nor to permit the Fall—and then to redeem some of the basis of that fallen state. Rather the first decree is: "God decreed to manifest His glory abroad in all its multifariousness and not for His own but for creatures' good, so that all things might respond to His wise command as to their ends, the praise of His name."

53. Barth, *Church Dogmatics*, II/2, pp. 123–184ff., 195; III/2, pp. 32–33; IV/1, sec. 57.

54. Cf. Schleiermacher, secs. 158, 163, Appendix; Ritschl, pp. 125ff.; Tillich, *ST* 3:151, 406–9; Pannenberg, *Jesus, God and Man*, pp. 272, 378–90; and Kaufman, pp. 305–6, 459, 471–72.

55. Typical of the difficulties all modern theologians, including this one, have with this whole matter of a final judgment for some and final restoration for others, is Aulen's solution: namely, "faith" must affirm *both!* "The possibilities of God's love must not be abridged and His radical opposition to sin must not be obscured. Under such circumstances, faith will reject both a rationally motivated and unconditionally maintained universal restoration . . . and a rationally motivated and unconditionally maintained so-called two-fold destiny" (Aulen, pp. 169–70). Aulen seems to get out of the quandary of asserting an apparent contradiction by adding the qualification "rationally motivated," which allows him to deny *both* sides of the contradiction.

Brunner illustrates this same "paradoxical" judgment about the dual destiny and universal redemption, both, as he points out, implied and even asserted in the New Testament: "Both voices are the word of God . . . We must listen to the voice which speaks of world judgment as to the voice of God Himself, in order that we may fear Him; we must listen to the voice which speaks of universal redemption as to the voice of God Himself, in order that we may love Him. Only through this indiminishable duality do we grasp the duality of God's being which yet is love: His holiness and His love" (Emil Brunner, *Eternal Hope*, pp. 183–84).

56. Rom. 5:15, 11:32; 1 Cor. 15:27–29; Phil. 2:9–11; John 10:16; Eph. 1:10. There is, of course, no question that the theme of a dual destiny for mankind has firm scriptural warrant. Our argument is that there *are* passages that indicate a universalist motif in the New Testament, i.e., that the redemptive love of God is directed at *all* creatures, and not just a few chosen ones, that it is a love that excludes none on whatever grounds, and that its aim is the reunion of all creatures with God.

57. "But God's act of grace is out of all proportion to Adam's wrongdoing" (Rom. 5:15).

58. The most important consideration in this connection is that the essence of the divine love, as portrayed throughout the New Testament, seems denied or negated by the traditional doctrine; that love is viewed in The New Testament as (a) the central character of God's will, and (b) as directed in mercy at the unworthy and not the worthy in order to redeem *them.* Such a view of the divine love in turn seems *denied* or *negated* either by (a) an arbitrary choice of some for salvation and others for retribution–for the latter are, as Reformation tradition put it, "hated by God" (Heppe, p. 148), and for no legitimate basis; or (b) by a view that some are chosen by their "faith" or "obedience"—a form, as the Reformers knew, of a merit doctrine (love comes to the worthy). In any case, it is plain, also through the gospel, how relative such distinctions are. Cf. Tillich, *ST* 3:407–9.

Chapter 12

1. The *grounds* for this ontological interpretation of historical passage in this volume have been multiple, a whole series, so to speak, of varied arguments arising from the analysis of different aspects of the experience of history, and of different ways of speaking about and inquiring into historical passage. This "ontology," then, has its sources in an analysis of (1) our most concrete experience of change; (2) our experience of communal political existence; (3) scientific and social scientific ways of talking about change and the future; (4) critical philosophy of history (the way—according to philosophers—historians talk about history); (5) speculative philosophy of history (the way speculative philosophers talk about history); and finally (6) the implications of certain central Christian symbols.

2. Both Whitehead and Tillich insist, rightly, that ontological categories by their very nature must apply to all of being, and not just to certain sections of it—as "ontic" categories do. With this we agree. Thus despite the fact that no effort has here been made to show that universal applicability, it is here recognized as an obligation—as yet unredeemed—if these categories are valid (Whitehead, PR, p. 4; Tillich, ST 1:20–21, 164–65.) In both of these philosophers, moreover, one finds that "universal" categories (ontological categories) are applied analogically to different realms of being, explicitly in Tillich (e.g., ST 3:313–26), and implicitly in Whitehead (cf. the use of the categories of prehension or "feeling," of "decision" or of "subjective aim," in which there is an *analogical* predication from an original usage in the human dimension to a parallel usage in other dimensions).

3. The passingness of temporality has led—as in Augustine—to a sense of its non-being; it has also led to a sense of time as the arena of new possibilities, of growth, of progress— since the decaying old is by time removed from being, and "room" is made for the new. Thus it is no accident that a sense of progress accompanied the radical temporalizing of the concept of being in the development of modern thought.

4. Spirit as that which *constitutes itself* in order to be is a recurrent and increasingly dominant theme in modern ontology: negative, in Hume's denial of the possibility of any experience of a substantial self; positive, in Kant's understanding of the moral act, in Hegel's definition of spirit, in Kierkegaard—and now in contemporary philosophy in Heidegger, Whitehead and Tillich (ST 3:32–50), as we have been.

5. As is well known, Tillich did not regard the presence of "questions" about the ground of finite being and knowing as constituting "proofs" (ST 1:204–10) because he viewed reason as both finite, confined to the subject-object realm, and estranged (*ibid.*, 1:81–83); White-head did, as we have seen, largely on the grounds of his "faith" in the ultimate coherence of all relevant reality as lying "together in a harmony that excludes mere arbitrariness" (SMW, p. 26).

6. Thus speculative philosophy, as Tillich says, has a "fate." For the intuition of an ultimate coherence, essential to the canons of coherence and of sufficient reason and so basic for all arguments for an ultimate factor in experienced becoming, is itself *historically* conditioned. In some ages such intuitions seem self-evident and well-nigh universal; in others, obscured. In the latter case, such arguments seem flights of speculative fancy unrelated to reality—as in much of our present. Our own interpretation is that the basic apprehension of the "logos" character of reality, on which speculative philosophy, and all natural theology, rest, is itself a response to the manifestation of the logos character of existence, a response in that sense to the general revelation of God as the necessary power of being and to God as the structure of providential possibility. Thus argument expresses a religious intuition responsive to the manifestation of the divine within passage rather than being mode of approaching that presence from a "neutral" position. So understood, arguments have a relative power and use in thematizing the experienced character of our existence in and through the being, the order and the love of God.

7. Whitehead, PR, pp. 337–38, 361.

8. Heppe, p. 256; Barth, *Church Dogmatics*, III/3, sec. 49, pp. 58ff. In this aspect of providence, as these references show, the issue is the work of providence as "preserving" the creature over time, i.e., against the non-being of passingness.

9. Reference here can be made to Augustine's (and later Thomas's, e.g., *Summa Theologica*, I, Question 105, Article 5) conception of a primary causality which works in and through secondary causes as the condition of their effectiveness (cf. chap. 7); and to Schleiermacher's doctrine that the absolute causality of God works through the reciprocal activity of the world as determining the self, and the free self as responding to the world (Schleiermacher, sec. 51 and 54).

10. Cf. Schleiermacher's definition of the "eternity" of God as that which conditions and makes possible every present and so temporality itself (ibid., sec. 52). Cf. also Augustine's conception of eternity (as true being) as the sole ground of the relative "non-being" or passingness characteristic of temporal finitude: e.g., *Tractates on the Gospel of St. John*, XXXVIII, 10; also VII, 1. This is, as we noted, in Whitehead one of the roles of "creativity" as transition, as the basis of the "leap" beyond the objectified entity into a new concrescing entity (PR, pp. 130, 320–22, 324).

11. Whitehead, PR, pp. 130–31.

12. Cf. Schleiermacher's persuasive argument that not only does the experience of being *caused* lead to an awareness of absolute dependence, but just as much the experience of *"being a cause,"* of freedom, point beyond itself to an absolute ground. Thus as Schleiermacher views the absolute causality of God in the reciprocity *both* of being determined and of determining (cf. Schleiermacher, sec. 4.3), so we are seeking to interpret in Points (1) and (2) the creative power of God *both* in the giving of destiny to freedom, *and* in the responding self-actualization of freedom. As we noted, in Whitehead the *primary* role for creativity is that of the "origination of self-actualization, namely, as the principle of 'conjunction out of disjunction,' i.e., of self-actualization as self-creation" (PR, pp. 31–32, 135, 339, 528).

13. We agree with Whitehead's dictum that all "reasons" must in the end stem from actuality, and neither from abstractions nor from mere possibility (PR, pp. 36–37, 64–65). This is the basis for our critique of his own notion of creativity as "the reason" either for transition (n. 10 above) or for self-actualization (n. 12 above), and for our insistence that only the actuality of God, as the power of being in transition and in self-creation, can be a "reason" for these aspects of experienced passage.

14. On "concurrence" as an aspect of providence, cf. Heppe, pp. 256, 258ff.; and on "accompanying," cf. Barth, vol. 3, pp. 3, pp. 90–154, esp. 90–107. In both of these concepts vis-à-vis providence, the issue is the providential work of God in relation to the freedom and autonomy of the creature.

15. "It is a contradiction in terms to assume that some explanatory fact can float into the actual world out of non-entity. . . . Every explanatory fact refers to the decision and the efficacy of an actual thing" (Whitehead, PR, p. 73).

16. Cf., for example, Niebuhr's view that there is a "general" revelation of the power of God on which we are "absolutely dependent," and a sense of being called, examined, and judged from beyond ourselves—which is the basis of conscience—both of which are shaped, clarified, and so more clearly defined as "God" by special revelation (*Nature and Destiny*, 1:125–36). Cf. also Calvin's view that a universal knowledge of God, available to all mankind but warped by idolatry, is refashioned into its true form by the revelation in scripture (*Institutes*, bk. I, chaps. VI and V; bk. II, chaps. VI.1.

17. Classical examples of such an "ontological" limitation on God by other metaphysical principles on which he works but which he did not "create," are, of course, the picture of the Demiourgos in Plato's *Timaeus*, the Unmoved Mover in Aristotle's *Metaphysics*, and in recent times Whitehead's God balanced by, dependent on, and cooperative with creativity and eternal objects: cf. PR, pp. 135, 392, 528.

18. For an analysis of the symbol of *ex nihilo* as indicating that all aspects of finite being arise from God, cf. the author's *Maker of Heaven and Earth*, pp. 47–58. For Whitehead's negative evaluation of *ex nihilo*, cf. PR, pp. 519–20.

19. "Both [God and the world] are in the grip of the ultimate metaphysical ground, the creative advance into novelty" (Whitehead PR, p. 529).

20. As Brunner rightly points out, creation and self-limitation are correlative concepts: "God limits Himself in order to create room for the creature . . . God creatures a creature, since He limits His absoluteness" Emil Brunner, *Dogmatics*, p. 172ff. Cf. also Kaufman, pp. 91–92, 145–46, 382–84. In this self-limitation, culminating, as noted, in the manifestation of God on the cross, there is a striking element of "non-being" in the divine, qualifying radically the absolute being of the classical tradition and showing again interesting relations with the conceptions of the "ultimate" as Nothingness in Buddhism.

21. Clearly our view is here in contrast, not only to the traditional view of God's being as transcendent to all change and so all real possibility, but also to that of Schleiermacher, for whom the distinction between actuality and possibility disappears in God (Schleiermacher, sec. 54). Tillich's description of God as "life" and as Spirit, and so as the ground of the process of the actualization and fulfillment of potential being, comes close to our conception (ST 1:241ff.); and in describing what is clearly his own view (dialectical realism) as a philosophical expression of "life," Tillich defines this view as follows—very close to the conception here presented: "Dialectical realism tries to unite the structural oneness of everything within the absolute with the undecided and unfinished manifoldness of the real" (ibid., 1:234–35). And yet Tillich also insisted that God transcends and unites *all* the ontological polarities, including that between actuality and potentiality (ibid., 1:273–74, 280) —which in the case of the passage from actuality to potentiality, we are here denying. For agreement with the position enunciated here, cf. Kaufman, pp. 157–58.

22. Cf. Kaufman, pp. 211ff.

23. As our discussion, that of Kaufman, and of course the very helpful arguments of both Whitehead and Hartshorne indicate, the *basis* for the divine experience and knowledge of the changing finite and so of historical passage itself lies ontologically *here*, in God's "changing relations" to the flux of events, and so finally in the reality of change in his own being. As Augustine's and Thomas's attempts to understand God's "knowledge" of the changing world without denying the divine unchangeability show, if God does not change and so is out of relation to changing actuality, then he can only "know" the world as "possible," i.e., through his original and eternal idea of it—and not in its actuality (cf. Augustine, *On the Trinity*, bks. XV, XIII, 33; Thomas, *Summa Theologica*, I, Question 14, Articles 5 and 6). That such a metaphysical position denies or at best makes unintelligible the biblical view of God as dynamically related to history in preservation, grace, judgment and promise—and so in "experience," "awareness" and "knowledge"—is evident.

24. The divine trinity of being (eternity), truth and love is fundamental for Augustine's conception of God, for his understanding of the relation of God to the creature, and so correspondingly for his conception of the creature. "For the essence of God, whereby He is, has altogether nothing changeable, neither in eternity, in truth, nor in will; since there truth is eternal, love eternal; and there love is true, eternity true; and there eternity is loved, and truth is loved" (*On the Trinity*, bk. XV, Preface). Cf. for the relation of this "trinity" to the creature, *City of God*, bk. XI, chap. XXIV: "In God's eternity is its life; in God's truth its light; in God's goodness its joy." And also chap. XXVI. It is this conception that we are seeking here to "reinterpret" in the light of the modern consciousness of history.

25. Calvin, *Institutes*, bk. I, chaps. I and II; Schleiermacher, secs. 35 and 50.

26. Tillich expresses the general position here enunciated with power and beauty in the introduction to *The Religious Situation*: "The present is the past" (ibid., p. 32); "the present is the future" (ibid., p. 33); and "the present is eternity" (ibid., p. 35); and he concludes: "We

may therefore combine our three questions and inquire after the eternal which presses on out of the past, in and through the present, towards future actualization" (ibid., p. 36).

27. Our categories of objective and subjective logos are, of course, taken from Tillich, *ST* 1:75–79. However, the same sense of an objective order in reality which the mind can grasp as the basis of all human cultural creativity is expressed in Whitehead: "That we fail to find in experience any elements intrinsically incapable of exhibition as examples of general theory is the hope of rationalism. This hope is not a metaphysical premise. It is the faith which forms the motive for the pursuit of all sciences alike, including metaphysics" (PR, p. 67).

BIBLIOGRAPHY

Abbott, Lyman. *Theology of an Evolutionist.* Boston: Houghton Mifflin, 1897.

Alves, Rubem. *A Theology of Human Hope.* St. Meinrad, Indiana: Abbey Press, 1972.

Augustine. *Basic Writings of St. Augustine,* edited by W. J. Oates. N.Y.: Random, 1948.

Aulen, Gustav. *The Faith of the Christian Church.* Philadelphia: Muhlenberg, 1948.

Barth, Karl. *Church Dogmatics.* Especially, volume 3, *The Doctrine of Creation,* part 3. Edinburgh: T. & T. Clark, 1967.

———. *The Epistle to the Romans.* 6th German ed. N.Y.: Oxford University, 1950.

———. *The Humanity of God.* Atlanta: John Knox, 1960.

Bendix, Reinhard. *Max Weber: An Intellectual Portrait.* London: Methuen, 1966.

Berdyaev, Nicolas. *The Beginning and the End.* N.Y.: Harper Torchbooks.

———. *The Meaning of History.* N.Y.: Scribner's, 1936.

Berger, Peter L. *The Sacred Canopy.* Garden City, N.Y.: Doubleday, 1967.

Berger, Peter L., and Luckmann, Thomas. *The Social Construction of Reality.* Garden City, N.Y.: Doubleday, Anchor, 1967.

Bergson, Henri. *The Two Sources of Morality and Religion.* N.Y.: H. Holt, 1935.

Berlin, Isaiah. *Historical Inevitability.* N.Y.: Oxford, 1955.

Bingham, June. *Courage to Change.* N.Y.: Scribner's, 1961.

Bloch, Ernst. *Man on His Own.* N.Y.: Herder and Herder, 1970.

———. *A Philosophy of the Future.* N.Y.: Herder and Herder, 1970.

———. *Das Prinzip Hoffnung.* Frankfurt am Main: Suhrkamp, 1959.

Boulding, Kenneth E. *The Meaning of the Twentieth Century.* N.Y.: Harper Colophon Books, 1965.

Brown, Norman O. *Life Against Death.* N.Y.: Random, Vintage, 1959.

———. *Love's Body.* N.Y.: Random, 1966.

Browning, Don S. *Generative Man.* Philadelphia: Westminster, 1973.

Brunner, Emil. *The Divine-Human Encounter.* Philadelphia: Westminster, 1943.

———. *Dogmatics: The Christian Doctrine of Creation and Redemption.* Vol. III. London: Lutterworth, 1952.

———. *Eternal Hope.* Philadelphia: Westminster, 1954.

Bultmann, Rudolf. *Essays Philosophical and Theological.* N.Y.: Macmillan, 1955.

———. *History and Eschatology.* Edinburgh: The University Press, 1951.

———. *Theology of the New Testament.* 2 vols. London: SCM, 1952–55.

Bultmann, Rudolf, et al. *Kerygma and Myth.* Edited by H. W. Bartsch, N.Y.: Harper Torchbooks, 1961.

Burtt, E. A., ed. *The English Philosophers from Bacon to Mill.* N.Y.: Modern Library, 1939.

Bury, J. B. *The Idea of Progress.* N.Y.: Dover, 1955.

Calvin, John. *Calvin: Commentaries.* Library of Christian Classics, vol. XXIII, edited by J. Haroutunian and L. P. Smith. Philadelphia: Westminster, 1968.

———. *Institutes of the Christian Religion.* Vol. 1. Translated by John Allen. Philadelphia: Presbyterian Board of Christian Education, 1936.

Cassirer, Ernst. *The Philosophy of the Enlightenment.* Boston: Beacon, 1951.

Chevalier, J. *La notion du nécessaire chez Aristote et chez son prédecesseurs.* Lyon: A. Ray, 1914.

434

Cochrane, C. N. *Christianity and Classical Culture.* London: Oxford University, 1944.

Cohn, Norman. *The Pursuit of the Millennium.* London: Palladin, 1970.

Collingwood, R. G. *An Essay on Metaphysics.* Oxford: Clarendon, 1940.

———. *The Idea of History.* Oxford: Clarendon, 1946.

Daedalus, vol. 96, no. 3 (Summer 1967): "Toward the Year 2000: Work in Progress."

Dewey, John. *Intelligence in the Modern World: John Dewey's Philosophy.* Edited by J. Ratner. N.Y.: Modern Library, 1939.

Dobzhansky, Theodosius. *Evolution, Genetics and Man.* N.Y.: John Wiley & Sons, 1965.

———. *Mankind Evolving.* New Haven: Yale University, 1962.

Donegan, Allan, and Donegan, Barbara. *Philosophy of History.* N.Y.: Macmillan, 1965.

Dowey, Edward A., jr. *The Knowledge of God in Calvin's Theology.* N.Y.: Columbia University, 1953.

Dray, W. H. *Philosophy of History.* Englewood, N.Y.: Prentice-Hall, 1964.

Drummond, Henry. *Natural Law in the Spiritual World.* N.Y.: James Pott & Co., 1884.

Eichrodt, Walther. *Theology of the Old Testament.* 2 vols. Philadelphia: Westminster, 1961–67.

Eiseley, Loren. *Darwin's Century.* Garden City, N.Y.: Doubleday, 1959.

Ellul, Jacques. *The Technological Society.* N.Y.: Random, Vintage, 1964.

Emmett, Dorothy. *Function, Purpose and Powers.* Philadelphia: Temple University, 1958.

Ferkiss, Victor. *Technological Man: The Myth and the Reality.* N.Y.: Braziller, 1969.

Fromm, Erich. *The Revolution of Hope.* N.Y.: Bantam, 1968.

Funk, R. W. *Journal for Theology and Church.* No. 6: *Apocalypticism.* N.Y.: Herder and Herder, 1969.

Gadamer, Hans-Georg. *Wahrheit und Methode.* 2nd ed. Tübingen: J. C. B. Mohr, 1965: *Truth and Method,* N.Y.: Seabury, 1975.

Gardiner, Patrick, ed. *Theories of History.* N.Y.: Free Press, 1959.

Gay, Peter. *The Enlightenment: An Interpretation: The Rise of Modern Paganism.* Vol. 1. N.Y.: Knopf, 1966.

Geertz, Clifford. *The Interpretation of Cultures.* N.Y.: Basic, 1973.

Gilkey, Langdon. *Catholicism Confronts Modernity.* N.Y.: Seabury, 1975.

———. "The Concept of Providence in Contemporary Theology." *Journal of Religion* 43 (1963): 171–92.

———. "The Contribution of Culture to the Reign of God." In *The Future as the Presence of Shared Hope,* edited by Maryellen Muckenhirn. N.Y.: Sheed & Ward, 1968. Pp. 34–58.

———. *Maker of Heaven and Earth.* N.Y.: Doubleday, 1959.

———. *Naming the Whirlwind.* Indianapolis: Bobbs-Merrill, 1969.

———. "Pannenberg's *Basic Questions in Theology.*" *Perspective* 14 (1973):34–55.

———. "Reinhold Niebuhr's Theology of History." *Journal of Religion* 54 (1974):360–86.

———. *Religion and the Scientific Future.* N.Y.: Harper & Row, 1970.

———. *Shantung Compound.* N.Y.: Harper & Row, 1964.

———. "The Universal and Immediate Presence of God." In *The Future of Hope,* by J. Moltmann et al. N.Y.: Herder and Herder, 1970. Pp. 81–109.

Gillespie, Charles C. *Genesis and Geology.* N.Y.: Harper Torchbooks, 1959.

Gilson, E. *The Christian Philosophy of St. Augustine.* N.Y.: Random, 1960.

Gouldner, Alvin. *The Coming Crisis of Western Sociology.* N.Y.: Avon, 1970.

Grant, Frederick C. *An Introduction to New Testament Thought.* Nashville: Abingdon, 1971.

Greene, John C. *The Death of Adam.* Ames, Ia: Iowa State University, 1959.

Gutierrez, Gustavo. *A Theology of Liberation.* Maryknoll, N.Y.: Orbis Books, 1972.

Habermas, Jürgen. *Erkenntnis und Interesse.* Frankfurt am Main: Suhrkamp, 1970: *Knowledge and Human Interests.* Boston: Beacon, 1971.

———. *Theorie und Praxis.* Neuwied, FRG: Luchterhand, 1969: *Theory and Practice.* Boston: Beacon, 1973.

———. *Toward a Rational Society.* Boston: Beacon, 1971.

Harnack, Adolf. *History of Dogma.* 7 vols. N.Y.: Russell & Russell, 1958.

Hartshorne, Charles. *Beyond Humanism.* Chicago: Willett, Clark and Co., 1937.

———. *Creative Synthesis and Philosophic Method.* La Salle, Ill.: Open Court, 1970.

———. *The Logic of Perfection.* La Salle, Ill.: Open Court, 1962.

———. *Reality as Social Process.* Glencoe, Ill.: Free Press, 1953.

Hazeldon, K., and Hefner, P. *Changing Man: The Threat and the Promise.* Garden City, N.Y.: Doubleday, 1967.

Hegel, G. W. F. *The Philosophy of History.* Translated by J. Sibree. N.Y.: Dover, 1956.

Heidegger, Martin. *Being and Time.* N.Y.: Harper & Bros., 1962.

Heilbroner, Robert L. *An Inquiry into the Human Prospect.* N.Y.: W. W. Norton, 1974.

Heppe, Heinrich. *Reformed Dogmatics.* London: George Allen & Unwin, 1950.

Herder, J. G. *Ideen zur Philosophie der Geschichte der Menschheit.* In *Johann Gottfried Herder, Schriften,* selected and introduced by Walter Flemmer. Munich: W. Goldmann, 1960.

Herzog, Frederick. *Liberation Theology.* N.Y.: Seabury, 1972.

Hill, Michael. *A Sociology of Religion.* N.Y.: Basic, 1973.

Himmelfarb, Gertrude. *Darwin and the Darwinian Revolution.* Garden City, N.Y.: Doubleday, 1959.

Huxley, Julian. *Religion without Revelation.* N.Y.: Harper & Row, 1957.

I-Ching. Translated by Richard Wilhelm and C. F. Baynes. Bollingen Series XIX. Princeton, N.J.: Princeton University, 1967.

Jaspers, Karl. *The Origin and Goal of History.* New Haven: Yale University, 1959.

Jay, Martin. *The Dialectical Imagination.* Boston: Little, Brown, 1973.

Jonas, Hans. *Augustin und das paulinische Freiheitsproblem.* Göttingen: Vandenhoeck & Ruprecht, 1930.

Kahn, Herman, and Weiner, A. J. *The Year 2000.* N.Y.: Macmillan, 1967.

Kant, Immanuel. *Idea for a Universal History from a Cosmopolitan Point of View.*

———. *Kant, On History.* Translated and edited by L. W. Beck. Indianapolis: Bobbs-Merrill, 1963.

———. *Religion Within the Limits of Reason Alone.* N.Y.: Harper Torchbooks, 1960.

Käsemann, Ernst. *Jesus Means Freedom.* Philadelphia: Fortress, 1968.

Kauffman, Gordon D. *Systematic Theology: A Historicist Perspective.* N.Y.: Scribner's, 1968.

Kuhn, Thomas. *The Structure of Scientific Revolutions.* Chicago: University of Chicago, 1962.

Kümmel, Werner Georg. *The Theology of the New Testament.* Nashville: Abingdon, 1973.

Leff, Gordon. *History and Social Theory.* Garden City, N.Y.: Doubleday, Anchor, 1971.

Levinas, Emmanuel. *Totalité et Infinité.* The Hague: Nijhoff, 1968.

Lonergan, Bernard. *Insight.* London: Longmans, 1964.

———. *Method in Theology.* N.Y.: Herder and Herder, 1972.

Löwith, Karl. *Meaning in History.* Chicago: University of Chicago, Phoenix, 1949.

———. *Nature, History and Existentialism.* Evanston, Ill.: Northwestern University, 1966.

———. *Von Hegel zu Nietzsche.* Stuttgart: W. Kolhammer, 1958.

Luckmann, Thomas. *Invisible Religion.* N.Y.: Macmillan, 1967.

Luther, Martin. *Bondage of the Will.* Translated by J. I. Parker and D. R. Johnston. Old Tappan, N.J.: Revell, 1957.

Mannheim, Karl. *Ideology and Utopia.* London: Routledge & Kegan Paul, 1936.

Marcuse, Herbert. *Eros and Civilization.* Boston: Beacon, 1955.

———. *One-Dimensional Man.* Boston: Beacon, 1964.

———. *Reason and Revolution.* Boston: Beacon, 1960.

Markus, R. A. *Saeculum: History and Theology in the Theology of St. Augustine.* Cambridge: At the University Press, 1970.

———, ed. *Augustine.* Garden City, N.Y.: Doubleday, Anchor, 1972.

Marx, Karl. *Karl Marx: Early Writings.* Translated and edited by T. B. Bottomore. N.Y.: McGraw-Hill, 1964.

———. *Karl Marx: Selected Writings in Sociology and Social Philosophy.* Translated by T. B. Bottomore. N.Y.: McGraw-Hill, 1956.

Meadows, Donella H., et al. *The Limits to Growth.* N.Y.: Universe Books, 1972.

Metz, J. B. *Theology of the World.* N.Y.: Herder and Herder, 1969.

Meyerhoff, Hans, ed. *The Philosophy of History in Our Time.* Garden City, N.Y.: Doubleday, Anchor, 1959.

Michalson, Carl. *The Hinge of History.* N.Y.: Scribner's, 1959.

———. *The Rationality of Faith.* N.Y.: Scribner's, 1963.

Moltmann, Jürgen. *The Crucified God,* N.Y.: Harper & Row, 1974.

———. *Religion, Revolution and the Future.* N.Y.: Scribner's, 1969.

———. *Revelation as History.* N.Y.: Macmillan, 1968.

———. *Theology of Hope.* N.Y.: Harper & Row, 1967.

Moltmann, Jürgen, et al. *The Future of Hope.* Edited by Frederick Herzog. N.Y.: Seabury, 1970.

Moore, Wilbert E. *Social Change.* Englewood, N.J.: Prentice-Hall, 1963.

Moore, W., and Cook, Robert, eds. *Readings in Social Change.* Englewood, N.J.: Prentice-Hall, 1967.

Niebuhr, Reinhold. *Beyond Tragedy.* N.Y.: Scribner's, 1937.

———. *Christian Realism and Political Problems.* N.Y.: Scribner's, 1953.

———. *Faith and History.* N.Y.: Scribner's, 1949.

———. *An Interpretation of Christian Ethics.* N.Y.: Harper, 1935.

_____. *Love and Justice.* Philadelphia: Westminster, 1957.

_____. *Man's Nature and His Communities.* N.Y.: Scribner's, 1965.

_____. *Moral Man and Immoral Society.* N.Y.: Scribner's, 1932.

_____. *The Nature and Destiny of Man.* 2 vols. N.Y.: Scribner's, 1941–43.

_____. *Reflections on the End of an Era.* N.Y.: Scribner's, 1934.

_____. "The Truth in Myths." In *The Nature of Religious Experience,* edited by J. S. Bixler. N.Y.: Harper & Bros., 1937.

Nisbet, Robert. *Social Change and History.* N.Y.: Oxford University, 1972.

_____. *The Sociological Tradition.* N.Y.: Basic, 1966.

Nygren, Anders. *Agape and Eros.* N.Y.: Harper & Row, 1969.

Ogden, Schubert. *The Reality of God.* N.Y.: Harper & Row, 1963.

Palmer, Richard. *Hermeneutics: Interpretative Theory in Schleiermacher, Dilthey, Heidegger and Gadamer.* Evanston, Ill.: Northwestern University, 1969.

Pannenberg, Wolfhart. *Basic Questions in Theology.* 2 vols. Philadelphia: Westminster, 1970–71.

_____. *Jesus: God and Man.* Philadelphia: Westminster, 1968.

_____. *Theology and the Kingdom of God.* Philadelphia: Westminster, 1969.

_____. ed. *Revelation As History.* N.Y.: Macmillan, 1968.

Parsons, Talcott. "Culture and Social System Revisited." In *The Idea of Culture in the Social Sciences,* edited by E. Schneider and C. Bonjean. N.Y.: Cambridge University, 1973.

Pelikan, J. *The Christian Tradition: Emergence of the Catholic Tradition.* Vol. 1. Chicago: University of Chicago, 1971.

Perrin, Norman. *The Kingdom of God in the Teaching of Jesus.* Philadelphia: Westminster, 1963.

_____. *The New Testament: An Introduction.* N.Y.: Harcourt Brace, 1974.

_____. *Rediscovering the Teaching of Jesus.* N.Y.: Harper & Row, 1967.

Polanyi, Michael. *Personal Knowledge.* N.Y.: Harper Torchbooks, 1964.

Popper, Karl. *The Poverty of Historicism.* N.Y.: Harper Torchbooks, 1969.

Prestige, G. L. *God in Patristic Thought.* London: William Huneman, 1936.

Przywara, E. *An Augustine Synthesis.* London: Sheed & Ward, 1945.

Ramsey, Ian. *Models and Mystery.* London: Oxford University, 1964.

_____. *Religious Language.* N.Y.: Macmillan, 1963.

Randall, John Herman, Jr. *Nature and Historical Experience.* N.Y.: Columbia University, 1958.

_____. *The Making of the Modern Mind.* Boston: Houghton Mifflin, 1940.

Rauschenbush, Walter. *Christianizing the Social Order.* N.Y.: Macmillan, 1915.

_____. *A Theology for the Social Gospel.* N.Y.: Macmillan, 1918.

Ricoeur, Paul. *The Symbolism of Evil.* N.Y.: Harper & Row, 1967.

Ritschl, Albrecht. *The Christian Doctrine of Justification and Reconciliation.* Translation of 3rd vol. of *Die christliche Lehre von der Rechtfertigung und Versöhnung.* Repr. of 1902 ed. Clifton, N.J.: Reference Book Pubs., 1966.

Robinson, J. M., and Cobb, J. B., eds. *Theology as History.* N.Y.: Harper & Row, 1967.

Rust, Eric. *Christian Understanding of History.* London: Lutterworth, 1947.

Schacht, Richard. *Alienation.* Garden City, N.Y.: Doubleday, Anchor, 1971.

Schleiermacher, Friedrich. *The Christian Faith.* 2nd German ed. Edinburgh: T. & T. Clark, 1948.

Schonfield, Andrew. "Thinking about the Future." *Encounter,* vol. 32, no. 2 (February 1969).

Schutz, Alfred. *On Phenomenology and Social Relations.* Edited by Helmut R. Wagner. Chicago: University of Chicago, 1970.

Schweitzer, Albert. *The Quest for the Historical Jesus.* London: A. & C. Black, 1948.

Shinn, Roger. *Christianity and the Problem of History.* St. Louis, Mo.: Bethany Press, 1964.

Simpson, George Gaylord. *The Meaning of Evolution.* N.Y.: NAL, Mentor, 1957.

Skinner, B. F. *Beyond Freedom and Dignity.* N.Y.: Knopf, 1971.

Steiner, George. *In Bluebeard's Castle.* New Haven: Yale University, 1971.

Tawney, R. H. *Religion and the Rise of Capitalism.* Harmondsworth: Penguin, 1940.

Tennant, F. R. *Philosophical Theology.* Cambridge: At the University Press, 1956.

TeSelle, Eugene. *Augustine, The Theologian.* N.Y.: Herder and Herder, 1970.

Tillich, Paul. *Biblical Reality and the Search for Ultimate Reality.* Chicago: University of Chicago, 1955.

_____. *The Courage to Be.* New Haven: Yale University, 1952.

_____. *The Interpretation of History.* N.Y.: Scribner's, 1936.

_____. *Love, Power and Justice.* N.Y.: Oxford University, 1954.

_____. *Political Expectation*. N.Y.: Harper & Row, 1971.

_____. *The Protestant Era*. Chicago: University of Chicago, 1948.

_____. *The Religious Situation*. N.Y.: Living Age, 1956.

_____. *Systematic Theology*. 3 vols. Chicago: University of Chicago, 1951–63.

_____. *The Theology of Culture*. N.Y.: Oxford University, 1959.

_____. "The World Situation." In *The Christian Answer*, edited by H. P. Van Dusen. N.Y.: Scribner's, 1945.

Tocqueville, Alexis de. *Democracy in America*. Edited by J. P. Mayor. Garden City, N.Y.: Doubleday, Anchor, 1969.

Toffler, Alvin. *Future Shock*. N.Y.: Bantam, 1971.

Torrance, T. F. *Calvin's Doctrine of Man*. London: Lutterworth, 1949.

Toulmin, Stephen. "Contemporary Scientific Mythology." In *Metaphysical Beliefs*, edited by A. MacIntyre. London: SCM, 1957.

Toynbee, Arnold, J. *A Study of History*. 12 vols. London: Oxford University, 1934–61.

Tracy, David. *Blessed Rage for Order*. N.Y.: Seabury, 1975.

Troeltsch, Ernst. *The Social Teaching of the Christian Churches*. 2 vols. N.Y.: Macmillan, 1949.

Unseld, Siegfried. *Ernst Bloch zu ehren*. Frankfurt am Main: Suhrkamp, 1965.

von Rad, Gerhard. *Old Testament Theology*. 2 vols. N.Y.: Harper & Row, 1962–66.

Walsh, W. H. *Philosophy of History*. N.Y.: Harper Torchbooks, 1967.

Whitehead, Alfred North. *Adventures of Ideas*. N.Y.: Macmillan, 1933.

_____. *Modes of Thought*. Cambridge, Ma.: Harvard University, 1938.

_____. *Process and Reality*. N.Y.: Macmillan, 1929.

_____. *Religion in the Making*. N.Y.: Macmillan, 1926.

_____. *Science and the Modern World*. N.Y.: Macmillan, 1926.

Willey, Basil. *Nineteenth Century Studies*. London: Chatto & Windus, 1950.

Winch, Peter. *The Idea of a Social Science and Its Relation to Philosophy*. London: Routledge & Kegan Paul, 1971.

Winter, Gibson. *Elements for a Social Ethic*. N.Y.: Macmillan, 1966.

_____. *Being Free*. N.Y.: Macmillan, 1970.

INDEX OF PERSONS

INDEX OF SUBJECTS